LYNCH

SYMPOS[

CLASSICAL SELECTIONS ON GREAT ISSUES

VOLUME VIII

SCIENCE, TECHNOLOGY, AND SOCIETY

Dewey
Bush
Oppenheimer
Lerner
Frederick W. Taylor
Aldous Huxley
H. G. Wells
Swift
Mary Shelley
Benét
Henry Adams
Muller
Mumford
Ellul
Russell
Nightingale
Childress
U.S. Atomic Energy Commission
Carson
C. S. Lewis
Annie Dillard
Gordon R. Taylor
Wiener
Turing

Copyright © 1997 by
Lynchburg College

University Press of America,® Inc.
4720 Boston Way
Lanham, Maryland 20706

12 Hid's Copse Rd.
Cummor Hill, Oxford OX2 9JJ

Co-published by arrangement with Lynchburg College

ISBN 0-7618-0835-3 (pbk: alk. ppr.)

SYMPOSIUM READINGS

Second Edition

Lynchburg College in Virginia

Compiled and Edited by the
following faculty members of Lynchburg College

Julius A. Sigler, Series Editor

**Julius A. Sigler, Professor of Physics
Volume Editor**

David Felty, Chaplain

James A. Huston, Dean and Professor Emeritus of History

Anne Marshall Huston, Professor Emeritus of Education and Human
Development

Joseph L. Nelson, Professor of Religion

R. Kendall North, Professor of Business Administration

Clifton W. Potter, Jr, Professor of History

Phillip H. Stump, Associate Professor of History

Thomas C. Tiller, Professor of Education and Human Development

and, for the first edition

Kenneth E. Alrutz, Assistant Professor of English
Virginia B. Berger, Professor Emeritus of Music
James L. Campbell, Professor of English
Robert L. Frey, Professor of History
Shannon McIntyre Jordan, Instructor in Philosophy
Jan G. Linn, Chaplain
Peggy S. Pittas, Associate Professor of Psychology

CONTENTS

PREFACE

The Symposium Readings were first developed by a group of Lynchburg College faculty members to be used in a unique senior capstone course, the Senior Symposium, which has been required of all seniors at Lynchburg College since 1976. The symposium is, loosely speaking, a great books great issues course whose aim is to integrate the fragmented knowledge acquired by students through the traditional courses offered by academic departments. A more complete description of the course and its philosophical underpinnings can be obtained by writing to the editor of the series.

More recently, another group of Lynchburg faculty proposed using the Symposium Readings to teach reading, writing, and speaking skills across the curriculum. The Lynchburg College Symposium Reading (LCSR) project evolved from their proposal. First funded by FIPSE, the project continues to evolve into an exciting part of the college curriculum. As various faculty experimented with the approach in their courses, it became apparent that a richer selection of readings would be required. Thus, the second edition. One might characterize the first edition as a largely male chorus, mostly white European males, punctuated by a few solo voices of women and minorities. The faculty who worked on the second edition has conscientiously tried to enrich the chorus, adding more voices of women, minorities, and third-world authors.

The editors do not claim that these ten volumes are in any way a canon. What constitutes a classic in an evolving field such as science and technology is at best an educated guess. Academic interests change, and in fact, discussions of a third edition, with different selections, are already underway. But that lies well in the future, to be done by the next generation of faculty.

ACKNOWLEDGMENTS

The following copyrighted materials have been used with the permission of the copyright holders:

John Dewey, *Democratic Faith and Education*, Copyright 1944, by The Antioch Review, Inc. First appeared in *Antioch Review*, Vol. 4, No. 2 (Summer, 1944). Reprinted by permission of the editors.

Reprinted with the permission of Simon & Schuster from *Science and the Common Understanding* by J. Robert Oppenheimer. Copyright 1954 by J. Robert Oppenheimer; copyright renewed ©1981 by Robert B. Meyner.

Reprinted with the permission of Simon & Schuster from *America as a Civilization* by Max Lerner. Copyright ©1957 by Max Lerner, copyright renewed © 1985 by Max Lerner.

From *The Abolition of Man* by C.S. Lewis. Reprinted by permission of HarperCollins Publishers Ltd.

From *The Impact of Science on Society* by Bertram Russell, Routledge (Unwin Hyman 1951), © Bertram Russell Peace Foundation. Reprinted by permission of Routledge Cheriton House.

From *Priorities in Biomedical Ethics*. ©1981 James F. Childress. Used by permission of Westminster John Knox Press.

From *Silent Spring*, by Rachel Carson. Houghton-Mifflin Co., ©1962 by Rachel L. Carson. Reprinted by permission of the publisher.

From *The Human Use of Human Beings*, by Norbert Weiner. Houghton-Mifflin Co., ©1950. Reprinted by permission of the publisher.

From *Brave New World*, by Aldous Huxley. Copyright 1932, 1960 by Aldous Huxley. Reprinted by permission of HarperCollins Publishers, Inc.

From *The Technological Order,* by Jacques Ellul, ed. Carl F. Stover (Detroit: Wayne State University Press, 1963). Reprinted by permission of Encyclopedia Brittanica, Inc.

From *The Children of Frankenstein*, by Herbert J. Muller. Copyright 1970, Indiana University Press.

By the Waters of Babylon by Stephen Vincent Benet. From: *The Selected Works of Stephen Vincent Benet*, Holt, Rhinehart & Winston, Inc. Copyright 1937 by Stephen Vincent Benet. Copyright renewed ©1964 by Thomas C. Benet, Stephanie B. Mahin and Rachel Benet Lewis. Reprinted by permission of Brandt & Brandt Literary Agents, Inc.

The editors also acknowledge with appreciation the advice and encouragement of faculty colleagues and the support of Dean Jacqueline Asbury. Special thanks are also expressed for the work of Mr. August Meidling, Mrs. Phyllis Lane and Mrs. Laurie Cassidy for their invaluable assistance in preparing these materials for publication.

INTRODUCTION TO VOLUME VIII

The greatest of the changes that science has brought us is the acuity of change; the greatest novelty the extent of novelty.

J. Robert Oppenheimer

Persons born in the twentieth century have witnessed what seem to be unparalleled changes in the world around them. These changes have occurred largely because of the scientific and technological revolutions which have characterized the past three centuries, particularly in the western world. Many authors have written about these changes and not always in positive terms. This volume provides a variety of viewpoints and insights into the ways in which science and technology have influenced and continue to influence the broader society.

The reader may be confused by the terms science and technology—terms which are often used interchangeably. Science is a particular way of studying and knowing the world. It is based upon a rational belief that an objective world exits and can be known. Science differs from other ways of knowing the world primarily in its insistence that its theories be experimentally testable in that world. In its purest form, scientists pursue their knowledge simply for the sake of knowing. Others, who might be called applied scientists, may seek the same knowledge in order to use it. Thus a scientist might try to understand the microscopic structure of a particular metal in order to create a theoretical understanding of all metals, while an applied scientist might study the same metal, using the same techniques, gaining the same knowledge, in an effort to create a harder form of steel, for example.

Technology is neither of these. The word technology originated from the Greek *tekhnē*, meaning skill. In anthropology, technology refers to the realm of tool-making. So a history of technology might begin with a study of the tools available in ancient cultures and, more importantly, with the knowledge associated with the crafting of those tools. In some sense the word still has that meaning. That is, one might use the term technology to refer to a particular set of tools or machines used in a particular way. i.e., "We must invest in new technology in order to be competitive." A diesel-electric locomotive represents a technology which replaced the older technology of steam locomotives. But technology has come to mean much more than a tool or a machine. Technology also refers to interrelated systems of science, machines, tools and the body of knowledge associated with them, applied to the solutions of particular problems. Thus our electrical power generating and distribution system is a technology. We can identify transportation technologies, communications technologies and defense technologies. Used in this way, Thomas Edison didn't just invent the electric lamp, a particular technological device for lighting, he (along with Westinghouse) invented the electric power industry. Electric technologies have changed people's lives in ways ranging from better lighting to better food preservation to communications and entertainment. In changing lives, the technology developed a dependence on the part of its users and it created the opportunity for ethical choices which had not previously existed on the part of the larger society.

For most of human history, technology was the province of tinkers or inventors. As recently as the 18th century, almost all technology was created by trial and error. James Watt invented the steam engine with no understanding of the science of heat which then developed in a futile attempt to devise substantially more efficient steam engines. That began to change in the late 18th century when the expatriate American, Benjamin Thompson, began a systematic study of the thermal properties of various fibers in an attempt to create the most efficient cloth for military uniforms. Thompson, later known as Count Rumford, was likely the first real scientist to pursue science for its utility.

By the middle of the 19th century, James Clerk Maxwell had published his theory of electromagnetism which demonstrated the interrelatedness of all known electromagnetic phenomena. This powerful theory also showed that light is an electromagnetic wave and predicted the existence of other, previously suspected, electromagnetic waves. In 1888, Heinrich Hertz verified the existence of such waves and by 1910, William Marconi had invented the wireless telegraph, an invention which would not have been possible without the understanding of the science of electromagnetism. The first commercial radio station (KDKA in Pittsburgh) began to broadcast in 1920, approximately fifty years after the publication of the theory. Modern technologies almost always develop from some scientific theory or discovery. Personal computers are possible because of the invention of the "chip." The chip is possible ultimately because of the work of scientists at Bell Laboratories who studied the electrical properties of crystals and, in the process, invented the transistor. The past century's rapid technological development has seen the time from scientific theory to invention to production compress, often to as short as a few weeks.

Since modern technologies and the problems they create are in fact modern, very few writings about technology have existed long enough to stand the test of time, which is often taken as one of the measures of a "classic" work. Those responsible for this series believe that most, if not all, of the works represented will still be read fifty years hence. This volume is organized in four sections.

The first section, entitled "In Praise of Science and Technology," articulates an enthusiastic optimism toward science and technology and their benefits for society. Taken from twentieth-century American authors, these writings are typical of an attitude that science and technology can solve all of the nation's (and by extension, the world's) problems. First, John Dewey poses an interesting argument for the relationship between science and democracy. Vannevar Bush argues that continued investment in and public support of science and technology are critical to the long term interests of the United States. The essay by Oppenheimer was originally delivered as one of a series of public lectures, invited by the British Broadcasting Company in the early fifties, to help a worried public understand the "new" physics which had created so many technological wonders and which had also created a new weapon of mass destruction. The selection from Max Lerner's brilliant *America as a Civilization* characterizes the growth and importance of technology in America, especially its impact on the workplace. Frederick Taylor applies principles taken from modern technology to improve the performance of factory workers.

Part II, "Visions of a Technological World," is comprised of selections taken from the world of fiction. Huxley, Wells, and Swift provide views of distopian societies, each based in some important way on science and technology. Huxley and Wells created worlds in which the machine has, in essence, taken over—a recurring theme in science fiction. The selection from *Brave New World* describes human cloning. The selection taken from *The Time Machine* treats the author's visit into the world of the distant future, where humans do not have to work and in which they have traded freedom for security. Swift satirizes the enlightenment view of science and technology. The selection from Mary Shelley's *Frankenstein* illustrates the attitude held by many scientists that certain things which are possible to do ought to be done because they are scientifically or technically "sweet." It also treats the unforeseen consequences of scientific and technological creation. Unfortunately, one cannot assume that today's students have even heard of these four novels. Most certainly have not read them. Steven Vincent Benét's sobering short story, "By the Waters of Babylon," also portrays a world which has been irrevocably changed by technology.

"Sounding the Alarm" provides philosophical discussions of the fears evidenced in Part II. Three selections taken from the work of Henry Adams address the driving force which created such wonders as Mont St Michel and Chartres and Adams' personal search for a new metaphor for the twentieth century—which he found in the dynamo. Herbert Muller, in a selection from *The Children of Frankenstein*, points out that new technologies not only create new opportunities, but also create new and often unforeseen ethical choices. Lewis Mumford argues that there are two different technologies which coexist, one which is powerful and controlling, the other weak and possibly controllable. Muller and Mumford not only worry that technology will always create unforeseen problems, but also that society may not be able to control technology and the problems it creates. Jacques Ellul is even more pessimistic, arguing that technology already controls man to the extent that nothing can be done to reverse the situation. Bertrand Russell explores the gains which science and technology have brought to humankind as well as the threats posed by that same science and technology.

Readings in the final section were chosen to illustrate an arbitrary selection of current technological issues. Although written in the middle of the 19th century, Florence Nightingale's appeal for more adequate public education in the science of health and application of that knowledge in the hospital and in the home illustrates an ongoing problem with scientific knowledge. Society continues to wrestle with the transmission of scientific understanding to the populace and with the use of practical scientific knowledge by the public, particularly in the fields of nutrition and health. James F. Childress, in "The Art of Technology Assessment," treats the difficult problem of determining the consequences of technologies before they are employed, with illustrations taken from his field of expertise, biomedical ethics. The "Reactor Safety Study," or "Rasmussen Report," as it is commonly known, is a relatively early attempt to apply risk-benefit analysis to nuclear energy, arguably the most hotly debated commercial technology of the century. Rachel Carson launched the modern environmental movement with the publication of *Silent Spring* in 1962. Her sobering account of the effects of pesticides in our environment, although controversial, nevertheless raised the sensitivity of the larger society to the effects of previously ignored pollutants on various ecosystems. In the selection from *The Abolition of Man*, C.S. Lewis struggled with the way the human attempt to conquer Nature has affected the very concept and definition of humanity. Annie Dillard's *Pilgrim at Tinker Creek* expresses a sense of awe and wonder in confronting the natural world. *The Biological Time Bomb*, published in 1968, forecast in a reasonably accurate fashion the subsequent development of modern biotechnologies. While Gordon Rattray Taylor marveled at the wonders of modern biology, he also noted the potential dangers its unbridled growth would create. No treatment of technology would be complete without some discussion of the impact of computers on modern society. Norbert Wiener, in a selection taken from *The Human Use of Human Beings*, defines the new science of cybernetics and discusses briefly the impact of the automatic machine on human work. A. M. Turing's definitive essay discusses the question of artificial intelligence and how one might determine whether or not a computer can "think."

Each of these readings illustrates aspects of the manner in which science and technology have altered society and the world in which society exists. We have become accustomed to new ideas and to new technologies accompanied by a frequency of change that would have been devastating to past societies. One corollary to the phenomenal success of science and technology has been our increasing tendency to assume that all problems can be solved by the methods of science and technology. Energy shortages, genetic engineering, the rise of computer-based technologies—all now cause doubt in some minds about the direction in which science and technology are taking us. Nevertheless, most assume that the answers to these and other problems lie within science and technology. If we run out of fossil fuels, scientists will invent a solution; if we pollute the oceans, science will find a way to clean them up. But more and more, scientists and engineers themselves realize that the solution to technological problems often lie outside the realm of science—in the realm of politics or in the world of moral choice. Perhaps the most significant issue in our lifetime will be the relationships among science, technology, and the larger society. Shall we be liberated by our technologies, or shall we be absorbed into a technological value system over which we have no control? Do we really have a choice?

Julius A. Sigler
Professor of Physics

The goal of life is living in agreement with nature.

Zeno, *Diogenes Laertius*

IN PRAISE OF SCIENCE AND TECHNOLOGY

John Dewey

Vannevar Bush

J. Robert Oppenheimer

Max Lerner

Frederick W. Taylor

It cannot be but that each generation succeeding to the knowledge acquired by all those who preceded it, adding to it their own acquisitions and discoveries, and handing the mass down for successive and constant accumulation, must advance the knowledge and well-being of mankind, not *infinitely*, as some have said, but *indefinitely*, and to a term which no one can fix and foresee. Indeed, we need look back half a century, to times which many now living remember well, and see the wonderful advances in the sciences and the arts which have been made within that period. Some of these have rendered the elements themselves subservient to the purposes of man, have harnessed them to the yoke of his labors, and effected the great blessings of moderating his own, of accomplishing what was beyond the feeble force, and extending the comforts of life to a much enlarged circle, to those who had before known its necessaries only.

Thomas Jefferson, *Report of the Rockfish Commissioners*, 1818

L'Avion est une machine sans doute, mais quel intstrument d'analyse! Cet instrument nous a fait découvrir le vrai visage de la terre . . . Nous voilà donc changés en physiciens, en biologistes, examinant ces civilisations qui ornent des fonds de vallées . . .Nous violà donc jugeant l'homme a l'échelle cosmique, l'ovservant a travers nos hublots, comme à travers des instruments d'étude. Nous voilà relisant notre histoire. The airplane is, without doubt, only a machine, but what an instrument of analysis! This instrument has made us see the real face of the earth. . . Up here we are changed into physicists, or biologists, examining the civilizations which garnish the depths of the valleys. . . .Up here we are judging man on a cosmic scale, observing him through our portholes, as through instruments of study. We are re-reading our own history.

Antoine de Saint-Exupéry, *Oevres d'Antoine de Saint-Exupéry*, 1953

The scientist was no longer thought of as a man in an ivory tower, gradually unraveling the secrets of nature for his own satisfaction, but as a miracle-worker who like Watt or Edison before him could bring about tremendous transformations of man's relation to his material surroundings.

James B. Conant, *Modern Science and Modern Man*, 1952

The real accomplishment of modern science and technology consists in taking ordinary men, informing them narrowly and deeply and then, through appropriate organization, arranging to have their knowledge combined with that or other specialized but equally ordinary men. This dispenses with the need for genius. The resulting performance, though less inspiring, is far more predictable.

John Kenneth Galbraith, *The New Industrial State*, 1967

Where there is the necessary technical skill to move mountains, there is no need for the faith that moves mountains.

Eric Hoffer, *The Passionate State of Mind*, 1955

THE DEMOCRATIC FAITH
AND EDUCATION

JOHN DEWEY

John Dewey (1859-1952) was the preeminent educational theorist of the twentieth century and a leading philosopher of pragmatism. He was a graduate of the University of Vermont and received the Ph.D. from The Johns Hopkins University. After teaching at the University of Minnesota and the University of Michigan, he served for ten years as head of the Department of Philosophy and Pedagogy at the University of Chicago. From 1904 until his retirement in 1930, he was professor of philosophy at Columbia University.

In "The Democratic Faith and Education" which first appeared in the *Antioch Review* for July 1944, his chief concern is how science and technology relate to democracy.

1. What four articles of faith does Dewey see as being "tragically frustrated" by the period of the 1940's?

2. Why have not the revolutions in science and technology brought all the benefits expected?

3. How does Dewey characterize science and technology?

4. What would Dewey do to correct the "state of imbalance . . . between our physical knowledge and our social-moral knowledge"? How would he deal with the unfortunate consequences of rapid developments in science and technology?

5. Can "scientific methods" be effective in creating understanding of human relationships and in developing plans and policies to minimize the problems created by science and technology?

6. What does Dewey think of the place of science and technology in the schools and the manner in which they are taught?

7. What is the relationship between democracy and science and technology?

THE DEMOCRATIC FAITH
AND EDUCATION

JOHN DEWEY

Not even the most far-seeing of men could have predicted, no longer ago than fifty years, the course events have taken. The expectations that were entertained by men of generous outlooks are in fact chiefly notable in that the actual course of events has moved, and with violence, in the opposite direction. The ardent and hopeful social idealist of the last century or so has been proved so wrong that a reaction to the opposite extreme has taken place. A recent writer has even proposed a confraternity of pessimists who should live together in some sort of social oasis. It is a fairly easy matter to list the articles of that old faith which, from the standpoint of today, have been tragically frustrated.

The first article on the list had to do with the prospects of the abolition of war. It was held that the revolution which was taking place in commerce and communication would break down the barriers which had kept the peoples of the earth alien and hostile and would create a state of interdependence which in time would insure lasting peace. Only an extreme pessimist ventured to suggest that interdependence might multiply points of friction and conflict.

Another item of that creed was the belief that a general development of enlightenment and rationality was bound to follow the increase in knowledge and the diffusion which would result from the revolution in science that was taking place. Since it had long been held that rationality and freedom were intimately allied, it was held that the movement toward democratic institutions and popular government which had produced in succession the British, American and French Revolutions was bound to spread until freedom and equality were the foundations of political government in every country of the globe.

A time of general ignorance and popular unenlightenment and a time of despotic and oppressive governmental rule were taken to be practically synonymous. Hence the third article of faith. There was a general belief among social philosophers that governmental activities were necessarily more or less oppressive; that governmental action tended to be an artificial interference with the operation of natural laws. Consequently the spread of enlightenment and democratic institutions would produce a gradual but assured withering away of the powers of the political state. Freedom was supposed to be so deeply rooted in the very nature of men that, given the spread of rational enlightenment, it would take care of itself with only a minimum of political action confined to insuring external police order.

The other article of faith to be mentioned was the general belief that the vast, the almost incalculable, increase in productivity resulting from the industrial revolution was bound to raise the general standard of living to a point where extreme poverty would be practically eliminated. It was believed that the opportunity to lead a decent, self-respecting, because self-sufficient, economic life would be assured to everyone who was physically and morally normal.

The course of events culminating in the present situation suffices to show without any elaborate argument how grievously these generous expectations have been disappointed. Instead of universal peace, there occurred two wars worldwide in extent and destructive beyond anything known in all history.

Instead of uniform and steady growth of democratic freedom and equality, we have seen the rise of powerful totalitarian states with thoroughgoing suppression of liberty of belief and expression, outdoing the most despotic states of previous history. We have an actual growth in importance and range of governmental action in legislation and administration as necessary means of rendering freedom on the part of the many an assured actual fact. Instead of promotion of economic security and movement toward the elimination of poverty, we now have a great increase in the extent and the intensity of industrial crises with great increase of inability of workers to find employment. Social instability has reached a point that may portend revolution if it goes on unchecked.

Externally it looks as if the pessimists had the best of the case. But before we reach a conclusion on that point, we have to inquire concerning the solidity of the premise upon which the idealistic optimists rested their case. This principle was that the more desirable goals in view were to be accomplished by a complex of forces to which in their entirety the name "Nature" was given. In practical effect, acceptance of this principle was equivalent to adoption of a policy of drift as far as human intelligence and effort were concerned. No conclusion is warranted until we have inquired how far failure and frustration are consequences of putting our trust in a policy of drift, a policy of letting "George" in the shape of Nature and Natural Law do the work which only human intelligence and effort could possibly accomplish. No conclusion can be reached until we have considered an alternative: What is likely to happen if we recognize that the responsibility for creating a state of peace internationally, and of freedom and economic security internally, has to be carried by deliberate cooperative human effort? Technically speaking the policy known as *laissez-faire* is one of limited application. But its limited and technical significance is one instance of a manifestation of widespread trust in the ability of impersonal forces, popularly called Nature, to do a work that has to be done by human insight, foresight, and purposeful planning.

Not all the men of the earlier period were of the idealistic type. The idealistic philosophy was a positive factor in permitting those who prided themselves upon being realistic to turn events so as to produce consequences dictated by their own private and class advantage. The failure of cooperative and collective intelligence and effort to intervene was an invitation to immediate short-term intervention by those who had an eye to their own profit. The consequences were wholesale destruction and waste of natural resources, increase of social instability, and mortgaging of the future to a transitory and brief present of so-called prosperity. If "idealists" were misguided in what they failed to do, "realists" were wrong in what they did. If the former erred in supposing that the drift (called by them progress or evolution) was inevitably toward the better, the latter were more actively harmful because their insistence upon trusting to natural laws was definitely in the interest of personal and class profit.

The omitted premise in the case of both groups is the fact that neither science nor technology is an impersonal cosmic force. They operate only in the medium of human desire, foresight, aim, and effort. Science and technology are transactions in which man and nature work together and in which the human factor is that directly open to modification and direction. That man takes part along with physical conditions in invention and use of the devices, implements, and machinery of industry and commerce, no one would think of denying.

But in practice, if not in so many words, it has been denied that man has any responsibility for the consequences that result from what he invents and employs. This denial is implicit in our widespread refusal to engage in large-scale collective planning. Not a day passes, even in the present crisis, when the whole idea of such planning is not ridiculed as an emanation from the brain of starry-eyed professors or of others equally inept in practical affairs. And all of this in the face of the fact that there is not a successful industrial organization that does not owe its success to persistent planning within a limited field—with an eye to profit—to say nothing of the terribly high price we have paid in the way of insecurity and war for putting our trust in drift.

Refusal to accept responsibility for looking ahead and for planning in matters national and international is based upon refusal to employ in social affairs, in the field of human relations, the methods of observation, interpretation, and test that are matters of course in dealing with physical things, and to which we owe the conquest of physical nature. The net result is a state of imbalance, of profoundly disturbed equilibrium between our physical knowledge and our social-moral knowledge. This lack of harmony is a powerful factor in producing the present crisis with all its tragic features. For physical knowledge and physical technology have far outstripped social or humane knowledge and human engineering. Our failure to use in matters of direct human concern the scientific methods which have revolutionized physical knowledge has permitted the latter to dominate the social scene.

The change in the physical aspect of the world has gone on so rapidly that there is probably no ground for surprise in the fact that our psychological and moral knowledge has not kept pace. But there is cause for astonishment in the fact that, after the catastrophe of war, insecurity, and the threat to democratic institutions have shown the need for moral and intellectual attitudes and habits which will correspond with the changed state of the world, there should be a definite campaign to make the scientific attitude the scapegoat for present evils, while a return to the beliefs and practices of a prescientific and pretechnological age is urged as the road to our salvation.

The organized attack made from time to time against science and against technology as inherently materialistic and as usurping the place properly held by abstract moral precepts—abstract because divorcing ends from the means by which they must be realized—defines the issue we now have to face. Shall we go backwards or shall we go ahead to discover and put into practice the means by which science and technology shall be made fundamental in the promotion of human welfare? The failure to use scientific methods in creating understanding of human relationships and interests and in planning measures and policies that correspond in human affairs to the technologies in physical use is easily explained in historical terms. The new science began with things at the furthest remove from human affairs, namely with the stars of the heavens. From astronomy the new methods went on to win their victories in physics and chemistry. Still later science was applied in physiological and biological subject-matter. At every state, the advance met determined resistance from the representatives of established institutions who felt their prestige was bound up with maintenance of old beliefs and found their class control of others being threatened. In consequence, many workers in science found that the easiest way in which to procure an opportunity to carry on their inquiries was to adopt an attitude of extreme specialization. The effect was equivalent to the position that their methods and conclusions were not and could not be "dangerous," since they had no point of contact with man's serious moral concerns. This position in turn served to perpetuate and confirm the older separation of man as man from the rest of nature and to intensify the split between the "material" and the moral and "ideal."

Thus it has come about that when scientific inquiry began to move from its virtually complete victories in astronomy and physics and its partial victory in the field of living things over into the field of human affairs and concerns, the interests and institutions which offered resistance to its earlier advance gathered themselves together for a final attack upon that aspect of science which in truth constitutes its supreme and culminating significance. On the principle that offense is the best defense, respect for science and loyalty to its outlook are attacked as the chief source of all our present social ills. One may read, for example, in current literature such a condescending concession as marks the following passage: "Of course, the scientific attitude, though often leading to such a catastrophe, is not to be condemned," the immediate context showing that the particular "catastrophe" in mind consists of "errors leading to war . . . derived from an incorrect theory of truth." Since these errors are produced by belief in the applicability of scientific method to human as well as physical facts, the remedy, according to this writer, is to abandon "the erroneous application of the methods and results of natural science to the problems of human life."

In three respects the passage is typical of such organized campaigns in active operation. There is first the assertion that such catastrophes as that of the recent war are the result of devotion to scientific method and conclusions. The denunciation of "natural" science as applied to human affairs carries, in the second place, the implication that man is outside of and above nature, and the consequent necessity of returning to the medieval prescientific doctrine of a supernatural foundation and outlook in all social and moral subjects. Then thirdly there is the assumption, directly contrary to fact, that the scientific method has at the present time been seriously and systematically applied to the problems of human life.

I dignify the passage quoted by this reference to it because it serves quite as well as a multitude of other passages from reactionaries to convey a sense of the present issues. It is true that the *results* of a natural science have had a large share, for evil as well as for good, in bringing the world to its present pass. But it is equally true that "natural" science has been identified with *physical* science in a sense in which the physical is set over against the human. It is true that the interests and institutions which are now attacking science are just the forces which in behalf of a supernatural center of gravity are those that strive to maintain this tragic split in human affairs. Now the issue, as is becoming clearer every day, is whether we shall go backward or whether we shall go forward toward recognition in theory and practice of the indissoluble unity of the humanistic and the naturalistic.

What has all this to do with education? The answer to this question may be gathered from the fact that those who are engaged in assault upon science center their attacks upon the increased attention given by our schools to science and to its application in vocational training. In a world which is largely what it is today because of science and technology they propose that education should turn its back upon even the degree of recognition science and technology have received. They propose we turn our face to the medievalism in which so-called "liberal" arts were identified with literary arts: a course natural to adopt in an age innocent of knowledge of nature, an age in which the literary arts were the readiest means of rising above barbarism through acquaintance with the achievements of Greek-Roman culture. Their proposal is so remote from the facts of the present world, it involves such a bland ignoring of actualities, that there is a temptation to dismiss it as idle vaporing. But it would be a tragic mistake to take the reactionary assaults so lightly. For they are an expression of just the forces that keep science penned up in a compartment labelled "materialistic and anti-human." They strengthen all the habits and institutions which render that which is morally "ideal" impotent in action and which leave the "material" to operate without humane direction.

Let me return for the moment to my initial statement that the basic error of social idealists was the assumption that something called "natural law" could be trusted, with only incidental cooperation by human beings, to bring about the desired ends. The lesson to be learned is that human attitudes and efforts are the strategic center for promotion of the generous aims of peace among nations; promotion of economic security; the use of political means in order to advance freedom and equality; and the worldwide cause of democratic institutions. Anyone who starts from this premise is bound to see that it carries with it the basic importance of education in creating the habits and the outlook that are able and eager to secure the ends of peace, democracy, and economic stability.

When this is seen, it will also be seen how little has actually been done in our schools to render science and technology active agencies in creating the attitudes and dispositions and in securing the kinds of knowledge that are capable of coping with the problems of men and women today. Externally a great modification has taken place in subjects taught and in methods of teaching them. But when the changes are critically examined it is found that they consist largely in emergency concessions and accommodation to the urgent conditions and issues of the contemporary world. The standards and the controlling methods in education are still mainly those of a prescientific and pretechnological age.

This statement will seem to many persons to be exaggerated. But consider the purposes which as a rule still govern instruction in just those subjects that are taken to be decisively "modern," namely science and vocational preparation. Science is taught upon the whole as a body of ready-made information and technical skills. It is not taught as furnishing in its method the pattern for all effective intelligent conduct. It is taught upon the whole not with respect to the way in which it actually enters into human life, and hence as a supremely humanistic subject, but as if it had to do with a world which is "external" to human concerns. It is not presented in connection with the ways in which it actually enters into every aspect and phase of present human life. And it is hardly necessary to add that still less is it taught in connection with what scientific knowledge of human affairs might do in overcoming sheer drift. Scientific method and conclusions will not have gained a fundamentally important place in education until they are seen and treated as supreme agencies in giving direction to collective and cooperative human behavior.

The same sort of thing is to be said about the kind of use now made in education of practical and vocational subjects so called. The reactionary critics are busy urging that the latter subjects be taught to the masses—who are said to be incapable of rising to the plane of the "intellectual" but who do the useful work which somebody has to do, and who may be taught by vocational education to do it more effectively. This view is of course an open and avowed attempt to return to that dualistic separation of ideas and action, of the "intellectual" and the "practical," of the liberal and servile arts, that marked the feudal age. And this reactionary move in perpetuation of the split from which the world is suffering is offered as a cure, a panacea, not a the social and moral quackery it actually is. As is the case with science, the thing supremely needful is to go forward. And the forward movement in the case of technology as in the case of science is to do away with the chasm which ancient and medieval educational practice and theory set up between the liberal and the vocational, not to treat the void, the hole, constituted by this chasm, as if it were a foundation for the creation of free society.

There is nothing whatever inherent in the occupations that are socially necessary and useful to divide them into those which are "learned" professions and those which are menial, servile, and illiberal. As far as such a separation exists in fact it is an inheritance from the earlier class structure of human relations. It is a denial of democracy. At the very time when an important, perhaps *the* important, problem in education is to fill education having an occupational direction with a genuinely liberal content, we have, believe it or not, a movement, such as is sponsored for example by President Hutchins, to cut vocational training off from any contact with what is liberating by relegating it to special schools devoted to inculcation of technical skills. Inspiring vocational education with a liberal spirit and filling it with a liberal content is not a utopian dream. It is a demonstrated possibility in schools here and there in which subjects usually labelled "practically useful" are taught charged with scientific understanding and with a sense of the social-moral applications they potentially possess.

If little is said in the foregoing remarks specifically upon the topic of democratic faith, it is because their bearing upon a democratic outlook largely appears upon their very face. Conditions in this country when the democratic philosophy of life and democratic institutions were taking shape were such as to encourage a belief that the latter were so natural to man, so appropriate to his very being, that if they were once established they would tend to maintain themselves. I cannot rehearse here the list of events that have given this naive faith a shock. They are contained in every deliberate attack upon democracy and in every expression of cynicism about its past failures and pessimism about its future—attacks and expressions which have to be taken seriously if they are looked at as signs of trying to establish democracy as an end in separation from the concrete means upon which the end depends.

Democracy is not an easy road to take and follow. On the contrary, it is, as far as its realization is concerned in the complex conditions of the contemporary world, a supremely difficult one. Upon the whole we are entitled to take courage from the fact that it has worked as well as it has done. But to this courage we must add, if our courage is to be intelligent rather than blind, the fact that successful maintenance of democracy demands the utmost in use of the best available methods to procure a social knowledge that is reasonably commensurate with our physical knowledge, and the invention and use of forms of social engineering reasonably commensurate with our technological abilities in physical affairs.

This then is the task indicated. It is, if we employ large terms, to humanize science. This task in the concrete cannot be accomplished save as the fruit of science, which is named technology, is also humanized. And the task can be executed in the concrete only as it is broken up into vital applications of intelligence in a multitude of fields to a vast diversity of problems so that science and technology may be rendered servants of the democratic hope and faith. The cause is capable of inspiring loyalty in thought and deed. But there has to be joined to aspiration and effort the formation of free, wide-ranging, trained attitudes of observation and understanding such as incorporate within themselves, as a matter so habitual as to be unconscious, the vital principles of scientific method. In this achievement science, education, and the democratic cause meet as one. May we be equal to the occasion, for it is our human problem. If a solution is found it will be through the medium of human desire, human understanding, and human endeavor.

SCIENCE: THE ENDLESS FRONTIER

VANNEVAR BUSH

Vannevar Bush (1890-1974), an electrical engineer, became the first director of the Office of Scientific Research and Development during World War II. In this position, he was responsible for mobilizing and coordinating the scientific aspects of the United States' war effort, a task that included the development of radar and the atomic bomb. After the war, as the excerpt from *Science - The Endless Frontier: A Report to the President,* demonstrates, he helped provide the impetus for the federal government's encouragement of science and basic research, thus launching what has become known as "big science."

1. Why did Bush feel that it is necessary for government to support major projects of scientific research?

2. What advantages accrue to society generally from scientific research?

3. How does scientific research help or hurt the basic economy according to Bush?

SCIENCE: THE ENDLESS FRONTIER

VANNEVAR BUSH

Science can be effective in the national welfare only as a member of a team, whether the conditions be peace or war. But without scientific progress no amount of achievement in other directions can insure our health, prosperity, and security as a nation in the modern world.

For The War Against Disease

We have taken great strides in the war against disease. The death rate for all diseases in the Army. including overseas forces, has been reduced from 14.1 per thousand in the last war to 0.6 per thousand in this war. In the last 40 years life expectancy has increased from 49 to 65 years, largely as a consequence of the reduction in the death rates of infants and children. But we are far from the goal. The annual deaths from one or two diseases far exceed the total number of American lives lost in battle during this war. A large fraction of these deaths in our civilian population cut short the useful lives of our citizens. Approximately 7,000,000 persons in the United States are mentally ill and their care costs the public over $175,000,000 a year. Clearly much illness remains for which adequate means of prevention and cure are not yet known.

The responsibility for basic research in medicine and the underlying sciences, so essential to progress in the war against disease, falls primarily upon the medical schools and universities. Yet we find that the traditional sources of support for medical research in the medical schools and universities, largely endowment income, foundation grants, and private donations are diminishing and there is no immediate prospect of a change in this trend. Meanwhile, the cost of medical research has been rising. If we are to maintain the progress in medicine which has marked the last 25 years, the Government should extend financial support to basic medical research in the medical schools and in universities.

For Our National Security

The bitter and dangerous battle against the U-boat was a battle of scientific techniques—and our margin of success was dangerously small. The new eyes which radar has supplied can sometimes be blinded by new scientific developments. V-2 was countered only by capture of the launching sites.

We cannot again rely on our allies to hold off the enemy while we struggle to catch up. There must be more—and more adequate—military research in peacetime. It is essential that the civilian scientists continue in peacetime some portion of those contributions to national security which they have made so effectively during the war. This can best be done through a civilian-controlled organization with close liaison with the Army and Navy, but with funds direct from Congress, and the clear power to initiate military research which will supplement and strengthen that carried on directly under the control of the Army and Navy.

And for the Public Welfare
One of our hopes is that after the war there will be full employment. To reach that goal the full creative and productive energies of the American people must be released. To create more jobs we must make new and better and cheaper products. We want plenty of new, vigorous enterprises. But new products and processes are not born full-grown. They are founded on new principles and new conceptions which in turn result from basic scientific research. Basic scientific research is scientific capital. Moreover, we cannot any longer depend upon Europe as a major source of this scientific capital. Clearly, more and better scientific research is one essential to the achievement of our goal of full employment.

How do we increase this scientific capital? First, we must have plenty of men and women trained in science, for upon them depends both the creation of new knowledge and its application to practical purposes. Second, we must strengthen the centers of basic research which are principally the colleges, universities, and research institutes. These institutions provide the environment which is most conducive to the creation of new scientific knowledge and least under pressure for immediate, tangible results. With some notable exceptions, most research in industry and in Government involves application of existing scientific knowledge to practical problems. It is only the colleges, universities, and a few research institutes that devote most of their research efforts to expanding the frontiers of knowledge.

Expenditures for scientific research by industry and Government increased from $140,000,000 in 1930 to $309,000,000 in 1940. Those for the colleges and universities increased from $20,000,000 to $31,000.000, while those for research institutes declined from $5,200,000 to $4,500,000 during the same period. If the colleges, universities, and research institutes are to meet the rapidly increasing demands of industry and Government for new scientific knowledge, their basic research should be strengthened by use of public funds.

For science to serve as a powerful factor in our national welfare, applied research both in Government and in industry must be vigorous. To improve the quality of scientific research within the Government, steps should be taken to modify the procedures for recruiting, classifying, and compensating scientific personnel in order to reduce the present handicap of governmental scientific bureaus in competing with industry and the universities for top-grade scientific talent. To provide coordination of the common scientific activities of these governmental agencies as to policies and budgets, a permanent Science Advisory Board should be created to advise the executive and legislative branches of Government on these matters.

The most important ways in which the Government can promote industrial research are to increase the flow of new scientific knowledge through support of basic research, and to aid in the development of scientific talent. In addition, the Government should provide suitable incentives to industry to conduct research (a) by clarification of present uncertainties in the Internal Revenue Code in regard to the deductibility of research and development expenditures as current charges against net income, and (b) by strengthening the patent system so as to eliminate uncertainties which now bear heavily on small industries and so as to prevent abuses which reflect discredit upon a basically sound system.

In addition, ways should be found to cause the benefits of basic research to reach industries which do not now utilize new scientific knowledge.

We Must Renew Our Scientific Talent

The responsibility for the creation of new scientific knowledge—and for most of its application—rests on that small body of men and women who understand the fundamental laws of nature and are skilled in the techniques of scientific research. We shall have rapid or slow advance on any scientific frontier depending on the number of highly qualified and trained scientists exploring it.

The deficit of science and technology students who, but for the war, would have received bachelor's degrees is about 150,000. It is estimated that the deficit of those obtaining advanced degrees in these fields will amount in 1955 to about 17,000—for it takes at least 6 years from college entry to achieve a doctor's degree or its equivalent in science or engineering. The real ceiling on our productivity of new scientific knowledge and its application in the war against disease, and the development of new products and new industries, is the number of trained scientists available.

The training of a scientist is a long and expensive process. Studies clearly show that there are talented individuals in every part of the population, but with few exceptions, those without the means of buying higher education go without it. If ability, and not the circumstance of family fortune, determines who shall receive higher education in science, then we shall be assured of constantly improving quality at every level of scientific activity. The Government should provide a reasonable number of undergraduate scholarships and graduate fellowships in order to develop scientific talent in American youth. The plans should be designed to attract into science only that proportion of youthful talent appropriate to the needs of science in relation to the other needs of the Nation for high abilities.

Including Those in Uniform

The most immediate prospect of making up the deficit in scientific personnel is to develop the scientific talent in the generation now in uniform. Even if we should start now to train the current crop of high-school graduates none would complete graduate studies before 1951. The Armed Services should comb their records for men who, prior to or during the war, have given evidence of talent for science. and make prompt arrangements, consistent with current discharge plans, for ordering those who remain in uniform, as soon as militarily possible, to duty at institutions here and overseas where they can continue their scientific education. Moreover, the Services should see that those who study overseas have the benefit of the latest scientific information resulting from research during the war.

The Lid Must Be Lifted

While most of the war research has involved the application of existing scientific knowledge to the problems of war, rather than basic research, there has been accumulated a vast amount of information relating to the application of science to particular problems. Much of this can be used by industry. It is also needed for teaching in the colleges and universities here and in the Armed Forces Institutes overseas. Some of this information must remain secret, but most of it should be made public as soon as there is ground for belief that the enemy will not be able to turn it against us in this war. To select that portion which should be made public, to coordinate its release, and definitely to encourage its publication. a Board composed of Army, Navy, and civilian scientific members should be promptly established.

A Program for Action

The Government should accept new responsibilities for promoting the flow of new scientific knowledge and the development of scientific talent in our youth. These responsibilities are the proper concern of the Government, for they vitally affect our health, our jobs, and our national security. It is in keeping also with basic United States policy that the Government should foster the opening of new frontiers and this is the modern way to do it. For many years the Government has wisely supported research in the agricultural colleges and the benefits have been great. The time has come when such support should be extended to other fields.

The effective discharge of these new responsibilities will require the full attention of some over-all agency devoted to that purpose. There is not now in the permanent governmental structure receiving its funds from Congress an agency adapted to supplementing the support of basic research in the colleges, universities, and research institutes, both in medicine and the natural sciences, adapted to supporting research on new weapons for both Services, or adapted to administering a program of science scholarships and fellowships.

Therefore I recommend that a new agency for these purposes be established. Such an agency should be composed of persons of broad interest and experience, having an understanding of the peculiarities of scientific research and scientific education. It should have stability of funds so that long-range programs may be undertaken. It should recognize that freedom of inquiry must be preserved and should leave internal control of policy, personnel and the method and scope of research to the institutions in which it is carried on. It should be fully responsible to the President and through him to the Congress for its program.

Early action on these recommendations is imperative if this Nation is to meet the challenge of science in the crucial years ahead. On the wisdom with which we bring science to bear in the war against disease, in the creation of new industries. and in the strengthening of our Armed Forces depends in large measure our future as a nation.

Scientific Progress Is Essential

We all know how much the new drug, penicillin, has meant to our grievously wounded men on the grim battlefronts of this war—the countless lives it has saved—the incalculable suffering which its use has prevented. Science and the great practical genius of this Nation made this achievement possible.

Some of us know the vital role which radar has played in bringing the Allied Nations to victory over Nazi Germany and in driving the Japanese steadily back from their island bastions. Again it was painstaking scientific research over many years that made radar possible.

What we often forget are the millions of pay envelopes on a peacetime Saturday night which are filled because new products and new industries have provided jobs for countless Americans. Science made that possible, too.

In 1939 millions of people were employed in industries which did not even exist at the close of the last war—radio, air conditioning, rayon and other synthetic fibers, and plastics are examples of the products of these industries. But these things do not mark the end of progress—they are but the beginning if we make full use of our scientific resources. New manufacturing industries can be started and many older industries greatly strengthened and expanded if we continue to study nature's laws and apply new knowledge to practical purposes.

Great advances in agriculture are also based upon scientific research. Plants which are more resistant to disease and are adapted to short growing seasons, the prevention and cure of livestock diseases, the control of our insect enemies, better fertilizers, and improved agricultural practices, all stem from painstaking scientific research.

Advances in science when put to practical use mean more jobs, higher wages, shorter hours, more abundant crops, more leisure for recreation, for study, for learning how to live without the deadening drudgery which has been the burden of the common man for ages past. Advances in science will also bring higher standards of living, will lead to the prevention or cure of diseases, will promote conservation of our limited national resources, and will assure means of defense against aggression. But to achieve these objectives—to secure a high level of employment, to maintain a position of world leadership, the flow of new scientific knowledge must be both continuous and substantial.

Our population increased from 75 million to 130 million between 1900 and 1940. In some countries comparable increases have been accompanied by famine. In this country, the increase has been accompanied by more abundant food supply, better living. more leisure, longer life, and better health. This is, largely, the product of three factors—the free play of initiative of a vigorous people under democracy, the heritage of great national wealth, and the advance of science and its application.

Science, by itself, provides no panacea for individual, social, and economic ills. It can be effective in the national welfare only as a member of a team. Whether the conditions be peace or war. But without scientific progress no amount of achievement in other directions can insure our health, prosperity, and security as a nation in the modern world.

Science Is a Proper Concern of Government

It has been basic United States policy that Government should foster the opening of new frontiers. It opened the seas to clipper ships and furnished land for pioneers. Although these frontiers have more or less disappeared, the frontier of science remains. It is in keeping with the American tradition —one which has made the United States great—that new frontiers shall be made accessible for development by all American citizens.

Moreover, since health, well-being, and security are proper concerns of Government, scientific progress is, and must be, of vital interest to Government. Without scientific progress the national health would deteriorate: without scientific progress we could not hope for improvement in our standard of living or for an increased number of jobs for our citizens; and without scientific progress we could not have maintained our liberties against tyranny.

Government Relations to Science—Past and Future

From early days the Government has taken an active interest in scientific matters. During the nineteenth century the Coast and Geodetic Survey,. the Naval Observatory, the Department of Agriculture, and the Geological Survey were established. Through the Land Grant College Acts the Government has supported research in state institutions for more than 80 years on I gradually increasing scale. Since 1900 a large number of scientific agencies have been established within the Federal Government, until in 1939 they numbered more than 40.

Much of the scientific research done by Government agencies is intermediate in character between the two types of work commonly referred to as basic and applied research. Almost all Government scientific work has ultimate practical objectives but, in many fields of broad national concern, it commonly involves long-term investigation of a fundamental nature. Generally speaking, the scientific agencies of Government are not so concerned with immediate practical objectives as are the laboratories of industry nor, on the other hand, are they as free to explore any natural phenomena without regard to possible economic applications as are the educational and private research institutions. Government scientific agencies have splendid records of achievement, but they are limited in function.

We have no national policy for science. The Government has only begun to utilize science in the nation's welfare. There is no body within the Government charged with formulating or executing a national science policy. There are no standing committees of the Congress devoted to this important subject. Science has been in the wings. It should be brought to the center of the stage—for in it lies much of our hope for the future.

There are areas of science in which the public interest is acute but which are likely to be cultivated inadequately if left without more support than will come from private sources. These areas—such as research on military problems, agriculture, housing, public health, certain medical research, and research involving expensive capital facilities beyond the capacity of private institutions—should be advanced by active Government support. To date, with the exception of the intensive war research conducted by the Office of Scientific Research and Development, such support has been meager and intermittent.

For reasons presented in this report we are entering a period when science needs and deserves increased support from public funds.

Freedom of Inquiry Must Be Preserved

The publicly and privately supported colleges, universities, and research institutes are the centers of basic research. They are the wellsprings of knowledge and understanding. As long as they are vigorous and healthy and their scientists are free to pursue the truth wherever it may lead, there will be a flow of new scientific knowledge to those who can apply it to practical problems in Government, in industry, or elsewhere.

Many of the lessons learned in the war-time application of science under Government can be profitably applied in peace. The Government is peculiarly fitted to perform certain functions, such as the coordination and support of broad programs on problems of great national importance. But we must proceed with caution in carrying over the methods which work in wartime to the very different conditions of peace. We must remove the rigid controls which we have had to impose, and recover freedom of inquiry and that healthy competitive scientific spirit so necessary for expansion of the frontiers of scientific knowledge.

Scientific progress on a broad front results from the free play of free intellects, working on subjects of their own choice, in the manner dictated by their curiosity for exploration of the unknown. Freedom of inquiry must be preserved under any plan for Government support of science.

* * * * *

SCIENCE AND THE PUBLIC WELFARE

Relation to National Security

In this war it has become clear beyond all doubt that scientific research is absolutely essential to national security. The bitter and dangerous battle against the U-boat was a battle of scientific techniques—and our margin of success was dangerously small. The new eyes which radar supplied to our fighting forces quickly evoked the development of scientific countermeasures which could often blind them. This again represents the ever continuing battle of techniques. The V-1 attack on London was finally defeated by three devices developed during this war and used superbly in the field. V-2 was countered only by capture of the launching sites.

The Secretaries of War and Navy recently stated in a joint letter to the National Academy of Sciences:

This war emphasizes three facts of supreme importance to national security: (1) Powerful new tactics of defense and offense are developed around new weapons created by scientific and engineering research: (2) the competitive time element in developing those weapons and tactics may be decisive; (3) war is increasingly total war, in which the armed services must be supplemented by active participation of every element of civilian population. To insure continued preparedness along farsighted technical lines, the research scientists of the country must be called upon to continue in peacetime some substantial portion of those types of contribution to national security which they have made so effectively during the stress of the present war.

There must be more—and more adequate—military research during peacetime. We cannot again rely on our allies to hold off the enemy while we struggle to catch up. Further, it is clear that only the Government can undertake military research; for it must be carried on in secret, much of it has no commercial value, and it is expensive. The obligation of Government to support research on military problems is inescapable.

Modern war requires the use of the most advanced scientific techniques. Many of the leaders in the development of radar are scientists who before the war had been exploring the nucleus of the atom. While there must be increased emphasis on science in the future training of officers for both the Army and

Navy, such men cannot be expected to be specialists in scientific research. Therefore, a professional partnership between the officers in the Services and civilian scientists is needed.

The Army and Navy should continue to carry on research and development on the improvement of current weapons. For many years the National Advisory Committee for Aeronautics has supplemented the work of the Army and Navy by conducting basic research on the problems of flight. There should now be permanent civilian activity to supplement the research work of the Services in other scientific fields so as to carry out in time of peace some part of the activities of the emergency wartime Office of Scientific Research and Development.

Military preparedness requires a permanent independent, civilian-controlled organization, having close liaison with the Army and Navy, but with funds directly from Congress and with the clear power to initiate military research which will supplement and strengthen that carried on directly under the control of the Army and Navy.

Science and Jobs

One of our hopes is that after the war there will be full employment, and that the production of goods and services will serve to raise our standard of living. We do not know yet how we shall reach that goal, but it is certain that it can be achieved only by releasing the full creative and productive energies of the American people.

Surely we will not get there by standing still, merely by making the same things we made before and selling them at the same or higher prices. We will not get ahead in international trade unless we offer new and more attractive and cheaper products.

Where will these new products come from? How will we find ways to make better products at lower cost? The answer is clear. There must be a stream of new scientific knowledge to turn the wheels of private and public enterprise. There must be plenty of men and women trained in science and technology for upon them depend both the creation of new knowledge and its application to practical purposes.

More and better scientific research is essential to the achievement of our goal of full employment.

The Importance of Basic Research

Basic research is performed without thought of practical ends. It results in general knowledge and an understanding of nature and its laws. This general knowledge provides the means of answering a large number of important practical problems, though it may not give a complete specific answer to any one of them. The function of applied research is to provide such complete answers. The scientist doing basic research may not be at all interested in the practical applications of his work, yet the further progress of industrial development would eventually stagnate if basic scientific research were long neglected.

One of the peculiarities of basic science is the variety of paths which lead to productive advance. Many of the most important discoveries have come as a result of experiments undertaken with very different purposes in mind. Statistically, it is certain that important and highly useful discoveries will result from some fraction of the undertakings in basic science; but the results of one particular investigation cannot be predicted with accuracy.

Basic research leads to new knowledge. It provides scientific capital. It creates the fund from which the practical applications of knowledge must be drawn. New products and new processes do not appear full-grown. They are founded on new principles and new conceptions, which in turn are painstakingly developed by research in the purest realms of science.

Today, it is truer than ever that basic research is the pacemaker of technological progress. In the nineteenth century, Yankee mechanical ingenuity, building largely upon the basic discoveries of European scientists, could greatly advance the technical arts. Now the situation is different.

A nation which depends upon others for its new basic scientific knowledge Will be slow in its industrial progress and weak in its competitive position in world trade regardless of its mechanical skill.

Centers of Basic Research

Publicly and privately supported colleges and universities and the endowed research institutes must furnish both the new scientific knowledge and the trained research workers. These institutions are uniquely qualified by tradition and by their special characteristics to carry on basic research. They are charged with the responsibility of conserving the knowledge accumulated by the past, imparting that knowledge to students, and contributing new knowledge of all kinds. It is chiefly in these institutions that scientists may work in an atmosphere which is relatively free from the adverse pressure of contention, prejudice, or commercial necessity. At their best they provide the scientific worker with a strong sense of solidarity and security, as well as a substantial degree of personal intellectual freedom. All of these factors are of great importance in the development of new knowledge, since much of new knowledge is certain to arouse opposition because of its tendency to challenge current beliefs or practice.

Industry is generally inhibited by preconceived goals, by its own clearly defined standards, and by the constant pressure of commercial necessity. Satisfactory progress in basic science seldom occurs under conditions prevailing in the normal industrial laboratory. There are some notable exceptions, it is true, but even in such cases it is rarely possible to match the universities in respect to the freedom which is so important to scientific discovery.

To serve effectively as the centers of basic research these institutions must be strong and healthy. They must attract our best scientists as teachers and investigators. They must offer research opportunities and sufficient compensation to enable them to compete with industry and government for the cream of scientific talent.

During the past 25 years there has been a great increase in industrial research involving the application of scientific knowledge to a multitude of practical purposes—thus providing new products, new industries, new investment opportunities, and millions of jobs. During the same period research within Government—again largely applied research—has also been greatly expanded. In the decade from 1930 to 1940 expenditures for industrial research increased from $116,000,000 to $240,000,000 and those for scientific research in Government rose from $24,000,000 to $69,000,000. During the same period expenditures for scientific research in the colleges and universities increased from $20,000,000 to $31,000,000, while those in the endowed research institutes declined from $5,200,000 to $4,500,000. These are the best estimates available. The figures have been taken from a variety of sources and arbitrary definitions have necessarily been applied, but it is believed that they may be accepted as indicating the following trends:

(a) Expenditures for scientific research by industry and Government—almost entirely applied research—have more than doubled between 1930 and 1940. Whereas in 1930 they were six times as large as the research expenditures of the colleges, universities, and research institutes, by 1940 they were nearly ten times as large.

(b) While expenditures for scientific research in the colleges and universities increased by one-half during this period, those for the endowed research institutes have slowly declined.

If the colleges, universities and research institutes are to meet the rapidly increasing demands of industry and Government for new scientific knowledge, their basic research should be strengthened by use of public funds.

Research Within the Government

Although there are some notable exceptions, most research conducted within governmental laboratories is of an applied nature. This has always been true and is likely to remain so. Hence Government, like industry, is dependent upon the colleges, universities, and research institutes to expand the basic scientific frontiers and to furnish trained scientific investigators.

Research within the Government represents an important part of our total research activity and needs to be strengthened and expanded after the war. Such expansion should be directed to fields of inquiry and service which are of public importance and are not adequately carried on by private organizations.

The most important single factor in scientific and technical work is the quality of personnel employed. The procedures currently followed within the Government for recruiting, classifying and compensating such personnel place the Government under a severe handicap in competing with industry and the universities for first-class scientific talent. Steps should be taken to reduce that handicap.

In the Government the arrangement whereby the numerous scientific agencies form parts of large departments has both advantages and disadvantages. But the present pattern is firmly established and there is much to be said for it. There is, however, a very real need for some measure of coordination of the common scientific activities of these agencies, both as to policies and budgets, and at present no such means exist.

A permanent Science Advisory Board should be created to consult with these scientific bureaus and to advise the executive and legislative branches of Government as to the policies and budgets of Government agencies engaged in scientific research.

This board should be composed of disinterested scientists who have no connection with the affairs of any Government agency.

Industrial Research

The simplest and most effective way in which the Government can strengthen industrial research is to support basic research and to develop scientific talent.

The benefits of basic research do not reach all industries equally or at the same speed. Some small enterprises never receive any of the benefits. It has been suggested that the benefits might be better utilized if "research clinics" for such enterprises were to be established. Businessmen would thus be able to make more use of research than they now do. This proposal is certainly worthy of further study.

One of the most important factors affecting the amount of industrial research is the income-tax law. Government action in respect to this subject will affect the rate of technical progress in industry, Uncertainties as to the attitude of the Bureau of Internal Revenue regarding the deduction of research and development expenses are a deterrent to research expenditure. These uncertainties arise from lack of clarity of the tax law as to the proper treatment of such costs.

The Internal Revenue Code should be amended to remove present uncertainties in regard to the deductibility of research and development expenditures as current charges against net income.

Research is also affected by the patent laws, They stimulate new invention and they make it possible for new industries to be built around new devices or new processes. These industries generate new jobs and new products, all of which contribute to the welfare and the strength of the country.

Yet, uncertainties in the operation of the patent laws have impaired the ability of small industries to translate new ideas into processes and products of value to the Nation. These uncertainties are, in part, attributable to the difficulties and expense incident to the operation of the patent system as it presently exists. These uncertainties are also attributable to the existence of certain abuses which have appeared in the use of patents. The abuses should be corrected. They have led to extravagantly critical attacks which tend to discredit a basically sound system.

It is important that the patent system continue to serve the country in the manner intended by the Constitution, for it has been a vital element in the industrial vigor which has distinguished this Nation.

The National Patent Planning Commission has reported on this subject. In addition, a detailed study, with recommendations concerning the extent to which modifications should be made in our patent laws is currently being made under the leadership of the Secretary of Commerce. It is recommended. therefore, that specific action with regard to the patent laws be withheld pending the submission of the report devoted exclusively to that subject.

International Exchange of Scientific Information

International exchange of scientific information is of growing importance. Increasing specialization of science will make it more important than ever that scientists in this country keep continually abreast of developments abroad. In addition, a flow of scientific information constitutes one facet of general international accord which should be cultivated.

The Government can accomplish significant results in several ways: by aiding in the arrangement of international science congresses, in the official accrediting of American scientists to such gatherings, in the official reception of foreign scientists of standing in this country, in making possible a rapid flow of technical information, including translation service, and possibly in the provision of international fellowships. Private foundations and other groups partially fulfill some of these functions at present, but their scope is incomplete and inadequate.

The Government should take an active role in promoting the international flow of scientific information.

The Special Need for Federal Support

We can no longer count on ravaged Europe as a source of fundamental knowledge. In the past we have devoted much of our best efforts to the application of such knowledge which has been discovered abroad. In the future we must pay increased attention to discovering this knowledge for ourselves particularly since the scientific applications of the future will be more than ever dependent upon such basic knowledge.

New impetus must be given to research in our country. Such new impetus can come promptly only from the Government. Expenditures for research in the colleges, universities, and research institutes will otherwise not be able to meet the additional demands of increased public need for research.

Further, we cannot expect industry adequately to fill the gap. Industry will fully rise to the challenge of applying new knowledge to new products. The commercial incentive can be relied upon for that. But basic research is essentially noncommercial in nature. It will not receive the attention it requires if left to industry.

For many years the Government has wisely supported research in the agricultural colleges and the benefits have been great. The time has come when such support should be extended to other fields.

In providing Government support, however, we must endeavor to preserve as far as possible the private support of research both in industry and in the colleges, universities, and research institutes. These private sources should continue to carry their share of the financial burden.

The Cost of a Program

It is estimated that an adequate program for Federal support of basic research in the colleges, universities, and research institutes and for financing important applied research in the public interest, will cost about 10 million dollars at the outset and may rise to about 50 million dollars annually when fully underway at the end of perhaps 5 years.

THE MEANS TO THE END

New Responsibilities for Government

One lesson is clear from the reports of the several committees attached as appendices. The Federal Government should accept new responsibilities for promoting the creation of new scientific knowledge and the development of scientific talent in our youth.

The extent and nature of these new responsibilities are set forth in detail in the reports of the committees whose recommendations in this regard are fully endorsed.

In discharging these responsibilities Federal funds should be made available. We have given much thought to the question of how plans for the use of Federal funds may be arranged so that such funds will not drive out of the picture funds from local governments, foundations, and private donors. We believe that our proposals will minimize that effect, but we do not think that it can be completely avoided. We submit, however, that the Nation's need for more and better scientific research is such that the risk must be accepted.

It is also clear that the effective discharge of these responsibilities will require the full attention of some over-all agency devoted to that purpose. There should be a focal point within the Government for a concerted program of assisting scientific research conducted outside of Government. Such an agency should furnish the funds needed to support basic research in the colleges and universities, should coordinate where possible research programs on matters of utmost importance to the national welfare, should formulate a national policy for the Government toward science, should sponsor the interchange of scientific information among scientists and laboratories both in this country and abroad, and should ensure that the incentives to research in industry and the universities are maintained. All of the committees advising on these matters agree on the necessity for such an agency.

The Mechanism

There are within Government departments many groups whose interests are primarily those of scientific research. Notable examples are found within the Departments of Agriculture, Commerce, Interior, and the Federal Security Agency. These groups are concerned with science as collateral and peripheral to the major problems of those Departments. These groups should remain where they are, and continue to perform their present functions, including the support of agricultural research by grants to the land grant colleges and experimental stations. Since their largest contribution lies in applying fundamental knowledge to the special problems of the Departments within which they are established.

By the same token these groups cannot be made the repository of the new and large responsibilities in science which belong to the Government and which the Government should accept. The recommendations in this report which relate to research within the Government, to the release of scientific information, to clarification of the tax laws, and to the recovery and development of our scientific talent now in uniform can be implemented by action within the existing structure of the Government. But nowhere in the governmental structure receiving its funds from Congress is there an agency adapted to supplementing the support of basic research in the universities, both in medicine and the natural sciences; adapted to supporting research on new weapons for both Services: or adapted to administering a program of science scholarships and fellowships.

A new agency should be established. therefore, by the Congress for the purpose. Such an agency, moreover, should be an independent agency devoted to the support of scientific research and advanced scientific education alone. Industry learned many years ago that basic research cannot often be fruitfully conducted as an adjunct to or a subdivision of an operating agency or department. Operating agencies have immediate operating goals and are under constant pressure to produce in a tangible way, for that is the test of their value. None of these conditions is favorable to basic research. Research is the exploration of the unknown and is necessarily speculative. It is inhibited by conventional approaches, traditions, and standards. It cannot be satisfactorily conducted in an atmosphere where it is gauged and tested by operating or production standards. Basic scientific research should not, therefore, be placed under an operating agency whose paramount concern is anything other than research. Research will always suffer when put in competition with operations. The decision that there should be a new and independent agency was reached by each of the committees advising in these matters.

I am convinced that these new functions should be centered in one agency. Science is fundamentally a unitary thing. The number of independent agencies should be kept to a minimum. Much medical progress, for example, will come from fundamental advances in chemistry. Separation of the sciences in tight compartments, as would occur if more than one agency were involved, would retard and not advance scientific knowledge as a whole.

Five Fundamentals

There are certain basic principles which must underlie the program of Government support for scientific research and education if such support is to be effective and if it is to avoid impairing the very things we seek to foster. These principles are as follows:

(1) Whatever the extent of support may be, there must be stability of funds over a period of years so that long-range programs may be undertaken.

(2) The agency to administer such funds should be composed of citizens selected only on the basis of their interest in and capacity to promote the work of the agency. They should be persons of broad interest in and understanding of the peculiarities of scientific research and education.

(3) The agency should promote research through contracts or grants to organizations outside the Federal Government. It should not operate any laboratories of its own.

(4) Support of basic research in the public and private colleges, universities, and research institutes must leave the internal control of policy, personnel, and the method and scope of the research to the institutions themselves. This is of the utmost importance.

(5) While assuring complete independence and freedom for the nature, scope, and methodology of research carried on in the institutions receiving public funds, and while retaining discretion in the allocation of funds among such institutions, the Foundation proposed herein must be responsible to the President and the Congress. Only through such responsibility can we maintain the proper relationship between science and other aspects of a democratic system. The usual controls of audits, reports, budgeting, and the like, should, of course, apply to the administrative and fiscal operations of the Foundation, subject, however, to such adjustments in procedure as are necessary to meet the special requirements of research.

Basic research is a long-term process—it ceases to be basic if immediate results are expected on short-term support. Methods should therefore be found which will permit the agency to make commitments of funds from current appropriations for programs of five years duration or longer. Continuity and stability of the program and its support may be expected (a) from the growing realization by the Congress of the benefits to the public from scientific research, and (b) from the conviction which will grow among those who conduct research under the auspices of the agency that good quality work will be followed by continuing support.

Military Research

As stated earlier in this report, military preparedness requires a permanent, independent, civilian-controlled organization, having close liaison with the Army and the Navy, but with funds direct from Congress and the clear power to initiate military research which will supplement and strengthen that directly under the control of the Army and Navy. As a temporary measure, the National Academy of Sciences has established the Research Board for National Security at the request of the Secretary of War and the Secretary of the Navy. This is highly desirable in order that there may be no interruption in the relations between scientists and military men after the emergency wartime Office of Scientific Research and Development goes out of existence. The Congress is now considering legislation to provide funds for this Board by direct appropriation.

I believe that, as a permanent measure, it would be appropriate to add to the other functions recommended in this report the responsibilities for civilian initiated and civilian-controlled military research. The function of such a civilian group would be primarily to conduct long-range scientific research on military problems—leaving to the Services research on the improvement of existing weapons.

Some research on military problems should be conducted, in time of peace as well as in war, by civilians independently of the military establishment. It is the primary responsibility of the Army and Navy to train the men, make available the weapons, and employ the strategy that will bring victory in combat. The Armed Services cannot be expected to be experts in all of the complicated fields which make it possible for a great nation to fight successfully in total war. There are certain kinds of research—such as research on the improvement of existing weapons—which can best be done within the military establishment. However, the job of long-range research involving application of the newest scientific discoveries to military needs should be the responsibility of those civilian scientists in the universities and in industry who are best trained to discharge it thoroughly and successfully. It is essential that both kinds of research go forward and that there be the closest liaison between the two groups.

Placing the civilian military research function in the proposed agency would bring it into close relationship with a broad program of basic research in both the natural sciences and medicine. A balance between military and other research could thus readily be maintained.

The establishment of the new agency, including a civilian military research group, should not be delayed by the existence of the Research Board for National Security, which is a temporary measure. Nor should the creation of the new agency be delayed by uncertainties in regard to the postwar organization of our military departments themselves. Clearly, the new agency, including a civilian military research group within it, can remain sufficiently flexible to adapt its operations to whatever may be the final organization of the military departments.

National Research Foundation

It is my judgment that the national interest in scientific research and scientific education can best be promoted by the creation of a National Research Foundation.

1. *Purposes*

The National Research Foundation should develop and promote a national policy for scientific research and scientific education, should support basic research in nonprofit organizations, should develop scientific talent in American youth by means of scholarships and fellowships, and should by contract and otherwise support long-range research on military matters.

The future of Thought, and therefore of History, lies in the hands of the physicists, and . . . the future historian must seek his education in the world of mathematical physics. A new generation must be brought up to think by new methods, and if our historical departments in the Universities cannot enter this next phase, the physical departments will have to assume this task alone.

Henry Adams, *The Degradation of the Democratic Dogma*, 1919

There floated through my mind a line from the Bhagavad-Gita in which Krishna is trying to persuade the Prince that he should do his duty: "I am become death, the shatterer of worlds." I think we all had this feeling more or less.

J. Robert Oppenheimer, 1945

It was through the Second World War that most of us suddenly appreciated for the first time the power of man's concentrated efforts to understand and control the forces of nature. We were appalled by what we saw.

Vannevar Bush, *Science is Not Enough*, 1967

When you see something that is technically sweet, you go ahead and do it and you argue about what to do about it only after you have had your technical success. That is the way it was with the atomic bomb.

J. Robert Oppenheimer, 1954

SCIENCE AND THE COMMON UNDERSTANDING

J. ROBERT OPPENHEIMER

J. Robert Oppenheimer (1904-1967) was a theoretical nuclear physicist who during World War II was the director of the Manhattan Project's Los Alamos National Laboratory. The force of his scientific insight and personality was crucial in the drive to develop the atomic bomb. After the war, he was named director of the Institute for Advanced Studies at Princeton. Ironically, his security clearance was subsequently revoked because of his vocal opposition to the development of the so-called "superbombs."

1. Would Oppenheimer's view of the nature of man be more like that of Hobbs or Locke? Why?

2. What does "The greatest of the changes that science has brought is the acuity of change...," imply to one? Have the years since this was written altered the validity of this statement?

3. One of the most common criticisms of science is that it lacks humanity. Do you find any support for this charge in Oppenheimer's writings?

4. After World War II, Oppenheimer was a powerful opponent of secrecy in science. His security clearance was revoked partly because of this attitude and partly because of his opposition to building the hydrogen bomb. Do scientists have a moral and professional responsibility to oppose what they consider inappropriate uses of research?

SCIENCE AND COMMON UNDERSTANDING

J. ROBERT OPPENHEIMER

THE SCIENCES AND MAN'S COMMUNITY

FOR some moments during these lectures we have looked together into one of the rooms of the house called "science." This is a relatively quiet room that we know as quantum theory or atomic theory. The great girders which frame it, the lights and shadows and vast windows—these were the work of a generation our predecessor more than two decades ago. It is not wholly quiet. Young people visit it and study in it and pass on to other chambers; and from time to time someone rearranges a piece of the furniture to make the whole more harmonious; and many, as we have done, peer through its windows or walk through it as sight-seers. It is not so old but that one can hear the sound of the new wings being built nearby, where men walk high in the air to erect new scaffoldings, not unconscious of how far they may fall. All about there are busy workshops where the builders are active, and very near indeed are those of us who, learning more of the primordial structure of matter, hope some day for chambers as fair and lovely as that in which we have spent the years of our youth and our prime.

It is a vast house indeed. It does not appear to have been built upon any plan but to have grown as a great city grows. There is no central chamber, no one corridor from which all others debouch. All about the periphery men are at work studying the vast reaches of space and the state of affairs billions of years ago; studying the intricate and subtle but wonderfully meet mechanisms by which life proliferates, alters, and endures; studying the reach of the mind and its ways of learning; digging deep into the atoms and the atoms within atoms and their unfathomed order. It is a house so vast that none of us know it, and even the most fortunate have seen most rooms only from the outside or by a fleeting passage, as in a king's palace open to visitors. It is a house so vast that there is not and need not be complete concurrence on where its chambers stop and those of the neighboring mansions begin.

It is not arranged in a line nor a square nor a circle nor a pyramid, but with a wonderful randomness suggestive of unending growth and improvisation. Not many people live in the house, relatively speaking—perhaps if we count all its chambers and take residence requirements quite lightly, one tenth of one per cent, of all the people in this world—probably, by any reasonable definition, far fewer. And even those who live here live elsewhere also, live in houses where the rooms are not labelled atomic theory or genetics or the internal constitution of the stars, but quite different names like power and production and evil and beauty and history and children and the word of God.

We go in and out; even the most assiduous of us is not bound to this vast structure. One thing we find throughout the house: there are no locks; there are no shut doors; wherever we go there are the signs and usually the words of welcome. It is an open house, open to all comers.

The discoveries of science, the new rooms in this great house, have changed the way men think of things outside its walls. We have some glimmering now of the depth in time and the vastness in space of the physical world we live in. An awareness of how long our history and how immense our cosmos touches us even in simple earthly deliberations. We have learned from the natural history of the earth and from the story of evolution to have a sense of history, of time and change. We learn to talk of ourselves, and of the nature of the world and its reality as not wholly fixed in a silent quiet moment, but as unfolding with novelty and alteration, decay and new growth. We have understood something of strange primitive cultures, and through this see the qualities of our own life in an altered perspective, and recognize its accidents as well as its inherent necessities. We are, I should think, not patriots less but patriots very differently for loving what is ours and understanding a little of the love of others for their lands and ways. We have begun to understand that it is not only in his rational life that man's psyche is intelligible, that even in what may appear to be his least rational actions and sentiments we may discover a new order. We have the beginnings of an understanding of what it is in man, and more in simple organisms, that is truly heritable, and rudimentary clues as to how the inheritance occurs. We know, in surprising detail, what is the physical counterpart of the act of vision and of other modes of perception. Not one of these new ideas and new insights is so little, or has so short a reach in its bearing on the common understanding but that it alone could make a proper theme for "Science and the Common Understanding." Yet we have been, bearing in mind my limited area of experience, in that one room of the part of the house where physics is, in which I have for some years worked and taught.

In that one room—in that relatively quiet room where we have been together—we have found things quite strange for those who have not been there before, yet reminiscent of what we have seen in other houses and known in other days. We have seen that in the atomic world we have been led by experience to use descriptions and ideas that apply to the large-scale world of matter, to the familiar world of our schoolday physics; ideas like the position of a body and its acceleration and its impulse and the forces acting on it; ideas like wave and interference; ideas like cause and probability. But what is new, what was not anticipated a half-century ago, is that, though to an atomic system there is a potential applicability of one or another of these ideas, in any real situation only some of these ways of description can be actual. This is because we need to take into account not merely the atomic system we are studying, but the means we use in observing it, and the fitness of these experimental means for defining and measuring selected properties of the system. All such ways of observing are needed for the whole experience of the atomic world; all but one are excluded in any actual experience. In the specific instance, there is a proper and consistent way to describe what the experience is; what it implies; what it predicts and thus how to deal with its consequences. But any such specific instance excludes by its existence the application of other ideas, other modes of prediction, other consequences. They are, we say, complementary to one another; atomic theory is in part an account of these descriptions and in part an understanding of the circumstances to which one applies, or another or another.

And so it is with man's life. He may be any of a number of things; he will not be all of them. He may be well versed, he may be a poet, he may be a creator in one or more than one science; he will not be all kinds of man or all kinds of scientist; and he will be lucky if he has a bit of familiarity outside the room in which he works.

So it is with the great antinomies that through the ages have organized and yet disunited man's experience: the antinomy between the ceaseless change and wonderful novelty and the perishing of all earthly things, and the eternity which inheres in every happening; in the antinomy between growth and order, between the spontaneous and changing and irregular and the symmetrical and balanced; in the related antinomy between freedom and necessity; between action, the life of the will, and observation and analysis and the life of reason; between the question "how?" and the questions "why?" and "to what end?"; between the causes that derive from natural law, from unvarying regularities in the natural world, and those other causes that express purposes and define goals and ends.

So it is in the antinomy between the individual and the community; man who is an end in himself and man whose tradition, whose culture, whose works, whose words have meaning in terms of other men and his relations to them. All our experience has shown that we can neither think, nor in any true sense live. without reference to these antinomic modes. We cannot in any sense be both the observers and the actors in any specific instance, or we shall fail properly to be either one or the other; yet we know that our life is built of these two modes, is part free and part inevitable, is part creation and part discipline, is part acceptance and part effort. We have no written rules that assign us to these ways; but we know that only folly and death of the spirit results when we deny one or the other, when we erect one as total and absolute and make the others derivative and secondary. We recognize this when we live as men. We talk to one another; we philosophize; we admire great men and their moments of greatness; we read; we study; we recognize and love in a particular act that happy union of the generally incompatible. With all of this we learn to use some reasonable part of the full register of man's resources.

We are, of course, an ignorant lot; even the best of us knows how to do only a very few things well; and of what is available in knowledge of fact, whether of science or of history, only the smallest part is in any one man's knowing.

The greatest of the changes that science has brought is the acuity of change; the greatest novelty the extent of novelty. Short of rare times of great disaster, civilizations have not known such rapid alteration in the conditions of their life, such rapid flowering of many varied sciences, such rapid changes in the ideas we have about the world and one another. What has been true in the days of a great disaster or great military defeat for one people at one time is true for all of us now, in the sense that our ends have little in common with our beginnings. Within a lifetime what we learned at school has been rendered inadequate by new discoveries and new inventions; the ways that we learn in childhood are only very meagerly adequate to the issues that we must meet in maturity.

In fact, of course, the notion of universal knowledge has always been an illusion; but it is an illusion fostered by the monistic view of the world in which a few great central truths determine in all its wonderful and amazing proliferation everything else that is true. We are not today tempted to search for these keys that unlock the whole of human knowledge and of man's experience. We know that we are ignorant; we are well taught it, and the more surely and deeply we know our own job the better able we are to appreciate the full measure of our pervasive ignorance. We know that these are inherent limits, compounded, no doubt, and exaggerated by that sloth and that complacency without which we would not be men at all.

But knowledge rests on knowledge; what is new is meaningful because it departs slightly from what was known before; this is a world of frontiers, where even the liveliest of actors or observers will be absent most of the time from most of them. Perhaps this sense was not so sharp in the village—that village which we have learned a little about but probably do not understand too well—the village of slow change and isolation and fixed culture which evokes our nostalgia even if not our full comprehension. Perhaps in the villages men were not so lonely; perhaps they found in each other a fixed community, a fixed and only slowly growing store of knowledge—a single world. Even that we may doubt, for there seem to be always in the culture of such times and places vast domains of mystery, if not unknowable, then imperfectly known, endless and open.

As for ourselves in these times of change, of ever-increasing knowledge, of collective power and individual impotence, of heroism and of drudgery, of progress and of tragedy, we too are brothers. And if we, who are the inheritors of two millennia of Christian tradition, understand that for us we have come to be brothers second by being children first, we know that in vast parts of the world where there has been no Christian tradition, and with men who never have been and never may be Christian in faith there is nevertheless a bond of brotherhood. We know this not only because of the almost universal ideal of human brotherhood and human community; we know it at first hand from the more modest, more diverse, more fleeting associations which are the substance of our life. The ideal of brotherhood, the ideal of fraternity in which all men, wicked and virtuous, wretched and fortunate, are banded together has its counterpart in the experience of communities, not ideal, not universal, imperfect, impermanent, as different from the ideal and as reminiscent of it as are the ramified branches of science from the ideal of a unitary, all-encompassing science of the eighteenth century.

Each of us knows from his own life how much even a casual and limited association of men goes beyond him in knowledge, in understanding, in humanity, and in power. Each of us, from a friend or a book or by concerting of the little we know with what others know, has broken the iron circle of his frustration. Each of us has asked help and been given it, and within our measure each of us has offered it. Each of us knows the great new freedom sensed almost as a miracle, that men banded together for some finite purpose experience from the power of their common effort. We are likely to remember the times of the last war, where the common danger brought forth in soldier, in worker, in scientist, and engineer a host of new experiences of the power and the comfort in even bleak undertakings, of common, concerted, co-operative life. Each of us knows how much he has been transcended by the group of which he has been or is a part; each of us has felt the solace of other men's knowledge to stay his own ignorance, of other men's wisdom to stay his folly, of other men's courage to answer his doubts or his weakness.

These are the fluid communities, some of long duration when circumstances favored—like the political party or many a trade union—some fleeting and vivid, encompassing in the time of their duration a moment only of the member's life; and in our world at least they are ramified and improvised, living and dying, growing and falling off almost as a form of life itself. This may be more true of the United States than of any other country. Certainly the bizarre and comical aspects impressed de Tocqueville more than a century ago when he visited our land and commented on the readiness with which men would band together: to improve the planting of a town, or for political reform, or for the pursuit or inter-exchange of knowledge, or just for the sake of banding together, because they liked one another or disliked someone else. Circumstances nay have exaggerated the role of the societies, of the fluid and yet intense communities in the United States; yet these form a common pattern for our civilization. It brought men together in the Royal Society and in the French Academy and in the Philosophical Society that Franklin founded, in family, in platoon, on a ship, in the laboratory, in almost everything but a really proper club.

If we err today—and I think we do—it is in expecting too much of knowledge from the individual and too much of synthesis from the community. We tend to think of these communities, no less than of the larger brotherhood of man. as made up of individuals, as composed of them as an atom is of its ingredients. We think similarly of general laws and broad ideas as made up of the instances which illustrate them, and from an observation of which we may have learned them.

Yet this is not the whole. The individual event, the act, goes far beyond the general law. It is a sort of intersection of many generalities, harmonizing them in one instance as they cannot be harmonized in general. And we as men are not only the ingredients of our communities; we are their intersection, making a harmony which does not exist between the communities except as we, the individual men, may create it and reveal it. So much of what we think, our acts, our judgments of beauty and of right and wrong, come to us from our fellow men that what would be left were we to take all this away would be neither recognizable nor human. We are men because we are part of, but not because only part of, communities; and the attempt to understand man's brotherhood in terms only of the individual man is as little likely to describe our world as is the attempt to describe general laws as the summary of their instances. These are indeed two complementary views, neither reducible to the other, no more reducible than is the electron as wave to the electron as particle.

And this is the mitigant of our ignorance. It is true that none of us will know very much; and most of us will see the end of our days without understanding in all its detail and beauty the wonders uncovered even in a single branch of a single science. Most of us will not even know, as a member of any intimate circle, anyone who has such knowledge; but it is also true that, although we are sure not to know everything and rather likely not to know very much, we can know anything that is known to man, and may, with luck and sweat, even find out some things that have not before been known to him. This possibility, which, as a universal condition of man's life is new, represents today a high and determined hope, not yet a reality; it is for us in England and in the United States not wholly remote or unfamiliar. It is one of the manifestations of our belief in equality, that belief which could perhaps better be described as a commitment to unparalleled diversity and unevenness in the distribution of attainments, knowledge, talent, and power.

This open access to knowledge, these unlocked doors and signs of welcome, are a mark of a freedom as fundamental as any. They give a freedom to resolve difference by converse, and, where converse does not unite, to let tolerance compose diversity. This would appear to be a freedom barely compatible with modern political tyranny. The multitude of communities, the free association for converse or for common purpose, are acts of creation. It is not merely that without them the individual is the poorer; without them a part of human life, not more nor less fundamental than the individual, is foreclosed. It is a cruel and humorless sort of pun that so powerful a present form of modern tyranny should call itself by the very name of a belief in community, by a word "communism" which in other times evoked memories of villages and village inns and of artisans concerting their skills, and of men of learning content with anonymity. But perhaps only a malignant end can follow the systematic belief that all communities are one community: that all truth is one truth; that all experience is compatible with all other; that total knowledge is possible; that all that is potential can exist as actual. This is not man's fate; this is not his path; to force him on it makes him resemble not that divine image of the all-knowing and all-powerful but the helpless, iron-bound prisoner of a dying world. The open society, the unrestricted access to knowledge, the unplanned and uninhibited association of men for its furtherance—these are what may make a vast, complex, ever-growing, ever-changing, ever more specialized and expert technological world nevertheless a world of human community.

So it is with the unity of science—that unity that is far more a unity of comparable dedication than a unity of common total understanding. This heartening phrase, "the unity of science," often tends to evoke a wholly false picture, a picture of a few basic truths, a few critical techniques, methods, and ideas, from which all discoveries and understanding of science derive; a sort of central exchange access to which will illuminate the atoms and the galaxies, the genes and the sense organs. The unity of science is based rather on just such a community as I have described. All parts of it are open to all of us, and this is no merely formal invitation. The history of science is rich in example of the fruitfulness of bringing two sets of techniques, two sets of ideas, developed in separate contexts for the pursuit of new truth. into touch with one another. The sciences fertilize each other; they grow by contact and by common enterprise. Once again, this means that the scientist may profit from learning about any other science; it does not mean that he must learn about them all. It means that the unity is a potential unity, the unity of the things that might be brought together and might throw light one on the other. It is not global or total or hierarchical.

Even in science, and even without visiting the room in its house called atomic theory, we are again and again reminded of the complementary traits in our own life, even in our own professional life. We are nothing without the work of others our predecessors, others our teachers, others our contemporaries. Even when, in the measure of our adequacy and our fullness, new insight and new order are created, we are still nothing without others. Yet we are more.

There is a similar duality in our relations to wider society. For society our work means many things: pleasure, we hope, for those who follow it; instruction for those who perhaps need it; but also and far more widely, it means a common power, a power to achieve that which could not be achieved without knowledge. It means the cure of illness and the alleviation of suffering; it means the easing of labor and the widening of the readily accessible frontiers of experience, of communication, and of instruction. It means, in an earthy way, the power of betterment—that riddled word. We are today anxiously aware that the power to change is not always, necessarily good.

As new instruments of war, of newly massive terror, add to the ferocity and totality of warfare, we understand that it is a special mark and problem of our age that man's ever-present preoccupation with improving his lot, with alleviating hunger and poverty and exploitation, must be brought into harmony with the over-riding need to limit and largely to eliminate resort to organized violence between nation and nation. The increasingly expert destruction of man's spirit by the power of police, more wicked if not more awful than the ravages of nature s own hand, is another such power, good only if never to be used.

We regard it as proper and just that the patronage of science by society is in large measure based on the increased power which knowledge gives. If we are anxious that the power so given and so obtained be used with wisdom and with love of humanity, that is an anxiety we share with almost everyone. But we also know how little of the deep new knowledge which has altered the face of the world, which has changed—and increasingly and ever more profoundly must change—man's views of the world, resulted from a quest for practical ends or an interest in exercising the power that knowledge gives. For most of us, in most of those moments when we were most free of corruption, it has been the beauty of the world of nature and the strange and compelling harmony of its order, that has sustained. inspirited, and led us. That also is as it should be. And if the forms in which society provides and exercises its patronage leave these incentives strong and secure, new knowledge will never stop as long as there are men.

We know that our work is rightly both an instrument and an end. A great discovery is a thing of beauty; and our faith—our binding, quiet faith—is that knowledge is good and good in itself. It is also an instrument; it is an instrument for our successors, who will use it to probe elsewhere and more deeply; it is an instrument for technology, for the practical arts, and for man's affairs. So it is with us as scientists; so it is with us as men. We are at once instrument and end, discoverers and teachers, actors and observers. We understand, as we hope others understand, that in this there is a harmony between knowledge in the sense of science, that specialized and general knowledge which it is our purpose to uncover, and the community of man. We, like all men, are among those who bring a little light to the vast unending darkness of man's life and world. For us as for all men, change and eternity, specialization and unity, instrument and final purpose, community and individual man alone, complementary each to the other, both require and define our bonds and our freedom.

AMERICA AS A CIVILIZATION

MAX LERNER

Max Lerner (1902-1992) was born in Minsk, Russia, and was brought to the United States when he was five years old. He received the A.B. degree from Yale University and began the study of law there. But then he went to Washington University in St. Louis for a master's degree, and to the Brookings Graduate School of Economics and Government in Washington, D.C., for the Ph.D. Long-time professor of American civilization at Brandeis University, he served as dean of the Graduate school there from 1954-56. He also taught at various times at Sarah Lawrence, Harvard, Williams College, Wellesley, Pomona College, University of Delhi, and Notre Dame. He was managing editor of the *Encyclopedia of the Social Sciences*, editor of the *Nation*, contributing editor of *The New Republic*, on the editorial board of *The American Scholar*, and editorial director of the newspaper *PM* and of the *New York Star*. For many years he wrote a daily world-wide syndicated column for the *New York Post* and *Los Angeles Times* Syndicate.

Lerner wrote many books and he edited works of Machiavelli, Thorstein Veblen, John Stuart Mill, Tocqueville, and others. He spoke at the Lynchburg College Senior Symposium on two occasions.

His highly acclaimed *America as a Civilization* (1957) was over twelve years in the writing. It was reissued on the twenty-fifth anniversary of its original publication.

1. Why has the emphasis in the United States been so much more on applied science and engineering than on "pure science"?

2. What has been the place of science in American civilization?

3. How does Lerner account for the Greek failure in technology and the American success in it?

4. What are the two imperatives upon which a great scientific civilization depends, according to Lerner? Do you agree? Can you think of exceptions?

5. What are the factors that make up the "characteristic pattern of American technology"?

6. According to Lerner, what were the "new work patterns which transformed the American work attitudes"?

7. What are the dangers that Lerner sees in the "three phases of the machine culture"? Can those dangers be avoided? If so, how?

AMERICA AS A CIVILIZATION

MAX LERNER

CHAPTER IV

The Culture of Science and the Machine

I. The Enormous Laboratory: Science and Power

AMERICA is a civilization founded on science and rooted in its achievements. Without science the whole ribbed frame of American technology, and with it American power, would have been impossible. America itself was born at the beginning of the great age of European science. Back of the flowering modern technology were the long centuries when the seed grew silently in the earth. The same expansive forces that produced the intellectual discoveries of that *saeculum mirabile* of European science—the seventeenth century—produced the American settlements as well. Europe reached out intellectually, as it reached out physically, for new frontiers. In England, the history of the Royal Society paralleled that of the plantation companies. The whole atmosphere surrounding the settlement and peopling of America was an atmosphere of scientific beginnings. Except in a climate of innovation the American experiment would have been impossible; conversely, it was in the intensely innovating social climate of America that invention was bound to flourish.

✻ ✻ ✻ ✻ ✻

The question about a civilization is not whether it uses science but how it uses science, what contributions it makes to it, what sciences are closest to its temper and civilization style. While the Greeks did important work in astronomy and physics, the characteristic Greek sciences were botany, zoology, biology, and mathematics, as befitted a people absorbed with the individual, the category, and their relations. The characteristic sciences of American technology turned out to be chemistry and physics, electronics and radiation, as befits a people absorbed with energy and speed, communication and power. In both cases the sciences are a key to the crucial civilization traits. In one case they are mainly the life sciences and the sciences of order, in the other the sciences of energy and power.

Spengler had at least a half-truth by the tail when, writing in his *Decline of the West* on the Faustian and Apollonian nature conceptions, he said that "force is the mechanical Nature-picture of Western man.... The primary ideas of this physics stood firm long before the first physicist was born." While this notion—that the science type in any civilization exists long before the science—has an element of poetry, it cannot be ignored. Veblen brushed the same problem in the 1920s when he linked the American "technology of physics and chemistry" (radiation and electronics had not yet emerged) with "absentee ownership" by and of corporations. And if you push absentee ownership and corporate power still further back, you get the "natural rights" of property.

Here, I think, we reach a significant relationship. The American conceptions of science went hand in hand with the American conceptions of nature: the Declaration of Independence, with its theory of the natural rights of the individual, was the forerunner of the great upsurge of American energy which led to the technological triumphs of the nineteenth century. The Federalist Papers are in themselves a microcosm of the forces in the American mind that were to shape the uses of science: on the one hand an equilibrium-politics, on the other a drive on purely pragmatic grounds to establish the principle of a central authority with the power to govern essential for survival. The two may seem inconsistent to the critical student of today, and their inconsistency has been shown in the creaking of the American governmental machine: yet the important fact is that they were both part of the eighteenth-century American mind, and the sense of natural law in the equilibrium principle coexisted with the empirical power sense in the principle of central authority.

These two—the sense of natural law and a power empiricism—have been the formative forces in American science and technology, as they have been in American political science and economics. The "reception" that the Americans gave the principles of John Locke, as Walton Hamilton has analyzed it and Merle Curti has traced it, is another instance of the transforming drive in the American civilization: for the Locke that emerged from American thinking on property was very different from the Locke that came into it from the English. It is in the nature of a civilization's "genius" that whatever material it borrows from others it transforms in its own image. When John Locke came out of the American transforming machine his name was Andrew Carnegie and Henry Ford. The Declaration of Independence became the "due process" decisions of the Supreme Court; Tom Paine's flaming pamphlet on natural law became the comfortable doctrines that bolstered property interests; the American idea of Nature turned into corporate ownership, and its servant was the technology of chemistry and physics. The congruity between American science and the driving spirit of American political and economic development was the congruity of *elan* and energy. The geography and resources of America invited a physics of force, and the role of Nature in American political thinking reflected it and prepared the ground for it. Out of the sciences of force came American technology and the machine process; and they in turn cast their spell back upon science.

This capacity for transforming science into technology, which accounts for so much of the success of American power, is not one to be taken for granted. The Greeks, for example, played a greater role in the history of scientific theory than the Americans. They took the great step from myth to science, just as Europeans in the seventeenth century took the final step in separating science from religion. Centuries before the Christian era there were thinkers in Thrace and Athens, in Sicily and on the coast of Asia Minor, who did basic thinking about biology and mathematics, about the nature of the world and the constitution of matter, upon which later centuries were built. At the height of the Greek achievement a Stagirite called Aristotle was able to synthesize what the Greeks knew of Nature and its workings into a system more comprehensive than any mind before or since. Yet Greek science, although it continued its achievements as science for several centuries after Aristotle, never took the crucial step from science to technology. To be sure, the Alexandrian world in the later Greek era had an impressive number of mechanical contrivances described by Hero, like the endless chain, the compound pulley, and the crane for lifting, some of which they put to practical use. Yet it remained true that Greek technology, however you measure its achievement, never explored and applied more than a small fraction of what Greek science might have made possible. It did not run machines, relieve labor of its burdens, increase man's productive capacity greatly, build a powerful industrial civilization. Why?

The clues to the Greek failure in technology may shed some light on the American success in it. Partly they lie in what may be called the slave syndrome. There is a British school of historians, including Benjamin Farmington and V. Gordon Children, who look to the slave system for the explanation of the arrested Greek development. They have pushed their thesis too hard in applying it to science, for it is obvious that the slave-based society of the Greek city-states was well developed by Plato's time, yet Greek science went on growing for several centuries in the work of Euclid, Archimedes, and others. But the heart of the matter is less in the failure of science to develop fully than in its failure to make the transition to technology. The thinking of the Greeks was done by free men and citizens; the work was done by foreigners and slaves. Where there is a contempt for work and trade and the sweat they entail, there is a separation from the sources of experience and Nature, and a blindness to those imperatives of practice that shape innovation. The American scientist or technician, no matter how famous and whether he works at industrial research or at a university, does not cut himself off from these sources of experience. Less a creator of world views than the ancient Greek or modern European scientist, he has been a discoverer of new ways of pushing old and new things to completion.

* * * * *

3. Big Technology and Neutral Technicians

THE AMERICANS DID NOT develop modern machine technology first, but they have carried it furthest and shown the most marked affinity for it. The sway of the machine is less disputed in America than that of any other institution, including the science which made it possible, the capitalism which has organized its use, and the democracy governing the distribution of the power that flows from it. Unlike the democratic idea, which is assigned to the realm of what ought to be, the empire of Big Technology is an integral part of the daily living and thinking of Americans. They pride themselves on their "production miracles," much as the English used to call their islands the "workshop of the world."

The Big Technology has been for Americans what the Cross was for the Emperor Constantine: *in hoc signo vincas*. It set the pace for an impressively swift and thorough conquest of a new environment and of world leadership. The American has been a machine-intoxicated man. The love affair (it has been nothing less) between the Americans and their Big Technology has been fateful, for it has joined the impersonal power of the machine to the dynamism of the American character. As by some tropism of the spirit the Americans have followed out the logic of technology all the way. The world has seen civilizations based on diverse principles: on beauty and an equipoise of living, on otherworldliness and the reality of the supernatural, on close personal allegiance, on military prowess, on ascetic control of the self. But in each case the principle was embodied in the life and outlook of an elite group Never before has the motive principle of a civilization spread so pervasively through all strata of its population, changing the lives of its ordinary people.

Veblen's ironic argument on the "merits of borrowing" (*Imperial Germany and the Industrial Revolution) is* now familiar: that England, where the Industrial Revolution was first given scope, paid the "penalty for taking the lead" by falling behind in the later industrial race, and that the borrowing countries—America, Germany, Japan, Russia—forged ahead because they started on a higher technological level, without the cluttering bric-a-brac of customs and vested interests which Britain had developed. Toynbee, an Englishman himself, ruefully approaches the same problem in terms of "hosts" and "parasites," quoting J. B. S. Haldane's "A step in evolution in any animal group is followed by an evolutionary advance on the part of their parasites." (*A Study of History,* Vol. IV, p. 430.) Yet one cannot fail to notice that aside from the Americans the other "parasites" or "borrowers," whatever they be called, do not make the same effective use of their borrowings or hosts; and that the Germans, the Japanese, even the Russians still seem technologically like bright and enterprising younger brothers of the Americans, trying hard to catch up with his skills. There is more complexity in the machine achievement of America than is dreamed of in the philosophy of Veblen and Toynbee.

What I have said above about the social climate that favored the development of the borrowed science in America applies even more to the flowering of the borrowed seeds of technology. The resources, the separating ocean which at first spurred self-sufficiency and then served as a carrier of commerce, the lack of institutional hindrances, the tinkering skill of the craftsmen and the organizing skill of the managers, the lure of profit, the growing population and markets, the Promethean sense throughout of the mastery of a continent: it was in the frame of these influences that the Big Technology came into its empire in America.

This technological flowering came early in America's industrial revolution, so that even before the Civil War the movement of America toward industrial pre-eminence was already recognized in Europe: the testimony of Adam Smith and Malthus was that the American living standard even in their day was higher than the European for the consumption levels of the comparable classes. While the financial leadership of Britain was to continue until the turn of the century there was little doubt about where the industrial pre-eminence belonged. Not the least of the factors spurring America on this path was, as Ray Ginger has pointed out, the scarcity and mobility of American labor. Since labor was scarce, wages high, and the turnover great, an industry like American textiles had to introduce labor-saving devices rapidly and avail itself of what labor it could get, including unskilled female operators for the looms. It was a case of labor necessity mothering technical invention.

More than anything else, this pace of technological change is what gives America its revolutionary character today. It is idle to talk of a second or a third Industrial Revolution in America. The changes in production and motive power, in transport and communications, on the farm and in the city, in the air and on the ground and under the ground, have been so unremitting as to merit somewhat

Trotsky's phrase, the "Permanent Revolution," which by a bold twist the editors of *Fortune* applied to the American technical and social scene. While the phrase is ripped out of its context of class meaning that Trotsky had intended, the vaguer idea of a continuing dynamism with far-reaching consequences still makes sense. The technological advance, through war and peace, through prosperity and slump, has been so constant as to become an element of the surrounding American atmosphere, easily taken for granted. The American is scarcely aware of the changes in the physical conditions of his living almost day to day; he takes a longer measurement of it by the span of generations when he compares his grandfather's daily life with his own, and that in turn with the life his grandchildren will live.

* * * * *

Item two is the use of precision machine tools, which have made possible the mass production not only of commodities but of machines themselves. Item three: the principle of interchangeable parts which allow the machine not only to be assembled but to be repaired with standardized ease. Item four: the "assembly line" or "belt line" method of processing an operation, first applied to iron and steel in the earlier foundries and to meat slaughtering in Cincinnati and Chicago, and then made famous by Ford in automobile manufacture. This has been modernized into a system of "continuous assembly," with conveyor belts and fork trucks both to feed the parts to the assembly line itself and also to take the finished product away; and with the whole factory laid out around the central assembly line, as around the heart arteries. Item five: the related principle of "automation," as applied to the process industries, especially to America's newest and greatest industrial segment, the chemical industries, in the form of the "continuous-flow" operation in chemical plants. In 1952 an entire napalm plant in Ohio required only four operators per shift, thus "missing 100 per cent automaticity by a hair, as a recent article on "The Factory of the Future" put it. Item six: the vacuum tube principle, which carries the automatic machine to its furthest reach in the "robot machines": already developed in the electronic calculators and the magnetic tape recorders, and likely to go much further in making the assembly line automatic and in revolutionizing not only the factory but the office as well.

* * * * *

Today the task of the American inventor has become harder. If he is a lone wolf he must find a laboratory to work in, the capital to make his invention "practical" and "marketable," the factory to produce it, and the sales organization to sell it. The days are over when a couple of bicycle fixers called Wilbur and Orville Wright got some pointers for the wing design of their plane by watching the flight of birds and then built a foot-square windbox for a couple of dollars to test the wings for the flight across the sand dunes of Kitty Hawk. Plane designers today need a wind tunnel costing millions, capable of testing the stresses on planes under conditions of supersonic speed. Many inventions today are therefore the product of corporate employees working in corporate laboratories with corporate research funds, seeking new processes and products that can be subjected to corporate mass-production methods and marketed under a corporate patent monopoly by corporate distributive mechanisms to a vast mass market for corporate profit, with the inventor getting sometimes only his employee pay, and sometimes a small royalty payment added.

Americans call these collective skills underlying their technology, as they call technology itself, by the expressive word *know-how*. More and more there has been a transfer of this know-how from the many workers who used to tend the machines to the many machines that now need ever fewer workers to tend them. The crucial technological skills are now located in a small elite group of engineers and technicians who design the machines and lay out the continuous-process operations, and who know what to do when the machines break down. They are in the highest demand in industry, and every year the graduates of professional engineering schools are eagerly grabbed up by the corporations. The ultimate goal of this process is, of course, the Aldous Huxley nightmare of an auto factory or chemical plant with no worker on the assembly line, directed only by other machines which direct and feed themselves and need only taping by man's hand to set them on their course. The goal of complete automation may never be reached but it is always being approached more closely.

This process has not, as expected, resulted in the much mooted "technological unemployment." There have been two other results. One is the steady shifting of workers from the unskilled (the earth-lifting machines have almost wholly done away with the pick-and-shovel man) to the semiskilled, and from the semiskilled in turn to the skilled and highly skilled, or the technicians. Since the latter group remains small, the second result has been a further shift of workers out of the industrial occupations themselves into the merchandizing, distributive, and white-collar groups of the corporations, the professions, and the government and Army bureaucracies.

* * * * *

Given these changes, and the changing patterns of work in America (which I shall discuss in the next section), there is a problem which has baffled students of American society, especially those who come to it from the experience of European history. Here (they argue) is a working population cut off from the soil, severed from its tools and from the idea of work as craft and calling: why does it not become the victim of revolutionary movements and demagogues? Granted that the unique conditions of American history have played hob with the idea of a self-conscious revolutionary proletariat, why has not America retraversed the experience of the Roman Empire, whose landless, rootless, tool-less population was used by adventurist leaders? Or the similar experience of Hitler's Germany?

Behind these questions there is the running theme of alienation and its political effects, which has been emphasized in the literature of Socialism and psychiatry from Marx to Erich Fromm. Most Americans, especially the industrial and white-collar classes, have been alienated from some crucial life experiences—from the soil, from independent enterprise, from the ownership of tools, from the sense of craft and the dignity of work, from the feeling of relation to the total product. One might expect this to turn the American into the "formless" man whom Nietzsche dreaded and whose emergence in the modern machine world Ortega y Gasset has described, and thus into easy material for either revolutionary or reactionary adventurers.

The catch is in the failure to see that men uprooted from one kind of social and institutional soil can become rooted in another. The loss of some of the old life values may affect the long-range survival of the culture, but what counts for the cohesion of a culture in the generations immediately ahead is whether people have (or think they have) what their culture has taught them to value. While the American has been alienated by the machine from his old role as independent farmer-artisan-entrepreneur, his culture still has a strong hold on him. The loss of a sense of independence in the productive processes has been replaced by a feeling of well-being in consumption and living standards. The pull of property, no longer in tools or productive land but in consumers' goods; the sense of power and pleasure in the means of sight and sound and movement placed at his disposal by the communications revolution; the glorying in what makes the world of drama and entertainment accessible; the whole range of popular culture; the feeling of access to new gradients of income and experience: these form the new soil in which the American has found new roots.

* * * * *

4. Work and the Automatic Factory

IN FEW RESPECTS has American culture been as radically transformed as in the relation of the machine to the industrial process, and of the worker to the machine and the job. One thinks back to Emerson's "the office of America is to liberate" and wonders how the assembly line fits into this office, and whether those who tend the machines and whose work is set to their pace have been liberated.

Many of the generalizations about work, as about other aspects of life in the Old Society of Jefferson and Jackson, and even of Lincoln and Bryan, are no longer true in the New Society. The greatest change has come about in the "gospel of work." Except for the ante-bellum South there were no Greek notions in America of work as a badge of dishonor, something belonging to a lower caste while the elite cultivates the mind or the graces of living. Freshly wrested from the frontier wilderness, the American land was a living reminder of the relation between work and survival; and as America grew in wealth it was a reminder also of the relation of work to its immediate rewards.

And to ultimate rewards also, for the religious spirit of America's Protestant sects reinforced the practical reasons for work by bringing God's reasons to bear as well. The American bourgeois spirit, which existed in its purest form where economic man met religious man, regarded idleness as sinful and the way of work as the good way. "Work. . . while it is day," said Jesus to his disciples. "For the night cometh, when no man can work." The American moralists found other ways of saying this, but the utilitarian reasons were strongly buttressed by religious sanctions. In the whole calendar of economic virtues, from Franklin's Poor Richard and Samuel Smiles and Richard Parton to Andrew Carnegie and Henry van Dyke, work was the primal source of all the others. Even the rich who did not have to work felt uneasy when they did not, and a life of complete leisure was more likely to be regarded as parasitism in the context of the Puritan tradition than anywhere else in the capitalist world. The great folk myths of America too, which expressed the proletarian spirit as Poor Richard expressed

the bourgeois spirit—the stories of Paul Bunyan and Mike Fink, of Casey Jones
and John Henry—are myths of mighty workers and their work prowess.

But as the myth has it, John Henry broke his heart when he tried to compete
with the monstrous strength of the steam crane. I take this as an allegory of the
dehumanizing of work in consequence of Big Technology.

The gospel of hard work took long to die. There has been no American
chronicler of the "condition of the working classes" to equal Engels or the
Hammonds for the condition of the English. But it is clear that Blake's "dark,
Satanic mills" do not apply to the factory experience of America, where labor
was scarce, technical innovation moved fast, and "scientific management" had
an early start. The American factories in the early nineteenth century were very
different from their European counterparts; the early factory owners tried to
avoid the excesses of the English and the European experience, including long
hours, child labor, poor pay, and scabrous working and living conditions. Eli
Whitney's factories were relatively comfortable places, with decent housing
provided for the workers in the vicinity. The Lowell mills were models of
comfort, and the girls who came to work in them were drawn to the work in
preference to the less interesting and more menial jobs of domestic work and
teaching. A few years' work at Lowell provided a young girl of good family
with money enough so that she could bring a respectable dowry and a dignified
background to her prospective husband. The idea behind the early American
factories, as Mitchell Wilson has pointed out, was that the American worker was
a dignified human being entitled to decent treatment.

The panic of 1837 changed the picture, driving many millowners and
manufacturers to the wall and giving them a reason for treating the workers in
a more exploitative way. The new tides of immigration, by providing a large
labor force whose living standards were lower, made the situation worse.
Toward the end of the century there were "sweatshops" in American garment
manufacture, there was child labor, and until 1923 there was a seventy-two-hour
week in the steel industry. Yet despite these changes the old Protestant-bourgeois
work ethic died in America for other reasons than applied to the dirty, crowded
factories and the long, exhausting hours of the English Industrial Revolution.

One might say that the old work ethic died because the work became
dehumanized and joyless, but this would miss the fact that joylessness in itself
might strengthen the Puritan work ethic, making work an end in itself. What did
happen was that, with the growth of the big corporation, work became
depersonalized; and with the change in the immigrant experience and
composition, hard work became associated with the foreign-born, the Negroes,
the illiterates, and the underlying social strata. The atmosphere of the Big
Money and the knowledge that so much of the income comes by way of what
the workers consider "easy rackets," all conspired to strip work of its
incentives. In the thinking both of the corporate employers and the trade-union
members work came to be expressed mainly in money terms. It was cut off
from a sense of creativeness and lost much of its dignity and meaning. The idea
of the dignity of work died not in the "dark, Satanic mills" but in the well-
lighted, ingeniously laid out, scientifically organized assembly-line plants, and
in the spacious headquarters and offices of the great American corporations.
What has replaced it on the employers' side is the ethic of efficiency and profit
and on the workers' side the ethic of security and success.

There is a triple process of transformation that has taken place in the American work pattern. The symbol of one phase was the white-collar worker; the removal of work, for an ever-growing section of those "gainfully employed," from industrial operations themselves to the stockroom, the fileroom, the office pool, the salesroom, the promotion and advertising office. This was part of the more general bureaucratization of economic life. The functional split in the work patterns carried with it a psychological split as well, with the white collar worker clinging to his sense of differentiated status and of superiority to the industrial worker. The second phase of the change was the assembly line, which came to dominate an ever-larger segment of what workers were still left in contact with the industrial processes themselves. The assembly line arose because of the need for connecting isolated machines and workers: this need was precisely the point at which industry became bureaucratized. The outcry against the assembly line misses the fact that a bureaucracy is the natural and necessary outgrowth of modern technology. The third, applying to those who still worked at the stationary machines and were the "machine tenders" proper, was monotony and anonymity, the carrying of the process of subdividing industrial operations so far that the worker became himself almost an interchangeable part in a factory world of interchangeable parts.

White-collar work, assembly-line work, anonymity: these were the new work patterns which transformed the American work attitudes.

* * * * *

6. The Culture of Machine Living

* * * * *

The danger in machine living itself is chiefly the danger of man's arrogance in exulting over the seemingly easy triumphs over Nature which he calls "progress," so that he cuts himself off increasingly from the organic processes of life itself. Thus with the soil: the erosion of the American earth is not, as some seem to believe, the result of the mechanization of agriculture; a farmer can use science and farm technology to the full, and he need not exhaust or destroy his soil but can replenish it, as has been shown in the TVA, which is itself a triumph of technology. But the machines have been accompanied by a greed for quick results and an irreverence for the soil which are responsible for destroying the balance between man and the environment. What is true of the soil is true of the household: the mechanized household appliances have not destroyed the home or undermined family life; rural electrification has made the farmer's wife less a drudge, and the mass production of suburban houses has given the white-collar family a better chance than it had for sun and living space. What threatens family life is not the "kitchen revolution" or the "housing revolution" but the restless malaise of the spirit, of which the machine is more product than creator.

Even in a society remarkable for its self-criticism the major American writers have not succumbed to the temptation of making the machine into a Devil. Most of the novelists have amply expressed the frustrations of American life, and some (Dreiser, Dos Passos, Farrell and Algren come to mind) have mirrored in their style the pulse beats of an urban mechanized civilization. But except for a few isolated works, like Elmer Rice's *Adding Machine* and Eugene O'Neill's *Dynamo,* the writers have refrained from the pathetic fallacy of ascribing the ills of the spirit to the diabolism of the machine. The greatest American work on technology and its consequences—Lewis Mumford's massive four-volume work starting with *Man and Technics* and ending with *The Conduct of Life*—makes the crucial distinction between what is due to the machine itself and what is due to the human institutions that guide it and determine its uses.

It is here, moving from machine living to cultural standardization, that the picture becomes bleaker. Henry Miller's phrase for its American form is "the air-conditioned nightmare." Someone with a satiric intent could do a withering take-off on the rituals of American standardization.

Most American babies (he might say) are born in standardized hospitals, with a standardized tag put around them to keep them from getting confused with other standardized products of the hospital. Many of them grow up either in uniform rows of tenements or of small-town or suburban houses. They are wheeled about in standard perambulators, shiny or shabby as may be, fed from standardized bottles with standardized nipples according to standardized formulas, and tied up with standardized diapers. In childhood they are fed standardized breakfast foods out of standardized boxes with pictures of standardized heroes on them. They are sent to monotonously similar schoolhouses, where almost uniformly standardized teachers ladle out to them standardized information out of standardized textbooks. They pick up the routine wisdom of the streets in standard slang and learn the routine terms which constrict the range of their language within dishearteningly narrow limits. They wear out standardized shoes playing standardized games, or as passive observers they follow through standardized newspaper accounts or standardized radio and TV programs the highly ritualized antics of grown-up professionals playing the same games. They devour in millions of uniform pulp comic books the prowess of standardized supermen.

As they grow older they dance to canned music from canned juke boxes, millions of them putting standard coins into standard slots to get standardized tunes sung by voices with standardized inflections of emotion. They date with standardized girls in standardized cars. They see automatons thrown on millions of the same movie and TV screens, watching stereotyped love scenes adapted from made-to-order stories in standardized magazines.

They spend the days of their years with monotonous regularity in factory, office, and shop, performing routinized operations at regular intervals. They take time out for standardized "coffee breaks" and later a quick standardized lunch, come home at night to eat processed or canned food, and read syndicated columns and comic strips. Dressed in standardized clothes they attend standardized club meetings, church services, and socials. They have standardized fun at standardized big-city conventions. They are drafted into standardized armies, and if they escape the death of mechanized warfare they die of highly uniform diseases, and to the accompaniment of routine platitudes they are buried in standardized graves and celebrated by standardized obituary notices.

Caricature? Yes, perhaps a crude one, but with a core of frightening validity in it. Every society has its routines and rituals, the primitive groups being sometimes more tyrannously restricted by convention than the industrial societies. The difference is that where the primitive is bound by the rituals of tradition and group life, the American is bound by the rituals of the machine, its products, and their distribution and consumption.

The role of the machine in this standardized living must be made clear. The machine mechanizes life, and since mass production is part of Big Technology, the machine also makes uniformity of life possible. But it does not compel such uniformity. The American who shaves with an electric razor and his wife who buys a standardized "home permanent" for her hair do not thereby have to wear a uniformly vacuous expression through the day. A newspaper that uses the press association wire stories and prints from a highly mechanized set of presses does not thereby have to take the same view of the world that every other paper takes. A novelist who uses a typewriter instead of a quill pen does not have to turn out machine-made historical romances.

The answer is that some do and some don't. What the machine and the mass-produced commodities have clone has been to make conformism easier. To buy and use what everyone else does, and live and think as everyone else does, becomes a short cut involving no need for one's own thinking. Those Americans have been captured by conformist living who have been capturable by it.

Cultural stereotypes are an inherent part of all group living, and they become sharper with mass living. There have always been unthinking people leading formless, atomized lives. What has happened in America is that the economics of mass production has put a premium on uniformity, so that America produces more units of more commodities (although sometimes of fewer models) than other cultures. American salesmanship has sought out every potential buyer of a product, so that standardization makes its way by the force of the distributive mechanism into every life. Yet for the person who has a personality pattern and style of his own, standardization need not mean anything more than a set of conveniences which leave a larger margin of leisure and greater scope for creative living. "That we may be enamored by the negation brought by the machine," as Frank Lloyd Wright has put it, "may be inevitable for a time. But I like to imagine this novel negation to be only a platform underfoot to enable a greater splendor of life to be ours than any known to Greek or Roman, Goth or Moor. We should know a life beside which the life they knew would seem not only limited in scale and narrow in range but pale in richness of the color of imagination and integrity of spirit."

Which is to say that technology is the shell of American life, but a shell that need not hamper or stultify the modes of living and thinking. The real dangers of the American mode of life are not in the machine or even in standardization as much as they are in conformism. The dangers do not flow from the contrivances that men have fashioned to lighten their burdens, or from the material abundance which, if anything, should make a richer cultural life possible. They flow rather from the mimesis of the dominant and successful by the weak and mediocre, from the intolerance of diversity, and from the fear of being thought different from one's fellows. This is the essence of conformism. It would be hard to make the connection between technology and conformism, unless one argues that men fashion their minds in the image of their surroundings, and that in a society of automatism, human beings themselves will become automatons. But this is simply not so. What relation there is between technology and conformism is far more subtle and less mystical. It is a double relation. On the one hand, as Jefferson foresaw, the simpler society of small-scale manufacture did not involve concentration of power in a small group, was not vulnerable to breakdown, and did not need drastic governmental controls; a society of big-scale industry has shown that it does. In that sense the big machines carry with them an imperative toward the directed society, which in turn—whether in war or peace—encourages conformism. On the second score, as De Tocqueville saw, a society in which there is no recognized elite group to serve as the arbiter of morals, thought, and style is bound to be a formless one in which the ordinary person seeks to heal his insecurity by attuning himself to the "tyranny of opinion"—to what others do and say and what they think of him. He is ruled by imitation and prestige rather than a sense of his own worth.

These are dangerous trends, but all of social living is dangerous. The notable fact is that in spite of its machines and standardization America has proved on balance less conformist than some other civilizations where the new technology has played less of a role. One thinks of the totalitarian experience of Italy, of Spain and Portugal, of Germany, of Russia and the East European countries, of Japan, of China. Some, like the Germans, the Japanese, and the Russian and Chinese Communists have been seized with an admiration for the machine; the others have had clerical and feudal traditions, and have lagged in industrial development. The totalitarian spirit can come to reside in a culture no matter what the shell of its technology is. There is no unvarying relation between machines and rigidity of living and thinking.

Americans have, it is true, an idolatry of production and consumption as they have an idolatry of success. But they have not idolized authority or submitted unquestioningly to human or supernatural oracles. They have had their cranks, eccentrics, and anarchists, and they still cling to individualism, even when it is being battered hard. It will take them some time before they can become "man in equipoise," balancing what science and the machine can do as against the demands of the life processes. But where they have failed, the failure has been less that of the machines they have wrought than of the very human fears, greeds, and competitive drives that have accompanied the building of a powerful culture.

It has been suggested that the American, like the Faustian, made a bargain with the Big Technology: a bargain to transform his ways of life and thought in the image of the machine, in return for the range of power and riches the machine would bring within his reach. It is a fine allegory. But truer than the Faustian bargain, with its connotations of the sale of one's soul to the Devil, is the image of Prometheus stealing fire from the gods in order to light a path of progress for men. The path is not yet clear, nor the meaning of progress, nor where it is leading: but the bold intent, the irreverence, and the secular daring have all become part of the American experience.

Technology—like science—is neutral all through, providing only means of control applicable to any purpose, indifferent to all.

John von Neumann, *Fortune*, 1955

At present the most unfounded and most harmful distortion is to ridicule Western civilization as materialistic and worship Eastern civilization as spiritual . . . . Modern civilization of the West, built on the foundation of the search for human happiness, not only has definitely increased material enjoyment to no small degree, but can also definitely satisfy the spiritual demands of mankind.

Hu Shih (1919)

Man masters nature not by force but by understanding. This is why science has succeeded where magic failed: because it has looked for no spell to cast over nature.

Jacob Bronowski, *Science and Human Values*, 1961

The practical utilization of the abundant store of energy locked up in every atom of matter is a problem which only the future can answer. Remember, at the dawn of electricity, it was looked on as a mere toy.

Henri Becquerel

THE PRINCIPLES OF SCIENTIFIC MANAGEMENT

FREDERICK W. TAYLOR

Frederick W. Taylor (1856-1915) is best known as the founder of scientific management. Despite his upper-class background, Taylor chose to study mechanics both in school and in the shop. He found that both machine shops and American industry generally operated chaotically and inefficiently. At first, he attempted to develop new tools to fit particular jobs, but eventually he expanded his efforts to include all aspects of the work place by insisting that management was a science.

1. Why does Taylor think efficiency is so important?

2. What will result from improving efficiency from the point of view of the worker?

3. What are the basic steps or principles of Taylor's scientific management?

4. What are the basic causes of inefficiency according to Taylor?

5. Do you object to thinking of the management of people as a science? Why or why not?

6. Why does Taylor think efficiency is so important?

7. What will result from improving efficiency from the point of view of the worker?

8. What are the basic steps or principles of Taylor's scientific management?

9. What are the basic causes of inefficiency according to Taylor?

10. Do you object to thinking of the management of people as a science? Why or why not?

THE PRINCIPLES OF SCIENTIFIC MANAGEMENT

FREDERICK W. TAYLOR

PRESIDENT ROOSEVELT, in his address to the Governors at the White House, prophetically remarked that "The conservation of our national resources is only preliminary to the larger question of national efficiency."

The whole country at once recognized the importance of conserving our material resources and a large movement has been started which will be effective in accomplishing this object. As yet, however, we have but vaguely appreciated the importance of "the larger question of increasing our national efficiency."

We can see our forests vanishing, our water-powers going to waste, our soil being carried by floods into the sea; and the end of our coal and our iron is in sight. But our larger wastes of human effort, which go on every day through such of our acts as are blundering, ill-directed, or inefficient, and which Mr. Roosevelt refers to as a lack of "national efficiency," are less visible, less tangible, and are but vaguely appreciated.

We can see and feel the waste of material things. Awkward, inefficient, or ill-directed movements of men, however, leave nothing visible or tangible behind them. Their appreciation calls for an act of memory, an effort of the imagination. And for this reason, even though our daily loss from this source is greater than from our waste of material things, the one has stirred us deeply, while the other has moved us but little.

As yet there has been no public agitation for "greater national efficiency," no meetings have been called to consider how this is to be brought about. And still there are signs that the need for greater efficiency is widely felt.

The search for better, for more competent men, from the presidents of our great companies down to our household servants, was never more vigorous than it is now. And more than ever before is the demand for competent men in excess of the supply.

What we are all looking for, however, is the ready-made, competent man; the man whom some one else has trained. It is only when we fully realize that our duty, as well as our opportunity, lies in systematically cooperating to train and to make this competent man, instead of in hunting for a man whom some one else has trained, that we shall be on the road to national efficiency.

In the past the prevailing idea has been well expressed in the saying that "Captains of industry are born, not made"; and the theory has been that if one could get the right man, methods could be safely left to him. In the future it will be appreciated that our leaders must be trained right as well as born right, and that no great man can (with the old system of personal management) hope to compete with a number of ordinary men who have been properly organized so as efficiently to cooperate.

In the past the man has been first; in the future the system must be first. This in no sense, however, implies that great men are not needed. On the contrary, the first object of any good system must be that of developing first-class men; and under systematic management the best man rises to the top more certainly and more rapidly than ever before.

This paper has been written: *First.* To point out, through a series of simple illustrations, the great loss which the whole country is suffering through inefficiency in almost all of our daily acts.

Second. To try to convince the reader that the remedy for this inefficiency lies in systematic management, rather than in searching for some unusual or extraordinary man.

Third. To prove that the best management is a true science, resting upon clearly defined laws, rules, and principles, as a foundation. And further to show that the fundamental principles of scientific management are applicable to all kinds of human activities, from our simplest individual acts to the work of our great corporations, which call for the most elaborate cooperation. And, briefly, through a series of illustrations, to convince the reader that whenever these principles are correctly applied, results must follow which are truly astounding.

This paper was originally prepared for presentation to The American Society of Mechanical Engineers. The illustrations chosen are such as, it is believed, will especially appeal to engineers and to managers of industrial and manufacturing establishments and also quite as much to all of the men who are working in these establishments. It is hoped, however, that it will be clear to other readers that the same principles can be applied with equal force to all social activities: to the management of our homes; the management of our farms; the management of the business of our tradesmen, large and small; of our churches, our philanthropic institutions, our universities and our governmental departments.

CHAPTER I

FUNDAMENTALS OF SCIENTIFIC MANAGEMENT

THE principal object of management should be to secure the maximum prosperity for the employer, coupled with the maximum prosperity for each employee.

The words "maximum prosperity" are used, in their broad sense, to mean not only large dividends for the company or owner, but the development of every branch of the business to its highest state of excellence, so that the prosperity may be permanent.

In the same way maximum prosperity for each employee means not only higher wages than are usually received by men of his class, but, of more importance still, it also means the development of each man to his state of maximum efficiency, so that he may be able to do, generally speaking, the highest grade of work for which his natural abilities fit him, and it further means giving him, when possible, this class of work to do.

It would seem to be so self-evident that maximum prosperity for the employer, coupled with maximum prosperity for the employee, ought to be the two leading objects of management, that even to state this fact should be unnecessary. And yet there is no question that, throughout the industrial world, a large part of the organization of employers, as well as employees, is for war rather than for peace, and that perhaps the majority on either side do not believe that it is possible so to arrange their mutual relations that their interests become identical.

The majority of these men believe that the fundamental interests of employees and employers are necessarily antagonistic. Scientific management, on the contrary, has for its very foundation the firm conviction that the true interests of the two are one and the same; that prosperity for the employer cannot exist through a long term of years unless it is accompanied by prosperity for the employee, and vice versa; and that it is possible to give the workman what he most wants—high wages—and the employer what he wants—a low labor cost—for his manufactures.

It is hoped that some at least of those who do not sympathize with each of these objects may be led to modify their views; that some employers, whose attitude toward their workmen has been that of trying to get the largest amount of work out of them for the smallest possible wages, may be led to see that a more liberal policy toward their men will pay them better; and that some of those workmen who begrudge a fair and even a large profit to their employers, and who feel that all of the fruits of their labor should belong to them, and that those for whom they work and the capital invested in the business are entitled to little or nothing, may be led to modify these views.

No one can be found who will deny that in the case of any single individual the greatest prosperity can exist only when that individual has reached his highest state of efficiency; that is, when he is turning out his largest daily output.

The truth of this fact is also perfectly clear in the case of two men working together. To illustrate: if you and your workman have become so skilful that you and he together are making two pairs of shoes in a day, while your competitor and his workman are making only one pair, it is clear that after selling your two pairs of shoes you can pay your workman much higher wages than your competitor who produces only one pair of shoes is able to pay his man, and that there will still be enough money left over for you to have a larger profit than your competitor.

In the case of a more complicated manufacturing establishment, it should also be perfectly clear that the greatest permanent prosperity for the workman, coupled with the greatest prosperity for the employer, can be brought about only when the work of the establishment is done with the smallest combined expenditure of human effort, plus nature's resources, plus the cost for the use of capital in the shape of machines, buildings, etc. Or, to state the same thing in a different way: that the greatest prosperity can exist only as the result of the greatest possible productivity of the men and machines of the establishment—that is, when each man and each machine are turning out the largest possible output; because unless, your men and your machines are daily turning out more work than others around you, it is clear that competition will prevent your paying higher wages to your workmen than are paid to those of your competitor. And what is true as to the possibility of paying high wages in the case of two companies competing close beside one another is, also true as to whole districts of the country and even as to nations which are in competition. In a word, that maximum prosperity can exist only as the result of maximum productivity. Later in this paper illustrations will be given of several companies which are earning large dividends and at the same time paying from 30 per cent. to 100 per cent. higher wages to their men than are paid to similar men immediately around them, and with whose employers they are in competition. These illustrations will cover different types of work, from the most elementary to the most complicated.

If the above reasoning is correct, it follows that the most important object of both the workmen and the management should be the training and development of each individual in the establishment, so that he can do (at his fastest pace and with the maximum of efficiency) the highest class of work for which his natural abilities fit him.

These principles appear to be so self-evident that many men may think it almost childish to state them. Let us, however, turn to the facts, as they actually exist in this country and in England. The English and American peoples are the greatest sportsmen in the world. Whenever an American workman plays, baseball, or an English workman plays cricket, it is safe to say that he strains every nerve to secure victory for his side. He does his very best to make the largest possible number of runs. The universal sentiment is so strong that any man who fails to give out all there is in him in sport is branded as a "quitter," and treated with contempt by those who are around him.

When the same workman returns to work on the following day, instead of using every effort to turn out the largest possible amount of work, in a majority of the cases this man deliberately plans to do as little as he safely can—to turn out far less work than he is well able to do—in many instances to do not more than one-third to one half of a proper day's work. And in fact if he were to do his best to turn out his largest possible day's work, he would be abused by his fellow-workers for so doing, even more than if he had proved himself a "quitter" in sport. Underworking, that is, deliberately working slowly so as to avoid doing a full day's work, "soldiering," as it is called in this country, "hanging it out," as it is called in England, "ca canae," as it is called in Scotland, is almost universal in industrial establishments, and prevails also to a large extent in the building trades; and the writer asserts without fear of contradiction that this constitutes the greatest evil with which the working-people of both England and America are now afflicted.

It will be shown later in this paper that doing away with slow working and "soldiering" in all its forms and so arranging the relations between employer and employee that each workman will work to his very best advantage and at his best speed, accompanied by the intimate cooperation with the management and the help (which the workman should receive) from the management, would result on the average in nearly doubling the output of each man and each machine. What other reforms, among those which are being discussed by these two nations, could do as much toward promoting prosperity, toward the diminution of poverty, and the alleviation of suffering? America and England have been recently agitated over such subjects as the tariff, the control of the large corporations on the one hand, and of hereditary power on the other hand, and over various more or less socialistic proposals for taxation, etc. On these subjects both peoples have been profoundly stirred, and yet hardly a voice has been raised to call attention to this vastly greater and more important subject of "soldiering," which directly and powerfully affects the wages, the prosperity, and the life of almost every working-man, and also quite as much the prosperity of every industrial establishment in the nation.

The elimination of "soldiering" and of the several causes of slow working would so lower the cost of production that both our home and foreign markets would be greatly enlarged, and we could compete on more than even terms with our rivals. It would remove one of the fundamental causes for dull times, for lack of employment, and for poverty, and therefore would have a more permanent and far-reaching effect upon these misfortunes than any of the curative remedies that are now being used to soften their consequences. It would insure higher wages and make shorter working hours and better working and home conditions possible.

Why is it, then, in the face of the self-evident fact that maximum prosperity can exist only as the result of the determined effort of each workman to turn out each day his largest possible day's work, that the great majority of our men are deliberately doing just the opposite, and that even when the men have the best of intentions their work is in most cases far from efficient?

There are three causes for this condition, which may be briefly summarized as: *First.* The fallacy, which has from time immemorial been almost universal among workmen, that a material increase in the output of each man or each machine in the trade would result in the end in throwing a large number of men out of work.

Second. The defective systems of management which are in common use, and which make it necessary for each workman to soldier, or work slowly, in order that he may protect his own best interests.

Third. The inefficient rule-of-thumb methods, which are still almost universal in all trades, and in practising which our workmen waste a large part of their effort.

CHAPTER II

THE PRINCIPLES OF SCIENTIFIC MANAGEMENT

THE writer has found that there are three questions uppermost in the minds of men when they become interested in scientific management.

First. Wherein do the principles of scientific management differ essentially from those of ordinary management?

Second. Why are better results attained under scientific management than under the other types?

Third. Is not the most important problem that of getting the right man at the head of the company? And if you have the right man cannot the choice of the type of management be safely left to him?

One of the principal objects of the following pages will be to give a satisfactory answer to these questions.

THE FINEST TYPE OF ORDINARY MANAGEMENT

Before starting to illustrate the principles of scientific management, or "task management" as it is briefly called, it seems desirable to outline what the writer believes will be recognized as the best type of management which is in common use. This is done so that the great difference between the best of the ordinary management and scientific management may be fully appreciated.

In an industrial establishment which employs say from 500 to 1000 workmen, there will be found in many cases at least twenty to thirty different trades. The workmen in each of these trades have had their knowledge handed down to them by word of mouth, through the many years, in which their trade has been developed from the primitive condition, in which our far-distant ancestors each one practised the rudiments, of many different trades to the present state of great and growing subdivision of labor, in which each man specializes upon some comparatively small class of work.

The ingenuity of each generation has developed quicker and better methods for doing every element of the work in every trade. Thus the methods which are now in use may in a broad sense be said to be an evolution representing the survival of the fittest and best of the ideas which have been developed since the starting of each trade. However, while this is true in a broad sense, only those who are intimately acquainted with each of these trades are fully aware of the fact that in hardly any element of any trade is there uniformity in the methods which are used. Instead of having only one way which is generally accepted as a standard, there are in daily use, say, fifty or a hundred different ways of doing each element of the work. And a little thought will make it clear that this must inevitably be the case, since our methods have been handed down from man to man by word of mouth, or have, in most cases, been almost unconsciously learned through personal observation. Practically in no instances have they been codified or systematically analyzed or described. The ingenuity and experience of each generation—of each decade, even, have without doubt handed over better methods to the next. This mass of rule-of-thumb or traditional knowledge may be said to be the principal asset or possession of every tradesman. Now, in the best of the ordinary types of management, the managers recognize frankly the fact that the 500 or 1000 workmen, included in the twenty to thirty trades, who are under them, possess this mass of traditional knowledge, a large part of which is not in the possession of the management. The management, of course, includes foremen and superintendents, who themselves have been in most cases first-class workers at their trades. And yet these foremen and superintendents know, better than any one else, that their own knowledge and personal skill falls far short of the combined knowledge and dexterity of all the workmen under them. The most experienced managers therefore frankly place before their workmen the problem of doing the work in the best and most economical way. They recognize the task before them as that of inducing each workman to use his best endeavors, his hardest work, all his traditional knowledge, his skill, his ingenuity, and his good-will—in a word, his "initiative," so as to yield the largest possible return to his employer. The problem before the management, then, may be briefly said to be that of obtaining the best *initiative* of every workman. And the writer uses the word "initiative" in its broadest sense, to cover all of the good qualities sought for from the men.

On the other hand, no intelligent manager would hope to obtain in any full measure the initiative of his workmen unless he felt that he was giving them something more than they usually receive from their employers. Only those among the readers of this paper who have been managers or who have worked themselves at a trade realize how far the average workman falls short of giving his employer his full initiative. It is well within the mark to state that in nineteen out of twenty industrial establishments the workmen believe it to be directly against their interests to give their employers their best initiative, and that instead of working hard to do the largest possible amount of work and the best quality of work for their employers, they deliberately work as slowly as they dare while they at the same time try to make those over them believe that they are working fast.

The writer repeats, therefore, that in order to have any hope of obtaining the initiative of his workmen the manager must give some *special incentive* to his men beyond that which is given to the average of the trade. This incentive can be given in several different ways, as, for example, the hope of rapid promotion or advancement; higher wages, either in the form of generous piecework prices or of a premium or bonus of some kind for good and rapid work; shorter hours of labor; better surroundings and working conditions than are ordinarily given, etc., and, above all, this special incentive should be accompanied by that personal consideration for, and friendly contact with, his workmen which comes only from a genuine and kindly interest in the welfare of those under him. It is only by giving a special inducement or "incentive" of this kind that the employer can hope even approximately to get the "initiative" of his workmen. Under the ordinary type of management the necessity for offering the workman a special inducement has come to be so generally recognized that a large proportion of those most interested in the subject look upon the adoption of some one of the modern schemes for paying men (such as piece work, the premium plan, or the bonus plan, for instance) as practically the whole system of management. Under scientific management, however, the particular pay system which is adopted is merely one of the subordinate elements.

Broadly speaking, then, the best type of management in ordinary use may be defined as management in which the workmen give their best *initiative* and in return receive some *special incentive* from their employers. This type of management will be referred to as the management of *"initiative and incentive"* in contradistinction to scientific management, or task management, with which it is to be compared.

The writer hopes that the management of "initiative and incentive" will be recognized as representing the best type in ordinary use, and in fact he believes that it will be hard to persuade the average manager that anything better exists in the whole field than this type. The task which the writer has before him, then, is the difficult one of trying to prove in a thoroughly convincing way that there is another type of management which is not only better but overwhelmingly better than the management of "initiative and incentive."

The universal prejudice in favor of the management of "initiative and incentive" is so strong that no mere theoretical advantages which can be pointed out will be likely to convince the average manager that any other system is better. It will be upon a series of practical illustrations of the actual working of the two systems that the writer will depend in his efforts to prove that scientific management is so greatly superior to other types. Certain elementary principles, a certain philosophy, will however be recognized as the essence of that which is being illustrated in all of the practical examples which will be given. And the broad principles in which the scientific system differs from the ordinary or "rule-of-thumb" system are so simple in their nature that it seems desirable to describe them before starting with the illustrations.

Under the old type of management success depends almost entirely upon getting the "initiative" of the workmen, and it is indeed a rare case in which this initiative is really attained. Under scientific management the "initiative" of the workmen (that is, their hard work, their good-will, and their ingenuity) is obtained with absolute uniformity and to a greater extent than is possible under the old system; and in addition to this improvement on the part of the men, the managers assume new burdens, new duties, and responsibilities never dreamed of in the past. The managers assume, for instance, the burden of gathering together all of the traditional knowledge which in the past has been possessed by the workmen and then of classifying, tabulating, and reducing this knowledge to rules, laws, and formulas which are immensely helpful to the workmen in doing their daily work. In addition to developing a *science* in this way. the management take on three other types of duties which involve new and heavy burdens for themselves.

These new duties are grouped under four heads:

First. They develop a science for each element of a man's work, which replaces the old rule-of-thumb method.

Second. They scientifically select and then train, teach, and develop the workman, whereas in the past he chose his own work and trained himself as best he could.

Third. They heartily cooperate with the men so as to insure all of the work being done in accordance with the principles of the science which has been developed.

Fourth. There is an almost equal division of the work and the responsibility between the management and the workmen. The management take over all work for which they are better fitted than the workmen, while in the past almost all of the work and the greater part of the responsibility were thrown upon the men.

It is this combination of the initiative of the workmen, coupled with the new types of work done by the management, that makes scientific management so much more efficient than the old plan.

Three of these elements exist in many cases, under the management of "initiative and incentive," in a small and rudimentary way, but they are, under this management, of minor importance, whereas under scientific management they form the very essence of the whole system.

The fourth of these elements, "an almost equal division of the responsibility between the management and the workmen," requires further explanation. The philosophy of the management of "initiative and incentive" makes it necessary for each workman to bear almost the entire responsibility for the general plan as well as for each detail of his work, and in many cases for his implements as well. In addition to this he must do all of the actual physical labor. The development of a science, on the other hand, involves the establishment of many rules, laws, and formulae which replace the judgment of the individual workman and which can be effectively used only after having been systematically recorded, indexed, etc. The practical use of scientific data also calls for a room in which to keep the books, records, etc., and a desk for the planner to work at. Thus all of the planning which under the old system was done by the workman, as a result of his personal experience, must of necessity under the new system be done by the management in accordance with the laws of the science; because even if the workman was well suited to the development and use of scientific data, it would be physically impossible for him to work at his machine and at a desk at the same time. It is also clear that in most cases one type of man is needed to plan ahead and an entirely different type to execute the work.

The man in the planning room, whose specialty under scientific management is planning ahead, invariably finds that the work can be done better and more economically by a subdivision of the labor; each act of each mechanic, for example, should be preceded by various preparatory acts done by other men. And all of this involves, as we have said, "an almost equal division of the responsibility and the work between the management and the workman."

To summarize: Under the management of "initiative and incentive" practically the whole problem is "up to the workman," while under scientific management fully one-half of the problem is "up to the management."

Perhaps the most prominent single element of modern scientific management is the task idea. The work of every workman is fully planned out by the management at least one day in advance, and each man receives in most cases complete written instructions, describing in detail the task which he is to accomplish, as well as the means to be used in doing the work. And the work planned in advance in this way constitutes, a task which is to be solved, as explained above, not by the workman alone, but in almost all cases, by the joint effort of the workman and the management. This task specifies not only what is to be done but how it is to be done and the exact time allowed for doing it. And whenever the workman succeeds in doing his task right, and within the time limit specified, he receives an addition of from 30 per cent. to 100 per cent. to his ordinary wages. These tasks are carefully planned, so that both good and careful work are called for in their performance, but it should be distinctly understood that in no case is the workman called upon to work at a pace which would be injurious to his health. The task is always so regulated that the man who is well suited to his job will thrive while working at this rate during a long term of years and grow happier and more prosperous, instead of being overworked. Scientific management consists very largely in preparing for and carrying out these tasks.

The writer is fully aware that to perhaps most of the readers of this paper the four elements which differentiate the new management from the old will at first appear to be merely high-sounding phrases; and he would again repeat that he has no idea of convincing the reader of their value merely through announcing their existence. His hope of carrying conviction rests upon demonstrating the tremendous force and effect of these four elements through a series of practical illustrations. It will be shown, first, that they can be applied absolutely to all classes of work, from the most elementary to the most intricate; and second, that when they are applied, the results must of necessity be overwhelmingly greater than those which it is possible to attain under the management of initiative and incentive.

The first illustration is that of handling pig iron, and this work is chosen because it is typical of perhaps the crudest and most elementary form of labor which is performed by man. This work is done by men with no other implements than their hands. The pig-iron handler stoops down, picks up a pig weighing about 92 pounds, walks for a few feet or yards and then drops it on to the ground or upon a pile. This work is so crude and elementary in its nature that the writer firmly believes that it would be possible to train an intelligent gorilla so as to become a more efficient pig-iron handler than any man can be. Yet it will be shown that the science of handling pig iron is so great and amounts to so much that it is impossible for the man who is best suited to this type of work to understand the principles of this science, or even to work in accordance with these principles without the aid of a man better educated than he is. And the further illustrations to be given will make it clear that in almost all of the mechanic arts the science which underlies each workman's act is so great and amounts to so much that the workman who is best suited actually to do the work is incapable (either through lack of education or through insufficient mental capacity) of understanding this science. This is announced as a general principle, the truth of which will become apparent as one illustration after another is given. After showing these four elements in the handling of pig iron, several illustrations will be given of their application to different kinds of work in the field of the mechanic arts, at intervals in a rising scale, beginning with the simplest and ending with the more intricate forms of labor.

One of the first pieces of work undertaken by us, when the writer started to introduce scientific management into the Bethlehem Steel Company, was to handle pig iron on task work. The opening of the Spanish War found some 80,000 tons of pig iron placed in small piles in an open field adjoining the works. Prices for pig iron had been so low that it could not be sold at a profit, and it therefore had been stored. With the opening of the Spanish War the price of pig iron rose, and this large accumulation of iron was sold. This gave us a good opportunity to show the workmen, as well as the owners and managers of the works, on a fairly large scale the advantages of task work over the old-fashioned day work and piece work, in doing a very elementary class of work.

The Bethlehem Steel Company had five blast furnaces, the product of which had been handled by a pig-iron gang for many years. This gang, at this time, consisted of about 75 men. They were good, average pig-iron handlers, were under an excellent foreman who himself had been a pig-iron handler, and the work was done, on the whole, about as fast and as cheaply as it was anywhere else at that time.

A railroad switch was run out into the field, right along the edge of the piles of pig iron. An inclined plank was placed against the side of a car, and each man picked up from his pile a pig of iron weighing about 92 pounds, walked up the inclined plank and dropped it on the end of the car.

We found that this gang were loading on the average about 12 ½ long tons per man per day. We were surprised to find, after studying the matter, that a first-class pig-iron handler ought to handle between 47 and 48 long tons per day, instead of 12 ½ tons. This task seemed to us so very large that we were obliged to go over our work several times before we were absolutely sure that we were right. Once we were sure, however, that 47 tons was a proper day's work for a first-class pig-iron handler, the task which faced us as managers under the modern scientific plan was clearly before us. It was our duty to see that the 80,000 tons of pig iron was loaded on to the cars at the rate of 47 tons per man per day, in place of 12 ½ tons, at which rate the work was then being done. And it was further our duty to see that this work was done without bringing on a strike among the men, without any quarrel with the men, and to see that the men were happier and better contented when loading at the new rate of 47 tons than they were when loading at the old rate of 12 ½ tons.

Our first step was the scientific selection of the workman. In dealing with workmen under this type of management, it is an inflexible rule to talk to and deal with only one man at a time, since each workman has his own special abilities and limitations, and since we are not dealing with men in masses, but are trying to develop each individual man to his highest state of efficiency and prosperity. Our first step was to find the proper workman to begin with. We therefore carefully watched and studied these 75 men for three or four days, at the end of which time we had picked out four men who appeared to be physically able to handle pig iron at the rate of 47 tons per day. A careful study was then made of each of these men. We looked up their history as far back as practicable and thorough inquiries were made as to the character, habits, and the ambition of each of them. Finally we selected one from among the four as the most likely man to start with. He was a little Pennsylvania Dutchman who had been observed to trot back home for a mile or so after his work in the evening about as fresh as he was when he came trotting down to work in the morning. We found that upon wages of $1.15 a day he had succeeded in buying a small plot of ground, and that he was engaged in putting up the walls of a little house for himself in the morning before starting to work and at night after leaving. He also had the reputation of being exceedingly "close," that is, of placing a very high value on a dollar. As one man whom we talked to about him said, "A penny looks about the size of a cart-wheel to him." This man we will call Schmidt.

The task before us, then, narrowed itself down to getting Schmidt to handle 47 tons of pig iron per day and making him glad to do it. This was done as follows. Schmidt was called out from among the gang of pig-iron handlers and talked to somewhat in this way: "Schmidt, are you a high-priced man?"

"Vell, I don't know vat you mean."

"Oh yes, you do. What I want to know is whether you are a high-priced man or not."

"Vell, I don't know vat you mean."

"Oh, come now, you answer my questions. What I want to find out is whether you are a high-priced man or one of these cheap fellows here. What I want to find out is whether you want to earn $1.85 a day or whether you are satisfied with $1.15, just the same as all those cheap fellows are getting."

"Did I vant $1.85 a day? Vas dot a high-priced man? Vell, yes, I vas a high-priced man."

"Oh, you're aggravating me. Of course you want $1.85 a day—every one wants it! You know perfectly well that that has very little to do with your being a high-priced man. For goodness' sake answer my questions, and don't waste any more of my time. Now come over here. You see that pile of pig iron?"

"Yes."

"You see that car?"

"Yes"

"Well, if you are a high-priced man, you will load that pig iron on that car to-morrow for $1.85. Now do wake up and answer my question. Tell me whether you are a high-priced man or not."

"Vell—did I got $1.85 for loading dot pig iron on dot car to-morrow?"

"'Yes, of course you do, and you get $1.85 for loading a pile like that every day right through the year. That is what a high-priced man does, and you know it just as well as I do."

"Vell, dot's all right. I could load dot pig iron on the car to-morrow for $1.85, and I get it every day, don't I?"

"Certainly you do—certainly you do."

"Vell, den, I vas a high-priced man."

"Now, hold on, hold on. You know just as well as I do that a high-priced man has to do exactly as he's told from morning till night. You have seen this man here before, haven't you?"

"No, I never saw him."

"Well, if you are a high-priced man, you will do exactly as this man tells you to-morrow, from morning till night. When he tells you to pick up a pig and walk, you pick it up and you walk, and when he tells you to sit down and rest, you sit down. You do that right straight through the day. And what's more, no back talk. Now a high-priced man does just what he's told to do, and no back talk. Do you understand that? When this man tells you to walk, you walk; when he tells you to sit down, you sit down, and you don't talk back at him. Now you come on to work here to-morrow morning and I'll know before night whether you are really a high-priced man or not."

This seems to be rather rough talk. And indeed it would be if applied to an educated mechanic, or even an intelligent laborer. With a man of the mentally sluggish type of Schmidt it is appropriate and not unkind, since it is effective in fixing his attention on the high wages which he wants and away from what, if it were called to his attention, he probably would consider impossibly hard work.

What would Schmidt's answer be if he were talked to in a manner which is usual under the management of "initiative and incentive?" say, as follows:

"Now, Schmidt, you are a first-class pig-iron handler and know your business well. You have been handling at the rate of 12 ½ tons per day. I have given considerable study to handling pig iron, and feel sure that you could do a much larger day's work than you have been doing. Now don't you think that if you really tried you could handle 47 tons of pig iron per day, instead of 12 ½ tons?"

What do you think Schmidt's answer would be to this?

Schmidt started to work and all day long, and at regular intervals, was told by the man who stood over him with a watch, "Now pick up a pig and walk. Now sit down and rest. Now walk—now rest," etc. He worked when he was told to work, and rested when he was told to rest, and at half past five in the afternoon had his 47 tons loaded on the car. And he practically never failed to work at this pace and do the task that was set him during the three years that the writer was at Bethlehem. And throughout this time he averaged a little more than $1.85 per day, whereas before he had never received over $1.15 per day, which was the ruling rate of wages at that time in Bethlehem. That is, he received 60 per cent. higher wages than were paid to other men who were not working on task work. One man after another was picked out and trained to handle pig iron at the rate of 47 tons per day until all of the pig iron was handled at this rate, and the men were receiving 60 per cent. more wages than other workmen around them.

The science which exists in most of the mechanic arts is, however, far simpler than the science of cutting metals. In almost all cases, in fact, the laws or rules which are developed are so simple that the average man would hardly dignify them with the name of a science. In most trades, the science is developed through a comparatively simple analysis and time study of the movements required by the workmen to do some small part of his work, and this study is usually made by a man equipped merely with a stop-watch and a properly ruled notebook. Hundreds of these " time-study men" are now engaged in developing elementary scientific knowledge where before existed only rule of thumb. Even the motion study of Mr. Gilbreth in bricklaying (described on pages 77 to 84) involves a much more elaborate investigation than that which occurs in most cases. The general steps to be taken in developing a simple law of this class are as follows:

First. Find, say, 10 or 15 different men (preferably in as many separate establishments and different parts of the country) who are especially skilful in doing the particular work to be analyzed.

Second. Study the exact series of elementary operations or motions which each of these men uses in doing the work which is being investigated, as well as the implements each man uses.

Third. Study with a stop-watch the time required to make each of these elementary movements and then select the quickest way of doing each element of the work.

Fourth. Eliminate all false movements, slow movements, and useless movements.

Fifth. After doing away with all unnecessary movements, collect into one series the quickest and best movements as well as the best implements.

This one new method, involving that series of motions. which can be made quickest and best, is then substituted in place of the ten or fifteen inferior series which were formerly in use. This best method becomes standard, and remains standard, to be taught first to the teachers (or functional foremen) and by them to every workman in the establishment until it is superseded by a quicker and better series of movements. In this simple way one element after another of the science is developed.

In the same way each type of implement used in a trade is studied. Under the philosophy of the management of "initiative and incentive" each workman is called upon to use his own best judgment, so as to do the work in the quickest time, and from this results in all cases a large variety in the shapes and types of implements which are used for any specific purpose. Scientific management requires, first, a careful investigation of each of the many modifications of the same implement, developed under rule of thumb; and second, after a time study has been made of the speed attainable with each of these implements, that the good points of several of them shall be united in a single standard implement, which will enable the workman to work faster and with greater ease than he could before. This one implement, then, is adopted as standard in place of the many different kinds before in use, and it remains standard for all workmen to use until superseded by an implement which has been shown, through motion and time study, to be still better.

With this explanation it will be seen that the development of a science to replace rule of thumb is in most cases by no means a formidable undertaking, and that it can be accomplished by ordinary, every-day men without any elaborate scientific training; but that, on the other hand, the successful use of even the simplest improvement of this kind calls for records, system, and cooperation where in the past existed only individual effort.

VISIONS OF A
TECHNOLOGICAL WORLD

Aldous Huxley

H. G. Wells

Jonathan Swift

Mary Shelley

Stephen Vincent Benét

By his very success in inventing labor-saving devices, modern man has manufactured an abyss of boredom that only the privileged class in earlier civilizations have ever fathomed.

Lewis Mumford, *The Conduct of Life*, 1951

The new electronic interdependence recreates the world in the image of a global village.

Marshall McLuhan, *The Medium is the Message*, 1967

I fear that the spinning wheel is not superior to the machine.

Jawaharlal Nehru

. . .Saw the heavens fill with commerce, argosies of magic sails,
Pilots of the purple twilight, dropping down with costly bales;
Heard the heavens fill with shouting, and there rained a ghastly dew
From the nations' airy navies grappling in the central blue. . .
Science moves, but slowly, slowly, creeping on from point to point. . .

Alfred, Lord Tennyson, *Locksley Hall*, 1832

BRAVE NEW WORLD

ALDOUS HUXLEY

Aldous Huxley (1894-1963) was born in England, the son of a physician and grandson of Thomas H. Huxley, and educated at Eton and Oxford. A siege of temporary blindness kept him from going to medical school, and he turned his attention to literature. As journalist, essayist, and novelist, he quickly became a prolific and renowned writer.

In the words of Huxley himself, "*Brave New World* presents a fanciful and somewhat ribald picture of a society, in which the attempt to recreate human beings in the likeness of termites has been pushed almost to the limits of the possible."

1. Do you see any parallels between the conditioning of children described by Huxley and any aspects of current society? Explain.

2. Implicit in *Brave New World* are at least two sharply different views of technology. Characterize them.

3. *Brave New World* was published in 1932. Has the relationship between technology and society developed in the way Huxley envisioned? Why or why not?

4. What aspects of *Brave New World* still seem far fetched, and what aspects already have come to pass or have been overtaken in the contemporary world?

5. Would you look forward to living in a society like that described in *Brave New World*? Is our society moving in that direction? What can be done either to accelerate or to stop that development?

6. What are the ethical implications of the cloning of human beings? Do you think cloning of humans ought to be allowed? Do you think it can be prevented?

BRAVE NEW WORLD

ALDOUS HUXLEY

Chapter One

A squat grey building of only thirty-four stories. Over the main entrance the words, CENTRAL LONDON HATCHERY AND CONDITIONING CENTRE, and, in a shield, the World State's motto, COMMUNITY, IDENTITY, STABILITY.

The enormous room on the ground floor faced towards the north. Cold for all the summer beyond the panes, for all the tropical heat of the rom itself, a harsh thin light glared through the windows, hungrily seeking some draped lay figure, some pallid shape of academic goose-flesh, but finding only the glass and nickel and bleakly shining porcelain of a laboratory. Wintriness responded to wintriness. The overalls of the workers were white, their hands gloved with a pale corpe-coloured rubber. The light was frozen, dead, a ghost. Only from the yellow barrels of the microscopes did it borrow a certain rich and living substance, lying along the polished tubes like butter, streak after luscious streak in long recessiondown the work tables.

"And this," said the Director opening the door, "is the Fertilizing Room."

Bent over their instruments, three hundred Fertilizers were plunged, as the Director of Hatcheries and Conditioning entered the room, in the scarcely breathing silence, the absent-minded, soliloquizing hum or whistle, of absorbed concentration. A troop of newly arrived students, very young, pink and callow, followed nervously, rather abjectly, at the Director's heels. Each of them carried a notebook, in which, whenever the great man spoke, he desperately scribbled. Straight from the horse's mouth. It was a rare privilege. The D.H.C. for Central London always made a point of personally conducting his new students round the various departments.

"Just to give you a general idea," he would explain to them. For of course some sort of general idea they must have, if they were to do their work intelligently—though as little of one, if they were to be good and happy members of society, as possible. For particulars, as every one knows, make for virtue and happiness; generalities are intellectually necessary evils. Not philosophers but fret-sawyers and stamp collectors compose the backbone of society.

"To-morrow," he would add, smiling at them with a slightly menacing geniality, "you'll be settling down to serious work. You won't have time for generalities. Meanwhile. . ."

Meanwhile, it was a privilege. Straight from the horse's mouth into the notebook. The boys scribbled like mad.

Tall and rather thin but upright, the Director advanced into the room. He had a long chin and big, rather prominent teeth, just covered, when he was not talking, by his full, floridly curved lips. Old, young? Thirty? Fifty? Fifty-five? It was hard to say. And anyhow the question didn't arise; in this year of stability, A.F. 632, it didn't occur to you to ask it.

"I shall begin at the beginning," said the D.H.C. and the more zealous students recorded his intention in their notebooks: *Begin at the beginning.* "These," he waved his hand, "are the incubtors." And opening an insulated door he showed them racks upon racks of numbered test-tubes. "The week's supply of ova. Kept," he explained, "at blood heat; whereas the male gametes," and here he opened another door, "they have to be kept at thirty-five instead of thirty-seven. Full blood heat sterilizes." Rams wrapped in theremogene beget no lambs.

Still leaning against the incubators he gave them, while the pencils scurried illegibly across the pages, a brief description of the modern fertilizing process; spoke first, of course, of its surgical introduction—"the operation undergone voluntarily for the good of Society, not to mention the fact that it carries a bonus amounting to six months' salary"; continued with some account of the technique for preserving the excised ovary alive and actively developing; passed on to a consideration of optimum temperature, salinity, viscosity; referred to the liquor in which the detached and ripened eggs were kept; and, leading his charges to the work tables, actually showed them how this liquor was drawn off from the test-tubes; how it was let out drop by drop onto the specially warmed slides of the microscopes; how the eggs which it contained were inspected for abnormalities, counted and transferred to a porous receptacle; how (and he now took them to watch the operation) this receptacle was immersed in a warm bouillon containing free-swimming spermatozoa—at a minimum concentration of one hundred thousand per cubic centimeter, he insisted; and how, after ten minutes, the container was liefted out of the liquor and its contents re-examined; how, if any of the eggs remained unfertilized, it was again immersed, and, if necessary, yet again; how the fertilized ova went back to the incubators; where the Alphas and Betas remained until definitely bottled; while the Gammas, Deltas and Epsilons were brought out again, after only thirty-six hours, to undergo Bokanovsky's Process.

"Bokanovsky's Process," repeated the Director, and the students underlined the words in their little notebooks.

One egg, one embryo, one-adult—normality. But a bokanovskified egg will bud, will proliferate, will divide. From eight to ninety-six buds, and every bud will grow into a perfectly formed embryo, and every embryo into a full-sized adult. Making ninety-six human beings grow where only one grew before. Progress.

"Essentially," the D.H.C. concluded, "bokanovskification consists of a series of arrests of development. We check the normal growth and, paradoxically enough, the egg responds by budding."

Responds by budding. The pencils were busy.

He pointed. On a very slowly moving band a rack-full of test-tubes was entering a large metal box, another rack-full was emerging. Machinery faintly purred. It took eight minutes for the tubes to go through, he told them. Eight minutes of hard X-rays being about as much as an egg can stand. A few died; of the rest, the least susceptible divided into two; most put out four buds; some eight; all were returned to the incubators, where the buds began to develop; then, after two days, were suddenly chilled, chilled and checked. Two, four, eight, the buds intheir turn budded; and having budded were dosed almost to death with alcohol; consequently burgeoned again and having budded—bud out of bud ot of bud—were thereafter—further arrest being generally fatal—left to develop in peace. By which time the original egg was in a fair way to becoming anything from eight to ninety-six embryos—a prodigious improvement, you will agree, on nature. Identical twins—but not in piddling twos and threes as in the old viviparous days, when an egg would sometimes accidentally divide; actually by dozens, by scores at a time.

"Scores," the Director repeated and flung out his arms, as though he were distributing largesse. "Scores."

But one of the students was fool enough to ask where the advantage lay.

"My good boy!" The Director wheeled sharply round on him. "Can't you see? Can't you *see?*" He raised a hand; his expression was solemn. "Bokanovsky's Process is one of the major instruments of social stability!"

Major instruments of social stability.

Standard men and women; in uniform batches. The whole of a small factory staffed with the products of a single bokanovskified egg.

"Ninety-six identical twins working ninety-six identical machines!" The voice was almost tremulous with enthusiasm. "You really know where you are. For the first time in history." He quoted the planetary motto. "Community, Identity, Stability." Grand words. "If we could bokanovskify indefinitely the whole problem would be solved."

Solved by standard Gammas, unvarying Deltas, uniform Epsilons. Millions of identical twins. The principle of mass production at last applied to biology.

"But, alas," the Director shook his head, "we *can't* bokanovskify indefinitely."

Ninety-six seemed to be the limit; seventy-two a good average. From the same ovary and with gametes of the same male to manufacture as many batches of identical twins as possible—that was the best (sadly a second best) that they could do. And even that was difficult.

"For in nature it takes thirty years for two hundred eggs to reach maturity. But our business is to stabilize the population at this moment, here and now. Dribbling out twins over a quarter of a century—what would be the use of that?"

Obviously, no use at all. But Podsnap's Technique had immensely accelerated the process of ripening. They could make sure of at least a hundred and fifty mature eggs within two years. Fertilze and bokanovskify—in other words, multiply by seventy-two—and you get an average of nearly eleven thousand brothers and sisters in a hundred and fifty batches of identical twins, all within two years of the same age.

"And in exceptional cases we can make one overay yield us over fifteen thousand adult individuals."

Beckoning to a fair-haired, ruddy young man who happened to be passing at the moment, "Mr. Foster," he called. The ruddy young man approached. "Can you tell us the record for a single ovary, Mr. Foster?

"Sixteen thousand and twelve in this Centre," Mr. Foster replied without hesitation. He spoke very quickly, had a vivacious blue eye, and took an evident pleasure in quoting figures. "Sixteen thousand and twelve; in one hundred and eighty-nine batches of identicals. But of course they've done much better," he rattled on, "in some of the tropical Centres. Singapore has often produced over sixteen thousand five hundred; and Mombasa has actually touched the seventeen thousand mark. But then they have unfair advantages. You should see the way a negro ovary responds to pituitary! It's quite astonishing, when you're used to working with European material. Still," he added, with a laugh (but the light of combat was in his eyes and the lift of his chin was challenging), "still, we mean to beat them if we can. I'm working on a wonderful Delta-Minuts ovary at this moment. Only just eighteen months old. Over twelve thousand seven hundred children already, either decanted or in embryo. And still going strong. We'll beat them yet."

"That's the spirit I like!" cried the Director, and clapped Mr Foster onthe shoulder. "Come along with us and give these boys the benefit of your expert knowledge."

Mr. Foster smiled modestly. "With pleasure." They went.

In the Bottling Room all was harmonious bustle and ordered activity. Flaps of fresh sow's peritoneum rady cut to the proper size came shooting up in little lfts from the Organ Store in the sub-basement. Whizz and then, click! the lift-hatches flew open; the bottle-liner had only to reach out a hand, take the flap, insert, smooth-down, and before the lined bottle had had time to travel out of reach along the endless band, whizz, click! another flap of peritoneum had shot up from the depths, ready to be slipped into yet another bottle, the next of that slow interminable procession on the band.

Next to the Linders stood the Matriculators. The procession advanced; one by one the eggs were transferred from their test-tubes to the larger containers; deftly the peritoneal lining was slit, the morula dropped into place, the saline solution poured in. . . and already the bottle had passed, and it was the turn of the labellers. Heredity, date of fertilization, membership of Bokanovsky Group—details were transferred from test-tube to bottle. No longer anonymous, but named, identified, the procession marched slowly on; on through an opening in the wall, slowly on; on through an opening in the wall, slowly on into the Social Predestination Room.

"Eighty-eight cubic metres of card-index," said Mr. Foster with relish as they entered.

"Containing *all* the relevant information," added the Director.

"Brought up to date every morning."

"And co-ordinated every afternoon."

"On the basis of which they make their calculations."

"So many individuals, of such and such quality," said Mr. Foster.

"Distributed in such and such quantities."

"The optimum Decanting Rate at any given moment."

"Unforeseen wastages promptly made good."

"Promptly," repeated Mr. Foster. "If you knew the amount of overtime I had to put in after the last Japanese earthquake!" He laughed good-humouredly and shook his head.

"The Predestinators send intheir figures to the Fertilizers."

"Who give them the embryos they ask for."

"And the bottles come in here to be predestinated in detail."

"After which they are sent down to the Embryo Store."

"Where we now proceed ourselves."

And opening a door Mr. Foster led the way down a staircase into the basement.

The temperature was still tropical. They descended into a thickening twilight. Two doors and a passage with a double turn insured the cellar against any possible infiltration of the day.

"Embryos are like photograph film," said Mr. Foster waggishly, as he pushed open the second door. "They can only stand red light."

And in effect the sultry darkness into which the students now followed him was visible and crimson, like the darkness of closed eyes on a summer's afternoon. The bulging flanks of row on receding row and tier above tier of bottles glinted with innumerable rubies, and among the rubies moved the dim red spectres of men and women with purple eyes and all the symptoms of lupus. The hum and rattle of machinery faintly stirred the air.

"Give them a few figures, Mr. Foster," said the Director, who was tired of talking.

Mr. Foster was only too happy to give them a few figures.

Two hundred and twenty metres long, two hundred wide, ten high. He pointed upwards. Like chickens drinking, the students lifted their eyes towards the distant ceiling.

Three tiers of racks: ground floor level, first gallery, second gallery.

The spidery steel-work of gallery above gallery faded away in all directions into the dark. Near them three red ghosts were busily unloading demijohns from a moving staircase.

The escalator from the Social Predestination Room.

Each bottle could be placed on one of fifteen racks, each rack, though you couldn't see it, was a conveyor travelling at the rate of thirty-three and a third centimetres an hour. Two hundred and sixty-seven days at eight metres a day. Two thousand one hundred and thirty-six metres in all. One circuit of the cellar at ground level, one on the first gallery, half on the second, and on the two hundred and sixty-seventh morning, daylight in the Decanting Room. Independent existence—so called.

"But in the interval," Mr. Foster concluded, "we've managed to do a lot to them. Oh, a very great deal." His laugh was knowing and triumphant.

"That's the spirit I like," said the Director once more. "Let's walk round. You tell them everything, Mr. Foster."

Mr. Foster duly told them.

Told them of the growing embryo on its bed of peritoneum. Made them taste the rich blood surrogate on which it fed. Explained why it had to be stimulated with placentin and thyroxin. Todl them of the *corpus luteum* extract. Showed them the jets through which at every twelfth metre from zero to 2040 it was automatically injected. Spoke of those gradually increasing doses of pituitary administered during the final ninety-six metres of their course. Described the artificial maternal circulation installed on every bottle at Metre 112; showed them the reservoir of blood-surrogate, the centrifugal pump that kept the liquid moving over the placenta and drove it through the synthetic lung and waste-product filter. Referred to the embryo's troublesome tendency to anaemia, to the massive doses of hog's stomach extract and foetal foal's liver with which, in sonequence, it had to be supplied.

Showed them the simple mechanism by means of which, during the last two metres out of every eight, all the embryos were simultaneously shaken into familiarity with movemet. Hinted at the gravity of the so-called "trauma of decanting," and enumerated the precautions taken to minimize, by a suitable training of the bottled embryo, that dangerous shock. Told them of the tests for sex carried out in the neighbourhood of metre 200. Explained the system of labelling—a T for the males, a circle for the females and for those who were destined to become freemartins a question mark, black on a white ground.

"For of course," said Mr. Foster, "in the vast majority of cases, fertility is merely a nuisance. One fertile ovary in twelve hundred—that would really be quite sufficient for our purposes. But we want to have a good choice. And of course one must always leave an enormous margin of safety. So we allow as many as thirty per cent of the female embryos to develop normally. The others get a dose of male sex-hormone every twenty-four metres for the rest of the course. Result: they're decanted as freemartins—structurally quite normal (except," he had to admit, "that they *do* have just the slightest tendency to grow beards), but sterile. Guaranteed sterile. Which rings us at last," continued Mr. Foster, "out of the realm of mere stavish imitation of nature into the much more interesting world of human invention."

He rubbed his hands. For of course, they didn't content themselves with merely hatching out embryos: any cow could do that.

"We also predestine and condition. We decant our babies as socialized human beings, as Alphas or Epsilons, as future sewage workers or future. . ." He was going to say "future World controllers," but correcting himself, said "future Directors of Hatcheries," instead.

The D.H.C. acknowledged the compliment with a smile.

They were passing Metre 320 on rack ll. A young Beta-Minus mechanic was busy with screwdriver and spanner on the blood-surrogate pump of a passing bottle. The hum of the electic motor deepened by fractions of a tone as he turned the nuts. Down, down. . .A final twist, a glance at the revolution counter, and he was done. He moved two paces down the line and began the same process onthe next pump.

"Reducing the number of revolutions per minute," Mr. Foster explained. "The surrogate goes round slower; therefore passes through the lung at longer intervals; therefore gives the embryo less oxygen. Nothing like oxygen-shortage for keeping an embryo below par." Again he rubbed his hands.

"But why do you want to keep the embryo below par?" asked an ingenuous student.

"Ass!" said the Director, breaking a long silence. "Hasn't it occurred to you that an Epsilon embryo must have an Epsilon environment as well as an Epsilon heredity?"

It evidently hadn't occurred to him. He was covered with confusion.

"The lower the caste," said Mr Foster, "the shorter the oxygen." The first organ affected was the brain. After that the skeleton. At seventy percent of normal oxygen you got dwarfs. At less than seventy eyeless monsters.

"Who are no use at all," concluded Mr. Foster.

Whereas (his voice became confidential and eager), if they could discover a technique for shortening the period of maturation what a triumph, what a benefaction to Society!

"Consider the horse."

They considered it.

Mature at six; the elephant at ten. While at thirteen a man is not yet sexually mature; and is only full-grown at twenty. Hence, of course, that fruit of delayed development, the human intelligence.

"But in Epsilons," said Mr. Foster very justly, "we don't need human intelligence."

Didn't need and didn't get it. But though the Epsilon mind was mature at ten, the Epsilon body was not fit to work till eighteen. Long years of superfluous and wasted immaturity. If the physical development could be speeded up till it was as quick, say, as a cow's, what an enormous saving to the Community!

"Enormous!" murmured the students. Mr. Foster's enthusiasm was infectious.

He became rather technical; spoke of the abnormal endocrine co-ordination which made men grow so slowly; postulated a germinal mutation to account for it. Could the effects of this germinal mutation be undone? Could the individual Epsilon embryo be made a revert, by a suitable technique, to the normality of dogs and cows? That was the problem. And it was all but solved.

Pilkington, at Mombasa, had produced individuals who were sexually mature at four and full-grown at six and a half. A scientific triumph. But socially useless. Six-year-old-men and women were too stupid to do even Epsilon work. And the process was an all-or-nothing one; either you failed to modify at all, or else you modified the whole way. They were still trying to find the ideal compromise between adults of twenty and adults of six. So far without success. Mr. Foster sighed and shook his head.

Their wanderings through the crimson twilight had brought thm to the neighbourhood of Metre 170 on Rack 9. From this point onwards Rack 9 was enclosed and the bottles performed the remainder of their journey in a kind of tunnel, interrupted here and there by openings two or three metres wide.

"Heat conditioning" said Mr. Foster.

Hot tunnels alternated with cool tunnels. Coolness was wedded to discomfort in the form of hard X-rays. By the time they were decanted, the embryos had a horror of cold. They were predestined to emigrate to the troics, to be miners and acetate silk spinners and steel workers. Later ontheir minds would be made to endorse the judgment of their bodies. "We condition them to thrive on heat," concluded Mr. Foster. "Our colleagues upstairs will teach them to love it."

"And that," put in the Diredtor sententiously, "that is the secret of happiness and virtue—liking what you've *got* to do. All conditioning aims at that, making people like their unescapable social destiny."

In a gap between two tunnels, a nurse was delicately probing with a long fine syringe into the gelatinous contents of a passing bottle. The students and their guides stood watching her for a few moments in silence.

"Well, Lenina," said Mr. Foster, when at last she withdrew the syringe and straightened herself up.

The girl turned with a start. One could see that, for all the lupus and the purple eyes, she was uncommonly pretty.

"Henry!" Her smile flashed redly at him—a row of coral teeth.

"Charming, charming," murmured the Director and, giving her two or three little pats, received in exchange a rather deferential smile for himself.

"What are you giving them?" asked Mr. Foster, making his tone very professional.

"Oh, the usual typhoid and sleeping sickness."

"Tropical workers start being inoculated at Metre 150," Mr. Foster explained to the students. "The embryos still have gills. We immunize the fish against the future man's diseases." Then, turning back to Lenina, "Ten to five on the roof this afternoon," he said, "as usual."

"Charming," said the Director once more, and, with a final pat, moved away after the others.

On Rack 10 rows of next generation's chemical workers were being trained in the toleration of lead, caustic soda, tar, chlorine. The first of a batch of two hundred and fifty embryonic rocket-plane engineers was just passing the eleven hundred metre mark on Rack 3. A special mechanism kept their containers in constant rotatoin. "To improve their sense of balance," Mr. Foster explained. "Doing repairs on the outside of a rocket in mid-air is a ticklish job. We slacken off the circulation when they're right way up, so that they're half starved, and double the flow of surrogate when they're upside down. They learn to associate topsy-turvydom with well-being; in fact, they're only truly happy when they're standing on their heads."

"And now," Mr. Foster went on, "I'd like to show you some very interesting conditioning for Alpha Plus Intellectuals. We have a big batch of them on Rack 5. First Gallery level," he called to two boys who had started to go down to the ground floor.

"They're round about Metre 900," he explained. "You can't really do any useful intellectual conditioning till the foetuses have lost their tails. Follow me."

But the Director had looked at his watch. "Ten to three," he said. "No time for the intellectual embryos, I'm afraid. We must go up to the Nurseries before the children have finished their afternoon sleep."

Mr. Foster was disappointed. "At least one glance at the Decanting Room," he pleaded.

"Very well then." The Director smiled indulgently. "Just one glance."

Chapter Sixteen

The room into which the three were ushered was the Controller's study.

"His fordship will be down in a amoment." The Gamma butler left them to themselves.

Helmholtz laughed aloud.

"It's more like a caffein-solution party than a trial," he said, and let himself fall into the most luxurious of the pneumatic arm-chairs. "Cheer up, Bernard," he added, catching sight of his friend's green unhappy face. But Bernard would not be cheered; without answering, without even looking at Helmholtz, he went and sat down on the most uncomfortable chair inthe room, carefully chosen in the obscure hope of somehow deprecating the wrath of the higher powers.

The Savage meanwhile wandered restlessly round the room, peering with a vague superficial inquisitiveness at the books in the shelves, at the soundd-track rolls and the reading machine bobbins intheir numbered pigeon-holes. On the table under the window lay a massive volume bound in limp black leather-surrogate, and stamped with large goldern T's. He picked it up and opened it. MY LIFE AND WORK, BY OUR FORD. The book had been published at Detroit by the Society for the Propagation of Fordian Knowledge. Idly he turned the pages, read a sentence here, a paragraph there, and had just come to the conclusion that the book didn't interest him, when the door opened, and the Resident World Controller for Western Europe walked briskly into the room.

Mustapha Mond shook hands with all three of them; but it was to the Savage that he addressed himself. "So you don't much like civilization, Mr. Savage," he said.

The Savage looked at him. He had been prepared to lie, to bluster, to remain sullenly unresponsive; but, reassured by the good-humoured intelligence of the Controller's face, he decided to tell the truth, straightforwardly. "No." He shook his head.

Bernard started and looked horrified. What would the Controller think? To be labeled as the friend of a man who said that he didn't like civilization—said it openly and, of all people, to the Controller—it was terrible. "But, John," he began. A look from Mustapha Mond reduced him to an abject silence.

"Of course," the Savage went on to admit, "there are some very nice things. All that music in the air, for instance. . ."

"Sometimes a thousand twangling instruments will hum about my ears and sometimes voices."

The Savage's face lit up with a sudden pleasure. "Have you read it too?" he asked. "I thought nobody knew about that book here, in England."

"Almost nobody. I'm one of the very few. It's prohibited, you see. But as I make the laws here, I can also break them. With impunity, Mr. Marx," he added, turning to Bernard. "Which I'm afraid you *can't* do."

Bernard sank into a yet more hopeless misery.

"But why is it prohibited?" asked the Savage. In the excitement of meeting a man who had read Shakespeare he had momentarily forgotten everything else.

The Controller shrugged his shoulders. "Because it's old; that's the chief reason. We haven't any use for old things here."

"Even when they're beautiful?"

"Particularly when they're beautiful. Beauty's attractive, and we don't want people to be attracted by old things. We want them to like the new ones."

"But the new ones are so stupid and horrible. Those plays, where there's nothing but helicopters flying about and you *feel* the people kissing." He made a grimace. "Goats and monkeys!" Only in Othello's words could he find an adequate vehicle for his contempt and hatred.

"Nice tame animals, anyhow," the Controller murmured parenthetically.

"Why don't you let them see *Othello* instead?"

"I've told you; it's old. Besides, they couldn't understand it."

Yes, that was true. He remembered how Helmholtz had laughed at *Romeo and Juliet*. "Well then," he said, after a pause, "something new that's like *Othello*, and that they could understand."

"That's what we've all been wanting to write," said Helmholtz, breaking a long silence.

"And it's what you never will write," said the Controller. "Because, if it were really like *Othello* nobody could understand it, however new it might be. And if it were new, it couldn't possibly be like *Othello*."

"Why not?"

"Yes, why not?" Helmholtz repeated. He too was forgetting the unpleasant realities of the situation. Green with anxiety and apprehension, only Bernard remembered them; the others ignored him. "Why not?"

"Because our world is not the same as Othello's world. You can't make flivvers without steel—and you can't make tragedies without social instability. The world's stable now. People are happy; they get what they want, and they never want what they can't get. They're well off; they're safe; they're never ill, they're not afraid of death; they're blissfully ignorant of passion and old age; they're plagued with no mothers or fathers; they've got no wives, or children or lovers to feel strongly about; they're so conditioned that they practically can't help behaving as they ought to behave. And if anything should go wrong, there's *soma*. Which you go and chuck out of the window in the name of liberty, Mr. Savage. *Liberty!*" He laughed. "Expecting Deltas to know what liberty is! And now expecting them to understand *Othello!* My good boy!"

The Savage was silent for a little. "All the same," he insisted obstinately, "*Othello's* good, *Othello's* better than those feelies."

"Of course it is," The Controller agreed. "But that's the price we have to pay for stability. You've got to choose between happiness and what people used to call high art. We've sacrificed the high art. We have the feelies and the scent organ instead."

"But they don't mean anything."

"The mean themselves; they mean a lot of agreeable sensations to the audience."

"But they're. . . they're told by an idiot."

The Controller laughed. "You're not being very polite to your friend, Mr. Watson. One of our most distinguished Emotional Engineers. . ."

"But he's right," said Helmholtz gloomily. "Because it *is* idiotic. Writing when there's nothing to say. . ."

"Precisely. But that requires the most enormous ingenuity. You're making flivvers out of the absolute minimum of steel—works of art out of practically nothing but pure sensation."

The Savage shook his head. "It all seems to me quite horrible."

"Of course it does. Actual happiness always looks pretty squalid in comparison with the over-compensations for misery. And, of course, stability isn't nearly so spectacular as instability. And being contented has none of the glamour of a good fight against misfortune, none of the picturesqueness of a struggle with temptation, or a fatal overthrow by passion or doubt. Happiness is never grand."

"I suppose not," said the Savage after a silence. "But need it be quite so bad as those twins?" He passed his hand over his eyes as though he were trying to wipe away the remembered image of those long rows of identical midgets at the assembling tables, those queued-up twin-herds at the entrance to the Brentford monorail station, those human maggots swarming round Linda's bed of death, the endlessly repeated face of his assailants. He looked at his bandaged left hand and shuddered. "Horrible!"

"But how useful! I see you don't like our Bokanovsky Groups; but, I assure you, they're the foundation on which every thing else is built. They're the gyroscope that stabilizes the rocket plane of state on its unswerving course." The deep voice thrillingly vibrated; the gesticulating hand implied all space and the onrush of the irresistible machine. Mustapha Mond's oratory was almost up to synthetic standards.

"I was wondering," said the Savage, "why you had them at all—seeing that you can get whatever you want out of those bottles. Why don't you make everybody an Alpha Double Plus while you're about it?"

Mustapha Mond laughed. "Because we have no wish to have our throats cut," he answered. "We believe in happiness and stability. A society of Alphas couldn't fail to be unstable and miserable. Imagine a factory staffed by Alphas—that is to say by separate and unrelated individuals of good heredity and conditioned so as to be capable (withing limits) of making a free choice and assuming responsibilities. Imagine it!" he repeated.

The Savage tried to imagine it, not very successfully.

"It's an absurdity. An Alpha-decanted, Alpha-conditioned man would go mad if he had to do Epsilon Semi-Moron work—go mad, or start smashing things up. Alphas can be completely socialized—but only on condition that you make them do Alpha work. Only an Epsilon can be expected to make Epsilon sacrifices, for the good reason that for him they aren't sacrifices; they're the line of least resistance. His conditioning has laid down rails along which he's got to run. He can't help himself; he's foredoomed. Even after decanting, he's still inside a bottle—an invisible bottle of infantile and embryonic fixations. Each one of us, of course," the Controller meditatively continued, "goes through life inside a bottle. But if we happen to be Alphas, our bottles are, relatively speaking, enormous. We should suffer acutely if we were confined in a narrower space. You cannot pour upper-caste champagne-surrogate into lower-caste bottles. It's obvious theoretically. But it has also been proved in actual practice. The result of the Cyprus experiment was convincing."

"What was that?" asked the Savage.

Mustapha Mond smiled. "Well, you can call it an experiment in rebottling if you like. It began in A.F. 473. The Controllers had the island of Cyprus cleared of all its existing inhabitants and re-colonized with a specially prepared batch of twenty-two thousand Alphas. All agricultural and industrial equipment was handed over to them and they were left to manage their own affairs. The result exactly fulfilled all the theoretical predictions. The land wasn't properly worked; there were strikes in all the factories; the laws were set at naught, orders disobeyed; all the people detailed for a spell of low-grade work were perpetually intriguing for high-grade jobs, and all the people with high-grade jobs were counter-intriguing at all costs to stay where they were. Within six years they were having a first-class civil war. When nineteen out of the twenty-two thousand had been killed, the survivors unanimously petitioned the World Controllers to resume the government of the island. Which they did. And that was the end of the only society of Alphas that the world has ever seen."

The Savage sighed, profoundly.

"The optimum population," said Mustapha Mond, "is modelled on the iceberg—eight-ninths below the water line, one-ninth above."

"And they're happy below the water line?"

"Happier than above it. Happier than your friend here, for example." He pointed.

"In spite of that awful work?"

"Awful? *They* don't find it so. On the contrary, they like it. It's light, it's childishly simple. No strain on the mind or the muscles. Seven and a half hours of mild, unexhausting labour, and then the *soma* ration and games and

unrestricted copulation and the feelies.   What more can they ask for?   True,"
he added, "they might ask for shorter hours.   And of course we could give them
shorter hours.   Technically it would be perfectly simple to reduce all lower-caste
working hours to three or four a day.   But would they be any the happier for
that?   No, they wouldn't.   The experiment was tried, more than a century and
a half ago.   The whole of Ireland was put on to the four-hour day.   What was
the result?   Unrest and a large increase in the consumption of *soma*; that was all.
Those three and a half hours of extra leisure were so far from being a source of
happiness, that people felt constrained to take a holiday from them.   The
Inventions Office is stuffed with plans for labour-saving processes.   Thousands
of them."   Mustapha Mond made a lavish gesture.   "And why don't we put
them into execution?   For the sake of the labourers; it would be sheer cruelty to
afflict them with excessive leisure.   It's the same with agriculture.   We could
synthesize every morsel of food, if we wanted to.   But we don't.   We prefer to
keep a third of the population on the land.   For their own sakes—because it takes
longer to get food out of the land than out of a factory.   Besides, we have our
stability to think of.   We don't want to change.   Every change is a menace to
stability.   That's another reason why we're so chary of applying new inventions.
Every discovery in pure science is potentially subversive; even science must
sometimes be treated as a possible enemy.   Yes, even science."

Science?   The Savage frowned.   He knew the word.   But what it exactly
signified he could not say.   Shakespeare and the old men of the pueblo had never
mentioned science, and from Linda he had only gathered the vaguest hints:
science was something you made helicopters with, something that caused you to
laugh at the Corn Dances, something that prevented you from being wrinkled
and losing your teeth.   He made a desperate effort to take the Controller's
meaning.

"Yes," Mustapha Mond was saying, "that's another item in the cost of
stability.   It isn't only art that's incompatible with happiness; it's also science.
Science is dangerous; we have to keep it most carefully chained and muzzled."

"What?" said Helmholtz, in astonishment.   "But we're always saying that
science is everything.   It's a hyponopaedic platitude."

"Three times a week between thirteen and seventeen," put in Bernard.

"And all the science propaganda we do at the College. . ."

"Yes; but what sort of science?" asked Mustapha Mond sarcastically.
"You've had no scientific training, so you can't judge."   I was a pretty good
physicist in my time.   Too good—goo enough to realize that all our science is
just a cookery book, with an orthodox theory of cooking that nobody's allowed
to question, and a list of recipes that mustn't be added to except by special
permission from the head cook.   I'm the head cook now.   But I was an
inquisitive young scullion once.   I started doing a bit of cooking on my own.
Unorthodox cooking, illicit cooking.   A bit of real science, in fact."   He was
silent.

"What happened?" asked Helmholtz Watson.

The Controller sighed.   "Very nearly what's going popping all around you?
That was when science first began to be controlled—after the Nine Years' War.
People were ready to have even their appetites controlled then.   Anything for a
quiet life.   We've gone on controlling ever since.   It hasn't been very good for
truth, of course.   But it's been very good for happiness.   One can't have

something for nothing. Happiness has got to be paid for. You're paying for it, Mr. Watson—paying because you happen to be too much interested in beauty. I was too much interested in truth; I paid too."

"But *you* didn't go to an island," said the Savage, breaking a long silence.

The Controller smiled. "That's how I paid. By choosing to serve happiness. Other people's—not mine. It's lucky," he added, after a pause, "that there are such a lot of islands in the world. I don't know what we should do without them. Put you all in the lethal chamber, I suppose. By the way, Mr. Watson, would you like a tropical climate? The Marquesas, for example; or Samoa? Or something rather more bracing?"

Helmholtz rose from his pneumatic chair. "I should like a thoroughly bad climate," he answered. "I believe one would write better if the climate were bad. If there were a lot of wind and storms, for example. . ."

The Controller nodded his approbation. "I like your spirit, Mr. Watson. I like it very much indeed. As much as I officially disapprove of it." He smiled. "What about the Falkland Islands?"

"Yes, I think that will do," Helmholtz answered. "And now if you don't mind, I'll go and see how poor Bernard's getting on."

Chapter Seventeen

"Art, science—you seem to have paid a fairly high price for your happiness," said the Savage, when they were alone. "Anything else?"

"Well, religion, of course," replied the Controller. "There used to be something called God—before the Nine Years' War. But I was forgetting; you know all about God, I suppose."

"Well. . ." The Savage hesitated. He would have liked to say something about solitude, about night, about the mesa lying pale under the moon, about the precipice, the plunge into shadowy darkness, about death. He would have liked to speak; but there were no words. Not even in Shakespeare.

THE TIME MACHINE

H. G. WELLS

H. G. Wells (1866-1946) was said by George Orwell to have had more influence on young people than any other writer between 1900 and 1920. He probably was the most prolific and the most widely read author of his time. A graduate of the South Kensington Normal School for Science in London, Wells was one of the first professional novelists to have had a formal education in science, and a primary concern of his was the role of science in society.

In essays and in fiction, he addressed questions of science and technology and the future of mankind, world government, and utopias. His *Outline of History* (1920) became an instant best seller. As early as 1903 he anticipated the tank as a battle weapon; in *War in the Air* (1908), he foresaw a world war with cities laid waste by aerial bombers; in *The World Set Free* (1913), he wrote of a war with atomic bombs to take place in the 1950's.

In these selections from *The Time Machine* (published in 1895), Wells looks at a society in which problems of population, war, and security have been overcome through the application of science and technology.

1. Do you think most people of today would be willing to trade freedom for security? Explain.

2. To what extent do you think that the application of science and technology can overcome current problems of population and food resources, war and peace, and energy?

3. If technology were able to solve the problems of population and food, war and peace, and energy, then what would we have? Compare your views with those of Wells.

THE TIME MACHINE

H. G. WELLS

The Time traveller (for so it will be convenient to speak of him) was expounding a recondite matter to us. His pale grey eyes shone and twinkled, and his usually pale face was flushed and animated. The fire burnt brightly, and the soft radiance of the incandescent lights in the lilies of silver caught the bubbles that flashed and passed in our glasses. Our chairs, being his patents, embraced and caressed us rather than submitted to being sat upon, and there was that luxurious after-dinner atmosphere, when thought runs gracefully free of the trammels of precision. And he put it to us in this way—marking the points with a lean forefinger—as we sat and lazily admired his earnestness over this new paradox (as we thought it) and his fecundity.

'You must follow me carefully. I shall have to controvert one or two ideas that are almost universally accepted. The geometry, for instance, they taught you at school is founded on a misconception.'

'Is not that rather a large thing to expect us to begin upon?' said Filby, an argumentative person with red hair.

'I do not mean to ask you to accept anything without reasonable ground for it. You will soon admit as much as I need from you. You know of course that a mathematical line, a line of thickness *nil*, has no real existence. They taught you that? Neither has a mathematical plane. These things are mere abstractions.'

'That is all right,' said the Psychologist.

'Nor having only length, breadth, and thickness, can a cube have a real existence.'

'There I object,' said Filby. 'Of course a solid body may exist. All real things—'

'So most people think. But wait a moment. Can an *instantaneous* cube exist?'

'Don't follow you,' said Filby.

'Can a cube that does not last for any time at all, have a real existence?'

Filby became pensive. 'Clearly,' the Time Traveller proceeded, 'any body must have extension in *four* directions: it must have Length, Breadth, Thickness, and—Duration. But through a natural infirmity of the flesh, which I will explain to you in a moment, we incline to overlook this fact. There are really four dimensions, three which we call the three planes of Space, and a fourth, Time. There is, however, a tendency to draw an unreal distinction between the former three dimensions and the latter, because it happens that our consciousness moves intermittently in one direction along the latter from the beginning to the end of our lives.'

'That,' said a very young man, making spasmodic efforts to relight his cigar over the lamp; 'that. . .very clear indeed.'

'Now, it is very remarkable that this is so extensively overlooked,' continued the Time Traveller, with a slight accession of cheerfulness. 'Really this is what is meant by the Fourth Dimension, though some people who talk about the Fourth Dimension do not know that mean it. It is only another way of looking at Time. *There is no difference between Time and any of the three dimensions of Space except that our consciousness moves along it.* But some foolish people have got hold of the wrong side of that idea. You have all heard what they have to say about this Fourth Dimension?'

'*I* have not,' said the Provincial Mayor.

'It is simply this. That Space, as our mathematicians have it, is spoken of as having three dimensions, which one may call Length, Breadth, and Thickness, and is always definable by reference to three planes, each at right-angles to the others. But some philosophical people have been asking why *three* dimensions particularly—why not another direction at right-angles to the other three?—and have even tried to construct a Four-Dimensional geometry. Professor Simon Newcomb was expounding this to the New York Mathematical Society only a month or so ago. You know how on a flat surface, which has only two dimensions, we can represent a figure of a three-dimensional solid, and similarly they think that by models of three dimensions they could represent one of four—if they could master the perspective of the thing. See?'

'I think so,' murmured the Provincial Mayor; and, knitting his brows, he lapsed into an introspective state, his lips moving as one who repeats mystic words. 'Yes, I think I see it now,' he said after some time, brightening in a quite transitory manner.

'Well, I do not mind telling you I have been at work upon this geometry of Four Dimensions for some time. Some of my results are curious. For instance, here is a portrait of a man at eight years old, another at fifteen, another at seventeen, another at twenty-three, and so on. All these are evidently sections, as it were, Three-Dimensional representations of his Four-Dimensional being, which is a fixed and unalterable thing.'

'Scientific people,' proceeded the Time Traveller, after the pause required for the proper assimilation of this, 'know very well that Time is only a kind of Space. Here is a popular scientific diagram, a weather record. This line I trace with my finger shows the movement of the barometer. Yesterday it was so high, yesterday night it fell, then this morning it rose again, and so gently upward to here. Surely the mercury did not trace this line in any of the dimensions of Space generally recognized? But certainly it traced such a line, and that line, therefore, we must conclude was along the Time-Dimension.'

'But,' said the Medical Man, staring hard at a coal in the fire, 'if Time is really only a fourth dimension of Space why is it, and why has it always been, regarded as something different? And why cannot we move about in Time as we move about I the other dimensions of Space'

The Time Traveller smiled. 'Are you so sure we can move freely in Space? Right and left we can go, backward and forward freely enough, and men always have done so. I admit we move freely in two dimensions. But how about up and down? Gravitation limits us there.'

'Not exactly,' said the Medical Man. 'There are balloons.'

'But before the balloons, save for spasmodic jumping and the inequalities of the surface, man had no freedom of vertical movement.'

'Still they could move a little up and down,' said the Medical Man.

'Easier, far easier down than up.'

'And you cannot move at all in Time, you cannot get away from the present moment.'

'My dear sir, that is just where you are wrong. That is just where the whole world has gone wrong. We are always getting away from the present moment. Our mental existences, which are immaterial and have no dimensions, are passing along the Time-Dimension with a uniform velocity from the cradle to the grave. Just as we should travel *down* if we began our existence fifty miles above the earths surface.'

'But the great difficulty is this,' interrupted the Psychologist. 'You *can* move about in all directions of Space, but you cannot move about I Time.'

'That is the germ of my great discovery. But you are wrong to say that we cannot move about in Time. For instance, if I am recalling an incident very vividly I go back to the instant of its occurrence: I become absent-minded, as you say. I jump back for a moment. Of course we have no means of staying back for any length of Time, any more than a savage or an animal has of staying six feet above the ground. But a civilized man is better off than the savage in this respect. He can go up against gravitation in a balloon, and why should he not hope that ultimately he may be able to stop or accelerate his drift along the Time-Dimension, or even turn about and travel the other way?'

'Oh, *this*,' began Filby, 'is all—'

'Why not?' said the Time Traveller.

'It's against reason,' said Filby.

'What reason?' said the Time Traveller.

'You can show black is white by argument,' said Filby, 'but you will never convince me.'

'Possibly not,' said the Time Traveller. 'But now you begin to see the object of my investigations into the geometry of the Four Dimensions. Long ago I had a vague inkling of a machine—'

'To travel through Time!' exclaimed the Very Young Man.

'That shall travel indifferently in any direction of Space and Time, as the driver determines.'

Filby contented himself with laughter.

'But I have experimental verification,' said the Time Traveller.

'It would be remarkably convenient for the historian,' the Psychologist suggested. 'One might travel back and verify the accepted account of the Battle of Hastings, for instance!'

'Don't you think you would attract attention?' said the Medical Man. 'Our ancestors had no great tolerance for anachronisms.'

'One might get one's Greek from the very lips of Homer and Plato,' the Very Young Man thought.

'In which case they would certainly plough you for the Little-go. The German scholars have improved Greek so much.'

'Then there is the future,' said the Very Young Man. 'Just think! One might invest all one's money, leave it to accumulate at interest, and hurry on ahead.'

'To discover a society,' said I, 'erected on a strictly communistic basis.'

'Of all the wild extravagant theories!' began the Psychologist.

'Yes, so it seemed to me, and so I never talked of it until—'

'Experimental verification!' cried I. 'You are going to verify *that*?'

'The experiment!' cried Filby, who was getting brain-weary.

'Let's see your experiment anyhow' said the Psychologist, 'though it's all humbug, you know.'

The Time Traveller smiled round at us. Then, still smiling faintly, and with his hands deep in his trousers pockets, he walked slowly out of the room, and we heard his slippers shuffling down the long passage to his laboratory.

The Psychologist looked at us. 'I wonder what he's got?'

'Some sleight-of-hand trick or other,' said the Medical Man, and Filby tried to tell us about a conjuror he had seen at Burslem, but before he had finished his preface the Time Traveller came back, and Filby's anecdote collapsed.

In the Golden Age

'In another moment we were standing face to face, I and this fragile thing out of futurity. He came straight up to me and laughed into my eyes. The absence from his bearing of any sign of fear struck me at once. Then he turned to the two others who were following him and spoke to them in a strange and very sweet and liquid tongue.

'There were others coming, and presently a little group of perhaps eight or ten of these exquisite creatures were about me. One of them addressed me. It came into my head, oddly enough, that my voice was too harsh and deep for them. So I shook my head, and pointing to my ears, shook it again. He came a step forward, hesitated, and then touched my hand. Then I felt other soft little tentacles upon my back and shoulders. They wanted to make sure I was real. There was nothing in this at all alarming. Indeed, there was something in these pretty little people that inspired confidence—a graceful gentleness, a certain child-like ease. And besides, they looked so frail that I could fancy myself flinging the whole dozen of them about like ninepins. But I made a sudden motion to warn them when I was their little pink hands feeling at the Time Machine. Happily then, when it was not too late, I thought of a danger I had hitherto forgotten, and reaching over the bars of the machine, I unscrewed the little levers that would set in motion, and put these in my pocket. Then I turned again to see what I could do in the way of communication.

'And then, looking more nearly into their features, I saw some further peculiarities in their Dresden china type of prettiness. Their hair, which was uniformly curly, came to a sharp end at the neck and cheek; there was not the faintest suggestion of it on the face, and their ears were singularly minute. The mouths were small, with bright red, rather thin lips, and the little chins ran to a point. The eyes were large and mild; and—this may seem egotism on my part—I fancied even then that there was a certain lack of the interest I might have expected in them.

'As they made no effort to communicate with me, but simply stood round me smiling and speaking in soft cooing notes to each other, I began the conversation. I pointed to the Time Machine and to myself. Then, hesitating for a moment how to express Time, I pointed to the sun. At once a quaintly pretty little figure in chequered purple and white followed my gesture, and then astonished me by imitating the sound of thunder.

'For a moment I was staggered, though the import of his gesture was plain enough. The question had come into my mind abruptly: were these creatures fools? You may hardly understand how it took me. You see, I had always anticipated that the people of the year Eight Hundred and Two Thousand odd would be incredibly in front of us in knowledge, art, everything. Then one of them suddenly asked me a question that showed him to be on the intellectual level of one of our five-year-old children—asked me, in fact, if I had come from the sun in a thunderstorm! It let loose the judgment I had suspended upon their clothes, their frail light limbs and fragile features. A flow of disappointment rushed across my mind. For a moment I felt that I had built the Time Machine in vain.

'I nodded, pointed to the sun, and gave them such a vivid rendering of a thunderclap as startled them. They all withdrew a pace or so and bowed. Then came one laughing towards me, carrying a chain of beautiful flowers altogether new to me, and put it about my neck. The idea was received with melodious applause; and presently they were all running to and fro with flowers and laughingly flinging them upon me until I was almost smothered with blossom. You who have never seen the like can scarcely imagine what delicate and wonderful flowers countless years of culture had created. Then someone suggested that their plaything should be exhibited in the nearest building, and so I was led past the sphinx of white marble, which had seemed to watch me all the while with a smile at my astonishment, towards a very grey edifice of fretted stone. As I went with them the memory of my confident anticipations of a profoundly grave and intellectual posterity came, with irresistible merriment, to my mind.

'The building had a huge entry, and was altogether of colossal dimensions. I was naturally most occupied with the growing crowd of little people, and with the big, open portals that yawned before me shadowy and mysterious. My general impression of the world I saw over their heads was of a tangled waste of beautiful bushes and flowers, a long-neglected and yet weedless garden. I saw a number of tall spikes of strange white flowers, measuring a foot perhaps across the spread of the waxen petals. They grew scattered, as if wild, among the variegated shrubs, but, as I say, I did not examine them closely at this time. The Time Machine was left deserted on the turf among the rhododendrons.

'The arch of the doorway was richly carved, but naturally I did not observe the carving very narrowly, though I fancied I saw suggestions of old Phoenician decorations as I passed through, and it struck me that they were very badly broken and weather-worn. Several more brightly-clad people met me in the doorway, and so we entered, I, dressed in dingy nineteenth-century garments, looking grotesque enough, garlanded with flowers, and surrounded by an eddying mass of bright, soft-coloured robes and shining white limbs, in a melodious whirl of laughter and laughing speech.

'The big doorway opened into a proportionately great hall hung with brown. The roof was in shadow, and the windows, partially glazed with coloured glass and partially unglazed, admitted a tempered light. The floor was made up of huge blocks of some very hard white metal, not plates nor slabs—blocks, and it was so much worn, as I judged by the going to and fro of past generations, as to be deeply channelled along the more frequented ways. Transverse to the length were innumerable tables made of slabs of polished stone, raised, perhaps, a foot from the floor, and upon these were heaps of fruits. Some I recognized as a kind of hypertrophied raspberry and orange, but for the most part they were strange.

'Between the tables was scattered a great number of cushions. Upon these my conductors seated themselves, signing for me to do likewise. With a pretty absence of ceremony they began to eat the fruit with their hands, flinging peel and stalks, and so forth, into the round openings in the sides of the tables. I was not loth to follow their example, for I felt thirsty and hungry. As I did so I surveyed the hall at my leisure.

'And perhaps the thing that struck me most was its dilapidated look. The stained-glass windows, which displayed only a geometrical pattern, were broken many places, and the curtains that hung across the lower end were thick with dust. And it caught my eye that the corner of the marble table near me was fractured. Nevertheless, the general effect was extremely rich and picturesque. There were, perhaps, a couple of hundred people dining in the hall, and most of them, seated as near to me as they could come, were watching me with interest, their little eyes shining over the fruit they were eating. All were clad in the same soft, and yet strong, silky material.

'Fruit, by the bye, was all their diet. These people of the remote future were strict vegetarians, and while I was with them, in spite of some carnal cravings, I had to be frugivorous also. Indeed, I found afterwards that horses, cattle, sheep, dogs, had followed the Ichthyosaurus into extinction. But the fruits were very delightful; one, in particularly, that seemed to be in season all the time I was there—a floury thing in a three-sided husk—was especially good, and I made it my staple. At first I was puzzled by all these strange fruits, and by the strange flowers I saw, but later I began to perceive their import.

'However, I am telling you of my fruit dinner in the distant future now. So soon as my appetite was a little checked I determined to make a resolute attempt to learn the speech of these new men of mine. Clearly that was the next thing to do. The fruits seemed a convenient thing to begin upon, and holding one of these up I began a series of interrogative sounds and gestures. I had some considerable difficulty in conveying my meaning. At first my efforts met with a stare of surprise or inextinguishable laughter, but presently a fair-haired little creature seemed to grasp my intention and repeated a name. They had to chatter and explain their business at great length to each other, and my first attempts to make their exquisite little sounds of the language caused an immense amount of genuine, if uncivil, amusement. However, I felt like a schoolmaster amidst children, and persisted, and presently I had a score of noun substantives at least at my command; and then I got to demonstrative pronouns, and even the verb 'to eat'. But it was slow work, and the little people soon tired and wanted to get away from my interrogations, so I determined, rather of necessity, to let them give their lessons in little doses when they felt inclined. And very little doses I found they were before long, for I never met people more indolent or more easily fatigued.'

The Sunset of Mankind

'A queer thing I soon discovered about my little hosts, and that was their lack of interest. They would come to me with eager cries of astonishment, like children, but, like children, they would soon stop examining me, and wander away after some other toy. The dinner and my conversational beginnings ended, I noted for the first time that almost all those who had surrounded me at first were gone. It is odd, too, how speedily I came to disregard these little people. I went out through the portal into the sunlit world again so soon as my hunger was satisfied. I was continually meeting more of these men of the future, who would follow me a little distance, chatter and laugh about me, and, having smiled and gesticulated in a friendly way, leave me again to my own devices.

'The calm of evening was upon the world as I emerged from the great hall, and the scene was lit by the warm glow of the setting sun. At first things were very confusing. Everything was so entirely different from the world I had known—even the flowers. The big building I had left was situated on the slope of a broad river valley, but the Thames had shifted, perhaps, a mile from its present position. I resolved to mount to the summit of a crest, perhaps a mile and a half away, from which I could get a wider view of this our planet in the year Eight Hundred and Two Thousand Seven Hundred and One, A.D. For that, I should explain, was the date the little dials of my machine recorded.

'As I walked I was watchful for every impression that could possibly help to explain the condition of ruinous spendour in which I found the world—for ruinous it was. A little way up the hill, for instance, was a great heap of granite bound together by masses of aluminium, a vast labyrinth of precipitous walls and crumbled heaps, amidst which were thick heaps of very beautiful pagoda-like plants—nettles possibly—but wonderfully tinted with brown about the leaves, and incapable of stinging. It was evidently the derelict remains of some vast structure, to what end built I could not determine. It was here that I was destined, at a later date, to have a very strange experience—the first intimation of a still stranger discovery—but of that I will speak in its proper place.

'Looking round, with a sudden thought, from a terrace on which I rested for a while, I realized that there were no small houses to be seen. Apparently, the single house, and possibly even the household, had vanished. Here and there among the greenery were palace-like buildings, but the house and the cottage, which form such characteristic features of our own English landscape, had disappeared.

'"Communism," said I to myself.

'And on the heels of that came another thought. I looked at the half-dozen little figures that were following me. Then, in a flash, I perceived that all had the same form of costume, the same soft hairless visage, and the same girlish rotundity of limb. It may seen strange, perhaps, that I had not noticed this before. But everything was so strange. Now, I saw the fact plainly enough. In costume, and in all the differences of texture and bearing that now mark off the sexes from each other, these people of the future were alike. And the children seemed to my eyes to be but the miniatures of their parents. I judged them that the children of that time were extremely precocious, physically at least, and I found afterwards abundant verification of my opinion.

'Seeing the ease and security in which these people were living, I felt that this close resemblance of the sexes was after all what one would expect; for the strength of the man and the softness of a woman, the institution of the family, and the differentiation of occupations are mere militant necessities of an age of physical force. Where population is balanced and abundant, much child-bearing becomes an evil rather than a blessing to the State: where violence comes but rarely and offspring are secure, there is less necessity—indeed there is no necessity—of an efficient family, and the specialization of the sexes with reference to their children's needs disappears. We see some beginnings of this even in our own time, and in this future age it was complete. This, I must remind you, was my speculation at the time. Later, I was to appreciate how far it fell short of the reality.

'While I was musing upon these things, my attention was attracted by a pretty little structure, like a well under a cupola. I thought in a transitory way of the oddness of wells still existing, and then resumed the thread of my speculations. There were no large buildings towards the top of the hill, and as my walking powers were evidently miraculous, I was presently left alone for the first time. With a strange sense of freedom an adventure I pushed on up to the crest.

'There I found a seat of some yellow metal that I did not recognize, corroded in places with a kind of pinkish rust and half-smothered in soft moss, the arm-rests cast and filed into the resemblance of griffins' heads. I sat down on it, and I surveyed the broad view of our own world under the sunset of that long day. It was as sweet and fair a view as I have ever seen. The sun had already gone below the horizon and the west was flaming gold, touched with some horizontal bars of purple and crimson. Below was the valley of the Thames, in which the river lay like a band of burnished steel. I have already spoken of the great palaces dotted about among the variegated greenery, some in ruins and some still occupied. Here and there rose a white or silvery figure in the waste garden of the earth, here and there came the sharp vertical line of some cupola or obelisk. There were no hedges, no signs of proprietary rights, no evidences of agriculture; the whole earth had become a garden.

'So watching, I began to put my interpretation upon the things I had seen, and as it shaped itself to me that evening, my interpretation was something in this way. (Afterwards I found I had got only a half truth—or only a glimpse of one facet of the truth):

'It seemed to me that I had happened upon humanity upon the wane. The ruddy sunset set me thinking of the sunset of mankind. For the first time I began to realize an odd consequence of the social effort in which we are at present engaged. And yet, come to think, it is a logical consequence enough. Strength is the outcome of need: security sets a premium on feebleness. The work of ameliorating the conditions of life—the true civilizing process that makes life more and more secure—had gone steadily on to a climax. One triumph of a united humanity over Nature had followed another. Things that are now mere dreams had become projects deliberately put in hand and carried forward. And the harvest was what I saw!

'After all, the sanitation and the agriculture of today are still in the rudimentary stage. The science of our time has attacked but a little department of the field of human disease, but, even so, it spreads its operations very steadily and persistently. Our agriculture and horticulture destroy a weed just here and there and cultivate perhaps a score or so of wholesome plants leaving eh greater number to fight out a balance as they can. We improve our favourite plants and animals—and how few they are—gradually by selective breeding; now a new and better peach, now a seedless grape, now a sweeter and larger flower, now a more convenient breed of cattle. We improve them gradually, because our ideals are vague and tentative, and our knowledge is very limited; because Nature, too, is shy and slow in our clumsy hands. Some day all this will be better organized, and still better. That is the drift of the current in spite of the eddies. The whole world will be intelligent, educated, and co-operating; things will move faster and faster towards the subjugation of Nature. In the end, wisely and carefully we shall readjust the balance of animal and vegetable life to suit our human needs.

'This adjustment, I say, must have been done, and done well: done indeed for all time, in the space of Time across which my machine had leapt. The air was free from gnats, the earth from weeds or fungi; everywhere were fruits and sweet and delightful flowers; brilliant butterflies flew hither and thither. The ideal of preventive medicine was attained. Disease had been stamped out. I saw no evidence of any contagious diseases during all my stay. And I shall have to tell you later that even the processes of putrefaction and decay had been profoundly affected by these changes.

'Social triumphs, too, had been effected. I saw mankind housed in splendid shelters, gloriously clothed, and as yet I had found them engaged in no toil. There were no signs of struggle, neither social nor economical struggle. The shop, the advertisement, traffic, all that commerce which constitutes the body of our world, was gone. It was natural on that golden evening that I should jump at the idea of a social paradise. The difficulty of increasing population had been met, I guessed, and population had ceased to increase.

'But with this change in condition comes inevitably adaptations to the change. What, unless biological science is a mass of errors, is the cause of human intelligence and vigour? Hardship and freedom: conditions under which the active, strong, and subtle survive and the weaker go to the wall; conditions that put a premium upon the loyal alliance of capable men, upon self-restraint, patience, and decision. And the institution of the family, and the emotions that arise therein, the fierce jealousy, the tenderness for offspring, parental self-devotion, all found their justification and support in the imminent dangers of the young. *Now*, where are these imminent dangers? There is a sentiment arising, and it will grow, against connubial jealousy, against fierce maternity, against passion of all sorts; unnecessary things now, and things that make us uncomfortable, savage survivals, discords in a refined and pleasant life.

'I thought of the physical slightness of the people, their lack of intelligence, and those big abundant ruins, and it strengthened my belief in a perfect conquest of Nature. For after the battle comes Quiet. Humanity had been strong, energetic, and intelligent, and had used all its abundant vitality to alter the conditions under which it lived. And now came the reaction of the altered conditions.

'Under the new conditions of perfect comfort and security, that restless energy that with us is strength would become weakness. Even in our own time certain tendencies and desires, once necessary to survival, are a constant source of failure. Physical courage and the love of battle, for instance, are no great help—may even be hindrances—to a civilized man. And in a state of physical balance and security, power, intellectual as well as physical, would be out of place. For countless years I judged there had been no danger of war or solitary violence, no danger from wild beasts, no wasting disease to require strength of constitution, no need of toil. For such a life, what we should call the weak are as well equipped as the strong, are indeed no longer weak. Better equipped indeed they are, for the strong would be fretted by an energy for which there was no outlet. No doubt the exquisite beauty of the buildings I saw was the outcome of the last surgings of the now purposeless energy of mankind before it settled down into perfect harmony with the conditions under which it lived—the flourish of that triumph which began the last great peace. This has ever been the fate of energy in security; it takes to art and to eroticism, and then come languour and decay.

'Even this artistic impetus would at last die away—had almost died in the Time I saw. To adorn themselves with flowers, to dance, to sing in the sunlight; so much was left of the artistic spirit, and no more. Even that would fade in the end into a contented inactivity. We are kept keen on the grindstone of pain and necessity, and it seemed to me that here was that hateful grindstone broken at last!

'As I stood there in the gathering dark I thought that in this simple explanation I had mastered the problem of the world—mastered the whole secret of these delicious people. Possibly the checks they had devised for the increase of population had succeeded too well, and their numbers had rather diminished than kept stationary. That would account for the abandoned ruins. Very simple was my explanation, and plausible enough—as most wrong theories are!'

Where is the Prince who can afford so to cover his country with troops for its defense, as that ten thousand men descending from the clouds, might not, in many places, do an infinite amount of mischief before a force could be brought together to repel them?

Benjamin Franklin (Dec. 6, 1783)

The whole of the developments and operations of analysis are now capable of being executed by machinery. . .As soon as an Analytical Engine exists, it will necessarily guide the future course of science.

Charles Babbage, *Passages from the Life of a Philosopher*, 1864

Our inventions are want to be pretty toys, which distract our attention from serious things. They are but an improved means to an unimproved end.

Henry David Thoreau, *Walden*, 1854

Technology is not an image of the world but a way of operating on reality. The nihilism of technology lies not only in the fact that it is the most perfect expression of the will to power. . .but also in the fact that it lacks meaning.

Octavio Paz, *Alternating Current*, 1967

GULLIVER'S TRAVELS

JONATHAN SWIFT

Gulliver's Travels, written between 1720 and 1725, is the best known work of one of the greatest satirists in world literature, Jonathan Swift (1667-1745). He is remembered for his genius and wit and for his satirical pieces in which, by grave humor, minute observation, and ludicrous exaggeration, he enforces a recognition of some momentous truth and the weakness of human nature.

Swift was born in Dublin, Ireland, some months after the death of his father who had come to Ireland from England to be steward of the King's Inn. With the help of an uncle, young Jonathan was educated at Kilkenny School. He entered Trinity College in Dublin at the age of 14 and graduated four years later, though he was censored for neglect of his studies and "tavern haunting."

An outbreak of political violence in Ireland in 1688 led him to go with his mother to England to live in the household of a distant relative, William Temple, at Moor Park, near London, where they remained for ten years. During this time he received an M.A. degree from Oxford and was ordained a priest in the Church of Ireland (Anglican).

While he gave some time to ecclesiastical pursuits, Swift devoted most of his time to writing. He was appointed dean of St. Patrick's Cathedral in 1713 and returned to Ireland shortly thereafter.

Two important influences on his life and writings were a girl, Hester Johnson (Stella), whom he met at Temple's and remained a close friend throughout his life (it was rumored that they married, but that is doubtful), and Esther Vanhomrigh (Vanessa), whom he met in London, who followed him to Ireland in the hope that he would marry her, but he never did.

Swift was an accomplished poet as well as a prose satirist, and his pen was a mighty weapon in his day. His writings included over 230 prose titles, some 300 poems, and 500 lettters. Though a Protestant, he was a great advocate for Ireland.

As will be seen in *Gulliver's Travels*, Swift was a strong critic of advancing technology and the pretensions of modern society—even in the early eighteenth century. Here he satirizes the attempt to apply so-called rational rules of mathematics and natural science to politics and human behavior.

1. What was the result of the visit of "certain persons" to Laputa?

2. How do you account for Swift's pessimism about the development of science and technology?

3. What was the nature of the grand Academy that Swift describes?

4. How might Swift's account apply to modern schools of science, technology, and agriculture?

GULLIVER'S TRAVELS

JONATHAN SWIFT

PART THREE

A VOYAGE TO LAPUTA, BALNIBARBI, LUGGNAG, GLUBBDUBDRIB, AND JAPAN

CHAPTER FOUR

* * * * *

The Sum of his Discourse was to this Effect. that about Forty Years ago, certain Persons went up to *Laputa,* either upon Business or Diversion; and after five Months Continuance, came back with a very little Smattering in Mathematicks, but full of Volatile Spirits acquired in that Airy Region. That these Persons upon their Return, began to dislike the Management of every Thing below; and fell into Schemes of putting all Arts, Sciences, Languages, and Mechanics upon a new Foot. To this end they procured a Royal Patent for erecting an Academy of PROJECTORS in *Lagado:* And the Humour prevailed so strongly among the People, that there is not a Town of any Consequence in the Kingdom without such an Academy. In these Colleges, the Professors contrive new Rules and Methods of Agriculture and Building, and new Instruments and Tools for all Trades and Manufacture, whereby, as they undertake, one man shall do the Work of Ten; a Palace may be built in a week, of Materials so durable as to last forever without repairing. All the Fruits of the Earth shall come to maturity at whatever Season we think fit to chuse, and increase an Hundred Fold more than they do at present; with innumerable other happy Proposals. The only Inconvenience is, that none of these Projects are yet brought to Perfection; and in the mean time, the whole Country lies miserably waste, the Houses in Ruins, and the People without Food or Cloaths. By all which, instead of being discouraged, they are Fifty Times more violently bent upon prosecuting their Schemes, driven equally on by Hope and Despair: That, as for himself, being not of an enterprizing Spirit, he was content to go on in the old Forms; to live in the Houses his Ancestors had built, and act as they did in every Part of Life without Innovation. That, some few other Persons of Quality and Gentry had done the same; but were looked on with an Eye of Contempt and ill Will, as Enemies to Art, ignorant, and ill Commonwealthsmen, preferring their own Ease and Sloth before the general Improvement of their Country.

His Lordship added, that he would not by any further Particulars prevent the Pleasure I should certainly take in viewing the grand Academy, whither he was resolved I should go. He only desired me to observe a ruined Building upon the Side of a Mountain about three Miles distant, of which he gave me this Account. That he had a very convenient Mill within Half a Mile of his House, turned by a Current from a large River, and sufficient for his own Family as well as a great Number of his Tenants. That, about seven Years ago, a Club of those Projectors came to him with Proposals to destroy this Mill, and build another on the Side of that Mountain, on the long Ridge whereof a long Canal must be cut for a Repository of Water, to be conveyed up by Pipes and Engines to supply the Mill: Because the Wind and Air upon a Height agitated the Water, and thereby made it fitter for Motion: And because the Water descending down a Declivity would turn the Mill with half the Current of a River whose Course is more upon a Level. He said, that being then not very well with the Court, and pressed by many of his Friends, he complyed with the Proposal; and after employing an Hundred Men for two Years, the Work miscarryed, the Projectors went off, laying the Blame intirely upon him; railing at him ever since, and putting others upon the same Experiment, with equal Assurance of Success, as well as equal Disappointment.

In a few Days we came back to Town; and his Excellency, considering the bad Character he had in the Academy, would not go with me himself, but recommended me to a Friend of his to bear me Company thither. My Lord was pleased to represent me as a great Admirer of Projects, and a Person of much Curiosity and easy Belief; which indeed was not without Truth; for I had myself been a Sort of Projector in my younger Days.

· CHAPTER FIVE

THIS Academy is not an entire single Building, but a Continuation of several Houses on both Sides of a Street; which growing waste, was purchased and applyed to that Use.

I was received Very kindly by the Warden, and went for many Days to the Academy. Every Room hath in it one or more Projectors; and I believe I could not be in fewer than five Hundred Rooms.

The first Man I saw was of a meagre Aspect, with sooty Hands and Face, his Hair and Beard long, ragged and singed in several Places. His Clothes, Shirt, and Skin were all of the same Colour. He had been eight Years upon a Project for extracting Sun-Beams out of Cucumbers, which were to be put into Vials hermetically sealed, and let out to warm the Air in raw inclement Summers. He told me, he did not doubt in Eight Years more, that he should be able to supply the Governors Gardens with Sun-shine at a reasonable Rate; but he complained that his Stock was low, and intreated me to give him something as an Encouragement to Ingenuity, especially since this had been a very dear Season for Cucumbers. I made him a small Present, for my Lord had furnished me with Money on purpose, because he knew their Practice of begging from all who go to see them.

I went into another Chamber, but was ready to hasten back, being almost overcome with a horrible Stink. My Conductor pressed me forward, conjuring me in a Whisper to give no Offence, which would be highly resented; and therefore I durst not so much as stop my Nose. The Projector of this Cell was the most ancient Student of the Academy. His Face and Beard were of a pale Yellow; his Hands and Clothes dawbed over with Filth. When I was presented to him, he gave me a very close embrace, (a Compliment I could well have excused.) His Employment from his first coming into the Academy, was an Operation to reduce human Excrement to its original Food, by separating the several Parts, removing the Tincture which it receives from the Gall, making the Odour exhale, and scumming off the Saliva. He had a weekly Allowance from the Society, of a Vessel filled with human Ordure, about the Bigness of a *Bristol* Barrel.

I saw another at work to calcine Ice into Gunpowder, who likewise shewed me a Treatise he had written concerning the Malleability of Fire, which he intended to publish.

There was a most ingenious Architect who had contrived a new Method for building Houses, by beginning at the Roof, and working downwards to the Foundations; which he justified to me by the like Practice of those two prudent Insects the Bee and the Spider.

There was a Man born blind, who had several Apprentices in his own Condition: Their Employment was to mix Colours for Painters, which their Master taught them to distinguish by feeling and smelling. It was indeed my Misfortune to find them at that Time not very perfect in their Lessons; and the Professor himself happened to be generally mistaken: This Artist is much encouraged and esteemed by the whole Fraternity.

In another Apartment I was highly pleased with a Projector, who had found a Device of plowing the Ground with Hogs, to save the Charges of Plows, Cattle, and Labour. The Method is this: In an Acre of Ground you bury at six Inches Distance, and eight deep, a Quantity of Acorns, Dates, Chesnuts, and other Masts or Vegetables whereof these Animals are fondest; then you drive six hundred or more of them into the Field, where in a few Days they will root up the whole Ground in search of their Food, and make it fit for sowing, at the same time manuring it with their Dung. It is true, upon Experiment they found the Charge and Trouble very great, and they had little or no Crop. However, it is not doubted that this Invention may be capable of great Improvement.

I went into another Room, where the Walls and Ceiling were all hung round with Cobwebs, except a narrow Passage for the Artist to go in and out. At my Entrance he called aloud to me not to disturb his Webs. He lamented the fatal Mistake the World had been so long in of using Silk-Worms, while we had such plenty of domestick Insects, who infinitely excelled the former, because they understood how to weave as well as spin. And he proposed farther, that by employing Spiders, the Charge of dying Silks would be wholly saved; whereof I was fully convinced when he shewed me a vast Number of Flies most beautifully coloured, wherewith he fed his Spiders; assuring us, that the Webs would take a Tincture from them; and as he had them of all hues, he hoped to fit every Body's Fancy, as soon as he could find proper Food for the Flies, of certain Gums, Oyls, and other glutinous Matter, to give a Strength and Consistence to the Threads.

There was an Astronomer who had undertaken to place a SunDial upon the great Weather-Cock on the Town-House, by adjusting the annual and diurnal Motions of the Earth and Sun, so as to answer and coincide with all accidental Turnings of the Wind.

I was complaining of a small Fit of the Cholick; upon which my Conductor led me into a Room, where a great Physician resided, who was famous for curing that Disease by contrary Operations from the same Instrument. He had a large Pair of Bellows, with a long slender Muzzle of Ivory. This he conveyed eight Inches up the Anus, and drawing in the Wind, he affirmed he could make the Guts as lank as a dried Bladder. But when the Disease was more stubborn and violent, he let in the Muzzle while the Bellows was full of Wind, which he discharged into the Body of the Patient; then withdrew the Instrument to replenish it, clapping his Thumb strongly against the Orifice of the Fundament;

and this being repeated three or four Times, the adventitious Wind would rush out, bringing the noxious along with it (like Water put into a Pump) and the Patient recovers. I saw him try both Experiments upon a Dog, but could not discern any Effect from the former. After the latter, the Animal was ready to burst, and made so violent a Discharge, as was very offensive to me and my Companions. The Dog died on the Spot, and we left the Doctor endeavouring to recover him by the same Operation.

I visited many other Apartments, but shall not trouble my Reader with all the Curiosities I observed, being studious of Brevity.

I had hitherto seen only one Side of the Academy, the other being appropriated to the Advancers of speculative Learning; of whom I shall say something when I have mentioned one illustrious Person more, who is called among them *the universal artist*. He told us, he had been Thirty Years employing his Thoughts for the Improvement of human Life. He had two large Rooms full of wonderful Curiosities, and Fifty Men at work. Some were condensing Air into a dry tangible Substance, by extracting the Nitre, and letting the aqueous or fluid Particles percolate: Others softening Marble for Pillows and Pin-cushions; others petrifying the Hoofs of a living Horse to preserve them from foundring. The Artist himself was at that Time busy upon two great Designs: The first, to sow Land with Chaff, wherein he affirmed the true seminal Virtue to be contained, as he demonstrated by several Experiments which I was not skilful enough to comprehend. The other was, by a certain Composition of Gums, Minerals, and Vegetables outwardly applied, to prevent the Growth of Wool upon two young Lambs; and he hoped in a reasonable Time to propagate the Breed of naked Sheep all over the Kingdom.

We crossed a Walk to the other Part of the Academy, where, as I have already said, the Projectors in speculative Learning resided.

The first Professor I saw was in a very large Room, with Forty Pupils about him. After Salutation, observing me to look earnestly upon a Frame, which took up the greatest Part of both the Length and Breadth of the Room, he said, perhaps I might wonder to see him employed in a Project for improving speculative Knowledge by practical and mechanical Operations. But the World would soon be sensible of its Usefulness; and he flattered himself, that a more noble exalted Thought never sprang in any other Man's Head. Every one knew how laborious the usual Method is of attaining to Arts and Sciences; whereas by his Contrivance, the most ignorant Person at a reasonable Charge, and with a little bodily Labour, may write Books in Philosophy, Poetry, Politicks, Law, Mathematicks and Theology, without the least Assistance from Genius or Study. He then led me to the Frame, about the Sides whereof all his Pupils stood in Ranks. It was Twenty Foot square, placed in the Middle of the Room. The Superficies was composed of several Bits of Wood, about the Bigness of a Dye, but some larger than others. They were all linked together by slender Wires. These Bits of Wood were covered on every Square with Papers pasted on them; and on these Papers were written all the Words of their Language in their several Moods, Tenses, and Declensions, but without any Order. The Professor then desired me to observe, for he was going to set his Engine at work. The Pupils at his Command took each of them hold of an Iron Handle, whereof there were Forty fixed round the Edges of the Frame; and giving them a sudden Turn, the whole Disposition of the Words was entirely changed. He then commanded

Six and Thirty of the Lads to read the several Lines softly as they appeared upon the Frame; and where they found three or four words together that might make Part of a Sentence, they dictated to the four remaining Boys who were Scribes. This Work was repeated three or four Times, and at every Turn the Engine was so contrived, that the Words shifted into new Places, as the square Bits of Wood moved upside down.

Six Hours a Day the young Students were employed in this Labour; and the Professor shewed me several Volumes in large Folio already collected, of broken Sentences, which he intended to piece together; and out of those rich Materials to give the World a Compleat Body of all Arts and Sciences; which however might be still improved, and much expedited, if the Publick would raise a Fund for making and employing five Hundred such Frames in *Lagado,* and oblige the Managers to contribute in common their several Collections. He assured me, that this Invention had employed all his Thoughts from his Youth; That he had emptyed the whole Vocabulary into his Frame, and made the strictest Computation of the General Proportion there is in Books between the Numbers of Particles, Nouns, and Verbs, and other Parts of Speech.

I made my humblest Acknowledgments to this illustrious Person for his great Communicativeness; and promised if ever I had the good Fortune to return to my native Country, that I would do him Justice, as the sole Inventor of this wonderful Machine, the Form and Contrivance of which I desired Leave to delineate upon Paper as in the Figure here annexed. I told him, although it were the Custom of our Learned in *Europe* to steal Inventions from each other, who had thereby at least this Advantage, that it became a Controversy which was the right Owner; yet I would take such Caution, that he should have the Honour entire without a Rival.

We next went to the School of Languages, where three Professors sat in Consultation upon improving that of their own Country. The first Project was to shorten Discourse by cutting Polysyllables into one, and leaving out Verbs and Participles; because in Reality all things imaginable are but Nouns.

The other, was a Scheme for entirely abolishing all Words whatsoever: And this was urged as a great Advantage in Point of Health as well as Brevity. For, it is plain, that every Word we speak is in some Degree a Diminution of our Lungs by Corrosion, and consequently contributes to the shortning of our Lives. An Expedient was therefore offered, that since Words are only Names for *Things, it* would be more convenient for all Men to carry about them, such *Things* as were necessary to express the particular Business they are to discourse on. And this invention would certainly have taken Place, to the great Ease as well as Health of the Subject, if the Women in Conjunction with the Vulgar and Illiterate had not threatened to raise a Rebellion, unless they might be allowed the Liberty to speak with their Tongues, after the Manner of their Forefathers: Such constant irreconcileable Enemies to Science are the common People. However, many of the most Learned and Wise adhere to the new Scheme of expressing themselves by *Things;* which hath only this Inconvenience attending it; that if a Man's Business be very great, and of various Kinds, he must be obliged in Proportion to carry a greater Bundle of *Things* upon his Back, unless he can afford one or Two strong Servants to attend him. I have often beheld two of those Sages almost sinking under the Weight of their Packs, like Pedlars among us; who when they met in the Streets would lay down their loads, open their Sacks, and hold Conversation for an Hour together; then put up their Implements, help each other to resume their Burthens, and take their Leave.

But, for short Conversations a Man may carry Implements in his Pockets and under his Arms, enough to supply him, and in his House he cannot be at a Loss; therefore the Room where Company meet who practice this Art, is full of all *Things* ready at Hand, requisite to furnish Matter for this Kind of artificial Converse.

Another great Advantage proposed by this Invention, was that it would serve as an universal Language to be understood in all civilized nations, whose Goods and Utensils are generally of the same Kind, or nearly resembling, so that their Uses might easily be comprehended. And thus, Embassadors would be qualified to treat with foreign Princes or Ministers of State, to whose Tongues they were utter Strangers.

I was at the Mathematical School, where the Master taught his Pupils after a Method scarce imaginable to us in *Europe*. The Proposition and Demonstration were fairly written on a thin Wafer, with Ink composed of a Cephalick Tincture. This the Student was to swallow upon a fasting Stomach, and for three Days following eat nothing but Bread and Water. As the Wafer digested, the Tincture mounted to his Brain, bearing the Proposition along with it. But the Success hath not hitherto been answerable, partly by some Error in the Quantum or Composition, and partly by the Perverseness of Lads; to whom this Bolus is so nauseous, that they generally steal aside, and discharge it upwards before it can operate; neither have they been yet persuaded to use so long an Abstinence as the Prescription requires.

God never planted a garden
But He placed a keeper there;
And the keeper ever razed the ground
And built a city where
God cannot walk at the eve of day,
Nor take the morning air.

Anne Spencer

FRANKENSTEIN

MARY SHELLEY

With the publication of *Frankenstein or The Modern Prometheus* in 1818 when she was only twenty years old, Mary Shelley (1797-1851) in effect founded a whole new genre of modern literature—science fiction—and introduced a new myth and a new metaphor into western literature—the creation of an uncontrollable monster.

She began writing the book when she was only eighteen, completed it within a year, and had it published anonymously a year later. It was an immediate success, and subsequently went through two additional editions (1823 and revised, 1831) and has been republished in new editions in 1963, 1965, and 1969. It has been the basis for numerous plays and motion pictures and the subject of hundreds of commentaries.

She was born Mary Wollstonecraft Godwin in London, the daughter of Mary Wollstonecraft, a writer and champion of women's rights (especially equality of education), who died ten days after the birth of her daughter, and William Godwin, a novelist of note and a political philosopher.

Percy Shelley, the great romantic lyric poet, became a friend of William Godwin, but when Godwin's daughter, at age sixteen, accompanied by her step-sister, Claire Clairmont, ran off to France and Switzerland with Shelley, then a married man, Godwin, contrary to his theory that legal marriage was not essential, was furious. Later a check from Shelley for £1,000 helped to appease the outraged father. In time he became completely reconciled.

After a little over a year back in England, Mary, her step-sister, and Shelley returned to Geneva where they met Lord Byron and his physician, a Dr. Polidori, who also became a novelist. During a siege of rainy weather, Mary, Shelley, Byron, and Polidori adopted a practice of reading German ghost stories. Then Byron suggested that each write a supernatural story. One night after an impressive ghost story and after listening to a conversation between Byron and Shelley on "the nature and principle of life," Mary had a vivid dream that became the basis for *Frankenstein*. She began the writing the next morning.

After an expedition to Chamonix and La Mer de Glace, Mary and Shelley returned to England where they were married within a month of the suicide of Shelley's first wife.

A few months later, Mary completed *Frankenstein*. With infant son and daughter, and again with the company of Claire, they settled in Italy. Their two little children died within six months of each other. Another son, Percy Florence, was born in 1819.

Shortly after the death of her husband by drowning at sea off Leghorn in 1822, Mary and her son returned to England. She wrote several more novels, but none ever had the impact of *Frankenstein*.

1. What point do you think Mary Shelley was trying to make through this novel?

2. In what way did Frankenstein's experiment go awry?

3. What led Frankenstein to undertake his project?

4. What was the reaction of Frankenstein when his creation came to life?

5. What does it mean to say that someone has created a "Frankenstein monster"? What examples of "Frankenstein monsters" in recent history and contemporary society can you suggest?

FRANKENSTEIN

MARY SHELLEY

CHAPTER II

WE were brought up together; there was not quite a year difference in our ages. I need not say that we were strangers to any species of disunion or dispute. Harmony was the soul of our companionship, and the diversity and contrast that subsisted in our characters drew us nearer together. Elizabeth was of a calmer and more concentrated disposition; but, with all my ardour, I was capable of a more intense application, and was more deeply smitten with the thirst for knowledge. She busied herself with following the aerial creations of the poets; and in the majestic and wondrous scenes which surrounded our Swiss home—the sublime shapes of the mountains; the changes of the seasons; tempest and calm; the silence of winter, and the life and turbulence of our Alpine summers,—she found ample scope for admiration and delight. While my companion contemplated with a serious and satisfied spirit the magnificent appearances of things, I delighted in investigating their causes. The world was to me a secret which I desired to divine. Curiosity, earnest research to learn the hidden laws of nature, gladness akin to rapture, as they were unfolded to me, are among the earliest sensations I can remember.

On the birth of a second son, my junior by seven years, my parents gave up entirely their wandering life, and fixed themselves in their native country. We possessed a house in Geneva, and a *campagne* on Belrive, the eastern shore of the lake, at the distance of rather more than a league from the city. We resided principally in the latter, and the lives of my parents were passed in considerable seclusion. It was my temper to avoid a crowd, and to attach myself fervently to a few. I was indifferent, therefore, to my schoolfellows in general; but I united myself in the bonds of the closest friendship to one among them. Henry Clerval was the son of a merchant of Geneva. He was a boy of singular talent and fancy. He loved enterprise, hardship, and even danger, for its own sake. He was deeply read in books of chivalry and romance. He composed heroic songs, and began to write many a tale of enchantment and knightly adventure. He tried to make us act plays, and to enter into masquerades, in which the characters were drawn from the heroes of Roncesvalles, of the Round Table of King Arthur, and the chivalrous train who shed their blood to redeem the holy sepulchre from the hands of the infidels.

No human being could have passed a happier childhood than myself. My parents were possessed by the very spirit of kindness and indulgence. We felt that they were not the tyrants to rule our lot according to their caprice, but the agents and creators of all the many delights which we enjoyed. When I mingled with other families, I distinctly discerned how peculiarly fortunate my lot was, and gratitude assisted the developement of filial love.

My temper was sometimes violent, and my passions vehement; but by some law in my temperature they were turned, not towards childish pursuits, but to an eager desire to learn, and not to learn all things indiscriminately. I confess that neither the structure of languages, nor the code of governments, nor the politics of various states, possessed attractions for me. It was the secrets of heaven and earth that I desired to learn; and whether it was the outward substance of things, or the inner spirit of nature and the mysterious soul of man that occupied me, still my enquiries were directed to the metaphysical, or, in its highest sense, the physical secrets of the world.

Meanwhile Clerval occupied himself, so to speak, with the moral relations of things. The busy stage of life, the virtues of heroes, and the actions of men, were his theme; and his hope and his dream was to become one among those whose names are recorded in story, as the gallant and adventurous benefactors of our species. The saintly soul of Elizabeth shone like a shrine-dedicated lamp in our peaceful home. Her sympathy was ours; her smile, her soft voice, the sweet glance of her celestial eyes, were ever there to bless and animate us. She was the living spirit of love to soften and attract: I might have become sullen in my study, rough through the ardour of my nature, but that she was there to subdue me to a semblance of her own gentleness. And Clerval—could aught ill entrench on the noble spirit of Clerval?—yet he might not have been so perfectly humane, so thoughtful in his generosity—so full of kindness and tenderness amidst his passion for adventurous exploit, had she not unfolded to him the real loveliness of beneficence, and made the doing good the end and aim of his soaring ambition.

I feel exquisite pleasure in dwelling on the recollections of childhood, before misfortune had tainted my mind, and changed its bright visions of extensive usefulness into gloomy and narrow reflections upon self. Besides, in drawing the picture of my early days, I also record those events which led, by insensible steps, to my after tale of misery: for when I would account to myself for the birth of that passion, which afterwards ruled my destiny, I find it arise, like a mountain river, from ignoble and almost forgotten sources; but, swelling as it proceeded, it became the torrent which, in its course, has swept away all my hopes and joys.

Natural philosophy is the genius that has regulated my fate; I desire, therefore, in this narration, to state those facts which led to my predilection for that science. When I was thirteen years of age, we all went on a party of pleasure to the baths near Thonon; the inclemency of the weather obliged us to remain a day confined to the inn. In this house I chanced to find a volume of the works of Cornelius Agrippa. I opened it with apathy; the theory which he attempts to demonstrate, and the wonderful facts which he relates, soon changed this feeling into enthusiasm. A new light seemed to dawn upon my mind; and, bounding with joy, I communicated my discovery to my father. My father looked carelessly at the titlepage of my book, and said, 'Ah! Cornelius Agrippa! My dear Victor, do not waste your time upon this; it is sad trash.'

If, instead of this remark, my father had taken the pains to explain to me, that the principles of Agrippa had been entirely exploded, and that a modern system of science had been introduced, which possessed much greater powers than the ancient, because the powers of the latter were chimerical, while those of the former were real and practical; under such circumstances, I should certainly have thrown Agrippa aside, and have contented my imagination, warmed as it was, by returning with greater ardour to my former studies. It is even possible, that the train of my ideas would never have received the fatal impulse that led to my ruin. But the cursory glance my father had taken of my volume by no means assured me that he was acquainted with its contents; and I continued to read with the greatest avidity.

When I returned home, my first care was to procure the whole works of this author, and afterwards of Paracelsus and Albertus Magnus. I read and studied the wild fancies of these writers with delight; they appeared to me treasures known to few beside myself. I have described myself as always having been embued with a fervent longing to penetrate the secrets of nature. In spite of the intense labour and wonderful discoveries of modern philosophers, I always came from my studies discontented and unsatisfied. Sir Isaac Newton is said to have avowed that he felt like a child picking up shells beside the great and unexplored ocean of truth. Those of his successors in each branch of natural philosophy with whom I was acquainted, appeared even to my boy's apprehensions, as tyros engaged in the same pursuit.

The untaught peasant beheld the elements around him, and was acquainted with their practical uses. The most learned philosopher knew little more. He had partially unveiled the face of Nature, but her immortal lineaments were still a wonder and a mystery. He might dissect, anatomise, and give names; but, not to speak of a final cause, causes in their secondary and tertiary grades were utterly unknown to him. I had gazed upon the fortifications and impediments that seemed to keep human beings from entering the citadel of nature, and rashly and ignorantly I had repined.

But here were books, and here were men who had penetrated deeper and knew more. I took their word for all that they averred, and I became their disciple. It may appear strange that such should arise in the eighteenth century; but while I followed the routine of education in the schools of Geneva, I was, to a great degree, self taught with regard to my favourite studies. My father was not scientific, and I was left to struggle with a child's blindness, added to a student's thirst for knowledge. Under the guidance of my new preceptors, I entered with the greatest diligence into the search of the philosopher's stone and the elixir of life; but the latter soon obtained my undivided attention. Wealth was an inferior object; but what glory would attend the discovery, if I could banish disease from the human frame, and render man invulnerable to any but a violent death!

Nor were these my only visions. The raising of ghosts or devils was a promise liberally accorded by my favourite authors, the fulfilment of which I most eagerly sought; and if my incantations were always unsuccessful, I attributed the failure rather to my own inexperience and mistake, than to a want of skill or fidelity in my instructors. And thus for a time I was occupied by exploded systems, mingling, like an unadept, a thousand contradictory theories, and floundering desperately in a very slough of multifarious knowledge, guided by an ardent imagination and childish reasoning, till an accident again changed the current of my ideas.

When I was about fifteen years old we had retired to our house near Belrive, when we witnessed a most violent and terrible thunder-storm. It advanced from behind the mountains of Jura; and the thunder burst at once with frightful loudness from various quarters of the heavens. I remained, while the storm lasted, watching its progress with curiosity and delight. As I stood at the door, on a sudden I beheld a stream of fire issue from an old and beautiful oak, which stood about twenty yards from our house; and so soon as the dazzling light vanished, the oak had disappeared, and nothing remained but a blasted stump. When we visited it the next morning, we found the tree shattered in a singular manner. It was not splintered by the shock, but entirely reduced to thin ribands of wood. I never beheld any thing so utterly destroyed.

Before this I was not unacquainted with the more obvious laws of electricity. On this occasion a man of great research in natural philosophy was with us, and, excited by this catastrophe, he entered on the explanation of a theory which he had formed on the subject of electricity and galvanism, which was at once new and astonishing to me. All that he said threw greatly into the shade Cornelius Agrippa, Albertus Magnus, and Paracelsus, the lords of my imagination; but by some fatality the overthrow of these men disinclined me to pursue my accustomed studies. It seemed to me as if nothing would or could ever be known. All that had so long engaged my attention suddenly grew despicable. By one of those caprices of the mind, which we are perhaps most subject to in early youth, I at once gave up my former occupations; set down natural history and all its progeny as a deformed and abortive creation; and entertained the greatest disdain for a would-be science, which could never even step within the threshold of real knowledge. In this mood of mind I betook myself to the mathematics, and the branches of study appertaining to that science, as being built upon secure foundations, and so worthy of my consideration.

Thus strangely are our souls constructed, and by such slight ligaments are we bound to prosperity or ruin. When I look back, it seems to me as if this almost miraculous change of inclination and will was the immediate suggestion of the guardian angel of my life—the last effort made by the spirit of preservation to avert the storm that was even then hanging in the stars, and ready to envelope me. Her victory was announced by an unusual tranquillity and gladness of soul, which followed the relinquishing of my ancient and latterly tormenting studies. It was thus that I was to be taught to associate evil with their prosecution, happiness with their disregard.

It was a strong effort of the spirit of good; but it was ineffectual. Destiny was too potent, and her immutable laws had decreed my utter and terrible destruction.

CHAPTER III

* * * * *

Such were my reflections during the first two or three days of my residence at Ingolstadt, which were chiefly spent in becoming acquainted with the localities, and the principal residents in my new abode. But as the ensuing week commenced, I thought of the information which M. Krempe had given me concerning the lectures. And although I could not consent to go and hear that little conceited fellow deliver sentences out of a pulpit, I recollected what he had said of M. Waldman, whom I had never seen, as he had hitherto been out of town.

Partly from curiosity, and partly from idleness, I went into the lecturing room, which M. Waldman entered shortly after. This professor was very unlike his colleague. He appeared about fifty years of age, but with an aspect expressive of the greatest benevolence; a few grey hairs covered his temples, but those at the back of his head were nearly black. His person was short, but remarkably erect; and his voice the sweetest I had ever heard. He began his lecture by a recapitulation of the history of chemistry, and the various improvements made by different men of learning, pronouncing with fervour the names of the most distinguished discoverers He then took a cursory view of the present state of the science, and explained many of its elementary terms. After having made a few preparatory experiments, he concluded with a panegyric upon modern chemistry, the terms of which I shall never forget:—

'The ancient teachers of this science,' said he, 'promised impossibilities, and performed nothing. The modern masters promise very little; they know that metals cannot be transmuted, and that the elixir of life is a chimera. But these philosophers, whose hands seem only made to dabble in dirt, and their eyes to pore over the microscope or crucible, have indeed performed miracles. They penetrate into the recesses of nature, and show how she works in her hiding places. They ascend into the heavens: they have discovered how the blood circulates, and the nature of the air we breathe. They have acquired new and almost unlimited powers; they can command the thunders of heaven, mimic the earthquake, and even mock the invisible world with its own shadows.'

Such were the professor's words—rather let me say such the words of fate, enounced to destroy me. As he went on, I felt as if my soul were grappling with a palpable enemy; one by one the various keys were touched which formed the mechanism of my being: chord after chord was sounded, and soon my mind was filled with one thought, one conception, one purpose. So much has been done, exclaimed the soul of Frankenstein,—more, far more, will I achieve: treading in the steps already marked, I will pioneer a new way, explore unknown powers, and unfold to the world the deepest mysteries of creation.

I closed not my eyes that night. My internal being was in a state of insurrection and turmoil; I felt that order would thence arise, but I had no power to produce it. By degrees, after the morning's dawn, sleep came. I awoke, and my yesternight's thoughts were as a dream. There only remained a resolution to return to my ancient studies, and to devote myself to a science for which I believed myself to possess a natural talent. On the same day, I paid M. Waldman a visit. His manners in private were even more mild and attractive than in public; for there was a certain dignity in his mien during his lecture, which in his own house was replaced by the greatest affability and kindness. I gave him pretty nearly the same account of my former pursuits as I had given to his fellow-professor. He heard with attention the little narration concerning my studies, and smiled at the names of Cornelius Agrippa and Paracelsus, but without the contempt that M. Krempe had exhibited. He said, that 'these were men to whose indefatigable zeal modern philosophers were indebted for most of the foundations of their knowledge. They had left to us, as an easier task, to give new names, and arrange in connected classifications, the facts which they in a great degree had been the instruments of bringing to light. The labours of men of genius, however erroneously directed, scarcely ever fail in ultimately turning to the solid advantage of mankind.' I listened to his statement, which was delivered without any presumption or affectation; and then added, that his lecture had removed my prejudices against modern chemists; I expressed myself in measured terms, with the modesty and deference due from a youth to his instructor, without letting escape (inexperience in life would have made me ashamed) any of the enthusiasm which stimulated my intended labours. I requested his advice concerning the books I ought to procure.

'I am happy,' said M. Waldman, 'to have gained a disciple; and if your application equals your ability, I have no doubt of your success. Chemistry is that branch of natural philosophy in which the greatest improvements have been and may be made: it is on that account that I have made it my peculiar study; but at the same time I have not neglected the other branches of science. A man would make but a very sorry chemist if he attended to that department of human knowledge alone. If your wish is to become really a man of science, and not merely a petty experimentalist, I should advise you to apply to every branch of natural philosophy, including mathematics.'

He then took me into his laboratory, and explained to me the uses of his various machines; instructing me as to what I ought to procure, and promising me the use of his own when I should have advanced far enough in the science not to derange their mechanism. He also gave me the list of books which I had requested; and I took my leave.

Thus ended a day memorable to me: it decided my future destiny.

CHAPTER IV

FROM this day natural philosophy, and particularly chemistry, in the most comprehensive sense of the term, became nearly my sole occupation. I read with ardour those works, so full of genius and discrimination, which modern enquirers have written on these subjects. I attended the lectures, and cultivated the acquaintance, of the men of science of the university; and I found even in M. Krempe a great deal of sound sense and real information, combined, it is true, with a repulsive physiognomy and manners, but not on that account the less valuable. In M. Waldman I found a true friend. His gentleness was never tinged by dogmatism; and his instructions were given with an air of frankness and good nature, that banished every idea of pedantry. In a thousand ways he smoothed for me the path of knowledge, and made the most abstruse enquiries clear and facile to my apprehension. My application was at first fluctuating and uncertain; it gained strength as I proceeded, and soon became so ardent and eager, that the stars often disappeared in the light of morning whilst I was yet engaged in my laboratory.

As I applied so closely, it may be easily conceived that my progress was rapid. My ardour was indeed the astonishment of the students, and my proficiency that of the masters. Professor Krempe often asked me, with a sly smile, how Cornelius Agrippa went on? whilst M. Waldman expressed the most heartfelt exultation in my progress. Two years passed in this manner, during which I paid no visit to Geneva, but was engaged, heart and soul, in the pursuit of some discoveries, which I hoped to make. None but those who have experienced them can conceive of the enticements of science. In other studies you go as far as others have gone before you, and there is nothing more to know; but in a scientific pursuit there is continual food for discovery and wonder. A mind of moderate capacity, which closely pursues one study, must infallibly arrive at great proficiency in that study; and I, who continually sought the attainment of one object of pursuit, and was solely wrapt up in this, improved so rapidly, that, at the end of two years, I made some discoveries in the improvement of some chemical instruments, which procured me great esteem and admiration at the university. When I had arrived at his point, and had become as well acquainted with the theory and practice of natural philosophy as depended on the lessons of any of the professors at Ingolstadt, my residence there being no longer conducive to my improvements, I thought of returning to my friends and my native town, when an incident happened that protracted my stay.

One of the phenomena which had peculiarly attracted my attention was the structure of the human frame, and, indeed, any animal endued with life. Whence, I often asked myself, did the principle of life proceed? It was a bold question, and one which has ever been considered as a mystery; yet with how many things are we upon the brink of becoming acquainted, if cowardice or carelessness did not restrain our enquiries. I revolved these circumstances in my mind, and determined thenceforth to apply myself more particularly to those branches of natural philosophy which relate to physiology. Unless I had been animated by an almost supernatural enthusiasm, my application to this study would have been irksome, and almost intolerable. To examine the causes of life, we must first have recourse to death. I became acquainted with the science of anatomy: but this was not sufficient; I must also observe the natural decay and corruption of the human body. In my education my father had taken the greatest precautions that my mind should be impressed with no supernatural horrors. I do not ever remember to have trembled at a tale of superstition, or to have feared the apparition of a spirit. Darkness had no effect upon my fancy; and a churchyard was to me merely the receptacle of bodies deprived of life, which, from being the seat of beauty and strength, had become food for the worm. Now I was led to examine the cause and progress of this decay, and forced to spend days and nights in vaults and charnel-houses. My attention was fixed upon every object the most insupportable to the delicacy of the human feelings. I saw how the fine form of man was degraded and wasted; I beheld the corruption of death succeed to the blooming cheek of life; I saw how the worm inherited the wonders of the eye and brain. I paused, examining and analysing all the minutiae of causation, as exemplified in the change from life to death, and death to life, until from the midst of this darkness a sudden light broke in upon me—a light so brilliant and wondrous, yet so simple, that while I became dizzy with the immensity of the prospect which it illustrated, I was surprised, that among so many men of genius who had directed their enquiries towards the same science, that I alone should be reserved to discover so astonishing a secret.

Remember, I am not recording the vision of a madman. The sun does not more certainly shine in the heavens, than that which I now affirm is true. Some miracle might have produced it, yet the stages of the discovery were distinct and probable. After days and nights of incredible labour and fatigue, I succeeded in discovering the cause of generation and life; nay, more, I became myself capable of bestowing animation upon lifeless matter.

The astonishment which I had at first experienced on this discovery soon gave place to delight and rapture. After so much time spent in painful labour, to arrive at once at the summit of my desires, was the most gratifying consummation of my toils. But this discovery was so great and overwhelming, that all the steps by which I had been progressively led to it were obliterated, and I beheld only the result. What had been the study and desire of the wisest men since the creation of the world was now within my grasp. Not that, like a magic scene, it all opened upon me at once: the information I had obtained was of a nature rather to direct my endeavours so soon as I should point them towards the object of my search, than to exhibit that object already accomplished. I was like the Arabian who had been buried with the dead, and found a passage to life, aided only by one glimmering, and seemingly ineffectual, light.

I see by your eagerness, and the wonder and hope which your eyes express, my friend, that you expect to be informed of the secret with which I am acquainted; that cannot be: listen patiently until the end of my story, and you will easily perceive why I am reserved upon that subject. I will not lead you on, unguarded and ardent as I then was, to your destruction and infallible misery. Learn from me, if not by my precepts, at least by my example, how dangerous is the acquirement of knowledge, and how much happier that man is who believes his native town to be the world, than he who aspires to become greater than his nature will allow.

When I found so astonishing a power placed within my hands, I hesitated a long time concerning the manner in which I should employ it. Although I possessed the capacity of bestowing animation, yet to prepare a frame for the reception of it, with all its intricacies of fibres, muscles, and veins, still remained a work of inconceivable difficulty and labour. I doubted at first whether I should attempt the creation of a being like myself, or one of simpler organization; but my imagination was too much exalted by my first success to permit me to doubt of my ability to give life to an animal as complex and wonderful as man. The materials at present within my command hardly appeared adequate to so arduous an undertaking; but I doubted not that I should ultimately succeed. I prepared myself for a multitude of reverses; my operations might be incessantly baffled, and at last my work be imperfect: yet, when I considered the improvement which every day takes place in science and mechanics, I was encouraged to hope my present attempts would at least lay the foundations of future success. Nor could I consider the magnitude and complexity of my plan as any argument of its impracticability. It was with these feelings that I began the creation of a human being. As the minuteness of the parts formed a great hindrance to my speed, I resolved, contrary to my first intention, to make the being of a gigantic stature; that is to say, about eight feet in height, and proportionably large. After having formed this determination, and having spent some months in successfully collecting and arranging my materials, I began.

No one can conceive the variety of feelings which bore me onwards, like a hurricane, in the first enthusiasm of success. Life and death appeared to me ideal bounds, which I should first break through, and pour a torrent of light into our dark world. A new species would bless me as its creator and source; many happy and excellent natures would owe their being to me. No father could claim the gratitude of his child so completely as I should deserve theirs. Pursuing these reflections, I thought, that if I could bestow animation upon lifeless matter, I might in process of time (although I now found it impossible) renew life where death had apparently devoted the body to corruption.

These thoughts supported my spirits, while I pursued my undertaking with unremitting ardour. My cheek had grown pale with study, and my person had become emaciated with confinement. Sometimes, on the very brink of certainty, I failed; yet still I clung to the hope which the next day or the next hour might realise. One secret which I alone possessed was the hope to which I had dedicated myself; and the moon gazed on my midnight labours, while, with unrelaxed and breathless eagerness, I pursued nature to her hiding-places. Who shall conceive the horrors of my secret toil, as I dabbled among the unhallowed damps of the grave, or tortured the living animal to animate the lifeless clay? My limbs now tremble, and my eyes swim with the remembrance; but then a resistless, and almost frantic, impulse, urged me forward; I seemed to have lost all soul or sensation but for this one pursuit. It was indeed but a passing trance, that only made me feel with renewed acuteness so soon as, the unnatural stimulus ceasing to operate, I had returned to my old habits. I collected bones from charnel-houses; and disturbed, with profane fingers, the tremendous secrets of the human frame. In a solitary chamber, or rather cell, at the top of the house, and separated from all the other apartments by a gallery and staircase, I kept my workshop of filthy creation: my eye-balls were starting from their sockets in attending to the details of my employment. The dissecting room and the slaughter-house furnished many of my materials; and often did my human nature turn with loathing from my occupation, whilst, still urged on by an eagerness which perpetually increased, I brought my work near to a conclusion.

The summer months passed while I was thus engaged, heart and soul, in one pursuit. It was a most beautiful season; never did the fields bestow a more plentiful harvest, or the vines yield a more luxuriant vintage: but my eyes were insensible to the charms of nature. And the same feelings which made me neglect the scenes around me caused me also to forget those friends who were so many miles absent, and whom I had not seen for so long a time. I knew my silence disquieted them; and I well remembered the words of my father: 'I know that while you are pleased with yourself, you will think of us with affection, and we shall hear regularly from you. You must pardon me if I regard any interruption in your correspondence as a proof that your other duties are equally neglected.'

I knew well therefore what would be my father's feelings; but I could not tear my thoughts from my employment, loathsome in itself, but which had taken an irresistible hold of my imagination. I wished, as it were, to procrastinate all that related to my feelings of affection until the great object, which swallowed up every habit of my nature, should be completed.

I then thought that my father would be unjust if he ascribed my neglect to vice, or faultiness on my part; but I am now convinced that he was justified in conceiving that I should not be altogether free from blame. A human being in perfection ought always to preserve a calm and peaceful mind, and never to allow passion or a transitory desire to disturb his tranquillity. I do not think that the pursuit of knowledge is an exception to this rule. If the study to which you apply yourself has a tendency to weaken your affections, and to destroy your taste for those simple pleasures in which no alloy can possibly mix, then that study is certainly unlawful, that is to say, not befitting the human mind. If this rule were always observed; if no man allowed any pursuit whatsoever to interfere with the tranquillity of his domestic affections, Greece had not been enslaved; Caesar would have spared his country; America would have been discovered more gradually; and the empires of Mexico and Peru had not been destroyed.

But I forget that I am moralising in the most interesting part of my tale; and your looks remind me to proceed.

My father made no reproach in his letters, and only took notice of my silence by enquiring into my occupations more particularly than before. Winter, spring, and summer passed away during my labours; but I did not watch the blossom or the expanding leaves—sights which before always yielded me supreme delight—so deeply was I engrossed in my occupation. The leaves of that year had withered before my work drew near to a close; and now every day showed me more plainly how well I had succeeded. But my enthusiasm was checked by my anxiety, and I appeared rather like one doomed by slavery to toil in the mines, or any other unwholesome trade, than an artist occupied by his favourite employment. Eery night I was oppressed by a slow fever, and I became nervous to a most painful degree; the fall of a leaf startled me, and I shunned my fellow-creatures as if I had been guilty of a crime. Sometimes I grew alarmed at the wreck I perceived that I had become; the energy of my purpose alone sustained me: my labours would soon end, and I believed that exercise and amusement would then drive away incipient disease; and I promised myself both of these when my creation should be complete.

CHAPTER V

IT was on a dreary night of November, that I beheld the accomplishment of my toils. With an anxiety that almost amounted to agony, I collected the instruments of life around me, that I might infuse a spark of being into the lifeless thing that lay at my feet. It was already one in the morning; the rain pattered dismally against the panes, and my candle was nearly burnt out, when, by the glimmer of the half-extinguished light, I saw the dull yellow eye of the creature open; it breathed hard, and a convulsive motion agitated its limbs.

How can I describe my emotions at this catastrophe, or how delineate the wretch whom with such infinite pains and care I had endeavoured to form? His limbs were in proportion, and I had selected his features as beautiful. Beautiful!—Great God! His yellow skin scarcely covered the work of muscles and arteries beneath; his hair was of a lustrous black, and flowing; his teeth of a pearly whiteness; but these luxuriances only formed a more horrid contrast with his watery eyes, that seemed almost of the same colour as the dun white sockets in which they were set, his shrivelled complexion and straight black lips.

The different accidents of life are not so changeable as the feelings of human nature. I had worked hard for nearly two years, for the sole purpose of infusing life into an inanimate body. For this I had deprived myself of rest and health. I had desired it with an ardour that far exceeded moderation; but now that I had finished the beauty of the dream vanished and breathless horror and disgust filled my heart. Unable to endure the aspect of the being I had created, I rushed out of the room, and continued a long time traversing my bed-chamber, unable to compose my mind to sleep. At length lassitude succeeded to the tumult I had before endured, and I threw myself on the bed in my clothes, endeavouring to seek a few moments of forgetfulness. But it was in vain: I slept, indeed, but I was disturbed by the wildest dreams. I thought I saw Elizabeth, in the bloom of health, walking in the streets of Ingolstadt. Delighted and surprised, I embraced her; but as I imprinted the first kiss on her lips, they became livid with the hue of death; her features appeared to change, and I thought that I held the corpse of my dead mother in my arms; a shroud enveloped her form, and I saw the grave-worms crawling in the folds of the flannel. I started from my sleep with horror; a cold dew covered my forehead, my teeth chattered, and every limb became convulsed: when, by the dim and yellow light of the moon, as it forced its way through the window shutters, I beheld the wretch—the miserable monster whom I had created. He held up the curtain of the bed; and his eyes, if eyes they may be called, were fixed on me. His jaws opened, and he muttered some inarticulate sounds, while a grin wrinkled his cheeks. He might have spoken, but I did not hear; one hand was stretched out, seemingly to detain me, but I escaped, and rushed down stairs. I took refuge in the courtyard belonging to the house which I inhabited; where I remained during the rest of the night, walking up and down in the greatest agitation, listening attentively, catching and fearing each sound as if it were to announce the approach of the demoniacal corpse to which I had so miserably given life.

Oh! no mortal could support the horror of that countenance. A mummy again endued with animation could not be so hideous as that wretch. I had gazed on him while unfinished; he was ugly then; but when those muscles and joints were rendered capable of motion, it became a thing such as even Dante could not have conceived.

I passed the night wretchedly. Sometimes my pulse beat so quickly and hardly, that I felt the palpitation of every artery; at others, I nearly sank to the ground through languor and extreme weakness. Mingled with this horror, I felt the bitterness of disappointment; dreams that had been my food and pleasant rest for so long a space were now become a hell to me; and the change was so rapid, the overthrow so complete!

Morning, dismal and wet, at length dawned, and discovered to my sleepless and aching eyes the church of Ingolstadt, its white steeple and clock, which indicated the sixth hour. The porter opened the gates of the court, which had that night been my asylum, and I issued into the streets, pacing them with quick steps, as if I sought to avoid the wretch whom I feared every turning of the street would present to my view. I did not dare return to the apartment which I inhabited, but felt impelled to hurry on, although drenched by the rain which poured from a black and comfortless sky.

I continued walking in this manner for some time, endeavouring, by bodily exercise, to ease the load that weighed upon my mind. I traversed the streets, without any clear conception of where I was, or what I was doing. My heart palpitated in the sickness of fear; and I hurried on with irregular steps, not daring to look about me:—

'Like one who, on a lonely road,
　　Doth walk in fear and dread,
And, having once turned round, walks on,
　　And turns no more his head;
Because he knows a frightful fiend
　　Doth close behind him tread.'

Coleridge's Ancient Mariner

CHAPTER X

* * * * *

It was nearly noon when I arrived at the top of the ascent. For some time I sat upon the rock that overlooks the sea of ice. A mist covered both that and the surrounding mountains. Presently a breeze dissipated the cloud, and I descended upon the glacier. The surface is very uneven, rising like the waves of a troubled sea, descending low, and interspersed by rifts that sink deep. The field of ice is almost a league in width, but I spent nearly two hours in crossing it. The opposite mountain is a bare perpendicular rock. From the side where I now stood Montanvert was exactly opposite, at the distance of a league; and above it rose Mont Blanc, in awful majesty. I remained in a recess of the rock, gazing on this wonderful and stupendous scene. The sea, or rather the vast river of ice, wound among its dependent mountains, whose aerial summits hung over its recesses. Their icy and glittering peaks shone in the sunlight over the clouds. My heart, which was before sorrowful, now swelled with something like joy; I exclaimed —'Wandering spirits, if indeed ye wander, and do not rest in your narrow beds, allow me this faint happiness, or take me, as your companion, away from the joys of life.'

As I said this, I suddenly beheld the figure of a man, at some distance, advancing towards me with superhuman speed. He bounded over the crevices in the ice, among which I had walked with caution; his stature, also, as he approached, seemed to exceed that of man. I was troubled: a mist came over my eyes, and I felt a faintness seize me; but I was quickly restored by the cold gale of the mountains. I perceived, as the shape came nearer (sight tremendous and abhorred?) that it was the wretch whom I had created. I trembled with rage and horror, resolving to wait his approach, and then close with him in mortal combat. He approached; his countenance bespoke bitter anguish, combined with disdain and malignity, while its unearthly ugliness rendered it almost too horrible for human eyes. But I scarcely observed this; rage and hatred had at first deprived me of utterance, and I recovered only to overwhelm him with words expressive of furious detestation and contempt.

'Devil,' I exclaimed, 'do you dare approach me? and do not you fear the fierce vengeance of my arm wreaked on your miserable head? Begone, vile insect! or rather, stay, that I may trample you to dust! and, oh! that I could, with the extinction of your miserable existence, restore those victims whom you have so diabolically murdered!'

'I expected this reception,' said the daemon. 'All men hate the wretched; how, then, must I be hated, who am miserable beyond all living things! Yet you, my creator, detest and spurn me, thy creature, to whom thou art bound by ties only dissoluble by the annihilation of one of us. You purpose to kill me. How dare you sport thus with life? Do your duty towards me, and I will do mine towards you and the rest of mankind. If you will comply with my conditions, I will leave them and you at peace; but if you refuse, I will glut the maw of death, until it be satiated with the blood of your remaining friends.'

'Abhorred monster! fiend that thou art! the tortures of hell are too mild a vengeance for thy crimes. Wretched devil! you reproach me with your creation; come on, then that I may extinguish the spark which I so negligently bestowed.'

My rage was without bounds; I sprang on him, impelled by all the feelings which can arm one being against the existence of another.

He easily eluded me, and said—

'Be calm! I entreat you to hear me, before you give vent to your hatred on my devoted head. Have I not suffered enough, that you seek to increase my misery? Life, although it may only be an accumulation of anguish, is dear to me, and I will defend it. Remember, thou hast made me more powerful than thyself; my height is superior to thine; my joints more supple. But I will not be tempted to set myself in opposition to thee. I am thy creature, and I will be even mild and docile to my natural lord and king, if thou wilt also perform thy part, the which thou owest me. Oh, Frankenstein, be not equitable to every other, and trample upon me alone, to whom thy justice, and even thy clemency and affection, is most due. Remember, that I am thy creature; I ought to be thy Adam; but I am rather the fallen angel, whom thou drivest from joy for no misdeed. Every where I see bliss, from which I alone am irrevocably excluded. I was benevolent and good; misery made me a fiend. Make me happy, and I shall again be virtuous.'

'Begone! I will not hear you. There can be no community between you and me; we are enemies. Begone, or let us try our strength in a fight, in which one must fall.'

'How can I move thee? Will no entreaties cause thee to turn a favourable eye upon thy creature, who implores thy goodness and compassion? Believe me, Frankenstein: I was benevolent; my soul glowed with love and humanity: but am I not alone, miserably alone? You, my creator, abhor me; what hope can I gather from your fellow-creatures, who owe me nothing? they spurn and hate me. The desert mountains and dreary glaciers are my refuge. I have wandered here many days; the caves of ice, which I only do not fear, are a dwelling to me, and the only one which man does not grudge. These bleak skies I hail, for they are kinder to me than your fellow-beings. If the multitude of mankind knew of my existence, they would do as you do, and arm themselves for my destruction. Shall I not then hate them who abhor me? I will keep no terms with my enemies. I am miserable, and they shall share my wretchedness. Yet it is in your power to recompense me, and deliver them from an evil which it only remains for you to make so great, that not only you and your family, but thousands of others, shall be swallowed up in the whirlwinds of its rage. Let your compassion be moved, and do not disdain me. Listen to my tale: when you have heard that, abandon or commiserate me, as you shall judge that I deserve. But hear me. The guilty are allowed, by human laws, bloody as they are, to speak in their own defence before they are condemned. Listen to me, Frankenstein. You accuse me of murder; and yet you would, with a satisfied conscience, destroy your own creature. Oh, praise the eternal justice of man! Yet I ask you not to spare me: listen to me; and then, if you can, and if you will, destroy the work of your hands.'

'Why do you call to my remembrance,' I rejoined, 'circumstances, of which I shudder to reflect, that I have been the miserable origin and author? Cursed be the day, abhorred devil, in which you first saw light! Cursed (although I curse myself) be the hands that formed you! You have made me wretched beyond expression. You have left me no power to consider whether I am just to you, or not. Begone! relieve me from the sight of your detested form.'

'Thus I relieve thee, my creator,' he said, and placed his hated hands before my eyes, which I flung from me with violence; 'thus I take from thee a sight which you abhor. Still thou canst listen to me, and grant me thy compassion. By the virtues that I once possessed, I demand this from you. Hear my tale; it is long and strange, and the temperature of this place is not fitting to your fine sensations; come to the hut upon the mountain. The sun is yet high in the heavens; before it descends to hide itself behind yon snowy precipices, and illuminate another world, you will have heard my story, and can decide. On you it rests, whether I quit for ever the neighbourhood of man, and lead a harmless life, or become the scourge of your fellow-creatures, and the author of your own speedy ruin.'

As he said this, he led the way across the ice: I followed. My heart was full, and I did not answer him; but, as I proceeded, I weighed the various arguments that he had used, and determined at least to listen to his tale. I was partly urged by curiosity, and compassion confirmed my resolution. I had hitherto supposed him to be the murderer of my brother, and I eagerly sought a confirmation or denial of this opinion. For the first time, also, I felt what the duties of a creator towards his creature were, and that I ought to render him happy before I complained of his wickedness. These motives urged me to comply with his demand. We crossed the ice, therefore, and ascended the opposite rock. The air was cold, and the rain again began to descend: we entered the hut, the fiend with an air of exultation, I with a heavy heart, and depressed spirits. But I consented to listen; and, seating myself by the fire which my odious companion had lighted, he thus began his tale.

BY THE WATERS OF BABYLON

STEPHEN VINCENT BENÉT

Stephen Vincent Benét (1898-1943) was known as a poet, a novelist, and a short-story writer. He was born to a military family and reared on army posts. Both his older brother, William Rose, and a sister, Laura, also became writers. Stephen published his first book at the age of seventeen, and wrote two others while an undergraduate at Yale. Civilian service in World War I interrupted his education, but he graduated from Yale in 1919 and earned a master's degree for which he submitted a volume of poems in lieu of a thesis. He spent two years in Paris, 1921-1923, on a fellowship to the Sorbonne and another two years in France, 1926-1928, on a Guggenheim fellowship.

Benét probably is best known for his epic poem, *John Brown's Body* (1928), which won a Pulitzer prize, and for the short story, *The Devil and Daniel Webster*. His *By the Waters of Babylon* (1937) is a fantasy that offers a sobering commentary on the human condition.

1. What do you think was Benét's purpose in writing this fantasy? What do the allegorical features represent?

2. Do you get any hint of what might have happened to create the "Place of the Gods"? If so, what?

3. Why do men bring about their own destruction with the very devices that should fill their needs abundantly?

4. Is man more the master or the victim of nature? Or is it more a question of some men being master and some victims of other men?

BY THE WATERS OF BABYLON

STEPHEN VINCENT BENÉT

THE NORTH and the west and the south are good hunting ground, but it is forbidden to go east. It is forbidden to go to any of the Dead Places except to search for metal and then he who touches the metal must be a priest or the son of a priest. Afterwards, both the man and the metal must be purified. These are the rules and the laws; they are well made. It is forbidden to cross the great river and look upon the place that was the Place of the Gods—this is most strictly forbidden. We do not even say its name though we know its name. It is there that spirits live, and demons—it is there that there are the ashes of the Great Burning. These things are forbidden—they have been forbidden since the beginning of time.

My father is a priest; I am the son of a priest. I have been in the Dead Places near us, with my father—at first, I was afraid. When my father went into the house to search for the metal, I stood by the door and my heart felt small and weak. It was a dead man's house, a spirit house. It did not have the smell of man, though there were old bones in a corner. But it is not fitting that a priest's son should show fear. I looked at the bones in the shadow and kept my voice still.

Then my father came out with the metal—a good, strong piece. He looked at me with both eyes but I had not run away. He gave me the metal to hold—I took it and did not die. So he knew that I was truly his son and would be a priest in my time. That was when I was very young—nevertheless my brothers would not have done it, though they are good hunters. After that, they gave me the good piece of meat and the warm corner by the fire. My father watched over me—he was glad that I should be a priest. But when I boasted or wept without a reason, he punished me more strictly than my brothers. That was right.

After a time, I myself was allowed to go into the dead houses and search for metal. So I learned the ways of those houses—and if I saw bones, I was no longer afraid. The bones are light and old—sometimes they will fall into dust if you touch them. But that is a great sin.

I was taught the chants and the spells—I was taught how to stop the running of blood from a wound and many secrets. A priest must know many secrets—that was what my father said. If the hunters think we do all things by chants and spells, they may believe so—it does not hurt them. I was taught how to read in the old books and how to make the old writings—that was hard and took a long time. My knowledge made me happy—it was like a fire in my heart. Most of all, I liked to hear of the Old Days and the stories of the gods. I asked myself many questions that I could not answer, but it was good to ask them. At night, I would lie awake and listen to the wind—it seemed to me that it was the voice of the gods as they flew through the air.

We are not ignorant like the Forest People—our women spin wool on the wheel, our priests wear a white robe. We do not eat grubs from the tree, we have not forgotten the old writings, although they are hard to understand. Nevertheless, my knowledge and my lack of knowledge burned in me—I wished to know more. When I was a man at last, I came to my father and said, "It is time for me to go on my journey. Give me your leave."

He looked at me for a long time, stroking his beard, then he said at last, "Yes. It is time." That night, in the house of the priesthood, I asked for and received purification. My body hurt but my spirit was a cool stone. It was my father himself who questioned me about my dreams.

He bade me look into the smoke of the fire and see—I saw and told what I saw. It was what I have always seen—a river and, beyond it, a great Dead Place and in it the gods walking. I have always thought about that. His eyes were stern when I told him—he was no longer my father but a priest. He said, "This is a strong dream."

"It is mine," I said, while the smoke waved and my head felt light. They were singing the Star song in the outer chamber and it was like the buzzing of bees in my head. He asked me how the gods were dressed and I told him how they were dressed. We know how they were dressed from the book, but I saw them as if they were before me. When I had finished, he threw the sticks three times and studied them as they fell.

"This is a very strong dream," he said. "It may eat you up."

"I am not afraid," I said and looked at him with both eyes. My voice sounded thin in my ears but that was because of the smoke.

He touched me on the breast and the forehead. He gave me the bow and the three arrows.

"Take them," he said. "It is forbidden to travel east. It is forbidden to cross the river. It is forbidden to go to the Place of the Gods. All these things are forbidden."

"All these things are forbidden," I said, but it was my voice that spoke and not my spirit. He looked at me again.

"My son," he said. "Once I had young dreams. If your dreams do not eat you up, you may be a great priest. If they eat you, you are still my son. Now go on your journey."

I went fasting, as is the law. My body hurt but not my heart. When the dawn came, I was out of sight of the village. I prayed and purified myself, waiting for a sign. The sign was an eagle. It flew east.

Sometimes signs are sent by bad spirits. I waited again on the flat rock, fasting, taking no food. I was very still—I could feel the sky above me and the earth beneath. I waited till the sun was beginning to sink. Then three deer passed in the valley, going east—they did not wind me or see me. There was a white fawn with them—a very great sign.

I followed them, at a distance, waiting for what would happen. My heart was troubled about going east, yet I knew that I must go. My head hummed with my fasting—I did not even see the panther spring upon the white fawn. But, before I knew it, the bow was in my hand. I shouted and the panther lifted his head from the fawn. It is not easy to kill a panther with one arrow but the arrow went through his eye and into his brain. He died as he tried to spring—he rolled over, tearing at the ground. Then I knew I was meant to go east—I knew that was my journey. When the night came, I made my fire and roasted meat.

It is eight suns' journey to the east and a man passes by many Dead Places. The Forest People are afraid of them but I am not. Once I made my fire on the edge of a Dead Place at night and, next morning, in the dead house, I found a good knife, little rusted. That was small to what came afterward but it made my heart feel big. Always when I looked for game, it was in front of my arrow, and twice I passed hunting parties of the Forest People without their knowing. So I knew my magic was strong and my journey clean, in spite of the law.

Toward the setting of the eighth sun, I came to the banks of the great river. It was half-a-day's journey after I had left the god-road—we do not use the god-roads now for they are falling apart into great blocks of stone, and the forest is safer going. A long way off, I had seen the water through trees but the trees were thick. At last, I came out upon an open place at the top of a cliff. There was the great river below, like a giant in the sun. It is very long, very wide. It could eat all the streams we know and still be thirsty. Its name is Ou-dis-sun, the Sacred, the Long. No man of my tribe had seen it, not even my father, the priest. It was magic and I prayed.

Then I raised my eyes and looked south. It was there, the Place of the Gods.

How can I tell what it was like—you do not know. It was there, in the red light, and they were too big to be houses. It was there with the red light upon it, mighty and ruined. I knew that in another moment the gods would see me. I covered my eyes with my hands and crept back into the forest.

Surely, that was enough to do, and live. Surely it was enough to spend the night upon the cliff. The Forest People themselves do not come near. Yet, all through the night, I knew that I should have to cross the river and walk in the places of the gods, although the gods ate me up. My magic did not help me at all and yet there was a fire in my bowels, a fire in my mind. When the sun rose, I thought, "My journey has been clean. Now I will go home from my journey." But, even as I thought so, I knew I could not. If I went to the place of the gods, I would surely die, but, if I did not go, I could never be at peace with my spirit again. It is better to lose one's life than one's spirit, if one is a priest and the son of a priest.

Nevertheless, as I made the raft, the tears ran out of my eyes. The Forest People could have killed me without fight, if they had come upon me then, but they did not come. When the raft was made, I said the sayings for the dead and painted myself for death. My heart was cold as a frog and my knees like water, but the burning in my mind would not let me have peace. As I pushed the raft from the shore, I began my death song—I had the right. It was a fine song.

"I am John, son of John," I sang.

"My people are the Hill People. They are the men. I go into the Dead Places but I am not slain.

I take the metal from the Dead Places but I am not blasted.   I   travel upon the god-roads and am not afraid. E-yah!

I have killed the panther, I have killed the fawn! E-yah!

I have come to the great river. No man has come there before. It is forbidden to go east, but I have gone, forbidden to go on the great river, but I am there.

Open your hearts, you spirits, and hear my song.

Now I go to the place of the gods, I shall not return.

My body is painted for death and my limbs weak, but my heart is big as I go to the place of the gods!"

All the same, when I came to the Place of the Gods, I was afraid, afraid. The current of the great river is very strong—it gripped my raft with its hands. That was magic, for the river itself is wide and calm. I could feel evil spirits about me, in the bright morning; I could feel their breath on my neck as I was swept down the stream. Never have I been so much alone—I tried to think of my knowledge, but it was a squirrels' heap of winter nuts. There was no strength in my knowledge any more and I felt small and naked as a new-hatched bird—alone upon the great river, the servant of the gods.

Yet, after a while, my eyes were opened and I saw. I saw both banks of the river—I saw that once there had been god-roads across it, though now they were broken and fallen like broken vines. Very great they were, and wonderful and broken—broken in the time of the Great Burning when the fire fell out of the sky. And always the current took me nearer to the Place of the Gods, and the huge ruins rose before my eyes.

I do not know the customs of rivers—we are the People of the hills. I tried to guide my raft with the pole but it spun around. I thought the river meant to take me past the Place of the Gods and out into the Bitter Water of the legends. I grew angry then—my heart felt strong. I said aloud, "I am a priest and the son of a priest!" The gods heard me—they showed me how to paddle with the pole on one side of the raft. The current changed itself—I drew near to the Place of the Gods.

When I was very near, my raft struck and turned over. I can swim in our lakes—I swam to the shore. There was a great spike of rusted metal sticking out into the river—I hauled myself up upon it and sat there, panting. I had saved my bow and two arrows and the knife I found in the Dead Place but that was all. My raft went whirling downstream toward the Bitter Water. I looked after it, and thought if it had trod me under, at least I would be safely dead. Nevertheless, when I had dried my bow-string and restrung it, I walked forward to the Place of the Gods.

It felt like ground underfoot; it did not burn me. It is not true what some of the tales say, that the ground there burns forever, for I have been there. Here and there were the marks and stains of the Great Burning, on the ruins, that is true. But they were old marks, and old stains. It is not true either, what some of our priests say, that it is an island covered with fogs and enchantments. It is not. It is a great Dead Place—greater than any Dead Place we know. Everywhere in it there are god-roads, though most are cracked and broken. Everywhere there are the ruins of the high towers of the gods.

How shall I tell what I saw? I went carefully, my strung bow in my hand, my skin ready for danger. There should have been the wailings of spirits and the shrieks of demons, but there were not. It was very silent and sunny where I had landed—the wind and the rain and the birds that drop seeds had done their work—the grass grew in the cracks of the broken stone. It is a fair island—no wonder the gods built there. If I had come there, a god, I also would have built.

How shall I tell what I saw? The towers are not all broken—here and there one still stands, like a great tree in a forest, and the birds nest high. But the towers themselves look blind, for the gods are gone. I saw a fish-hawk, catching fish in the river. I saw a little dance of white butterflies over a great heap of broken stones and columns. I went there and looked about me—there was a carved stone with cut-letters, broken in half. I can read letters but I could not understand these. They said UBTREAS. There was also the shattered image of a man or a god. It had been made of white stone and he wore his hair tied back like a woman's. His name was ASHING, as I read on the cracked half of a stone. I thought it wise to pray to ASHING, though I do not know that god.

How shall I tell what I saw? There was no smell of man left, on stone or metal. Nor were there many trees in that wilderness of stone. There are many pigeons, nesting and dropping in the towers —the gods must have loved them, or, perhaps, they used them for sacrifices. There are wild cats that roam the god-roads, green-eyed, unafraid of man. At night they wail like demons but they are not demons. The wild dogs are more dangerous, for they hunt in a pack, but them I did not meet till later. Everywhere there are the carved stones, carved with magical numbers or words.

I went North—I did not try to hide myself. When a god or a demon saw me, then I would die, but meanwhile I was no longer afraid. My hunger for knowledge burned in me—there was so much that I could not understand. After awhile, I knew that my belly was hungry. I could have hunted for my meat, but I did not hunt. It is known that the gods did not hunt as we do—they got their food from enchanted boxes and jars. Sometimes these are still found in the Dead Places—once, when I was a child and foolish, I opened such a jar and tasted it and found the food sweet. But my father found out and punished me for it strictly, for, often, that food is death. Now, though, I had long gone past what was forbidden, and I entered the likeliest towers, looking for the food of the gods.

I found it at last in the ruins of a great temple in the mid-city. A mighty temple it must have been, for the roof was painted like the sky at night with its stars—that much I could see, though the colors were faint and dim. It went down into great caves and tunnels—perhaps they kept their slaves there. But when I started to climb down, I heard the squeaking of rats, so I did not go—rats are unclean, and there must have been many tribes of them, from the squeaking. But near there, I found food, in the heart of a ruin, behind a door that still opened. I ate only the fruits from the jars—they had a very sweet taste. There was drink, too, in bottles of glass—the drink of the gods was strong and made my head swim. After I had eaten and drunk, I slept on the top of a stone, my bow at my side.

When I woke, the sun was low. Looking down from where I lay, I saw a dog sitting on his haunches. His tongue was hanging out of his mouth; he looked as if he were laughing. He was a big dog, with a gray-brown coat, as big as a wolf. I sprang up and shouted at him but he did not move—he just sat there as if he were laughing. I did not like that. When I reached for a stone to throw, he moved swiftly out of the way of the stone. He was not afraid of me; he looked at me as if I were meat. No doubt I could have killed him with an arrow, but I did not know if there were others. Moreover, night was falling.

I looked about me—not far away there was a great, broken god-road, leading North. The towers were high enough, but not so high, and while many of the dead-houses were wrecked, there were some that stood. I went toward this god-road, keeping to heights of the ruins, while the dog followed. When I had reached the god-road, I saw that there were others behind him. If I had slept later, they would have come upon me asleep and torn out my throat. As it was, they were sure enough of me; they did not hurry. When I went into the dead-house, they kept watch at the entrance—doubtless they thought they would have a fine hunt. But a dog cannot open a door and I knew, from the books, that the gods did not like to live on the ground but on high.

I had just found a door I could open when the dogs decided to rush. Ha! They were surprised when I shut the door in their faces—it was a good door, of strong metal. I could hear their foolish baying beyond it but I did not stop to answer them. I was in darkness—I found stairs and climbed. There were many stairs, turning around till my head was dizzy. At the top was another door—I found the knob and opened it. I was in a long small chamber—on one side of it was a bronze door that could not be opened, for it had no handle. Perhaps there was a magic word to open it but I did not have the word. I turned to the door in the opposite side of the wall. The lock of it was broken and I opened it and went in.

Within, there was a place of great riches. The god who lived there must have been a powerful god. The first room was a small ante-room—I waited there for some time, telling the spirits of the place that I came in peace and not as a robber. When it seemed to me that they had had time to hear me, I went on. Ah, what riches! Few, even, of the windows had been broken—it was all as it had been. The great windows that looked over the city had not been broken at all though they were dusty and streaked with many years. There were coverings on the floors, the colors not greatly faded, and the chairs were soft and deep. There were pictures upon the walls, very strange, very wonderful—I remember one of a bunch of flowers in a jar—if you came close to it, you could see nothing but bits of color, but if you stood away from it, the flowers might have been picked yesterday. It made my heart feel strange to look at this picture—and to look at the figure of a bird, in some hard clay, on a table and see it so like our birds. Everywhere there were books and writings, many in tongues that I could not read. The god who lived there must have been a wise god and full of knowledge. I felt I had right there, as I sought knowledge also.

Nevertheless, it was strange. There was a washing-place but no water—perhaps the gods washed in air. There was a cooking-place but no wood, and though there was a machine to cook food, there was no place to put fire in it. Nor were there candles or lamps—there were things that looked like lamps but they had neither oil nor wick. All these things were magic, but I touched them and lived—the magic had gone out of them. Let me tell one thing to show. In the washing-place, a thing said "Hot" but it was not hot to the touch—another thing said "Cold" but it was not cold. This must have been a strong magic but the magic was gone. I do not understand—they had ways—I wish that I knew.

It was close and dry and dusty in their house of the gods. I have said the magic was gone but that is not true—it had gone from the magic things but it had not gone from the place. I felt the spirits about me, weighing upon me. Nor had I ever slept in a Dead Place before—and yet, tonight, I must sleep there. When I thought of it, my tongue felt dry in my throat, in spite of my wish for knowledge. Almost I would have gone down again and faced the dogs, but I did not.

I had not gone through all the rooms when the darkness fell. When it fell, I went back to the big room looking over the city and made fire. There was a place to make fire and a box with wood in it, though I do not think they cooked there. I wrapped myself in a floor-covering and slept in front of the fire—I was very tired.

Now I tell what is very strong magic. I woke in the midst of the night. When I woke, the fire had gone out and I was cold. It seemed to me that all around me there were whisperings and voices. I closed my eyes to shut them out. Some will say that I slept again, but I do not think that I slept. I could feel the spirits drawing my spirit out of my body as a fish is drawn on a line.

Why should I lie about it? I am a priest and the son of a priest. If there are spirits, as they say, in the small Dead Places near us, what spirits must there not be in that great Place of the Gods? And would not they wish to speak? After such long years? I know that I felt myself drawn as a fish is drawn on a line. I had stepped out of my body—I could see my body asleep in front of the cold fire, but it was not I. I was drawn to look out upon the city of the gods.

It should have been dark, for it was night, but it was not dark. Everywhere there were lights—lines of light—circles and blurs of light—ten thousand torches would not have been the same. The sky itself was alight—you could barely see the stars for the glow in the sky. I thought to myself "This is strong magic" and trembled. There was a roaring in my ears like the rushing of rivers. Then my eyes grew used to the light and my ears to the sound. I knew that I was seeing the city as it had been when the gods were alive.

That was a sight indeed—yes, that was a sight: I could not have seen it in the body—my body would have died. Everywhere went the gods, on foot and in chariots—there were gods beyond number and counting and their chariots blocked the streets. They had turned night to day for their pleasure—they did not sleep with the sun. The noise of their coming and going was the noise of many waters. It was magic what they could do—it was magic what they did.

I looked out of another window—the great vines of their bridges were mended and the god-roads went East and West. Restless, restless, were the gods and always in motion! They burrowed tunnels under rivers—they flew in the air. With unbelievable tools they did giant works—no part of the earth was safe from them, for, if they wished for a thing, they summoned it from the other side of the world. And always, as they labored and rested, as they feasted and made love, there was a drum in their ears—the pulse of the giant city, beating and beating like a man's heart.

Were they happy? What is happiness to the gods? They were great, they were mighty, they were wonderful and terrible. As I looked upon them and their magic, I felt like a child—but a little more, it seemed to me, and they would pull down the moon from the sky. I saw them with wisdom beyond wisdom and knowledge beyond knowledge. And yet not all they did was well done—even I could see that—and yet their wisdom could not but grow until all was peace.

Then I saw their fate come upon them and that was terrible past speech. It came upon them as they walked the streets of their city. I have been in the fights with the Forest People—I have seen men die. But this was not like that. When gods war with gods, they use weapons we do not know. It was fire falling out of the sky and a mist that poisoned. It was the time of the Great Burning and the Destruction. They ran about like ants in the streets of their city—poor gods, poor gods! Then the towers began to fall. A few escaped—yes, a few. The legends tell it. But, even after the city had become a Dead Place, for many years the poison was still in the ground. I saw it happen, I saw the last of them die. It was darkness over the broken city and I wept.

All this, I saw. I saw it as I have told it, though not in the body. When I woke in the morning, I was hungry, but I did not think first of my hunger for my heart was perplexed and confused. I knew the reason for the Dead Places but

I did not see why it had happened. It seemed to me it should not have happened, with all the magic they had. I went through the house looking for an answer. There was so much in the house I could not understand—and yet I am a priest and the son of a priest. It was like being on one side of the great river, at night, with no light to show the way.

Then I saw the dead god. He was sitting in his chair, by the window, in a room I had not entered before and, for the first moment, I thought that he was alive. Then I saw the skin on the back of his hand—it was like dry leather. The room was shut, hot and dry—no doubt that had kept him as he was. At first I was afraid to approach him—then the fear left me. He was sitting looking out over the city—he was dressed in the clothes of the gods. His age was neither young nor old—I could not tell his age. But there was wisdom in his face and great sadness. You could see that he would have not run away. He had sat at his window, watching his city die —then he himself had died. But it is better to lose one's life than one's spirit—and you could see from the face that his spirit had not been lost. I knew, that, if I touched him, he would fall into dust—and yet, there was something unconquered in the face.

That is all of my story, for then I knew he was a man—I knew then that they had been men, neither gods nor demons. It is a great knowledge, hard to tell and believe. They were men—they went a dark road, but they were men. I had no fear after that—I had no fear going home, though twice I fought off the dogs and once I was hunted for two days by the Forest People. When I saw my father again, I prayed and was purified. He touched my lips and my breast, he said, "You went away a boy. You come back a man and a priest." I said, "Father, they were men! I have been in the Place of the Gods and seen it! Now slay me, if it is the law—but still I know they were men."

He looked at me out of both eyes. He said, "The law is not always the same shape—you have done what you have done. I could not have done it in my time, but you come after me. Tell!"

I told and he listened. After that, I wished to tell all the people but he showed me otherwise. He said, "Truth is a hard deer to hunt. If you eat too much truth at once, you may die of the truth. It was not idly that our fathers forbade the Dead Places." He was right—it is better the truth should come little by little. I have learned that, being a priest. Perhaps, in the old days, they ate knowledge too fast.

Nevertheless, we make a beginning. It is not for the metal alone we go to the Dead Places now—there are the books and the writings. They are hard to learn. And the magic tools are broken—but we can look at them and wonder. At least, we make a beginning. And, when I am chief priest we shall go beyond the great river. We shall go to the Place of the Gods—the place new-york—not one man but a company. We shall look for the images of the gods and find the god ASHING and the others—the gods Lincoln and Biltmore and oses. But they were men who built the city, not gods or demons. They were men. I remember the dead man's face. They were men who were here before us. We must build again.

genetics today

I have seen
The old gods go
And the new gods come.

Day by day
And year by year
The idols fall
And the idols rise.

Today
I worship the hammer.

Carl Sandburg, *The Hammer*, 1910

SOUNDING THE ALARM

Henry Adams

Herbert J. Muller

Lewis Mumford

Jacques Ellul

Bertrand Russell

A student who can weave his technology into the fabric of society can claim to have a liberal education; a student who cannot weave his technology into the fabric of society cannot claim even to be a good technologist.

Lord Eric Ashby, *Technology and the Academics*, 1958

The pace of science forces the pace of technique. Theoretical physics forces atomic energy on us; the successful production of the fission bomb forces upon us the manufacture of the hydrogen bomb. We do not choose our problems, we do not choose our products; we are pushed, we are forced—by what? By a system which has no purpose and goal transcending it, and which makes man its appendix.

Erich Fromm, *The Sane Society*, 1955

We have genuflected before the god of science only to find that it has given us the atomic bomb, producing fears and anxieties that science can never mitigate.

Martin Luther King, Jr., *Strength Through Love*, 1963

"Men have forgotten a truth," said the fox. "You are responsible forever after for anything you tame."

Antoine de Saint-Exupéry

If we had a reliable way to label our toys good and bad, it would be easy to regulate technology wisely. But we can rarely see far enough ahead to know which road leads to damnation. Whoever concerns himself with big technology, either to push it forward or to stop it, is gambling in human lives.

Freemon J. Dyson, *Disturbing the Universe*, 1979

There is a lurking fear that some things are not meant "to be known," that some inquiries are too dangerous for human beings to make.

Carl Sagan, *Broca's Brain*, 1979

I have seen the science I worshiped and the aircraft I loved, destroying the civilization I expected them to serve.

Charles A. Lindbergh, *Time*, 1967

Science without conscience is the soul's perdition.

François Rabelais, *Gargantua and Pantagruel*, 1532

All the steam in the world could not, like the Virgin, build Chartres. . . . Symbol or energy, the Virgin had acted as the greatest force the Western world ever felt. . .

Henry Adams, *The Education of Henry Adams*, 1907

MONT-SAINT-MICHEL AND CHARTRES

THE EDUCATION OF HENRY ADAMS

PRAYER TO THE VIRGIN OF CHARTRES

HENRY ADAMS

Henry Brooks Adams (1838-1918) was a grandson of President John Quincy Adams and a great-grandson of President John Adams. A philosopher-historian who taught for a time at Harvard, Adams was particularly impressed with the rise of science and technology. Living under the burden of being an Adams, Henry's life was filled with personal tragedy and a constant feeling that he was not living up to the family name.

Adams was tremendously impressed with the magnificent beauty and overpowering force of the great Gothic cathedrals of Europe, particularly the Cathedral of Chartres. In this excerpt from the book, *Mont-Saint-Michel and Chartres* (1905), Adams attempts to explain the power of the "Virgin of Chartres."

The Education of Henry Adams was written in 1906 as a sequel to *Mont-Saint-Michel and Chartres*. It was originally distributed only to Henry Adams' friends for comment. In the excerpt reproduced below, Adams concludes that the power of his age was represented by the great dynamos which powered American industry. Adams goes on to apply the laws of physics to the movement of human history.

Adams puts the image of the Virgin together with the image of the Dynamo in these poems which are two prayers, one to the Virgin of Chartres and one to the modern Dynamo, with a postscript prayer to the Virgin once again.

1. Why did Adams believe the Gothic cathedrals were important to twentieth-century America?

2. Why did the people in twelfth-century France spend such huge amounts of money on cathedrals like the one at Chartres?

3. What did the Virgin demand from the people?

4. In our society of today, what might fill the role or take the place of the Virgin of Chartres?

5. What is a dynamo? Why did Adams believe the dynamo represented his age?

6. Why did the people of early twentieth-century United States spend so much money on dynamos?

7. What did the dynamo demand from the people?

8. What do the Virgin and the Dynamo represent to their respective societies?

9. What does Adams mean by the "Abyss of Ignorance"?

10. Adams refers to his age as the Age of Multiplicity and to the twelfth century as the Age of Unity. Why does he do this? How does the Virgin create unity and the Dynamo, multiplicity?

11. Do you think Adams successfully applies the laws of physics to human history? Why or why not?

12. In which image did Adams see salvation, the Virgin or the Dynamo?

13. What does Adams fear about the Dynamo?

14. Does it make any sense to pray to the Dynamo?

15. Why was the Virgin Mary the Dynamo of the Middle Ages?

16. What was the difference between the power of the Virgin and the power of the Dynamo?

17. Was the Dynamo moral?

18. How does Adams see the future of the world?

19. Does the poem make you sad, happy, or what emotion?

MONT-SAINT-MICHEL AND CHARTRES

HENRY ADAMS

Chapter VI

THE VIRGIN OF CHARTRES

We must take ten minutes to accustom our eyes to the light, and we had better use them to seek the reason why we come to Chartres rather than to Rheims or Amiens or Bourges, for the cathedral that fills our ideal. The truth is, there are several reasons; there generally are, for doing the things we like; and after you have studied Chartres to the ground, and got your reasons settled, you will never find an antiquarian to agree with you; the architects will probably listen to you with contempt; and even these excellent priests, whose kindness is great, whose patience is heavenly, and whose good opinion you would so gladly gain, will turn from you with pain, if not with horror. The Gothic is singular in this; one seems easily at home in the Renaissance; one is not too strange in the Byzantine; as for the Roman, it is ourselves; and we could walk blindfolded through every chink and cranny of the Greek mind; all these styles seem modern, when we come close to them; but the Gothic gets away. No two men think alike about it, and no woman agrees with either man. The Church itself never agreed about it, and the architects agree even less than the priests. To most minds it casts too many shadows; it wraps itself in mystery; and when people talk of mystery, they commonly mean fear. To others, the Gothic seems hoary with age and decrepitude, and its shadows mean death. What is curious to watch is the fanatical conviction of the Gothic enthusiast, to whom the twelfth century means exuberant youth, the eternal child of Wordsworth, over whom its immortality broods like the day; it is so simple and yet so complicated; it sees so much and so little; it loves so many toys and cares for so few necessities; its youth is so young, its age so old, and its youthful yearning for old thought is so disconcerting, like the mysterious senility of the baby that—
Deaf and silent, reads the eternal deep,
Haunted forever by the eternal mind.
One need not take it more seriously than one takes the baby itself. Our amusement is to play with it, and to catch its meaning in its smile; and whatever Chartres may be now, when young it was a smile. To the Church, no doubt, its cathedral here has a fixed and administrative meaning, which is the same as that of every other bishop's seat and with which we have nothing whatever to do. To us, it is a child's fancy; a toy-house to please the Queen of Heaven—to please her so much that she would be happy in it—to charm her till she smiled.

The Queen Mother was as majestic as you like; she was absolute; she could be stern; she was not above being angry; but she was still a woman, who loved grace, beauty, ornament—her toilette, robes, jewels—who considered the arrangements of her palace with attention, and liked both light and colour; who kept a keen eye on her Court, and exacted prompt and willing obedience from king and arch-bishops as well as from beggars and drunken priests. She protected her friends and punished her enemies. She required space, beyond what was known in the Courts of kings, because she was liable at all times to have ten thousand people begging her for favours—mostly inconsistent with law—and deaf to refusal. She was extremely sensitive to neglect, to disagreeable impressions, to want of intelligence in her surroundings. She was the greatest artist, as she was the greatest philosopher and musician and theologist, that ever lived on earth, except her Son, Who, at Chartres, is still an Infant under her guardianship. Her taste was infallible; her sentence eternally final. This church was built for her in this spirit of simple-minded, practical, utilitarian faith—in this singleness of thought, exactly as a little girl sets up a doll-house for her favourite blonde doll. Unless you can go back to your dolls, you are out of place here. If you can go back to them, and get rid for one small hour of the weight of custom, you shall see Chartres in glory.

The palaces of earthly queens were hovels compared with these palaces of the Queen of Heaven at Chartres, Paris, Laon, Noyon, Rheims, Amiens, Rouen, Bayeux, Coutances—a list that might be stretched into a volume. The nearest approach we have made to a palace was the Merveille at Mont-Saint-Michel, but no Queen had a palace equal to that. The Merveille was built, or designed, about the year 1200; toward the year 1500, Louis XI built a great castle at Loches in Touraine, and there Queen Anne de Bretagne had apartments which still exist, and which we will visit. At Blois you shall see the residence which served for Catherine de Medicis till her death in 1589. Anne de Bretagne was trebly queen, and Catherine de Medicis took her standard of comfort from the luxury of Florence. At Versailles you can see the apartments which the queens of the Bourbon line occupied through their century of magnificence. All put together, and then trebled in importance, could not rival the splendour of any single cathedral dedicated to Queen Mary in the thirteenth century; and of them all, Chartres was built to be peculiarly and exceptionally her delight.

One has grown so used to this sort of loose comparison, this reckless waste of words, that one no longer adopts an idea unless it is driven in with hammers of statistics and columns of figures. With the irritating demand for literal exactness and perfectly straight lines which lights up every truly American eye, you will certainly ask when this exaltation of Mary began, and unless you get the dates, you will doubt the facts. It is your own fault if they are tiresome; you might easily read them all in the "Iconographie de la Sainte Vierge," by M. Rohault de Fleury, published in 1878. You can start at Byzantium with the Empress Helena in 326, or with the Council of Ephesus in 431. You will find the Virgin acting as the patron saint of Constantinople and of the Imperial residence, under as many names as Artemis or Aphrodite had borne. As Godmother, Deipara, Pathfinder, she was the chief favourite of the Eastern Empire, and her picture was carried at the head of every procession and hung on the wall of every hut and hovel, as it is still wherever the Greek Church goes. In the year 610, when Heraclius sailed from Carthage to dethrone Phocas at Constantinople, his ships carried the image of the Virgin at their mastheads. In 1143, just before the flèche on the Chartres clocher was begun, the Basileus John Comnenus died, and so devoted was he to the Virgin that, on a triumphal entry into Constantinople, he put the image of the Mother of God in his chariot, while he himself walked. In the Western Church the Virgin had always been highly honoured, but it was not until the crusades that she began to overshadow the Trinity itself. Then her miracles became more frequent and her shrines more frequented, so that Chartres, soon after 1100, was rich enough to build its western portal with Byzantine splendour. A proof of the new outburst can be read in the story of Citeaux. For us, Citeaux means Saint Bernard, who joined the Order in 1112, and in 1115 founded his Abbey of Clairvaux in the territory of Troyes. In him, the religious emotion of the half-century between the first and second crusades (1095-1145) centred as in no one else. He was a French precursor of Saint Francis of Assisi who lived a century later. If we were to plunge into the story of Citeaux and Saint Bernard we should never escape, for Saint Bernard incarnates what we are trying to understand, and his mind is further from us than the architecture. You would lose hold of everything actual, if you could comprehend in its contradictions the strange mixture of passion and caution, the austerity, the self-abandonment, the vehemence, the restraint, the love, the hate, the miracles, and the scepticism of Saint Bernard. The Cistercian Order, which was founded in 1098, from the first put all its churches under the special protection of the Virgin, and Saint Bernard in his time was regarded as the apple of the Virgin's eye. Tradition as old as the twelfth century, which long afterwards gave to Murillo the subject of a famous painting, told that once, when he was reciting before her statue the "Ave Maris Stella," and came to the words, "Monstra te esse Matrem," the image, pressing its breast, dropped on the lips of her servant three drops of the milk which had nourished the Saviour. The same miracle, in various forms, was told of many other persons, both saints and sinners; but it made so much impression on the mind of the age that, in the fourteenth century, Dante, seeking in Paradise for some official introduction to the foot of the Throne, found no intercessor with the Queen of Heaven more potent than Saint Bernard. You can still read Bernard's hymns to the Virgin, and even his sermons, if you like. To him she was the great mediator. In the eyes of a culpable humanity, Christ was too sublime, too terrible, too just, but not even the weakest human frailty could fear to approach his Mother. Her attribute was humility; her love and pity were infinite. "Let him deny your mercy who can say that he has ever asked it in vain."

Saint Bernard was emotional and to a certain degree mystical, like Adam de Saint-Victor, whose hymns were equally famous, but the emotional saints and mystical poets were not by any means allowed to establish exclusive rights to the Virgin's favour. Abélard was as devoted as they were, and wrote hymns as well. Philosophy claimed her, and Albert the Great, the head of scholasticism, the teacher of Thomas Aquinas, decided in her favour the question: "Whether the Blessed Virgin possessed perfectly the seven liberal arts." The Church at Chartres had decided it a hundred years before by putting the seven liberal arts next her throne, with Aristotle himself to witness; but Albertus gave the reason: "I hold that she did, for it is written, 'Wisdom has built herself a house, and has sculptured seven columns.' That house is the blessed Virgin; the seven columns are the seven liberal arts. Mary, therefore, had perfect mastery of science." Naturally she had also perfect mastery of economics, and most of her great churches were built in economic centres. The guilds were, if possible, more devoted to her than the monks; the bourgeoisie of Paris, Rouen, Amiens, Laon, spend money by millions to gain her favour. Most surprising of all, the great military class was perhaps the most vociferous. Of all inappropriate haunts for the gentle, courteous, pitying Mary, a field of battle seems to be the worst, if not distinctly blasphemous; yet the greatest French warriors insisted on her leading them into battle, and in the actual mêlée when men were killing each other, on every battlefield in Europe, for at least five hundred years, Mary was present, leading both sides. The battle cry of the famous Constable du Guesclin was "Notre-Dame-Guesclin"; "Notre-Dame-Coucy" was the cry of the great Sires de Coucy; "Notre-Dame-Auxerre"; "Notre-Dame-Sancerre"; "Notre-Dame-Hainault"; "Notre-Dame-Gueldres"; "Notre-Dame-Bourbon"; "Notre-Dame-Bearn"—all well-known battle cries. The King's own battle at one time cried, "Notre-Dame-Saint-Denis-Montjoie"; the Dukes of Burgundy cried, "Notre-Dame-Bourgogne"; and even the soldiers of the Pope were said to cry, "Notre-Dame-Saint-Pierre."

The measure of this devotion, which proves to any religious American mind, beyond possible cavil, its serious and practical reality, is the money it cost. According to statistics, in the single century between 1170 and 1270, the French built eighty cathedrals and nearly five hundred churches of the cathedral class, which would have cost, according to an estimate made in 1840, more than five thousand millions to replace. Five thousand million francs is a thousand million dollars and this covered only the great churches of a single century. The same scale of expenditure had been going on since the year 1000, and almost every parish in France had rebuilt its church in stone; to this day France is strewn with the ruins of this architecture, and yet the still preserved churches of the eleventh and twelfth centuries, among the churches that belong to the Romanesque and Transition period, are numbered by hundreds until they reach well into the thousands. The share of this capital which was—if one may use a commercial figure—invested in the Virgin cannot be fixed, any more than the total sum given to religious objects between 1000 and 1300; but in a spiritual and artistic sense, it was almost the whole, and expressed an intensity of conviction never again reached by any passion, whether of religion, of loyalty, of patriotism, or of wealth; perhaps never even paralleled by any single economic effort, except in war. Nearly every great church of the twelfth and thirteenth centuries belonged to Mary, until in France one asks for the church of Notre Dame as though it meant cathedral; but, not satisfied with this, she contracted the habit of requiring in all churches a chapel of her own, called in English the "Lady Chapel," which was apt to be as large as the church but was always meant to be handsomer; and there, behind the high altar, in her own private apartment, Mary sat, receiving her innumerable suppliants, and ready at any moment to step up upon the high altar itself to support the tottering authority of the local saint.

Expenditure like this rests invariably on an economic idea. Just as the French of the nineteenth century invested their surplus capital in a railway system in the belief that they would make money by it in this life, in the thirteenth they trusted their money to the Queen of Heaven because of their belief in her power to repay it with interest in the life to come. The investment was based on the power of Mary as Queen rather than on any orthodox Church conception of the Virgin's legitimate station. Papal Rome never greatly loved Byzantine empresses or French queens. The Virgin of Chartres was never wholly sympathetic to the Roman Curia. To this day the Church writers—like the Abbé Bulteaur or M. Rohault de Fleury—are singularly shy of the true Virgin of majesty, whether at Chartres or at Byzantium or wherever she is seen.

The fathers Martin and Cahier at Bourges alone felt her true value. Had the Church controlled her, the Virgin would perhaps have remained prostrate at the foot of the Cross. Dragged by a Byzantine Court, backed by popular insistence and impelled by overpowering self-interest, the Church accepted the Virgin throned and crowned, seated by Christ, the Judge throned and crowned; but even this did not wholly satisfy the French of the thirteenth century who seemed bent on absorbing Christ in His Mother, and making the Mother the Church, and Christ the Symbol.

The Church had crowned and enthroned her almost from the beginning, and could not have dethroned her if it would. In all Christian art—sculpture or mosaic, painting or poetry—the Virgin's rank was expressly asserted. Saint Bernard, like John Comnenus, and probably at the same time (1120-40), chanted hymns to the Virgin as Queen—

O salutaris Virgo Stella Maris	O saviour Virgin, Star of Sea,
Generans prolem, Æquitatis solem,	Who bore for child the Son of
Lucis auctorem, Retinens pudorem,	Justice,
Suscipe laudem!	The source of Light, Virgin always
	Hear our praise!

Celi Regina l'er quam medicina	Queen of Heaven who have given
Datur ægrotis, Gratia devotis,	Medicine to the sick, Grace to the
Gaudium mœstis, Mundo lux	devout,
cœlestis,	Joy to the sad, Heaven's light to the
Spesque salutis;	world
	And hope of salvation;

Aula regalis, Virgo specialis,	Court royal, Virgin typical,
Posce medelam Nobis et tutelam,	Grant us cure and guard,
Suscipe vota. Precibusque cuncta	Accept our vows, and by prayers
Pelle molestra!	Drive all griefs away!

As the lyrical poet of the twelfth century, Adam de Saint-Victor seems to have held rank higher if possible than that of Saint Bernard, and his hymns on the Virgin are certainly quite as emphatic an assertion of her majesty—

Imperatrix supernorum!	Empress of the highest,
Superatrix infernorum?	Mistress over the lowest,
Eligenda via cœli,	Chosen path of Heaven,
Retinenda spe fideli,	Held fast by faithful hope,
Separatoes a te longe	Those separated from you far,
Revocatos ad te junge	Recalled to you, unite
Tuorum collegio!	In your fold!

To delight in the childish jingle of the mediæval Latin is a sign of a futile mind, no doubt, and I beg pardon of you and of the Church for wasting your precious summer day on poetry which was regarded as mystical in its age and which now sounds like a nursery rhyme; but a verse or two of Adam's hymn on the assumption of the Virgin completes the record of her rank, and goes to complete also the documentary proof of her majesty at Chartres—

Salve, Mater Salvatoris!
Vas electrum! Vas honoris!
   Vas coelestis Gratiae!
Ab aeterno Vas provisum!
Vas insigne! Vas excisum
   Manu sapientiae!

Salve, Mater pietatis,
Et totius Trinitatis
   Nobile Triclinium!
Verbi tamen incarnati
Speciale majestati
   Praeparans hospitium!

O Maria! Stella maris!
Dignitate singularis,
Super omnes ordinaris
   Ordines coelestium!
In supremo sita poli
Nos commenda tuae proli,
Ne terrores sive doli
   Nos supplantent hostium!
Hail, Mother of Divinity!

Mother of our Saviour, hail!
Chosen vessel! Sacred Grail!
   Font of celestial grace!
From eternity forethought!
By the hand of Wisdom wrought!
   Precious, faultless Vase!

Hail, Temple of the Trinity!
   Home of the Triune God!
In whom the Incarnate Word had birth,
The King! to wqhom you gave on earth
   Imperial abode.

Oh, Maria! Constellation!
Inspiration! Elevation!
Rule and Law and Ordination
   Of the angels' host!
Highest height of God's Creation,
Pray your Son's commiseration,
Lest, by fear or fraud, salvation
   For our souls be lost!

Constantly—one might better say at once, officially, she was addressed in these terms of supreme majesty: "Imperatrix supernorum!" "Cœli Regina!" "Aula regalis!" but the twelfth century seemed determined to carry the idea out to its logical conclusion in defiance of dogma. Not only was the Son absorbed int he Mother, or represented as under her guardianship, but the Father fared no better, and the Holy Ghost followed. The poets regarded the Virgin as the "Templum Trinitatis"; "totius Trinitatis nobile Triclinium." She was the refectory of the Trinity—the "Triclinium"—because the refectory was the largest room and contained the whole of the members, and was divided in three parts by two rows of columns. She was the "Templum Trinitatis," the Church itself, with its triple aisle. The Trinity was absorbed in her.

This is a delicate subject in the Church, and you must feel it with delicacy, without brutally insisting on its necessary contradictions. All theology and all philosophy are full of contradictions quite as flagrant and far less sympathetic. This particular variety of religious faith is simply human, and has made its appearance in one form or another in nearly all religions; but though the twelfth century carried it to an extreme, and at Chartres you see it in its most charming expression, we have got always to make allowances for what was going on beneath the surface in men's minds, consciously or unconsciously, and for the latent scepticism which lurks behind all faith. The Church itself never quite accepted the full claims of what was called Mariolatry. One may be sure, too, that the bourgeois capitalist and the student of the schools, each from his own point of view, watched the Virgin with anxious interest. The bourgeois had put an enormous share of his capital into what was in fact an economical speculation, not unlike the South Sea Scheme, or the railway system of our own time; except that in one case the energy was devoted to shortening the road to Heaven; in the other, to shortening the road to Paris; but no serious schoolman could have felt entirely convinced that God would enter into a business partnership with man, to establish a sort of joint-stock society for altering the operation of divine and universal laws. The bourgeois cared little for the philosophical doubt if the economical result proved to be good, but he watched this result with his usual practical sagacity, and required an experience of only about three generations (1200-1300) to satisfy himself that relics were not certain in their effects; that the Saints were not always able or willing to help; that Mary herself could not certainly be bought or bribed; that prayer without money seemed to be quite as efficacious as prayer with money; and that neither the road to Heaven nor Heaven itself had been made surer or brought nearer by an investment of capital which amounted to the best part of the wealth of France. Economically speaking, he became satisfied that his enormous money-investment had proved to be an almost total loss, and the reaction on his mind was as violent as the emotion. For three hundred years it prostrated France. The efforts of the bourgeoisie and the peasantry to recover their property, so far as it was recoverable, have lasted to the present day and we had best take care not to get mixed in those passions.

If you are to get the full enjoyment of Chartres, you must, for the time, believe in Mary as Bernard and Adam did, and feel her presence as the architects did, in every stone they placed, and every touch they chiseled. You must try first to rid your mind of the traditional idea that the Gothic is an intentional expression of religious gloom. The necessity for light was the motive of the Gothic architects. They needed light and always more light, until they sacrificed safety and common sense in trying to get it. They converted their walls into windows, raised their vaults, diminished their piers, until their churches could no longer stand. You will see the limits at Beauvais; at Chartres we have not got so far, but even here, in places where the Virgin wanted it—as above the high altar—the architect has taken all the light there was to take. For the same reason, fenestration became the most important part of the Gothic architect's work, and at Chartres was uncommonly interesting because the architect was obliged to design a new system, which should at the same time satisfy the laws of construction and the taste and imagination of Mary. No doubt the first command of the Queen of Heaven was for light, but the second, at least equally imperative, was for colour. Any earthly queen, even though she were not Byzantine in taste, loved colour; and the truest of queens—the only true Queen of Queens—had richer and finer taste in colour than the queens of fifty earthly kingdoms, as you will see when we come to the immense effort to gratify her in the glass of her windows. Illusion for illusion—granting for the moment that Mary was an illusion—the Virgin Mother in this instance repaid to her worshipers a larger return for their money than the capitalist has ever been able to get, at least in this world, from any other illusion of wealth which he has tried to make a source of pleasure and profit.

The next point on which Mary evidently insisted was the arrangement for her private apartments, the apse, as distinguished from her throne-room, the choir; both being quite distinct from the hall, or reception-room of the public, which was the nave with its enlargements in the transepts. This arrangement marks the distinction between churches built as shrines for the deity and churches built as halls of worship for the public. The difference is chiefly in the apse, and the apse of Chartres is the most interesting of all apses from this point of view.

The Virgin required chiefly these three things, or, if you like, these four: space, light, convenience; and colour decoration to unite and harmonize the whole. This concerns the interior; on the exterior she required statuary, and the only complete system of decorative sculpture that existed seems to belong to her churches—Paris, Rheims, Amiens, and Chartres.   Mary required all this magnificence at Chartres for herself alone, not for the public. As far as one can see into the spirit of the builders, Chartres was exclusively intended for the Virgin, as the Temple of Abydos was intended for Osiris. The wants of man, beyond a mere roof-cover, and perhaps space to some degree, enter to no very great extent into the problem of Chartres. Man came to render homage or to ask favours. The Queen received him in her palace, where she alone was at home, and alone gave commands.

The artist's second thought was to exclude from his work everything that could displease Mary; and since Mary differed from living queens only in infinitely greater majesty and refinement, the artist could admit only what pleased the actual taste of the great ladies who dictated taste at the Courts of France and England, which surrounded the little Court of the Counts of Chartres.   What they were—these women of the twelfth and thirteenth centuries—we shall have to see or seek in other directions; but Chartres is perhaps the most magnificent and permanent monument they left of their taste, and we can begin here with learning certain things which they were not.

In the first place, they were not in the least vague, dreamy, or mystical in a modern sense—far from it! They seemed anxious only to throw the mysteries into a blaze of light; not so much physical, perhaps—since they, like all women, liked moderate shadow for their toilettes—but luminous in the sense of faith. There is nothing about Chartres that you would think mystical, who know your Lohengrin, Siegfried, and Parsifal. If you care to make a study of the whole literature of the subject, read M. Mâle's "Art Religieux du XIII Sièle en France," and use it for a guide-book. Here you need only note how symbolic and how simple the sculpture is, on the portals and porches. Even what seems a grotesque or an abstract idea is no more than the simplest child's personification. On the walls you may have noticed the *Ane qui vielle*—the ass playing the lyre; and on all the old churches you can see "bestiaries," as they were called, of fabulous animals, symbolic or not; but the symbolism is as simple as the realism of the oxen at Laon. It gave play to the artist in his effort for variety of decoration, and it amused the people—probably the Virgin also was not above being amused—now and then it seems about to suggest what you would call an esoteric meaning, that is to say, a meaning which each one of us can consider private property reserved for our own amusement, and from which the public is excluded; yet, in truth, in the Virgin's churches the public is never excluded, but invited. The Virgin even had the additional charm to the public that she was popularly supposed to have no very marked fancy for priests as such; she was a queen, a woman, and a mother, functions, all which priests could not perform. Accordingly, she seems to have had little taste for mysteries of any sort, and even the symbols that seem most mysterious were clear to every old peasant-woman in her church. The most pleasing and promising of them all is the woman's figure you saw on the front of the cathedral in Paris; her eyes bandaged; her head bent down, her crown falling; without cloak or royal robe; holding in her hand a guidon or banner with its staff broken in more than one place. On the opposite pier stands another woman, with royal mantle, erect and commanding. The symbol is so graceful that one is quite eager to know its meaning; but every child in the Middle Ages would have instantly told you that the woman with the falling crown meant only the Jewish Synagogue, as the one with the royal robe meant the Church of Christ.

Another matter for which the female taste seemed not much to care was theology in the metaphysical sense. Mary troubled herself little about theology except when she retired into the south transept with Pierre de Dreux. Even there one finds little said about the Trinity, always the most metaphysical subtlety of the Church. Indeed, you might find much amusement here in searching the cathedral for any distinct expression at all of the Trinity as a dogma recognized by Mary. One cannot take seriously the idea that the three doors, the three portals, and the three aisles express the Trinity, because, in the first place, there was no rule about it; churches might have what portals and aisles they pleased; both Paris and Bourges have five; the doors themselves are not allotted to the three members of the Trinity, nor are the portals; while another more serious objection is that the side doors and aisles are not of equal importance with the central, but mere adjuncts and dependencies, so that the architect who had misled the ignorant public into accepting so black a heresy would have deserved the stake, and would probably have gone to it. Even this suggestion of trinity is wanting in the transepts, which have only one aisle, and in the choir, which has five, as well as five or seven chapels, and, as far as an ignorant mind can penetrate, no triplets whatever. Occasionally, no doubt, you will discover in some sculpture or window, a symbol of the Trinity, but this discovery itself amounts to an admission of its absence as a controlling idea, for the ordinary worshiper must have been at least as blind as we are, and to him, as to us, it would have seemed a wholly subordinate detail. Even if the Trinity, too, is anywhere expressed, you will hardly find here an attempt to explain its metaphysical meaning—not even a mystic triangle.

The church is wholly given up to the Mother and the Son. The Father seldom appears; the Holy Ghost still more rarely. At least, that is the impression made on an ordinary visitor who has no motive to be orthodox; and it must have been the same with the thirteenth-century worshiper who came here with his mind absorbed in the perfections of Mary. Chartres represents, not the Trinity, but the identity of the Mother and Son. The Son represents the Trinity, which is thus absorbed in the Mother. The idea is not orthodox, but this is no affair of ours. The Church watches over its own.

The Virgin's wants and tastes, positive and negative, ought now to be clear enough to enable you to feel the artist's sincerity in trying to satisfy them; but first you have still to convince yourselves of the people's sincerity in employing the artists. This point is the easiest of all, for the evidence is express. In the year 1145 when the old flèche was begun—the year before Saint Bernard preached the second crusade at Vézelay—Abbot Haimon, of Saint-Pierre-sur-

Dives in Normandy, wrote to the monks of Tutbury Abbey in England a famous letter to tell of the great work which the Virgin was doing in France and which began at the Church of Chartres. "Hujus sacræ institutionis ritus apud Carnotensem ecclesiam est inchoatus." From Chartres it had spread through Normandy, where it produced among other things the beautiful spire which we saw at Saint-Pierre-sur-Dives. "Postremo per totam fere Normanniam longe lateque convaluit ac loca per singula Matri misericordiæ dicata præcipue occupavit." The movement affected especially the palaces devoted to Mary, but ran through all Normandy, far and wide. Of all Mary's miracles, the best attested, next to the preservation of her church, is the building of it; not so much because it surprises us as because it surprised even more the people of the time and the men who were its instruments. Such deep popular movements are always surprising, and at Chartres the miracle seems to have occurred three times, coinciding more or less with the dates of the crusades, and taking the organization of a crusade, as Archbishop Hugo of Rouen described it in a letter to Bishop Thierry of Amiens. The most interesting part of this letter is the evident astonishment of the writer, who might be talking to us today, so modern is he—

> The inhabitants of Chartres have combined to aid in the construction of their church by transporting the materials; or Lord was rewarded their humble zeal by miracles which have roused the Normans to imitate the piety of their neighbours. . . Since then the faithful of our diocese and of other neighbouring regions have formed associations for the same object; they admit no one into their company unless he has been to confession, has renounced enmities and revenges, and has reconciled himself with his enemies. That done, they elect a chief, under whose direction they conduct their waggons in silence and with humility.

The quarries at Berchères-l'Evêque are about five miles from Chartres. The stone is excessively hard, and was cut in blocks of considerable size, as you can see for yourselves; blocks which required great effort to transport and lay in place. The work was done with feverish rapidity, as it still show, but it is the solidest building of the age, and without a sign of weakness yet. The Abbot told, with more surprise than pride, of the spirit which was built into the cathedral with the stone—

> Who has ever seen—Who has ever heard tell, in times past, that powerful princes of the world, that men brought up in honour and in wealth, that nobles, men and women, have bent their proud and haughty necks to the harness of carts, and that, like beasts of burden, they have dragged to the abode of Christ these waggons, loaded with wines, grains, oil, stone, wood, and all that is necessary for the wants of life, or for the construction of the church? But while they draw these burdens, there is one thing admirable to observe; it is that often when a thousand persons and more are attached to the chariots—so great is the difficulty—yet they march in such silence that not a murmur is heard, and truly if one did not see the thing with one's eyes, one might believe that among such a multitude there was hardly a person present. When they halt on the road, nothing is heard but the confession of sins, and pure and suppliant prayer to God to obtain

pardon. At the voice of the priests who exhort their hearts to peace, they forget all hatred, discord is thrown far aside, debts are remitted, the unity of hearts is established. But if any one is so far advanced in evil as to be unwilling to pardon an offender, or if he rejects the counsel of the priest who has piously advised him, his offering is instantly thrown from the wagon as impure, and he himself ignominiously and shamefully excluded from the society of the holy. There one sees the priests who preside over each chariot exhort every one to penitence, to confession of faults, to the resolution of better life? There one sees old people, young people, little children, calling on the Lord with a suppliant voice, and uttering to Him, from the depth of the heart, sobs and sighs with words of glory and praise! After the people, warned by the sound of trumpets and the sight of banners, have resumed their road, the march is made with such ease that no obstacle can retard it. . . . When they have reached the church they arrange the wagons about it like a spiritual camp, and during the whole night they celebrate the watch by hymns and canticles. On each waggon they light tapers and lamps; they place there the infirm and sick, and bring them the precious relics of the Saints for their relief. Afterwards the priests and clerics close the ceremony by processions which the people follow with devout heart, imploring the clemency of the Lord and of his Blessed Mother for the recovery of the sick.

Of course, the Virgin was actually and constantly present during all this labour, and gave her assistance to it, but you would get no light on the architecture from listening to an account of her miracles, nor do they heighten the effect of popular faith. Without the conviction of her personal presence, men would not have bene inspired; but, to us, it is rather the inspiration of the art which proves the Virgin's presence, and we can better see the conviction of it in the work than in the words. Every day, as the work went on, the Virgin was present, directing the architects, and it is this direction that we are going to study, if you have now got a realizing sense of what it meant. Without this sense, the church is dead. Most persons of a deeply religious nature would tell you emphatically that nine churches out of ten actually were dead-born, after the thirteenth century, and that church architecture became a pure matter of mechanism and mathematics; but that is a question for you to decide when you come to it; and the pleasure consists not in seeing the death, but in feeling the life.

Now let us look about!

THE EDUCATION OF HENRY ADAMS

HENRY ADAMS

Chapter XXV

THE DYNAMO AND THE VIRGIN

Until the Great Exposition of 1900 closed its doors in November, Adams haunted it, aching to absorb knowledge, and helpless to find it. He would have liked to know how much of it could have been grasped by the best-informed man in the world. While he was thus meditating chaos, Langley came by, and showed it to him. At Langley's behest, the Exhibition dropped its superfluous rags and stripped itself of the skin, for Langley knew what to study, and why, and how; while Adams might as well have stood outside in the night, staring at the Milky Way. Yet Langley said nothing new, and taught nothing that one might not have learned from Lord Bacon, three hundred years before; but though one should have known the "Advancement of Science" as well as one knew the "Comedy of Errors," the literary knowledge counted for nothing until some teacher should show how to apply it. Bacon took a vast deal of trouble in teaching King James I and his subjects, American or other, towards the year 1620, that true science was the development or economy of forces; yet an elderly American in 1900 knew neither the formula nor the forces: or even so much as to say to himself that his historical business in the Exposition concerned only the economies or developments of force since 1893, when he began the study at Chicago.

Nothing in education is so astonishing as the amount of ignorance it accumulates in the form of inert facts. Adams had looked at most of the accumulations of art in the storehouses called Art Museums; yet he did not know how to look at the art exhibits of 1900. He had studied Karl Marx and his doctrines of history with profound attention, yet he could not apply them at Paris. Langley, with the ease of a great master of experiment, threw out of the field every exhibit that did not reveal a new application of force, and naturally threw out, to begin with, almost the whole art exhibit. Equally, he ignored almost the whole industrial exhibit. He led his pupil directly to the forces. His chief interest was in new motors to make his airship feasible, and he taught Adams the astonishing complexities of the new Daimler motor, and of the automobile, which, since 1893, had become a nightmare at a hundred kilometres an hour, almost as destructive as the electric tram which was only ten years older; and threatening t become as terrible as the locomotive steam-engine itself, which was almost exactly Adams's own age.

Then he showed his scholar the great hall of dynamos, and explained how little he knew about electricity or force of any kind, even of his own special sun, which spouted heat in inconceivable volume, but which, as far as he knew, might spout less or more, at any time, for all the certainty he felt in it. To him, the dynamo itself was but an ingenious channel for conveying somewhere the heat latent in a few tons of poor coal hidden in a dirty engine-house carefully kept out of sight; but to Adams the dynamo became a symbol of infinity. As he grew accustomed to the great gallery of machines, he began to feel the forty-foot dynamos as a moral force, much as the early Christians felt the Cross. The planet itself seemed less impressive, in its old-fashioned, deliberate, annual or daily revolution, than this huge wheel, revolving within arm's-length at some vertiginous speed, and barely murmuring—scarcely humming an audible warning to stand a hair's-breadth further for respect of power—while it would not wake the baby lying close against its frame. Before the end, one began to pray to it; inherited instinct taught the natural expression of man before silent and infinite force. Among the thousand symbols of ultimate energy, the dynamo was not so human as some, but it was the most expressive.

Yet the dynamo, next to the steam-engine, was the most familiar of exhibits. For Adams's objects its value lay chiefly in its occult mechanism. Between the dynamo in the gallery of machines and the engine-house outside, the break of continuity amounted to abysmal fracture for a historian's objects. No more relation could he discover between the steam and the electric current than between the Cross and the cathedral. The forces were interchangeable if not reversible, but he could see only an *absolute fiat* in electricity as in faith. Langley could not help him. Indeed, Langley seemed to be worried by the same trouble, for he constantly repeated that the new forces were anarchical, and specially that he was not responsible for the new rays, that were little short of parricidal in their wicked spirit towards science. His own rays, with which he had doubled the solar spectrum, were altogether harmless and beneficent; but Radium denied its God—or, what was to Langley the same thing, denied the truths of his Science. The force was wholly new.

A historian who asked only to learn enough to be as futile as Langley or Kelvin, made rapid progress under this teaching, and mixed himself up in the tangle of ideas until he achieved a sort of Paradise of ignorance vastly consoling to his fatigued senses. He wrapped himself in vibrations and rays which were new, and he would have hugged Marconi and Branly had he met them, as he hugged the dynamo; while he lost his arithmetic in trying to figure out the equation between the discoveries and the economies of force. The economies, like the discoveries, were absolute, super-sensual, occult; incapable of expression in horse-power. What mathematical equivalent could he suggest as the value of a Branly coherer? Frozen air, or the electric furnace, had some scale of measurement, no doubt, if somebody could invent a thermometer adequate to the purpose; but X-rays had played no part whatever in man's consciousness, and the atom itself had figured only as a fiction of thought. In these seven years man had translated himself into a new universe which had no common scale of measurement with the old. He had entered a supersenual world, in which he could measure nothing except by chance collisions of movements imperceptible to his senses, perhaps even imperceptible to his instruments, but perceptible to each other, and so to some known ray at the end of the scale. Langley seemed prepared for anything, even for an indeterminable number of universes interfused—physics stark mad in metaphysics.

Historians undertake to arrange sequences—called stories, or histories—assuming in silence a relation of cause and effect. These assumptions, hidden in the depths of dusty libraries, have been astounding, but commonly unconscious and childlike; so much so, that if any captious critic were to drag them to light, historians would probably reply, with one voice, that they had never supposed themselves required to know what they were talking about. Adams, for one, had toiled in vain to find out what he meant. He had even published a dozen volumes of American history for no other purpose than to satisfy himself whether, by the severest process of stating, with the least possible comment, such facts as seemed sure, in such order as seemed rigorously consequent, he could fix for a familiar moment a necessary sequence of human movement. The result had satisfied him as little as at Harvard College. Where he saw sequence, other men saw something quite different, and no one saw the same unit of measure. He cared little about his experiments and less about his statesmen, who seemed to him quite as ignorant as himself and, as a rule, no more honest; but he insisted on a relation of sequence, and if he could not reach it by one method, he would try as many methods as science knew. Satisfied that the sequence of men led to nothing and that the sequence of their society could lead no further, while the mere sequence of time was artificial, and the sequence of thought was chaos, he turned at last to the sequence of force: and thus it happened that, after ten years' pursuit, he found himself lying in the Gallery of Machines at the Great Exposition of 1900, his historical neck broken by the sudden irruption of forces totally new.

Since no one else showed much concern, an elderly person without other cares had no need to betray alarm. The year 1900 was not the first to upset schoolmasters. Copernicus and Galileo had broken many professorial necks about 1500; Columbus had stood the world on its head towards 1500; but the nearest approach to the revolution of 1900 was that of 310, when Constantine set up the Cross. The rays that Langley disowned, as well as those which he fathered, were occult, supersensual, irrational; they were a revelation of mysterious energy like that of the Cross; they were what, in terms of mediaeval science, were called immediate modes of the divine substance.

The historian was thus reduced to his last resources. Clearly if he was bound to reduce all these forces to a common value, this common value could have no measure but that of their attraction on his own mind. He must treat them as they had been felt; as convertible, reversible, interchangeable attractions on thought. He made up his mind to venture it; he would risk translating rays into faith. Such a reversible process would vastly amuse a chemist, but the chemist could not deny that he, or some of his fellow physicists, could feel the force of both. When Adams was a boy I Boston, the best chemist in the place had probably never heard of Venus except by way of scandal, or of the Virgin except as idolatry; neither had he heard of dynamos or automobiles or radium; yet his mind was ready to feel the force of all, though the rays were unborn and the women were dead.

Here opened another totally new education, which promised to be by far the most hazardous of all. The knife-edge along which he must crawl, like Sir Lancelot in the twelfth century, divided two kingdoms of force which had nothing in common but attraction. They were as different as a magnet is from gravitation, supposing one knew what a magnet was, or gravitation, or love. The force of the Virgin was still felt at Lourdes, and seemed to be as potent as

X-rays: but in America neither Venus nor Virgin ever had value as force—at most as sentiment. No American had ever been truly afraid of either.

This problem in dynamics gravely perplexed an American historian. The Woman had once been supreme; in France she still seemed potent, not merely as a sentiment, but as a force. Why was she unknown in America? For evidently America was ashamed of her, and she was ashamed of herself, otherwise they would not have strewn fig-leaves so profusely all over her. When she was a true force, she was ignorant of fig-leaves, but the monthly-magazine-made American female had not a feature that would have been recognized by Adam. The trait was notorious, and often humorous, but any one brought up among Puritans knew that sex was sin. In any previous age, sex was strength. Neither art nor beauty was needed. Every one, even among Puritans, knew that neither Diana of the Ephesians nor any of the Oriental goddesses was worshiped for her beauty. She was goddess because of her force; she was the animated dynamo; she was reproduction—the greatest and most mysterious of all energies; all she needed was to be fecund. Singularly enough, not one of Adams's many schools of education had ever drawn his attention to the opening lines of Lucretius, though they were perhaps the finest in all Latin literature, where the poet invoked Venus exactly aw Dante invoked the Virgin—

"Quae quoniam rerum naturam *sola* gubernas."

The Venus of Epicurean philosophy survived in the Virgin of the Schools—

"Donna, sei tanto grande, e tanto vali,

Che qual vuol grazia, e a te non ricorre,

Sua disianza vuol volar senz' ali."

All this was to American thought as though it had never existed. The true American knew something of the facts, but nothing of the feelings: he read the letter, but he never felt the law. Before this historical chasm, a mind like that of Adams felt itself helpless; he turned from the Virgin to the Dynamo as though he were a Branly coherer. On one side, at the Louvre and at Chartres, as he knew by the record of work actually done and still before his eyes, was the highest energy ever known to man, the creator of four-fifths of his noblest art, exercising vastly more attraction over the human mind than all the steam-engines and dynamos ever dreamed of; and yet this energy was unknown to the American mind. An American Virgin would never dare command; an American Venus would never dare exist.

The question, which to any plain American of the nineteenth century seemed as remote as it did to Adams, drew him almost violently to study, once it was posed; and on this point Langleys were as useless as though they were Herbert Spencers or dynamos. The idea survived only as art. There one turned as naturally as though the artist were himself a woman. Adams began to ponder, asking himself whether he knew of any American artist who had ever insisted on the power of sex, as every classic had always done; but he could think only of Walt Whitman; Bret Harte, as far as the magazines would let him venture; and one or two painters, for the flesh-tones. All the rest had used sex for sentiment, never for force; to them, Eve was a tender flower, and Herodias an unfeminine horror. American art, like the American language and American education, was as far as possible sexless. Society regarded this victory over sex as its greatest triumph, and the historian readily admitted it, since the moral issue, for the moment, did not concern one who was studying the relations of unmoral force. He cared nothing for the sex of the dynamo until he could measure its energy.

Vaguely seeking a clue, he wandered through the art exhibit, and, in his stroll, stopped almost every day before St. Gaudens's General Sherman, which had been given the central post of honor. St. Gaudens himself was in Paris, putting on the work his usual interminable last touches, and listening to the usual contradictory suggestions of brother sculptors. Of all the American artists who gave to American art whatever life it breathed in the seventies, St. Gaudens was perhaps the most sympathetic, but certainly the most inarticulate. General Grant or Don Cameron had scarcely less instinct of rhetoric than he. All the others—the Hunts, Richardson, John La Farge, Stanford White—were exuberant; only St. Gaudens could never discuss or dilate on an emotion, or suggest artistic arguments for giving to his work the forms that he felt. He never laid down the law, or affected the despot, or became brutalized like Whistler by the brutalities of his world. He required no incense; he was no egoist; his simplicity of thought was excessive; he could not imitate, or give any form but his own to the creations of his hand. No one felt more strongly than he the strength of other men, but the idea that they could affect him never stirred an image in his mind.

This summer his health was poor and his spirits were low. For such a temper, Adams was not the best companion, since his own gaiety was not *folle*; but he risked going now and then to the studio on Mont Parnasse to draw him out for a stroll in the Bois de Boulogne, or dinner as pleased his moods, and in return St. Gaudens sometimes let Adams go about in his company.

Once St. Gaudens took him down to Amiens, with a party of Frenchmen, to see the cathedral. Not until they found themselves actually studying the sculpture of the western portal, did it dawn on Adams's mind that, for his purposes, St. Gaudens on that spot had more interest to him than the cathedral itself. Great men before great monuments express great truths, provided they are not taken too solemnly. Adams never tired of quoting the supreme phrase of his idol Gibbon, before the Gothic cathedrals: "I darted a contemptuous look on the stately monuments of superstition." Even in the footnotes of his history, Gibbon had never inserted a bit of humor more human than this, and one would have paid largely for a photograph of the fat little historian, on the background of Notre Dame of Amiens, trying to persuade his readers—perhaps himself—that he was darting a contemptuous look on the stately monument, for which he felt in fact the respect which every man of his vast study and active mind always feels before objects worthy of it; but besides the humor, one felt also the relation. Gibbon ignored the Virgin, because in 1789 religious monuments were out of fashion. In 1900 his remark sounded fresh and simple as the green fields to ears that had heard a hundred years of other remarks, mostly no more fresh and certainly less simple. Without malice, one might find it more instructive than a whole lecture of Ruskin. One sees what one brings, and at that moment Gibbon brought the French Revolution. Ruskin brought reaction against the Revolution. St. Gaudens had passed beyond all. He liked the stately monuments much more than he liked Gibbon or Ruskin; he loved their dignity; their unity; their scale; their lines; their lights and shadows; their decorative sculpture; but he was even less conscious than they of the force that created it all—the Virgin, the Woman—by whose genius "the stately monuments of superstition" were built, through which she was expressed. He would have seen more meaning in Isis with the cow's horns, at Edfoo, who expressed the same thought. The art remained, but the energy was lost even upon the artist.

Yet in mind and person St. Gaudens was a survival of the 1500; he bore the stamp of the Renaissance, and should have carried an image of the Virgin round his neck, or stuck in his hat, like Louis XI. In mere time he was a lost soul that had strayed by chance into the twentieth century, and forgotten where it came from. He writhed and cursed at his ignorance, much as Adams did at his own, but in the opposite sense. St. Gaudens was a child of Benvenuto Cellini, smothered in an American cradle. Adams was a quintessence of Boston, devoured by curiosity to think like Benvenuto. St. Gaudens's art was starved from birth, and Adams's instinct was blighted from babyhood. Each had but half of a nature, and when they came together before the Virgin of Amiens they ought both to have felt in her the force that made them one; but it was not so. To Adams she became more than ever a channel of force; to St. Gaudens she remained as before a channel of taste.

For a symbol of power, St. Gaudens instinctively preferred the horse, as was plain in his horse and Victory of the Sherman monument. Doubtless Sherman also felt it so. The attitude was so American that, for at least forty years, Adams had never realized that any other could be in sound taste. How many years had he taken to admit a notion of what Michael Angelo and Rubens were driving at? He could not say; but he knew that only since 1895 had he begun to feel the Virgin or Venus as force, and not everywhere even so. At Chartres—perhaps at Lourdes—possibly at Cnidos if one could still find there the divinely named Aphrodite of Praxiteles—but otherwise one must look for force to the goddesses of Indian mythology. The idea died out long ago in the German and English stock. St. Gaudens at Amiens was hardly less sensitive to the force of the female energy than Mattthew Arnold at the Grande Chartreuse. Neither of them felt goddesses as power—only as reflected emotion, human expression, beauty, purity, taste, scarcely even as sympathy. They felt a railway train as power; yet they, and all other artists, constantly complained that the power embodied in a railway train could never be embodied in art. All the steam in the world could not, like the Virgin, build Chartres.

Yet in mechanics, whatever the mechanicians might think, both energies acted as interchangeable forces on man, and by action on man all known force may be measured. Indeed, few men of science measured force in any other way. After once admitting that a straight line was the shortest distance between two points, no serious mathematician cared to deny anything that suited his convenience, and rejected no symbol, unproved or unprovable, that helped him to accomplish work. The symbol was force as a compass-needle or a triangle was force, as the mechanist might prove by losing it, and nothing could be gained by ignoring their value. Symbol or energy, the Virgin had acted as the greatest force the Western world ever felt, and had drawn man's activities to herself more strongly than any other power, natural or supernatural, had ever done; the historian's business was to follow the track of the energy; to find where it came from and where it went to; its complex source and shifting channels; its values, equivalents, conversions. It could scarcely be more complex than radium; it could hardly be deflected, diverted, polarized, absorbed more perplexingly than other radiant matter. Adams knew nothing about any of them, but as a mathematical problem of influence on human progress, though all were occult, all reacted on his mind, and he rather inclined to think the Virgin easiest to handle.

The pursuit turned out to be long and tortuous, leading at last into the vast forests of scholastic science. From Zeno to Descartes, hand in hand with Thomas Aquinas, Montaigne, and Pascal, one stumbled as stupidly as though one were still a German student of 1860. Only with the instinct of despair could one force one's self into this old thicket of ignorance after having been repulsed at a score of entrances more promising and more popular. Thus far, no path had led anywhere, unless perhaps to an exceedingly modest living. Forty-five years of study had proved to be quite futile for the pursuit of power; one controlled no more force in 1900 than in 1850, although the amount of force controlled by society had enormously increased. The secret of education still hid itself somewhere behind ignorance, and one fumbled over it as feebly as ever. In such labyrinths, the staff is a force almost more necessary than the legs; the pen becomes a sort of blind-man's dog, to keep him from falling into the gutters. The pen works for itself, and acts like a hand, modeling the plastic material over and over again to the form that suits it best. The form is never arbitrary, but is a sort of growth like crystallization, as any artist knows too well; for often the pencil or pen runs into side-paths and shapelessness, loses its relations, stops or is bogged. Then it has to return on its trail, and recover, if it can, its line of force. The result of a year's work depends more on what is struck out than on what is left in; on the sequence of the main lines of thought, than on their play or variety. Compelled once more to lean heavily on this support, Adams covered more thousands of pages with figures as formal as though they were algebra, laboriously striking out, altering, burning, experimenting, until the year had expired, the Exposition had long been closed, and winter drawing to its end, before he sailed from Cherbourg, on January 19, 1901, for home.

* * * * *

CHAPTER XXIX
THE ABYSS OF IGNORANCE (1902)

The years hurried past, and gave hardly time to note their work. Three or four months, though big with change, come to an end before the mind can catch up with it. Winter vanished; spring burst into flower; and again Paris opened its arms, though not for long. Mr. Cameron came over, and took the castle of Inverlochy for three months, which he summoned his friends to garrison. Lochaber seldom laughs, except for its children, such as Camerons, McDonalds, Campbells and other products of the mist; but in the summer of 1902 Scotland put on fewer airs of coquetry than usual. Since the terrible harvest of 1879 which one had watched sprouting on its stalks on the Shropshire hillsides, nothing had equaled the gloom. Even when the victims fled to Switzerland, they found the Lake of Geneva and the Rhine not much gayer, and Carlsruhe no more restful than Paris; until at last, in desperation, one drifted back to the Avenue of the Bois de Boulogne, and, like the Cuckoo, dropped into the nest of a better citizen. Diplomacy has its uses. Reynolds Hitt, transferred to Berlin, abandoned his attic to Adams, and there, for long summers to come, he hid in ignorance and silence.

Life at last managed of its own accord to settle itself into a working arrangement. After so many years of effort to find one's drift, the drift found the seeker, and slowly swept him forward and back, with a steady progress oceanwards. Such lessons as summer taught, winter tested, and one had only to watch the apparent movement of the stars in order to guess one's declination. The process is possible only for men who have exhausted auto-motion. Adams never knew why, knowing nothing of Faraday, he began to mimic Faraday's trick of seeing lines of force al about him, where he had always seen lines of will. Perhaps the effect of knowing no mathematics is to leave the mind to imagine figures—images—phantoms; one's mind is a watery mirror at best; but, once conceived, the image became rapidly simple, and the lines of force presented themselves as line of attraction. Repulsions counted only as battle of attractions. By this path, the mind stepped into the mechanical theory of the universe before knowing it, and entered a distinct new phase of education.

This was the work of the dynamo and the Virgin of Chartres. Like his masters, since thought began, he was handicapped by the eternal mystery of Force—the sink of all science. For thousands of years in history, he found that Force had been felt as occult attraction—love of God and lust for power in a future life. After 1500, when this attraction began to decline, philosophers fell back on some *vis a tergo*—instinct of danger from behind, like Darwin's survival of the fittest; and one of the greatest minds, between Descartes and Newton—Pascal—saw the master-motor of man in *ennui*, which was also scientific: "I have often said that all the troubles of man come from his not knowing how to sit still." Mere restlessness forces action. "So passes the whole of life. We combat obstacles in order to get repose, and, when got, the repose is insupportable; for we think either of the troubles we have, or of those that threaten us; and even if we felt safe on every side, *ennui* would of its own accord spring up from the depths of the heart where it is rooted by nature, and would fill the mind with its venom."

"If goodness lead him not, yet weariness
    May toss him to My breast."

Ennui, like Natural Selection, accounted for change, but failed to account for direction of change. For that, an attractive force was essential; a force from outside; a shaping influence. Pascal and all the old philosophies called this outside force God or Gods. Caring but little for the name, and fixed only on tracing the Force, Adams had gone straight to the Virgin at Chartres, and asked her to show him God, face to face, as she did for St. Bernard. She replied, kindly as ever, as though she were still the young mother of to-day, with a sort of patient pity for masculine dulness: "My dear outcast, what is it you see? This is the Church of Christ! If you seek him through me, you are welcome, sinner or saint; but he and I are one. We are Love! We have little or nothing to do with God's other energies which are infinite, and concern us the less because our interest is only in man, and the infinite is not knowable to man. Yet if you are troubled by your ignorance, you see how I am surrounded by the masters of the schools! Ask them!"

The answer sounded singularly like the usual answer of British science which had repeated since Bacon that one must not try to know the unknowable, though one was quite powerless to ignore it; but the Virgin carried more conviction, for her feminine lack of interest in all perfections except her own was honester than the formal phrase of science; since nothing was easier than to follow her advice, and turn to Thomas Aquinas, who, unlike modern physicists, answered at once and plainly: "To me," said St. Thomas, "Christ and the Mother are one Force—Love—simple, single, and sufficient for all human wants; but Love is a human interest which acts even on man so partially that you and I, as philosophers, need expect no share in it. Therefore we turn to Christ and the Schools who represent all other Force. We deal with Multiplicity and call it God. After the Virgin has redeemed by her personal Force as Love all that is redeemable I man, the Schools embrace the rest, and give it For, Unity, and Motive."

This chart of Force was more easily studied than any other possible scheme, for one had but to do what the Church was always promising to do—abolish in one flash of lightning not only man, but also the Church itself, the earth, the other planets, and the sun, in order to clear the air; without affecting mediaeval science.   The student felt warranted in doing what the church threatened—abolishing his solar system altogether—in order to look at God as actual; continuous movement, universal cause, and interchangeable force. This was pantheism, but the Schools were pantheist; at least as pantheistic as the *Energetik* of the Germans; and their duty was the ultimate energy, whose thought and act were one.

Rid of man and his mind, the universe of Thomas Aquinas seemed rather more scientific than that of Haeckel or Ernst Mach.   Contradiction for contradiction, Attraction for attraction, Energy for energy, St. Thomas's idea of God had merits. Modern science offered not a vestige of proof, or a theory of connection between its forces, or any scheme of reconciliation between thought and mechanics; while St. Thomas at least linked together the joints of his machine. As far as a superficial student could follow, the thirteenth century supposed mind to be a mode of force directly derived from the intelligent prime motor, and the cause of all form and sequence in the universe—therefore the only proof of unity.   Without thought in the unit, there could be no unity; without unity no orderly sequence or ordered society. Thought alone was Form. Mind and Unity flourished or perished together.

This education startled even a man who had dabbled in fifty educations all over the world; for, if he were obliged to insist on a Universe, he seemed driven to the Church. Modern science guaranteed no unity. The student seemed to feel himself, like all his predecessors, caught, trapped, meshed in this eternal drag-net of religion.

In practice the student escapes this dilemma in two ways: the first is that of ignoring it, as one escapes most dilemmas; the second is that the Church rejects pantheism as worse than atheism, and will have nothing to do with the pantheist at any price. In wandering through the forests of ignorance, one necessarily fell upon the famous old bear that scared children at play; but, even had the animal shown more logic than its victim, one had learned fro Socrates to distrust, above all other traps, the trap of logic—the mirror of the mind. Yet the search for a unit of force led into catacombs of thought where hundreds of thousands of educations had found their end. Generation after generation of painful and honest-minded scholars had been content to stay in these labyrinths forever, pursuing ignorance in silence, in company with the most famous teachers of all time. Not one of them had ever found a logical highroad of escape.

Adams cared little whether he escaped or not, but he felt clear that he could not stop there, even to enjoy the society of Spinoza and Thomas Aquinas. True, the Church alone had asserted unity with any conviction, and the historian alone knew what oceans of blood and treasure the assertion had cost; but the only honest alternative to affirming unity was to deny it; and the denial would require a new education. At sixty-five years old a new education promised hardly more than the old.

Possibly the modern legislator or magistrate might no longer know enough to treat as the Church did the man who denied unity, unless the denial took the form of a bomb; but no teacher would know how to explain what he thought he meant by denying unity. Society would certainly punish the denial if ever any one learned enough to understand it. Philosophers, as a rule, cared little what principles society affirmed or denied, since the philosopher commonly held that though he might sometimes be right by good luck on some one point, no complex of individual opinions could possibly be anything but wrong; yet, supposing society to be ignored, the philosopher was no further forward. Nihilism had no bottom. For thousands of years every philosopher had stood on the shore f this sunless sea, diving for pearls and never finding them. Al had seen that, since they could not find bottom, they must assume it. The Church claimed to have found it, but, since 1450, motives for agreeing on some new assumption of Unity, broader and deeper than that of the Church, had doubled I force until even the universities and schools, like the Church and State, seemed about to be driven into an attempt to educate, though specially forbidden to do it.

Like most of his generation, Adams had taken the word of science that the new unit was as good as found. It would not be an intelligence—probably not even a consciousness—but it would serve. He passed sixty years waiting for it, and at the end of that time, on reviewing the ground, he was led to think that the final synthesis of science and its ultimate triumph was the kinetic theory of gases; which seemed to cover all motion in space, and to furnish the measure of time. So far as he understood it, the theory asserted that any portion of space is occupied by molecules of gas, flying in right lines at velocities varying up to a mile in a second, and colliding with each other at intervals varying up to 17,750,000 times in a second. To this analysis—if one understood it right—all matter whatever was reducible, and the only difference of opinion in science regarded the doubt whether a still deeper analysis would reduce the atom of gas to pure motion.

Thus, unless one mistook the meaning of motion, which might well be, the scientific synthesis commonly called Unity was the scientific analysis commonly called Multiplicity. The two things were the same, all forms being shifting phases of motion. Granting this ocean of colliding atoms, the last hope of humanity, what happened if one dropped the sounder into the abyss—let it go—frankly gave up Unity altogether? What was Unity? Why was one to be forced to affirm it?

Here everybody flatly refused help. Science seemed content with its old phrase of "larger synthesis," which was well enough for science, but meant chaos for man. One would have been glad to stop and ask no more, but the anarchist bomb bade one go on, and the bomb is a powerful persuader. One could not stop, even to enjoy the charms of a perfect gas colliding seventeen million times in a second, much like an automobile in Paris. Science itself had been crowded so close to the edge of the abyss that its attempts to escape were as metaphysical as the leap, while an ignorant old man felt no motive for trying to escape, seeing that the only escape possible lay I the form of *vis a tergo* commonly called Death. He got out his Descartes again; dipped into his Hume and Berkeley; wrested anew with his Kant; pondered solemnly over his Hegel and Schopenhauer and Hartmann; strayed gaily away with his Greeks—all merely to ask what Unity meant, and what happened when one denied it.

Apparently one never denied it. Every phiosopher, whether sane or insane, naturally affirmed it. The utmost flight of anarchy seemed to ahve stoped with the assertion of two principles, and even these fitted into each other, like good and evil, light and darkness. Pessimism itself, blackas it might be painted, had been content to turn the universe of contradictions into the human thought as one Will, and treat it as representation.   Metaphysics insisted on treating the universe as one thought or treating thought as one universe; and philosophers agreed, like kinetic gas, that the universe could be known only as motion of mind, and therefore as unity. One could know it only as one's self; it was psychology.

Of all forms of pessimism, the metaphysical form was, for a historian, the least enticing. Of all studies, the one he would rather have avoided was that of his own mind. He knew no tragedy so heartrnedig as introspection, and the more, because—as Mephistopheles said of Marguerite—he was not the first. Nearly all the highest intelligence known to history had drowned itself in the reflection of its own thought, and the bovine survivors had rudely told the truth about it, without affecting the intelligent. One's own time had nto been exempt. Even since 1870 friends by scores had fallen victims to it. Within five-and-twenty years, a new library had grown out of it. Harvard College was a focus of the study; France supported hospitals for it; England publshed magazines of it. Nothing was easier than to take one's mind in one's hand, and ask one's psychological friends what they made of it, and the more because it mattered so little to either party, since their minds, whatever they were, had pretty nearly ceased to reflect, and let them do what they liked with the small remnant, they could scarcely do anything very new with it. All one asked was to learn what they hoped to do.

Unfortunately the pursuit of ignorance in silence had, by this time, led the weary plgrim into such mountains of ignorance that he could no longer see any path whatever, and could not even understand a signpost. He failed to fathom the depths of the new psychology, which proved to him that, on that side as on the mathematical side, his power of thought was atrophied, if, indeed, it ever existed. Since he could not fathom the science, he could only ask the simplest of questions: Did the new psychology hold that the ψυχή—soul or mind—was or was not a unit? He gathered from the books that the psychologists had, in a few cases, distinguished several personalities in the same mind, each conscious and constant, individual and exclusive. The fact seemed scarcely surprising, since it had been a habit of mind from earliest recorded time, and equally familiar to the last acquaintance who had taken a drug or caught a fever, or eaten a Welsh rarebit before bed; for surely no one could follow the action of a vivid dream, and still need to be told that the actors evoked by his mind were not himself, but quite unknown to all he had ever recognized as self. The new psychology went further, and seemed convinced that it had actually split personality not only into dualism, but also into complex groups, like telephonic centres and systems, that might be isolated and called up at will, and whose physical action might be occult in the sense of strangeness to any known form of force. Dualism seemed to have become as common as binary stars. Alternating personalities turned up constantly, even among one's friends. The facts seemed certain, or at least as certain as other facts; all they needed was explanation.

This was not the business of the searcher of ignorance, who felt himself in no way responsible for causes. To his mind, the compound υχή took at once the form of a bicycle-rider, mechanically balancing himself by inhibiting all his inferior personalities, and sure to fall into the sub-conscious chaos below, if one of his inferior personalities got on top. The only absolute truth was the sub-conscious chaos below, which every one could feel when he sought it.

Whether the psychologists admitted it or not, mattered little to the student who, by the law o his profession, was engaged in studying his own mind. On him, the effect was surprising. He woke up with a shudder as though he had himself fallen off his bicycle. If his mind were really this sort of magnet, mechanically dispersing its lines of force when it went to sleep, and mechanically orienting them when it woke up—which was normal, the dispersion or orientation? The mind, like the body, kept its unity unless it happened to lose balance, but the professor of physics, who slipped on a pavement and hurt himself, knew no more than an idiot what knocked him down, though he did know—what the idiot could hardly do—that his normal condition was idiocy, or want of balance, and that his sanity was unstable artifice. His normal thought was dispersion, sleep, dream, inconsequence; the simultaneous action of different thought-centres without central control. His artificial balance was acquired habit. He was an acrobat, with a dwarf on his back, crossing a chasm on a slack-rope, and commonly breaking his neck.

By that path of newest science, one saw no unity ahead—nothing but a dissolving mind—and the historian felt himself driven back on thought as one continuous Force, without Race, Sex, School, Country, or Church. This has been always the fate of rigorous thinkers, and has always succeeded in making them famous, as it did Gibbon, Buckle, and Auguste Comte. Their method made what progress the science of history knew, which was little enough, but they did at last fix the law that, if history ever meant to correct the errors she made in detail, she must agree on a scale for the whole. Every local historian might defy this law till history ended, but its necessity would be the same for man as for space or time or force, and without it the historian would always remain a child in science.

Any schoolboy could see that man as a force must be measured by motion, from a fixed pont. Psychology helped here by suggesting a unit—the point of history when man held the highest idea of himself as a unit in a unified universe. Eight or ten years of study had led Adams to think he might use the century 1150-1250, expressed in Amiens Cathedral and the Works of Thomas Aquinas, as the unit from which he might measure motion down to his own time, without assuming anything as true or untrue, except relation. The movement might be studied at once in philosophy and mechanics. Setting himself to the task, he began a volume which he mentally knew as "Mont-Saint-Michel and Chartres: a Study of Thirteenth-Century Unity." From that point he proposed to fix a position for himself, which he could label: "The Education of Henry Adams: a Study of Twentieth-Century Multiplicity." With the help of these two points of relation, he hoped to project his lines forward and backward indefinitely, subject to correction from any one who should know better. Thereupon, he sailed for home.

CHAPTER XXXI
THE GRAMMAR OF SCIENCE (1903)

OF all the travels made by man since the voyages of Dante, this new exploration along the shores of Multiplicity and Complexity promised to be the longest, though as yet it had barely touched two familiar regions—race and sex. Even within these narrow seas the navigator lost his bearings and followed the winds as they blew. By chance it happened that Raphael Pumpelly helped the winds; for, being in Washington on his way to Central Asia he fell to talking with Adams about these matters, and said that Willard Gibbs thought he got most help from a book called the "Grammar of Science," by Karl Pearson. To Adams's vision, Willard Gibbs stood on the same plane with the three or four greatest minds of his century, and the idea that a man so incomparably superior should find help anywhere filled him with wonder. He sent for the volume and read it. From the time he sailed for Europe and reached his den on the Avenue du Bois until he took his return steamer at Cherbourg on December 26, he did little but try to find out what Karl Pearson could have taught Willard Gibbs.

Here came in, more than ever, the fatal handicap of ignorance in mathematics. Not so much the actual tool was needed, as the right to judge the product of the tool. Ignorant as one was of the finer values of French or German, and often deceived by the intricacies of thought hidden in the muddiness bf the medium, one could sometimes catch a tendency to intelligible meaning even in Kant or Hegel; but one had not the right to a suspicion of error where the tool of thought was algebra. Adams could see in such parts of the "Grammar" as he could understand, little more than an enlargement of Stallo's book already twenty years old. He never found out what it could have taught a master like Willard Gibbs.

Yet the book had a historical value out of all proportion to its science. No such stride had any Englishman before taken in the lines of English thought. The progress of science was measured by the success of the "Grammar," when, for twenty years past, Stallo had been deliberately ignored under the usual conspiracy of silence inevitable to all thought which demands new thought machinery. Science needs time to reconstruct its instruments, to follow a revolution in space; a certain lag is inevitable; the most active mind cannot instantly swerve from its path; but such revolutions ate portentous, and the fall or rise of half-a-dozen empires interested a student of history less than the rise of the "Grammar of Science," the more pressingly because, under the silent influence of Langley, he was prepared to expect it.

For a number of years Langley had published in his Smithsonian Reports the revolutionary papers that foretold the overflow of nineteenth-century dogma, and among the first was the famous address of Sir William Crookes on psychical research, followed by a series of papers on Roentgen and Curie, which had steadily driven the scientific lawgivers of Unity into the open; but Karl Pearson was the first to pen them up for slaughter in the schools. The phrase is not stronger than that with which the "Grammar of Science" challenged the fight: "Anything more hopelessly illogical than the statements with regard to Force and Matter current in elementary textbooks of science, it is difficult to imagine," opened Mr. Pearson, and the responsible author of the "elementary textbook," as he went on to explain, was Lord Kelvin himself. Pearson shut out of science everything which the nineteenth century had brought into it. He told his scholars that they must put up with a fraction of the universe! and a very small fraction at that—the circle reached by the senses, where sequence could be taken for granted—much as the deep-sea fish tales for granted the circle of light which he generates. "Order and reason, beauty and benevolence, are characteristics and conceptions which we find solely associated with the mind of man." The assertion, as a broad truth, left one's mind in some doubt of its bearing, for order and beauty seemed to be associated also in the mind of a crystal, if one's senses were to be admitted as judge; but the historian had no interest in the universal truth of Pearson's or Kelvin's or Newton's laws; he sought only their relative drift or direction, and Pearson went on to say that these conceptions must stop: "Into the chaos beyond sense-impressions we cannot scientifically project them." We cannot even infer them: "In the chaos behind sensations, in the 'beyond' of sense-impressions, we cannot infer necessity, order or routine, for these are concepts formed by the mind of man on this side of sense-impressions"; but we must infer chaos: "Briefly chaos is all that science can logically assert of the supersensuous." The kinetic theory of gas is an assertion of ultimate chaos. In plain words, Chaos was the law of nature; Order was the dream of man.

No one means all he says, and yet very few say all they mean, for words are slippery and thought is viscous; but since Bacon and Newton, English thought had gone on impatiently protesting that no one must try to know the unknowable at the same time that every one went on thinking about it. The result was as chaotic as kinetic gas; but with the thought a historian had nothing to do. He sought only its direction. For himself he knew, that, in spite of all the Englishmen that ever lived, he would be forced to enter supersensual chaos if he meant to find out what became of British science—or indeed of any other science. From Pythagoras to Herbert Spencer, every one had done it, although commonly science had explored an ocean which it preferred to regard as Unity or a Universe, and called Order. Even Hegel, who taught that every notion included its own negation, used the negation only to reach a "larger synthesis," till he reached the universal which thinks itself, contradiction and all. The Church alone had constantly protested that anarchy was not order, that Satan was not God, that pantheism was worse than a theism, and that Unity could not be proved as a contradiction. Karl Pearson seemed to agree with the Church, but every one else, including Newton, Darwin and Clerk Maxwell, had sailed gaily into the super-sensual, calling it:—

> "One God, one Law, one Element, And one far-off, divine event, To which the whole creation moves."

Suddenly, in 1900, science raised its head and denied.

Yet, perhaps, after all, the change had not been so sudden as it seemed. Real and actual, it certainly was, and every newspaper betrayed it, but sequence could scarcely be denied by one who had watched its steady approach, thinking the change far more interesting to history than the thought. When he reflected about it, he recalled that the flow of tide had shown itself at least twenty years before; that it had become marked as early as 1893; and that the man of science must have been sleepy indeed who did not jump from his chair like a scared dog when, in 1858 Mme. Curie threw on his desk the metaphysical bomb she called radium. There remained no hole to bide in. Even metaphysics swept back over science with the green water of the deep-sea ocean and no one could longer hope to bar out the unknowable, for the unknowable was known.

The fact was admitted that the uniformitarians of one's youth had wound about their universe a tangle of contradictions meant only for temporary support to be merged in "larger synthesis," and had waited for the larger synthesis in silence and in vain. They had refused to hear Stallo. They had betrayed little interest in Crookes. At last their universe had been wrecked by rays, and Karl Pearson undertook to cut the wreck loose with an axe leaving science adrift on a sensual raft in the midst of a supersensual chaos. The confusion seemed, to a mere passenger, worse than that of 1600 when the astronomers upset the world; it resembled rather the convulsion of 310 when the *Civitas Dei* cut itself loose from the *Civitas Romae,*and the Cross took the place of the legions; but the historian accepted it all alike; he knew that his opinion was worthless; only, in this case, be found himself on the raft, personally and economically concerned in its drift.

English thought had always been chaos and multiplicity itself, in which the new step of Karl Pearson marked only a consistent progress; but German thought had affected system, unity, and abstract truth, to a point that fretted the most patient foreigner, and to Germany the voyager in strange seas of thought alone might resort with confident hope of renewing his youth. Turning his back on Karl Pearson and England, he plunged into Germany, and had scarcely crossed the Rhine when he fell into libraries of new works bearing the names of Ostwald, Ernst Mach, Ernst Haeckel, and others less familiar, among whom Haeckel was easiest to approach, not only because of being the oldest and clearest and steadiest spokesman of nineteenth-century mechanical convictions, but also because in 1902 he had published a vehement renewal of his faith. The volume contained only one paragraph that concerned a historian; it was that in which Haeckel sank his voice almost to a religious whisper in avowing with evident effort, that the "proper essence of substance appeared to him more and more marvelous and enigmatic as he penetrated further into the knowledge of its attributes—matter and energy—and as he learned to know their innumerable phenomena and their evolution." Since Haeckel seemed to have begun the voyage into multiplicity that Pearson had forbidden to Englishmen, he should have been a safe pilot to the point, at least, of a "proper essence of substance" in its attributes of matter and energy; but Ernst Mach seemed to go yet one step further, for he rejected matter altogether, and admitted but two processes in nature—change of place and interconversion of forms. Matter was Motion—Motion was Matter—the thing moved.

A student of history bad no need to understand these scientific ideas of very great men; he sought only the relation with the ideas of their grandfathers, and their common direction towards the ideas of their grandsons. He had long ago reached, with Hegel, the limits of contradiction; and Ernst Mach scarcely added a shade of variety lo the identity of opposites; but both of them seemed to be in agreement with Karl Pearson on the facts of the supersensual universe which could be known only as unknowable.

With a deep sigh of relief, the traveler turned back to France. There he felt safe. No Frenchman except Rabelais and Montaigne had ever taught anarchy other than as path to order. Chaos would be unity in Paris even in child of the guillotine. To make this assurance mathematically sure, the highest scientific authority ;D France was a great mathematician, M. Poincaré of the Institute, who published in 1902 a small volume called "La Science et l'Hypothèse," which purported to be relatively readable. Trusting to its external appearance, the traveler timidly bought it, and greedily devoured it, without understanding a single consecutive page, but catching here and there a period that startled him to the depths of his ignorance, for they seemed to show that M. Poincaré was troubled by the same historical landmarks which guided or deluded Adams himself: "[In science] we are led," said Mr. Poincaré, "to act as though a simple law, when other things were equal, must be more probable than a complicated law. Half a century ago one frankly confessed it, and proclaimed that nature loves simplicity. She has since given us too often the lie. To-day this tendency is no longer avowed, and only as much of it is preserved as is indispensable so that science shall not become impossible."

Here at last was a fixed point beyond the chance of confusion with self-suggestion. History and mathematics agreed. Had M. Poincaré shown anarchistic tastes, his evidence would have weighed less heavy but he seemed to be the only authority in science who felt what a historian felt so strongly—the need of unity in a universe. "Considering everything we have made some approach towards unity. We have not gone as fast as we hoped fifty years ago; we have not always taken the intended road; but definitely we have gained much ground." This was the most clear and convincing evidence of progress yet offered to the navigator of ignorance; but suddenly he fell on another view which seemed to him quite irreconcilable with the first: "Doubtless if our means of investigation should become more and more penetrating, we should discover the simple under the complex; then the complex under the simple; then anew the simple under the complex; and so on without ever being able to foresee the last term."

A mathematical paradise of endless displacement promised eternal bliss to the mathematician, but turned the historian green with horror. Made miserable by the thought that he knew no mathematics, he burned to ask whether M. Poincaré knew any history, since he began by begging the historical question altogether, and assuming that the past showed alternating phases of simple and complex—the precise point that Adams, after fifty years of effort, found himself forced to surrender; and then going on to assume alternating phases for the future which, for the weary Titan of Unity, differed in nothing essential from the kinetic theory of a perfect gas.

Since monkeys first began to chatter in trees, neither man nor beast had ever denied or doubted Multiplicity, Diversity, Complexity, Anarchy, Chaos. Always and everywhere the Complex had been true and the Contradiction had been certain. Thought started by it. Mathematics itself began by counting one—two—three; then imagining their continuity, which M. Poincaré was still exhausting his wits to explain or defend; and this was his explanation: "In short, the mind has the faculty of creating symbols, and it is thus that it has constructed mathematical continuity which is only a particular system of symbols." With the same light touch, more destructive in its artistic measure than the heaviest-handed brutality of Englishmen or Germans, he went on to upset relative truth itself: "How should I answer the question whether Euclidian Geometry is true? It has no sense!... Euclidian Geometry is, and will remain, the most convenient."

Chaos was a primary fact even in Paris—especially in Paris—as it was in the Book of Genesis; but every thinking being in Paris or out of it had exhausted thought in the effort to prove Unity, Continuity, Purpose, Order, Law, Truth, the Universe, God, after having begun by taking it for granted, and discovering, to their profound dismay, that some minds denied it. The direction of mind, as a single force of nature, had been consistent since history began. Its own unity had created a universe the essence of which was abstract Truth; the Absolute; God! To Thomas Aquinas, the universe was still a person; to Spinoza, a substance; to Kant, Truth was the essence of the "I"; an innate conviction; a categorical imperative; to Poincaré, it was a convenience; and to Karl Pearson, a medium of exchange.

The historian never stopped repeating to himself that he knew nothing about it; that he was a mere instrument of measure, a barometer, pedometer, radiometer; and that his whole share in the matter was restricted to the measurement of thought-motion as marked by the accepted thinkers. He took their facts for granted. He knew no more than a firefly about rays—or about race—or sex—or ennui—or a bar of music—or a pang of love—or a grain of musk—or of phosphorus—or conscience—or duty—or the force of Euclidian geometry—or non-Euclidian—or heat—or light—or osmosis—or electrolysis—or the magnet—or ether—or vis *inertiae*—or gravitation—or cohesion—or elasticity—or surface tension—or capillary attraction—or Brownian motion—or of some scores, or thousands, or millions of chemical attractions, repulsions or indifferences which were busy within and without him; or, in brief, of Force itself, which, he was credibly informed, bore some dozen definitions in the textbooks, mostly contradictory. and all, as he was assured, beyond his intelligence; but summed up in the dictum of the last and highest science, that Motion seems to be Matter and Matter seems to be Motion, yet "we are probably incapable of discovering" what either is. History had no need to ask what either might be; all it needed to know was the admission of ignorance; the mere fact of multiplicity baffling science. Even as to the fact, science disputed, but radium happened to radiate something that seemed to explode the scientific magazine, bringing thought, for the time, to a standstill; though, in the line of thought-movement in history, radium was merely the next position, familiar and inexplicable since Zeno and his arrow: continuous from the beginning of time, and discontinuous at each successive point. History set it down on the record—pricked its position on the chart—and waited to be led, or misled, once more.

The historian must not try to know what is truth, if be values his honesty; for, if he cares for his truths, he is certain to falsify his facts. The laws of history only repeat the lines of force or thought. Yet though his will be iron, he cannot help now and then resuming his humanity or simianity in face of a fear. The motion of thought had the same value as the motion of a cannonball seen approaching the observer on a direct line through the air. One could watch its curve for five thousand years. Its first violent acceleration in historical times had ended in the catastrophe of 310. The next swerve of direction occurred towards 1500. Galileo and Bacon gave a still newer curve to it, which altered its values; but all these changes had never altered the continuity. Only in 1900, the continuity snapped.

Vaguely conscious of the cataclysm, the world sometimes dated it from 1893, by the Roentgen rays, or from 1898, by the Curies' radium; but in 1904, Arthur Balfour announced on the part of British science that the human race without exception had lived and died in a world of illusion until the last year of the century. The date was convenient, and convenience was truth.

The child born in 1900 would, then, be born into a new world which would not be a unity but a multiple. Adams tried to imagine it, and an education that would fit it. He found himself in a land where no one had ever penetrated before; where order was an accidental relation obnoxious to nature; artificial compulsion imposed on motion; against which every free energy of the universe revolted; and which, being merely occasional, resolved itself back into anarchy at last. He could not deny that the law of the new multiverse e%plained much that had been most obscure, especially the persistently fiendish treatment of man by man; the perpetual effort of society to establish law, and the perpetual revolt of society against the law it had established; the perpetual building up of authority by force, and the perpetual appeal to force to overthrow it; the perpetual symbolism of a higher law, and the perpetual relapse to a lower one; the perpetual victory of the principles of freedom, and their perpetual conversion into principles of power; but the staggering problem was the outlook ahead into the despotism of artificial order which nature abhorred. The physicists had a phrase for it, unintelligible to the vulgar: "All that we win is a battle—lost in advance—with the irreversible phenomena in the background of nature."

All that a historian won was a vehement wish to escape. He saw his education complete and was sorry he ever began it. As a matter of taste, he greatly preferred his eighteenth-century education when God was a father and nature a mother, and all was for the best in a scientific universe. He repudiated all share in the world as it was to be, and yet he could not detect the point where his responsibility began or ended.

As history unveiled itself in the new order, man's mind had behaved like a young pearl oyster, secreting its universe to suit its conditions until it had built up a shell of *nacre* that embodied all its notions of the perfect. Man knew it was true because be made it, and he loved it for the same reason. He sacrificed millions of lives to acquire his unity, but he achieved it, and justly thought it a work of art. The woman especially did great things, creating her deities on a higher level than the male, and, in the end, compelling the man to accept the Virgin as guardian of the man's God. The man's part in his Universe was secondary, but the woman was at home there, and sacrificed herself without limit to make it habitable, when man permitted it, as sometimes happened for brief intervals of war and famine; but she could not provide protection against forces of nature. She did not think of her universe as a raft to which the limpets stuck for life in the surge of a supersensual chaos; she conceived herself and her family as the centre and flower of an ordered universe which she knew to be unity because she had made it after the image of her own fecundity; and this creation of hers was surrounded by beauties and perfections which she knew to be real because she herself had imagined them.

Even the masculine philosopher admired and loved and celebrated her triumph, and the greatest of them sang it in the noblest of his verses:—

"Alma Venus, coeli subter labentia signa
Quae mare navigerum, quae terras frugiferenteis
Concelebras ....
Quae quoniam rerum naturam sola gubernas,
Nec sine te quidquam dias in luminis oras
Exoritur, neque fit laetum neque amabile quidquam;
Te sociam studeo!"

Neither man nor woman ever wanted to quit this Eden of their own invention, and could no more have done it of their own accord than the pearl oyster could quit its shell; but although the oyster might perhaps assimilate or embalm a grain of sand forced into its aperture, it could only perish in face of the cyclonic hurricane or the volcanic upheaval of its bed. Her supersensual chaos killed her.

Such seemed the theory of history to be imposed by science on the generation born after 1900. For this theory, Adams felt himself in no way responsible. Even as a historian he had made it his duty always to speak with respect of everything that had ever been thought respectable—except an occasional statesman; but he had submitted to force all his life and he meant to accept it for the future as for the past. All his efforts bad been turned only to the search for its channel. He never invented his facts: they were furnished him by the only authorities he could find. As for himself, according to Helmholz, Ernst Mach, and Arthur Balfour, he was henceforth to be a conscious ball of vibrating motions, traversed in every direction by infinite lines of rotation or vibration, rolling at the feet of the Virgin at Chartres or of M. Poincaré in an attic at Paris, a centre of supersensual chaos. The discovery did not distress him. A solitary man of sixty-five years or more, alone in a Gothic cathedral or a Paris apartment, need fret himself little about a few illusions more or less. He should have learned his lesson fifty years earlier; the times had long passed when a student could stop before chaos or order; he had no choice but to march with his world.

Nevertheless, he could not pretend that his mind felt flattered by this scientific outlook. Every fabulist has told how the human mind has always struggled like a frightened bird to escape the chaos which caged it; how—appearing suddenly and inexplicably out of some unknown and unimaginable void; passing half its known life in the mental chaos of sleep;

victim even when awake, to its own ill-adjustment, to disease, to age, to external suggestion, to nature s compulsion; doubting its sensations, and, in the last resort, trusting only to instruments and averages—after sixty or seventy years of growing astonishment, the mind wakes to find itself looking blankly into the void of death. That it should profess itself pleased by this performance was all that the highest rules of good breeding could ask; but that it should actually be satisfied would prove that it existed only as idiocy.

Satisfied, the future generation could scarcely think itself, for even when the mind existed in a universe of its own creation. it had never been quite at ease. As far as one ventured to interpret actual science, the mind had thus far adjusted itself by an infinite series of infinitely delicate adjustments forced on it by the infinite motion of an infinite chaos of motion; dragged at one moment into the unknowable and unthinkable, then trying to scramble back within its senses and to bar the chaos out, but always assimilating bits of it, until at last, in 1900, a new avalanche of unknown forces had fallen on it, which required new mental powers to control. If this view was correct, the mind could gain nothing by flight or by fight; it must merge in its supersensual multiverse or succumb to it.

* * * * *

CHAPTER XXXIV
A LAW OF ACCELERATION (1904)

IMAGES are not arguments, rarely even lead to proof, but the mind craves them, and, of late more than ever, the keenest experimenters find twenty images better than one, especially if contradictory; since the human mind has already learned to deal in contradictions.

The image needed here is that of a new centre, or preponderating mass, artificially introduced on earth in the midst of a system of attractive forces that previously made their own equilibrium, and constantly induced to accelerate its motion till it shall establish a new equilibrium. A dynamic theory would begin by assuming that all history, terrestrial or cosmic, mechanical or intellectual, would be reducible to this formula if we knew the facts.

For convenience, the most familiar image should come first; and this is probably that of the comet, or meteoric streams, like the Leonids and Perseids; a complex of minute mechanical agencies, reacting within and without, and guided by the sum of forces attracting or deflecting it. Nothing forbids one to assume that the man-meteorite might grow, as an acorn does, absorbing light, heat, electricity—or thought; for, in recent times, such transference of energy has become a familiar idea; but the simplest figure, at first, is that of a perfect comet—say that of 1843—which drops from space, in a straight line, at the regular acceleration of speed, directly into the sun, and after wheeling sharply about it, in heat that ought to dissipate any known substance, turns back unharmed, in defiance of law, by the path on which it came. The mind, by analogy, may figure as such a comet, the better because it also defies law.

Motion is the ultimate object of science, and measures of motion are many; but with thought as with matter, the true measure is mass in its astronomic sense—the sum or difference of attractive forces. Science has quite enough trouble in measuring its material motions without volunteering help to the historian, but the historian needs not much help to measure some kinds of social movement; and especially in the nineteenth century, society by common accord agreed in measuring its progress by the coal-output. The ratio of increase in the volume of coal-power may serve as dynamometer.

The coal-output of the world, speaking roughly, doubled every ten years between 1840 and 1900, in the form of utilized power, for the ton of coal yielded three or four times as much power in 1900 as in 1840. Rapid as this rate of acceleration in volume seems, it may be tested in a thousand ways without greatly reducing it. Perhaps the ocean steamer is nearest unity and easiest to measure, for any one might hire, in 1905, for a small sum of money, the use of 30,000 steam-horse-power to cross the ocean, and by halving his figure every ten years, he got back to 234 horse-power for 1835, which was accuracy enough for his purposes. In truth, his chief trouble came not from the ratio in volume of heat, but from the intensity, since he could get no basis for a ratio there. All ages of history have known high intensities, like the iron-furnace, the burning-glass, the blow-pipe; but no society has e-er used high intensities on any large scale till now, nor can a mere bystander decide what range of temperature is now in common use. Loosely guessing that science controls habitually the whole range from absolute zero to 3000° Centigrade, one might assume for convenience, that the ten-year ratio for volume could be used temporarily for intensity; and still there remained a ratio to guessed for other forces than heat. Since 1800 scores of new forces had been discovered; old forces had been raised to higher powers, as could be measured in the navy-gun; great regions of chemistry had been opened up, and connected with other regions of physics. Within ten years a new universe of force had been revealed in radiation. Complexity had extended itself on immense horizons, and arithmetical ratios were useless for any attempt at accuracy. The force evolved seemed more like explosion than gravitation, and followed closely the curve of steam; but, at all events, the ten-year ratio seemed carefully conservative. Unless the calculator was prepared to be instantly overwhelmed by physical force and mental complexity, he must stop there.

Thus, taking the year 1900 as the starting point for carrying back the series, nothing was easier than to assume a ten-year period of retardation as far back as 1820, but beyond that point the statistician failed, and only the mathematician could help. Laplace would have found it child's-play to fix a ratio of progression in mathematical science between Descartes, Leibnitz, Newton, and himself. Watt could have given in pounds the increase of power between Newcomen's engines and his own. Volta and Benjamin Franklin would have stated their progress as absolute creation of power. Dalton could have measured minutely his advance on Boerhaave. Napoleon I must have had a distant notion of his own numerical relation to Louis XIV. No one in 1789 doubted the progress of force, least of all those who were to lose their heads by it.

Pending agreement between these authorities, theory may assume what it likes—say a fifty, or even a five-and-twenty-year period of reduplication for the eighteenth century, for the period matters little until the acceleration itself is admitted. The subject is even more amusing in the seventeenth than in the eighteenth century, because Galileo and Kepler, Descartes, Huygens, and Isaac Newton took vast pains to fix the laws of acceleration for moving bodies, while Lord Bacon and William Harvey were content with showing experimentally the fact of acceleration in knowledge; but from their combined results a historian might be tempted to maintain a similar rate of movement back to 1600, subject to correction from the historians of mathematics.

The mathematicians might carry their calculations back as far as the fourteenth century when algebra seems to have become for the first time the standard measure of mechanical progress in Western Europe; for not only Copernicus and Tycho Brahe, but even artists like Leonardo, Michael Angelo, and Albert Dürer worked by mathematical processes, and their testimony would probably give results more exact than that of Montaigne or Shakespeare; but, to save trouble, one might tentatively carry back the same ratio of acceleration, or retardation, to the year 1400, with the help of Columbus and Gutenberg, so taking a uniform rate during the whole four centuries (1400-1800), and leaving to statisticians the task of correcting it.

Or better, one might, for convenience, use the formula of squares to serve for a law of mind. Any other formula would do as well, either of chemical explosion, or electrolysis, or vegetable growth, or of expansion or contraction in innumerable forms; but this happens to be simple and convenient. Its force increases in the direct ratio of its squares. As the human meteoroid approached the sun or centre of attractive force, the attraction of one century squared itself to give the measure of attraction in the next.

Behind the year 1400, the process certainly went on, but the progress became so slight as to be hardly measurable. What was gained in the east or elsewhere, cannot be known; but forces, called loosely Greek fire and gunpowder, came into use in the west in the thirteenth century, as well as instruments like the compass, the blow-pipe, clocks and spectacles, and materials like paper; Arabic notation and algebra were introduced, while metaphysics and theology acted as violent stimulants to mind. An architect might detect a sequence between the Church of St. Peter's at Rome, the Amiens Cathedral, the Duomo at Pisa, San Marco at Venice, Sancta Sofia at Constantinople and the churches at Ravenna. All the historian dares affirm is that a sequence is manifestly there, and be has a right to carry back his ratio, to represent the fact, without assuming its numerical correctness. On the human mind as a moving body, the break in acceleration in the Middle Ages is only apparent; the attraction worked through shifting forms of force, as the sun works by light or heat, electricity, gravitation, or what not, on different organs with different sensibilities, but with invariable law.

The science of prehistoric man has no value except to prove that the law went back into indefinite antiquity. A stone arrowhead is as convincing as a steam-engine. The values were as clear a hundred thousand years ago as now, and extended equally over the whole world. The motion at last became infinitely slight, but cannot be proved to have stopped. The motion of Newton's comet at aphelion may be equally slight. To evolutionists may be left the processes of evolution; to historians the single interest is the law of reaction between force and force— between mind and nature—the law of progress.

The great division of history into phases by Turgot and Comte first affirmed this law in its outlines by asserting the unity of progress, for a mere phase interrupts no growth, and nature shows innumerable such phases. The development of coal-power in the nineteenth century furnished the first means of assigning closer values to the elements; and the appearance of supersensual forces towards 1900 made this calculation a pressing necessity; since the next step became infinitely serious.

A law of acceleration, definite and constant as any law of mechanics, cannot be supposed to relax its energy to suit the convenience of man. No one is likely to suggest a theory that man's convenience had been consulted by nature at any time, or that Nature has consulted the convenience of any of her creations, except perhaps the *Terebratula*. In every age man has bitterly and justly complained that nature hurried and hustled him, for inertia almost invariably has ended in tragedy. Resistance is its law, and resistance to superior mass is futile and fatal.

Fifty years ago. science took for granted that the rate of acceleration could not last. The world forgets quickly, but even today the habit remains of founding statistics on the faith that consumption will continue nearly stationary. Two generations, with John Stuart Mill, talked of this stationary period, which was to follow the explosion of new power. All the men who were elderly in the forties died in this faith, and other men grew old nursing the same conviction, and happy in it; while science, for fifty years, permitted, or encouraged, society to think that force would prove to be limited in supply. This mental inertia of science lasted through the eighties before showing signs of breaking up; and nothing short of radium fairly wakened men to the fact, long since evident, that force was inexhaustible. Even then the scientific authorities vehemently resisted.

Nothing so revolutionary had happened since the year 300. Thought had more than once been upset, but never caught and whirled about in the vortex of infinite forces. Power leaped from every atom, and enough of it to supply the stellar universe showed itself running to waste at every pore of matter. Man could no longer hold it off. Forces grasped his wrists and flung him about as though he had hold of a live wire or a runaway automobile; which was very nearly the exact truth for the purposes of an elderly and timid single gentleman in Paris, who never drove down the Champs Ulysses without expecting an accident, and commonly witnessing one; or found himself in the neighborhood of an official without calculating the chances of a bomb. So long as the rates of progress held good, these bombs would double in force and number every ten years.

Impossibilities no longer stood in the way. One's life had fattened on impossibilities. Before the boy was six years old, he had seen four impossibilities made actual—the ocean-steamer, the railway, the electric telegraph, and the Daguerreotype; nor could he ever learn which of the four had most hurried others to come. He had seen the coal-output of the United States grow from nothing to three hundred million tons or more. What was far more serious, he had seen the number of minds, engaged in pursuing force—the truest measure of its attraction—increase from a few scores or hundreds, in 1838, to many thousands in 1905, trained to sharpness never before reached, and armed with instruments amounting to new senses of indefinite power and accuracy, while they chased force into hiding-places where Nature herself had never known it to be, making analyses that contradicted being, and syntheses that endangered the elements. No one could say that the social mind now failed to respond to new force, even when the new force annoyed it horribly. Every day Nature violently revolted, causing so-called accidents with enormous destruction of property and life, while plainly laughing at man, who helplessly groaned and shrieked and shuddered, but never for a single instant could stop. The railways alone approached the carnage of war; automobiles and fire-arms ravaged society, until an earthquake became almost a nervous relaxation. An immense volume of force had detached itself from the unknown universe of energy, while still vaster reservoirs, supposed to be infinite, steadily revealed themselves, attracting mankind with more compulsive course than all the Pontic Seas or Gods or Gold that ever existed, and feeling still less retiring ebb.

In 1850, science would have smiled at such a romance as this, but, in 1900, as far as history could learn, few men of science thought it a laughing matter. If a perplexed but laborious follower could venture to guess their drift, it seemed in their minds a toss-up between anarchy and order. Unless they should be more honest with themselves in the future than ever they were in the past, they would be more astonished than their followers when they reached the end. If Karl Pearson's notions of the universe were sound, men like Galileo, Descartes, Leibnitz, and Newton should have stopped the progress of science before 1700, supposing them to have been honest in the religious convictions they expressed. In 1900 they were plainly forced back on faith in a unity unproved and an order they had themselves disproved. They had reduced their universe to a series of relations to themselves. They had reduced themselves to motion in a universe of motions, with an acceleration, in their own case, of vertiginous violence. With the correctness of their science, history had no right to meddle, since their science now lay in a plane where scarcely one or two hundred minds in the world could follow its mathematical processes; but bombs educate vigorously, and even wireless telegraphy or airships might require the reconstruction of society. If any analogy whatever existed between the human mind, on one side, and the laws of motion, on the other, the mind had already entered a field of attraction so violent that it must immediately pass beyond, into new equilibrium, like the Comet of Newton, to suffer dissipation altogether, like meteoroids in the earth's atmosphere. If it behaved like an explosive, it must rapidly recover equilibrium; if it behaved like a vegetable, it must reach its limits of growth; and even if it acted like the earlier creations of energy—the saurians and sharks—it must have nearly reached the limits of its expansion. If science were to go on doubling or quadrupling its complexities every ten years, even mathematics would soon succumb. An average mind had succumbed already in 1850; it could no longer understand the problem in 1900.

Fortunately, a student of history had no responsibility for the problem; he took it as science gave it, and waited only to be taught. With science or with society, he had no quarrel and claimed no share of authority. He had never been able to acquire knowledge, still less to impart it; and if he had, at times, felt serious differences with the American of the nineteenth century, he felt none with the American of the twentieth. For this new creation, born since 1900, a historian asked no longer to be teacher or even friend; he asked only to be a pupil, and promised to be docile, for once, even though trodden under foot; for he could see that the new American—the child of incalculable coal-power, chemical power, electric power, and radiating energy, as well as of new forces yet undetermined—must be a sort of God compared with any former creation of nature. At the rate of progress since 1800, every American who lived into the year 2000 would know how to control unlimited power. He would think in complexities unimaginable to an earlier mind. He would deal with problems altogether beyond the range of earlier society. To him the nineteenth century would stand on the same plane with the fourth—equally childlike—and he would only wonder how both of them, knowing so little, and so weak in force, should have done so much. Perhaps even he might go back, in 1964, to sit with Gibbon on the steps of Ara Coeli.

Meanwhile he was getting education. With that, a teacher who had failed to educate even the generation of 1870, dared not interfere. The new forces would educate. History saw few lessons in the past that would be useful in the future; but one, at least, it did see. The attempt of the American of 1800 to educate the American of 1900 had not often been surpassed for folly; and since 1800 the forces and their complications had increased a thousand times or more. The attempt of the American of 1900 to educate the American of 2000, must be even blinder than that of the Congressman of 1800, except so far as he had learned his ignorance. During a million or two of years, every generation in turn had toiled with endless agony to attain and apply power, all the while betraying the deepest alarm and horror at the power they created. The teacher of 1900, if foolhardy, might stimulate; if foolish, might resist; if intelligent, might balance, as wise and foolish have often tried to do from the beginning; but the forces would continue to educate, and the mind would continue to react. All the teacher could hope was to teach it reaction.

Even there his difficulty was extreme. The most elementary books of science betrayed the inadequacy of old implements of thought. Chapter after chapter closed with phrases such as one never met in older literature: "The cause of this phenomenon is not understood"; "science no longer ventures to explain causes"; "the first step towards a causal explanation still remains to be taken"; "opinions are very much divided"; "in spite of the contradictions involved"; "science gets on only by adopting different theories, sometimes contradictory." Evidently the new American would need to think in contradictions, and instead of Kant's famous four antinomies, the new universe would know no law that could not be proved by its anti-law.

To educate—one's self to begin with—had been the effort of one's life for sixty years; and the difficulties of education had gone on doubling with the coal-output, until the prospect of waiting another ten years, in order to face a seventh doubling of complexities, allured one's imagination but slightly. The law of acceleration was definite, and did not require ten years more study except to show whether it held good. No scheme could be suggested to the new American, and no fault needed to be found, or complaint made; but the next great influx of new forces seemed near at hand, and its style of education promised to be violently coercive. The movement from unity into multiplicity, between 1200 and 1900, was unbroken in sequence, and rapid in acceleration. Prolonged one generation longer, it would require a new social mind. As though thought were common salt in indefinite solution it must enter a new phase subject to new laws. Thus far, since five or ten thousand years, the mind had successfully reacted, and nothing yet proved that it would fail to react—but it would need to jump.

PRAYER TO THE VIRGIN OF CHARTRES

Gracious Lady:—

Simple as when I asked your aid before;
  Humble as when I prayed for grace in vain
Seven hundred years ago; weak, weary, sore
  In heart and hope, I ask your help again.

You, who remember all, remember me;
  An English scholar of a Norman name,
I was a thousand who then crossed the sea
  To wrangle in the Paris schools for fame.

When your Byzantine portal was still young
  I prayed there with my master Abailard;
When Ave Maris Stella was first sung,
  I helped to sing it here with Saint Bernard.

When Blanche set up your gorgeous Rose of France
  I stood among the servants of the Queen;
And when Saint Louis made his penitence,
  I followed barefoot where the King had been.

For centuries I brought you all my cares,
  And vexed you with the murmurs of a child;
You heard the tedious burden of my prayers;
  You could not grant them, but at least you smiled.

If then I left you, it was not my crime,
  Or if a crime, it was not mine alone.
All children wander with the truant Time.
  Pardon me Too! You pardoned once your Son!

For He said to you:—"Wist ye not that I
  Must be about my Father's business?" So,
Seeking his Father he pursued his way
  Straight to the Cross towards which we all must go.

So I too wandered off among the host
  That racked the earth to find the father's clue.
I did not find the Father, but I lost
  What now I value more, the Mother—You!

I thought the fault was yours that foiled my search;
  I turned and broke your image on its throne,

Cast down my idol, and resumed my march
    To claim the father's empire for my own.

Crossing the hostile sea, our greedy band
    Saw rising hills and forests in the blue;
Our father's kingdom in the promised land!
    —West seized it, and dethroned the father too.

And now we are the Father, with our brood,
    Ruling the Infinite, not Three but One;
We made our world and saw that it was good;
Ourselves we worship, and we have no Son.

Yet we have Gods, for even our strong nerve
    Falters before the Energy we own.
Which shall be master? Which of us shall serve?
    Which wears the fetters? Which shall bear the crown?

Brave though we be, we dread to face the Sphinx,
    Or answer the old riddle she still asks.
Strong as we are, our reckless courage shrinks
    To look beyond the piece-work of our tasks.

But when we must, we pray, as in the past
    Before the Cross on which your Son was nailed.
Listen, dear lady! You shall hear the last
    Of the strange prayers Humanity has wailed.

PRAYER TO THE DYNAMO

Mysterious Power! Gentle Friend!
    Despotic Master! Tireless Force!
You and We are near the End.
Either You or We must bend
    To bear the martyrs' Cross.

We know ourselves, what we can bear
    As men; our strength and weakness too;
Down to the fraction of a hair;
And know that we, with all our care
    And knowledge, know not you.

You come in silence, Primal Force,
    We know not whence, or when, or why;
You stay a moment in your course
To play; and lo! You leap across
    To Alpha Centauri!

We know not whether you are kind,
    Or cruel in your fiercer mood;
But be you Matter, be you Mind,
We think we know that you are blind,
    And we alone are good.

We know that prayer is thrown away,
    For you are only force and light;
A sifting current; night and day;
We know this well, and yet we pray,
    For prayer is infinite,

Like you! Within the finite sphere
    That bounds the impotence of thought,
We search an outlet everywhere
But only find that we are here
    And that you are—are not!

What are we then? The lords of space?
    The master-mind whose tasks you do?
Jockey who rides you in the race?
Or are we atoms whirled apace,
    Shaped and controlled by you?

Still silence? Still no end in sight?
    No sound in answer to our cry?
Then, by the God we now hold tight,
Though we destroy soul, life and light,
    Answer you shall—or die!

We are no beggars! What we care we
    For hopes or terrors, love or hate?
What for the universe? We see
Only our certain destiny
    And the last word of Fate.

Seize, then, the Atom! Rack his joints!
    Tear out of him his secret spring!
Grind him to nothing!—though he points
To us, and his life-blood anoints
    Me—the dead Atom-King!

———————————————

A curious prayer, dear lady! Is it not?
    Strangely unlike the prayers I prayed to you!
Stranger because you find me at this spot,
    Here, at your feet, asking your help anew.

Strangest of all, that I have ceased to strive,
    Ceased even care what new coin fate shall strike.
In truth it does not matter. Fate will give
    Some answer; and all answers are alike.

So, while we slowly rack and torture death
    And wait for what the final void will show,
Waiting I feel the energy of faith
    Not in the future science, but in you!

The man who solves the Infinite, and needs
    The force of solar systems for his play,
Will not need me, nor greatly care what deeds
    Made me illustrious in the dawn of day.

He will send me, dethroned, to claim my rights,
Fossil survival of an age of stone,
Among the cave-men and the troglodytes
    Who carved the mammoth on the mammoth's bone.

He will forget my thought, my acts, my fame,
    As we forget the shadows of the dusk,
Or catalogue the echo of a name
    As we the scratches on the mammoth's tusk.

But when, like me, he too has trod the track
    Which leads him up to power above control,
He too will have no choice but wander back
    And sink in helpless hopelessness of soul,

Before your majesty of race and love,
    The purity, the beauty and the faith;
The depth of tenderness beneath above,
    The glory of the life and of the death.

When your Byzantine portal still was young
    I came here with my master Abailard;
When Ave Maris Stella was first sung,
    I joined to sing it here with Saint Bernard.

When Blanche set up your glorious Rose of France,
    In scholar's robes I waited on the Queen;
When good Saint Louis did his penitence,
    My prayer was deep like his: my faith as keen.

What loftier prize seven hundred years shall bring,
    What deadlier struggles for a larger air,
What immortality our strength shall wring
    From Tie and Space, we may—or may not—care;

But years, or ages, or eternity,
    Will find me still in thought before your throne,
Pondering the mystery of Maternity,
    Soul within Soul—Mother and Child in One!

Help me to see! Not with my mimic sight—
    With yours! Which carried radiance, like the sun,
Giving the rays you was with—light in light—
    Tying all suns and stars and worlds in one.

Help me to know! Not with my mocking art—
    With you, who knew yourself unbound by laws;
Gave God your strength, your life, your sight, your heart,
    And took from him the Thought that Is—the Cause.

Help me to feel! not with my insect sense—
    With yours that felt all life alive in you;
Infinite heart beating at your expense;
    Infinite passion breathing the breath you drew!

Help me to bear! not my own baby load,
    But yours; who bore the failure of the light,
The strength, the knowledge and the thought of God—
    The futile folly of the Infinite!

The means by which we live have outdistanced the ends for which we live. Our scientific power has outrun our spiritual power. We have guided missiles and misguided men.

Martin Luther King, Jr., *Strength Through Love*, 1963

Progress was all right; it only went on too long.

James Thurber

There will one day spring from the brain of science a machine or force so fearful in its potentialities, so absolutely terrifying that even man, the fighter, who will dare torture and death in order to inflict torture and death, will be appalled, and so abandon war forever. What man's mind can create, man's character can control.

Thomas Alva Edison

The age of innocent faith in science and technology may be over. . .every major advance in the technological competence of man has enforced revolutionary changes in the economic and social structures of society.

Barry Commoner

The question is not so much whether we are masters or slaves of our machines, but whether machines will still serve the world and its things, or if, on the contrary, they and the automatic motion of their processes have begun to rule and even destroy world and things.

Hannah Arendt, *The Human Condition*, 1958

I am myself and what is around me, and if I do not save it, it shall not save me.

José Ortegá y Gasset, *Meditations on Quixote* (1911)

Wisdom entereth not into a malicious mind, and science without conscience is but the ruin of the soul.

François Rabelais, *Gargantua and Pantagruel*, 1532

THE CHILDREN OF FRANKENSTEIN

HERBERT J. MULLER

Herbert J. Muller (1905-1980), author of *Children of Frankenstein: A Primer on Modern Technology and Human Value,* was professor of English and government at Indiana University. He is well known for his writings on the impact of science and technology on humanity.

1. What are the good and bad points of the Industrial Revolution according to Muller?

2. In what ways do you agree or disagree with Muller's criticism of modern technology? What is the "fourth dimension"?

3. How can we control technology according to Muller? Do you agree?

4. To what extent do Muller's attitudes toward technology resemble or differ from other writers in this theme?

5. What is the connection between Mary Shelley's *Frankenstein* and Herbert Muller's *Children of Frankenstein*?

THE CHILDREN OF FRANKENSTEIN

HERBERT J. MULLER

1
Definitions, Premises, and Basic Issues

According to my dictionary, technology is "the science or study of the practical or industrial arts." In modern usage emphasis has been on industrial techniques, based on the machine. I am using the term in a broader sense to cover as well the distinctive practices that have been generated by the rise of industrialism. These include large-scale organization throughout our society, professionalism in all activities, and the ways of thinking and doing indicated by such typically modern terms as "system," "systematic" methods, and "methodology." Modern technology may be broadly defined as the elaborate development of standardized, efficient means to practical ends. A comparable definition is Kenneth Galbraith's, "the systematic application of scientific or other organized knowledge to practical tasks." Jacques Ellul prefers to call all this simply "technique." In any case—it is well to keep in mind that the term is not so precise or "scientific" as it may sound.

Practical arts or skills have of course always been vitally important as a means of providing for the material necessities of life. At the dawn of man's history we find him chipping flints, inaugurating his career ever after as a tool-maker—a career in which he would have far more success than in his quest of wisdom and virtue. A historical survey may make clearer the "naturalness" of technology, the continuities through the long ages, and the unquestionable progress that man has made in this fundamental endeavor. Not until our century, however, did men begin to write the history of technology, and the obvious reason why historians have so belatedly recognized its importance is the novelty of the supreme importance of modern technology. This is not only vastly superior in efficiency to the technology of pre-industrial societies but essentially different in kind, and has had many unprecedented consequences.

The fantastic pace of change, due initially to the increasingly systematic "invention of invention" as the Industrial Revolution gathered momentum. has in our time been steadily accelerated by the many billions spent on "R & D," research and development. The most conspicuous result has been the immense power over nature, now including the conquest of outer space, that man has achieved by what are being called "megatechnics." But most important for my purposes is the range of influence of modern technology. It is a commonplace that our society is dominated by science and technology, so much so that some writers (such as Jacques Barzun) have attacked C. P. Snow's thesis of the "two cultures"—by maintaining that we really have only one culture. I think we have at least two, as the very complaints about science and technology suggest; but there is no question of their dominion. Hence many writers are echoing Ellul's insistence that our whole way of life is "unnatural." The extraordinary progress of technology is regarded as a problem, and though most men still celebrate the progress, it has certainly created problems such as past societies never had to worry over. As some scientist remarked, it has taught us how to become gods before we have learned to be men.

My primary concern is the systematic neglect or abuse of what I consider essential human values. (It is significant that values are regularly called "human" these days even though the term is strictly redundant—only human beings can have conscious values.) To be sure, anything that people want or think is good may be called a human value. Like Spinoza, I assume that people do not desire something because it is good, but that it is considered good because people desire it. Although money is often called a "false" value, it is plainly a real one. As plainly, however, it is only a means to some end. So too is our marvelous technology. The matrix of our problems, especially in America, is the common assumption in effect that it is an end in itself—an assumption fortified by the immense energy that goes into it, the worship of efficiency as the sovereign ideal, the boasts about our material wealth and power, and the national goal of steady economic growth. True, we cannot absolutely separate means and ends, since the achievement of necessary means may be satisfying in and for itself. As the end for many Americans has been not so much a pile of money as the game of money-making, so the mastery of technology may be its own reward, affording the satisfactions of a problem solved, a truth found, an adventure consummated, a craftsman's aim achieved—all amounting to a kind of esthetic satisfaction, in keeping with the definition of technology as a study of the practical "arts." Yet I assume that we still can and must roughly distinguish means and ends, both for our personal purposes and for purposes of sizing up our society. The distinction is all the more necessary because of our fabulous wealth of efficient means. And I am committed to the simple, old-fashioned assumption that the proper end for man is the good life.

Once upon a time men believed, or at least were constantly told, that their main business on earth was the salvation of their immortal soul, through the service of God. In America today the popular word for the good life is "happiness." This seems to me a quite normal goal, but the question remains what people mean by the term. The American pursuit of happiness can often look like a compulsive, joyless effort to escape boredom, and in any case a people blessed with far more material advantages than any other society has ever enjoyed is not clearly the happiest people on earth. One plain reason is a paltry conception of the good life, or what I have called the highest standard of low living in all history. But this only forces the basic question. What, then, is the good life?

The whole history of thought and culture may be summed up as an endless disagreement over this question. I take it that men never can or will agree on just what is the good life, unless the human race reaches the state of a universal anthill that Ellul and others predict. Neither do I wish for anything like complete agreement, in view of the rich, diverse potentialities of human nature and the manifold personal differences in interest and capacity. Yet the history of thought and culture also suggests that we can arrive at a general agreement on certain basic goods. They begin with the elementary goods of physical well-being, through health and the satisfaction of hunger and other physiological needs. They include the basic goods of social life, beginning with family life and broadening into simple comradeliness, fellow-feeling, and love. They include as well cultural goods—the satisfactions of natural curiosity, of the esthetic sense, and of the related craftsman's or creative impulse. These may be suspect to the man on the street for the same reason they are often called "higher," that they involve pleasures of the mind, but the powers of mind are precisely what distinguish man from other animals. All men normally enjoy using their heads, as children conspicuously do, and all known societies have made some provision for the cultivation of these goods. To some extent they are always known to the man on the street too. No Americans are as purely materialistic, or as narrowly practical, as they are often reputed to be. Though always inclined to ask where does it get you, they do all kinds of things that get them nowhere—except into a pleasurable state of mind.

Since most of us are conscientious relativists these days, and I have myself always shied away from high talk about the eternal verities, I venture some more elementary ideas. I am now operating on the premise that there *are* permanent, absolute values, at least so long as we assume that life is worthwhile. We cannot absolutely prove that it is, inasmuch as many men have decided otherwise, even to killing themselves; but this is the assumption that the rest of us perforce operate on, and these values are what warrant that assumption. They may be given some scientific warrant too in the common assumptions about the basic needs and drives of man, and lately the attention to the universals of culture, long neglected by anthropologists because of their stress on the more conspicuous diversity of cultures. I prefer, however, to emphasize their basis in common experience. They are absolute goods in that they are good for their own sake, they do not require either religious or scientific sanction, and they do not have to be demonstrated because men conscious of them simply know they are good. If they are not good enough to make life worthwhile for all men, the plainest reason is the deprivation of some basic good, such as health, or the frustration of some basic need And especially on these needs I have not sought the authority of psychologists and social scientists. Usually concentrating on the obvious physiological drives, such as hunger, sex, and self-preservation, they have paid much less attention to natural curiosity, the esthetic sense, creative activity, and the desire for self-realization through such normal interests, if only because these are harder to deal with by any respectable methodology. I am assuming that the "higher" goods are also sprung from vital needs, and that life is seriously impoverished when people, however well-fed and well-sexed, have limited capacities or opportunities for enjoying them.

In insisting on the reality and importance of what may also be called "spiritual" values, I am expressing not merely my personal opinion as an English professor but something like the judgment of the human race, apparent in all known societies. It remains apparent as we approach the more complicated question of "civilized" values, another of my major concerns. The rise of civilization, with its seemingly artificial life, may nevertheless be regarded as a natural outgrowth of the absolute goods, a more conscious, elaborate, refined realization of human potentialities, or an extension and enrichment of consciousness, the seat of all human values. Similarly its "high" culture was a more deliberate pursuit of truth, beauty, and goodness, sometimes holiness. The historic outcome was the growth of learning, the flowering of literature and the fine arts, in time the rise of philosophy, the higher religions, and pure science itself—the astonishing belief in the sovereign value of a disinterested pursuit of truth, an absolute value that scientists may overlook because many of them taboo value-judgments on principle. The fuller consciousness that men had grown to amplified as well such simple goods as fellow-feeling, which flowered into the no less astonishing ideal of universal brotherhood. In this fuller consciousness disagreements over the good life also became more marked, but first we should note the broad agreement on what were the great works of art and thought—an agreement the more significant because today we know far more about the history of civilization, and the values of all other civilizations, than men ever did or could in the great societies of the past.

With distinctively civilized values, however, we can no longer talk easily of permanence or absoluteness. They came very late in the history of man, and we have learned that civilization is a precarious adventure. Most of its high culture, moreover, was never made available to most people, in particular the illiterate peasant masses, who made do with their prehistoric kind of folk culture. At that anthropologists insist that we have no right to regard civilized societies as superior to the primitive ones they study, and some writers offer variations on the perennial theme of primitivism, the belief harking back to antiquity that the values of civilization are not worth its costs. To me they are worth it; but I would argue only that the great works of art and thought provide a richer experience than primitive or folk art (which I enjoy too), and that almost all people who have learned to appreciate them value this experience, as both a component of the good life and a possible guide to better conceptions of it.

More complex issues are raised by the distinctive values of our own civilization, above all the ideals of personal freedom, and the rights, opportunities, and incentives it has extended to the individual. In my efforts to write the history of freedom I was soon forced to question the congenial belief embedded in American tradition, that men have not only a natural right to freedom but a natural passion for it. On the historic record the great majority of men through the long ages manifested no such passion, they put up with what now looks like oppressive servitude, and they hardly dreamed of the rights and opportunities that most Americans take for granted as their birthright. Here I am arguing only that on the record man nevertheless has some potentialities for freedom, that once people have known and enjoyed more freedom they generally recognize it as a precious good, and that they have sound reason for this value judgment. Similarly with the ideals of individuality and self-realization that have come to be considered essential for the good life. They became conscious ideals with only a few peoples in the past, notably the ancient Greeks, and only in modern times have they been held up to the common people; there was no worry in past societies over the pressures to conformism that alarm contemporaries because the leaders of these societies wanted nothing more than conformity or unquestioning obedience in the common people. I assume only that these ideals have a biological basis in the fact that man is the most highly individualized of animals, as well as a historical basis in the wider range of choice and self-expression developed by civilization, and that on the record of Western civilization, and the basis of our own experience, there is again good reason for the common belief that they are precious ideals.

The excuse for all these elementary observations, at any rate, is that they may help as we begin to size up the social and cultural consequences of modern technology, the themes to be developed in later chapters. Most obviously it is by far the most efficient means yet devised by man to provide for the absolute goods of physical well-being, beginning with the bread man needs before he can realize that he cannot live on bread alone. Because these are "material" goods it has become all too easy to disparage them, and hard to realize that before our times untold millions of people starved to death, many more millions all through history had to get along without enough bread—as in the non-Western world they still do. Almost all of us enjoy many other of our abundant material goods. Readers may forgive the repetition of the commonplace that it is quite possible to lead the good life in a comfortable home with plumbing, central heating, electrical appliances, even a garage. Very few critics of modern civilization actually spurn all these comforts and conveniences, and I know of none who are putting on hair shirts. Today the drive of the whole non-Western world to modernize confirms the judgment of the human race that the basic material goods are absolute goods. Those who think the human race is wrong—as no doubt it can be—might look harder at their own experience.

Almost as plain, but also often overlooked by critics, are the cultural goods that have flowed out of modern technology. It provided the wealth that made possible the effort of nations to educate their entire populace, as no pre-industrial society could do even if its rulers had dreamed of such a thing. It also provided the incentive because of the needs of industry; a predominantly agricultural society can get along with an illiterate peasantry, as all did in the past, but an industrial society has to have not merely laborers but many kinds of literate workers. Likewise modern technology has made much more widely available a wealth of cultural goods in paperbacks, musical albums, photographs and reproductions of paintings, the better offerings of the mass media, etc. To the extent of their interest and capacity, ordinary people may now share in the values of civilization as the vast majority never did in the past. And because of the ample provision for both material needs and the uses of the mind they enjoy more effective freedom, freedom not only from want but to want, with more opportunities for self-realization, a much wider range of choices and a greater power of choice.

What they commonly choose, however, brings up the depressing products of modern technology—the superabundance of trivial goods that have been made into needs, the flood of trash in the mass media, the incessant, high-powered advertising of a vulgar conception of the good life, and so on *ad nauseam*. I shall be obliged to return to such too familiar complaints about the uses of our wealth and power, and of literacy. At this point I return to my premise of absolute goods. Because men can agree on them they can also agree on some absolute evils. No one would deny, for example, that the pollution of our rivers and the air we breathe is a bad thing. No one would argue either that dropping nuclear bombs on people is good for them. A nuclear war would be bad for everybody, except maybe the "victors"—and people are beginning to realize tardily that in an all-out war there would be no victors, only some wretched survivors. Then the question arises: Why all the pollution? Why has the richest, most powerful nation in all history only begun to do something about it? Why must it go on making bigger and better nuclear bombs when it already has many more than enough to blast the whole earth? I am brought to the compulsions of modern technology, the reasons why it so often neglects or even outrages essential human values, and why it has also drastically limited human freedom.

From the beginning the Industrial Revolution introduced new compulsions. It would condemn millions of people to the routines of factory work, force them day in and day out to go through the same mechanical operations. In a real sense slaves to their machines when at work, they also had to live where machines were at home and so lived in dreary places like Gary, Indiana, once described as a city inhabited by four blast furnaces and a hundred thousand people. In various ways people have been subjected to the compulsions of the new technology in the interests of efficiency and economy, conceived in terms of money values, too often without regard to human costs. I shall have to elaborate the tiresome theme of how our technology has tended to standardize and regiment people, mechanize and dehumanize life, generate massive pressures against the individual it had helped to liberate.

More paradoxical, at once subtler and more tyrannical, are the compulsions resulting from the astoundingly rapid progress of technology since World War II. Together with a wealth of new wonders, from television to space ships, this has created the "affluent society," one so much wealthier than any in the past that it is different in kind. As has often been said, the primary function of Americans today is to be consumers. They must keep on consuming faithfully, arduously, to the end of their days. If most of them appear to be doing their duty gladly enough, it nevertheless illustrates the odd kind of tyranny of our economy; if they didn't keep on buying the latest model, and all kinds of superfluous goods or gadgets, our economy would collapse. To assist them we have built up an immense advertising industry, which spends many billions on strictly unproductive but now essential purposes. One of the forms of propaganda required by an advanced technological society, it is a reminder that the immense power man has achieved is increasingly a power over not only nature but people, through ways of manipulating people. These may be for their own good, but thereby they raise again the question of what is good for people, and what people are good for.

* * * * *

4
The Industrial Revolution

In 1835, when a "railway mania" was exciting Britain, the editor of the journal John Bull was much alarmed by the latest invention. "Railroads, if they succeed," he warned, "will give an unnatural impetus to society, destroy all the relations which exist between man and man, overthrow all mercantile regulations, and create. at the peril of life, all sorts of confusion and distress." Needless to say, railroads did succeed. A generation later Britishers rejoiced in the thousands of miles of them that crisscrossed their land. Although trains had been invented chiefly to transport freight, they had soon attracted droves of passengers, and by the end of the century would be carrying well over a billion riders a year. Europeans on the Continent had been as pleased to imperil life by building railways, and Americans were simply thrilled when their first transcontinental railroad was completed in 1869. Everywhere the locomotive, whistling through the countryside at sixty miles an hour, was the most popular symbol of the new powers man was acquiring in an industrial age. The editor, long since forgotten, would have seemed a ludicrous old fogey.

Yet he was quite right. It is now hard to realize that before the railway era the great majority of people the world over spent their entire life in the region where they were born, never leaving the village except perhaps to go to the nearest market town, always remaining set in their traditional ways. The railroad accordingly did represent an "unnatural impetus," and a profoundly disruptive one. It signaled the end of the old social and political order as it broke down both geographical and social barriers by carrying ever more millions of passengers, drawn from all classes. It became the popular symbol of a technological revolution that was in fact destroying the traditional relations between men and creating "all sorts of confusion and distress." Even its literal peril to life was dramatized upon the inauguration of the first railroad: a director was run over by the train, prophetically named the Rocket. Today we can better understand the disruption of a traditional society by industrialism, for this is the drama being enacted all over the non—western world as it seeks to "modernize."

More to the point, the editor of *John Bull* still spoke for many respectable people of his day, and indeed for the vast majority of mankind throughout history. Men had always tended to resist fundamental change, any radical innovation. Though the Industrial Revolution had started at least fifty years before the editor wrote, it had proceeded slowly enough to obscure the deepest change taking place, also symbolized by the railroad. This was again the attitude toward change itself, now in daily life as well as government. It was the growing disposition to accept innovation, even to welcome it. Not only thinkers but ordinary people were calling change "progress." The once novel faith in progress was on its way to becoming common sense. But then we must add that that stodgy editor is still not really a stranger in our revolutionary world. Although change has long since become routine, most people welcome only superficial novelty—the latest models, gadgets, thrills. They still resent and resist any call for fundamental change in their ways of thinking; as Bertrand Russell once observed, most people would sooner die than think, and in fact do so. Especially in America they do not at all welcome radically new ideas; despite our boasts about our greatness, Americans seem more afraid of radicals or revolutionaries in our midst than are any other people in the world. And none more so than the business leaders who keep on revolutionizing the economy, accelerating the drive of our technology—the most influential radicals of our day.

This brings up a deeper paradox. The Industrial Revolution was the work of many inventive, enterprising, daring individuals. At first largely confined to a few districts in England, it was a natural, understandable development of what had started in the Elizabethan Age, but it was by no means inevitable, automatic, or predetermined by any known iron laws of history. Although broadly anticipated by Francis Bacon, its actual course was foretold by no thinker of the time, including Adam Smith, the most acute analyst in the days when machines were growing up. Yet by the same token the Industrial Revolution as a whole was quite unplanned. Its pioneers did not get together and say, Let us try for a change a society based on the machine. Like the inventor of the railroad, and the medieval burghers before them, they were unconscious revolutionaries who hardly foresaw, much less intended, the profound changes their innovations would bring throughout the whole society. The revolution illustrated the "vast, impersonal forces" of history that today we hear so much about. Slowly as it moved in the first fifty years, it came to seem impersonal and automatic as one invention called out another, and the impetus given it by the railroad made it well nigh as irresistible as irreversible. Basically the whole process was by no means so "rational" as historians of technology now make it appear. And all along society was even slower to realize the changes that were coming over it, to deal adequately with the problems they created. It illustrated the difficulties men always have in understanding and catching up with the history they have somehow made—difficulties that we now call cultural lag, but that in spite of our knowingness are as great as ever because of the terrific drive of our technology.

With these ironies in mind, let us review a few of the inventions that started revolutionizing life in a society that had known and valued machines since its beginning. James Watt's steam engine deserves its textbook fame as the key invention, no less because he only improved an engine long used to pump water out of mines. A pupil of a maker of "philosophical-instruments," Watt did not build on new scientific knowledge, but like the technicians of the past merely experimented in a practical spirit. Although he went broke on his early experiments with engines, he persevered, in 1769 patented one good for pumping, and then spent twenty years adding improvements that made it capable of driving all kinds of machinery, in factories as well as mines. Powerful, regular, and itself movable, it had a great advantage over water power in its independence of geography and season: henceforth industry could grow up in any region. Watt helped to sell his engine by establishing a standard measure called "horsepower," though without realizing that the animal would be replaced by the "iron horse"; as an old man he rejected the new-fangled idea of a steam carriage on railways. By that time the steam engine had nevertheless become the prime-mover of a new industrial age, now called the Age of Steam.

One reason why it took half a century to become the main source of industrial power was that the early engines had to be made by hand and could not be made to precise standards. The Age of Steam got really under way with the development of the machine tool industry, which signaled a fantastic development by turning out "machines that make machines," or breeding monsters like Frankenstein's; by 1850 all the basic ones were invented or perfected. The challenge of engines also led to the rise of a new profession, engineering, destined to take its place among the major professions.

Another early key to the Industrial Revolution that deserves its textbook reputation was the textile industry. A series of inventions known to most people (including me) only by name if at all—the water frame, the jenny, the mule—was climaxed by the power loom of Edmund Cartwright, a clergyman turned inventor to meet the increasing need of inventions. This made the industry the first major one to be revolutionized; machinery now did the work, making nonsense of the original meaning of "manufacture"—to make by hand. Likewise it accentuated the essential difference between modern machines and tools or neolithic machines. Whereas the latter required skilled craftsmen, most of the modern ones were automatic, requiring only operators to keep them going. Cotton manufacturers could accordingly begin producing for mass consumption, in foreign markets too. They did most to make Britain, already the greatest trading nation, the "workshop of the world." A grateful House of Commons awarded Cartwright in his old age 10,000 pounds for the benefits he had conferred on his country.

A title was enough for Richard Arkwright, the most enterprising of the early textile manufacturers, who had started out as a barber's apprentice. Described by Carlyle as "that bag-cheeked, pot-bellied, much enduring, much inventing barber," he had to endure the loss of his patent for the water frame, an invention he had stolen from other men; but he earned both a fortune and the title Sir Richard by developing the major social invention required by the new technology—the factory system. Unlike the spinning jenny, but like other of the new machines, his water frame was much too big and heavy to be installed in a worker's cottage, or to be powered by hand or foot; so he and his partners built cotton mills run by water power, in which they employed hundreds of workers. Factories had indeed long been known in Europe, in particular arms factories for its professional armies, but now many more were needed because they were the natural home of the machine. In his mills Arkwright mastered the new art of managing large establishments with machine processes, teaching workers (as he put it) "to conform to the regular celerity of the machine." He employed mostly children because they were not only cheap labor but quicker at learning this strange habit; men with skills were apt to make poor machine-tenders. Arkwright's title, still a rare honor for a businessman, perhaps did not entitle him to be considered one of the "real noblemen" envisaged by Saint-Simon; but in any case it foreshadowed the increasing prestige businessmen would win in the new society.

With his partners Arkwright heralded as well a new era of capitalism, primarily industrial. Such partnerships were common in the early days of the Industrial Revolution, inasmuch as few men had at once the capital to set up a mill and the technical and commercial skills needed to run it successfully. With the growth of industry small firms grew into joint-stock companies as other men were induced to invest their savings, and from mid-century on such companies became the standard form of business organization, producing the bulk of manufactured goods. The "organizational revolution" was under way, a major consequence of the new technology that would culminate in giant corporations, and with them big organizations all throughout the society. Capitalism was also equipped with a philosophy, such as it had lacked in the heyday of the Fuggers. In *The Wealth of Nations* Adam Smith had advanced his novel theory of laissez faire or free private enterprise, based on what is technically called the principle of the self-regulating market. The theory was that unregulated competition in self-interest best produced the goods people wanted, and that a free market would regulate itself, as if by an "unseen hand," because the incompetent would be weeded out, only those would succeed who knew how to produce the goods cheaply; granting a free rein to self-interest thus benefited the whole society. The new creed, which rationalized common business practice, was admirably suited to the interests of a rising business class that in England had to contend with an often hostile landed aristocracy in control of the government. In America, where business met much less opposition, the new theory became a gospel long before the end of the century. Here economic freedom would be hailed as the most fundamental freedom, the heart of the American Way of Life.

Early in the century America had contributed its pioneer in the factory system, Eli Whitney. Best known to schoolboys for his cotton gin, he also ran a small arms factory in which he introduced the manufacture of interchangeable parts, the rudiments of the assembly line. Harking back to the printing press, his ingenious "American system" speeded up the mass production more characteristic of the new age. And among the new industries to adopt it was harvesting machinery, dating from Cyrus McCormick's invention of the mechanical reaper in 1834, which started the revolutionizing of agriculture too by the machine. Immediately it was another reminder that it took a lot of bold persons to create the "vast, impersonal forces" that made the Industrial Revolution. Twelve years after McCormick's invention, an observer in America—the celebrated land of opportunity and enterprise—marveled at a factory that was daring enough to manufacture a hundred reapers. "It was difficult indeed," he reported, "to find parties with sufficient boldness or pluck and energy to undertake the hazardous enterprise of building reapers, and quite as difficult to prevail upon farmers to take their chances of cutting their grain with them, or to look favorably upon such innovation."

Because of such attitudes the "unnatural impetus" of railroads takes on more importance, warranting another new name—the Railway Age. While in England they soon became a "mania" as a profitable source of investment, elsewhere they brought countries to what is now called the "take-off" stage in modernizing. They not only constituted a big new industry, a booming market for iron and coal, but stimulated the growth of all other industries. Whereas transport of goods had been slow and expensive, except for towns located on rivers or the sea, railroads could swiftly deliver all raw materials and finished products, giving manufacturers a much wider choice both in sites for their factories and in markets for their goods. And outside of Britain they gave still more impetus to industrialism by bringing in the aid of government. In America the government lavished huge grants of public lands on the transcontinental railroad builders, as well as generous loans for every mile of track they finished; such public enterprise enabled these entrepreneurs to make fortunes with little personal investment, at as little personal risk. On the Continent the railroad systems were generally planned when not built by the state.

Hence the revolution that had started in Britain now spread to all of Europe. Some countries took to industrialism much more slowly than others, remaining "backward," but everywhere it introduced the same tendencies—more use of mechanical power, more material goods, more standardization of products, and more business. By the end of the century a machine civilization was well on its way to becoming the first civilization in history in which most people would make their living through business instead of agriculture. Likewise it was becoming the first predominantly urban civilization, in which most people in the advanced industrial countries would live in or about the city instead of the village.

We may now pause over an early climax of the Industrial Revolution, the Great Exposition of London in 1851. Held in the Crystal Palace, a monumental building of iron and glass designed especially for the occasion (though not by an architect), it was still more dazzling as the first international exhibition of the wonders being produced by industry. The London *Economist* described the Palace as a temple erected to the honor of "the mightiest empire of the globe—the empire in which industry is most successfully cultivated, and in which its triumphs have been greatest." This was simple fact, no mere boast, but Victorians might be more edified by the deeper significance the *Economist* pointed out in the exhibits in this temple. They testified to the "honor" in which "humble industry" was now held, the "moral improvement" already apparent, the "devotion to peace," the promise of a still more peaceful future—all in all, the "irresistible assurances that a yet higher destiny awaits our successors even on earth."

So we are brought to the social consequences of the Industrial Revolution. Since it has become all too easy to resist the complacent assurances of the *Economist*, I should note first of all that its editor had some good reasons for his complacence. Men had obviously achieved much more of the power over nature that the human race had always cherished, and they could rightly expect to acquire ever more power, and with it more wealth. In his *Communist Manifesto* Karl Marx himself had already been pleased to grant that the bourgeois economy was by far the most productive in history. Unlike others it was producing an abundance of cheap goods; its main market was ordinary people, not the rich. Although economists are still debating to what extent, if any, real wages went up in the early decades of industrialism, by mid-century the trend was clearly upward; workers were on their way to the highest standard of living in history. C. P. Snow has reminded the literary world of a simple truth too often overlooked, that for all its evils the Industrial Revolution was the only hope of the poor—the great majority of mankind who had lived in poverty ever since the rise of civilization. With the prospects of increasing plenty it was not unreasonable to hope for increasing peace too. Marx could dream of his classless society, in which industrialism would provide an abundance for all.

In view of such real gains we may discount somewhat the admitted evils of early industrialism—the many women and children working twelve or fourteen hours a day in factories and mines, the many men slaving at starvation wages, the foul living conditions to which all were condemned in the industrial towns or city slums. Herbert Heaton, an economic historian, has observed that these were ancient forms of evil, taken for granted in the past, and that the revolutionary development was the realization that they were evils. It was the growing indignation over them, the belief that they were remediable, and then the positive resolve to do something about them. We know much more about them than we do about the lot of workers in the past because of a series of full, detailed reports by Royal Commissions and Committees of Inquiry; these were the main source not only of Marx's documentation of the evils of capitalism but of the indignation of many bourgeois, and of government enterprise in a series of laws to check the worst abuses. And the spreading faith in progress that may seem ludicrous in the *Economist's* hymn to the Great Exposition had much to do with the concerted efforts at reform, which in the past had been rare and sporadic. It was not merely a complacent belief in an automatic material progress, but an active will to improve life on earth. Among the many inspired by the faith in progress had been Robert Owen, an early industrialist who by his own success demonstrated that the current evils of the factory system were economically unnecessary, and who preached that "the new powers which men are about to acquire" made any poverty unnecessary.

Workers themselves were stirred by the new spirit. The violent uprisings that had broken out as early as the Middle Ages could be called the beginning of class war against the bourgeois, but the still unbaptized "proletariat" had then had no political program. In the 1830's the great Chartist movement swept over England, leading to enough riots by workers to look like a revolution, but also gathering more than a million signatures to a petition for a "People's Charter" of democratic government. If this owed most to the democratic ideals proclaimed by the American and French Revolutions, it also owed much to the Industrial Revolution. The industrial proletariat was the fastest growing class in England, it was concentrated in cities, and as Marx would say, it was being "armed" by the bourgeois. It was growing more literate and class-conscious, learning from the successful efforts of the bourgeois to wrest political rights from the ruling aristocracy. So it began its protracted struggle for the right to organize in labor unions, the right to vote, and the right to free public education. By the end of the century it had largely won these rights in the advanced industrial countries. With their rising standard of living, workers thereby had the means to more effective freedom than they had enjoyed in any previous society.

Yet they always had to struggle, in America especially against the almost solid opposition of the ruling business class. Although the most shocking abuses of the early years have been eliminated, there remain plenty of evils. We are still struggling with the basic problems created by the triumph of industrialism. I think we still need to dwell on the neglect of elementary human values that was so glaring at the outset.

To begin with, most of the workers long remained wretchedly poor. This was a repetition of an old story, beginning with the rise of civilization, but it was more demoralizing in a society that was acquiring far more wealth and power than any before it. Another common kind of victim of industrial progress was the hand-weaver, the many men left with useless skills, fighting a doomed battle against machines, in their fury now and then smashing them. Comfortable economists, always at home with abstractions, would point out that the new technology caused only "temporary dislocations," inasmuch as its victims would in time be absorbed by new industries, but the dislocations were always painful for human beings, who usually lacked the means of promptly moving into new jobs. Later on economists also grew aware of the "business cycle," the periodic panics of depressions that came with the new economy, throwing men out of work for no fault of their own; but they regarded this cycle coolly as a kind of natural law of business and proposed no means of preventing depressions, nor of taking care of their victims. And despite the accelerating industrial progress, and the gradual rise of real wages, there always remained millions of very poor people. Americans have only begun to realize belatedly how many millions of them there are in our most affluent society. An increasing abundance of material goods made more glaring an elementary failure of industrialism: all along it failed to provide a great many workers with the minimum necessities of a decent life—an adequate diet, adequate medical care, decent homes, pleasant surroundings.

Living conditions were most appalling in the new industrial towns, the heralds of the first predominantly urban civilization in history. In the same year when the editor of *John Bull* was alarmed by the prospect of railroads, Alexis de Tocqueville reported on the city of Manchester, the foremost center of industrialism: "From this foul drain the greatest stream of human industry flows out to fertilize the whole world. From this filthy sewer pure gold flows. Here humanity attains its most complete development and its most brutish, here civilization works its miracles and civilized man is turned almost into a savage." The smoke-filled towns were the drabbest, grimiest, and ugliest in all history. As they went about "making a new Heaven and a new Earth—both black," they made little or no provision for sanitation and recreation, parks and playgrounds, or any open space where people could gather and relax. The industrial slums that started growing up in the old cities too made drabness, filthiness, and ugliness seem still more like a natural, normal condition of industrial progress. Respectable people were not shocked by the foul surroundings in which men were learning to live, and could hope to live with any contentment only by virtue of deadened senses, with the help of gin.

One might excuse such failings by saying that it would naturally take men some time to learn how to live with machines and factories. Thus municipal government in Britain was quite unprepared for the new conditions, and lacked anyway the authority to deal with them; in time it would acquire the authority, make some provision for the elementary needs of a decent civic life. Yet the slums would remain, above all in wealthy America, and with them other root evils that would grow worse. Industry soon began polluting rivers and the atmosphere; not until American cities were smog-bound did people begin to realize, too late, how intolerable the pollution had become. Likewise people grew so inured to ugliness that they seemed quite unaware of it—as most Americans still seem unaware of the commercial blight on their landscape, once known as God's own country. Progressive industrial man has never shown the respect for the natural environment that his benighted ancestors did in creating and tending the landscape of Europe.

Hence the obvious question: Why all such neglect or even contempt of elementary human values? The immediate answer seems to me as obvious: it was due to the vaunted free private enterprise that created industrialism, for the sake of private profit. So in fairness I would again first acknowledge the very real enterprise of the pioneers in the Industrial Revolution, and the technical ingenuity and resourcefulness of their followers in building up industry, producing the goods that people did indeed want. No other class at the time was so enterprising. In America, where businessmen were given most freedom and opportunity, they rewarded the nation by conquering a continent. Having a particular need of machinery for this purpose, they responded by developing a genius for mechanizing, organizing, and standardizing their far-flung operations. In but a generation after the Civil War they made America the greatest industrial power on earth. Allan Nevins has called them "the heroes of our material growth"—the growth that Americans have always been proud of.

Yet the heroes also distinguished themselves by exploitation, plunder, and fraud, on a colossal scale unknown in Britain. They made this generation the most flagrant in the nation's history for routine corruption, in both government and business; they thoroughly earned another name for themselves, the "robber barons." With the help of the Republican Party, which ruled the country in their interests to the end of the century, they also made America the most backward of the industrial countries in social legislation to protect workers against the abuses of private enterprise and the hazards of industry—just as the interests of business had helped to make it the last "Christian" nation to abolish slavery. The economic freedom they prized, no less because the authors of the Constitution had neglected to mention it, was a freedom only for themselves, the men on top; they fought bitterly the enterprise of workers who sought to achieve more freedom for themselves by organizing in labor unions. They forced the basic issue that is still with us, in an era of much bigger business.

5
The "Neotechnic" Phase

Toward the end of the nineteenth century the Industrial Revolution entered a new phase, which in his pioneering *Technics and Civilization* Lewis Mumford called "neotechnic" to distinguish it from the long initial phase he called "paleotechnic" and regarded as on the whole a "disastrous interlude." Men now began mastering their new technology. They not only developed much more rapidly all kinds of practical possibilities but realized more of the ideal possibilities of the machine, feeling more at home with it. They exercised more social control over their technology, in the interests of long neglected human values. Mumford added, however, that barbarous paleotechnic ideals still largely dominated industry and politics, and in a review of his book written twenty-five years later he played down the successes of the neotechnic phase. In my somewhat broader treatment of modern technology I should stress still more both the persistence of old problems and the emergence of new ones. On all counts we may get a perspective on the further gains made in our own time, and also on the much worse problems confronting us.

* * * * *

6
"Post-Industrial" Society

Having at last reached our own time, the generation since World War II, I feel obliged to begin by recording more history. Much of it will already seem like ancient history to young people under twenty-five, who now make up almost half the population of America. They must find it hard to realize what occurred to me only a few years ago, when I noted that in this one generation we have lived through more radical, sweeping, startling changes than past civilizations had experienced in a thousand years. These changes incidentally included a host of new technical marvels—radar, television, wonder drugs, transistors, computers, jets, sputniks, intercontinental missiles, etc.—most of which did not startle me when I first saw or heard of them; I suppose young people too soon learned to take them as a matter of course. We have all grown used to the momentous events on the world stage, such as the dawn of the Atomic Age, the emergence of the Soviet as a world power rivaling America, the Cold War, the conquest of outer space, and the revolt and rise of the whole non-Western world, the dozens of new nations in the United Nations. It is already unnecessary to use quotation marks with once sensational phrases like the population explosion and the knowledge explosion. In our society exploding appears to be a normal mode of expansion.

All these changes were due to technology. In alliance with science, it is now unmistakably the basic determinant of our history.

The upshot was the now notorious "military-industrial complex," another new power in the land. This oligarchy was due simply to the requirements of military technology—not to any theory of either capitalism or socialism. Even so President Eisenhower warned against it as a possible menace to democracy in his farewell address to the nation. Although conservatives have been most fearful of bureaucratic power, they have otherwise expressed little alarm over this extreme example of it, the immense power exercised by a small inner group not directly responsible to the public, the possibly life-or-death decisions made often in secrecy without public debate. In view of the obsession with the Cold War most Americans do not complain either because their government has been directing our fabulous technology primarily to military purposes.

With some absent-minded exceptions, businessmen have been outgrowing their suspicion of another government enterprise, described by Daniel Moynihan as the "most powerful development" of this generation—a more wholesome effort to avert depressions and promote steady economic growth by new fiscal policies based on forecasts of economic advisers. Although growth was at first retarded by periodic "recessions," which were hard on unemployed workers even when they were given the still gentler name of "rolling readjustments," post-industrial society has so far been able to prevent the severe depressions that for a century were regular occurrences. Businessmen and Congressmen are much less horrified by "government planning," which they had regarded as something that only the Russians did, hence *ipso facto* an un-American activity bad for business (They never objected, of course, to extensive planning by big corporations.) Similarly they are less frightened by deviations from archaic notions of "sound fiscal policy," the fetish of the balanced budget that hobbled the Eisenhower administration. Altogether, it appears that the economy is under far better control than it ever was in the palmy days of free private enterprise; though laymen might wonder how it would fare without the big war business.

Ordinary Americans have mostly welcomed a quite different reason for the expansion of government—the growth of the Welfare State, dating from the New Deal. This has been much slower and spottier than the growth of the Warfare State. Congressmen who voted billions for military defense expenditures without batting an eye were still disposed to regard expenditures on public welfare services as reckless extravagance; so for years the nation spent on these services a smaller proportion of its growing national income than it had been spending, while a supposedly alarming increase in the federal debt was actually a decrease in relation to this income. Public demand for them grew, however, if only because an affluent society could plainly afford them. The necessity of keeping up with the Russians finally persuaded Congress of the need of federal aid to education, at first to turn out more scientists and engineers. More tardily the government began to respond to the crying public needs of decent housing and adequate medical care, which private enterprise was either unable or indisposed to provide except at a cost beyond the means of many Americans. At length the government launched a piddling but unprecedented "war" on poverty—the poverty that had persisted all through the triumphant progress of industrialism, and that in a land of unparalleled wealth and abundance had at last come to seem both unnecessary and unjust. President Johnson announced that the national goal was the Great Society.

But perhaps the most significant change in post-industrial society has come about through the vast sums that the government has poured into research and development, especially in the universities (The last time I looked, the sums had reached $17 billion a year.) As I noted at the outset, the "knowledge industry" has become the biggest business in America. Daniel Bell predicts that the university will become the primary institution of the new society, more important even than the big corporation, and that all the major institutions will be intellectual, not business institutions. If businessmen may long retain more prestige as well as wealth, a new professional elite of brainworkers will make the major decisions about policy.

So all of us in the universities might rejoice in our new eminence. All, that is, except maybe those engaged in the old-fashioned business of liberal education, concentrated on human values. When Clark Kerr writes, in the kind of language now popular, that the "production, distribution, and consumption" of knowledge accounts for 29 per cent of the gross national product, and is growing at about twice the rate of the economy, teachers of the humanities may be reminded that their product represents an insignificant fraction of the GNP. The billions are going chiefly to science and technology. Bell emphasizes "the new centrality of *theoretical* knowledge, the primacy of theory over empiricism," or one might add over the common sense of businessmen; but what about *philosophical* knowledge? It appears that political scientists now distinguish between political theory and political philosophy, which in my innocence I had thought were virtually synonymous. Theory is what goes with the study of political behavior, the current vogue; it eschews value judgments and has outmoded philosophy. I remain more concerned with philosophy, the issues of the good state and its service of the good life.

In government the host of technicians and experts, who have given the name of "technocratic" to our society, raise a cluster of questions. By definition a technocrat is a technician who has been endowed with power, enough to influence when not to make important political decisions, and he is rarely elected to office. Some thinkers argue that technocracy dooms democracy, makes it already a mere appearance, or let us say an incidental nuisance to experts. Others might rejoice that the status of the new elite is based upon knowledge and skill, not success in pursuing economic or political self-interest; but what are their ruling values? Are their ends primarily the interests of people, or of system? Specifically, Secretary of Defense Robert McNamara developed an influential cost-effectiveness analysis for making key decisions, or what is called "value-engineering"; and does this technique take into account values other than economy? Can any such technique promote wisdom—an imprecise term, but a quality especially needed in a technological society with tremendous power at its disposal? At the moment all such questions are obscured by the Cold War. Daniel Bell has remarked the irony that whereas thinkers from Saint-Simon on who hailed industrialism assumed that the "new men" it would make leaders of would be hostile to the wasteful military spirit, it is primarily war that has elevated the technocrats. But if or when the obsession with the Cold War lifts, what then will come out of all the system?

Since I shall return to such questions, I shall say here only that I do not think the answers are simple, clear, or foreordained. As for the cultural values of the good life, government need not serve as their principal custodian or promoter; enough if it maintains the conditions that make it possible for people to cultivate these values. Immediately I am more concerned with the issues forced by postwar society regarded simply as an affluent society, in which most people have as never before the means to pursue the good life.

Among many other things, the affluent society has produced the historically novel type of the teenager, with whole industries catering to his tastes, and tending to make him not an endearing type. It also produced the education explosion that has sent millions of teenagers to college, most of them with the primary goal of becoming "well-adjusted" to such a society. With the coming of automation it holds out the prospect of increasing leisure in which to enjoy the abundance. This apparent boon is regarded, rather oddly, as a "problem"; but the problem seems less odd when one considers a favorite means of passing the time—staring at TV. A society in which the vast majority own a television set has made it the most popular and influential of the mass media, and so raises the issue of mass culture and the notions of the good life it inculcates. Meanwhile the big networks suggest some reservations about the prediction that the university will replace the corporation as the primary institution, and an intellectual class will make the major decisions affecting public policy. As the networks keep making their own decisions with little interference from government, so the big corporations have been holding their own. They too have been directing our fabulous technology, in the interests of private profit. Hence they force another basic question: How well is big business serving the public interest?

For the time being, all these issues may be illustrated by the mammoth automobile industry. Although invented in Europe its product became distinctively American as the most popular status symbol, transformed American life more than has any other single product, and indeed has had a deeper, more lasting influence on people than had any historic conqueror. After Henry Ford achieved the mass production of the standardized Model T, a sturdy, economical car once beloved, he had to meet the competition of another wizard, Alfred Sloan, who built up General Motors by producing a range of fancier cars at higher prices, featuring annual new models. Since the war GM has dominated the industry, producing more than half the cars. In the early days of the industry Ford and other entrepreneurs had had a real passion for making automobiles, but Sloan had a more effective strategy. As he explained in *My Years with General Motors:* "The primary object of the corporation. . . was to make money, not just to make motor cars." He knew it would make more money by turning out cars with excess power and chrome, not just sturdy, well-designed, efficient cars. His kind of commercial rather than mechanical efficiency also included careful planning to assure a 20 per cent return on capital, with such success that GM actually averaged a higher return, almost double the national average, once hitting a record 50 per cent; though this did not lead to lower prices for consumers.

To these record profits government contributed by spending lavishly on services for the automobile—one kind of public service that conservatives whole-heartedly favored. Congress under frugal President Eisenhower approved a federal highway program costing many billions, while states spent more billions to speed the traffic on superhighways and freeways, and cities ate their heart out to provide more parking space. By now more than a hundred billion dollars a year goes into automobiles and their servicing—gas, tires, repairs, insurance and finance, maintenance of highways, etc. Americans own enough cars for every man, woman, and child in the country to ride in the front seat, since some ten million families have at least two of them.

The transformation of the country began when the automobile brought modern life to Main Street, the tractor to the farm: except in some backwoods districts, the villager and the farmer were no longer "hayseeds" or "yokels." The many shiny highways everywhere with all their accessories—gas stations, roadside stands, lunchrooms, billboards, etc.—have changed the face of the countryside. The automobile stimulated the mass migration to the suburbs, which have been spreading fast all over the land, changing cities into undefined "metropolitan areas." As it created such other novelties as supermarkets, shopping centers, and drive-ins, suburbanites grew absolutely dependent on it. It took fathers to work, mothers to the store, youngsters to school. Teenagers used it to make love in or to go on joy-rides. And from the beginning it had brought joy to the hearts of Americans, an exhilarating sense of freedom and power as they drove, and of possible social mobility too.

Some by-products of their pleasure, however, illustrate a neglect of human values that has become more conspicuous in the affluent society. The most publicized is the slaughter on the highways, realizing the "peril to life" that the editor of *John Bull* feared in the railroad: many more Americans have been killed by automobiles than were killed in both world wars. The automobile industry has contributed to the slaughter by its primary concern with what made money, including excessive power rather than safety. Highway engineers have been more responsible after their fashion but in the interest only of efficiency and economy, bulldozing their way through landscape and cityscape without regard for natural beauty or civic concerns. Business interests have shown less respect for the landscape as they defiled it with garish billboards, designed to attract attention by not blending into it. The automobile itself ends up in the junkyards that provide more eyesores, speeding the transformation of the country into "God's own junkyard."

The migration to the suburbs it promoted was more rational—except that one reason for it is another basic irrationality of a technological society, the blight of the American city. In the most urban of civilizations, and the richest nation on earth, one might reasonably expect to find beautiful cities, spacious, airy, comfortable; but in fact most of the big ones have notoriously been growing dirtier and shoddier, more congested and polluted, more unfit to live in. The automobile has been chiefly responsible for the congestion and pollution; ever more highways are built to enable more drivers to get into the heart of the city. Hence the people who have fled the city do not really escape it. They help to enact one of the most absurd daily spectacles in affluent America: millions of people driving to and from work, one to an automobile, bumper to bumper, often through smog, often tense and irritable—unable even to absorb the message of all the billboards and neon signs. Lewis Mumford summed up the whole story in a protest that this "Sacred Cow of the American Way of Life is overfed and bloated; that the milk she supplies is poisonous; that the pasturage this species requires wastes acres of land that could be used for more significant human purposes; and that the vast herd of sacred cows, allowed to roam everywhere, like their Hindu counterparts, are trampling down the vegetation, depleting the wild life, and turning both urban and rural areas into a single smudgy wasteland, whose fancy sociological name is Megalopolis."

Still, the Sacred Cow evidently remains a primary need of Americans in their pursuit of happiness. Granted that the industry spends hundreds of millions to create their needs by advertising, there is no question that most Americans like their cars big, powerful, and ostentatious. As certainly they want all the services that government lavishes on the automobile; as taxpayers they are more willing to pay for highway programs than for better schools. They seldom protest against all the bulldozing, the erosion of the heart of cities by parking areas. Once behind the wheel, they do not mind all the ugliness along the highways. Ultimately, in short, the American people must be blamed for the neglect of human values. They may complain about this or that, chiefly about the taxes they have to pay for having it so good; but apparently they would rather have life this way than support a national effort to make America fit for civilized living. Their primary duty remains consuming, buying instead of merely making a living to the end of their days. suitably marked by a costly funeral. Theirs not to question why—theirs only to go and buy.

So regarded, Americans scarcely look like a great people—the kind of people needed to create a Great Society, or to appreciate one. They support rather the forecast of Aldous Huxley, that technology is preparing them for life in something like Brave New World—a benevolent totalitarian state in which almost everybody will be kept happy and hollow. Automation will provide the machinery for running such a world. The technocratic elite is learning how to govern it. Big business is able and willing to cooperate by producing the needed superfluity of material goods. Admen will keep the people consuming and conforming, television will keep them entertained. Experts in motivational research—another new kind of technician—will condition them more perfectly to a state of mindless happiness, while wonder drugs will keep them tranquil, remove the uneasiness of such mind as they have left. In *Post-Historic Man* Roderick Seidenberg foresees a society in which all individuality and spontaneity will be ironed out and consciousness itself will finally disappear.

Again I do not think that the trend toward such a state is irresistible, for reasons I will go into at the end; there is much more to be said about the American people. Meanwhile the clearest reason is frightening, quite apart from the constant possibility of nuclear war. To the peoples of the non-Western world—the great majority of mankind—worries over the possibility of a Brave New World are simply academic. Stirred by the rising expectations of the fruits of modern technology, they will have to struggle indefinitely with the problems of scarcity, in India even with the threat of mass starvation. The affluence of America and western Europe is steadily widening the gulf between the few haves and the many more have-not nations, while the population explosion aggravates the difficulties and kindles other explosive possibilities. Americans may still dream of going their own way toward ever more affluence, ease, and comfort, their notion of happiness; but they can never hope for the security and stability of a Brave New World so long as the aroused non-Western world suffers from acute want. If consciousness is doomed to disappear, it can be trusted to remain painful enough for the foreseeable future. Today the problem in America is to alert it to the worldwide consequences of modern technology.

* * * * *

12
Higher Education

So let us consider C.P. Snow's celebrated, much abused lecture "The Two Cultures," the sciences and the humanities. His thesis was that these cultures, alike essential to an adequate education today, are unfortunately separated by mutual incomprehension, to some extent even by hostility. Critics were quick to point out that there are more than two cultures—one could easily make out two dozen—and that there is as little communication within them as between them. Sir Charles was more vulnerable because of his complacence over science and technology. He took for granted the greater importance and value of science, dwelling chiefly on the faults of literary people; he said very little about the values of literature, the reasons why scientists ought to be better acquainted with it. But after such qualifications his basic thesis seems to me clearly valid. Most specialists in science do not have an adequate grounding in the humanities; most specialists in the humanities do not know enough about the fundamentals of science and technology. And the current stress on research and development is widening and deepening the gulf between them.

In a following lecture Snow recognized the social sciences as a "third culture," a potential bridge between the other two. Ideally they could serve as a mediator because their subject is man and society. Actually, however, they are generally taught and practiced as sciences, not as humanistic studies, and if anything they have been tending to widen the gulf, arouse more suspicion or hostility among literary people, for reasons I suggested previously. Similarly with the study of engineering. Eric Ashby has said that it could unite science and humanism because it is inseparable from men and communities, concerned with the application of science to their needs. In fact most students of technology acquire very little humanistic culture, and they tend to be more indifferent to it than are students of the natural sciences. And technical or vocational studies have been attracting a larger proportion of the students flooding our colleges than have either the humanities or the natural sciences. They might be grouped in another separate culture, distinctive in its incomprehension of both the other two. Too many of their graduates are cultural illiterates.

The best excuse for such narrowness, all the practical training that students need to fit them for their profession, may now look antiquated. As long ago as 1897 John Dewey pointed out a peculiar difficulty of education today:

The only possible adjustment which we can give to the child under existing conditions is that which arises through putting him in complete possession of all his powers. With the advent of democracy and modern industrial conditions, it is impossible to foretell definitely just what civilization will be twenty years from now. Hence it is impossible to prepare the child for any precise set of conditions.

Since Dewey wrote, the much faster pace of technological change has made his comment still more pertinent, above all for college students. For years engineers and other technical students who went into business have never used much of the supposedly practical training they got, but today much of it is strictly obsolescent, in process of being outmoded by the latest innovations. Many technical students are being prepared thoroughly, meticulously, for a "set of conditions" that is ceasing to exist. They may find themselves in not only a rut but the wrong rut. In this view, as Robert Hutchins argues, a liberal education may be considered the most practical kind. The humanities in particular are supposed to put students in a fuller possession of all their powers.

But we therefore need to look more closely into their claims, which traditionalists may too easily take for granted. Students in the humanities also concentrate on specialized subject matter, and while it will not be simply superseded as scientific theories and engineering techniques often are, one may ask what purpose is served by all the knowledge or "book learning" they acquire. It is clearly useful for students who are going on to become teachers or scholars in their subject, but what of the many more who are going out into the world? Specifically, the guardians of the humanities might ponder some pointed questions asked by a responsible business leader who wanted to know more about their value. Just why are they considered so important? "Speaking quite practically, what can the humanities do for me, for my family, for my business, for my community? . . . Do they make people better? Do they make people happier? Do they make people more capable? How do you know?"

He could read many resounding answers. To cite a few random examples, the humanities preserve our rich cultural heritage; they are "the very soul of our culture," the heart of the "civilizing process"; they elevate the spirit by giving us "a sense of man's innate worth and of his infinite capacities;" they further our understanding "of such enduring values as justice, freedom, virtue, beauty, and truth"; they are a "storehouse of wisdom" that enables us to make better judgments; they endow us with purpose and "concern for man's ultimate destiny"; they "help men to live more fully and creatively and to expand their dignity, self-direction, and freedom"; and scientists themselves are wont to say that without a knowledge of the humanities "science would lack vision, inspiration, and purpose." Or the businessman might ponder Cardinal Newman's classic statement of the ideal values of a liberal education:

It aims at raising the intellectual tone of society, at cultivating the public mind, at purifying the national taste, at supplying true principles to popular enthusiasm and fixed aims to popular aspiration, at giving enlargement and sobriety to the ideas of the age, at facilitating the exercise of political power, and refining the intercourse of private life. It is the education which gives a man a clear conscious view of his own opinions and judgments, a truth in developing them, an eloquence in expressing them, and a force in urging them. It teaches him to see things as they are, to go right to the point, to disentangle a skein of thought, to detect what is sophistical, and to discard what is irrelevant. It prepares him to fill any post with credit, and to master any subject with facility. It shows him how to accommodate himself to others, how to throw himself into their state of mind, how to bring before them his own, how to influence them, how to come to an understanding with them, how to bear with them. He is at home in any society, he has common ground with every class: he knows when to speak and when to be silent; he is able to converse, he is able to listen; he can ask a question pertinently, and gain a lesson seasonably, when he has nothing to impart himself: he is ever ready, yet never in the way: he is a pleasant companion, and a comrade you can depend upon: he knows when to be serious and when to trifle, and he has a sure tact which enables him to trifle with gracefulness and to be serious with effect. He has the repose of a mind which lives in itself, while it lives in the world, and which has resources for its happiness at home when it cannot go abroad. He has a gift which serves him in public, and supports him in retirement, without which good fortune is but vulgar, and with which failure and disappointment have a charm. The art which tends to make a man all this is in the object which it pursues as useful as the art of wealth or the art of health, though it is less susceptible of method, and less tangible, less certain, less complete in its result.

Still, Newman paid this tribute at a time when Oxford and Cambridge were offering a routine classical education that now looks pretty sterile. The important question remains unanswered: Do the humanities today actually achieve these high goals, or come anywhere near them? As the businessman asked, *"How do you know?"*

The honest answer is that we don't know. I doubt that we can know, since the lofty objectives ascribed to the humanities do not lend themselves to measurement. As it is, we go on giving examinations that test chiefly a student's knowledge of a particular subject, scarcely his wisdom, vision, creativity, humanity, soulfulness, or what not. We do not know either what kind of subject matter would help most in attaining the lofty objectives, but go on teaching all the traditional subjects in more or less traditional ways. As an English teacher I am disposed to believe that a proper command of language and literature could contribute most to self-realization, or broadly to a fuller realization of both our common humanity and one's personal identity, but the history of literary studies offers no convincing evidence that they make men more humane, and recent history gives more reason for doubt; Dr. Goebbels was only one of the many German doctors of letters who welcomed Hitler. I am sure only that many students specializing in the humanities achieve at most a mastery of a particular subject, or rather of some subdivision of it. Their studies have made them more capable in some respects, and we must hope on the whole better people. but we must wonder how much they can contribute.

* * * * *

21
Coda: The Problem of Human Nature

Yet we of course can and must talk about human nature, as we do about "man," "mankind," the "human condition," and our "common humanity." Biologically man is a distinct species, with the same structure and needs that he had fifty thousand years ago. "It is absolutely certain," writes Rene Dubos, "that all of his physiological needs and drives, his potentialities and limitations, his responses to environmental stimuli, are still determined by the same twenty thousand pairs of genes that controlled his life when he was a palaeolithic hunter or a neolithic farmer." Dubos explains that we know very little about the pathological effects on man of a polluted, crowded environment and the stresses of modern life because the problems they create appear chiefly late in life, past the reproductive age that could call into play the mechanisms of natural selection; but he is certain that the new environment and ways of life have had deleterious effects. Likewise biologists and sociologists know hardly anything about man's adaptive potentialities, which would require studies of long-range consequences; but again it is certain that man cannot adapt himself successfully to any kind of life in any kind of environment. Meanwhile technology keeps plunging on in ignorance, in ways largely determined by economic expediency, with little regard for the basic nature and needs of man. So the accelerating pace of change may make one wonder: Just how much change can man stand? Can he adapt himself successfully to a continuously revolutionary world?

As a humanistic scientist who believes that "quiet, privacy, independence, initiative, and open space" are "real biological necessities," Dubos recalls me to my own premises. At the outset I stated my belief that despite the conspicuous diversity of cultures and relativity of values we *can* talk of absolute values, permanent as long as man exists; or in other words, these derive from "human nature." The psychologist William Maslow maintains that even the "higher" human needs, as for friendship, love, dignity, self-respect, and self-fulfillment, are biological in origin, and human nature has been sold short because they have not been so considered by most scientists; but in any case they have long been vital needs. As for our own society, he attributes the growing discontent and rebelliousness of young people to the frustration of the idealism natural to them. Academic psychology, economics, and most social science offer them a limited view of human nature, with emphasis on the lower or material needs. The dominant positivistic and behavioristic theories reduce the highest values and virtues to mere appearances or illusions. The whole society operates on a low conception of human nature. "How could young people not be disappointed and disillusioned?" Maslow concludes. "What else could be the result of *getting* all the material and animal gratifications and then *not being happy*, as they were led to expect, not only by the theorists, but also by the conventional wisdom of parents and teachers, and the insistent grey lies of the advertisers?"

The youth also best exemplify the peculiar complication of human nature today. A person's genes determine not primarily his traits but his potentialities; man is distinguished by the remarkable range of his potentialities, most of which the individual never realizes or develops. Our technological society has carried much further the ambiguous tendencies that arose with civilization, which at once widened the range of opportunities for self-realization and for most people narrowed it by a division of labor as well as inequality of opportunity. Young people now have an extraordinary range of choice in profession, habitat, and way of life, while most of them also feel impelled to become specialists and conform to the requirements of a technological society, in an urban environment becoming increasingly uniform. And collective man, always at once creator and creature of his culture, has become both to a more marked extent. While developing immense power to change the environment that shapes his nature, and now more power to change his nature directly, technological man—the most thoroughly conditioned creature of his culture—feels impelled to go on acquiring still more power, however dangerous, and to use it for purposes that many young people find revolting. They have been growing more aware of rich potentialities unrealized in the American way of life. Change is now so rapid that it has taken only a few years to create a wide gap between the generations.

In this view of human nature "alienation" can become more meaningful as a neglect or frustration of higher needs. First I would repeat that it is not a plight peculiar to modern man. By virtue of his plastic nature and his powers of choice, man has always been capable of stupid, perverted, self-defeating, possibly fatal behavior, as his whole history abundantly proves. Yet alienation in modern America is in some respects historically new. It may spring from mechanical routines to which man is not clearly adapted, biologically or psychologically. The many symptoms of it in ordinary people, including the feelings of emptiness and impotence, are quite different from the fatalistic resignation to which the peasant masses were always prone And the very achievements of America, in creating opportunities and incentives for self-fulfillment, have alienated many people because they have higher expectations, make higher demands on their society than people did in the past.

Hence the question now is, are Americans likely to get more alienated in the years ahead? Much will depend on what the nation does about-all its serious problems, including the manmade scene. Whether in particular the many millions of poor, above all the blacks, remain alienated or get more so depends wholly on whether it recognizes its debt to them. Their prospects are dimmer because the problem in my present terms is to improve not merely their material but their spiritual condition, by building up their self-respect, enabling them to have more feeling of dignity, giving them more opportunities for self-fulfillment, bringing them into the society as full-fledged members; and this calls for more patience, humility, tact, and concern for the higher needs than are displayed by either most technologists or most prosperous Americans. While not at all confident that the nation will commit itself to a serious effort to eliminate poverty, discrimination, and social injustice, I take it that at best the problem will not be solved by the year 2000. When dealing with such problems one may realize, as William James did in his later years, that for the purposes of a lifetime human nature isn't so damn plastic after all.

As for the subtler "alienation" of prosperous Americans, I would not venture a prediction. Increasing wealth might fortify their complacence and their hedonistic tendencies, or it might intensify their underlying discontents and anxieties. If the latter, it might produce more violent outbursts of irrationality and inhumanity, or more concern for basic human values and higher human needs. Most likely the affluence will have all these effects on people, and then some, but in proportions impossible to predict with assurance in a society changing so rapidly. All I should say is that our hope lies in the growing awareness of these conflicting tendencies, the persistent criticism of our society, and the characteristic theme of "challenges." Having announced that alienation is "almost total," Erich Fromm nevertheless writes *The Revolution of Hope: Toward a Humanized Technology*. Maslow believes that a "Humanist Revolution" is under way in all fields of thought, with a centering of concern on human needs. Ralph Siu, a fervent technologist, likewise believes that we are on the threshold of an "Age of Holistic Humanism." If so, people may in time grow better adapted to affluence and leisure, as over the ages they have to toil.

At least the symptoms of alienation might lessen the fear that we are headed toward Brave New World. They belie the assumption of Huxley and other critics that people are growing ever more content with their affluence, their mindless role as consumers, or the satisfaction of merely material needs. In this respect "human nature" does appear to be resisting the trend toward Brave New World. But here we run into all the other technological threats to humanistic ideals. In particular they threaten the ideals of individuality and personal freedom, the most obvious basis for resistance to the whole trend.

As I have said, these ideals cannot on the historic record be considered an absolute need of man, or permanent values, but are nevertheless clearly, basic potentialities of human nature. All societies have enabled the individual to achieve some measure of self-fulfillment through the development of skills. Since our own civilization has developed the fullest consciousness of selfhood, the value of self-realization, and then of personal freedom as a necessary means to this end, these possibilities of human life can for us be regarded as among the higher needs of man. "The excellent becomes the permanent," Aristotle observed, "—once seen it is never completely lost." Or in historical terms, human nature is a product of a development that has included some values the human race has hung on to. Hence the widespread alarm over the trend to uniformity and the pressures to conformity is quite "natural" even though it is historically novel. No less natural are the fears of increasing organization. As Roderick Seidenberg sees it, organization breeds organization, it accomplishes what used to be the work of creative individuals, it steadily shrinks the autonomy of the individual, and it moves inexorably toward uniformity and universality, the ideal of frictionless mechanism or perfect efficiency Lewis Mumford agrees that already the foundations have been laid for a society that could produce Seidenberg's "post-historic man," lacking all individuality:

If the goal of human history is a uniform type of man, reproducing at a uniform rate, in a uniform environment, kept at constant temperature, pressure, and humidity, living a uniformly lifeless existence, with his uniform physical needs satisfied by uniform goods, all inner waywardness brought into conformity by hypnotics and sedatives, or by surgical extirpation, a creature under constant mechanical pressure from incubator to incinerator, most of the problems of human development would disappear. Only one problem would remain: Why should anyone, even a machine, bother to keep this kind of creature alive?

There is no immediate prospect, however, of any such uniformity in society or human nature. Granted all the plain pressures against the individual, the signs of resistance to them have become plainer too, especially among the many critical or rebellious young people. If this may be a passing fashion, the individual remains very much alive in ordinary capacities. Even in systems analysis he is still considered real and important as a means of "feedback." Administrators of public welfare programs soon learn . . .that they are not dealing with atomized mass-men, for they run into plenty of positive opinions from spokesmen of local groups or communities, and they make plainest that the technological threats to individuality are not all simply threats.

A planned society need not be totalitarian, and if the experience of the Soviets means anything, it cannot be totally or permanently planned. Karl Mannheim's idea of "planning for freedom" may be questionable, but at least planning is not necessarily fatal to freedom and individuality, any more than would be a program for eliminating poverty; some planners want to get rid of much unnecessary interference with people. Neither, to repeat, is organization necessarily fatal. This is obviously necessary not only for accomplishing the massive action called for by some problems, but for combatting the organizations of vested interests, as the young radicals have discovered. While feeling most strongly that the "Establishment" is hostile to the ideal of self-determination, these radicals are also learning that the old-time uncompromising individualist, or the loner like Thoreau, cannot hope to be effective today, that in organized movements they have to provide for cooperativeness and tolerance of diverse opinion, and that in these movements they can nevertheless enjoy more sense of personal freedom and self-fulfillment. (No class, incidentally, is more addicted to "groupism" than the hippies.) On a national scale the extraordinary number of diverse organizations—public, private, professional—likewise afford the individual opportunities for self-fulfillment, and suggest that the real problem is to develop a different kind of individualist. Nor is rationality or intelligence so blind or ultimately stupid as Seidenberg pictures it. Intelligence can of course be sensitive to its own abuses, just as what men used to call "reason" can be aware of its limitations and its excesses. It is reason or intelligence that warns us against the dangers of organization, the common excesses of technical rationality, the trends toward Brave New World. Human nature as it has developed has some capacity for reasonableness, which is the necessary basis for what hope we can muster.

In any case Seidenberg is looking ahead thousands of years, to a future we need not worry about at the moment. Thus he sees society becoming ever more unified, moving toward a state of complete and permanent stability; but we have to deal with the realities of a divided people and dynamic change, a highly uncertain future. He likewise argues that freedom must disappear for the sake of perfect justice, since injustice would make impossible the frictionless mechanism to which organization aspires; but we still have plenty of social injustice to cope with, for millions of Americans it remains the chief threat to their effective freedom, and we can count indefinitely on ample friction. For such reasons too there is little or no prospect of Brave New World in the near future. Meanwhile it is too easy to blame everything on technology. Our most serious problems are political and moral, strictly up to us. With these problems we could do with more utopian thinking, appealing to the best in the American people, whose tradition has it that human nature can be improved by democratic institutions, or appealing to the many who still are concerned with the higher human needs.

But so far I have been writing with an eye chiefly to the nature of Americans in their man-made scene. For the sake of perspective I wish finally to take a brief look at the rest of mankind, specifically the non-Western world, which remains the most obvious reason why we will not have to worry about Brave New World for a long time to come. It also throws some light on the nature of man, who has grown capable of much more rapid adaptation to change, but at enough biological and psychological cost to make one wonder how much change he can stand. Today the disorders all over the world, including the student revolts, suggest that the whole human race may be facing a crisis.

Herman Kahn and Anthony Wiener forecast that by the year 2000 Japan will have joined the United States and the Western democracies as post-industrial societies; so presumably it will know all the blessings and the problems of affluence. A few countries, including the Soviet Union and several of its satellites, will have reached the early post-industrial stage, and more the mass-consumption stage. But such large countries as China, India, Pakistan, Indonesia, Brazil, and Nigeria, with an estimated total population then of over 3 billion, will still be only partially industrialized and will have a per capita income ranging from only $200 to $600. Behind them will still be most of Africa, two-thirds of the Arab world, and some scattered small countries, with a total population of 750 million, greater than that of the post-industrial countries. Hence an island of wealth will be surrounded by "misery." Although the poor countries will have a higher standard of living, they will be much farther behind the affluent ones than they now are.

This prospect, which will give Americans more trouble than they realize even though they have begun to learn that we have fewer friends in the world than ever, is still not bringing out the best in them. The $30 billion we have spent on aid to pre-industrial countries represent much less than one per cent of the national income, and of late the foreign aid program has been steadily whittled as nominally Christian politicians and voters complain of "give-aways." Apparently they do not know that American business has profited from the program, inasmuch as about 80 per cent of the aid is spent here. Now more of it is being tied to exports, while seldom giving the poor countries better opportunities to export their products. Although the disappointing results of the aid program have been largely due to the common inefficiency and corruption of government in the poor nations, and the selfishness of their wealthy class, they have also been due to politics at home. Backed by Congress, our aid missions have usually favored industrialization projects more than projects for improving agriculture; these might lead to competition with U.S. farm products. In short, Uncle Sam has been neither the Santa Claus nor the sucker portrayed in cartoons. Not to mention that a people very proud of their own Revolution remain about the least capable of understanding or tolerating revolutions in the rest of the world.

I shall not go into the staggering economic and political problems of the new nations, except to say that they cannot be solved by any magic of free private enterprise, or merely economic rationality. My concern here is some questions raised by their recognition of the goods of modern technology, their confirmation of its apparently irresistible drive, and the consequences of their efforts to modernize, in the name of "progress." They have already made enough progress to produce a growing uniformity, immediately recognizable in their airports and in the new buildings and boulevards of their capitals. Industrial societies are bound to be much more alike than agricultural, handicraft societies. Railroads, automobiles, cement factories, steel mills, power plants, and all kinds of machinery and machine products are everywhere basically the same, alike under Communism or capitalism. People grown used to them might be expected to be more alike.

Yet industrialism by no means requires the total elimination of traditional cultures. When Japan, for example, developed a factory system, it was quite different from the American system. A worker employed by a company assumed he would work for it the rest of his life and would not quit to take a higher paid job in another factory, while the company felt as obligated to him, only under extreme circumstances discharging him or even laying him off temporarily. Still by far the most successful of the non-Western countries in modernizing, Japan accordingly refutes the assumption of Jacques Ellul that technology is wholly autonomous and automatically imposes its requirements. In India, where Nehru gave up Gandhi's opposition to industrialism, leaders are still trying to adapt it to their traditional culture; some resent the term "underdeveloped" because it implies that economic growth and technological advance are the supreme goals for a nation. Although leaders are typically eager to modernize, few of the non-Western peoples set such store by economic values as Americans do, or assume that economic motives are the most powerful. [Americans might be bewildered by the attitude of peasants in Java. When the price of coconuts goes up, they are likely to bring fewer instead of more coconuts to market, for the sensible reason that the higher price makes it unnecessary for them to work as hard to satisfy their needs.] They are not simply awed either by American know-how or modes of efficiency, which are usually not suited to their culture and environment.

For such reasons they are likely to be handicapped in industrializing, especially because their traditional ways often conflict with the regular habits and technical rationality it requires. Nevertheless their leaders also have a potential advantage in being aware of the evils that can come with it. Although most of them now tend to be arrogant and short-sighted in the exercise of their new powers, the "developing" nations (to use the politer term) may hope to escape the inhumanity of early or "palaeolithic" industrialism, and to retain more respect for esthetic and other human values than most Americans appear to have. Kahn and Wiener, who remarked that the "Sensate" culture of the West has been spreading over the whole world, consider it an open question whether this trend will continue in the next generation. The tendencies to "Late Sensate" are certainly much less conspicuous in the non-Western world.

In the very long run, if or when all countries reach the post-industrial stage, I suppose it is conceivable that there might be an almost complete uniformity, and "human nature" will everywhere be more literally the same. Even by the year 2000 there may be a considerable degree of drab uniformity, especially if television "unifies" peoples. In my own travels abroad I have been mostly depressed by the changes that have taken place in just thirty years, because of both technology and tourism. Yet it seems to me unlikely that the world will ever have but one culture, any more than that all people will speak the same language and worship the same God. Countries with advanced technology can still retain much of their traditional culture and have different styles of living, as European countries do; my generalizations about the nature of Americans and their man-made scene would not all apply in Europe. In the non-Western world an intense nationalism—a sentiment that Americans think of as just human nature, but that was actually acquired under Western domination—creates a more conscious pride in traditional values or native variations, and strengthens a resolve to be not just like Americans.

Unfortunately it also heightens the dangers of war—the all too real possibility that there may be no long run for modern man. The non-Western world throws into relief the most tragic aspect of the failures of America in its professed role as leader of the "free world." As an Italian historian remarked to Walter Lippmann, we have come down off the pedestal and entered history, joined all the other nations that have insoluble problems and suffer defeats; yet the tragedy remains that there is no nation clearly fit to take our place or carry the torch for the non-Western world. Despite de Gaulle's dreams of *gloire,* France is no more ready or able than Great Britain, West Germany, or Japan. The Soviet Union still adheres to a narrow conception of its own national interests; it antagonized most of the world by its ruthless suppression of the Czechs. The future may belong to teeming China, but who would now look to it for world leadership? Or to India, Pakistan, Indonesia, Egypt, Nigeria? By the year 2000 there will no doubt be surprising changes in the status and the alignment of nations, but the critical period is the coming generation, during which the danger of a nuclear explosion will be most acute; and as we face it, the fact is that no nation on earth has both the material means and the will to provide the enlightened aid needed by the poor countries.

Otherwise the plainest lesson for Americans in the turbulent drama of the non-Western world is the need of not only more sympathetic understanding of the different ways of other peoples, but more self-understanding, a more critical attitude toward their own accepted values and notions of the good life, or simply more awareness that their own nature is not just human nature, their ways are too often a perversion or defiance of the developed higher needs of man. Else there is also a real possibility that America—the pace-setter in technology, and the country in which above all it has run wild—may go down as the greatest failure in history, or that it will be spared this ignominy only because history will have come to an end.

AUTHORITARIAN AND DEMOCRATIC TECHNICS

LEWIS MUMFORD

Lewis Mumford (1895-1970), an outstanding social critic, philosopher, journalist, and historian, has written a four volume philosophy of civilization. The first volume, *Technics and Civilization,* is considered a classic. Other outstanding works of his include *The City in History* (1961), *Technics and Human Development* (1967) and *The Pentagon of Power 1970).*

This paper, first presented at a convocation of the Fund for the Republic, was published in *Technology and Culture (Vol. V, No. 1).*

1. Differentiate between what Mumford calls authoritarian and democratic technics and give examples of each. Which is preferable and why? Does the preference have universal application?

2. How can the preferred technics be maximized?

3. According to Mumford, what caused the development of authoritarian technics? What may be the final consequences of their spread?

4. How does Mumford see technology as affecting the individual?

5. How does Mumford's view on technology differ from Muller's? From Vannevar Bush's?

AUTHORITARIAN AND DEMOCRATIC TECHNICS

LEWIS MUMFORD

"Democracy" is a term now confused and sophisticated by indiscriminate use, and often treated with patronizing contempt. Can we agree, no matter how far we might diverge at a later point, that the spinal principle of democracy is to place what is common to all men above that which any organization, institution, or group may claim for itself? This is not to deny the claims of superior natural endowment, specialized knowledge, technical skill, or institutional organization: all these may, by democratic permission, play a useful role in the human economy. But democracy consists in giving final authority to the whole, rather than the part; and only living human beings, as such, are an authentic expression of the whole, whether acting alone or with the help of others.

Around this central principle clusters a group of related ideas and practices with a long foreground in history, though they are not always present, or present in equal amounts, in all societies. Among these items are communal self-government, free communication as between equals, unimpeded access to the common store of knowledge, protection against arbitrary external controls, and a sense of individual moral responsibility for behavior that affects the whole community. All living organisms are in some degree autonomous, in that they follow a life-pattern of their own; but in man this autonomy is an essential condition for his further development. We surrender some of our autonomy when ill or crippled: but to surrender it every day on every occasion would be to turn life itself into a chronic illness. The best life possible—and here I am consciously treading on contested ground—is one that calls for an ever greater degree of self-direction, self-expression, and self-realization. In this sense, personality, once the exclusive attribute of kings, belongs on democratic theory to every man. Life itself in its fullness and wholeness cannot be delegated.

In framing this provisional definition I trust that I have not, for the sake of agreement, left out anything important. Democracy, in the primal sense I shall use the term, is necessarily most visible in relatively small communities and groups. whose members meet frequently face to face, interact freely, and are known to each other as persons. As soon as large numbers are involved, democratic association must be supplemented by a more abstract, depersonalized form. Historical experience shows that it is much easier to wipe out democracy by an institutional arrangement that gives authority only to those at the apex of the social hierarchy than it is to incorporate democratic practices into a well-organized system under centralized direction. which achieves the highest degree of mechanical efficiency when those who work it have no mind or purpose of their own.

The tension between small-scale association and large-scale organization. between personal autonomy and institutional regulation, between remote control and diffused local intervention, has now created a critical situation. If our eyes had been open, we might long ago have discovered this conflict deeply embedded in technology itself.

I wish it were possible to characterize technics with as much hope of getting assent, with whatever quizzical reserves you may still have, as in this description of democracy. But the very title of this paper is, I confess, a controversial one; and I cannot go far in my analysis without drawing on interpretations that have not yet been adequately published, still less widely discussed or rigorously criticized and evaluated. My thesis, to put it bluntly, is that from late neolithic times in the Near East, right down to our own day, two technologies have recurrently existed side by side: one authoritarian, the other democratic, the first system-centered, immensely powerful, but inherently unstable, the other man-centered, relatively weak, but resourceful and durable. If I am right, we are now rapidly approaching a point at which, unless we radically alter our present course, our surviving democratic technics will be completely suppressed or supplanted, so that every residual autonomy will be wiped out, or will be permitted only as a playful device of government, like national balloting for already chosen leaders in totalitarian countries.

The data on which this thesis is based are familiar; but their significance has, I believe, been overlooked. What I would call democratic technics is the small-scale method of production, resting mainly on human skill and animal energy but always, even when employing machines, remaining under the active direction of the craftsman or the farmer, each group developing its own gifts, through appropriate arts and social ceremonies, as well as making discreet use of the gifts of nature. This technology had limited horizons of achievement, but, just because of its wide diffusion and its modest demands, it had great powers of adaptation and recuperation. This democratic technics has underpinned and firmly supported every historical culture until our own day, and redeemed the constant tendency of authoritarian technics to misapply its powers. Even when paying tribute to the most oppressive authoritarian regimes, there yet remained within the workshop or the farmyard some degree of autonomy, selectivity, creativity. No royal mace, no slave-driver's whip, no bureaucratic directive left its imprint on the textiles of Damascus or the pottery of fifth-century Athens.

If this democratic technics goes back to the earliest use of tools, authoritarian technics is a much more recent achievement: it begins around the fourth millennium B.C. in a new configuration of technical invention, scientific observation, and centralized political control that gave rise to the peculiar mode of life we may now identify, without eulogy, as civilization. Under the new institution of kingship, activities that had been scattered, diversified. cut to the human measure, were united on a monumental scale into an entirely new kind of theological-technological mass organization. In the person of an absolute ruler, whose word was law, cosmic powers came down to earth, mobilizing and unifying the efforts of thousands of men, hitherto all-too autonomous and too decentralized to act voluntarily in unison for purposes that lay beyond the village horizon.

The new authoritarian technology was not limited by village custom or human sentiment: its herculean feats of mechanical organization rested on ruthless physical coercion. forced labor and slavery, which brought into existence machines that were capable of exerting thousands of horsepower centuries before horses were harnessed or wheels invented. This centralized technics drew on inventions and scientific discoveries of a high order: the written record, mathematics and astronomy, irrigation and canalization: above all, it created complex human machines composed of specialized, standardized, replaceable, interdependent parts—the work army, the military army, the bureaucracy. These work armies and military armies raised the ceiling of human achievement: the first in mass construction, the second in mass destruction, both on a scale hitherto inconceivable. Despite its constant drive to destruction, this totalitarian technics was tolerated, perhaps even welcomed, in home territory, for it created the first economy of controlled abundance: notably, immense food crops that not merely supported a big urban population but released a large trained minority for purely religious. scientific, bureaucratic, or military activity. But the efficiency of the system was impaired by weaknesses that were never overcome until our own day.

To begin with, the democratic economy of the agricultural village resisted incorporation into the new authoritarian system. So even the Roman Empire found it expedient, once resistance was broken and taxes were collected to consent to a large degree of local autonomy in religion and government. Moreover, as long as agriculture absorbed the labor of some 90 per cent of the population, mass technics were confined largely to the populous urban centers. Since authoritarian technics first took form in an age when metals were scarce and human raw material, captured in war, was easily convertible into machines, its directors never bothered to invent inorganic mechanical substitutes. But there were even greater weaknesses: the system had no inner coherence: a break in communication, a missing link in the chain of command, and the great human machines fell apart. Finally, the myths upon which the whole system was based—particularly the essential myth of kingship—were irrational, with their paranoid suspicions and animosities and their paranoid claims to unconditional obedience and absolute power. For all its redoubtable constructive achievements, authoritarian technics expressed a deep hostility to life.

By now you doubtless see the point of this brief historical excursus. That authoritarian technics has come back today in an immensely magnified and adroitly perfected form. Up to now, following the optimistic premises of nineteenth-century thinkers like Auguste Comte and Herbert Spencer, we have regarded the spread of experimental science and mechanical invention as the soundest guarantee of a peaceful, productive, above all democratic, industrial society. Many have even comfortably supposed that the revolt against arbitrary political power in the seventeenth century was causally connected with the industrial revolution that accompanied it. But what we have interpreted as the new freedom now turns out to be a much more sophisticated version of the old slavery: for the rise of political democracy during the last few centuries has been increasingly nullified by the successful resurrection of a centralized authoritarian technics—a technics that had in fact for long lapsed in many parts of the world.

Let us fool ourselves no longer. At the very moment Western nations threw off the ancient regime of absolute government, operating under a once-divine king, they were restoring this same system in a far more effective form in their technology, reintroducing coercions of a military character no less strict in the organization of a factory than in that of the new drilled, uniformed, and regimented army. During the transitional stages of the last two centuries, the ultimate tendency of this system might be in doubt, for in many areas there were strong democratic reactions; but with the knitting together of a scientific ideology, itself liberated from theological restrictions or humanistic purposes, authoritarian technics found an instrument at hand that has now given it absolute command of physical energies of cosmic dimensions. The inventors of nuclear bombs, space rockets. and computers are the pyramid builders of our own age: psychologically inflated by a similar myth of unqualified power, boasting through their science of their increasing omnipotence, if not omniscience. moved by obsessions and compulsions no less irrational than those of earlier absolute systems: particularly the notion that the system itself must be expanded, at whatever eventual cost to life.

Through mechanization, automation, cybernetic direction, this authoritarian technics has at last successfully overcome its most serious weakness: its original dependence upon resistant, sometimes actively disobedient servomechanisms, still human enough to harbor. purposes that do not always coincide with those of the system.

Like the earliest form of authoritarian technics, this new technology is marvelously dynamic and productive: its power in every form tends to increase without limits, in quantities that defy assimilation and defeat control. whether we are thinking of the output of scientific knowledge or of industrial assembly lines. To maximize energy, speed, or automation, without reference to the complex conditions that sustain organic life, have become ends in themselves. As with the earliest forms of authoritarian technics, the weight of effort, if one is to judge by national budgets, is toward absolute instruments of destruction, designed for absolutely irrational purposes whose chief by-product would be the mutilation or extermination of the human race. Even Ashurbanipal and Genghis Khan performed their gory operations under normal human limits.

The center of authority in this new system is no longer a visible personality, an all-powerful king: even in totalitarian dictatorships the center now lies in the system itself, invisible but omnipresent: all its human components, even the technical and managerial elite, even the sacred priesthood of science, who alone have access to the secret knowledge by means of which total control is now swiftly being effected, are themselves trapped by the very perfection of the organization they have invented. Like the pharaohs of the Pyramid Age, these servants of the system identify its goods with their own kind of well-being: as with the divine king, their praise of the system is an act of self-worship; and again like the king, they are in the grip of an irrational compulsion to extend their means of control and expand the scope of their authority. In this new systems-centered collective, this Pentagon of power, there is no visible presence who issues commands: unlike Job's God, the new deities cannot be confronted, still less defied. Under the pretext of saving labor, the ultimate end of this technics is to displace life, or rather, to transfer the attributes of life to the machine and the mechanical collective, allowing only so much of the organism to remain as may be controlled and manipulated.

Do not misunderstand this analysis. The danger to democracy does not spring from any specific scientific discoveries or electronic inventions. The human compulsions that dominate the authoritarian technics of our own day date back to a period before even the wheel had been invented. The danger springs from the fact that, since Francis Bacon and Galileo defined the new methods and objectives of technics, our great physical transformations have been effected by a system that deliberately eliminates the whole human personality, ignores the historical process, overplays the role of the abstract intelligence, and makes control over physical nature, ultimately control over man himself, the chief purpose of existence. This system has made its way so insidiously into Western society that my analysis of its derivation and its intentions may well seem more questionable—indeed more shocking—than the facts themselves.

Why has our age surrendered so easily to the controllers, the manipulators, the conditioners of an authoritarian technics? The answer to this question is both paradoxical and ironic. Present-day technics differs from that of the overtly brutal, half-baked authoritarian systems of the past in one highly favorable particular: it has accepted the basic principle of democracy, that every member of society should have a share in its goods. By progressively fulfilling this part of the democratic promise, our system has achieved a hold over the whole community that threatens to wipe out every other vestige of democracy.

The bargain we are being asked to ratify takes the form of a magnificent bribe. Under the democratic-authoritarian social contract, each member of the community may claim every material advantage, every intellectual and emotional stimulus he may desire, in quantities hardly available hitherto even for a restricted minority: food, housing, swift transportation, instantaneous communication, medical care, entertainment, education. But on one condition: that one must not merely ask for nothing that the system does not provide, but likewise agree to take everything offered, duly processed and fabricated, homogenized and equalized, in the precise quantities that the system, rather than the person, requires. Once one opts for the system no further choice remains. In a word, if one surrenders one's life at source, authoritarian technics will give back as much of it as can be mechanically graded, quantitatively multiplied, collectively manipulated and magnified.

"Is this not a fair bargain?" those who speak for the system will ask. "Are not the goods authoritarian technics promises real goods? Is this not the horn of plenty that mankind has long dreamed of, and that every ruling class has tried to secure, at whatever cost of brutality and injustice, for itself?" I would not belittle, still less deny, the many admirable products this technology has brought forth, products that a self-regulating economy would make good use of. I would only suggest that it is time to reckon up the human disadvantages and costs, to say nothing of the dangers, of our unqualified acceptance of the system itself. Even the immediate price is heavy; for the system is so far from being under effective human direction that it may poison us wholesale to provide us with food or exterminate us to provide national security, before we can enjoy its promised goods. Is it really humanly profitable to give up the possibility of living a few years at Walden Pond, so to say, for the privilege of spending a lifetime in *Walden Two*? Once our authoritarian technics consolidates its powers, with the aid of its new forms of mass control, its panoply of tranquilizers and sedatives and aphrodisiacs, could democracy in any form survive? That question is absurd: life itself will not survive, except what is funneled through the mechanical collective. The spread of a sterilized scientific intelligence over the planet would not, as Teilhard de Chardin so innocently imagined, be the happy consummation of divine purpose: it would rather ensure the final arrest of any further human development.

Again: do not mistake my meaning. This is not a prediction of what *will* happen, but a warning against what *may* happen.

What means must be taken to escape this fate? In characterizing the authoritarian technics that has begun to dominate us, I have not forgotten the great lesson of history: prepare for the unexpected! Nor do I overlook the immense reserves of vitality and creativity that a more humane democratic tradition still offers us. What I wish to do is to persuade those who are concerned with maintaining democratic institutions to see that their constructive efforts must include technology itself. There, too, we must return to the human center. We must challenge this authoritarian system that has given to an under-dimensioned ideology and technology the authority that belongs to the human personality. I repeat: life cannot be delegated.

Curiously, the first words in support of this thesis came forth, with exquisite symbolic aptness, from a willing agent—but very nearly a classic victim!—of the new authoritarian technics. They came from the astronaut, John Glenn, whose life was endangered by the malfunctioning of his automatic controls, operated from a remote center. After he barely saved his life by personal intervention, he emerged from his space capsule with these ringing words; "Now let man take over!"

That command is easier to utter than obey. But if we are not to be driven to even more drastic measures than Samuel Butler suggested in *Erewhon,* we had better map out a more positive course: namely, the reconstitution of both our science and our technics in such a fashion as to insert the rejected parts of the human personality at every stage in the process. This means gladly sacrificing mere quantity in order to restore qualitative choice, shifting the seat of authority from the mechanical collective to the human personality and the autonomous group, favoring variety and ecological complexity, instead of stressing undue uniformity and standardization, above all, reducing the insensate drive to extend the system itself, instead of containing it within definite human limits and thus releasing man himself for other purposes. We must ask, not what is good for science or technology, still less what is good for General Motors or Union Carbide or IBM or the Pentagon, but what is good for man: not machine-conditioned, system-regulated, mass-man, but man in person, moving freely over every area of life.

There are large areas of technology that can be redeemed by the democratic process, once we have overcome the infantile compulsions and automatism that now threaten to cancel out our real gains. The very leisure that the machine now gives in advanced countries can be profitably used, not for further commitment to still other kinds of machine, furnishing automatic recreation, but by doing significant forms of work, unprofitable or technically impossible under mass production: work dependent upon special skill, knowledge, aesthetic sense. The do-it-yourself movement prematurely got bogged down in an attempt to sell still more machines; but its slogan pointed in the right direction, provided we still have a self to do it with. The glut of motor cars that is now destroying our cities can be coped with only if we redesign our cities to make fuller use of a more efficient human agent: the walker. Even in childbirth, the emphasis is already happily shifting from an officious, often lethal. authoritarian procedure, centered in hospital routine. to a more human mode, which restores initiative to the mother and to the body's natural rhythms.

The replenishment of democratic technics is plainly too big a subject to be handled in a final sentence or two: but I trust I have made it clear that the genuine advantages our scientifically based technics has brought can be preserved only if we cut the whole system back to a point at which it will permit human alternatives, human interventions, and human destinations for entirely different purposes from those of the system itself. At the present juncture, if democracy did not exist, we would have to invent it, in order to save and recultivate the spirit of man.

THE TECHNOLOGICAL ORDER

JACQUES ELLUL
Translated from the French by John Wilkinson

Jacques Ellul (1912-   ) is Professor of History and Contemporary Sociology at the University of Bordeaux in France.   He is also a prominent Protestant layman who has been active in the ecumenical movement.   In his writings, he has produced a powerful critique of technology which each of us needs to consider because it says a great deal about our freedom in a technological society.

1.   What negative characteristics does technology have according to Ellul? Consider these characteristics carefully; they are not easy to understand. What examples of each can you identify in modern society?

2.   From Ellul's point of view, why does technology destroy human values?

3.   What does Ellul say can be done to avoid the negative consequences of technology?   Do you agree?   If not, what do you think can be done to avoid the negative aspects of technology that Ellul identifies?

4.   Can technological progress ever be good according to Ellul?   Do you agree?

5.   Why does technology create change?   What type of changes does technology create?

THE TECHNOLOGICAL ORDER

JACQUES ELLUL

I.   I refer the reader to my book *The Technological Society* for an account of my general theses on this subject. I shall confine myself here to recapitulating the points which seem to me to be essential to a sociological study of the problem:

1.   Technique has become the new and specific milieu in which man is required to exist, one which has supplanted the old milieu, namely, that of nature.

2.   This new technical milieu has the following characteristics:
   a. It is artificial;
   b. It is autonomous with respect to values, ideas, and the state;
   c. It is self-determining in a closed circle. Like nature, it is a closed organization which permits it to be self-determinative independently of all human intervention;
   d. It grows according to a process which is causal but not directed to ends;
   e. It is formed by an accumulation of means which have established primacy over ends;
   f. All its parts are mutually implicated to such a degree that it is impossible to separate them or to settle any technical problem in isolation.

3.   The development of the individual techniques is an "ambivalent" phenomenon.

4.   Since Technique has become the new milieu, all social phenomena are situated in it. It is incorrect to say that economics, politics, and the sphere of the cultural are influenced or modified *by* Technique; they are rather situated in it, a novel situation modifying all traditional social concepts. Politics, for example, is not modified by Technique as one factor among others which operate upon it; the political world is today *defined* through its relation to the technological society. Traditionally. politics formed a part of a larger social whole; at the present the converse is the case.

5.   Technique comprises organizational and psychosociological techniques. It is useless to hope that the use of techniques of organization will succeed in compensating for the effects of techniques in general; or that the use of psychosociological techniques will assure mankind ascendancy over the technical phenomenon. In the former case, we will doubtless succeed in averting certain technically induced crises, disorders, and serious social disequilibrations; but this will but confirm the fact that Technique constitutes a closed circle. In the latter case, we will secure human psychic equilibrium in the technological milieu by avoiding the psychobiologic pathology resulting from the individual techniques taken singly and thereby attain a certain happiness. But these results will come about through the *adaptation of human beings to the technical milieu.* Psychosociological techniques result in the *modification* of men in order to render them happily subordinate to their new environment, and by no means imply any kind of human domination over Technique.

6.   The ideas, judgments, beliefs, and myths of the man of today have already been essentially modified by his technical milieu. It is no longer possible to reflect that, on the one hand, there are techniques which may or may not have

an effect on the human being; and, on the other, there is the human being himself who is to attempt to invent means to master his techniques and subordinate them to his own ends by *making a choice* among them. Choices and ends are both based on beliefs, sociological presuppositions, and myths which are a function of the technological society. Modern man's state of mind is completely dominated by technical values, and his goals are represented only by such progress and happiness as is to be achieved through techniques. Modern man in choosing is already incorporated within the technical process and modified in his nature by it. He is no longer in his traditional state of freedom with respect to judgment and choice.

II. To understand the problem posed to us, it is first of all requisite to disembarrass ourselves of certain fake problems.

1. We make too much of the disagreeable features of technical development—for example, urban overcrowding, nervous tension, air pollution, and so forth. I am convinced that all such inconveniences will be done away with by the ongoing evolution of Technique itself, and indeed, that it is only by means of such evolution that this can happen. The inconveniences we emphasize are always dependent on technical solutions, and it is only by means of techniques that they can be solved. This fact leads to the following two considerations:

   a. Every solution to some technical inconvenience is able only to reinforce the system of techniques *in their ensemble;*
   b. Enmeshed in a process of technical development like our own, the possibilities of human survival are better served by more technique than less, a fact which contributes nothing, however, to the resolution of the basic problem.

2. We hear too often that morals are being threatened by the growth of our techniques. For example, we hear of greater moral decadence in those environments most directly affected technically—say, in working class or urbanized milieux. We hear, too, of familial disintegration as a function of techniques. The falseness of this problem consists in contrasting the technological environment with the moral values inculcated by Society itself. The presumed opposition between ethical problematics and technological systematics probably at the present is, and certainly in the long run will be, false. The traditional ethical milieu and the traditional moral values are admittedly in process of disappearing, and we are witnessing the creation of a *new* technological ethics with its own values. We are witnessing the evolution of a morally consistent system of imperatives and virtues, which tends to replace the traditional system. But man is not necessarily left thereby on a morally inferior level, although a moral relativism is indeed implied—an attitude according to which everything is well, *provided* that the individual obeys some ethic or other. We *could* contest the value of this development *if* we had a clear and adequate concept of what good-in-itself is. But such judgments are impossible on the basis of our general morality. On that level, what we are getting is merely a substitution of a new technological morality for a traditional one which Technique has rendered obsolete.

3. We dread the "sterilization" of art through technique. We hear of the artist's lack of freedom, calm, and the impossibility of meditation in the

technological society. This problem is no more real than the two preceding. On the contrary, the best artistic production of the present is a result of a close connection between art and Technique. Naturally, new artistic form, expression, and ethic are implied, but this fact does not make art less art than what we traditionally called such. What assuredly is *not* art is a fixation in congealed forms, and a rejection of technical evolution as exemplified, say, in the neoclassicism of the nineteenth century or in present-day "socialist realism." The modern cinema furnishes an artistic response comparable to the Greek theater at its best; and modern music, painting, and poetry express, not a canker, but an authentic esthetic expression of mankind plunged into a new technical milieu.

4.   One last example of a false problem is our fear that the technological society is completely *eliminating* instinctive human values and powers. It is held that systematization, organization, "rationalized" conditions of labor, overly hygienic living conditions, and the like have a tendency to repress the forces of instinct. For some people the phenomenon of "beatniks," *"blousons noirs,"* and "hooligans" is explained by youth's violent reaction and the protestation of youth's vital force to a society which is overorganized, overordered, overregulated, in short, technicized. But here too, even if the facts are established beyond question, it is very likely that a superior conception of the technological society will result in the integration *of* these instinctive, creative, and vital forces. Compensatory mechanisms an already coming into play; the increasing appreciation of the aesthetic eroticism of authors like Henry Miller and the rehabilitation of the Marquis de Sade are good examples. The same holds for music like the new jazz forms which are "escapist" and exaltative of instinct; *item*, the latest dances. All these things represent a process of *"defoulement"* which is finding its place in the technological society. In the same way, we are beginning to understand that it is impossible indefinitely to repress or expel religious tendencies and to bring the human race to a perfect rationality. Our fears for our instincts *are* justified to the degree that Technique, instead of provoking conflict, tends rather to *absorb* it, and to *integrate* instinctive and religious forces by giving them a place within its structure, whether it be by an adaptation of Christianity or by the creation of new religious expressions like myths and mystiques which are in full compatibility with the technological society. The Russians have gone farthest in creating a "religion" compatible with Technique by means of their transformation of communism into a religion.

III. What, then, is the real problem posed to men by the development of the technological society? It comprises two parts: 1. Is man able to remain master in a world of means?   2. Can a new civilization appear inclusive of Technique?

1.   The answer to the first question, and the one most often encountered, seems obvious: Man, who exploits the ensemble of means, is the master of them. Unfortunately, this manner of viewing matters is purely theoretical and superficial. We must remember the autonomous character of Technique. We must likewise not lose sight of the fact that the human individual himself is to an ever greater degree the *object of* certain techniques and their procedures. He is the object *of* pedagogical techniques, psychotechniques, vocational guidance testing, personality and intelligence testing, industrial and group aptitude testing, and so on. In these cases (and in countless others) most men are treated as a collection of objects. But, it might be objected, these techniques are exploited

by other men, and the exploiters at least remain masters. In a certain sense this is true; the exploiters are masters of the particular techniques they exploit. But they, too, are subjected to the action of yet other techniques—as, for example, propaganda. Above all, they are spiritually taken over by the technological society; they believe in what they do; they are the most fervent adepts of that society. They themselves have been profoundly technicized. They never in any way affect *to* despise Technique, which *to* them is a thing good in itself. They never pretend *to* assign values *to* Technique, which *to* them is in itself an entity working out its own ends. They never claim to subordinate it to any value because for them Technique is value.

It may be objected that these individual techniques have as their end the best adaptation *of* the individual, the best utilization *of* his abilities, and, in the long run, his happiness. This, in effect, is the objective and the justification *of* all techniques. (One ought not, *of* course, to confound man's "happiness" with capacity for mastery with, say, freedom.) If the first of all values is happiness, it is likely that man, thanks to his techniques, will be in a position to attain to a certain state *of* this good. But happiness does not contain everything it is thought to contain, and the *absolute disparity between happiness and freedom* remains an ever real theme for our reflections. To say that man should remain *subject* rather than *object* in the technological society means two things—namely, that he be capable of giving direction and orientation to Technique, and that, to this end, he be able to master it.

Up to the present he has been able to do neither. As to the first, he is content passively to participate in technical progress, to accept whatever direction it takes automatically, and to admit its autonomous meaning. In the circumstances he can either proclaim that life is an absurdity without meaning or value; *or* he can predicate a number of indefinitely sophisticated values. But neither attitude accords with the fact of the technical phenomenon any more than it does with the other. Modern declarations of the absurdity of life are not based on modern technological efflorescence. which none (least of all the existentialists) think an absurdity. And the predication of values is a purely theoretical matter, since these values are not equipped with any means for putting them into practice. It is easy to reach agreement on what they are, but it is quite another matter to make them have any effect whatever on the technological society, or to cause them to be accepted in such a way that techniques must evolve in order to realize them. The values spoken of in the technological society are simply there to justify what is; *or* they are generalities without consequence; *or* technical progress realizes them automatically as a matter of course. Put otherwise, neither of the above alternatives is to be taken seriously.

The second condition *that man be subject rather than object*—that is, the imperative that he exercise mastery over technical development—is facilely accepted by everyone. But factually it simply does not hold. Even more embarrassing than the question How? is the question Who? We must ask ourselves realistically and concretely just who is in a position to choose the values which give Technique its justification and to exert mastery over it. If such a person or persons are to be found, it must be in the Western world (inclusive of Russia). They certainly are not to be discovered in the bulk of the world's population which inhabits Africa and Asia, who are, as yet, scarcely confronted by technical problems, and who, in any case, are even less aware of the questions involved than we are.

Is the arbiter we seek to be found among the *philosophers,* those thinking specialists? We well know the small influence these gentry exert upon our society, and how the technicians of every order distrust them and rightly refuse to take their reveries seriously. Even if the philosopher could make his voice heard, he would still have to contrive means of mass education so as to communicate an effective message to the masses.

Can the *technician* himself assume mastery over Technique? The trouble here is that the technician is *always* a specialist and cannot make the slightest claim to have mastered any technique but his own. Those for whom Technique bears its meaning in itself will scarcely discover the values which lend meaning to what they are doing. They will not even look for them. The only thing they can do is to apply their technical specialty and assist in its refinement. They cannot in *principle* dominate the totality *of* the technical problem or envisage it in its global dimensions. *Ergo,* they are completely incapable *of* mastering it.

Can the *scientist* do it? There, *if* anywhere, is the great hope. Does not the scientist dominate our techniques? Is he not an intellectual inclined and fit to put basic questions? Unfortunately, we are obliged to re-examine our hopes here when we look at things as they are. We see quickly enough that the scientist is as specialized as the technician, as incapable of general ideas, and as much out of commission as the philosopher. Think of the scientists who, on one tack or another, have addressed themselves to the technical phenomenon: Einstein, Oppenheimer, Carrel. It is only too clear that the ideas these gentlemen have advanced in the sphere of the philosophic or the spiritual are vague, superficial, and contradictory *in extremis.* They really ought to stick to warnings and proclamations for, as soon as they assay anything else, the other scientists and the technicians rightly refuse to take them seriously, and they even run the risk of losing their reputations as scientists.

Can the *politician* bring it off? In the democracies the politicians are subject to the wishes of their constituents who are primarily concerned with the happiness and well-being which they think Technique assures them. Moreover, the further we get on, the more a conflict shapes up between the politicians and the technicians. We cannot here go into the matter which is just beginning to be the object of serious study. But it would appear that the power of the politician is being (and will continue to be) outclassed by the power of the technician in modern states. Only dictatorships can impose their will on technical evolution. But, on the one hand, human freedom would gain nothing thereby, and, on the other, a dictatorship thirsty for power has no recourse at all but to push toward an excessive development *of* various techniques at its disposal.

Any of us? An individual can doubtless seek the soundest attitude to dominate the techniques at his disposal. He can inquire after the values to impose on techniques in his use of them, and search out the way to follow in order to remain a man in the fullest sense of the word within a technological society. All this is extremely difficult, but it is far from being useless, since it is apparently the only solution presently possible. But the individual's efforts are powerless to resolve in any way the technical problem in its universality; to accomplish this would mean that *all* men adopt the same values and the same behavior.

2.   The second real problem posed by the technological society is whether or not a new civilization can appear which is inclusive of Technique. The elements of this question are as difficult as those of the first. It would obviously be vain to deny all the things that can contribute something useful to a new civilization: security, ease of living, social solidarity, shortening of the work week, social security, and so forth. But a civilization in the strictest sense of the term is not brought into being by all these things.

A threefold contradiction resides between civilization and Technique of which we must be aware if we are to approach the problem correctly:

a.   The technical world is the world of material things; it is put together out of material things and with respect to them. When Technique displays any interest in man, it does so by converting him into a material object. The supreme and final authority in the technological society is fact, at once ground and evidence. And when we think on man as he exists in this society it can only be as a being immersed in a universe of objects, machines, and innumerable material things. Technique indeed guarantees him such material happiness as material objects can. But, the technical society is not, and cannot be, a genuinely humanist society since it puts in first place not man but material things. It can only act on man by lessening him and putting him in the way of the quantitative. The radical contradiction referred to exists between technical perfection and human development because such perfection is only to be achieved through quantitative development and necessarily aims exclusively at what is measurable. Human excellence, on the contrary, is of the domain of the qualitative and aims at what is not measurable. Space is lacking here to argue the point that spiritual values cannot evolve as a function of material improvement. The transition from the technically quantitative to the humanly qualitative is an impossible one. In our times, technical growth monopolizes all human forces, passions, intelligences, and virtues in such a way that it is in practice nigh impossible to seek and find anywhere any distinctively human excellence. And if this search is impossible, there cannot be any civilization in the proper sense of the term.

b.   Technical growth leads to a growth of power in the sense of technical means incomparably more effective than anything ever before invented, power which has as its object only power, in the widest sense of the word. The possibility of action becomes limitless and absolute. For example, we are confronted for the first time with the possibility of the annihilation of all life on earth, since we have the means to accomplish it. In every sphere of action we are faced with just such absolute possibilities. Again, by way of example, governmental techniques, which amalgamate organizational, psychological, and police techniques, tend to lend to government absolute powers. And here I must emphasize a great law which I believe to be essential to the comprehension of the world in which we live—namely, that when power becomes absolute, values disappear. When man is able to accomplish anything at all, there is no value which can be proposed to him; when the means of action are absolute, no goal of action is imaginable. Power eliminates in proportion to its growth, the boundary between good and evil, between the just and the unjust. We are familiar enough with this phenomenon in totalitarian societies. The distinction between good and evil disappears beginning with the moment that the ground of action (for example, the *raison d'etre,* or the instinct of the proletariat) claims to have absolute power and thus to incorporate *ipso facto* all value. Thus it is that the growth of technical means tending to absolutism forbids the appearance of values, and condemns to sterility our search for the ethical and the spiritual. Again, where Technique has place, there is the implication of the impossibility of the evolution of civilization.

c. The third and final contradiction is that Technique can never engender freedom. Of course, Technique frees mankind from a whole collection of ancient constraints. It is evident, for example, that it liberates him from the limits imposed on him by time and space; that man, through its agency, is free (or at least tending to become free) from famine, excessive heat and cold, the rhythms of the seasons, and from the gloom of night; that the race is freed from certain social constraints through its commerce with the universe, and from its intellectual limitations through its accumulation of information. But is this what it means really to be free? Other constraints as oppressive and rigorous as the traditional ones are imposed on the human being in today's technological society through the agency of Technique. New limits and technical oppressions have taken the place of the older, natural constraints, and we certainly cannot aver that much has been gained. The problem is deeper—the operation of Technique is the contrary of freedom, an operation of determinism and necessity. Technique is an ensemble of rational and efficient practices; a collection of orders, schemas, and mechanisms. All of this expresses very well a necessary order and a determinate process, but one into which freedom, unorthodoxy, and the sphere of the gratuitous and spontaneous cannot penetrate. All that these last could possibly introduce is discord and disorder. The more technical actions increase in society, the more human autonomy and initiative diminish. The more the human being comes to exist in a world of ever increasing demands (fortified with technical apparatus possessing its own laws to meet these demands), the more he loses any possibility of free choice and individuality in action. This loss is greatly magnified by Technique's character of self-determination, which makes its appearance among us as a kind of fatality and as a species of perpetually exaggerated necessity. But where freedom is excluded in this way, an authentic civilization has little chance. Confronted in this way by the problem, it is clear to us that no solution can exist, in spite of the writings of all the authors who have concerned themselves with it. They all make an unacceptable premise, namely, rejection of Technique and return to a pretechnical society. One may well regret that some value or other of the past, some social or moral form, has disappeared; but, when one attacks the problem of the technical society, one can scarcely make the serious claim to be able to revive the past, a procedure which, in any case, scarcely seems to have been, globally speaking, much of an improvement over the human situation of today. All we know with certainty is that it was different, that the human being confronted other dangers, errors, difficulties, and temptations. Our duty is to occupy ourselves with the dangers, errors, difficulties, and temptations of modern man in the modern world. All regret for the past is vain; every desire to revert to a former social stage is unreal. There is no possibility of turning back, of annulling, or even of arresting technical progress. What is done is done. It is our duty to find our place in our present situation and in no other. Nostalgia has no survival value in the modern world and can only be considered a flight into dreamland.

We shall insist no further on this point. Beyond it, we can divide into two great categories the authors who search for a solution to the problem posed by Technique: the first class is that of those who hold that the problem will solve itself; the second, of those who hold that the problem demands a great effort or even a great modification of the whole man. We shall indicate a number of examples drawn from each class and beg to be excused for choosing to cite principally French authors.

Politicians, scientists, and technicians are to be found in the first class. In general, they consider the problem in a very concrete and practical way. Their general notion seems to be that technical progress resolves all difficulties *pari passu* with their appearance, and that it contains within itself the solution to everything. The sufficient condition for them, therefore, is that technical progress be not arrested; everything which plagues us today will disappear tomorrow.

The primary example of these people is furnished by the Marxists, for whom technical progress is the solution to the plight of the proletariat and all its miseries, and to the problem posed by the exploitation of man by man in the capitalistic world. Technical progress, which is for Marx the motive force of history, *necessarily* increases the forces of production, and simultaneously produces a progressive conflict between forward-moving factors and stationary social factors like the state, law, ideology, and morality, a conflict occasioning the periodic disappearance of the outmoded factors. Specifically, in the world of the present, conflict necessitates the disappearance of the structures of capitalism, which are so constituted as to be completely unable to absorb the economic results of technical progress, and are hence obliged to vanish. When they do vanish, they of necessity make room for a socialist structure of society corresponding perfectly to the sound and normal utilization of Technique. The Marxist solution to the technical problems is therefore an automatic one since the transition to socialism is in *itself* the solution. Everything is *ex hypothesi* resolved in the socialist society, and humankind finds therein its maturation. Technique, integrated into the socialist society, "changes sign": from being destructive it becomes constructive; from being a means of human exploitation it becomes humane; the contradiction between the infrastructures and the suprastructures disappears. In other words, all the admittedly difficult problems raised in the modern world belong to the structure of capitalism and not to that of Technique. On the one hand, it *suffices* that social structures become socialist for social problems to disappear; and, on the other, society must *necessarily* become socialist by the very movement of Technique. Technique, therefore, carries in itself the response to all the difficulties it raises.

A second example of this kind of solution is given by a certain number of technicians—for example, Frisch. All difficulties, according to Frisch, will inevitably be resolved by the technical growth which will bring the technicians to power. Technique admittedly raises certain conflicts and problems, but their cause is that the human race remains attached to certain political ideologies and moralities and loyal to certain outmoded and antiquated humanists whose sole visible function is to provoke discord of heart and head, thereby preventing men from adapting themselves and from entering resolutely into the path of technical progress. *Ergo,* men are subject to distortions of life and consciousness which have their origin, *not* in Technique, but in the conflict between Technique and the false values to which men remain attached. These fake values, decrepit sentiments, and outmoded notions must inevitably be eliminated by the invincible progress of Technique. In particular, in the political domain, the majority of crises arise from the fact that men are still wedded to certain antique political forms and ideas—for example, democracy. All problems will be resolved if power is delivered into the hands of the technicians who alone are capable of directing Technique in its entirety and making of it a positive instrument for human service. This is all the more true in that, thanks to the so-called "human techniques" (for example, propaganda), they will be in a position to take account of the human factor in the technical context. The technocrats will be able to use the totality of Technique without destroying the human being, but rather by treating him as he should be treated so as to become simultaneously useful and happy. General power accorded to the technicians become technocrats is the only way out for Frisch, since they are the only ones possessing the necessary competence; and, in any case, they are being carried to power by the current of history, the fact which alone offers a quick enough solution to technical problems. It is impossible to rely on the general improvement of the human species, a process which would take too long and would be too chancy. For the generality of men, it is necessary to take into account that Technique establishes an inevitable discipline, which, on the one hand, they must accept, and, on the other, the technocrats will humanize.

The third and last example (it is possible that there are many more) is furnished by the economists, who, in very different ways, affirm the thesis of the automatic solution. Fourastié is a good example of such economists. For him, the first thing to do is to draw up a balance between that which Technique is able to deliver and that which it may destroy. In his eyes there is no real problem: what Technique can bring to man is incomparably superior to that which it threatens. Moreover, if difficulties *do* exist, they are only temporary ones which will be resolved beneficially, as was the case with the similar difficulties of the last century. Nothing decisive is at stake; man is in no mortal danger. The contrary is the case: Technique produces the foundation, infrastructure, and suprastructure which will enable man really to become man. What we have known up to now can only be called the *prehistory* of a human race so overwhelmed by material cares, famine, and danger that the truly human never had an opportunity to develop into a civilization worthy of the name. Human intellectual, spiritual, and moral life will, according to Fourastié, never mature except when life is able to start from a complete satisfaction of its material needs, complete security, including security from famine and disease. The growth of Technique, therefore, initiates the genuinely human history of the whole man. This new type of human being will clearly be different from what we have hitherto known; but this fact should occasion no complaint or fear. The new type cannot help being superior to the old in every way, *after* all the traditional (and exclusively material) obstacles to his development have vanished. Thus progress occurs automatically, and the inevitable role of Technique will be that of guaranteeing such material development as allows the intellectual and spiritual maturation of what has been up to now only potentially present in human nature.

The orientation of the other group of doctrines affirms, on the contrary, that man is dangerously imperiled by technical progress; and that human will, personality, and organization must be set again to rights if society is to be able to guard against the imminent danger. Unfortunately, these doctrines share with their opposites the quality of being too optimistic, in that they affirm that their thesis is even feasible and that man is really capable of the rectifications proposed. I will give three very different examples of this, noting that the attitude in question is generally due to philosophers and theologians.

The orientation of Einstein, and the closely related one of Jules Romains, are well known—namely, that the human being must get technical progress back again into his own hands, admitting that the situation is so complicated and the data so overwhelming that only some kind of "superstate" can possibly accomplish the task. A sort of spiritual power integrated into a world government in possession of indisputable moral authority might be able to master the progression of techniques and to direct human evolution. Einstein's suggestion is the convocation *of* certain philosopher-scientists, whereas Romain's idea is the establishment *of* a "Supreme Court *of* Humanity." Both of these bodies would be organs of meditation, of moral quest, before which temporal powers would be forced to bow. (One thinks, in this connection, of the role of the papacy in medieval Christianity vis-a-vis the temporal powers.)

A second example of this kind of orientation is given by Bergson, at the end of his work, *The Two Sources of Morality and Religion*. According to Bergson, initiative can only proceed from humanity, since in Technique there is no *"force des choses."* Technique has conferred disproportionate power on the human being, and a disproportionate extension to his organism. But "in this disproportionately magnified body, the soul remains what it was, i.e., too small to fill it and too feeble to direct it. Hence the void between the two." Bergson goes on to say that "this enlarged body awaits a supplement of soul, the mechanical demands the mystical," and "that Technique will never render service proportionate to its powers unless humanity, which has bent it earthwards, succeeds by its means in reforming itself and looking heavenwards." This means that humanity has a task to perform, and that man must grow proportionately to his techniques, but that he must will it and *force* himself to make the experiment. This experiment is, in Bergson's view, a possibility, and is even favored by that technical growth which allows more material resources to men than ever before. The required "supplement of soul" is, therefore, of the order of the possible and will suffice for humans to establish mastery over Technique. The same position, it may be added, has in great part been picked up by E. Mounier.

A third example is afforded by a whole group of theologians, most of them Roman Catholic. Man, in his actions in the domain of the technical, is but obeying the vocation assigned him by his Creator. Man, in continuing his work of technical creation, is pursuing the work of his Creator. Thanks to Technique, this man, who was originally created "insufficient," is becoming "adolescent." He is summoned to new responsibilities in this world which do not transcend his powers since they correspond exactly to what God expects of him. Moreover, it is God Himself who through man is the Creator of Technique, which is something not to be taken in itself but in its relation to its Creator. Under such conditions, it is clear that Technique is neither evil nor fraught with evil consequences. On the contrary, it is good and cannot be dangerous to men. It can only become evil to the extent that man turns from God; it is a danger only if its true nature is misapprehended. All the errors and problems visible in today's world result uniquely from the fact that man no longer recognizes his vocation as God's collaborator. If man ceases to adore the "creature" (i.e., Technique) in order to adore the true God; if he turns Technique to God and to His service, the problems must disappear. All of this is considered the more true in that the world transformed by technical activity must become the point of departure and the material support of the new creation which is to come at the end of time.

Finally, it is necessary to represent by itself a doctrine which holds at the present a place of some importance in the Western world—that is, that of Father Teilhard de Chardin, a man who was simultaneously a theologian and a scientist. His doctrine appears as an intermediate between the two tendencies already sketched. For Chardin, evolution in general, since the origin of the universe, has represented a constant progression. First of all, there was a motion toward a diversification of matter and of beings; then there supervened a motion toward Unity—that is, a higher Unity. In the biological world, every step forward has been effected when man has passed from a stage of "dispersion" to a stage of "concentration." At the present, technical human progress and the spontaneous movement of life are in agreement and in mutual continuity. They are evolving together toward a higher degree of organization, and this movement manifests the influence of Spirit. Matter, left to itself, is characterized by a necessary and continuous degradation. But, on the contrary, we note that progress, advancement, improvement do exist, and, hence, a power contradicting the spontaneous movement of matter, a power of creation and progress exists which is the opposite of matter—that is, it is Spirit. Spirit has contrived Technique as a means of organizing dispersed matter, in order simultaneously to express progress and to combat the degradation of matter. Technique is producing at the same time a prodigious demographic explosion—that is, a greater density of human population. By all these means it is bringing forth "communion" among men; and, likewise, creating from inanimate matter a higher and more organized form of matter which is taking part in the ascension of the cosmos toward God. Granting that it is true that every progression in the physical and biological order is brought about by a condensation of the elements of the preceding period, what we are witnessing today, according to Chardin, is a condensation, a concentration of the whole human species. Technique, in producing this, possesses a function of unification *inside* humanity, so that humanity becomes able thereby to have access to a sort of unity. Technical progress is, therefore, synonymous with "socialization," this latter being but the political and economic sign of communion among men, the temporary expression of the "condensation" of the human species into a whole. Technique is the irreversible agent of this condensation; it prepares the new step forward which humanity must make. When men cease to be individual and separate units, and all together form a total and indissoluble communion, then humanity will be a single body. This material concentration is always accompanied by a spiritual concentration—that is, a maturation of the spirit, the commencement of a new species of life. Thanks to Technique, there is socialization, the progressive concentration on a planetary scale of disseminated spiritual personalities into a suprapersonal unity. This mutation leads to another Man, spiritual and unique, and means that humanity in its ensemble and in its unity, has attained the supreme goal, that is, its fusion with that glorious Christ who must appear at the end of time. Thus Chardin holds that in technical progress man is "Christified," and that technical evolution tends inevitably to the "edification" of the cosmic Christ.

It is clear that in Chardin's grandiose perspective, the individual problems, difficulties, and mishaps of Technique are negligible. It is likewise clear how Chardin's doctrine lies midway between the two preceding ones: on the one hand, it affirms a natural and involuntary ascension of man, a process inclusive of biology, history, and the like, evolving as a kind of will of God in which Technique has its proper place; and, on the other, it affirms that the evolution in question implies consciousness, and an intense *involvement* on the part of man who is proceeding to socialization and thus *committing* himself to this mutation.

We shall not proceed to a critique of these different theories, but content ourselves with noting that all of them appear to repose on a too superficial view of the technical phenomenon; and that they are *practically* inapplicable because they presuppose a certain number of *necessary* conditions which are not given. None of these theories, therefore, can be deemed satisfactory.

IV. It does not seem that at the present we are in a position to give a satisfactory reply to the complex of technical problems. All that appears possible is to inquire into the above-mentioned *necessary* conditions for a possible solution.

In any case, it seems to me that we can set forth the following thesis: The further technical progress advances, the more the social problem of mastering this progress becomes one of an ethical and spiritual kind. In proportion to the degree that man extricates himself from the domain of the material, dominates it, and multiplies thereby the means of exploiting matter, the problem ceases to be one of human possibilities and limits and becomes one rather of knowing which man (or group of men) will exploit technical means, and what will be the enabling moral and spiritual qualities. (In this point I am not far from that, for example, of Bergson.) It is essential not to consider the problem resolved once this has been said; the current attitude is false according to which, once a matter has been pronounced a matter of morality, it is something simple and also automatically resolvable. On the contrary, the more decision depends on a man or a group of them, the more difficult it appears, if we take a realistic view of the matter and refuse to admit *a priori* that man is good, democratic, liberal, reasonable, and so on. The difficulty resides in the following points:

a.   It is impossible to trust the spontaneous employment which men will make of the available technical means;

b.   Man, as we have already indicated, is *integrated* into the technological process;

c.   If we desire to preserve man's freedom, dignity, and responsibility, it is precluded to act upon him by technical means, like psychology, and so forth. To transform a man into a reasonable being and a good exploiter of techniques *through* certain psychological procedures is precisely to destroy him as a spiritual and ethical subject.

We are thus caught in a dilemma before the decisive question, the question which may well be the penultimate one.

With this preliminary, what are these necessary conditions? I shall note them as they appear to me at the present, starting from that which is more general and working toward that which is more particular.

1.   The first thing needed is a correct diagnosis and an effort to achieve a genuine consciousness of the problem. It is necessary to see the situation clearly and to pose the problem correctly if it be desired to know just what is to be done and if adequate answers are to be forthcoming. Inexact formulation of the problem affords no hope of getting a solution. The diagnostic element, on which I do not insist, must be accompanied by a becoming conscious—by passing from the intellectual to the existential, which means that mankind must accept the fact that his existence is "engaged" and involved in this venture, and that his very freedom is at stake. It is necessary to become conscious of the fact that in every domain Technique has established stricter and stricter domination over the human being. But this consciousness must not be negative—no scientific determinism or divine fatalism before which man can only bow and confess himself unfree. On the contrary, it must be recognized that man *qua* free is subject to constraints and determinations which his vocation to be free must make him combat and rise clear of. *But*, to the extent that man clings to the illusion of the present that he is free (and uses the vocabulary of freedom), conceiving liberty as inalienable, *or,* to the extent that he holds to the conviction that all will be well though he sees that the Technique actually diminishes the area of freedom, and dreams that possibilities of freedom still exist—in all these cases, his natural inertia is leading him to accept a condition of slavery and to pay for his technological happiness with his freedom. It is only by making men conscious to what degree they have become slaves in becoming "happy," that there is any hope of regaining liberty by asserting themselves, perhaps at the cost of much sacrifice, over the Technique which has come to dominate them. Short of attaining to such consciousness, there is no reason for any human being to lift a finger to secure mastery over his technology.

2.   A second essential element consists in ruthlessly destroying the "myth" of Technique—that is, the whole ideological construction and the tendency to consider technology something possessing sacred character. Intellectuals attempt to insert the technical phenomenon into the framework of their respective intellectual or philosophical systems by attributing to it a quality of supreme excellence; for example, when they demonstrate that Technique is an instrument of freedom, or the means of ascent to historical destiny, or the execution of a divine vocation, and the like. All such constructions have the result of glorifying and sanctifying Technique and of putting the human being at the disposal of some indisputable historical law or other. A further aspect of this element is the

sacred—that is, the human tendency spontaneously to attribute sacred value to what so manifestly possesses transcendent power. Technique, in this view, is not solely an ensemble of material elements, but that which gives meaning and value to life, allowing man not only to live but to live well. Technique is intangible and unattackable precisely because *everything* is subject and subordinate to it. Man unconsciously invests with a holy prestige that against which he is unable to prevail. It seems to me that the only means to mastery over Technique is by way of "desacralization" and "deideologization." This means that *all* men must be shown that Technique is nothing more than a complex of material objects, procedures, and combinations, which have as their sole result a modicum of comfort, hygiene, and ease; and that it possesses nothing worthy of the trouble of devoting one's whole life to it, or of commanding an excessive respect, or of reposing in it one's success and honor, or of massacring one's fellow men. Men must be convinced that technical progress is not humanity's supreme adventure, but a commonplace fabrication of certain objects which scarcely merit enthusiastic delirium even when they happen to be Sputniks. As long as man worships Technique, there is as good as no chance at all that he will ever succeed in mastering it.

3.   A consequence of this is that, in practice, it is necessary to teach man in his employment of Techniques a certain detachment, an independence with respect to them—and humor. It is, naturally, very difficult to accomplish this; and, above all, to get him to give up his illusions, not pretending to be completely free with respect to automobiles, television sets, or jobs, when the plain fact is that he is totally enslaved to them. Man must be capable of questioning at every step his use of his technical goods, able to refuse them and to force them to submit to determining factors other than the technical—say, the spiritual. He must be able to exploit all these goods without becoming unduly attached to them and without becoming convinced that even his most imposing technical conquests are to be taken seriously. Such recommendations must, of course, appear scandalous to contemporary eyes. To affirm that these things have no importance at all in respect to truth and freedom, that it is a matter of no *real* importance whether man succeeds in reaching the moon, or curing disease with antibiotics, or upping steel production, is really a scandal. As long as man does not learn to use technical objects in the right way he must remain their slave.   What I am saying refers to Technique itself and *not* to the individual's use of individual techniques. These two problems are situated on different levels. But, if the *individual* cannot attain personal liberty with respect to technical objects, there is no chance that he will be able to respond to the general problem of Technique. Let us recall once more that what we are setting forth are certain necessary conditions for finding a solution to this general problem.

4.   Everything we have said presupposes an effort at reflection which might be thought of as philosophic. If we admit that the technical adventure is a genuine novelty for the human race, that all that it has excogitated up to now can scarcely be of any use to it at the present; if we admit that it can only be by means of a fundamental and arduous search that we will be able to extricate ourselves from the mess we are in, a *truly* philosophic reflection will be necessary.   But modern philosophic systems, like existentialism and phenomenology, have small utility because they limit themselves into desuetude

with their assertions that philosophy *in principle* can have no purchase on Technique. How, in the nature of things, can a philosophy which is nothing more than a research into the meaning of words, get any grip on the technical phenomenon? Preoccupation with "semantics" is the reason why modern philosophy immures itself in a refusal to come to grips with Technique. As Ducasse has put it in his *Les Techniques et le philosophe:* "Between the refusal of the philosophers, who claim to open up existence to themselves while evading the technical nature of the existent, and the hypocritical humility of the technicians manifested by an ambition stronger than their discipline, some very peculiar enterprises get under way, which might be termed pseudophilosophics and pseudotechniques, respectively, and which usurp in man the place of philosophy's absent mediation." Authentic philosophy of real meaning would bring us to precisely that possibility of mediation between man and the technical phenomenon without which any legitimate attitude is inconceivable. But for such a philosophy to exist would mean that philosophy would first have to cease to be a purely academic technique with a hermetically sealed vocabulary, to become again the property of *every* man who thinks while he is engaged in the business of being alive.

5.   Finally, it is necessary to point out the importance of the relation between the technicians and those who try to pose the technical problem. None of the preceding is more difficult than this, since the technicians have become an authoritarian and closed world. They are armed with good consciences, but likewise with the conviction of their essential rightness and the persuasion that *all* discourse and reflection of a nontechnical nature are verbalisms of no importance. To get them to engage in the dialogue or to question their own creation is an almost superhuman task, the more so that he who will enter this dialogue must be completely aware of what he wants, just what the technician is driving at, and what the technician is able to grasp of the problem. But, as long as such interchange does not take place, nothing will happen, since influencing Technique necessarily means influencing the technicians. It seems to me that this dialogue can only come about by making contact which will represent a *permanent* and *basic* confrontation between Technique's pretensions to resolve all human problems and the human will to escape technical determinism.

Such, I think, are the five conditions necessary that an opening on the technical problem can even become a possibility.

Note on the Theme: Technical Progress Is Always Ambiguous

It cannot be maintained that technical progress is in itself either good or bad. In the evolution of Technique, contradictory elements are always indissolubly connected. Let us consider these elements under the following four rubrics:

1.   All technical progress exacts a price;
2.   Technique raises more problems than it solves;
3.   Pernicious effects are inseparable from favorable effects; and
4.   Every technique implies unforeseeable effects.

1.   ALL TECHNICAL PROGRESS EXACTS A PRICE

What is meant here is not that technical progress exacts a price in money or in intellectual effort, but that, when technical progress adds something, on the one hand, it inevitably subtracts something on the other. It is always difficult to interpret satisfactorily the bald statement that "technical progress is an established fact," because some people cling to traditional social forms, tending to deny any value at all to such progress, and deeming that nothing can be called progress if it casts doubt on established social values. Other persons, on the contrary, hold that Technique produces extraordinary things of a prodigious novelty, bringing about the consequent disappearance of all sorts of valueless junk.

The fact is that, viewed objectively, technological progress produces values of unimpeachable merit, while simultaneously destroying values no less important. As a consequence, it cannot be maintained that there is absolute progress or absolute regress.

Let me give a few simple examples of this reciprocal action. In the first place, let us consider the fact that modern man, thanks to hygiene in particular and to technical progress in general, enjoys a greater life span than ever before. Life expectancy in France today is approximately sixty years, compared, say, to thirty-five years in 1890 and thirty years about 1800. But, even with this indubitable extension of the average life span, all physicians are in agreement that, proportionate to this extension, life has become very much more precarious—that is, our general state of health has become very much more fragile. Human beings of the present have neither the same resistance as their ancestors to disease or to natural conditions nor the same endurance; they suffer from a certain nervous "fragility" and a loss of general vitality, sensitiveness of the senses, and so on. In the sixty years during which such studies have been carried out, regression in all these respects has been marked. Thus, though we live longer, we live a reduced life with nothing resembling the vital energy of our ancestors. It is clear that diminution, on the one hand, has been accompanied by augmentation, on the other.

In the sphere of labor, the technical progress of the present has effected a considerable economy of muscular effort; but at the same time this progress has come to demand a greater and greater nervous effort so that tension and wear and tear on our nerves have inversely increased. Here, again, a kind of equilibrium has asserted itself between savings and expense.

To take an instance from the sphere of economics, technical progress allows the creation of new industries. But a just view of the matter would compel us to take into consideration the accompanying destruction of resources. To take a French example, the so-called Lacq case is beginning to be well known. An industrial complex for the exploitation of sulphur and natural gas has been established at Lacq, a simple technical fact. But, from the economic point of view, this is far from being the case, since a serious agricultural problem has arisen because of the excessive destruction of farm products in the region. Up to now, the government has not seen fit to take the matter seriously, although it has been officially estimated in reports to the Chamber that, for 1960, agricultural losses have aggregated two billion francs. Now the vineyards of Jurancon are being attacked by the sulfurous gases and are disappearing, a not inconsiderable economic loss.

To calculate from the economist's point of view the profits of an industry of this kind, it would at the minimum be necessary to deduct the value of what has been destroyed—in this case two billion francs. It would likewise be necessary to deduct the very considerable expenses of all the necessary protective devices, hospitals (which, incidentally, have not yet been constructed), schools—in short, of the whole urban complex which has not yet been brought into being but which is nevertheless indispensable. We must *whole*. The Lacq enterprise, counting all the expenses of which we have been speaking, must be reckoned a "deficit" enterprise.

Our last example has to do with the problem of the intellectual culture of the masses. True, today's technical means permit a mass culture to exist. Television allows people who never visited a theater in their lives to see performances of the great classics. *Paris-Match,* through its articles, allows masses of people who would be in total ignorance without such articles to attain to a certain literary (and even to a certain aesthetic) culture. But, on the other side of the ledger, it must be recorded that this same technical progress leads to an ever increasing cultural superficiality. Technical progress absolutely forbids certain indispensable conditions of a genuine culture—namely, reflection and opportunity for assimilation. We are indeed witnessing the creation of knowledge, since we are in possession of the means of knowing what we could never have known before; but it is, nevertheless, a superficial development because it is one which is purely *quantitative.*

The intellectual no longer has any time to meditate on a book and must choose between two alternatives: *either* he reads through a whole collection of books rapidly, of which a little later but a few fragments survive—scattered bits of vague knowledge; *or* he takes a year to peruse a few books thoroughly. I should like to know who today has the time to take Pascal or Montaigne seriously. To do them justice would require months and months; but today's Technique forbids any such thing. Exactly the same holds for the problem of the "Musee Imaginaire," which Malraux has put so well. We can be in contact with the whole painting and sculpture of humanity; but this availability has no cultural value comparable to that enjoyed by Poussin, who, in his voyage to Rome, passed several years in studying, statue by statue, the ensemble of artistic works at his disposal. He clearly knew nothing of Polynesian or Chinese art, but what he did know had infinitely more educational value for him because it penetrated his personality slowly.

So, once again, we see that Technique allows us to progress quantitatively to the level of culture spoken of, but at the same time interdicts us from making any progress in depth. In the circumstances, is it really possible to speak of "culture" at all? All technical progress exacts a price. We cannot believe that Technique brings us nothing; but we must not think that what it brings it brings free of charge.

2. THE PROBLEMS POSED BY TECHNICAL PROGRESS

The second aspect of the ambiguity of technical progress concerns the following point: When Technique evolves, it does so by solving a certain number of problems, and by raising others.

The further we advance into the technological society, the more convinced we become that, in any sphere whatever, there are nothing but technical problems. We conceive all problems in their technical aspect, and think that solutions to them can only appear by means of further perfecting techniques. In a certain sense, we are right; it is true that Technique permits us to solve the majority of the problems we encounter. But we are compelled to note (perhaps not often enough) that each technical evolution raises new problems, and that, as a consequence, there is never *one* technique which solves *one* problem. The technological movement is more complicated; one technique solves one problem, but at the same time creates others.

Let us take some simple examples of this fact. We are well acquainted with the details of the gravest sociological problem faced by the nineteenth century—that is, that of the proletariat, a problem which we are only now in process of solving (with difficulty). The phenomenon of the proletariat is not to be considered a simple one, and Marx himself did not describe it as "merely" the exploitation of the workers by certain wicked capitalists. His explanation of the "proletarian condition" was very much more profound; he demonstrated that the proletariat was a result of the division and the mechanization of labor. He expressly states that "it is necessary to pass through the stage represented by the proletariat." For Marx therefore, the problem is not, say, a moral one, with "bad guys exploiting good guys." Marx never puts the problem in this way: he always poses it as lying outside good or bad moral qualities, external to value judgments, and on the level of fact. And the fact is the fact of the division of labor, and of the machine, giving rise to a society in which exploitation is inevitable—that is, drawing off surplus values. The phenomenon of the proletariat is, therefore, even in the Marxian analysis, the result of technical progress. The machine and the division of labor allowed, from the economic point of view, an extraordinary expansion, but, at the same time, and as a result of the same movement, posed the social problem which it has taken a whole century to resolve.

Let us consider in the same way the extension of the above problem as it appears in the questions which will eventually but certainly be posed by the so-called automation. Again, automation is not just another simple economic fact; indeed, we are gradually coming to realize that it will entail difficulties which, from our present point of view, can only be characterized as insurmountable. First of all, automation implies a production of goods in a relatively constant series of types. This means that when production has been automated, it is no longer possible to vary types, so that an unavoidable condition of immobilism with regard to production must ensue. An automated production line, considered in its full context of operation, is so expensive that amortization must occur over terms so long that the exclusive production of certain types of goods without any possibility of modification must be a consequence. *But,* up to the present, no commercial market of the capitalist world is suited to the absorption of the production of an unchanging line of goods. No presently existing Western economic organization, *on the commercial plane,* is prepared to find an answer to automated production.

Another difficulty of automation is the fact that it will result in a massive diminution of the necessary labor force. The simplistic reaction to this problem will clearly be to hold that the solution is easy. It is not necessary to cut down on the number of the workers, but only to diminish the number of daily working hours of each. This solution is quite clearly impossible for a very simple reason. Automation cannot be applied to any arbitrarily selected industry or production, and this for reasons which are basic and not due to the temporary exigencies of, say, the money market. Certain kinds of production can and will be automated;

certain others cannot and will never be automated. Consequently, it is not possible to cut down working hours over the working class as a whole. There are industrial sectors in which the workers would conceivably work one hour per day, whereas in others the workers would have to continue working a normal day of eight hours. Hence, as a result of automation, there will be extended sectors of the economy emptied of manpower, while other sectors will continue on the normal standard.

Diebold estimates that in the single year 1955-1956, in the United States, automation reduced the total number of working hours by 7 percent. In the automated plants of the Ford Motor Company there was a reduction of personnel by 25 percent; and in 1957, in industrial branches in which automation gained most (in particular in the manufacture of electric bulbs and in the very highly automated chemical industry), it was possible to dispense with the services of eight hundred thousand workers. In other words, automation does not result in labor saving favorable to the workers, but is expressed through unemployment and employment disequilibration.

It might be alleged that the situation is true of capitalist countries but cannot be identical in socialist. This statement is not exact; in socialist countries the problem likewise is posed, primarily because of socialist egalitarianism. The problem is the same for the Soviet Union, for example, where automation is commencing, as for the United States. There will be specialized workers in some industries who will be freed from the necessity to work in one way or another, while in other branches of industry the eight-hour day will have to remain force, a situation clearly unacceptable to the egalitarian theories of socialism.

A second problem is bound to arise in connection with the *retraining* of the "liberated" workers for jobs in new industrial sectors in which there is a shortage of manpower. But such retraining more often than not presents enormous difficulties, since the disemployed worker is generally semiskilled (or unskilled) and a completely new apprenticeship is implied of such a nature as to steer him toward other branches of industry.

A third difficulty occasioned by automation is the problem of *wages*. The wage problem produced by automation has, up till now, not been solved. How is it possible to fix a wage scale for automated industrial plants? It cannot be done on the piecework plan—machines do all the work. It cannot be done on the basis of time put in on the job. If it is desired to reduce unemployment by reducing the work day to, say, two or three hours, a given worker would only be employed for a very short period each day. Should such a worker, then, be paid according to a wage schedule which pays him for two hours of work at the equivalent of a worker who must work eight? The injustice of such a procedure is clear. How, then, should wages be calculated in an automated industry? One is forced to the admission that the relation between wages and productivity, on the one hand, and between wages and job time, on the other, must disappear. Wages will be calculated only as a function of the purchasing power given to the worker (with a view to maximum consumption) by dividing the total production value by the total number of workers. Such a method is really the only one feasible. Since 1950, in Russia, it has actually been tried twice. But the results were unsatisfactory, and it very soon became necessary to return to the system of hourly wages, since, in the present state of affairs, the necessary calculations prove unfeasible. But then the difficulties mentioned above (inherent in calculating either according to job time or according to production) return, and, at the moment, wage calculation in automated industries is completely shrouded in uncertainties.

Still another problem is presented by the fact that modern economic crises most often result from a "distortion" between the different economic sectors—more exactly, from unequal growth of the different sectors. Here automation must prove to be an economic factor much to be feared. There will not only be disparity of economic growth between the automated and the nonautomated industrial sectors, but still more between industry and agriculture. *Either* capitalist countries must look forward to an increase of crises due to automation, *or* they must adopt planning aimed at rectifying the distortions (and planning by authoritarian measures, as in the Soviet Union). At the present time even the Soviet planners find that their planning is insufficient to meet the problems of automation, since it is not "flexible" enough, on the one hand, and not "extensive" enough to re-equilibrate the out-of-phase sectors, on the other.

Here, then, are a number of problems (and there are a great many others) with which we must expect to be confronted by the fact of automation, all of which furnish us with examples of our thesis that Technique raises, in proportion to its progress, problems of greater and greater difficulty.

Let me indicate one final example of this, that is, the problem of overpopulation, resulting from the application of medical and prophylactic health techniques, the final result of which is the suppression of infant mortality and the prolongation of human life. The phenomenon of overpopulation, in its turn, produces the tragic phenomenon of underconsumption. A century hence, all of us *without exception* will be menaced by a general underconsumption which will afflict the whole human race, if the expansion of the world's population increases. Here we are confronted by a problem clearly provoked by certain techniques, certain *positive techniques*.

The common factor of all these examples is that technical progress raises whole complexes of problems which we are in no position to solve. Examples of such problems are literally innumerable.

3. THE EVIL EFFECTS OF TECHNIQUE ARE INSEPARABLE FROM THE GOOD

An idea frequently to be encountered in superficial inquiries concerning Technique is the following: "At bottom, everything depends on the way Technique is employed; mankind has only to use Technique for the good and avoid using it for the bad." A common example of this notion is the usual recommendation to employ techniques for the beneficent purposes of peace and eschew them for the maleficent purposes of war. All then will go well.

Our thesis is that technical progress contains simultaneously the good *and* the bad. Consider automation, the problem which we have just been discussing. It is indisputable that technological unemployment is the result of mechanical progress. It cannot be otherwise. All mechanical progress necessarily entails a saving of labor and, consequently, a necessary technological unemployment. Here we have an ill-omened effect indissolubly connected with one which is in itself beneficial. The progress of mechanization necessarily entails unemployment. The technological unemployment so produced can be resolved by either of two means, which are the only two means economically or politically possible—namely, spreading it out either in *space* or in *time.*

A capitalist economist holds that the solution to unemployment is "that technological unemployment ultimately dies out of itself." This means that the workers who have been "freed" (the optimistic formula for unemployment) because of technical advances will ultimately find jobs, either by directing themselves toward industries with manpower shortages or through the fact that new inventions will produce new opportunities of employment and new vocations. The standard example cited in defense of this thesis is that of the vocational opportunities connected with the invention of the automobile. Admittedly, this technological device did suppress a certain number of vocations, but it brought innumerable others into being, with the final result that a vast number of persons are now employed by the servicing required by this industry. Hence the machine in question has actually created employment.

All of this is indeed true. It is, nevertheless, a terribly heartless view of the situation, because it neglects to mention the *interim* period. It is all very well to say that the worker rendered jobless will, *with the lapse of a certain time,* again find employment . . . and that, after he has been reclassified, unemployment will die out. But, humanly speaking, what is the situation of the unemployed worker in the interim? Here the problem of spreading out unemployment in time is posed.

In the Soviet Union, unemployment of a technological nature (which not only exists but springs from the same sources) is spread out in space. By this I mean that when in one place new machines are applied and workers "liberated" the affected workers will, without having to wait very long, receive a work card which tells them in effect: "Two thousand kilometers from here a job has been assigned to you; you are hereby directed to remove yourself to such and such a factory." In one way, such a procedure seems a little less inhuman; but, in another way, it seems just as inhuman as the time procedure of the capitalists, since no account is taken of one's attachments to family, friends, locality, and so on. The human being is only a pawn to be moved about. It is hard to tell, between the capitalist and the socialist ways of handling the problem, which solution presents the worse indecencies.

A further example of the inseparable mingling of good and bad effects is furnished by the noteworthy study of the American sociological historian, J. U. Nef, concerning "industry and war." Nef shows how industrialism—that is, the development of industry taken as a whole—necessarily prods industrialized societies in the direction of war. His analysis has nothing to do with the inner essence of industrialism; the phenomena described by him lie purely at the level of the human being.

First, industrialism gives an increasing population the means to live. It is a law sociologically irrefutable that, the denser the population, the greater the number of wars. This phenomenon is known as a *practical* matter to all sociologists, but only Nef has studied it carefully.

Second, industrialism creates the media of the press, transmission of information, and transport, and finally the means of making war, all of which make it more and more difficult and even almost impossible to distinguish between the aggressor and the aggressed. At the present, no one knows (and perhaps no one can know) which side has commenced hostilities, a fact not solely due to armaments, but also to facility of transport. The extraordinary rapidity of transport allows an aggression to be launched within twenty-four hours, or even less, without anyone being able to foresee it. Here the influence of the press is extremely important, since the press function is to confuse and addle the facts so that no one is able to gain any correct intelligence of them.

Finally, Nef indicates that the new means of destruction created by industrialism have greatly reduced the trouble, the difficulties, and the anguish implied in the act of killing people. A bombardier or artillerist has no feeling at all of killing anyone; he is, in fact, able to reach the conclusion that he has killed someone only with the aid of a syllogism. In hand-to-hand combat all the tiresome difficulties of conscience about the evil of murder keep obtruding themselves. In such ways, then, positive elements of industry result essentially (by very complex expedients) in favoring war and even in provoking it, even if no one has the *intention* of using Technique "badly."

Let us consider, as a final example of the relation between good effects and bad effects, the press and information.

It seems to be a simple matter, for example, to distinguish between information and propaganda. But closer study of the problem reveals that it is practically impossible to make such a distinction. Considering but a few elements of the situation, the problem of information is today no longer that of the necessity *of* transmitting *honest* information—everybody agrees on this point. On the moral level it is a commonplace that we ought to transmit true information. I merely inquire, How do we get it? To remain on the *moral* level is simply not to understand the situation. The *concrete* situation, to take but a single example, is something like the following: Over the wires and into the offices of the Associated Press pass daily up to three hundred thousand words of world news, approximately equal to an enormous volume of one thousand pages. From this mass of words, it is necessary for the Associated Press, in competition with all the other world agencies, to choose, cut, and re-expedite as quickly as possible, perhaps a twentieth part of the whole to its subscribers. How is it possible to select from such a flood just what should be retained, what is true, what is possibly false, and so on? The editors have no criteria, they are at the mercy of whatever comes in, and (even when they judge in good faith and knowledge) they must essentially judge subjectively. Then again, even if the editor had only true news, how should he assign it a coefficient of importance? To do so is his business, and here the stereotypes of the editor are true enough: The Catholic editor will deem the news of the latest Vatican Council of great significance, information which has not the slightest importance to the Communist editor. What we have to do with here is not a question of bad faith, but of a difference of perspective on the world. The result is that we never know, even under the most favorable circumstances, if a given piece of information is subjective. And we must always bear in mind that this information, whatever it is, has been worked over by at least four or five different pairs of hands.

My reasons for maintaining that good effects are inseparable from bad are now, I trust, clear. And, as communications improve, the freer will be the flow of the news and the more available to all agencies concerned. These factors will play an ever greater role, making the difficulties of editing proportionately more difficult, and the chance of selecting absurd rather than sound news ever greater.

4. ALL TECHNICAL PROGRESS CONTAINS UNFORESEEABLE EFFECTS

The final aspect of the ambiguity of technical progress resides in the following state of affairs: When scientists carry out their researches in one or another discipline and hit upon new technical means, they generally see clearly in what sphere the new technique will be applicable. Certain results are expected and gotten. *But* there are always secondary effects which had not been anticipated, which in the primary stage of the technical progress in question could not *in principle* have been anticipated. This unpredictability arises from the fact that predictability implies complete possibility of experimenting in *every* sphere, an inconceivable state of affairs.

The most elementary example is furnished by drugs. You have a cold in the head; you take an aspirin. The headache disappears, but aspirin has other actions besides doing away with headaches. In the beginning we were totally oblivious of these side effects; but, I should imagine, by now everyone has read articles warning against the use of aspirin because of its possible dangerous effects, say, on the blood picture. Grave hemorrhages have appeared in people who habitually took two or three aspirins daily. Yet aspirin was thought the perfect remedy a scant ten years ago—on the ground that no side effects were to be feared. Now such effects begin to appear even in what was, and is, probably the most harmless of all drugs.

Another spectacular example is that of DDT, a chemical which in 1945 was thought to be a prodigiously successful means for the destruction of all kinds of vermin and insects. One of the most admirable things about DDT was that it was said to be completely innocuous toward human beings. DDT was sprinkled over the whole surface of the globe. Then, by accident, it was discovered that in certain areas veal cattle were wasting away and dying. Research revealed that DDT in oily solution causes anemia. Cattle had been dusted with DDT in order to get rid of insects; they had subsequently licked themselves clean and ingested the DDT. The chemical in question passed into their milk and by this route found its way into oily solution, that is, in the milk fat. Calves suckled by such cows died of anemia, and it is needless to say that the same milk was ingested by human infants. Identical problems are potentially raised by *all* chemicals consumed by animals or men. Recall the recent example of thalidomide.

This is an example of the so-called secondary effects, effects which are essentially unpredictable and only revealed after the technique in question has been applied on a grand scale—that is, when it is no longer possible to retrace one's steps.

Another interesting example is furnished by the psychosociological studies of the particular psychology of big city dwellers, where, once more, we are confronted with the effect of the technical environment on the human being. One of the principal elements of big city life is the feeling of isolation, loneliness, absence of human contacts, and so on. One of the leading ideas of Le Corbusier in his *Maison des Hommes* was the admission that "big city dwellers do not know one another." "Let us create," said Le Corbusier, "great blocks of dwellings where people will meet one another as they did in the village, with everything (grocer, baker, butcher) included in the block so that people will get to know one another and a community will come into being." The result of Le Corbusier's creation was exactly the opposite of what had been planned;

problems of loneliness and isolation in such blocks of dwellings proved to be much more tragic than in the normal and traditional city.

Then it was held (and this is the penultimate word in city planning) that it was necessary to rediscover groupings *on a human scale,* not on the scale of a block with, say, five thousand separate dwelling units. In the works and writings of sociologists and of city planners of perhaps seven or eight years ago we read: "At bottom, the only ones who understood what a city was were the people of the Middle Ages, who knew how to create a true city corresponding to the demands of a genuine city-planning technique, that is, a human community centered about a small square surrounded by small houses, toward which converged the (straight) city streets, etc." The new city planners, in keeping with these theories, applied them to the suburbs of Chicago and, in particular, to the well-known "village" of Park Forest. There, it was thought, was to be found the distinctively human formula, one which really allows the human being his full scope. But, the most recent sociological and psychological analyses show this model community to represent nothing less than a new and unexpected difficulty. This time, people are traumatized because they are perpetually under the eyes and under the surveillance of their neighbors. The affected group is indeed much reduced in size; but no one dares to budge, because everybody knows just what everybody else is up to, a frightfully constricting situation, to say the least. It is clear that, even with the best intentions and with the application of hyper-modern and profound research in psychology and sociology, we only succeed in coming to results in every case which could not possibly have been anticipated.

I shall give one last example of these unforeseeable effects, this time from agriculture—namely, the massive cultivation of certain plants like corn and cotton. The cultivation of these plants in the "new countries" seems to represent undeniable progress. The deforestation of land too heavily forested is a felicitous operation, profitable from every point of view, and, consequently, represents technical progress. But it could not have been anticipated that corn and cotton are plants which not only impoverish the soil, but even annihilate it by the twofold action of removing certain natural elements and destroying the relation between the humus and the soil particles. Both these last are destroyed by the roots of cotton and corn to the degree that, after thirty or forty years of cultivation of these agricultural products, the soil is transformed into a veritable dust bowl. A strong wind need only to pass over it to reduce it to bare rock.

The phenomenon is world wide, and is to be encountered in the United States, Brazil, and Russia, among others. It is a bone of contention between Khrushchev and certain Soviet agricultural specialists. Khrushchev essentially emphasizes the cultivation of corn, as is well known; but many Soviet specialists insist that this emphasis is a very dangerous one. It allows a very rapid economic progress for, say, twenty years, only to be followed by a destruction of hitherto fertile lands which may last for centuries.

The inquiries of Castro and Vogt have shown that, at the present, in certain regions 20 percent of cultivated land is threatened with destruction in this way. If this factor is considered in connection with that of population growth, a very considerable difficulty seems to lurk in the offing. If arable land continues to diminish in extent beyond possibility of recovery, our chances of survival diminish correspondingly. Here we have an example of typical and unpredictable secondary effects, effects which in corn and cotton agriculture do not reveal themselves except after thirty years of experience. It is again impossible, therefore, to say whether technical progress is in essence good or bad.

We are launched into a world of an astonishing degree of complexity; at every step we let loose new problems and raise new difficulties. We succeed progressively in solving these difficulties, but only in such a way that when one has been resolved we are confronted by another. Such is the progress of technology in our society. All I have been able to do is to give a few fragmentary examples. What would be necessary in order to comprehend the problem in its entirety is a systematic and detailed study of all these points.

THE IMPACT OF SCIENCE ON SOCIETY

BERTRAND RUSSELL

Bertrand Russell (1872-1970) has been called "the most profound of mathematicians, the most brilliant of philosophers, and the most lucid of popularizers." He has been called many other things by persons who disagreed with his philosophy or his views on public policy.

He was the grandson of Lord John Russell, British Foreign Secretary during the American Civil War.

Russell's early education was at home by governesses and tutors from whom he acquired a thorough knowledge of French and German. His higher education was at Trinity College, Cambridge.

He served brief terms as lecturer or professor at Trinity, Harvard, National University of Peking, University of Chicago, and the University of California at Los Angeles. But he devoted most of his effort to his writing. He wrote some forty books on mathematics, science, and philosophy. In 1950 he won the Nobel Prize for literature.

1. What does Russell consider the two most important discoveries in scientific technique in the late Middle Ages? Why?

2. What were the consequences of other advances in scientific technique?

3. How have changes come about in the manner of influencing public opinion? Do the people have more or less power since the development of modern communications? How do Russell's views compare with the situation portrayed in Orwell's *1984*?

4. How have scientific techniques affected human freedom?

5. If Russell is right in saying that modern communications and weapons have made centralized governments more powerful, and rebellion much more difficult, how do you account for the successful uprisings in Poland, East Germany, Czechoslovakia and Romania in recent years? How do you account for the long-standing civil wars in what was Yugoslavia?

6. And if he is right in saying that communications have been the chief factor in limiting empires, how do you account for the fact that the Roman Empire endured much longer than did the Russian or the British or the Soviet?

7. How would you weigh the advantages and disadvantages of modern technology?

THE IMPACT OF SCIENCE ON SOCIETY

BERTRAND RUSSELL

Chapter II
General Effects of Scientific Technique

SCIENCE, ever since the time of the Arabs, has had two functions: (1) to enable us to *know* things, and (2) to enable us to *do* things. The Greeks, with the exception of Archimedes, were only interested in the first of these. They had much curiosity about the world, but, since civilized people lived comfortably on slave labor, they had no interest in technique. Interest in the practical uses of science came first through superstition and magic. The Arabs wished to discover the philosopher's stone, the elixir of life, and how to transmute base metals into gold. In pursuing investigations having these purposes, they discovered many facts in chemistry, but they did not arrive at any valid and important general laws, and their technique remained elementary.

However, in the late Middle Ages two discoveries were made which had a profound importance: they were gunpowder and the mariner's compass. It is not known who made these discoveries—the only thing certain is that it was *not* Roger Bacon.

The main importance of gunpowder, at first, was that it enabled central governments to subdue rebellious barons. Magna Carta would have never been won if John had possessed artillery. But although in this instance we may side with the barons against the king, in general the Middle Ages suffered from anarchy, and what was needed was a way of establishing order and respect for law. At that time, only royal power could achieve this. The barons had depended upon their castles, which could not stand against guns. That is why the Tudors were more powerful than earlier kings. And the same kind of change occurred at the same time in France and Spain. The modern power of the State began in the late fifteenth century and began as a result of gunpowder. From that day to this, the authority of States has increased, and throughout it has been mainly improvement in weapons of war that has made the increase possible. This development was begun by Henry VII, Louis XI, and Ferdinand and Isabella. It was artillery that enabled them to succeed.

The mariner's compass was equally important. It made possible the age of discovery. The New World was opened to white colonists; the route to the East round Cape of Good Hope made possible the conquest of India, and brought about important contacts between Europe and China. The importance of sea power was enormously increased, and through sea power Western Europe came to dominate the world. It is only in the present century that this domination has come to an end.

Nothing of equal importance occurred in the way of new scientific technique until the age of steam and the industrial revolution. The atom bomb has caused many people during the last seven years to think that scientific technique may be carried too far. But there is nothing new in this. The industrial revolution caused unspeakable misery both in England and in America. I do not think any student of economic history can doubt that the average of happiness in England in the early nineteenth century was lower than it had been a hundred years earlier; and this was due almost entirely to scientific technique.

Let us consider cotton, which was the most important example of early industrialization. In the Lancashire cotton mills (from which Marx and Engels derived their livelihood), children worked from twelve to sixteen hours a day; they often began working at the age of six or seven. Children had to be beaten to keep them from falling asleep while at work; in spite of this, many failed to keep awake and rolled into the machinery, by which they were mutilated or killed. Parents had to submit to the infliction of these atrocities upon their children, because they themselves were in a desperate plight. Handicraftsmen had been thrown out of work by the machines; rural laborers were compelled to migrate to the towns by the Enclosure Acts, which used Parliament to make landowners richer by making peasants destitute; trade unions were illegal until 1824; the government employed *agents provocateurs* to try to get revolutionary sentiments out of wage-earners, who were then deported or hanged.

Such was the first effect of machinery in England.

Meanwhile the effects in the United States had been equally disastrous.

At the time of the War of Independence, and for some years after its close, the Southern States were quite willing to contemplate the abolition of slavery in the near future. Slavery in the North and West was abolished by a unanimous vote in 1787, and Jefferson, not without reason, hoped to see it abolished in the South. But in the year 1793 Whitney invented the cotton gin, which enabled a Negro to clean fifty pounds of fiber a day instead of only one, as formerly. "Laborsaving" devices in England had caused children to have to work fifteen hours a day; "laborsaving" devices in America inflicted upon slaves a life of toil far more severe than what they had to endure before Mr. Whitney's invention. The slave trade having been abolished in 1808, the immense increase in the cultivation of cotton after that date had to be made possible by importing Negroes from the less southerly States in which cotton could not be grown. The deep South was unhealthy, and the slaves on the cotton plantations were cruelly overworked. The less Southern slave States thus became breeding-grounds for the profitable Southern graveyards. A peculiarly revolting aspect of the traffic was that a white man who owned female slaves could beget children by them, who were his slaves, and whom, when he needed cash, he could sell to the plantations, to become (in all likelihood) victims of hookworm, malaria, or yellow fever.

The ultimate outcome was the Civil War, which would almost certainly not have occurred if the cotton industry had remained unscientific.

There were also results in other continents. Cotton goods could find a market in India and Africa; this was a stimulus to British imperialism. Africans had to be taught that nudity is wicked; this was done very cheaply by missionaries. In addition to cotton goods we exported tuberculosis and syphilis, but for them there was no charge.

I have dwelt upon the case of cotton because I want to emphasize that evils due to a new scientific technique are no new thing. The evils I have been speaking of ceased in time: child labor was abolished in England, slavery was abolished in America, imperialism is now at an end in India. The evils that persist in Africa have now nothing to do with cotton.

Steam, which was one of the most important elements in the industrial revolution, had its most distinctive sphere of operation in transport—steamers and railways. The really large-scale effects of steam transportation did not develop fully till after the middle of the nineteenth century, when they led to the opening of the Middle West of America and the use of its grain to feed the industrial populations of England and New England. This led to a very general increase of prosperity, and had more to do than any other single cause with Victorian optimism. It made possible a very rapid increase in population in every civilized country—except France, where the Code Napoleon had prevented it by decreeing equal division of a man's property among all his children, and where a majority were peasant proprietors owning very little land.

This development was not attended with the evils of early industrialism, chiefly, I think, because of the abolition of slavery and the growth of democracy. Irish peasants and Russian serfs, who were not self-governing, continued to suffer. Cotton operatives would have continued to suffer if English landowners had been strong enough to defeat Cobden and Bright.

The next important stage in the development of scientific technique is connected with electricity and oil and the internal-combustion engine.

Long before the use of electricity as a source of power, it was used in the telegraph. This had two important consequences: first, messages could now travel faster than human beings; secondly, in large organizations detailed control from a center became much more possible than it had formerly been.

The fact that messages could travel faster than human beings was useful, above all, to the police. Before the telegraph, a highwayman on a galloping horse could escape to a place where his crime had not yet been heard of, and this made it very much harder to catch him. Unfortunately, however, the men whom the police wish to catch are frequently benefactors of mankind. If the telegraph had existed, Polycrates would have caught Pythagoras, the Athenian government would have caught Anaxagoras, the Pope would have caught William of Occam, and Pitt would have caught Tom Paine when he fled to France in 1792. A large proportion of the best Germans and Russians have suffered under Hitler and Stalin; many more would have escaped but for the rapid transmission of messages. The increased power of the police therefore, is not wholly a gain.

Increase of central control is an even more important consequence of the telegraph. In ancient empires satraps or proconsuls in distant provinces could rebel, and had time to entrench themselves before the central government knew of their disaffection. When Constantine proclaimed himself Emperor at York and marched on Rome, he was almost under the walls of the city before the Roman authorities knew he was coming. Perhaps if the telegraph had existed in those days the Western world would not now be Christian. In the War of 1812, the battle of New Orleans was fought after peace had been concluded, but neither army was aware of the fact. Before the telegraph, ambassadors had an independence which they have now completely lost, because they had to be allowed a free hand if swift action was necessary in a crisis.

It was not only in relation to government, but wherever organizations covering large areas were concerned, that the telegraph effected a transformation. Read, for instance, in Hakluyt's *Voyages,* the accounts of attempts to foster trade with Russia that were made by English commercial interests in the time of Elizabeth. All that could be done was to choose an energetic and tactful emissary, give him letters, goods, money, and leave him to make what headway he could. Contact with his employers was possible only at long intervals, and their instructions could never be up to date.

The effect of the telegraph was to increase the power of the central government and diminish the initiative of distant subordinates. This applied not only to the State, but to every geographically extensive organization. We shall find that a great deal of scientific technique has a similar effect. The result is that fewer men have executive power, but those few have more power than such men had formerly.

In all these respects, broadcasting has completed what the telegraph began.

Electricity as a source of power is much more recent than the telegraph, and has not yet had all the effects of which it is capable. As an influence on social organization its most notable feature is the importance of power stations, which inevitably promote centralization. The philosophers of Laputa could reduce a rebellious dependency to submission by interposing their floating island between the rebels and the sun. Something very analogous can be done by those who control power stations, as soon as a community has become dependent upon them for lighting and heating and cooking. I lived in America in a farmhouse which depended entirely upon electricity, and sometimes, in a blizzard, the wires would be blown down. The resulting inconvenience was almost intolerable. If we had been deliberately cut off for being rebels, we should soon have had to give in.

The importance of oil and the internal-combustion engine in our present technique is obvious to everybody. For technical reasons, it is advantageous if oil companies are very large, since otherwise they cannot afford such things as long pipe lines. The importance of oil companies in the politics of the last thirty years has been very generally recognized. This applies especially to the Middle East and Indonesia. Oil is a serious source of friction between the West and the U.S.S.R., and tends to generate friendliness towards communism in some regions that are strategically important to the West.

But what is of most importance in this connection is the development of flying. Airplanes have increased immeasurably the power of governments. No rebellion can hope to succeed unless it is favored by at least a portion of the air force. Not only has air warfare increased the power of governments, but it has increased the disproportion between great and small Powers. Only great Powers can afford a large air force, and no small Power can stand out against a great Power which has secure air supremacy.

This brings me to the most recent technical application of physical knowledge—I mean the utilization of atomic energy. It is not yet possible to estimate its peaceful uses. Perhaps it will become a source of power for certain purposes, thus carrying further the concentration at present represented by power stations. Perhaps it will be used as the Soviet Government says it intends to use it—to alter physical geography by abolishing mountains and turning deserts into lakes. But as far as can be judged at present, atomic energy is not likely to be as important in peace as in war.

War has been, throughout history, the chief source of social cohesion; and since science began, it has been the strongest incentive to technical progress. Large groups have a better chance of victory than small ones, and therefore the usual result of war is to make States larger. In any given state of technique there is a limit to size. The Roman Empire was stopped by German forests and African deserts; the British conquests in India were halted by the Himalayas; Napoleon was defeated by the Russian winter. And before the telegraph large empires tended to break up because they could not be effectively controlled from a center.

Communications have been hitherto the chief factor limiting the size of empires. In antiquity the Persians and the Romans depended upon roads, but since nothing traveled faster than a horse, empires became unmanageable when the distance from the capital to the frontier was very great. This difficulty was diminished by railways and the telegraph, and is on the point of disappearing with the improvement of the long-range bomber. There would now be no technical difficulty about a single world-wide Empire. Since war is likely to become more destructive of human life than it has been in recent centuries, unification under a single government is probably necessary unless we are to acquiesce in either a return to barbarism or the extinction of the human race.

There is, it must be confessed, a psychological difficulty about a single world government. The chief source of social cohesion in the past, I repeat, has been war: the passions that inspire a feeling of unity are hate and fear. These depend upon the existence of an enemy, actual or potential. It seems to follow that a world government could only be kept in being by force, not by the spontaneous loyalty that now inspires a nation at war. I will return to this problem at a later stage.

So far, I have been considering only techniques derived from physics and chemistry. These have, up to the present, been the most important, but biology, physiology, and psychology are likely in the long run to affect human life quite as much as physics and chemistry.

Take first the question of food and population. At present the population of the globe is increasing at the rate of about 20 millions a year. Most of this increase is in Russia and Southeast Asia. The population of Western Europe and the United States is nearly stationary. Meanwhile, the food supply of the world as a whole threatens to diminish, as a result of unwise methods of cultivation and destruction of forests. This is an explosive situation. Left to itself, it must lead to a food shortage and thence to a world war. Technique, however, makes other issues possible.

Vital statistics in the West are dominated by medicine and birth control: the one diminishes the deaths, the other the births. The result is that the average age in the West increases: there is a smaller percentage of young people and a larger percentage of old people. Some people consider that this must have unfortunate results, but speaking as an old person, I am not sure.

The danger of a world shortage of food may be averted for a time by improvements in the technique of agriculture. But, if population continues to increase at the present rate, such improvements cannot long suffice. There will then be two groups, one poor with an increasing population, the other rich with a stationary population. Such a situation can hardly fail to lead to world war. If there is not to be an endless succession of wars, population will have to become stationary throughout the world, and this will probably have to be done, in many countries, as a result of governmental measures. This will require an extension of scientific technique into very intimate matters. There are, however, two other possibilities. War may become so destructive that, at any rate for a time, there is no danger of overpopulation; or the scientific nations may be defeated and anarchy may destroy scientific technique.

Biology is likely to affect human life through the study of heredity. Without science, men have changed domestic animals and food plants enormously in advantageous ways. It may be assumed that they will change them much more, and much more quickly, by bringing the science of genetics to bear. Perhaps, even, it may become possible artificially to induce desirable mutations in genes. (Hitherto the only mutations that can be artificially caused are neutral or harmful.) In any case, it is pretty certain that scientific technique will very soon effect great improvements in the animals and plants that are useful to man.

When such methods of modifying the congenital character of animals and plants have been pursued long enough to make their success obvious, it is probable that there will be a powerful movement for applying scientific methods to human propagation. There would at first be strong religious and emotional obstacles to the adoption of such a policy. But suppose (say) Russia were able to overcome these obstacles and to breed a race stronger, more intelligent, and more resistant to disease than any race of men that has hitherto existed, and suppose the other nations perceived that unless they followed suit they would be defeated in war, then either the other nations would voluntarily forgo their prejudices, or, after defeat, they would be compelled to forgo them. Any scientific technique, however beastly, is bound to spread if it is useful in war—until such time as men decide that they have had enough of war and will henceforth live in peace. As that day does not seem to be at hand, scientific breeding of human beings must be expected to come about. I shall return to this subject in a later chapter.

Physiology and psychology afford fields for scientific technique which still await development. Two great men, Pavlov and Freud, have laid the foundation. I do not accept the view that they are in any essential conflict, but what structure will be built on their foundations is still in doubt.

I think the subject which will be of most importance politically is mass psychology. Mass psychology is, scientifically speaking, not a very advanced study, and so far its professors have not been in universities: they have been advertisers, politicians, and, above all, dictators. This study is immensely useful to practical men, whether they wish to become rich or to acquire the government. It is, of course, as a science, founded upon individual psychology, but hitherto it has employed rule-of-thumb methods which were based upon a kind of intuitive common sense. Its importance has been enormously increased by the growth of modern methods of propaganda. Of these the most influential is what is called "education." Religion plays a part, though a diminishing one; the press, the cinema, and the radio play an increasing part.

What is essential in mass psychology is the art of persuasion. If you compare a speech of Hitler's with a speech of (say) Edmund Burke, you will see what strides have been made in the art since the eighteenth century. What went wrong formerly was that people had read in books that man is a rational animal, and framed their arguments on this hypothesis. We now know that limelight and a brass band do more to persuade than can be done by the most elegant train of syllogisms. It may be hoped that in time anybody will be able to persuade anybody of anything if he can catch the patient young and is provided by the State with money and equipment.

This subject will make great strides when it is taken up by scientists under a scientific dictatorship. Anaxagoras maintained that snow is black, but no one believed him. The social psychologists of the future will have a number of classes of school children on whom they will try different methods of producing an unshakable conviction that snow is black. Various results will soon be arrived at. First, that the influence of home is obstructive. Second, that not much can be done unless indoctrination begins before the age of ten. Third, that verses set to music and repeatedly intoned are very effective. Fourth, that the opinion that snow is white must be held to show a morbid taste for eccentricity. But I anticipate. It is for future scientists to make these maxims precise and discover exactly how much it costs per head to make children believe that snow is black, and how much less it would cost to make them believe it is dark gray.

Although this science will be diligently studied, it will be rigidly confined to the governing class. The populace will not be allowed to know how its convictions were generated. When the technique has been perfected, every government that has been in charge of education for a generation will be able to control its subjects securely without the need of armies or policemen. As yet there is only one country which has succeeded in creating this politician's paradise.

The social effects of scientific technique have already been many and important, and are likely to be even more noteworthy in the future. Some of these effects depend upon the political and economic character of the country concerned; others are inevitable, whatever this character may be. I propose in this chapter to consider only the inevitable effects.

The most obvious and inescapable effect of scientific technique is that it makes society more organic, in the sense of increasing the interdependence of its various parts. In the sphere of production, this has two forms. There is first the very intimate interconnection of individuals engaged in a common enterprise, e.g. in a single factory; and secondly there is the relation, less intimate but still essential, between one enterprise and another. Each of these becomes more important with every advance in scientific technique.

A peasant in an unindustrialized country may produce almost all his own food by means of very inexpensive tools. These tools, some of his clothes, and a few things such as salt are all that he needs to buy. His relations with the outer world are thus reduced to a minimum. So long as he produces, with the help of his wife and children, a little more food than the family requires, he can enjoy almost complete independence, though at the cost of hardship and poverty. But in a time of famine he goes hungry, and probably most of his children die. His liberty is so dearly bought that few civilized men would change places with him. This was the lot of most of the population of civilized countries till the rise of industrialism.

Although the peasant's lot is in any case a hard one, it is apt to be rendered harder by one or both of two enemies: the moneylender and the landowner. In any history of any period, you will find roughly the following gloomy picture: "At this time the old hardy yeoman stock had fallen upon evil days. Under threat of starvation from bad harvests, many of them had borrowed from urban landowners, who had none of their traditions, their ancient piety, or their patient courage. Those who had taken this fatal step became, almost inevitably, the slaves or serfs of members of the new commercial class. And so the sturdy farmers, who had been the backbone of the nation, were submerged by supple men who had the skill to amass new wealth by dubious methods." You will find substantially this account in the history of Attica before Solon, of Latium after the Punic Wars, of England in the early nineteenth century, of Southern California as depicted in Norris' *Octopus,* of India under the British Raj, and of the reasons which have led Chinese peasants to support communism. The process, however regrettable, is an unavoidable stage in the integration of agriculture into a larger economy.

By way of contrast with the primitive peasant, consider the agrarian interests in modern California or Canada or Australia or the Argentine. Everything is produced for export, and the prosperity to be brought by exporting depends upon such distant matters as war in Europe or Marshall Aid or the devaluation of the pound. Everything turns on politics, on whether the Farm Bloc is strong in Washington, whether there is reason to fear that Argentina may make friends with Russia, and so on. There may still be nominally independent farmers, but in fact they are in the power of the vast financial interests that are concerned in manipulating political issues. This interdependence is in no degree lessened—perhaps it is even increased—if the countries concerned are socialist, as, for example, if the Soviet Government and the British Government make a deal to exchange food for machinery. All this is the effect of scientific technique in agriculture. Malthus, at the beginning of the nineteenth century, wrote: "In the wildness of speculation it has been suggested (of course more in jest than in earnest) that Europe should grow its corn in America, and devote itself solely to manufactures and commerce." It turned out that the speculation was by no means "wild."

So much for agriculture. In industry, the integration brought about by scientific technique is much greater and more intimate.

One of the most obvious results of industrialism is that a much larger percentage of the population live in towns than was formerly the case. The town dweller is a more social being than the agriculturist, and is much more influenced by discussion. In general, he works in a crowd, and his amusements are apt to take him into still larger crowds. The course of nature, the alternations of day and night, summer and winter, wet or shine, make little difference to him; he has no occasion to fear that he will be ruined by frost or drought or sudden rain. What matters to him is his human environment, and his place in various organizations especially.

Take a man who works in a factory, and consider how many organizations affect his life. There is first of all the factory itself, and any larger organization of which it may be a part. Then there is the man's trade union and his political party. He probably gets house room from a building society or public authority. His children go to school. If he reads a newspaper or goes to a cinema or looks at a football match, these things are provided by powerful organizations. Indirectly, through his employers, he is dependent upon those from whom they buy their raw material and those to whom they sell their finished product. Above all, there is the State, which taxes him and may at any moment order him to go and get killed in war, in return for which it protects him against murder and theft so long as there is peace, and allows him to buy a fixed modicum of food.

The capitalist in modern England, as he is never weary of telling us, is equally hemmed in. Half, or more than half, of his profits go to a government that he detests. His investing is severely controlled. He needs permits for everything, and has to show cause why he should get them. The government has views as to where he should sell. His raw material may be very difficult to get, particularly if it comes from a dollar area. In all dealings with his employees he has to be careful to avoid stirring up a strike. He is haunted by fear of a slump, and wonders whether he will be able to keep up the premiums on his life insurance. He wakes in the night in a cold sweat, having dreamed that war has broken out and his factory and his house and his wife and his children have all been wiped out. But, although his liberty is destroyed by such a multiplicity of organizations, he is busy trying to make more of them: new armed units, Western Union, Atlantic Pact, lobbies, and fighting unions of manufacturers. In nostalgic moments he may talk about *laisser faire,* but in fact he sees no hope of safety except in new organizations to fight existing ones that he dislikes, for he knows that as an isolated unit he would be powerless, and as an isolated State his country would be powerless.

The increase of organization has brought into existence new positions of power. Every body has to have executive officials, in whom, at any moment, its power is concentrated. It is true that officials are usually subject to control, but the control may be slow and distant. From the young lady who sells stamps in a post office all the way up to the Prime Minister, every official is invested, for the time being, with some part of the power of the State. You can complain of the young lady if her manners are bad, and you can vote against the Prime Minister at the next election if you dis-approve of his policy. But both the young lady and the Prime Minister can have a very considerable run for their money before (if ever) your discontent has any effect. This increase in the power of officials is a constant source of irritation to everybody else. In most countries they are much less polite than in England; the police, especially in America for instance, seem to think you must be a rare exception if you are not a criminal. This tyranny of officials is one of the worst results of increasing organization, and one against which it is of the utmost importance to find safeguards if a scientific society is not to be intolerable to all but an insolent aristocracy of Jacks-in-office. But for the present I am concerned with description, not with schemes of reform.

The power of officials is, usually, distinct from that of people who are theoretically in ultimate control. In large corporations, although the directors are nominally elected by the shareholders, they usually manage, by various devices, to be in fact self-perpetuating, and to acquire new directors, when necessary, by co-option more or less disguised as election. In British politics, it is a commonplace that most Ministers find it impossible to cope with their civil servants, who in effect dictate policy except on party questions that have been prominently before the public. In many countries the armed forces are apt to get out of hand and defy the civil authorities. Of the police I have already spoken, but concerning them there is more to be said. In countries where the communists enter coalition governments, they always endeavor to make sure of control of the police. When once this is secured, they can manufacture plots, make arrests, and extort confessions freely. By this means they pass from being participants in a coalition to being the whole government. The problem of causing the police to obey the law is a very difficult one; it is, for example, very far from being solved in America, where confessions are apt to be extorted by "third degree" from people who may well be innocent.

The increased power of officials is an inevitable result of the greater degree of organization that scientific technique brings about. It has the drawback that it is apt to be irresponsible, behind-the-scenes, power, like that of emperors' eunuchs and kings' mistresses in former times. To discover ways of controlling it is one of the most important political problems of our time. Liberals protested, successfully, against the power of kings and aristocrats; socialists protested against the power of capitalists. But unless the power of officials can be kept within bounds, socialism will mean little more than the substitution of one set of masters for another: all the former power of the capitalist will be inherited by the official. In 1942, when I lived in the country in America, I had a part-time gardener, who spent the bulk of his working day making munitions. He told me with triumph that his union had secured the "closed shop." A little while later he told me, without triumph, that the union dues had been raised and that the extra money went wholly to increase the salary of the secretary of the union. Owing to what was practically a war situation between labor and capital any agitation against the secretary could be represented as treachery. This little story illustrates the helplessness of the public against its own officials, even where there is nominally complete democracy.

One of the drawbacks to the power of officials is that they are apt to be quite remote from the things they control. What do the men in the Education Office know about education? Only what they dimly remember of their public school and university some twenty or thirty years ago. What does the Ministry of Agriculture know about mangel-wurzels? Only how they are spelled. What does the Foreign Office know about modern China? After I had returned from China in 1921, I had some dealings with the permanent officials who determined British Far Eastern policy, and found their ignorance unsurpassed except by their conceit. America has invented the phrase "yes-men" for those who flatter great executives. In England we are more troubled by "no-men," who make it their business to employ clever ignorance in opposing and sabotaging every scheme suggested by those who have knowledge and imagination and enterprise. I am afraid our "no-men" are a thousand times more harmful than the American "yes-men." If we are to recover prosperity, we shall have to find ways of emancipating energy and enterprise from the frustrating control of constitutionally timid ignoramuses.

Owing to increase of organization, the question of the limits of individual liberty needs completely different treatment from that of nineteenth-century writers such as Mill. The acts of a single man are as a rule unimportant, but the acts of groups are more important than they used to be. Take, for example, refusal to work. If one man, on his own initiative, chooses to be idle, that may be regarded as his own affair; he loses his wages, and there is an end of the matter. But if there is a strike in a vital industry, the whole community suffers. I am not arguing that the right to strike should be abolished; I am only arguing that, if it is to be preserved, it must be for reasons concerned with this particular matter, and not on general grounds of personal liberty. In a highly organized country there are many activities which are important to everybody, and without which there would be widespread hardship. Matters should be so arranged that large groups seldom think it to their interest to strike. This can be done by arbitration and conciliation, or, as under the dictatorship of the proletariat, by starvation and police action. But in one way or another it must be done if an industrial society is to prosper.

War is a more extreme case than strikes, but raises very similar questions of principle. When two men fight a duel, the matter is trivial, but when 200 million people fight 200 million other people the matter is serious. And with every increase of organization war becomes more serious. Until the present century, the great majority of the population, even in nations engaged in such contests as the Napoleonic Wars, were still occupied with peaceful pursuits, and as a rule little disturbed in their ordinary habits of life. Now, almost everybody, women as well as men, are set to some kind of war work. The resulting dislocation makes the peace, when it comes, almost worse than the war. Since the end of the late war, throughout Central Europe, enormous numbers, men, women, and children, have died in circumstances of appalling suffering, and many millions of survivors have become homeless wanderers, uprooted, without work, without hope, a burden equally to themselves and to those who feed them. This sort of thing is to be expected when defeat introduces chaos into highly organized communities.

The right to make war, like the right to strike, but in a far higher degree, is very dangerous in a world governed by scientific technique. Neither can be simply abolished, since that would open the road to tyranny. But in each case it must be recognized that groups cannot, in the name of freedom, justly claim the right to inflict great injuries upon others. A regards war, the principle of unrestricted national sovereignty, cherished by liberals in the nineteenth century and by the Kremlin in the present day, must be abandoned. Means must be found of subjecting the relations of nations to the rule of law, so that a single nation will no longer be, as at present, the judge in its own cause. If this is not done, the world will quickly return to barbarism. If that case, scientific technique will disappear along with science, and men will be able to go on being quarrelsome because their quarrels will no longer do much harm. It is, however, just possible that mankind may prefer to survive and prosper rather than to perish in misery, and, if so, national liberty will have to be effectively restrained.

As we have seen, the question of freedom needs a completely fresh examination. There are forms of freedom that are desirable, and that are gravely threatened; there are other forms of freedom that are undesirable, but that are very difficult to curb. There are two dangers, both rapidly increasing. Within any given organization, the power of officials, or of what may be called the "government," tends to become excessive, and to subject individuals to various forms of tyranny. On the other hand, conflicts between different organizations become more and more harmful as organizations acquire more power over their members. Tyranny within and conflict without are each other's counterpart. Both spring from the same source: the lust for power. A State which is internally despotic will be externally warlike, in both respects because the men who govern the State desire the greatest attainable extent and intensity of control over the lives of other men. The resultant twofold problem, of preserving liberty internally and diminishing it externally, is one that the world must solve, and solve soon, if scientific societies are to survive.

Let us consider for a moment the social psychology involved in this situation.

Organizations are of two kinds, those which aim at getting something done, and those which aim at preventing something from being done. The Post Office is an example of the first kind; a fire brigade is an example of the second kind. Neither of these arouses much controversy, because no one objects to letters' being carried, and incendiaries dare not avow a desire to see buildings burnt down. But when what is to be prevented is something done by human beings, not by Nature, the matter is otherwise. The armed forces of one's own nation exist—so each nation asserts—to *prevent* aggression by other nations. But the armed forces of other nations exist—or so many people believe to *promote* aggression. If you say anything against the armed forces of your own country, you are a traitor, wishing to see your fatherland ground under the heel of a brutal conqueror. If, on the other hand, you defend a potential enemy State for thinking armed forces necessary to its safety, you malign your own country, whose unalterable devotion to peace only perverse malice could lead you to question. I heard all this said about Germany by a thoroughly virtuous German lady in 1936, in the course of a panegyric on Hitler.

The same sort of thing applies, though with slightly less force, to other combatant organizations. My Pennsylvania gardener would not publicly criticize his trade union secretary for fear of weakening the union in contest with capitalists. It is difficult for a man of ardent political convictions to admit either the shortcomings of politicians of his own Party or the merits of those of the opposite Party.

And so it comes about that, whenever an organization has a combatant purpose, its members are reluctant to criticize their officials, and tend to acquiesce in usurpations and arbitrary exercises of power which, but for the war mentality, they would bitterly resent. It is the war mentality that gives officials and governments their opportunity. It is therefore only natural that officials and governments are prone to foster war mentality.

The only escape is to have the greatest possible number of disputes settled by legal process, and not by a trial of strength. Thus here again the preservation of internal liberty and external control go hand in hand, and both equally depend upon what is *prima facie* a restraint upon liberty, namely an extension of the domain of law and of the public force necessary for its enforcement.

In what I have been saying so far in this chapter I feel that I have not sufficiently emphasized the gains that we derive from scientific technique. It is obvious that the average inhabitant of the United States at the present day is very much richer than the average inhabitant of England in the eighteenth century, and this advance is almost entirely due to scientific technique. The gain in the case of England is not so great, but that is because we have spent so much on killing Germans. But even in England there are enormous material advances. In spite of shortages, almost everybody has as much to eat as is necessary for health and efficiency. Most people have warmth in winter and adequate light after sunset. The streets, except in time of war, are not pitch dark at night. All children go to school. Everyone can get medical attendance. Life and property are much more secure (in peacetime) than they were in the eighteenth century. A much smaller percentage of the population lives in slums. Travel is vastly easier, and many more amusements are available than in former times. The improvement in health would in itself be sufficient to make this age preferable to those earlier times for which some people feel nostalgic. On the whole, I think, this age is an improvement on all its predecessors except for the rich and privileged.

Our advantages are due entirely, or almost entirely, to the fact that a given amount of labor is more productive than it was in pre-scientific days. I used to live on a hilltop surrounded by trees, where I could pick up firewood with the greatest ease. But to secure a given amount of fuel in this way cost more human labor than to have it brought across half England in the form of coal, because the coal was mined and brought scientifically, whereas I could employ only primitive methods in gathering sticks. In old days, one man produced not much more than one man's necessaries; a tiny aristocracy lived in luxury, a small middle class lived in moderate comfort, but the great majority of the population had very little more than was required in order to keep alive. It is true that we do not always spend our surplus of labor wisely. We are able to set aside a much larger proportion for war than our ancestors could. But almost all the large-scale disadvantages of our time arise from failure to extend the domain of law to the settlement of disputes which, when left to the arbitrament of force, have become, through our very efficiency, more harmful than in previous centuries. This survival of formerly endurable anarchy must be dealt with if our civilization is to survive. Where liberty is harmful, it is to law that we must look.

SOME ISSUES IN SCIENCE AND TECHNOLOGY

Florence Nightingale

James F. Childress

U.S. Atomic Energy Commission

Rachel Carson

C. S. Lewis

Annie Dillard

Gordon Rattray Taylor

Norbert Wiener

A. M. Turing

What is life? It is the flash of a firefly in the night. It is the breath of a buffalo in the wintertime. It is the little shadow which runs across the grass and loses itself in the sunset.

Crowfoot, *Last Words*, 1890

A culture is no better than its woods.

W. H. Auden, *Bucolics*

Ye marshes, how candid and simple and
  nothing-withholding and free
Ye publish yourselves to the sky and offer
  yourselves to the sea!

Sidney Lanier, *The Marshes of Glynn*, 1877

We can never have enough of nature. We must be refreshed by the sight of inexhaustible vigor, vast and titanic features, the sea-coast with its wrecks, the wilderness with its living and its decaying trees, the thundercloud, and the rain which lasts three weeks and produces freshets. We need to witness our own limits transgressed, and some life pasturing freely where we never wander.

Henry David Thoreau, *Walden*, 1854

American science is a thing of the future, and not of the present or past; and the proper course of one in my position is to consider what must be done to create a science of physics in the country, rather than to call telegrams, electric lights, and such conveniences by the name of science.

Henry Augustus Rowland (1883)

Man was formed by his struggle with exterior forces and it is only easy for him to discern things which are outside of himself.

José Ortegá y Gasset, *The Modern Theme* (1923)

NOTES ON NURSING: WHAT IT IS, AND WHAT IT IS NOT (1859)

FLORENCE NIGHTINGALE

Florence Nightingale (1820-1910) generally is regarded as the founder of trained nursing as a profession for women. She was born on May 20, 1820, in Florence, Italy, where her English parents were temporarily in residence. Back in England, she grew up in favorable surroundings. She received a broad education, mostly from her father, in Greek, Latin, French, German, Italian, history, mathematics, and philosophy. At the age of seventeen she felt a strong "call" for service, though it was another nine years before she figured out what form this should take.

In the company of her parents and her sister she traveled widely in Europe. She visited hospitals whenever she could. Three years of study of Parliamentary Reports made her something of an expert on hospitals and public health. In 1851 she went to an institution of nursing at Kaiserswerth, in Germany, where she spent three months in observation and study. Later she began further studies in Paris, but after only two weeks she had to give those up on account of illness. In 1853 she was appointed superintendent of the Institution for the Care of Sick Gentlewomen, a small private hospital in London, where her reforms and administration earned for her an outstanding reputation.

At the outbreak of the Crimean War in 1854, she immediately offered her services. The secretary of state for war asked her to form a company of female nurses for service in the war zone. On November 5 she arrived with thirty-eight nurses at the British Army hospital in the Selimye barracks at Scutari, Turkey, across the Bosporus from Constantinople. At first she encountered strong opposition from the local commander and most of the medical officers. Immediately she set her nurses to cleaning up the place. Six months after her arrival, the mortality rate at the hospital had dropped from 42 percent to 2.2 percent. Soon she was widely acclaimed. In May 1855 she transferred to Balaklava in the Crimea. There she contracted the "Crimea fever," but remained at her post throughout.

After the war she was greeted in England as a heroine. A public subscription raised a sum of 45,000 pounds for her. She used this to found the Nightingale School of Nursing at St. Thomas's Hospital, the first of its kind in the world. During the ensuing years she devoted herself to nurses training, the training of midwives, the improvement of British military medical service, public health, and related activities.

From 1857 she lived as an invalid. Nevertheless she continued her voluminous work from her sick room where she continued to work day and night. By 1901 she was almost totally blind. In 1907 she became the first woman ever to receive the Order of Merit from the King. She died in August 1910 at the age of ninety.

Florence Nightingale wrote extensively on the basis of her experience, her study, and the application of statistics to medical reports. The selection reproduced here is from a small book published in 1859. "These notes," she said, "are by no means intended... as a manual to teach nurses to nurse,... but simply to give hints for thought to women who have personal charge of the health of others."

1. How does Florence Nightingale compare the popular attitude about the laws of the physical universe to that about the laws of hygiene?

2. What does Nightingale consider to be the essential points for making a house healthy? What is the importance of each? Are all those points still valid?

3. How do you account for her insistence on cleanliness and sanitation at a time before the germ theory of disease had even been proposed?

4. What was so revolutionary about her ideas on ventilation?

5. Nightingale's recommendations on diet were given many years before there was any notion of food calories, vitamins, or cholesterol. How do her recommendations stand up today?

6. What is Nightingale's advice to those who visit the sick? To what extent do you agree or disagree? Explain.

7. How do you account for the early opposition to having women as nurses in military hospitals? What is Nightingale's attitude about "women's rights?"

NOTES ON NURSING:
WHAT IT IS AND WHAT IT IS NOT

FLORENCE NIGHTINGALE

Macaulay somewhere says, that it is extraordinary that, whereas the laws of the motions of the heavenly bodies, far removed as they are from us, are perfectly well understood, the laws of the human mind, which are under our observation all day and every day, are no better understood than they were two thousand years ago.

But how much more extraordinary is it that, whereas what we might call the coxcombries of education—e.g., the elements of astronomy—are now taught to every school-girl, neither mothers of families of any class, nor school-mistresses of any class, nor nurses of children, nor nurses of hospitals, are taught anything about those laws which God has assigned to the relations of our bodies with the world in which He has put them. In other words, the laws which make these bodies, into which He has put our minds, healthy or unhealthy organs of those minds, are all but unlearnt. Not but that these laws—the laws of life—are in a certain measure understood, but not even mothers think it worth their while to study them—to study how to give their children healthy existences. They call it medical or physiological knowledge, fit only for doctors.

Another objection.

We are constantly told—"but the circumstances which govern our children's healths are beyond our control. What can we do with winds? There is the east wind. Most people can tell before they get up in the morning whether the wind is in the east."

To this one can answer with more certainty than to the former objections. Who is it who knows when the wind is in the east? Not the Highland drover, certainly, exposed to the east wind, but the young lady who is worn out with the want of exposure to fresh air, to sunlight, &c. Put the latter under as good sanitary circumstances as the former, and she too will not know when the wind is in the east.

I. Ventilation and Warming

The very first canon of nursing, the first and the last thing upon which a nurse's attention must be fixed, the fist essential to a patient, without which all the rest you can do for him is as nothing, with which I had almost said you may leave all the rest alone, is this: TO KEEP THE AIR HE BREATHES AS PURE AS THE EXTERNAL AIR, WITHOUT CHILLING HIM. Yet what is so little attended to? Even where it is thought of at all, the most extraordinary misconceptions reign about it. Even in admitting air into the patient's room or ward, few people ever think, where that air comes from. It may come from a corridor into which other wards are ventilated, from a hall, always unaired, always full of the fumes of gas, dinner, of various kinds of mustiness; from an underground kitchen, sink, washhouse, water-closet, or even, as I myself have had sorrowful experience, from open sewers loaded with filth; and with this the patient's room or ward is aired, as it is called—poisoned, it should rather be said. Always air from the air without, and that, too, through those windows,

through which the air comes freshest. From a closed court, especially if the
wind do not blow that way, air may come as stagnant as any from a hall·or
corridor.

Again, a thing I have often seen both in private houses and institutions. A
room remains uninhabited; the fireplace is carefully fastened up with a board;
the windows are never opened; probably the shutters are kept always shut;
perhaps some kind of stores are kept in the room; no breath of fresh air can by
possibility enter into that room, nor any ray of sun. The air is as stagnant,
musty, and corrupt as it can be possibility be made. It is quite ripe to breed
small-pox, scarlet-fever, diphtheria, or anything else you please.

Yet the nursery, ward, or sick room adjoining will positively be aired by
having the door opened into that room. Or children will be put into that room,
without previous preparation, to sleep.

A short time ago a man walked into a back-kitchen in Queen square, and cut
the throat of a poor consumptive creature, sitting by the fire. The murderer did
not deny the act, but simply said, "It's all right." Of course he was mad.

The extraordinary confusion between cold and ventilation, even in the minds
of well educated people, illustrates this. To make a room cold is by no means
necessarily to ventilate it. Nor is it at all necessary, in order to ventilate a
room, to chill it. Yet, if a nurse finds a room close, she will open the door into
a cold room, without a fire, or an open window in it, by way of improving the
ventilation. The safest atmosphere of all for a patient is a good fire and an open
window, excepting in extremes of temperature. (Yet no nurse can ever be made
to understand this.) To ventilate a small room without draughts of course
requires more care than to ventilate a large one.

Another extraordinary fallacy is the dread of night air. What air can we
breathe at night but night air? The choice is between pure night air from without
and foul night air from within. Most people prefer the latter. An unaccountable
choice. What will they say if it is proved to be true that fully one-half of all the
disease we suffer from is occasioned by people sleeping with their windows
shut? An open window most nights in the year can never hurt any one. This
is not to say that light is not necessary for recovery. In great cities, night air is
often the best and purest air to be had in the twenty-four hours. I could better
understand in towns shutting the windows during the day than during the night,
for the sake of the sick. The absence of smoke, the quiet, all tend to making
night the best time for airing the patients. One of our highest medical authorities
on Consumption and Climate has told me that the air in London is never so good
as after ten o'clock at night.

Always air your room, then, from the outside air, if possible. Windows are
made to open; doors are made to shut—a truth which seems extremely difficult
of apprehension. I have seen a careful nurse airing her patient's room through
the door, near to which were two gaslights, (each of which consumes as much
air as eleven men,) a kitchen, a corridor, the composition of the atmosphere in
which consisted of gas, paint, foul air, never changed, full of effluvia, including
a current of sewer air from an ill-placed sink, ascending in a continual stream
by a well-staircase, and discharging themselves constantly into the patient's
room. The window of the said room, if opened, was all that was desirable to
air it. Every room must be aired from without—every passage from without.
But the fewer passages there are in a hospital the better.

* * * * *

If the nurse be a very careful one, she will, when the patient leaves his bed, but not his room, open the sheets wide, and throw the bed-clothes back, in order to air his bed. And she will spread the wet towels or flannels carefully out upon a horse, in order to dry them. Now either these bed-clothes and towels are not dried and aired, or they dry and air themselves into the patient's air. And whether the damp and effluvia do him most harm in his air or in his bed, I leave to you to determine, for I cannot.

Even in health people cannot repeatedly breathe air in which they live with impunity, on account of its becoming charged with unwholesome matter from the lungs and skin. In disease where everything given off from the body is highly noxious and dangerous, not only must there be plenty of ventilation to carry off the effluvia, but everything which the patient passes must be instantly removed away, as being more noxious than even the emanations from the sick....

II. Health of Houses

There are five essential points in securing the health of houses:
1.   Pure air.
2.   Pure water.
3.   Efficient drainage.
4.   Cleanliness.
5.   Light.
Without these, no house can be healthy. And it will be unhealthy just in proportion as they are deficient.

1. To have pure air, your house be so constructed as that the outer atmosphere shall find its way with ease to every corner of it. House architects hardly ever consider this. The object in building a house is to obtain the largest interest for the money, not to save doctors' bills to the tenants. But, if tenants should ever become so wise as to refuse to occupy unhealthy constructed houses, and if Insurance Companies should ever come to understand their interest so thoroughly as to pay a Sanitary Surveyor to look after the houses where their clients live, speculative architects would speedily be brought to their senses. As it is, they build what pays best. And there are always people foolish enough to take the houses they build. And if in the course of time the families die off, as is so often the case, nobody ever thinks of blaming any but Providence for the result. Ill-informed medical men aid in sustaining the delusion, by laying the blame on "current contagions." Badly constructed houses do for the healthy what badly constructed hospitals do for the sick. Once insure that the air in a house is stagnant, and sickness is certain to follow.

2. Pure water is more generally introduced into houses than it used to be, thanks to the exertions of the sanitary reformers. Within the last few years, a large part of London was in the daily habit of using water polluted by the drainage of its sewers and water closets. This has happily been remedied. But, in many parts of the country, well water of a very impure kind is used for domestic purposes. And when epidemic disease shows itself, persons using such water are almost sure to suffer.

3. It would be curious to ascertain by inspection, how many houses in London are really well drained. Many people would say, surely all or most of them. But many people have no idea in what good drainage consists. They think that a sewer in the street, and a pipe leading to it from the house is good drainage. All the while the sewer may be nothing but a laboratory from which epidemic disease and ill health is being distilled into the house. No house with any untrapped drain pipe communicating immediately with a sewer, whether it be from water closet, sink, or gully-grate, can ever be healthy. An untrapped sink may at any time spread fever or pyaemia among the inmates of a palace.

The ordinary oblong sink is an abomination. That great surface of stone, which is always left wet, is always exhaling into the air. I have known whole houses and hospitals smell of the sink. I have met just as strong a stream of sewer air coming up the back staircase of a grand London house from the sink, as I have ever met at Scutari; and I have seen the rooms in that house all ventilated by the open doors, and the passages all unventilated by the closed windows, in order that as much of the sewer air as possible might be conducted into and retained in the bed-rooms. It is wonderful.

Another great evil in house construction is carrying drains underneath the house. Such drains are never safe. All house drains should begin and end outside the walls. Many people will readily admit, as a theory, the importance of these things. But how few are there who can intelligently trace disease in their households to such causes! Is it not a fact, that when scarlet fever, measles, or small-pox appear among the children, the very first thought which occurs is, "where" the children can have "caught" the disease? And the parents immediately run over in their minds all the families with whom they may have been. They never think of looking at home for the source of the mischief. If a neighbour's child is seized with small-pox, the first question which occurs is whether it had been vaccinated. No one would undervalue vaccination; but it becomes of doubtful benefit to society when it leads people to look abroad for the source of evils which exist at home.

4. Without cleanliness, within and without your house, ventilation is comparatively useless. In certain foul districts of London, poor people used to object to open their windows and doors because of the foul smells that came in. Rich people like to have their stables and dunghill near their houses. But does it ever occur to them that with many arrangements of this kind it would be safer to keep the windows shut than open? You cannot have the air of the house pure with dung-heaps under the windows. These are common all over London. And yet people are surprised that their children, brought up in large "well-aired" nurseries and bed-rooms suffer from children's epidemics. If they studied Nature's laws in the matter of children's health, they would not be so surprised.

There are other ways of having filth inside a house besides having dirt in heaps. Old papered walls of years' standing, dirty carpets, uncleansed furniture, are just as ready sources of impurity to the air as if there were a dung-heap in the basement. People are so unaccustomed from education and habits to consider how to make a home healthy, that they either never think of it at all, and take every disease as a matter of course, to be "resigned to" when it comes "as from the hand of Providence;" or if they ever entertain the idea of preserving the health of their household as a duty, they are very apt to commit all kinds of "negligences and ignorances" in performing it.

5. A dark house is always an unhealthy house, always an ill-aired house, always a dirty house. Want of light stops growth, and promotes scrofula, rickets, &c., among the children.

People lose their health in a dark house, and if they get ill they cannot get well again in it. More will be said about this farther on.

Three out of many "negligences and ignorances" in managing the health of house generally, I will here mention as specimens 1) That the female head in charge of any building does not think it necessary to visit every hole and corner of it every day. How can she expect those who are under her to be more careful to maintain her house in a healthy condition than she who is in charge of it? 2) That it is not considered essential to air, to sun, and to clean rooms while uninhabited; which is simply ignoring the first elementary notion of sanitary things, and laying the ground ready for all kinds of diseases. 3) That the window, and one window, is considered enough to air a room. Have you never observed that any room without a fire-place, would you cram it up not only with a chimney-board, but perhaps with a great wisp of brown paper, in the throat of the chimney—to prevent the soot from coming down, you say? If your chimney is foul, sweep it; but don't expect that you can ever air a room with only one aperture; don't suppose that to shut up a room is the way to keep it clean. It is the best way to foul the room and all that is in it. Don't imagine that if you, who are in charge, don't look to all these things yourself, those under you will be more careful than you are. It appears as if the part of a mistress now is to complain of her servants, and to accept their excuses—not to show them how there need be neither complaints made nor excuses.

But again, to look to all these things yourself does not mean to do them yourself. "I always open the windows," the head in charge often says. If you do it, it is by so much the better, certainly, than if it were not done at all. But can you not insure that it is done when not done by yourself? Can you insure that it is not undone when your back is turned? This is what being "in charge" means. And a very important meaning it is, too. The former only implies that just what you can do with your own hands is done. The latter that what ought to be done is always done.

And now, you think these things trifles, or at least exaggerated. But what you "think" or what I "think" matters little. Let us see what God thinks of them. God always justifies His ways. While we are thinking, He has been teaching. I have known cases of hospital pyaemia quite as severe in handsome private houses as in any of the worst hospitals, and from the same cause, viz., foul air. Yet nobody learnt the lesson. Nobody learnt *anything* at all from it. They went on *thinking*—thinking that the sufferer had scratched his thumb, or that it was singular that "all the servants" had "whitlows," or that something was "much about this year; there is always sickness in our house." This is a favourite mode of thought—leading not to inquire what is the uniform cause of these general "whitlows," but to stifle all inquiry. In what sense is "sickness" being "always there," a justification of its being "there" at all?

I will tell you what was the cause of this hospital pyaemia being in that large private house. It was that the sewer air from an ill-placed sink was carefully conducted into all the rooms by sedulously opening all the doors, and closing all the passage windows. It was that the slops were emptied into the foot pans!—it was that the utensils were never properly rinsed—it was that the chamber crockery was rinsed with dirty water—it was that the beds were never properly shaken, aired, picked to pieces, or changed. It was that the carpets and curtains were always musty—it was that the furniture was always dusty—it was that the papered walls were saturated with dirt—it was that the floors were never cleaned—it was that the uninhabited rooms were never sunned, or cleaned, or aired—it was that the cupboards were always reservoirs of foul air—it was that the windows were always tight shut up at night—it was that no window was ever systematically opened even in the day, or that the right window was not opened. A person gasping for air might open a window for himself. But the servants were not taught to open the windows, to shut the doors; or they opened the windows upon a dank well between high walls, not upon the airier court; or they opened the room doors into the unaired halls and passages, by way of airing the rooms. Now all this is not fancy, but fact. In that handsome house I have known in one summer three cases of hospital pyaemia, one of phlebitis, two of consumptive cough; all the *immediate* products of foul air. When, in temperate climates, a house is more unhealthy in summer than in winter, it is a certain sign of something wrong. Yet nobody learns the lesson. Yes, God always justifies His ways. He is teaching while you are not learning. This poor body loses his finger, that one loses his life. And all fro the most easily preventible causes.

The houses of the grandmothers and great grandmothers of this generation, at least the country houses, with front door and back door always standing open, winter and summer, and a thorough draught always blowing through—with all the scrubbing, and cleaning, and polishing, and scouring which used to go on, the grandmothers, and still more the great grandmothers, always out of doors and never with a bonnet on except to go to church, these things entirely account for the fact so often seen of a great grandmother, who was a tower of physical vigour descending into a grandmother perhaps a little less vigorous but still sound as a bell and healthy to the core, into a mother languid and confined to her carriage and house, and lastly into a daughter sickly and confined to her bed. For, remember, even with a general decrease of mortality you may often find a race thus degenerating and still oftener a family. You may see poor little feeble washed-out rags, children of a noble stock, suffering morally and physically, throughout their useless, degenerate lives, and yet people who are going to marry and to bring more such into the world, will consult nothing but their own convenience as to where they are to live, or how they are to live.

With regard to the health of houses where there is a sick person, it often happens that the sick room is made a ventilating shaft for the rest of the house. For while the house is kept as close, unaired, and dirty as usual, the window of the sick room is kept a little open always, and the door occasionally. Now, there are certain sacrifices which a house with one sick person in it does make to that sick person: it ties up its knocker; it lays straw before it in the street. Why can't it keep itself thoroughly clean and unusually well aired, in deference to the sick person?

We must not forget what, in ordinary language, is called "Infection:"—a thing of which people are generally so afraid that they frequently follow the very practice in regard to it which they ought to avoid. Nothing used to be considered so infectious or contagious as small-pox; and people not very long ago used to cover up patients with heavy bed clothes, while they kept up large fires and shut the windows. Small-pox, of course, under this *regime*, is very "infectious." People are somewhat wiser now in their management of this disease. They have ventured to cover the patients lightly and to keep the windows open; and we hear much less of the "infection" of small-pox than we used to do. But do people in our days act with more wisdom on the subject of "infection" in fevers—scarlet fever, measles, &c.—than their forefathers did with small-pox? Does not the popular idea of "infection" involve that people should take greater care of themselves than of the patient? That, for instance, it is safer not to be too much with the patient, not to attend too much to his wants? Perhaps the best illustration of the utter absurdity of this view of duty in attending on "infectious" diseases is afforded by what was very recently the practice, if it is not so even now, in some of the European lazarets—in which the plague-patient used to be condemned to the horrors of filth, overcrowding, and want of ventilation, while the medical attendant was ordered to examine the patient's tongue through an opera-glass and to toss him a lancet to open his abscesses with?

True nursing ignores infection, except to prevent it. Cleanliness and fresh air from open windows, with unremitting attention to the patient, are the only defence a true nurse either asks or needs.

Wise and humane management of the patient is the best safeguard against infection.

There are not a few popular opinions, in regard to which it is useful at times to ask a question or two. For example, it is commonly thought that children must have what are commonly called "children's epidemics," "current contagions," &c., in other words, that they are born to have measles, hooping-cough, perhaps even scarlet fever, just as they are born t cut their teeth, if they live.

Now, do tell us, why must a child have measles?

Oh because, you say, we cannot keep it from infection—other children have measles—and it must take them—and it is safer that it should.

But why must other children have measles? And if they have, why must yours have them too?

If you believed in and observed the laws for preserving the health of houses which inculcate cleanliness ventilation, white-washing, and other means, and which, by the way, *are laws*, as implicitly as you believe in the popular opinion, for it is nothing more than an opinion, that your child must have children's epidemics, don't you think that upon the whole your child would be more likely to escape altogether?

* * * * *

VI. Taking Food

Every careful observer of the sick will agree in this that thousands of patients are annually starved in the midst of plenty, from want of attention to the ways which alone make it possible for them to take food. This want of attention is as remarkable in those who urge upon the sick to do what is quite impossible to them, as in the sick themselves who will not make the effort to do what is perfectly possible to them.

For instance, to the large majority of very weak patients it is quite impossible to take any solid food before 11 A.M., nor than, if their strength is still further exhausted by fasting till that hour. For weak patients have generally feverish nights and, in the morning, dry mouths; and, if they could eat with those dry mouths, it would be the worse for them. A spoonful of beef-tea, of arrowroot and wine, of egg flip, every hour, will give them the requisite nourishment, and prevent them from being to much exhausted to take at a later hour the solid food, which is necessary for their recovery. And every patient who can swallow at all can swallow these liquid things, if he chooses. But how often do we hear a mutton-chop, an egg, a bit of bacon, ordered to a patient for breakfast, to whom (as a moments consideration would show us) it must be quite impossible to masticate such things at that hour.

Again, a nurse is ordered to give a patient a tea-cup full of some article of food every three hours. The patient's stomach rejects it. If so, try a table-spoon full every hour; if this will not do, a tea-spoon full every quarter of an hour.

I am bound to say, that I think more patients are lost by want of care and ingenuity in these momentous minutiae in private nursing than in public hospitals. And I think there is more of the *entente cordiale* to assist one another's hands between the doctor and his head nurse in the latter institutions, than between the doctor and the patient's friends in the private house.

If we did but know the consequences which may ensue, in very weak patients, from ten minutes' fasting or repletion (I call it repletion when they are obliged to let too small an interval elapse between taking food and some other exertion, owing to the nurse's unpunctuality), we should be more careful never to let this occur. In very weak patients there is often a nervous difficulty of swallowing, which is so much increased by any other call upon their strength that, unless they have their food punctually at the minute, which minute again must be arranged so as to fall in with no other minute's occupation, they can take nothing till the next respite occurs—so that an unpunctuality or delay of ten minutes may very well turn out to be one of two or three hours. And why is it not as easy to be punctual to a minute Life often literally hangs upon these minutes.

In acute cases, where life or death is to be determined in a few hours, these matters are very generally attended to, especially in Hospitals; and the number of cases is large where the patient is, as it were, brought back to life by exceeding care on the part of the Doctor or Nurse, or both, in ordering and giving nourishment with minute selection and punctuality.

But in chronic cases, lasting over months and years, where the fatal issue is often determined at last by mere protracted starvation, I had rather not enumerate the instances which I have known where a little ingenuity, and a great deal of perseverance, might, in all probability, have averted the result. The consulting the hours when the patient can take food, the observation of the times, often varying, when he is most faint, the altering seasons of taking food, in order to anticipate and prevent such times—all this, which requires observation, ingenuity, and perseverance (and these really constitute the good Nurse), might save more lives than we wont of.

To leave the patient's untasted food by his side, from meal to meal, in hopes that he will eat it in the interval is simply to prevent him from taking any food at all. I have known patients literally incapacitated from taking one article of food after another, by this piece of ignorance. Let the food come at the right time, and be taken away, eaten or uneaten, at the right time; but never let a patient have "something always standing" by him, if you don't wish to disgust him of everything.

On the other hand, I have known a patient's life saved (he was sinking for want of food) by the simple question, put to him by the doctor, "But is there no hour when you feel you could eat?" "Oh, yes," he said, "I could always take something at __ o'clock and __ o'clock." The thing was tried and succeeded. Patients very seldom, however, can tell this, it is for you to watch and find it out.

A patient should, if possible, not see or smell either the food of others, or a greater amount of food than he himself can consume at one time, or even hear food talked about or see it in the raw state. I know of no exception to the above rule. The breaking of it always induces a greater or less incapacity of taking food.

In hospital wards it is of course impossible to observe all this; and in single wards, where a patient must be continuously and closely watched, it is frequently impossible to relieve the attendant, so that his or her own meals can be taken out of the ward. But it is not the less true that, in such cases, even where the patient is not himself aware of it, his possibility of taking food is limited by seeing the attendant eating meals under his observation. In some cases the sick are aware of it, and complain. A case where the patient was supposed to be insensible, but complained as soon as able to speak, is now present to my recollection.

Remember, however, that the extreme punctuality in well-ordered hospitals, the rule that nothing shall be done in the ward while the patients are having their meals, go far to counterbalance what unavoidable evil there is in having patients together. I have often seen the private nurse go on dusting or fidgeting about in a sick room all the while the patient is eating, or trying to eat.

That the more alone an invalid can be when taking food, the better, is unquestionable; and, even if he must be fed, the nurse should not allow him to talk, or talk to him, especially about food, while eating.

When a person is compelled, by the pressure of occupation, to continue his business while sick, it ought to be a rule WITHOUT ANY EXCEPTION WHATEVER, that no one shall bring business to him or talk to him while he is taking food, nor go on talking to him on interesting subjects up to the last moment before his meals, nor make an engagement with him immediately after, so that there be any hurry of mind while taking them.

Upon the observance of these rules, especially the first, often depends the patient's capability of taking food at all, or, if he is amiable and forces himself to take food, of deriving any nourishment from it.

A nurse should never put before a patient milk that is sour, meat or soup that is turned, an egg that is bad, or vegetables underdone. Yet often I have seen these things brought in to the sick in a state perfectly perceptible to every nose or eye except the nurse's. It is here that the clever nurse appears; she will not bring in the peccant article, but, not to disappoint the patient, she will whip up something else in a few minutes. Remember that sick cookery should half do the work of your poor patient's weak digestion. But if you further impair it with your bad articles, I know not what is to become of him or of it.

If the nurse is an intelligent being, and not a mere carrier of diets to and from the patient, let her exercise her intelligence in these things. How often we have known a patient eat nothing at all in the day, because one meal was left untasted (at that time he was incapable of eating), at another the milk was sour, the third was spoiled by some other accident. And it never occurred to the nurse to extemporize some expedient—it never occurred to her that as he had had no solid food that day he might eat a bit of toast (say) with his tea in the evening, or he might have some meal an hour earlier. A patient who cannot touch his dinner at two, will often accept it gladly, if brought to him at seven. But somehow nurses never "think of these things." One would imagine they did not consider themselves bound to exercise their judgment; they leave it to the patient. Now I am quite sure that it is better for a patient rather to suffer these neglects than to try to teach his nurse to nurse him, if she does not know how. It ruffles him, and if he is ill he is in no condition to teach, especially upon himself. The above remarks apply much more to private nursing than to hospitals.

I would say to the nurse, have a rule of thought about your patient's diet; consider, remember how much he has had, and how much he ought to have to-day. Generally, the only rule of the private patient's diet is what the nurse has to give. It is true she cannot give him what she has not got; but his stomach does not wait for her convenience, or even her necessity. If it is used to having its stimulus at one hour to-day, and tomorrow it does not have it, because she has failed in getting it, he will suffer. She must be always exercising her ingenuity to supply defects, and to remedy accidents which will happen among the best contrivers, but from which the patient does not suffer the less, because "they cannot be helped."

One very minute caution—take care not to spill into your patient's saucer, in other words, take care that the outside bottom rim of his cup shall be quite dry and clean; if, every time he lifts his cup to his lips, he has to carry the saucer with it, or else to drop the liquid upon, and to soil his sheet, or his bed-gown, or pillow, or if he is sitting up, his dress, you have no idea what a difference this minute want of care on your part makes to his comfort and even to his willingness for food.

VII. What Food?

I will mention one or two of the most common errors among women in charge of sick respecting sick diet. One is the belief that beef tea is the most nutritive of all articles. Now, just try and boil down a lb. Of beef into beef tea, evaporate your beef tea, and see what is left of your beef. You will find that there is barely a teaspoonful of solid nourishment to half a pint of water in beef tea—nevertheless there is a certain reparative quality in it, we do not know what, as there is in tea—but it may safely be given in almost any inflammatory disease, and is as little to be depended upon with the healthy or convalescent where much nourishment is required. Again, it is an ever ready saw that an egg is equivalent to a lb. Of meat—whereas it is not at all so. Also, it is seldom noticed with how many patients, particularly of nervous or bilious temperament, eggs disagree. All puddings made with eggs, are distasteful to them in consequence. An egg, whipped up with wine, is often the only form in which they can take this kind of nourishment. Again, if the patient has attained to eating meat, it is supposed that to give him meat is the only thing needful for his recovery; whereas scorbutic sores have been actually known to appear among sick persons living in the midst of plenty in England, which could be traced to no other source than this, viz.: that the nurse, depending on meat alone, had allowed the patient to be without vegetables for a considerable time, these latter being so badly cooked that he always left them untouched. Arrowroot is another grand dependence of the nurse. As a vehicle for wine, and as a restorative quickly prepared, it is all very well. But it is nothing but starch and water. Flour is both more nutritive, and less liable to ferment, and is preferable wherever it can be used.

Again, milk and the preparations from milk, are a most important article of food for the sick. Butter is the lightest kind of animal fat, and though it wants the sugar and some of the other elements which there are in milk, yet it is most valuable both in itself and in enabling the patient to eat more bread. Flour, oats, groats, barley, and their kind, are, as we have already said, preferable in all their preparations to all the preparations of arrowroot, sago, tapioca, and their kind. Cream, in many long chronic diseases, is quite irreplaceable by any other article whatever. It seems to act in the same manner as beef tea, and to most it is much easier of digestion than milk. In fact, it seldom disagrees. Cheese is not usually digestible by the sick, but it is pure nourishment for repairing waste; and I have seen sick, and not a few either, whose craving for cheese shewed how much it was needed by them.

But, if fresh milk is so valuable a food for the sick, the least change or sourness in it, makes it of all articles, perhaps, the most injurious; diarrhoea is a common result of fresh milk allowed to become at all sour. The nurse therefore ought to exercise her utmost care in this. In large institutions for the sick, even the poorest, the utmost care is exercised. Wenham Lake ice is used for this express purpose every summer, while the private patient, perhaps, never tastes a drop of milk that is not sour, all though the hot weather, so little does the private nurse understand the necessity of such care. Yet, if you consider that the only drop of real nourishment in your patient's tea is the drop of milk, and how much almost all English patients depend upon their tea, you will see the great importance of not depriving your patient of this drop of milk. Buttermilk, a totally different thing, is often very useful, especially in fevers.

In laying down rules of diet, by the amounts of "solid nutriment" in different kinds of food, it is constantly lost sight of what the patient requires to repair his waste, what he can take and what he can't. You cannot diet a patient from a book, you cannot make up the human body as you would make up a prescription—so many parts "carboniferous," so many parts "nitrogenous" will constitute a perfect diet for the patient. The nurse's observation here will materially assist the doctor—the patient's "fancies" will materially assist the nurse. For instance, sugar is one of the must nutritive of all articles, being pure carbon, and is particularly recommended in some books. But the vast majority of all patients in England, young and old, male and female, rich and poor, hospital and private, dislike sweet things—and while I have never known a person take to sweets when he was ill who disliked them when he was well, I have known many fond of them when in health, who in sickness would leave off anything sweet, even to sugar in tea—sweet puddings, sweet drinks, are their aversion; the furred tongue almost always likes what is sharp or pungent. Scorbutic patients are an exception, they often crave for sweetmeats and jams.

Jelly is another article of diet in great favour with nurses and friends of the sick; even if it could be eaten solid, it would not nourish, but it is simply the height of folly to take 1/8 oz. of gelatine and make it into a certain bulk by dissolving it in water and then to give it to the sick, as if the mere bulk represented nourishment. It is now known that jelly does not nourish, that it has a tendency to produce diarrhoea—and to trust to it to repair the waste of a diseased constitution is simply to starve the sick under the guise of feeding them. If 100 spoonfuls of jelly were given in the course of the day, you would have given one spoonful of gelatine, which spoonful has no nutritive power whatever.

And, nevertheless, gelatine contains a large quantity of nitrogen, which is one of the most powerful elements in nutrition; on the other hand, beef tea may be chosen as an illustration of great nutrient power in sickness, co-existing with a very small amount of solid nitrogenous matter.

Dr. Christison says that "every one will be struck with the readiness with which" certain classes of "patients will often take diluted meat juice or beef tea repeatedly, when they refuse all other kinds of food." This is particularly remarkable in "cases of gastric fever, in which," he says, "little or nothing else besides beef tea or diluted meat juice" has been taken for weeks or even months, "and yet a pint of beef tea contains scarcely 1/4 oz. of anything but water"—the result is so striking that he asks what is its mode of action? "Not simply nutrient—1/4 oz. of the most nutritive material cannot nearly replace the daily wear and tear of the tissues in any circumstances Possibly," he says, "it belongs to a new denomination of remedies."

It has been observed that a small quantity of beef tea added to other articles of nutrition augments their power out of all proportion to the additional amount of solid matter.

The reason why jelly should be in nutritious and beef tea nutritious to the sick, is a secret yet undiscovered, but it clearly shows that careful observation of the sick is the only clue to the best dietary.

Chemistry has as yet afforded little insight into the dieting of sick. All that chemistry can tell us is the amount of "carboniferous" or "nitrogenous" elements discoverable in different dietetic articles. It has given us lists of dietetic substances, arranged in the order of their richness in one or other of these principles; but that is all. In the great majority of cases, the stomach of the patient is guided by other principles of selection than merely the amount of carbon or nitrogen in the diet. No doubt, in this as in other things, nature has very definite rules for her guidance, but these rules can only be ascertained by the most careful observation at the bedside. She there teaches us that living chemistry, the chemistry of reparation, is something different from the chemistry of the laboratory. Organic chemistry is useful, as all knowledge is, when we come face to face with nature; but it by no means follows that we should learn in the laboratory any one of the reparative processes going on in disease.

Again, the nutritive power of milk and of the preparations from milk, is very much undervalued; there is nearly as much nourishment in half a pint of milk as there is in a quarter of a lb. of meat. But this is not the whole question or nearly the whole. The main question is what the patient's stomach can assimilate or derive nourishment from, and of this the patient's stomach is the sole judge. Chemistry cannot tell this. The patient's stomach must be its own chemist. The diet which will keep the healthy man healthy, will kill the sick one. The same beef which is the most nutritive of all meat and which nourishes the healthy man, is the least nourishing of all food to the sick man, whose half-dead stomach can assimilate no part of it, that is, make no food out of it. On a diet of beef tea healthy men on the other hand speedily lose their strength.

I have known patients live for many months without touching bread, because they could not eat baker's bread. These were mostly country patients, but not all. Homemade bread or brown bread is a most important article of diet for many patients. The use of aperients may be entirely superseded by it. Oat cake is another.

To watch for the opinions, then, which the patient's stomach gives, rather than to read "analyses of foods," is the business of all those who have to settle what the patient is to eat—perhaps the most important thing to be provided for him after the air he is to breathe.

Now the medical man who sees the patient only once a day or even only once or twice a week, cannot possibly tell this without the assistance of the patient himself, or of those who are in constant observation on the patient. The utmost the medical man can tell is whether the patient is weaker or stronger at this visit than he was at the last visit. I should therefore say that incomparably the most important office of the nurse, after she has taken care of the patient's air, is to take care to observe the effect of his food, and report it to the medical attendant.

It is quite incalculable the good that would certainly come from such *sound* and close observation in this almost neglected branch of nursing, or the help it would give to the medical man.

A great deal too much against tea is said by wise people, and a *great deal* too much of tea is given to the sick by foolish people. When you see the natural and almost universal craving in English sick for the "tea," you cannot but feel that nature knows what she is about. But a little tea or coffee restores them quite as much as a great deal, and a great deal of tea and especially of coffee impairs the little power of digestion they have. Yet a nurse, because she sees how one or two cups of tea or coffee restores her patient, thinks that three or four cups will do twice as much. This is not the case at all; it is however certain that there is nothing yet discovered which is a substitute to the English patient for his cup of tea; he can take it when he can take nothing else, and he often can't take anything else if he has it not. I should be very glad if any of the abusers of tea would point out what to give to an English patient after a sleepless night, instead of tea. If you give it at 5 or 6 o'clock in the morning, he may even sometimes fall asleep after it, and get perhaps his only two or three hours' sleep during the twenty-four. At the same time you never should give tea or coffee to the sick, as a rule, after 5 o'clock in the afternoon. Sleeplessness in the early night is from excitement generally and is increased by tea or coffee; sleeplessness which continues to the early morning is from exhaustion often, and is relieved by tea. The only English patients I have ever known refuse tea, have been typhus cases, and the first sign of their getting better was their craving again for tea. In general, the dry and dirty tongue always prefers tea to coffee, and will quite decline milk, unless with tea. Coffee is a better restorative than tea, but a greater impairer of the digestion. Let the patient's taste decide. You will say that, in cases of great thirst, the patient's craving decides that it will drink a great deal of tea, and that you cannot help it. But in these cases be sure that the patient requires diluents for quite other purposes than quenching the thirst; he wants a great deal of some drink, not only of tea, and the doctor will order what he is to have, barley water or lemonade, or soda water and milk, as the case may be.

Lehman, quoted by Dr. Christison, says that, among the well and active "the infusion of 1 oz. of roasted coffee daily will diminish the waste" going on in the body "by one-fourth," and Dr. Christison adds that tea has the same property. Now this is actual experiment. Lehman weighs the man and finds the fact from his weight. It is not deduced from any "analysis" of food. All experience among the sick shows the same thing.

Cocoa is often recommended to the sick in lieu of tea or coffee. But independently of the fact that English sick very generally dislike cocoa; it has quite a different effect from tea or coffee. It is an oily starchy nut having no restorative power at all, but simply increasing fat. It is pure mockery of the sick, therefore, to call it a substitute for tea. For any renovating stimulus it has, you might just as well offer them chestnuts instead of tea.

An almost universal error among nurses is in the bulk of the food and especially the drinks they offer to their patients. Suppose a patient ordered 4 oz. brandy during the day, how is he to take this if you make it into four pints with diluting it? the same with tea and beef tea, with arrowroot, milk, &c. You have not increased the nourishment, you have not increased the renovating power of these articles, by increasing their bulk—you have very likely diminished both by giving the patient's digestion more to do, and most likely of all, the patient will leave half of what he has been ordered to take, because he cannot swallow the bulk with which you have been pleased to invest it. It requires very nice observation and care (and meets with hardly any) to determine what will not be too thick or strong for the patient to take, while giving him no more than the bulk which he is able to swallow.

* * * * *

XII. Chattering Hopes and Advices

The sick man to his advisers.

"My advisers! Their name is legion.   * * * Somehow or other, it seems a provision of the universal destinies, that every man, woman, and child should consider him, her, or itself privileged especially to advise me. Why? That is precisely what I want to know." And this is what I have to say to them. I have been advised to go to every place extant in and out of England—to take every kind of exercise by every kind of cart, carriage—yes, and even swing(!) and dumb-bell (!) in existence; to imbibe every different kind of stimulus that ever has been invented. And this when those best fitted to know, viz., medical men, after long and close attendance, had declared any journey out of the question, had prohibited any kind of motion whatever, had closely laid down the diet and drink. What would my advisers say, were they the medical attendants, and I the patient left their advice, and took the casual adviser's? But the singularity in Legion's mind is this: it never occurs to him that everybody else is doing the same thing, and that I the patient *must* perforce say, in sheer self-defence, like Rosalind, "I could not do with all."

"Chattering Hopes" may seem an odd heading. But I really believe there is scarcely a greater worry which invalids have to endure than the incurable hopes of their friends. There is no one practice against which I can speak more strongly from actual personal experience, wide and long, of its effects during sickness observed both upon others and upon myself. I would appeal most seriously to all friends, visitors, and attendants of the sick to leave off this practice of attempting to "cheer" the sick by making light of their danger and by exaggerating their probabilities of recovery.

Far more now than formerly does the medical attendant tell the truth to the sick who are really desirous to hear it about their own state.

How intense is the folly, then, to say the least of it, of the friend, be he even a medical man, who thinks that his opinion, given after a cursory observation, will weigh with the patient, against the opinion of the medical attendant, given, perhaps, after years of observation, after using every help to diagnosis afforded by the stethoscope, the examination of pulse, tongue, &c.; and certainly after much more observation than the friend can possibly have had.

Supposing the patient to be possessed of common sense—how can the "favourable" opinion, if it is to be called an opinion at all, of the casual visitor "cheer" him—when different from that of the experienced attendant? Unquestionably the latter may, and often does, turn out to be wrong. But which is most likely to be wrong?

The fact is, that the patient is not "cheered" at all by these well-meaning, most tiresome friends. On the contrary, he is depressed and wearied. If, on the one hand, he exerts himself to tell each successive member of this too numerous conspiracy, whose name is legion, why he does not think as they do—in what respect he is worse—what symptoms exist that they know nothing of—he is fatigued instead of "cheered" and his attention is fixed upon himself. In general, patients who are really ill, do not want to talk about themselves. Hypochondriacs do, but again I say we are not on the subject of hypochondriacs.

If, on the other hand, and which is much more frequently the case, the patient says nothing, but the Shakespearian "Oh!" "Ah!" "Go to !" and "In good sooth!" in order to escape from the conversation about himself the sooner, he is depressed by want of sympathy. He feels isolated in the midst of friends. He feels what a convenience it would be, if there were any single person to whom he could speak simply and openly, without pulling the string upon himself of this shower-bath of silly hopes and encouragements; to whom he could express his wishes and directions without that person persisting in saying, "I hope that it will please God yet to give you twenty years" or, "You have a long life of activity before you." How often we see at the end of biographies or of cases recorded in medical papers, "after a long illness A. died rather suddenly, or, unexpectedly both to himself and to others." "Unexpectedly" to others, perhaps, who did not see, because they did not look; but by no means "unexpectedly to himself," as I feel entitled to believe, both from the internal evidence in such stories, and from watching similar cases; there was every reason to expect that A. would die, and he knew it; but he found it useless to insist upon his own knowledge to his friends.

In these remarks I am alluding neither to acute cases which terminate rapidly nor to "nervous" cases.

By the first much interest in their own danger is very rarely felt. In writings of fiction, whether novels or biographies, these death-beds are generally depicted as almost seraphic in lucidity of intelligence. Sadly large has been my experience in death-beds, and I can only say that I have seldom or never seen such. Indifference, excepting with regard to bodily suffering, or to some duty the dying man desires to perform, is the far more usual state.

The "nervous case," on the other hand, delights in figuring to himself and others a fictitious danger.

But the long chronic case, who knows too well himself, and who has been told by his physician that he will never enter active life again, who feels that every month he has to give up something he could do the month before—oh! spare such sufferers your chattering hopes. You do not know how you worry and weary them. Such real sufferers cannot bear to talk of themselves, still less to hope for what they cannot at all expect.

So also as to all the advice showered so profusely upon such sick, to leave off some occupation, to try some other doctor, some other house, climate, pill, powder, or specific; I say nothing of the inconsistency—for these advisers are sure to be the same persons who exhorted the sick man not to believe his own doctor's prognostics, because "doctors are always mistaken," but to believe some other doctor, because "this doctor is always right." Sure also are these advisers to be the persons to bring the sick man fresh occupation, while exhorting him to leave his own.

Wonderful is the face with which friends, lay and medical, will come in and worry the patient with recommendations to do something or other, having just as little knowledge as to its being feasible, or even safe for him, as if they were to recommend a man to take exercise, not knowing he had broken his leg. What would the friend say, if *he* were the medical attendant, and if the patient, because some *other* friend had come in, because somebody, anybody, nobody, had recommended something, anything, nothing, were to disregard his orders, and take that other body's recommendation? But people never think of this.

A celebrated historical personage has related the commonplaces which, when on the eve of executing a remarkable resolution, were showered in nearly the same words by every one around successively for a period of six months. To these the personage states that it was found least trouble always to reply the same thing, viz., that it could not be supposed that such a resolution had been taken without sufficient previous consideration. To patients enduring every day for years from every friend or acquaintance, either by letter or *viva voce*, some torment of this kind, I would suggest the same answer. It would indeed be spared, if such friends and acquaintances would but consider for one moment, that it is probable the patient has heard such advice at least fifty times before, and that, had it been practicable, it would have been practised long ago. But of such consideration there appears to be no chance. Strange, though true, that people should be just the same in these things as they were a few hundred years ago!

To me these commonplaces, leaving their smear upon the cheerful, single-hearted, constant devotion to duty, which is so often seen in the decline of such sufferers, recall the slimy trail left by the snail on the sunny southern garden-wall loaded with fruit.

No mockery in the world is so hollow as the advice showered upon the sick. It is of no use for the sick to say anything, for what the adviser wants is, not to know the truth about the state of the patient, but to turn whatever the sick may say to the support of his own argument, set forth, it must be repeated, without any inquiry whatever into the patient's real condition. "But it would be impertinent or indecent in me to make such an inquiry," says the adviser. True; and how much more impertinent is it to give your advice when you can know nothing about the truth, and admit you could not inquire into it.

To nurses I say—these are the visitors who do your patient harm. When you hear him told: 1) that he has nothing the matter with him, and that he wants cheering, 2) that he is committing suicide, and that he wants preventing, 3) that he is the tool of somebody who makes use of him for a purpose, 4) that he will listen to nobody, but is obstinately bent upon his own way; and 5) that he ought to be called to a sense of duty, and is flying in the face of Providence—then know that your patient is receiving all the injury that he can receive from a visitor.

How little the real sufferings of illness are known or understood. How little does any one in good health fancy him or even *her*self into the life of a sick person.

Do, you who are about the sick or who visit the sick, try and give them pleasure, remember to tell them what will do so. How often in such visits the sick person has to do the whole conversation, exerting his own imagination and memory, while you would take the visitor, absorbed in his own anxieties, making no effort of memory or imagination, for the sick person. "Oh! my dear, I have so much to think of, I really quite forgot to tell him that; besides, I thought he would know it," says the visitor to another friend. How could "he know it?" Depend upon it, the people who say this are really those who have little "to think of." There are many burthened with business who always manage to keep a pigeon-hole in their minds, full of things to tell the "invalid."

I do not say, don't tell him your anxieties—I believe it is good for him and good for you too; but if you tell him what is anxious, surely you can remember to tell him what is pleasant too.

A sick person does so enjoy hearing good news—for instance, of a love and courtship, while in progress to a good ending. If you tell him only when the marriage takes place, he loses half the pleasure, which God knows he has little enough of; and ten to one but you have told him of some love-making with a bad ending.

A sick person also intensely enjoys hearing of any *material* good, any positive or practical success of the right. He has so much of books and fiction, of principles, and precepts, and theories; do, instead of advising him with advice he has heard at least fifty times before, tell him of one benevolent act which has really succeeded practically—it is like a day's health to him.

You have no idea what the craving of sick with undiminished power of thinking, but little power of doing, is to hear of good practical action, when they can no longer partake in it.

Do observe these things with the sick. Do remember how their life is to them disappointed and incomplete. You see them lying there with miserable disappointments, from which they can have no escape but death, and you can't remember to tell them of what would give them so much pleasure, or at least an hour's variety.

They don't want you to be lachrymose and whining with them, they like you to be fresh and active and interested, but they cannot bear absence of mind, and they are so tired of the advice and preaching they receive from everybody, no matter whom it is, they see.

There is no better society than babies and sick people for one another. Of course you must manage this so that neither shall suffer from it, which is perfectly possible. If you think, the "air of the sick room" bad for the baby, why it is bad for the invalid too, and, therefore, you will of course correct it for both. It freshens up a sick person's whole mental atmosphere to see "the baby." And a very young child, if unspoiled, will generally adapt itself wonderfully to the ways of a sick person, if the time they spend together is not too long.

If you knew how unreasonably sick people suffer from reasonable causes of distress, you would take more pains about all these things. An infant laid upon the sick bed will do the sick person, thus suffering, more good than all your logic. A piece of good news will do the same. Perhaps you are afraid of "disturbing" him. You say there is no comfort for his present cause of affliction. It is perfectly reasonable. The distinction is this, if he is obliged to act, do not "disturb" him with another subject of thought just yet; help him to do what he wants to do; but, if he *has* done this, or if nothing can be done, then "disturb" him by all means. You will relieve more effectually, unreasonable suffering from reasonable causes by telling him "the news," showing him "the baby," or giving him something new to think of or to look at than by all the logic in the world.

It has been very justly said that the sick are like children in this, that there is no *proportion* in events to them. Now it is your business as their visitor to restore this right proportion for them—to show them what the rest of the world is doing. How can they find it out otherwise? You will find them far more open to conviction than children in this. And you will find that their unreasonable intensity of suffering from unkindness, from want of sympathy, &c., will disappear with their freshened interest in the bid world's events. But then you must be able to give them real interests, not gossip.

Summary

To sum up: the answer to two of the commonest objections urged, one by women themselves, the other by men, against the desirableness of sanitary knowledge for women, *plus* a caution, comprises the whole argument for the art of nursing.

1)   It is often said by men, that it is unwise to teach women anything about these laws of health, because they will take to physicking—that there is a great deal too much of amateur physicking as it is, which is indeed true. One eminent physician told me that he had known more calomel given, both at a pinch and for a continuance, by mothers, governesses, and nurses, to children than he had ever heard of a physician prescribing in all his experience. Another says, that women's only idea in medicine is calomel and aperients. This is undeniably too often the case. There is nothing ever seen in any professional practice like the reckless physicking by amateur females. But this is just what the really

experienced and observing nurse does not do; she neither physics herself or others. And to cultivate in things pertaining to health observation and experience in women who are mothers, governesses or nurses, is just the way to do away with amateur physicking, and if the doctors did but know it, to make the nurses obedient to them—helps to them instead of hindrances. Such education in women would indeed diminish the doctor's work—but no one really believes that doctors wish that there should be more illness, in order to have more work.

2) It is often said by women, that they cannot know anything of the laws of health, or what to do to preserve their children's health, because they can know nothing of "Pathology," or cannot "dissect,"—a confusion of ideas which it is hard to attempt to disentangle. Pathology teaches the harm that disease has done. But it teaches nothing more. We know nothing of the principle of health, the positive of which pathology is the negative, except from observation and experience. And nothing but observation and experience will teach us the ways to maintain or to bring back the state of health. It is often thought that medicine is the curative process. It is no such thing; medicine is the surgery of functions, as surgery proper is that of limbs and organs. Neither can do anything but remove obstructions; neither can cure; nature alone cures. Surgery removes the bullet out of the limb, which is an obstruction to cure, but nature heals the wound. So it is with medicine; the function of an organ becomes obstructed; medicine, so far as we know, assists nature to remove the obstruction, but does nothing more. And what nursing has to do in either case, is to put the patient in the best condition for nature to act upon him. Generally, just the contrary is done. You think fresh air, and quiet and cleanliness extravagant, perhaps dangerous, luxuries, which should be given to the patient only when quite convenient, and medicine the *sine qua non*, the panacea. If I have succeeded in any measure in dispelling this illusion, and in showing what true nursing is, and what it is not, my object will have been answered.

Now for the caution:

3) It seems a commonly received idea among men and even among women themselves that it requires nothing but a disappointment in love, the want of an object, a general disgust, or incapacity for other things, to turn a woman into a good nurse.

This reminds one of the parish where a stupid old man was set to be schoolmaster because he was "past keeping the pigs."

Apply the above receipt for making a good nurse to making a good servant. And the receipt will be found to fail.

Yet popular novelists of recent days have invented ladies disappointed in love or fresh out of the drawing-room turning into the war-hospitals to find their wounded lovers, and when found, forthwith abandoning their sickward for their lover, as might be expected. Yet in the estimation of the authors, these ladies were none the worse for that, but on the contrary were heroines of nursing.

What cruel mistakes are sometimes made by benevolent men and women in matters of business about which they can know nothing and think they know a great dead.

The everyday management of a large ward, let alone of a hospital—the knowing what are the laws of life and death for men, and what the laws of health for wards—(and wards are healthy or unhealthy, mainly according to the knowledge or ignorance of the nurse)—are not these matters of sufficient importance and difficulty to require learning by experience and careful inquiry, just as much as any other art? They do not come by inspiration to the lady disappointed in love, nor to the poor workhouse drudge hard up for a livelihood.

And terrible is the injury which has followed to the sick from such wild notions!

In this respect (and why is it so?), in Roman Catholic countries, both writers and workers are, in theory at least, far before ours. They would never think of such a beginning for a good working Superior or Sister of Charity. And many a Superior has refused to admit a *Postulant* who appeared to have no better "vocation" or reasons for offering herself than these.

It is true we can make "no vows." But is a "vow" necessary to convince us that the true spirit for learning any art, most especially an art of charity, aright, is not a disgust to everything or something else? Do we really place the love of our kind (and of nursing, as one branch of it) so low as this? What would the Mère Angélique of Port Royal, what would our own Mrs. Fry have said to this?

NOTE: I would earnestly ask my sisters to keep clear of both the jargons now current everywhere (for they are equally jargons); of the jargon, namely, about the "rights" of women, which urges women to do all that men do, including the medical and other professions, merely because men do it, and without regard to whether this is the best that women can do; and of the jargon which urges women to do nothing that men do, merely because they are women, and should be "recalled to a sense of their duty as women," and because "this is women's work" and "that is men's," and "these are things which women should not do," which is all assertion, and nothing more. Surely woman should bring the best she has, *whatever* that is, to the work of God's world, without attending to either of these cries. For what are they, both of them, the one *just* as much as the other, but listening to the "what people will say," to opinion, to the "voices from without?" And as a wise man has said, no one has ever done anything great or useful by listening to the voices from without.

You do not want the effect of your good things to be, "How wonderful for a *woman*!" nor would you be deterred from good things by hearing it said, "Yes, but she ought not to have done this, because it is not suitable for a woman." But you want to do the thing that is good, whether it is "suitable for a woman" or not.

It does not make a thing good, that it is remarkable that a woman should have been able to do it. Neither does it make a thing bad, which would have been good had a man done it, that it has been done by a woman.

Oh, leave these jargons, and go your way straight to God's work, in simplicity and singleness of heart.

Endnotes

1.   The health of carriages, especially close carriages, is not of sufficient universal importance to mention here, otherwise than cursorily. Children, who are always the most delicate test of sanitary conditions, generally cannot enter a close carriage without being sick—and very lucky for them that it is so. A close carriage, with the horse-hair cushions and linings always saturated with organic matter, if to this be added the windows up, is one of the most unhealthy of human receptacles. The idea of taking an *airing* in it is something preposterous. Dr. Angus Smith has shown that a crowded railway carriage, which goes at the rate of 30 miles an hour, is as unwholesome as the strong smell of a sewer, or as a back yard in one of the most unhealthy courts off one of the most unhealthy streets in Manchester.

2.   In the diseases produced by bad food, such as scorbutic dysentery and diarrhoea, the patient's stomach often craves for and digests things, some of which certainly would be laid down in no dietary that ever was invented for sick, and especially not for such sick. These are fruit, pickles, jams, gingerbread, fat of ham or bacon, suet, cheese, butter, milk. These cases I have seen not by ones, nor by tens, but by hundreds. And the patient's stomach was right and the book was wrong. The articles craved for, in these cases, might have been principally arranged under the two heads of fat and vegetable acids.
There is often a marked difference between men and women in this matter of sick feeding. Women's digestion is generally slower.

3.   In making coffee, it is absolutely necessary to buy it in the berry and grind it at home. Otherwise you may reckon upon its containing a certain amount of chicory, *at least*. This is not a question of the taste, or of the wholesomeness of chicory. It is that chicory has nothing at all of the properties for which you give coffee. And therefore you may as well not give it.
Again, all laundresses, mistresses of dairy-farms, head nurses, (I speak of the good old sort only—women who unite a good deal of hard manual labour with the head-work necessary for arranging the day's business, so that none of it shall tread upon the heels of something else,) set great value, I have observed, upon having a high-priced tea. This is called extravagant. But these women are "extravagant" in nothing else. And they are right in this. Real tea-leaf tea alone contains the restorative they want; which is not to be found in sloc-leaf tea.
The mistresses of houses, who cannot even go over their own house once a day, are incapable of judging for these women. For they are incapable themselves, to all appearance, of the spirit of arrangement (no small task) necessary for managing a large ward or dairy.

4.   There are, of course, cases, as in first confinements, when an assurance from the doctor or experienced nurse to the frightened suffering woman that there is nothing unusual in her case, that she has nothing to fear but a few hours' pain, may cheer her most effectually. This is advice of quite another order. It is the advice of experience to utter inexperience. But the advice we have been referring to is the advice of inexperience to bitter experience; and, in

general, amounts to nothing more than this, that you think I shall recover from consumption because somebody knows somebody somewhere who has recovered from fever.

I have heard a doctor condemned whose patient did not, alas! recover, because another doctor' s patient of a *different* sex, of a *different* age, recovered from a *different* disease, in a *different* place. Yes, this is really true. If people who make these comparisons did but know (only they do not care to know), the care and preciseness with which such comparisons require to be made, (and are made) in order to be of any value whatever, they would spare their tongues. In comparing the deaths of one hospital with those of another, any statistics are justly considered absolutely valueless which do not give the ages, the sexes, and the diseases of all the cases. It does not seem necessary to mention this. It does not seem necessary to say that there can be no comparison between old men with dropsies and young women with consumptions. Yet the cleverest men and the cleverest women are often heard making such comparisons, ignoring entirely sex, age, disease, place—in fact, *all* the conditions essential to the question. It is the merest *gossip*.

5.   A small pet animal is often an excellent companion for the sick, for long chronic cases especially. A pet bird in a cage is sometimes the only pleasure of an invalid confined for years to the same room. If he can feed and clean the animal himself, he ought always to be encouraged to do so.

6.   I have known many ladies who, having once obtained a "blue pill" prescription from a physician, gave and took it as a common aperient two or three times a week—with what effect may be supposed. In one case I happened to be the person to inform the physician of it, who substituted for the prescription a comparatively harmless aperient pill. The lady came to me and complained that it "did not suit her half so well. "

If women will take or give physic, by far the safest plan is to send for "the doctor" every time—-for I have known ladies who both gave and took physic, who would not take the pains to learn the names of the commonest medicines, and confounded, e.g., colocynth with colchicum. This *is* playing with sharp-edged tools "with a vengeance. "

There are excellent women who will write to London to their physician that there is much sickness in their neighbourhood in the country, and ask for some prescription from him, which they used to like themselves, and then give it to all their friends and to all their poorer neighbours who will take it. Now, instead of giving medicine, of which you cannot possibly know the exact and proper application, nor all its consequences, would it not be better if you were to persuade and help your poorer neighbours to remove the dung-hill from before the door, to put in a window which opens, or an Arnott's ventilator, or to cleanse and limewash the cottages? Of these things the benefits are sure. The benefits of the inexperienced administration of medicines are by no means so sure.

Homeopathy has introduced one essential amelioration in the practice of physic by amateur females; for its rules are excellent, its physicking comparatively harmless—the "globule" is the one grain of folly which appears to be necessary to make any good thing acceptable. Let then women, if they will give medicine, give homoeopathic medicine. It won't do any harm.

An almost universal error among women is the supposition that everybody must have the bowels opened once in every twenty-four hours, or must fly immediately to aperients. The reverse is the conclusion of experience.

This is a doctor's subject, and I will not enter more into it; but will simply repeat, do not go on taking or giving to your children your abominable "coruses of aperients," without calling in the doctor.

It is very seldom indeed, that by choosing your diet, you cannot regulate your own bowels; and every woman may watch herself to know what kind of diet will do this; I have known deficiency of meat to produce constipation, quite as often as deficiency of vegetables; baker's bread much oftener than either. Home made brown bread will oftener cure it than anything else.

I have no doubt that it is possible to give a new direction to technological development, a direction that will lead it back to the real needs of man, and that also means, *to the actual size of man.* Man is small, and, therefore, small is beautiful. To go for giantism is to go for self-destruction.

E.F. Schumacher, *Small is Beautiful,* 1973

THE ART OF
TECHNOLOGY ASSESSMENT

JAMES F. CHILDRESS

James F. Childress, professor of religious studies and medical education at the University of Virginia, was born in 1940 at Mount Airy, North Carolina. He received a B.A. degree from Guilford College, and the B.D., M.A. and Ph.D. from Yale. He has been a member of the faculty at the University of Virginia since 1968, with an interim as professor of Christian ethics at Georgetown University, 1975-1979, and has served as visiting professor at the University of Chicago, Princeton, and the College of Physicians and Surgeons at Columbia. He has written broadly on issues of ethics in science and medicine, and is widely regarded as one of the very best thinkers in the area of biomedical ethics.

1. How does Childress think that the opening lines of Dickens' *A Tale of Two Cities* apply to modern technology and society?

2. What is Childress' criticism of "technological determinism"?

3. What is "technology assessment" and what is its function?

4. What should be the reasonable approach to human control over nature?

5. What principles and values would Childress apply to technology assessment?

6. How can one accept the principles of proportionality or utility without accepting utilitarianism?

THE ART OF TECHNOLOGY ASSESSMENT

JAMES F. CHILDRESS

Technology, Assessment, and Control

"It was the best of times, it was the worst of times, it was the age of wisdom, it was the age of foolishness." These Words, which Charles Dickens uses for the French Revolution in *A Tale of Two Cities,* could easily apply to our discourse about technology. Positive and negative superlatives abound. We are quick to applaud or to disapprove. Rarely do we grasp the ambiguity of technology and the necessity of subtle and nuanced evaluations. Our public policies will not be responsible until we grasp this ambiguity and deal with it in relation to moral principles and values.

In the late 1950s and early 1960s, many commentators declared that the modern world had lost interest in, or the capacity to answer, big questions such as the meaning of life and the goals of our institutions. Social scientists such as Daniel Bell announced the "end of ideology," philosophers such as Peter Laslett observed that "political philosophy is dead," and theologians such as Harvey Cox noted the decline of religion. According to Cox, the secular city was emerging, and its inhabitants would be pragmatic and profane, interested only in what will work in this world. All these interpretations converged: individuals and communities are no longer interested in, or able to deal with, ideology, metaphysics, and mystery. Some interpreters even went so far as to say that the important issues are merely technical and can be handled by the technicians or experts. President Kennedy expressed this viewpoint in the early '60s, when he held that the real issue today is the management of industrial society—a problem of ways and means, not of ideology. As he put it, "the fact of the matter is that most of the problems, or at least many of them, that we now face are technical problems, are administrative problems [requiring] . . . very sophisticated judgments which do not lend themselves to the great sort of 'passionate movements' which have stirred this country so often in the past."

The obituaries for ideology, social and political philosophy, and religion were premature—as the events of the last twenty years have demonstrated. In the rapid growth of various religious communities and in the conflicts over civil rights, the war in Vietnam, abortion, and technology, it became clear that interest in the big questions was only dormant or overlooked in the rush to embrace new trends.

For the most part, those who wrote the obituaries for meaning and value in the modern world were quite sanguine about technological society and the technocrats who would run it without worrying about larger perspectives. But while they praised technological man, others such as Jacques Ellul, viewed him with distrust and disdain. However, their debates lacked subtlety and discrimination largely because the protechnologists and the antitechnologists tended to agree that the issue was technology as such (or at least modern technology as such}. As a result, they obscured the importance of assessing and controlling particular technologies.

Unfortunately, these global perspectives endure. Two examples can be found in recent books. In *The Republic of Technology: Reflections on Our Future Community*, Daniel Boorstin, the Librarian of Congress, connects the growth of technology with the (alleged) decline of ideology: "Technology dilutes and dissolves ideology.... More than any other modern people we have been free of the curse of ideology." Holding that we are most human when we are making and using tools, Boorstin is enthusiastic about technology as such.

An example of a global perspective that is negative toward technology (at least within one area of medicine) is Stanley Reiser's *Medicine and the Reign of Technology*. Reiser, a historian of medicine, traces the development of various diagnostic technologies such as the stethoscope and concludes that they have increasingly alienated physicians from patients. Because they provide external, objective signs, the physician no longer relies on his own personal contact with the patient for diagnosis. Thus, the physician concentrates on the measurable aspects of illness rather than on human factors. "Accuracy, efficiency, and security are purchased at a high price," Reiser contends, "When that price is impersonal medical care and undermining the physician's belief in his own medical powers." The physician, he says, "must rebel against this reign of technology."

It is interesting that both Boorstin and Reiser choose "political" metaphors and images when they discuss technology: "republic," "reign," and "rebellion." And despite their different responses to technology, both appear to hold a form of technological determinism, either hard or soft. Technology determines social relationships, for example, between patient and physician. Not only are there problems with this determinism which makes technology an independent variable, but it is not accurate or helpful to approach technology as such, to offer global praise or blame. More precise and discriminate judgements are required if we are to reap the benefits and avoid the evils of particular technologies. One attempt in the last fifteen years to provide a way to control technologies through public policy is *technology assessment*. I want to examine the art of technology assessment, its possibilities and its limitations.

For our purposes, "technology" can be defined as the "systematic application of scientific knowledge and technical skills for the control of matter, energy, etc., for practical purposes." I shall concentrate on biomedical technologies: the technologies, (techniques, drugs, equipment, and procedures) used by professionals in delivering medical care. Examples include insulin, the totally implantable artificial heart, kidney dialysis, CAT scanners, and in vitro fertilization.

We assess technologies in order to be able to "control" them responsibly through our public policies. Public policy is a purposive course or pattern of action or inaction by government officials. Public policies designed to "control" technologies may operate in many different ways. The most typical and common controls are the allocation of funds (e.g., the decision to give research on cancer priority) and regulation or prohibition (e.g., the prohibition of the use of Laetrile). But it is also possible to permit and even to fund a technology while trying to control its side effects through other measures.

Control cannot be properly directed without an assessment of technology. The phrase "technology assessment" was apparently first used in 1966 by Philip Yeager, counsel for the House Committee on Science and Astronautics, in a report by the House Subcommittee on Science, Research and Development, chaired by Congressman Emilio Q. Dadderio (D-Conn.), later the first head of the Office of Technology Assessment. Basically, technology assessment is a comprehensive approach, considering all the possible or probable consequences, intended and unintended effects, of a technology on society. It is thus multidisciplinary and interdisciplinary.

Against some interpreters and practitioners of technology assessment, I would argue that it is "an art form," not a science. As an art form, it is basically the work of imagination which is indispensable for judgment-making. All sorts of methods can be used, and technology assessment should not be identified with any particular methods. Before policy-makers had access to systems analysts, and the like, they consulted astrologers, and, on the whole, Hannah Arendt once suggested it would be better if they still consulted astrologers! I want to show that technology assessment can be more than a narrow technique and that, as a broad approach, drawing on several different methods it is an indispensable art.

Theological Convictions

Technology assessments will draw on theological (or quasi-theological) convictions as well as on moral principles and values. Before turning to the latter, I want to indicate how general theological convictions provide perspectives on and engender attitudes toward technology, often through perspectives on and attitudes toward nature. It should be noted that Christian (and Jewish) convictions reflect certain tensions which may be creative or destructive.

On the one hand, the Christian tradition affirms the goodness of creation, holding that nature is not an enemy to be assaulted. On the other hand, it also leads to what Max Weber called "the disenchantment of the world" or "the rationalization of the world." Its stress on God's transcendence tends to exclude spirits in nature who need to be approached with awe, and it thus frees nature for man's dominion.

Another tension can be seen in the distinction between sovereignty over nature and stewardship of nature. Although the Christian tradition has sometimes engendered (or at least supported) attitudes of human sovereignty over nature, its dominant theme is human stewardship, deputyship, or trusteeship. While the sovereign is not accountable, the trustee is accountable to God and for what happens to nature. Human action takes place within a context in which humans are ultimately responsible to God as the sovereign Lord of life, Creator, Preserver, and Redeemer. Within this perspective of trusteeship, we cannot be satisfied with a short-term view of responsibility. For example, there is penultimate responsibility to and for future generations: it is not legitimate to slight this responsibility by asking, What has posterity ever done for us? And there is penultimate responsibility to and for nonhuman nature, not only because "nature bats last!"

Some theological critics reject the image of stewardship or trusteeship because it involves *dominium tarrae*. But it is irresponsible to neglect or to repudiate human control over nature. The issue is not control (technology) but, rather, the ends, effects, and means of control (technology). This control is not total or unlimited: it is not absolute dominion. It is limited and constrained by nature itself, by moral principles and rules, and by ultimate loyalty and responsibility to God. It is not necessary or desirable to conceive these limits and constraints in terms of "rights" (e.g., rights of trees) as though we can imagine moral requirements only when we can invoke rights. However, important rights are—and they are very important—we can conceive moral limits on our control of nature without appealing to them.

The ends of *dominium terrae* are also subject to criticism. If there is a hierarchy of interests, and if human interests are dominant, they should not be construed narrowly—for example, in terms of material goods. Nor should they exclude the goods of nature which are not reducible to human interests. Theologically, the propensity of human beings to construe their interests narrowly and to exclude nonhuman interests or goods is explained in terms of sin. Because humanity is fallen, its control over nature will frequently be misdirected and even destructive. In addition, as we will see when we discuss process later, procedures and mechanisms for reducing the effects of sin are indispensable; even though they cannot eradicate sin, they can lessen its destructiveness.

According to some theological critics, the image of stewardship or trusteeship is also suspect because it appears to separate human beings and nonhuman nature. To be sure, this image depends on a distinction between humanity and nature, but it does not imply an invidious separation. Humanity is part of nature. But, created in the image of God, it is a distinctive, even unique, part of nature. In addition, there may be a hierarchy of value with humanity at the apex. However much we need to emphasize the continuity between humanity and nature, discontinuity, at least as distinction, is still evident and important. Even as part of nature, humanity can still be a steward and trustee for nature.

Furthermore, to distinguish humanity and nature is not to deny their interdependence. Humanity should recognize its solidarity, its community of interests, with nature, because what affects nonhuman nature also affects humanity. It is not necessary or desirable, however, to focus on oneness or organic harmony or to develop a process theology in order to support an adequate ethic. It is possible, for example, to develop adequate limits on human control over nature from a perspective of conflict between humanity and nature in a fallen world. As Gerhard Liedke argues, such a perspective would hold that nonhuman nature is more than material, for, at the very least, it is a rival partner in a conflict. And it needs protection to ensure its participation as an equal in this conflict. Furthermore, recognizing nature in this way is compatible with an attitude of awe and wonder that supports limits on human control over nature.

Although general theological (or quasi-theological) convictions provide perspectives and engender attitudes, they are not by themselves sufficient for the assessment of technologies. For such a task, we need an ethical bridgework or framework to connect these convictions, perspectives, and attitudes with judgments about technologies. Such a bridgework or framework will consist, in part, of general principles and values. But theological convictions, along with the perspectives they provide and the attitudes they engender, do not merely serve as warrants for moral principles and values. They also shape interpretations of situations to which we apply principles and values. Consider, for example, beliefs about death in debates about technologies to prolong and extend life. If a society views death as an enemy, always to be opposed, it will be inclined to provide funds to develop life-prolonging and life-extending technologies and to use them even when the expected quality of life is poor. An adequate critique would thus include convictions, perspectives, and attitudes that shape interpretations of situations, as well as moral principles and values.

Because it is not possible here to establish all the important connections between theological convictions, moral principles and values, and interpretations of situations, I shall assume several principles and values in order to trace their implications for the assessment of technologies. Unless a single principle or value is accepted as overriding, conflicts and dilemmas are inevitable. As Guido Calabresi and Philip Bobbitt emphasize in *Tragic Choices*, tragedy is largely a cultural phenomenon: it depends on the principles and values of the individual or the society. This point was underlined during a 1979 visit to the People's Republic of China with an interdisciplinary and interprofessional delegation interested in ethics, public policy, and health care. Frequently members of our delegation asked Chinese policy makers, health care professionals, and others how they handle some of our "problems" such as refusal of treatment. The most common response was: "That's not a problem here. It doesn't exist here." Sometimes this response reflected the state of technological development: often, however, it reflected the unimportance of some Western principles and values such as autonomy, privacy, (for which there is no Chinese word), and other ingredients of individualism.

Principles and Values in Technology Assessment

I now want to indicate how technology assessment might proceed and, in particular, what principles and values it ought to consider. Nothing in its logic requires that it be as narrow as it sometimes is. Its practitioners need not be what John Stuart Mill called "one-eyed men" attending only to the "business" side of life.

1. Any technology assessment depends to a great extent on the principle of proportionality—proportion between the probable good and bad effects of technologies. This principle is expressed in various methods used to assess technologies, for example, cost-benefit analysis and risk-benefit analysis, which are only "new names for very old ways of thinking" (as William James said of pragmatism). They represent attempts to systematize, formalize, and frequently to quantify what we ordinarily do. For example, outside Canton, patients in a commune hospital formed their own risk-benefit analysis of traditional Chinese herbal medicine and Western medicine, both of which were available. They said, "Chinese medicine might not help you, but it won't hurt you: Western medicine might help you, but it also might hurt you."

I shall concentrate on *risk* and *benefit*, viewing risk as one sort of cost, i.e., cost as threat to safety, health, and life. The terms "risk" and "benefit" are perhaps not the best. Risk includes both amount or magnitude of harm and probability of harm. When we juxtapose benefit and risk, we are likewise interested in the magnitude and probability of benefit. It would be more accurate then to say that we need to balance the probability and magnitude of harm and the probability and magnitude of benefit. But since that expression is too cumbersome. I will use the common formulation of *risk-benefit analysis*.

Risk-benefit analysis involves what has been called "statistical morality." Risks are everywhere, and one major question is how far we are willing to go in order to reduce the risks of premature mortality, morbidity, and trauma. Let us concentrate on mortality and ask the troubling question: How much is it worth to save a life (really to postpone death, since lives are never really saved)? Or what is the value of a life? Consider the controversy over the Pinto. Apparently in 1973 Ford officials decided not to install a safety device that would prevent damage to the Pinto's gasoline tank in rear-end collisions. According to some reports, this device would have cost eleven dollars per vehicle or 137 million dollars for the whole production run. It is not accurate to say that Ford valued human life at eleven dollars. Rather, using a figure of approximately $200,000 per life, it concluded that the safety device should not be used because its costs outweighed its benefits.

Economists propose two different ways to determine the value of life. First, discounted future earnings. This approach tends to give priority to young adult white males. Thus a program to encourage motorcyclists to wear helmets would be selected over a cervical cancer program. Second, a willingness to pay. The question is not how much we would be willing to pay in order to avoid certain death, but how much we would be willing to pay to reduce the risk of death. How is willingness to pay determined? By finding out how much all those who are affected would be willing to pay, summing up the individual amounts and then dividing by the anticipated number of deaths prevented. While it might be possible to study actual behavior (e.g., in the workplace), one promising approach uses opinion polls to determine, for example, how much a community would be willing to pay in taxes for a technology that would reduce the chances of death after a heart attack.

Although it may be impossible to avoid valuing lives (at least implicitly} in technology assessment, criticisms abound. Religious critics contend that life has infinite or absolute value. But their criticism is nor serious insofar as it is directed against policies that do not do everything possible to reduce the risk of death. Judaism and Christianity, to take two examples, do not hold that life is an absolute value superior to all other values. Both traditions honor martyrs who refuse to value life more highly than other goods such as obedience to the divine will. Furthermore, there is a difference between negative and positive duties, and the duty not to kill is more stringent than the duty to save lives.

Other critics hold that it is immoral to put a value on life. But we all have life plans and risk budgets. Our life plans consist of aims, ends, and values, and our risk budgets indicate the risks to our health and survival we are willing to accept in order to realize some other goods. Health and survival are conditional, not final, values. A society might justly choose to put more of its budget into goods other than health and survival, as I argued in *Priorities in Biomedical Ethics*. Such a choice may be more political, i.e., to he resolved through the political process in terms of the community's values, or even aesthetic. One way to make this choice is to determine a community's willingness to pay for different goods.

An extension of these religious and moral objections opposes the calculation of consequences. Utilitarianism has sometimes been depicted as "ethics in cold blood." But, as I will argue later, consequences are always morally relevant even if they are not always morally decisive. This objection to calculation of consequences may simply be an objection to doing self-consciously and openly what we have to do. For example, Steven Rhoads argues that we should do a little dissembling since to put a public value on life would shock the community and perhaps lead to callousness. In effect, he offers consequentialist grounds for not openly pursuing consequentialism.

These various objections to valuing lives do not hold. For the most part, they are not even aimed at the right targets. And it would be useful for us as individuals and members of a community to ask how much we are willing to spend to reduce the risk of death (in brief, to put a value on life).

It is obvious that value considerations determine what counts as benefit and what counts as harm. They also determine how much particular benefits and harms count, how much weight they should have in the calculation. An adequate risk-benefit analysis needs to keep in play a wide range of values to identify, weigh, and balance benefits and harms. Analysts tend to prefer the hard, quantifiable variables, rather than the soft variables that are less susceptible to quantification. But a "narrow" cost or risk-benefit analysis fails to convey the richness of our moral values and principles.

2.   Value considerations not only shape our perceptions of benefits and harms, they also "dictate the manner in which uncertainty as to the potential adverse consequences will be resolved." To some analysts, the absence of evidence that harm will result is taken as evidence that the harm will not result, and so forth. The resolution of uncertainty, then, will reflect the value judgments of the analyst, whether he uses his own values or reflects the society's values. Description and evaluation cannot be separated even in the determination of the probability of harm because of "opposing dispositions or outlooks toward the future" such as confidence and hope or fear and anxiety.

In the face of uncertainty, a procedural suggestion seems justified. In the past, technology has been presumed innocent until proven guilty. ("Guilt" and "innocence" are used metaphorically to refer to risk-benefit analysis.) But in the light of our experiences in the last twenty years, we cannot be satisfied with this approach: we should, perhaps, presume that technology is guilty until proven innocent. The burden of proof and of going forward should be placed on the advocates of a technology who hold that its benefits will outweigh its harms. Such a shift in the *onus probandi* would not signal opposition to technological development. It would only indicate that we have not been sufficiently attentive to the harmful side effects and second-order consequences in technological development and that we intend to correct this deficiency.

A version of this procedure is mandated for the Food and Drug Administration, which cannot approve drugs for use outside research until they have been shown to be safe and efficacious. In effect, research may go forward (within the limits sketched in Chapter 3 of my *Priorities in Biomedical Ethics* [Philadelphia: Westminst, 1981], "Human Subjects in Research"), research may even be funded (in accord with priorities sketched in Chapter 4 of the same book, "Allocating Health Care Resources"), but let's not introduce a technology until we have determined with a reasonable degree of assurance that its probable benefits outweigh its probable harms. This procedure will not harass or arrest technology.

3.   It is not sufficient for a technology to have a favorable risk-benefit ratio; its proponents should also show that its risk-benefit ratio is more favorable than

alternative technologies or even no technology at all. For example, if both X and Y have favorable risk-benefit ratios, they may not be equally acceptable if Y's ratio is more favorable. Many critics of technology call on society to consider alternative technologies, particularly technologies that emphasize the values of smallness and the integrity of person, community, and nature. To a great extent, the issue is again the range of values that should be invoked for risk-benefit analysis.

4.   We should seek to minimize risks even by *some* reduction in the probability and amount of the benefit we seek, if that is the only way to minimize the risks. Because we have duties to do no harm and to benefit others, we are responsible for balancing harms and benefits in an imperfect world. But, *ceteris paribus,* the principle of not harming others (including imposing risks) takes priority over the principle of benefiting others: thus, we should minimize risks even at some reduction in the magnitude and/or probability of the benefit. Although this principle is sound, it is difficult to specify how far we should go to minimize risks short of making it impossible to realize the benefit we seek.

5.   In the long run, "the reversibility of an action should . . . be counted as a major benefit; its irreversibility a major cost." Thus, reversibility of a technology and its effects should be preferred over irreversibility. Why should reversibility have this privileged position? Surely, if we could realize the ideal social order on earth, we would prefer that it be irreversible and imperishable. But precisely because of the *uncertainties* about probabilities and magnitudes of benefits and harms, we should be particularly cautious about technologies with apparently irreversible effects. The "preservation of future options" IS an important goal, and it requires, for example, special concern about the destruction of an animal species and about nuclear waste.

Let me summarize these points about the principle of proportionality, the first consideration in technology assessment. We should balance the probabilities and amounts of benefits and harms. Value considerations will influence all aspects of the balance, including what counts as benefits and harms, how much they count, and how uncertainty is to be resolved. If lives are valued in public policy by determining how much people are willing to pay, the process of valuing lives is not inherently objectionable and may even be illuminating. Procedurally, the advocates of a technology should demonstrate its innocence before it is implemented and should show that its risk-benefit ratio is more favorable than any alternative technologies. We should minimize risks when we reduce (within limits) the probability and amount of benefit. Finally, reversibility is a benefit, irreversibility a cost.

Limiting Principles

Many flaws in contemporary technology assessments can be traced to the perspective of utilitarianism—the moral, social, and political doctrine that acts and policies are to be judged by their consequences and effects. It is an end-result view of life. After my praise for the principle of proportionality, the reader may wonder whether I am not at least a "closet utilitarian." After all, isn't the principle of proportionality roughly what the utilitarians mean by the principle of utility—maximizing net benefit relative to harm? Any adequate moral, social, or political theory must include the principle of proportionality or the principle of utility. In a world that is not ideal, it is impossible always to do good and to avoid harm. Often doing good produces at least the risk of harm. The principle of proportionality or utility requires that we weigh and balance these benefits and harms when they come into conflict and that we try to produce a net benefit (or, when considering only bad states of affairs, the best of the alternatives). Whatever we call this principle it is required by any adequate morality.

But we can accept the principle of proportionality or utility without accepting utilitarianism, which may be stated more sharply as the doctrine that right and wrong are determined *only* by the consequences of acts or policies. It makes the utility the only principle (act-utilitarianism) or the *primary* principle (rule-utilitarianism). And it distorts many technology assessments by restricting the range of relevant moral considerations. In particular, it concentrates on aggregative rather than distributive matters and it ignores other moral limits such as "rights" (which it frequently translates into "interests").

Utilitarian assessors sum up the interests of various individuals and groups to be affected by the technology, and they use this summation to determine our policy toward that technology. Although they may take account of wider and wider ranges of impacts and interests, they frequently overlook how burdens and harms are distributed. "Acceptable level of risk" of a technology, for example, should not be considered only in terms of the summed-up interests of the society. Principles of justice require that we consider the distribution of risks and benefits.

This issue can be sharpened by an examination of four possible patterns of distribution of risks and benefits. (1) The risks and benefits may fall on the same party. For example, in most therapy, the patient bears the major risks and stands to gain the major benefits. (2) One party may bear the risks, while another party gains the benefits. For example, in nontheraputic research, the subject bears risks, while others in the future will gain the benefits. Or we may gain the benefits of some technologies that will adversely affect future generations. (3) Both parties may bear the risks, while only one party gains the benefits. For example, a nuclear-powered artificial heart would benefit the user but would impose risks on other parties as well as on the user. (4) Both parties may gain the benefits, while only one party bears the risks. For example, persons in the vicinity of a nuclear power plant may bear significantly greater risks than other persons who also benefit from the plant. These patterns suggest the importance of considerations of distributive justice. As an Advisory Committee on the Biological Effects of Ionizing Radiations reports:

For medical radiation, as well as for certain uses of radiation in energy production, the problem of balancing benefits and costs is complicated by issues of ethics and discrimination. As an example, increased years of life expectation or increased economic productivity can be a useful measure of health benefit in some contexts. If, however, these parameters are used to balance the benefit-cost equation against the elderly with limited life expectancy or those with limited productivity, important values of society will have been overlooked.

Utilitarianism in technology assessment often fails to take account of other limits because of its particular view of rationality. Max Weber drew classic distinctions between types of social action: "goal-rational" (*zweckrational*), "value-rational" (*wertrational*), affective, and traditional types of action. For our purposes the first two, which I introduced in Chapter 4 of *Priorities in Biomedical Ethics,* are the most important. Value-rational conduct involves "a conscious belief in the absolute value of some ethical, aesthetic, religious, or other form of behavior, entirely for its own sake and independently of any prospects of external success." Goal-rational conduct involves reasoning about means to ends. It is a form of "instrumental rationality," involving the choice of effective (and efficient) means to given ends. It has been dominant not only in technology but also in technology assessment. By stressing limits, I have tried to include another type of rationality that may modify instrumental rationality by setting boundaries and constraints on the pursuit of goals.

Instrumental rationality tends to exclude value-rational considerations because they do not fit easily into the schema of means and ends. Just as I suggested about policies of the allocation of resources, we might choose policies toward technologies not because they *achieve* certain goals, but because they *express* certain values. They are expressive, symbolic, or representative. This range of considerations frequently involves *gestures,* not only *tasks.* For example, we might approach nature to make it serve our needs, or to express a certain attitude toward or relationship with it. As Laurence Tribe indicates, technology assessors typically ask what are society's current values regarding nature and they treat nonhuman life merely in relation to those values. But suppose society asked seriously, How should we value nature, including wildlife? And suppose the society came to the conclusion that it should treat nature with respect. Although this conclusion would not necessarily imply that the society would never give human interests priority over nature, "the very process of according nature a fraternal rather than an exploited role would shape the community's identity and at least arguably alter its moral character." As Tribe suggests, the decision maker's own identity might be at stake, for in choosing policies toward technologies, "the decision-maker chooses not merely how to achieve his ends but what they are to be and who he is to become." Who are we and who shall we be? These are considerations of agent-morality that do and should influence our technology assessments.

Process

One critical issue in technology assessment is often overlooked: process. Process is largely a matter of who should decide—that is, who should make the assessment, and how. It is possible to argue that technology assessors do not overlook process. Rather, they judge processes by their results. They ask whether particular processes "pay off" in producing the best possible outcomes—that is, the best possible predictions, evaluations, and controls of technology. When this judgment of processes by their results is combined with the view that we should judge technologies by their predicted consequences for human interests as measured by preferences, there is one obvious conclusion: the *experts* should make the assessment. This viewpoint simply perpetuates the myth of the end of ideology even while trying to control technology.

Its critics are numerous and vocal. Many of them are concerned with processes of evaluation and decision-making in some independence of their results. In technology assessment, the demand for public participation has become widespread and has encouraged the language of "participatory technology." The World Council of Churches Church and Society Conference on "Faith, Science and the Future" at the Massachusetts Institute of Technology in July 1979 emphasized a just, participatory and sustainable society. As the general secretary of the WCC, Philip Potter, put it in his address at the MIT conference, "a just and sustainable society is impossible without a society which is participatory." He continued:

In the present situation of science and technology, they are not really participatory, or rather they are forced to be biased on the side of those who wield economic and political power. There is little sign that they are on the side of the oppressed, the deprived and the marginalized, or simply the people.

It is no exaggeration to claim that "the central issue in technology assessment concerns democratic theory." Involving the public, and especially the individuals and groups affected by the technology, expresses the value of equal concern and respect. It should be built not so much on anticipated results as on the right to treatment as an equal. Processes of public participation in technology assessment are essential to embody this right to treatment as an equal, as one whose wishes, choices, and actions count. In addition, fairness, a principle derived from the principle of equal concern and respect applies to specific procedures that may be used for public participation (e.g., adversary hearings and public forums). These values and principles are independent of the results of the procedures and processes.

Emphasizing that technology requires a "new ethics of long-range responsibility," Hans Jonas notes the "insufficiency of representative government to meet the new demands on its normal principles and by its normal mechanics." In a lighter vein, H. L. Mencken once said, "I do not believe in democracy, but I admit that it provides the only really amusing form of government ever endured by mankind." He went on to describe democracy as "government by orgy, an orgy of public opinion." Obviously, it is necessary to devise procedures and mechanisms that can both satisfy independent principles and values and sustain effective and disciplined public participation in technology assessment. The creation of such procedures and mechanisms may presuppose that we transcend interest-group liberalism.

Temporal Perspective

As currently practiced, technology assessment tends to "find opportunities for making judgments and taking action only at those points in which a new development in technology occurs." Why? Perhaps because the utilitarianism back of much technology assessment is forward-looking, or because many assessors believe that what we now have is good, or because they believe that we cannot undo what has already been done. Whatever the reason, technology assessment for the most part predicts and evaluates for the future and is less interested in the evaluation of technologies already developed. Langdon Winner argues that we need not only technology assessment, but also "technology criticism," which can look at the past and the present as well as the future, which can look at long-term trends of technological development as well as at particular technologies, and which can look at the society as well as at the technologies it produces.

Winner's concerns are legitimate, but technology assessment, properly understood, can encompass them. It should be an ongoing process, dealing not only with the introduction of a technology but also with its impact as it is implemented. For example, there was no systematic assessment of the technology of renal dialysis in the 1950s and 1960s, but it has received careful scrutiny since its introduction, widespread use, and funding by the Government. While it is difficult to make adjustments once societal momentum has reached a certain point, we have learned, and are continuing to learn from the experience with dialysis, and our experience may improve our policies in other areas. Among the numerous questions that remain about dialysis are whether it is worth the cost (already over one billion dollars a year), whether the money could have spent better elsewhere, and whether we are able to cope with the successes of technologies (e.g., prolongation of life vs. quality of life of dialysis patients).

Nevertheless, our struggle with these questions, and others may illuminate present and future technology assessments.

Another point needs to be made about temporal orientation. Historical perspective may bring a cautionary tone to discussions of technology assessment. In a fine essay, entitled "Technology Assessment from the Stance of a Medieval Historian," Lynn White, Jr., directs our attention away from the easily measured factors to what he calls the "imponderables" and insists that technology assessment requires "cultural analysis" since the impact of a technology is filtered through the culture and the society. Among his several case studies is alcohol, which was distilled from wine as a pharmaceutical at Salerno, the site of Europe's most famous medical school. How, he asks, could anyone have offered an assessment of alcohol in the twelfth century? Alcohol was praised in medieval literature as a pharmaceutical with beneficial effects for chronic headaches, stomach trouble, cancer, arthritis, sterility, falling or graying hair, and bad breath. It was supposed to be good for people who had a "cold temperament." But then widespread drunkenness and disorder became problems. To shorten the history, we have problems of traffic deaths and cirrhosis of the liver. White observes, "a study group eight centuries ago, equipped with entire foresight, would have failed at an assessment of alcohol as we today fail."

Although White's point is not always clear, it appears to be that technologies touch on many aspects of life (e.g., psychological and sociological factors) that cannot be determined with great precision. What will happen in the interactions between technologies and society, culture, and psyches is an "imponderable." His lesson is salutary. History is ironic, and we can only be modest about (a) our ability to *predict* effects, (b) our ability to *assess* effects, and (c) our ability to *control* effects. It is true, as a character in *Death Trap* puts it, that "nothing recedes like success." While modesty is in order because our abilities are indeed limited, we have no choice but to try to predict, to assess, and to control in the light of moral principles and values.

Write 5pts you consider noteworthy

If the federal government had been around when the Creator was putting His hand to this state, Indiana wouldn't be here. It'd still be waiting for an environmental impact statement.

Ronald Reagan, *Speaking My Mind*, 1989

The chessboard is the world, the pieces are the phenomena of the universe, the rules of the game are what we call the laws of Nature. The player on the other side of the board is hidden from us. We know that his play is always fair, just and patient. But we also know, to our cost, that he never overlooks a mistake, or makes the smallest allowance for ignorance.

T. H. Huxley, *A Liberal Education*, 1868

Physics does not change the nature of the world it studies, and no science of behavior can change the essential nature of man, even though both sciences yield technologies with a vast power to manipulate their subject matters.

B. F. Skinner, *Cumulative Record*, 1972

REACTOR SAFETY STUDY

U.S. ATOMIC ENERGY COMMISSION

The Atomic Energy Commission was created in 1946 to serve as both controller and regulator of the nuclear industry. The AEC was given the responsibility of maintaining U.S. nuclear superiority and at the same time was required to develop peaceful uses for nuclear energy. Thus the agency not only supported the early development of commercial nuclear power plants, it also oversaw the laboratories which designed and the plants which manufactured nuclear weapons. By the mid-fifties, both the AEC and the Joint Committee on Atomic Energy, its congressional watchdog, were aggressively promoting the commercial use of nuclear reactors. Because of the inherent conflict posed by the dual roles of promoting and regulating the nuclear industry, the AEC was increasingly under fire during the sixties and the seventies. As a result of this legitimate criticism and as a result of a series of nuclear incidents, the AEC was replaced by the Nuclear Regulatory Commission, which as its name implies, is a regulatory agency, in the late seventies. This report, published in 1974, was developed and written by an impressive group of nuclear scientists, under the direction of Norman Rasmussen of MIT, to provide an independent estimate of the possibility of serious or catastrophic nuclear accidents. The report was attacked by anti-nuclear forces before it was published. This summary of the report is reproduced here to illustrate some of the issues associated with risk-benefit analysis and to stimulate discussion of nuclear issues.

1. Do you think that the development of nuclear power should be encouraged? Why or why not?

2. In recent years, nuclear power plants have been built much more quickly in France than in the United States. By the late 1990's France derived more than 90 percent of its electrical energy from nuclear power, while in the United States less than 10 percent of the electrical energy was derived from nuclear power plants. How do you account for the differences?

3. Why are people so much more fearful of nuclear power plants than of oil rigs and gas lines and coal mines, where there have been far more casualties?

4. In view of the subsequent accidents in nuclear power plants at Three Mile Island and at Chernobyl, do you think this report is still valid?

5. What would you consider an acceptable level of risk in the development of various forms of energy and in maintaining various systems of transportation?

6. Critics often refer to nuclear energy as a "Faustian bargain." What do they mean?

REACTOR SAFETY STUDY

U.S. ATOMIC ENERGY COMMISSION

INTRODUCTION AND RESULTS

The Reactor Safety Study was sponsored by the U.S. Atomic Energy Commission to estimate the public risks that could be involved in potential accidents in commercial nuclear power plants of the type now in use. It was performed under the independent direction of Professor Norman C. Rasmussen of the Massachusetts Institute of Technology. The risks had to be estimated, rather than measured, because although there are about 50 such plants now operating, there have been no nuclear accidents to date. The methods used to develop these estimates are based on those developed by the Department of Defense and the National Aeronautics and Space Administration in the last 10 years.

The objective of the study was to make a realistic estimate of these risks and to compare them with nonnuclear risks to which our society and its individuals are already exposed. This information will be of help in determining the future use of nuclear power as a source of electricity.

The basic conclusion of this study is that the risks to the public from potential accidents in nuclear power plants are very small. This is based on the following considerations:

(1) The consequences of potential reactor accidents are no larger, and in many cases, are much smaller than those of nonnuclear accidents. These consequences are smaller than people have been led to believe by previous studies that deliberately maximized risk estimates.

(2) The likelihood of reactor accidents is much smaller than many nonnuclear accidents having similar consequences. All nonnuclear accidents examined in this study, including fires, explosions, toxic chemical releases, dam failures, airplane crashes, earthquakes, hurricanes and tornadoes, are much more likely to occur and can have consequences comparable to or larger than nuclear accidents.

Figures 3-4, 3-5, and 3-6 compare nuclear reactor accident risks for the 100 plants expected to be operating by about 1980 with risks from other man-made and natural phenomena. [An example of the numerical meaning of Figures 3-4 to 3-6 can be seen by selecting a vertical consequence line and reading the likelihood that various types of accidents would cause that consequence. For instance, in Figure 3-4, 100 plants would cause this consequence with a likelihood of one in 10,000 per year. Chlorine releases are about 100 times more likely, or about one in 100; fires are about 1,000 times more likely, or about one in 10 per year; air crashes are about 5,000 times more likely, or about one per 2 years.] These figures indicate the following:

(1) Figure 3-4 and 3-5 show the likelihood and number of fatalities from both nuclear and a variety of non-nuclear accidents. These figures indicate that non-

nuclear events are about 10,000 times more likely to produce large accidents than nuclear plants.

(2) Figure 3-6 shows the likelihood and dollar value of property damage associated with nuclear and non-nuclear accidents. Nuclear plants are about 100 to 1,000 times less likely to cause comparable large dollar value accidents than other sources. Property damage is associated with three effects: (a) the cost of temporarily moving people away from contaminated areas, (b) the denial of use of real property during the few weeks to a few months during which the radioactivity is cleaned up, and (c) the cost of assuring that people are not exposed to potential sources of radioactivity in food and water supplies. This latter cost reflects the efforts required to survey agricultural products, plus the loss of products which might be contaminated.

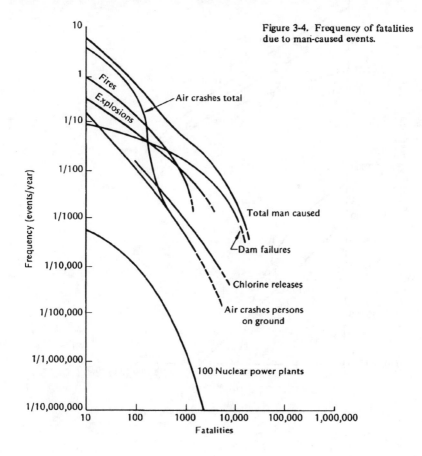

Figure 3-4. Frequency of fatalities due to man-caused events.

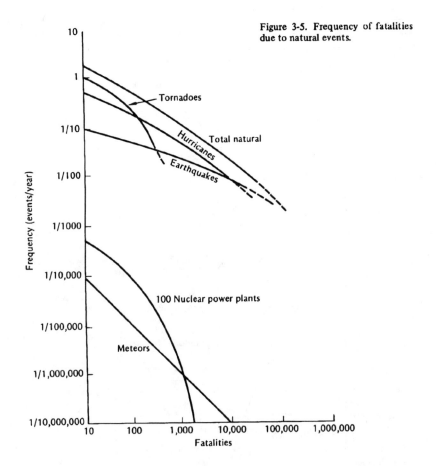

Figure 3-5. Frequency of fatalities due to natural events.

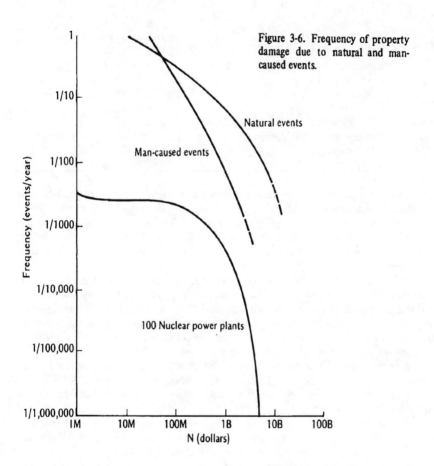

Figure 3-6. Frequency of property damage due to natural and man-caused events.

Table 3-7. Risk of Fatality by Various Causes

Accident Type	Total Number	Individual Chance per Year
Motor vehicle	55,791	1 in 4,000
Falls	17,827	1 in 10,000
Fires and hot substances	7,451	1 in 25,000
Drowning	6,181	1 in 30,000
Firearms	2,309	1 in 100,000
Air travel	1,778	1 in 100,000
Falling objects	1,271	1 in 160,000
Electrocution	1,148	1 in 160,000
Lightning	160	1 in 2,000,000
Tornadoes	91	1 in 2,500,000
Hurricanes	93	1 in 2,500,000
All accidents	111,992	1 in 1,600
Nuclear reactor accidents (100 plants)	0	1 in 300,000,000

In addition to the over-all risk information in Figures 3-4 through 3-6, it is useful to consider the risk to individuals of being fatally injured by various types of accidents. The bulk of the information shown in Table 3-7 is taken from the 1973 U.S. Statistical Abstract and applies to the year 1969, the latest year for which this data has been tabulated. The nuclear risks are very small compared to other possible causes of fatal injuries.

In addition to fatalities and property damage, a number of other health effects can be caused by nuclear accidents. These include injuries and long-term health effects such as cancers, genetic effects, and thyroid gland illness. The injuries expected in potential accidents would be about twice as large as the fatalities shown in Figures 3-4 and 3-5; however, such injuries would be insignificant compared to the 8 million injuries caused annually by other accidents. The number of cases of genetic effects and long-term cancers are predicted to be much smaller than the normal incidence rate of these diseases. Even for a large, very unlikely accident, the small increases in these diseases would not be detected.

Thyroid illnesses that might result from a large accident are the formation of nodules on the thyroid gland that can be treated by medical procedures and rarely lead to serious consequences. For most accidents, the number of nodules caused would be small compared to their normal incidence rate. The number that might be produced in very unlikely accidents would be comparable to their normal rate of occurrence. These would be observed during a period of 10 to 20 years following the accident and would be about equal to their normal incidence in the people exposed.

While the study has presented the estimated risks from nuclear power plant accidents and compared them with other risks that exist in our society, it has made no judgment on the acceptability of nuclear risks. Though the study believes nuclear accident risks are very small, the judgment as to what level of risk society should accept is a broader one than can be made here.

QUESTIONS AND ANSWERS ABOUT THE STUDY

This section of the summary presents more information about the details of the study than was covered in the introduction. It is presented in question and answer format for ease of reference.

Who did this study and how much effort was involved?

The study was done principally at the Atomic Energy Commission headquarters by a group of scientists and engineers who had the skills needed to carry out the study's tasks. They came from a variety of organizations including the Atomic Energy Commission, the national laboratories, private laboratories, and universities. About 10 people were Atomic Energy Commission employees. The director of the study was Professor Norman C. Rasmussen of the Department of Nuclear Engineering of the Massachusetts Institute of Technology, who served as an Atomic Energy Commission consultant during the course of the study. The staff director who had day-to-day responsibility for the project was Mr. Saul Levine of the Atomic Energy Commission. The study was started in the summer of 1972 and took two years to complete. A total of 60 people, various consultants, 50 man years of effort and $3 million were involved.

What kind of nuclear power plants are covered by the study?

The study considered large power reactors of the pressurized water and boiling water type being used in the United States today. This present generation of reactors are all water cooled and, therefore, the study limited itself to this type. Although high-temperature gas-cooled and liquid-metal fast-breeder reactor designs are now under development, no large reactors of this type are expected to operate in this decade; thus they were not considered.

Nuclear power plants produce electricity by the fissioning (or splitting) of uranium atoms. The nuclear reactor fuel in which the uranium atoms fission is in a large steel vessel. The reactor fuel consists of about 100 tons of uranium. The uranium is inside metal rods about 0.5 inch in diameter and about 12 feet long. These rods are formed into fuel bundles of about 50 to 200 rods each. Each reactor contains several hundred bundles. The vessel is filled with water which is needed both to cool the fuel and to maintain the fission chain reaction.

The heat released in the uranium by the fission process heats the water and forms steam; the steam turns a turbine to generate electricity. Similarly, coal and oil plants generate electricity using fossil fuel to boil water.

Today's nuclear power plants are very large. A typical plant has an electrical capacity of 1,000,000 kilowatts, or 1,000 megawatts. This is enough electricity for a city of about 500,000 people.

Can a nuclear power plant explode like an atom bomb?

No. It is impossible for nuclear power plants to explode like a nuclear weapon. The laws of physics do not permit this because the fuel contains only a small fraction (3-5 per cent) of the special type of uranium (uranium-235) used in weapons.

How is risk defined?

The idea of risk involves both the likelihood and consequences of an event. Thus, to estimate the risk involved in driving an automobile, one would need to know the likelihood of an accident in which, for example, an individual could be (a) injured or (b) killed. Thus, there are two different consequences, injury or fatality, each with its own likelihood. For injury, an individual's chance per year is one in 130 and for fatality, it is one in 4,000. This type of data concerns the risk to individuals and can affect attitudes and habits that individuals have toward driving.

However, from an over-all societal viewpoint, different types of data are of interest. Here, 1.5 million injuries per year and 55,000 fatalities per year due to automobile accidents represent the kind of information that might be of use in making decisions on highway and automobile safety.

The same type of logic applies to reactors. From the viewpoint of a person living in the general vicinity of a reactor, the likelihood of being killed in any one year in a reactor accident is one chance in 300,000,000 and the likelihood of being injured in any one year in a reactor accident is one chance in 150,000,000.

From a broader societal viewpoint, one individual of the 15 million people living in the vicinity of 100 reactors might be killed and 2 individuals might be injured every 25 years. This type of information might be of some use to the Congress or other decision makers in thinking about the over-all risk to society from reactor accidents.

What causes the risks associated with nuclear power plant accidents?

The risks from nuclear power plants are due to the radioactivity formed by the fission process. In normal operation nuclear power plants release only minute amounts of this radioactivity under controlled conditions. In the event of highly unlikely accidents, larger amounts of radioactivity could be released that could cause significant risks.

The fragments of the uranium atom that remain after it fissions are radioactive. These radioactive atoms are called fission products. They disintegrate further with the release of nuclear radiations. Many of them decay away quickly, in a matter of minutes or hours, to nonradioactive forms. Others decay away more slowly and require months and, in a few cases, many years to decay. The fission products accumulating in the fuel rods include both gases and solids. Included are iodine, gases like krypton and xenon, and solids like cesium and strontium.

How can radioactivity be released?

The only way that potentially large amounts of radioactivity can be released is by melting the fuel in the reactor core. The fuel removed from a reactor after use and stored at the plant site contains considerable amounts of radioactivity. However, accidental releases from such fuel were found to be very small compared to potential releases of radioactivity from the full reactor core.

The safety design of reactors includes a series of systems to prevent the overheating of fuel and to control potential releases of radioactivity from the fuel. Thus, to get an accidental release of radioactivity to the environment there must be a series of sequential failures that cause the fuel to overheat and release its radioactivity. There must also be failures in the systems designed to remove and contain the radioactivity.

The study has examined thousands of potential paths by which radioactive releases could occur and has identified those that determine the risks. This involved defining the ways in which the fuel in the core could melt and the ways in which systems to control the release of radioactivity could fail.

How might a core-melt accident occur?

It is significant that not once in some 200 reactor years of commercial operation of reactors of the type considered in the report has there ever been fuel melting. To melt the fuel requires that a failure in the cooling system occur that allows the fuel to heat up to its melting point, about 5,000°F.

To those unfamiliar with the characteristics of reactors, it might seem that all that is required to prevent fuel from overheating is a system to promptly stop, or shutdown, the fission process at the first sign of trouble. Although reactors have such systems, they alone are not enough since the radioactive decay of the fuel continues to generate heat (called *decay heat)* that must be removed even after the fission process stops. Thus, redundant decay heat-removal systems are also provided in reactors. In addition, emergency core cooling systems (ECCS) are provided to cope with a series of potential but unlikely accidents.

The Reactor Safety Study has defined two broad types of situations that might potentially lead to a melting of the reactor core: the loss of coolant accident and transients. In the event of a loss of coolant (LOCA) the normal cooling water is lost from the cooling systems and core melting would be prevented by the use of the emergency core cooling system. However, melting could potentially occur in a loss of coolant if the emergency core cooling system failed to operate.

The term *transient* refers to any one of a number of conditions that can occur in a plant that require the reactor to be shut down. Following shutdown, the decay heat removal systems operate to keep the core from overheating. Certain failures in either the shutdown or the decay heat removal systems have the potential to cause melting of the core.

What features are provided in reactors to cope with a core-melt accident?

Nuclear power plants have numerous systems to prevent core melting. Furthermore, there are inherent physical processes and additional features that remove and contain the radioactivity released from the molten fuel should core melting occur. Although there are features provided to keep the containment building from being damaged for some time after the core melts, the containment will ultimately fail, causing a release of radioactivity .

An essentially leak-tight containment building is provided to prevent the initial dispersion of the air-borne radioactivity into the environment. Although the containment will fail a number of hours after the core melts, until that time, the radioactivity released from the fuel will be deposited by natural processes on the surfaces inside the containment. In addition, plants are provided with systems to contain and trap the radioactivity released within the containment building. These systems include such things as water sprays and pools to wash radioactivity out of the building atmosphere and filters to trap radioactive particles prior to their release. Since the containment buildings are made essentially leak tight, the radioactivity is contained as long as the building remains intact. Even if the building were to have sizable leaks, large amounts of the radioactivity would be removed by the systems provided for that purpose or would be deposited on interior surfaces of the building by natural processes.

Even though the containment building would be expected to remain intact for some time following a core melt, eventually the molten mass would be expected to eat its way through the concrete floor into the ground below. Following this, most of the radioactive gases will be trapped in the soil; however, a small amount would escape to the surface and be released. Almost all of the nongaseous radioactivity would be trapped in the soil.

It is possible to postulate highly unlikely core-melt accidents in which the containment building fails by overpressurization or by missiles created by the accident. Such accidents could release a larger amount of air-borne radioactivity and have more serious consequences. The consequences of these less likely accidents have been included in the study's results ·shown in Figures 3-4 to 3-6.

How might the loss of coolant accident lead to a core melt?

Loss of coolant accidents are postulated to result from failures in the normal reactor cooling water system and plants are designed to cope with such failures. The water in the reactor cooling systems is at a very high pressure (between 50 to 100 times the pressure in a car tire) and if a rupture were to occur in the pipes, pumps, valves, or vessels that contain it, then a "blow out" would happen. In this case the water would flash to steam and blow out of the hole. This could be serious since the fuel could melt if additional cooling were not supplied in a rather short time.

The loss of normal cooling in the event of a loss of coolant accident would stop the chain reaction so that the amount of heat produced would drop almost instantly to a few percent of its operating level. However, after this sudden drop the amount of heat being produced would decrease much more slowly and would be controlled by the decay of the radioactivity in the fuel. Though this decrease in heat generation is helpful, it would not be enough to prevent the fuel from melting unless additional cooling were supplied. To deal with this situation, reactors have emergency core-cooling systems, the function of which is to provide cooling for just such events. These systems have pumps, pipes, valves, and water supplies capable of dealing with breaks of various sizes. They are also designed to be redundant so that if some components fail to operate, the core can still be cooled.

The study has reviewed a large number of potential sequences of events following loss of coolant accidents of various sizes. In almost all of the cases, the loss of coolant accident must be followed by multiple failures in the emergency core-cooling system for the core to melt. The principal exception to this is the massive failure of the large pressure vessel that contains the core. However, the accumulated experience with pressure vessels indicates that the chance of such a failure is indeed very small. In fact, the study found that the likelihood of pressure vessel failure is so small that it does not contribute to the overall risk from reactor accidents.

How might a reactor transient lead to a core melt?

The term *reactor transient* refers to a number of events that require the reactor to be shut down. These range from normal shutdown for such things as refueling to such unplanned but expected events as loss of power to the plant from the utility transmission lines. The reactor is designed to cope with unplanned transients by automatically shutting down. Following shutdown, cooling systems would be operated to remove the heat produced by the radioactivity in the fuel. There are several different cooling systems capable of removing this heat, but if they all should fail, the heat being produced would be sufficient to eventually boil away all the cooling water and melt the core.

In addition to the above pathway to core melt, it is also possible to postulate core melt resulting from the failure of the reactor shutdown systems following a transient event. In this case, it would be possible for the pressure to increase enough so that the normal reactor cooling system might rupture. This would create a loss of coolant accident and could lead to core melting.

How likely is a core-melt accident?

This Reactor Safety Study carefully examined the various paths leading to core melt. Using methods developed in recent years for estimating the likelihood of such accidents, a probability of occurrence was determined for each core melt accident identified. These probabilities were combined to obtain the total probability of melting the core. The value obtained was one in 17,000 per reactor per year. With 100 reactors operating, as is anticipated for the United States by about 1980, this means that one such accident would occur, on the average, every one and three-quarters centuries.

It is important to note that a melting of the core in a nuclear power plant does not necessarily involve an accident with serious public consequences. One of the major findings of the study is that only about one in 10 potential core melt accidents, occurring on the average of once every 17 centuries, might produce measurable health effects.

What is the nature of the health effects that a core-melt accident might produce?

It is possible for a core-melt accident to release enough radioactivity so that some fatalities might occur within a short time (a few weeks) after the accident.

Other people may be exposed to radiation levels that would produce observable effects requiring medical attention but from which they would recover completely. In addition, some people may receive even lower exposures, which produce no noticeable effects but may increase the incidence of certain diseases over a period of many years. The observable effects that occur shortly after the accident are called *short-term* or *acute* effects.

The *delayed* or *latent* effects of radiation exposure can cause some increase in the incidence of diseases such as cancer, genetic effects, and thyroid gland illnesses in the exposed population. These effects would appear as an increase in these diseases over a 10- to 20-year period following the exposure. Such effects would be difficult to notice because the increase is usually small compared with the normal incidence rate of these diseases.

The study has conservatively estimated the increased incidence of potentially fatal cancers over the 20 years following an accident. This has been done by following a procedure that estimates the number by extrapolating data from high dose rates to low dose rates. It is generally believed that this procedure probably overestimates the effect considerably, but it is not possible to do experiments with large enough populations to determine these very small effects. The number of latent cancers are predicted to be very small compared with the normal incidence of cancer. Thyroid illness refers to small lumps on the thyroid gland that can be felt by an examining physician; they are treated by medical procedures that sometimes involve simple surgery and rarely lead to serious consequences. For very large potential reactor accidents, the increase in nodules would be about equal to their normal incidence rate.

Radiation is recognized as one of the factors that can produce genetic effects which appear as defects in a subsequent generation. From the total population exposure caused by the accident, the expected increase in congenital defects in subsequent generations can be estimated. These effects are predicted to be very small compared with their normal incidence rate.

What are the most likely consequences of a core-melt accident?

The most likely core-melt accident would occur on the average of one every 17,000 years per plant. The size of the consequences of such an accident are given in Table 3-8.

Table 3-8. Consequences of the
Most Likely Core-Melt Accident

	Consequences
Fatalities	< 1
Injuries	< 1
Latent fatalities	< 1
Thyroid nodules	~4
Genetic defects	< 1
Property damage[a]	$100,000

[a]This does not include damage that might occur to the plant.

How does the annual risk from nuclear accidents compare to other common risks?

Considering the 15 million people who live within 20 miles of current or planned United States reactor sites, and based on current accident rates in the United States, the annual number of fatalities and injuries expected from various sources are shown in Table 3-9.

Table 3-9. Annual Fatalities and Injuries Expected among the 15 Million People Living within 20 Miles of United States Reactor Sites

Accident Type	Fatalities	Injuries
Automobile	4,200	375,000
Falls	1,500	75,000
Fire	560	22,000
Electrocution	90	—
Lightning	8	—
Reactors (100 plants)	0.3	6

What is the number of fatalities and injuries expected as a result of a core-melt accident?

A core-melt accident is similar to many other types of major accidents such as fires, explosions, dam failures, and the like, in that a wide range of consequences is possible depending on the exact conditions under which the accident occurs. In the case of a core melt, the consequences depend mainly on three factors; the amount of radioactivity released, the way it is dispersed by the prevailing weather conditions, and the number of people exposed to the radiation. With these three factors known it is possible to make a reasonable estimate of the consequences.

The study calculated the health effects and the probability of occurrence for 4,800 possible combinations of radioactive release magnitude, weather type, and population exposed. The probability of a given release was determined from a careful examination of the likelihood of various reactor-system failures. The probability of various weather conditions was obtained from weather data collected at many reactor sites. The probability of various numbers of people being exposed was obtained from United States census data for current and planned United States reactor sites. These thousands of calculations were carried out with the aid of a large digital computer.

These calculations showed that the probability of accidents having 10 or more fatalities is predicted to be about I in 250,000 per plant per year. The probability of 100 or more fatalities is predicted to be about 1 in 1,000,000 and for 1,000 or more, 1 in 100,000,000. The largest calculated value was 2,300 fatalities with a probability of about one in a billion.

The estimates given above are based on the assumption that evacuation procedures would be used to move most of the people out of the path of the airborne radioactivity. Experience has shown that evacuations have been successfully carried out in a large number of nonnuclear accident situations. Since nuclear power plants have evacuation plans prepared and since there is warning time before radioactivity would be released to the environment, it seems highly likely that evacuation would be effective in the case of nuclear accidents.

Table 3-10. Probability of Major Man-Caused and Natural Events

Type of Events	Probability of 100 or More Fatalities	Probability of 1,000 or More Fatalities
Man-caused		
Airplane crash	1 in 2 years	1 in 2,000 years
Fire	1 in 7 years	1 in 200 years
Explosion	1 in 16 years	1 in 120 years
Toxic gas	1 in 100 years	1 in 1,000 years
Natural		
Tornado	1 in 5 years	very small
Hurricanes	1 in 5 years	1 in 25 years
Earthquake	1 in 20 years	1 in 50 years
Meteorite impact	1 in 100,000 years	1 in 1,000,000 years
Reactors		
100 plants	1 in 10,000 years	1 in 1,000,000 years

If we consider a group of 100 similar plants then the chance of an accident causing 10 or more fatalities is 1 in 2,500 per year or, on the average, one such accident every 25 centuries. For accidents involving 1,000 or more fatalities the number is I in 1,000,000 or once in a million years. Interestingly, this is just the probability that a meteor would strike a United States population center and cause 1000 fatalities.

Table 3-10 can be used to compare the likelihood of a nuclear accident to nonnuclear accidents that could cause the same consequences. These include man-caused as well as natural events. Many of these probabilities are obtained from historical records but others are so small that no such event has ever been observed. In the latter cases the probability has been calculated using techniques similar to those used for the nuclear plant.

With regard to injuries from potential nuclear power plant accidents, the number of injuries that could require medical attention shortly after an accident is about two times larger than the number of fatalities predicted.

What is the magnitude of the latent or long term health effects?

As with the short term effects the magnitude of latent cancers, treatable latent thyroid illness, and genetic effects vary with the exact accident conditions. Table 3-11 illustrates the potential size of such events. The first column shows the consequences that would be produced by core-melt accidents, the most likely of which has one chance in 17,000 per plant per year of occurring. The second column shows the consequences for an accident that has a chance of 1 in million of occurring. The third column shows the normal incidence rate.

In these accidents, only the production of thyroid nodules would be observed and this only in the case of an exceedingly unlikely accident. These nodules are easily diagnosed and treatable by medical or surgical procedures. The other effects are too small to be discernable above the high normal incidence of these two diseases.

Table 3-11. Magnitude of Latent Health Effects Expected in a 20-Year Period for an Accident That Produces 100 Fatalities

| Effect | Chance per Plant per Year | | Normal[a] Incidence Rate |
	One in 17,000	One in 1,000,000	
Latent cancers	<1	450	64,000
Thyroid illness	4	12,000	20,000
Genetic effects	<1	450	100,000

[a]This is the normal incidence that would be expected for people in the vicinity of any one reactor.

What type of property damage might a core-melt accident produce?

A serious nuclear accident would cause no physical damage to property beyond the plant site but may contaminate it with radioactivity. At high levels of contamination, people would have to be moved temporarily from their homes until the radioactivity either decayed away or was removed. At levels lower than this, but involving a larger area, people might take simple actions to reduce possible contamination, but would continue being able to live in the area. The principal concern in this larger area would be to monitor farm produce to keep the amount of radioactivity ingested through the food chain small. Farms in this area would have to have their produce monitored and any produce above a safe level could not be used.

The most likely core-melt accident, having a likelihood of one in 17,000 per plant per year, would result in little or no contamination. The probability of an accident that requires temporary evacuation of 20 square miles is one in 170,000 per reactor per year. Ninety per cent of all core-melt accidents would be expected to be less severe than this. The largest accident might require temporary evacuation from 400 square miles. In an accident such as this, agricultural products, particularly milk, would have to be monitored for a month or two over an area about 100 times as large until the iodine decayed away. After that, the area requiring monitoring would be very much smaller.

What would be the cost of a core-melt accident?

As with the other consequences, the cost will depend upon the exact circumstances of the accident. The cost calculated by the Reactor Safety Study included the cost of moving and housing the people that were evacuated, the cost caused by denial of land use and the cost associated with the denial of use of reproducible assets such as dwellings and factories. The most likely core-melt accident, having a likelihood of one in 17,000 per plant per year, would cause property damage of about $100,000. The chance of an accident causing $100,000,000 damage would be about one in 50,000 per plant per year. Such an accident would be expected on the average to occur once every 5 centuries for 100 operating reactors. The probability would be about one in 1,000,000 per plant per year of causing damage of about $2 to 3 billion. The maximum value would be predicted to be about $4 to 6 billion with a probability of about one in 1,000,000,000 per plant per year.

This property damage risk from nuclear accidents can be compared to other risks in several ways. The largest man-caused events that have occurred are fires. In recent years there have been an average of three fires with damage in excess of $10 million every year. About once every two years there is a fire with damage in the $50 to $100-million range. There have been four hurricanes in the last 10 years which caused damage in the range of $0.5 to $5 billion. Recent earthquake estimates suggest a $1 billion earthquake can be expected in the United States about once every 50 years.

A comparison of the preceding costs shows that, though a severe reactor accident would be very costly, it would not be significantly larger than a number of serious accidents with which our society deals quite often, and the probability of such a nuclear accident is, of course, estimated to be much smaller than the other events.

What will be the chance of a reactor melt down in the year 2000 if we have 1,000 reactors operating?

One might be tempted to take the per plant probability of a particular reactor accident and multiply it by 1,000 to estimate the chance of an accident in the year 2000. This is not a valid calculation, however, because it assumes that the reactors to be built during the next 25 years will be the same as those being built today. Experience with other technologies such as automobiles and aircraft show that as more units are built and more experience is gained the overall safety record in terms of the probability of accidents per unit decreases. There are already changes in plants now being constructed that appear to be improvements over the plants analyzed in the study.

How do we know that the study has included all accidents in the analysis?

The study devoted a large amount of its effort to ensuring that it covered all potential accidents important in determining the public risk. It relied heavily on over 20 years of experience that exists in the identification and analysis of potential reactor accidents. It also went considerably beyond earlier analyses that have been performed by considering a large number of potential failures that had never before been analyzed. For example, failure of reactor systems that can lead to core melt and the failure of systems that affect the consequences of core melt have been analyzed. The consequences of the failure of the massive steel reactor vessel were considered for the first time. The likelihood that various external forces such as earthquakes, floods, and tornadoes could cause accidents were also analyzed.

In addition there are further factors that give a high degree of confidence that all significant accidents have been included. These are: (a) the identification of all significant sources of radioactivity located at nuclear power plants, (b) the fact that a large release of radioactivity can occur only if reactor fuel melts, and (c) knowledge of the factors that can cause fuel to melt. This type of approach led to the screening of thousands of potential accident paths to identify those that would determine the public risk.

Whereas there is no way of proving that all possible accident sequences which contribute to public risk have been considered in this study, the systematic approach used in identifying possible accident sequences make it very unlikely that an accident which would contribute to the overall risk was overlooked.

Table 3-12. Comparison of Consequences from Accidents in a 500-Megawatt Reactor as Calculated in WASH-740 and as Predicted by WASH-1400

	WASH-740	WASH-1400	
Parameter	Peak	Peak	Average
Acute deaths	3,400	92	0.05
Acute illness	43,000	200	0.01
Total dollar damage (billions)	7[a]	1.7[b]	0.5[b]
Approximate chance per reactor year		One in a billion	One in ten thousand

[a]This is the value predicted in 1957 dollars. [b]The values shown are in 1973 dollars. In 1957 dollars, these values should be about two-thirds of that shown.

How do your calculations of reactor accidents compare with those of earlier studies that predicted much larger consequences?

The principal earlier study of reactor accidents (WASH-740) was published by the Atomic Energy Commission in 1957, before any commercial nuclear power plants were operating. Thus, this study was necessarily vague about the engineering details of reactor accidents. The purpose of that study was to essentially maximize the consequences that could occur in an accident. This was done because it was to serve as a basis for the Congress to use in establishing adequate indemnification of the public in the event that an accident occurred. Thus, WASH-740 served as the basis for the Price-Anderson Act which provides such indemnification.

The reactor used for the WASH-740 study was one that generated 500 million watts (megawatts) of thermal energy as opposed to today's reactor of about 3,200 megawatts. To compare the earlier estimates with the more realistic approach used in this study, calculations were made for a 500 megawatt reactor using the reactor safety study model. The results are presented in Table 3-12. The differences between these two sets of results can in large part be explained as follows:

(1) This study used actual population data from the census bureau for the areas in the vicinity of actual reactor sites. The WASH-740 study used an estimated population that was much higher.

(2) The WASH-740 study assumed that 50 per cent of all the core radioactivity would be released to the environment. This study, using available experimental data, finds it physically impossible to attain total core releases as large as those used in WASH-740.

(3) The WASH-740 calculation made no provisions for the evacuation of people. Experience shows that evacuation is highly likely and would significantly reduce the consequences of an accident should it occur.

(4) The radioactivity released in a potential reactor accident would be in the form of a plume such as can be seen from smoke stacks. The radioactivity has sufficient heat associated with it to cause the plume to rise, thus reducing the concentration of radioactivity near the ground. This has some effect in reducing consequences. The calculations of the WASH-740 study did not include this effect.

What techniques were used in performing the study?

The latest methodologies, developed over the past ten years by the Department of Defense and National Aeronautics and Space Administration, were used in this study. These techniques are called *event trees* and *fault trees* and help to define potential accident paths and their likelihood of occurrence.

An event tree defines an initial failure within the plant. It then examines the course of events which follow as determined by the operation or failure of various systems that are provided to prevent the core from melting and to prevent the release of radioactivity to the environment. Event trees were used in this study to define thousands of potential accident paths that were examined to determine their likelihood of occurrence and the amount of radioactivity that they might release.

Fault trees were used to determine the likelihood of failure of the various systems identified in the event tree accident paths. A fault tree starts with the definition of an undesired event, such as failure of a system to operate, and then determines, using engineering and mathematical logic, the ways in which the system can fail. Using data covering (a) the failure of components such as pumps, pipes and valves, (b) the likelihood of operator errors, and (c) the likelihood of maintenance errors, it is possible to estimate the likelihood of system failure, even where no data on total system failure exist.

The likelihood and the size of radioactive releases from potential accident paths were used in combination with the likelihood of various weather conditions and population distributions in the vicinity of the reactor to calculate the consequences of the various potential accidents.

How will the results of the study affect safety decision-making?

This study, using an over-all methodology directed toward risk assessment, has developed new insights that contribute to a better understanding of reactor safety. However, many of the techniques used were developed and used only for the purpose of over-all risk assessment and are not directly applicable for optimizing safety designs or evaluating the acceptability of specific designs or reactor site locations. Though the techniques developed in the Study may someday be useful for such purposes, considerable additional development is needed before they can assist effectively in safety decision-making.

Decision-making processes in many fields, and especially in safety, are quite complex and should not lightly be changed. This is especially true where a good safety record has already been obtained, as is so far true for nuclear power plants. The use of quantitative techniques in decision-making associated with risk is still in its early stages and is highly formative. It appears that for the near future considerable additional development is needed in quantitative techniques before they can be used effectively in safety decision-making processes.

Knowledge of physical science will not console me for ignorance of morality in time of affliction, but knowledge of morality will always console me for ignorance of physical science.

Blaise Pascal, *Pensées*, 1670

SILENT SPRING

RACHEL CARSON

Silent Spring (1962) probably was the most important influence in setting off the movement for environmental protection, not only in the United States, but around the world in the 1960's.

Rachel Carson (1907-1964) was born in Springdale, Pennsylvania. She developed a keen interest in wildlife during her childhood. She received the A.B. degree from Pennsylvania College for Women and a master's from Johns Hopkins. After serving for six years on the zoology staff at the University of Maryland, and summer sessions at Johns Hopkins, she joined the U.S. Bureau of Fisheries, later the U.S. Fish and Wildlife Service as a biologist, and remained for twenty-eight years.

She won many awards for her writing. Her book, *The Sea Around Us*, published in 1951, won the National Book Award. Her other works included *Under the Sea-wind* (1941) and *The Edge of the Sea* (1955).

Silent Spring was the basis for a symposium held in Philadelphia in 1984, the proceedings of which were published by the American Chemical Society in 1987 as *Silent Spring Revisited*.

1. Aside from nuclear war, what does Carson consider to be the "central problem of our age"? Do you agree?

2. Which is a greater threat to peoples of the world, destruction of crops by certain insects, or destruction of those insects with DDT? How would you deal with this problem?

3. How does the battle against harmful insects and other "pests" with chemical insecticides and pesticides differ from the battle against harmful bacteria or germs with antibiotics?

4. What are "systemic insecticides" and what is their significance?

5. What has been the significance of the development of synthetic insecticides since World War II?

6. How does Darwin's principle of natural selection and the survival of the fittest relate to the use of insecticides?

7. What would Carson have us do about insects that destroy crops and trees and insects that carry dangerous diseases? What would you recommend?

SILENT SPRING

RACHEL CARSON

3. Elixirs of Death

FOR THE FIRST TIME in the history of the world, every human being is now subjected to contact with dangerous chemicals, from the moment of conception until death. In the less than two decades of their use, the synthetic pesticides have been so thoroughly distributed throughout the animate and inanimate world that they occur virtually everywhere. They have been recovered from most of the major river systems and even from streams of groundwater flowing unseen through the earth. Residues of these chemicals linger in soil to which they may have been applied a dozen years before. They have entered and lodged in the bodies of fish, birds, reptiles, and domestic and wild animals so universally that scientists carrying on animal experiments find it almost impossible to locate subjects free from such contamination. They have been found in fish in remote mountain lakes, in earthworms burrowing in soil, in the eggs of birds—and in man himself. For these chemicals are now stored in the bodies of the vast majority of human beings, regardless of age. They occur in the mother's milk, and probably in the tissues of the unborn child.

All this has come about because of the sudden rise and prodigious growth of an industry for the production of man-made or synthetic chemicals with insecticidal properties. This industry is a child of the Second World War. In the course of developing agents of chemical warfare, some of the chemicals created in the laboratory were found to be lethal to insects. The discovery did not come by chance: insects were widely used to test chemicals as agents of death for man.

The result has been a seemingly endless stream of synthetic insecticides. In being man-made—by ingenious laboratory manipulation of the molecules, substituting atoms, altering their arrangement—they differ sharply from the simpler inorganic insecticides of prewar days. These were derived from naturally occurring minerals and plant products—compounds of arsenic, copper, lead, manganese, zinc, and other minerals, pyrethrum from the dried flowers of chrysanthemums, nicotine sulphate from some of the relatives of tobacco, and rotenone from leguminous plants of the East Indies.

What sets the new synthetic insecticides apart is their enormous biological potency. They have immense power not merely to poison but to enter into the most vital processes of the body and change them in sinister and often deadly ways. Thus, as we shall see, they destroy the very enzymes whose function is to protect the body from harm, they block the oxidation processes from which the body receives its energy, they prevent the normal functioning of various organs, and they may initiate in certain cells the slow and irreversible change that leads to malignancy.

Yet new and more deadly chemicals are added to the list each year and new uses are devised so that contact with these materials has become practically worldwide. The production of synthetic pesticides in the United States soared from 124,259,000 pounds in 1947 to 637,666,000 pounds in 1960—more than a fivefold increase. The wholesale value of these products was well over a quarter of a billion dollars. But in the plans and hopes of the industry this enormous production is only a beginning.

A Who's Who of pesticides is therefore of concern to us all. If we are going to live so intimately with these chemicals—eating and drinking them, taking them into the very marrow of our bones—we had better know something about their nature and their power.

Although the Second World War marked a turning away from inorganic chemicals as pesticides into the wonder world of the carbon molecule, a few of the old materials persist. Chief among these is arsenic, which is still the basic ingredient in a variety of weed and insect killers. Arsenic is a highly toxic mineral occurring widely in association with the ores of various metals, and in very small amounts in volcanoes, in the sea, and in spring water. Its relations to man are varied and historic. Since many of its compounds are tasteless, it has been a favorite agent of homicide from long before the time of the Borgias to the present. Arsenic was the first recognized elementary carcinogen (or cancer-causing substance), identified in chimney soot and linked to cancer nearly two centuries ago by an English physician. Epidemics of chronic arsenical poisoning involving whole populations over long periods are on record. Arsenic-contaminated environments have also caused sickness and death among horses, cows, goats, pigs, deer, fishes, and bees; despite this record arsenical sprays and dusts are widely used. In the arsenic-sprayed cotton country of southern United States beekeeping as an industry has nearly died out. Farmers using arsenic dusts over long periods have been afflicted with chronic arsenic poisoning; livestock have been poisoned by crop sprays or weed killers containing arsenic. Drifting arsenic dusts from blueberry lands have spread over neighboring farms, contaminating streams, fatally poisoning bees and cows, and causing human illness. "It is scarcely possible . . . to handle arsenicals with more utter disregard of the general health than that which has been practiced in our country in recent years," said Dr. W. C. Hueper, of the National Cancer Institute, an authority on environmental cancer. "Anyone who has watched the dusters and sprayers of arsenical insecticides at work must have been impressed by the almost supreme carelessness with which the poisonous substances are dispensed."

Modern insecticides are still more deadly. The vast majority fall into one of two large groups of chemicals. One, represented by DDT, is known as the "chlorinated hydrocarbons." The other group consists of the organic phosphorus insecticides, and is represented by the reasonably familiar malathion and parathion. All have one thing in common. As mentioned above, they are built on a basis of carbon atoms, which are also the indispensable building blocks of the living world, and thus classed as "organic." To understand them, we must see of what they are made, and how, although linked with the basic chemistry of all life, they lend themselves to the modifications which make them agents of death.

The basic element, carbon, is one whose atoms have an almost infinite capacity for uniting with each other in chains and rings and various other configurations, and for becoming linked with atoms of other substances. Indeed, the incredible diversity of living creatures from bacteria to the great blue whale is largely due to this capacity of carbon. The complex protein molecule has the carbon atom as its basis, as have molecules of fat, carbohydrates, enzymes, and vitamins. So, too, have enormous numbers of nonliving things, for carbon is not necessarily a symbol of life.

Some organic compounds are simply combinations of carbon and hydrogen. The simplest of these is methane, or marsh gas, formed in nature by the bacterial decomposition of organic matter under water. Mixed with air in proper proportions, methane becomes the dreaded "fire damp" of coal mines. Its structure is beautifully simple, consisting of one carbon atom to which four hydrogen atoms have become attached:

Chemists have discovered that it is possible to detach one or all of the hydrogen

```
      H       H
        \   /
          C
        /   \
      H       H
```

atoms and substitute other elements. For example, by substituting one atom of chlorine for one of hydrogen we produce methyl chloride:

```
      H       Cl
        \   /
          C
        /   \
      H       H
```

Take away three hydrogen atoms and substitute chlorine and we have the anesthetic chloroform:

```
      H       Cl
        \   /
          C
        /   \
     Cl       Cl
```

Substitute chlorine atoms for all of the hydrogen atoms and the result is carbon tetrachloride, the familiar cleaning fluid:

```
     Cl       Cl
        \   /
          C
        /   \
     Cl       Cl
```

In the simplest possible terms, these changes rung upon the basic molecule of methane illustrate what a chlorinated hydrocarbon is. But this illustration gives little hint of the true complexity of the chemical world of the hydrocarbons, or of the manipulations by which the organic chemist creates his infinitely varied materials. For instead of the simple methane molecule with its single carbon atom, he may work with hydrocarbon molecules consisting of many carbon atoms, arranged in rings or chains, with side chains or branches, holding to themselves with chemical bonds not merely simple atoms of hydrogen or chlorine but also a wide variety of chemical groups. By seemingly slight changes the whole character of the substance is changed; for example, not only what is attached but the place of attachment to the carbon atom is highly important. Such ingenious manipulations have produced a battery of poisons of truly extraordinary power.

DDT (short for dichloro-diphenyl-trichloro-ethane) was first synthesized by a German chemist in 1874, but its properties as an insecticide were not discovered until 1939. Almost immediately DDT was hailed as a means of stamping out insect-borne disease and winning the farmers' war against crop destroyers overnight. The discoverer, Paul Muller of Switzerland, won the Nobel Prize.

DDT is now so universally used that in most minds the product takes on the harmless aspect of the familiar. Perhaps the myth of the harmlessness of DDT rests on the fact that one of its first uses was the wartime dusting of many thousands of soldiers, refugees, and prisoners, to combat lice. It is widely believed that since so many people came into extremely intimate contact with DDT and suffered no immediate ill effects the chemical must certainly be innocent of harm. This understandable misconception arises from the fact that—unlike other chlorinated hydrocarbons—DDT *in powder form* is not readily absorbed through the skin. Dissolved in oil, as it usually is, DDT is definitely toxic. If swallowed, it is absorbed slowly through the digestive tract; it may also be absorbed through the lungs. Once it has entered the body it is stored largely in organs rich in fatty substances (because DDT itself is fat-soluble) such as the adrenals, testes, or thyroid. Relatively large amounts are deposited in the liver, kidneys, and the fat of the large, protective mesenteries that enfold the intestines.

This storage of DDT begins with the smallest conceivable intake of the chemical (which is present as residues on most foodstuffs) and continues until quite high levels are reached. The fatty storage depots act as biological magnifiers, so that an intake of as little as 1/10 of 1 part per million in the diet results in storage of about 10 to 15 parts per million, an increase of one hundredfold or more. These terms of reference, so commonplace to the chemist or the pharmacologist, are unfamiliar to most of us. One part in a million sounds like a very small amount—and so it is. But such substances are so potent that a minute quantity can bring about vast changes in the body. In animal experiments, 3 parts per million has been found to inhibit an essential enzyme in heart muscle; only 5 parts per million has brought about necrosis or disintegration of liver cells; only 2.5 parts per million of the closely related chemicals dieldrin and chlordane did the same.

This is really not surprising. In the normal chemistry of the human body there is just such a disparity between cause and effect. For example, a quantity of iodine as small as two ten-thousandths of a gram spells the difference between health and disease. Because these small amounts of pesticides are cumulatively stored and only slowly excreted, the threat of chronic poisoning and degenerative changes of the liver and other organs is very real.

Scientists do not agree upon how much DDT can be stored in the human body. Dr. Arnold Lehman, who is the chief pharmacologist of the Food and Drug Administration, says there is neither a floor below which DDT is not absorbed nor a ceiling beyond which absorption and storage ceases. On the other hand, Dr. Wayland Hayes of the United States Public Health Service contends that in every individual a point of equilibrium is reached, and that DDT in excess of this amount is excreted. For practical purposes it is not particularly important which of these men is right. Storage in human beings has been well investigated, and we know that the average person is storing potentially harmful amounts. According to various studies, individuals with no known exposure (except the inevitable dietary one) store an average of 5.3 parts per million to 7.4 parts per million; agricultural workers 17.1 parts per million; and workers in insecticide plants as high as 648 parts per million! So the range of proven storage is quite wide and, what is even more to the point, the minimum figures are above the level at which damage to the liver and other organs or tissues may begin.

One of the most sinister features of DDT and related chemicals is the way they are passed on from one organism to another through all the links of the food chains. For example, fields of alfalfa are dusted with DDT; meal is later prepared from the alfalfa and fed to hens; the hens lay eggs which contain DDT. Or the hay, containing residues of 7 to 8 parts per million, may be fed to cows. The DDT will turn up in the milk in the amount of about 3 parts per million, but in butter made from this milk the concentration may run to 65 parts per million. Through such a process of transfer, what started out as a very small amount of DDT may end as a heavy concentration. Farmers nowadays find it difficult to obtain uncontaminated fodder for their milk cows, though the Food and Drug Administration forbids the presence of insecticide residues in milk shipped in interstate commerce.

The poison may also be passed on from mother to offspring. Insecticide residues have been recovered from human milk in samples tested by Food and Drug Administration scientists. This means that the breast-fed human infant is receiving small but regular additions to the load of toxic chemicals building up in his body. It is by no means his first exposure, however: there is good reason to believe this begins while he is still in the womb. In experimental animals the chlorinated hydrocarbon insecticides freely cross the barrier of the placenta, the traditional protective shield between the embryo and harmful substances in the mother's body. While the quantities so received by human infants would normally be small, they are not unimportant because children are more susceptible to poisoning than adults. This situation also means that today the average individual almost certainly starts life with the first deposit of the growing load of chemicals his body will be required to carry thenceforth.

All these facts—storage at even low levels, subsequent accumulation, and occurrence of liver damage at levels that may easily occur in normal diets, caused Food and Drug Administration scientists to declare as early as 1950 that it is "extremely likely the potential hazard of DDT has been underestimated." There has been no such parallel situation in medical history. No one yet knows what the ultimate consequences may be.

Chlordane, another chlorinated hydrocarbon, has all these unpleasant attributes of DDT plus a few that are peculiarly its own. Its residues are long persistent in soil, on foodstuffs, or on surfaces to which it may be applied. Chlordane makes use of all available portals to enter the body. It may be absorbed through the skin, may be breathed in as a spray or dust, and of course is absorbed from the digestive tract if residues are swallowed. Like all other chlorinated hydrocarbons, its deposits build up in the body in cumulative fashion. A diet containing such a small amount of chlordane as 2.5 parts per million may eventually lead to storage of 75 parts per million in the fat of experimental animals.

So experienced a pharmacologist as Dr. Lehman has described chlordane in 1950 as "one of the most toxic of insecticides—anyone handling it could be poisoned." Judging by the carefree liberality with which dusts for lawn treatments by suburbanites are laced with chlordane, this warning has not been taken to heart. The fact that the suburbanite is not instantly stricken has little meaning, for the toxins may sleep long in his body, to become manifest months or years later in an obscure disorder almost impossible to trace to its origins. On the other hand, death may strike quickly. One victim who accidentally spilled a 25 per cent industrial solution on the skin developed symptoms of poisoning within 40 minutes and died before medical help could be obtained. No reliance can be placed on receiving advance warning which might allow treatment to be had in time.

Heptachlor, one of the constituents of chlordane, is marketed as a separate formulation. It has a particularly high capacity for storage in fat. If the diet contains as little as 7/10 of I part per million there will be measurable amounts of heptachlor in the body. It also has the curious ability to undergo change into a chemically distinct substance known as heptachlor epoxide. It does this in soil and in the tissues of both plants and animals. Tests on birds indicate that the epoxide that results from this change is more toxic than the original chemical, which in turn is four times as toxic as chlordane.

As long ago as the mid-1930's a special group of hydrocarbons, the chlorinated naphthalenes, was found to cause hepatitis, and also a rare and almost invariably fatal liver disease in persons subjected to occupational exposure. They have led to illness and death of workers in electrical industries; and more recently, in agriculture, they have been considered a cause of a mysterious and usually fatal disease of cattle. In view of these antecedents, it is not surprising that three of the insecticides that are related to this group are among the most violently poisonous of all the hydrocarbons. These are dieldrin, aldrin, and endrin.

Dieldrin, named for a German chemist, Diels, is about 5 times as toxic as DDT when swallowed but 40 times as toxic when absorbed through the skin in solution. It is notorious for striking quickly and with terrible effect at the nervous system, sending the victims into convulsions. Persons thus poisoned recover so slowly as to indicate chronic effects. As with other chlorinated hydrocarbons, these long-term effects include severe damage to the liver. The long duration of its residues and the effective insecticidal action make dieldrin one of the most used insecticides today, despite the appalling destruction of wildlife that has followed its use. As tested on quail and pheasants, it has proved to be about 40 to so times as toxic as DDT.

There are vast gaps in our knowledge of how dieldrin is stored or distributed in the body, or excreted, for the chemists' ingenuity in devising insecticides has long ago outrun biological knowledge of the way these poisons affect the living organism. However, there is every indication of long storage in the human body, where deposits may lie dormant like a slumbering volcano, only to flare up in periods of physiological stress when the body draws upon its fat reserves. Much of what we do know has been learned through hard experience in the antimalarial campaigns carried out by the World Health Organization. As soon as dieldrin was substituted for DDT in malaria-control work (because the malaria mosquitoes had become resistant to DDT), cases of poisoning among the spraymen began to occur. The seizures were severe—from half to all (varying in the different programs) of the men affected went into convulsions and several died. Some had convulsions as long as *four months* after the last exposure.

Aldrin is a somewhat mysterious substance, for although it exists as a separate entity it bears the relation of alter ego to dieldrin. When carrots are taken from a bed treated with aldrin they are found to contain residues of dieldrin. This change occurs in living tissues and also in soil. Such alchemistic transformations have led to many erroneous reports, for if a chemist, knowing aldrin has been applied, tests for it he will be deceived into thinking all residues have been dissipated. The residues are there, but they are dieldrin and this requires a different test.

Like dieldrin, aldrin is extremely toxic. It produces degenerative changes in the liver and kidneys. A quantity the size of an aspirin tablet is enough to kill more than 400 quail. Many cases of human poisonings are on record, most of them in connection with industrial handling.

Aldrin, like most of this group of insecticides, projects a menacing shadow into the future, the shadow of sterility. Pheasants fed quantities too small to kill them nevertheless laid few eggs, and the chicks that hatched soon died. The effect is not confined to birds. Rats exposed to aldrin had fewer pregnancies and their young were sickly and short-lived. Puppies born of treated mothers died within three days. By one means or another, the new generations suffer for the poisoning of their parents. No one knows whether the same effect will be seen in human beings, yet this chemical has been sprayed from airplanes over suburban areas and farmlands.

Endrin is the most toxic of all the chlorinated hydrocarbons. Although chemically rather closely related to dieldrin, a little twist in its molecular structure makes it 5 times as poisonous. It makes the progenitor of all this group of insecticides, DDT, seem by comparison almost harmless. It is 15 times as poisonous as DDT to mammals, 30 times as poisonous to fish, and about 300 times as poisonous to some birds.

In the decade of its use, endrin has killed enormous numbers of fish, has fatally poisoned cattle that have wandered into sprayed orchards, has poisoned wells, and has drawn a sharp warning from at least one state health department that its careless use is endangering human lives.

In one of the most tragic cases of endrin poisoning there was no apparent carelessness; efforts had been made to take precautions apparently considered adequate. A year-old child had been taken by his American parents to live in Venezuela. There were cockroaches in the house to which they moved, and after a few days a spray containing endrin was used. The baby and the small family dog were taken out of the house before the spraying was done about nine o'clock one morning. After the spraying the floors were washed. The baby and dog were returned to the house in mid-afternoon. An hour or so later the dog vomited, went into convulsions, and died. At 10 P.M. on the evening of the same day the baby also vomited, went into convulsions, and lost consciousness. After that fateful contact with endrin, this normal, healthy child became little more than a vegetable—unable to see or hear, subject to frequent muscular spasms, apparently completely cut off from contact with his surroundings. Several months of treatment in a New York hospital failed to change his condition or bring hope of change. "It is extremely doubtful," reported the attending physicians, "that any useful degree of recovery will occur."

The second major group of insecticides, the alkyl or organic phosphates, are among the most poisonous chemicals in the world. The chief and most obvious hazard attending their use is that of acute poisoning of people applying the sprays or accidentally coming in contact with drifting spray, with vegetation coated by it, or with a discarded container. In Florida, two children found an empty bag and used it to repair a swing. Shortly thereafter both of them died and three of their playmates became ill. The bag had once contained an insecticide called parathion, one of the organic phosphates; tests established death by parathion poisoning. On another occasion two small boys in Wisconsin, cousins, died on the same night. One had been playing in his yard when spray drifted in from an adjoining field where his father was spraying potatoes with parathion; the other had run playfully into the barn after his father and had put his hand on the nozzle of the spray equipment.

The origin of these insecticides has a certain ironic significance. Although some of the chemicals themselves—organic esters of phosphoric acid—had been known for many years, their insecticidal properties remained to be discovered by a German chemist, Gerhard Schrader, in the late 1930's. Almost immediately the German government recognized the value of these same chemicals as new and devastating weapons in man's war against his own kind, and the work on them was declared secret. Some became the deadly nerve gases. Others, of closely allied structure, became insecticides.

The organic phosphorus insecticides act on the living organism in a peculiar way. They have the ability to destroy enzymes—enzymes that perform necessary functions in the body. Their target is the nervous system, whether the victim is an insect or a warm-blooded animal. Under normal conditions, an impulse passes from nerve to nerve with the aid of a "chemical transmitter" called acetylcholine, a substance that performs an essential function and then disappears. Indeed, its existence is so ephemeral that medical researchers are unable, without special procedures, to sample it before the body has destroyed it. This transient nature of the transmitting chemical is necessary to the normal functioning of the body. If the acetylcholine is not destroyed as soon as a nerve impulse has passed, impulses continue to flash across the bridge from nerve to nerve, as the chemical exerts its effects in an ever more intensified manner. The movements of the whole body become uncoordinated: tremors, muscular spasms, convulsions, and death quickly result.

This contingency has been provided for by the body. A protective enzyme called cholinesterase is at hand to destroy the transmitting chemical once it is no longer needed. By this means a precise balance is struck and the body never builds up a dangerous amount of acetylcholine. But on contact with the organic phosphorus insecticides, the protective enzyme is destroyed, and as the quantity of the enzyme is reduced that of the transmitting chemical builds up. In this effect, the organic phosphorus compounds resemble the alkaloid poison muscarine, found in a poisonous mushroom, the fly amanita.

Repeated exposures may lower the cholinesterase level until an individual reaches the brink of acute poisoning, a brink over which he may be pushed by a very small additional exposure. For this reason it is considered important to make periodic examinations of the blood of spray operators and others regularly exposed.

Parathion is one of the most widely used of the organic phosphates. It is also one of the most powerful and dangerous. Honeybees become "wildly agitated and bellicose" on contact with it, perform frantic cleaning movements, and are near death within half an hour. A chemist, thinking to learn by the most direct possible means the dose acutely toxic to human beings, swallowed a minute amount, equivalent to about .00424 ounce. Paralysis followed so instantaneously that he could not reach the antidotes he had prepared at hand, and so he died. Parathion is now said to be a favorite instrument of suicide in Finland. In recent years the State of California has reported an average of more than 200 cases of accidental parathion poisoning annually. In many parts of the world the fatality rate from parathion is startling: 100 fatal cases in India and 67 in Syria in 1958, and an average of 336 deaths per year in Japan.

Yet some 7,000,000 pounds of parathion are now applied to fields and orchards of the United States—by hand sprayers, motorized   blowers and dusters, and by airplane. The amount used on California farms alone could, according to one medical authority, "provide a lethal dose for 5 to 10 times the whole world's population."

One of the few circumstances that save us from extinction by this means is the fact that parathion and other chemicals of this group are decomposed rather rapidly. Their residues on the crops to which they are applied are therefore relatively short-lived compared with the chlorinated hydrocarbons. However, they last long enough to create hazards and produce consequences that range from the merely serious to the fatal. In Riverside, California, eleven out of thirty men picking oranges became violently ill and all but one had to be hospitalized. Their symptoms were typical of parathion poisoning. The grove had been sprayed with parathion some two and a half weeks earlier; the residues that reduced them to retching, half-blind, semiconscious misery were sixteen to nineteen days old. And this is not by any means a record for persistence. Similar mishaps have occurred in groves sprayed a month earlier, and residues have been found in the peel of oranges six months after treatment with standard dosages.

The danger to all workers applying the organic phosphorus insecticides in fields, orchards, and vineyards, is so extreme that some states using these chemicals have established laboratories where physicians may obtain aid in diagnosis and treatment. Even the physicians themselves may be in some danger, unless they wear rubber gloves in handling the victims of poisoning. So may a laundress washing the clothing of such victims, which may have absorbed enough parathion to affect her.

Malathion, another of the organic phosphates, is almost as familiar to the public as DDT, being widely used by gardeners, in household insecticides, in mosquito spraying, and in such blanket attacks on insects as the spraying of nearly a million acres of Florida communities for the Mediterranean fruit fly. It is considered the least toxic of this group of chemicals and many people assume they may use it freely and without fear of harm. Commercial advertising encourages this comfortable attitude.

The alleged "safety" of malathion rests on rather precarious ground, although—as often happens—this was not discovered until the chemical had been in use for several years. Malathion is "safe" only because the mammalian liver, an organ with extraordinary protective powers, renders it relatively harmless. The detoxification is accomplished by one of the enzymes of the liver. If, however, something destroys this enzyme or interferes with its action, the person exposed to malathion receives the full force of the poison.

Unfortunately for all of us, opportunities for this sort of thing to happen are legion. A few years ago a team of Food and Drug Administration scientists discovered that when malathion and certain other organic phosphates are administered simultaneously a massive poisoning results—up to 50 times as severe as would be predicted on the basis of adding together the toxicities of the two. In other words, 1/100 of the lethal dose of each compound may be fatal when the two are combined.

This discovery led to the testing of other combinations. It is now known that many pairs of organic phosphate insecticides are highly dangerous, the toxicity being stepped up or "potentiated" through the combined action. Potentiation seems to take place when one compound destroys the liver enzyme responsible for detoxifying the other. The two need not be given simultaneously. The hazard exists not only for the man who may spray this week with one insecticide and next week with another; it exists also for the consumer of sprayed products. The common salad bowl may easily present a combination of organic phosphate insecticides. Residues well within the legally permissible limits may interact.

The full scope of the dangerous interaction of chemicals is as yet little known, but disturbing findings now come regularly from scientific laboratories. Among these is the discovery that the toxicity of an organic phosphate can be increased by a second agent that is not necessarily an insecticide. For example, one of the plasticizing agents may act even more strongly than another insecticide to make malathion more dangerous. Again, this is because it inhibits the liver enzyme that normally would "draw the teeth" of the poisonous insecticide.

What of other chemicals in the normal human environment? What, in particular, of drugs? A bare beginning has been made on this subject, but already it is known that some organic phosphates (parathion and malathion) increase the toxicity of some drugs used as muscle relaxants, and that several others (again including malathion) markedly increase the sleeping time of barbiturates.

In Greek mythology the sorceress Medea, enraged at being supplanted by a rival for the affections of her husband Jason, presented the new bride with a robe possessing magic properties. The wearer of the robe immediately suffered a violent death. This death-by-indirection now finds its counterpart in what are known as "systemic insecticides." These are chemicals with extraordinary properties which are used to convert plants or animals into a sort of Medea's robe by making them actually poisonous. This is done with the purpose of killing insects that may come in contact with them, especially by sucking their juices or blood.

The world of systemic insecticides is a weird world, surpassing the imaginings of the brothers Grimm—perhaps most closely akin to the cartoon world of Charles Addams. It is a world where the enchanted forest of the fairy tales has become the poisonous forest in which an insect that chews a leaf or sucks the sap of a plant is doomed. It is a world where a flea bites a dog, and dies because the dog's blood has been made poisonous, where an insect may die from vapors emanating from a plant it has never touched, where a bee may carry poisonous nectar back to its hive and presently produce poisonous honey.

The entomologists' dream of the built-in insecticide was born when workers in the field of applied entomology realized they could take a hint from nature: they found that wheat growing in soil containing sodium selenate was immune to attack by aphids or spider mites. Selenium, a naturally occurring element found sparingly in rocks and soils of many parts of the world, thus became the first systemic insecticide.

What makes an insecticide a systemic is the ability to permeate all the tissues of a plant or animal and make them toxic. This quality is possessed by some chemicals of the chlorinated hydrocarbon group and by others of the organophosphorus group, all synthetically produced, as well as by certain naturally occurring substances. In practice, however, most systemics are drawn from the organophosphorus group because the problem of residues is somewhat less acute.

Systemics act in other devious ways. Applied to seeds, either by soaking or in a coating combined with carbon, they extend their effects into the following plant generation and produce seedlings poisonous to aphids and other sucking insects. Vegetables such as peas, beans, and sugar beets are sometimes thus protected. Cotton seeds coated with a systemic insecticide have been in use for some time in California, where 25 farm laborers planting cotton in the San Joaquin Valley in 1959 were seized with sudden illness, caused by handling the bags of treated seeds.

In England someone wondered what happened when bees made use of nectar from plants treated with systemics. This was investigated in areas treated with a chemical called schradan. Although the plants had been sprayed before the flowers were formed, the nectar later produced contained the poison. The result, as might have been predicted, was that the honey made by the bees also was contaminated with schradan.

Use of animal systemics has concentrated chiefly on control of the cattle grub, a damaging parasite of livestock. Extreme care must be used in order to create an insecticidal effect in the blood and tissues of the host without setting up a fatal poisoning. The balance is delicate and government veterinarians have found that repeated small doses can gradually deplete an animal's supply of the protective enzyme cholinesterase, so that without warning a minute additional dose will cause poisoning.

There are strong indications that fields closer to our daily lives are being opened up. You may now give your dog a pill which, it is claimed, will rid him of fleas by making his blood poisonous to them. The hazards discovered in treating cattle would presumably apply to the dog. As yet no one seems to have proposed a human systemic that would make us lethal to a mosquito. Perhaps this is the next step.

So far in this chapter we have been discussing the deadly chemicals that are being used in our war against the insects. What of our simultaneous war against the weeds?

The desire for a quick and easy method of killing unwanted plants has given rise to a large and growing array of chemicals that are known as herbicides, or, less formally, as weed killers. The story of how these chemicals are used and misused will be told in Chapter 6; the question that here concerns us is whether the weed killers are poisons and whether their use is contributing to the poisoning of the environment.

The legend that the herbicides are toxic only to plants and so pose no threat to animal life has been widely disseminated, but unfortunately it is not true. The plant killers include a large variety of chemicals that act on animal tissue as well as on vegetation. They vary greatly in their action on the organism. Some are general poisons, some are powerful stimulants of metabolism, causing a fatal rise in body temperature, some induce malignant tumors either alone or in partnership with other chemicals, some strike at the genetic material of the race by causing gene mutations. The herbicides, then, like the insecticides, include some very dangerous chemicals, and their careless use in the belief that they are "safe" can have disastrous results.

Despite the competition of a constant stream of new chemicals issuing from the laboratories, arsenic compounds are still liberally used, both as insecticides (as mentioned above) and as weed killers, where they usually take the chemical form of sodium arsenite. The history of their use is not reassuring. As roadside sprays, they have cost many a farmer his cow and killed uncounted numbers of wild creatures. As aquatic weed killers in lakes and reservoirs they have made public waters unsuitable for drinking or even for swimming. As a spray applied to potato fields to destroy the vines they have taken a toll of human and nonhuman life.

In England this latter practice developed about 1951 as a result of a shortage of sulfuric acid, formerly used to burn off the potato vines. The Ministry of Agriculture considered it necessary to give warning of the hazard of going into the arsenic-sprayed fields, but the warning was not understood by the cattle (nor, we must assume, by the wild animals and birds) and reports of cattle poisoned by the arsenic sprays came with monotonous regularity. When death came also to a farmer's wife through arsenic-contaminated water, one of the major English chemical companies (in 1959) stopped production of arsenical sprays and called in supplies already in the hands of dealers, and shortly thereafter the Ministry of Agriculture announced that because of high risks to people and cattle restrictions on the use of arsenites would be imposed. In 1961, the Australian government announced a similar ban. No such restrictions impede the use of these poisons in the United States, however.

Some of the "dinitro" compounds are also used as herbicides. They are rated as among the most dangerous materials of this type in use in the United States. Dinitrophenol is a strong metabolic stimulant. For this reason it was at one time used as a reducing drug, but the margin between the slimming dose and that required to poison or kill was slight—so slight that several patients died and many suffered permanent injury before use of the drug was finally halted.

A related chemical, pentachlorophenol, sometimes known as "penta," is used as a weed killer as well as an insecticide, often being sprayed along railroad tracks and in waste areas. Penta is extremely toxic to a wide variety of organisms from bacteria to man. Like the dinitros, it interferes, often fatally, with the body's source of energy, so that the affected organism almost literally burns itself up. Its fearful power is illustrated in a fatal accident recently reported by the California Department of Health. A tank truck driver was preparing a cotton defoliant by mixing diesel oil with pentachlorophenol. As he was drawing the concentrated chemical out of a drum, the spigot accidentally toppled back. He reached in with his bare hand to regain the spigot. Although he washed immediately, he became acutely ill and died the next day.

While the results of weed killers such as sodium arsenite or the phenols are grossly obvious, some other herbicides are more insidious in their effects. For example, the now famous cranberry-weed-killer aminotriazole, or amitrol, is rated as having relatively low toxicity. But in the long run its tendency to cause malignant tumors of the thyroid may be far more significant for wildlife and perhaps also for man.

Among the herbicides are some that are classified as "mutagens," or agents capable of modifying the genes, the materials of heredity. We are rightly appalled by the genetic effects of radiation; how then, can we be indifferent to the same effect in chemicals that we disseminate widely in our environment?

THE ABOLITION OF MAN

C. S. LEWIS

C.S. Lewis (1898-1963) was a prolific writer of science fiction and children's stories, a notable literary critic, and a highly influential apologist of twentieth century Christianity.

He was a fellow of Magdalene College, Oxford, and later professor of medieval and renaissance literature at Cambridge.

The Abolition of Man, published in 1947, carried the subtitle: *Reflections on Education with Special Reference to the Teaching of English in the Upper Forms of Schools*, but the chief concern of Lewis here is what the struggle of Man against Nature does to the struggle of Man against Man.

1. In what sense is Man the possessor of increasing power over Nature?

2. What is the *Tao* to which Lewis refers?

3. What does Lewis mean by "the abolition of man"?

4. What new Natural Philosophy does Lewis propose?

5. Can man ever really "conquer" Nature?

THE ABOLITION OF MAN

C. S. LEWIS

III
THE ABOLITION OF MAN

It came burning hot into my mind, whatever he said
and however he flattered, when he got me home to
his house, he would sell me for a slave.

BUNYAN

'MAN'S conquest of Nature' is an expression often used to describe the progress of applied science. 'Man has Nature whacked' said someone to a friend of mine not long ago. In their context the words had a certain tragic beauty, for the speaker was dying of tuberculosis. 'No matter,' he said, 'I know I'm one of the casualties. Of course there are casualties on the winning as well as on the losing side. But that doesn't alter the fact that it is winning.' I have chosen this story as my point of departure in order to make it clear that I do not wish to disparage all that is really beneficial in the process described as 'man's conquest,' much less all the real devotion and self-sacrifice that has gone to make it possible. But having done so I must proceed to analyse this conception a little more closely. In what sense is Man the possessor of increasing power over Nature?

Let us consider three typical examples: the aeroplane, the wireless, and the contraceptive. In a civilized community, in peace-time, anyone who can pay for them may use these things. But it cannot strictly be said that when he does so he is exercising his own proper or individual power over Nature. If 1 pay you to carry me, I am not therefore myself a strong man. Any or all of the three things I have mentioned can be withheld from some men by other men—by those who sell, or those who allow the sale, or those who own the sources of production, or those who make the goods. What we call Man's power is, in reality, a power possessed by some men which they may, or may not, allow other men to profit by. Again, as regards the powers manifested in the aeroplane or the wireless, Man is as much the patient or subject as the possessor, since he is the target both for bombs and for propaganda. And as regards contraceptives, there is a paradoxical, negative sense in which all possible future generations are the patients or subjects of a power wielded by those already alive. By contraception simply, they are denied existence; by contraception used as a means of selective breeding, they are, without their concurring voice, made to be what one generation, for its own reasons, may choose to prefer. From this point of view, what we call Man's power over Nature turns out to be a power exercised by some men over other men with Nature as its instrument.

It is, of course, a commonplace to complain that men have hitherto used badly, and against their fellows, the powers that science has given them. But that is not the point I am trying to make. I am not speaking of particular corruptions and abuses which an increase of moral virtue would cure: I am considering what the thing called 'Man's power over Nature' must always and essentially be. No doubt, the picture could be modified by public ownership of raw materials and factories and public control of scientific research. But unless we have a world state this will still mean the power of one nation over others. And even within the world state or the nation it will mean (in principle) the power of majorities over minorities, and (in the concrete) of a government over the people. And all long-term exercises of power, especially in breeding, must mean the power of earlier generations over later ones.

The latter point is not always sufficiently emphasized, because those who write on social matters have not yet learned to imitate the physicists by always including Time among the dimensions. In order to understand fully what Man's power over Nature, and therefore the power of some men over other men, really means, we must picture the race extended in time from the date of its emergence to that of its extinction. Each generation exercises power over its successors: and each, in so far as it modifies the environment bequeathed to it and rebels against tradition, resists and limits the power of its predecessors. This modifies the picture which is sometimes painted of a progressive emancipation from tradition and a progressive control of natural processes resulting in a continual increase of human power. In reality, of course, if any one age really attains, by eugenics and scientific education, the power to make its descendants what it pleases, all men who live after it are the patients of that power. They are weaker, not stronger: for though we may have put wonderful machines in their hands we have pre-ordained how they are to use them. And if, as is almost certain, the age which had thus attained maximum power over posterity were also the age most emancipated from tradition, it would be engaged in reducing the power of its predecessors almost as drastically as that of its successors. And we must also remember that, quite apart from this, the later a generation comes—the nearer it lives to that date at which the species becomes extinct—the less power it will have in the forward direction, because its subjects will be so few. There is therefore no question of a power vested in the race as a whole steadily growing as long as the race survives. The last men, far from being the heirs of power, will be of all men most subject to the dead hand of the great planners and conditioners and will themselves exercise least power upon the future. The real picture is that of one dominant age—let us suppose the hundredth century A.D.—which resists all previous ages most successfully and dominates all subsequent ages most irresistibly, and thus is the real master of the human species. But even within this master generation (itself an infinitesimal minority of the species) the power will be exercised by a minority smaller still. Man's conquest of Nature, if the dreams of some scientific planners are realized, means the rule of a few hundreds of men over billions upon billions of men. There neither is nor can be any simple increase of power on Man's side. Each new power won by man is a power *over* man as well. Each advance leaves him weaker as well as stronger. In every victory, besides being the general who triumphs, he is also the prisoner who follows the triumphal car.

I am not yet considering whether the total result of such ambivalent victories is a good thing or a bad. I am only making clear what Man's conquest of Nature really means and especially that final stage in the conquest, which, perhaps, is not far off. The final stage is come when Man by eugenics, by pre-natal conditioning, and by an education and propaganda based on a perfect applied psychology, has obtained full control over himself. *Human* nature will be the last part of Nature to surrender to Man. The battle will then be won. We shall have 'taken the thread of life out of the hand of Clotho' and be henceforth free to make our species whatever we wish it to be. The battle will indeed be won. But who, precisely, will have won it?

For the power of Man to make himself what he pleases means, as we have seen, the power of some men to make other men what *they* please. In all ages, no doubt, nurture and instruction have, in some sense, attempted to exercise this power. But the situation to which we must look forward will be novel in two respects. In the first place, the power will be enormously increased. Hitherto the plans of educationalists have achieved very little of what they attempted and indeed, when we read them—how Plato would have every infant 'a bastard nursed in a bureau,' and Elyot would have the boy see no men before the age of seven and, after that, no women, and how Locke wants children to have leaky shoes and no turn for poetry—we may well thank the beneficent obstinacy of real mothers, real nurses, and (above all) real children for preserving the human race in such sanity as it still possesses. But the man-moulders of the new age will be armed with the powers of an omnicompetent state and an irresistible scientific technique: we shall get at last a race of conditioners who really can cut out all posterity in what shape they please. The second difference is even more important. In the older systems both the kind of man the teachers wished to produce and their motives for producing him were prescribed by the Tao—a norm to which the teachers themselves were subject and from which they claimed no liberty to depart. They did not cut men to some pattern they had chosen. They handed on what they had received: they initiated the young neophyte into the mystery of humanity which over-arched him and them alike. It was but old birds teaching young birds to fly. This will be changed. Values are now mere natural phenomena. Judgements of value are to be produced in the pupil as part of the conditioning. Whatever *Tao* there is will be the product, not the motive, of education. The conditioners have been emancipated from all that. It is one more part of Nature which they have conquered. The ultimate springs of human action are no longer, for them, something given. They have surrendered—like electricity: it is the function of the Conditioners to control, not to obey them. They know how to *produce* conscience and decide what kind of conscience they will produce. They themselves are outside, above. For we are assuming the last stage of Man's struggle with Nature. The final victory has been won. Human nature has been conquered—and, of course, has conquered, in whatever sense those words may now bear.

The Conditioners, then, are to choose what kind of artificial *Tao* they will, for their own good reasons, produce in the Human race. They are the motivators, the creators of motives. But how are they going to be motivated themselves? For a time, perhaps, by survivals, within their own minds, of the old 'natural' *Tao*. Thus at first they may look upon themselves as servants and guardians of humanity and conceive that they have a 'duty' to do it 'good.' But it is only by confusion that they can remain in this state. They recognize the concept of duty as the result of certain processes which they can now control. Their victory has consisted precisely in emerging from the state in which they were acted upon by those processes to the state in which they use them as tools. One of the things they now have to decide is whether they will, or will not, so condition the rest of us that we can go on having the old idea of duty and the old reactions to it. How can duty help them to decide that? Duty itself is up for trial: it cannot also be the judge. And 'good' fares no better. They know quite well how to produce a dozen different conceptions of good in us. The question is which, if any, they should produce. No conception of good can help them to decide. It is absurd to fix on one of the things they are comparing and make it the standard of comparison.

To some it will appear that I am inventing a factitious difficulty for my Conditioners. Other, more simple-minded, critics may ask 'Why should you suppose they will be such bad men?' But I am not supposing them to be bad men. They are, rather, not men (in the old sense) at all. They are, if you like, men who have sacrificed their own share in traditional humanity in order to devote themselves to the task of deciding what 'Humanity' shall henceforth mean. 'Good' and 'bad,' applied to them, are words without content: for it is from them that the content of these words is henceforward to be derived. Nor is their difficulty factitious. We might suppose that it was possible to say 'After all, most of us want more or less the same things—food and drink and sexual intercourse, amusement, art, science, and the longest possible life for individuals and for the species. Let them simply say, This is what we happen to like, and go on to condition men in the way most likely to produce it. Where's the trouble?' But this will not answer. In the first place, it is false that we all really like the same things. But even if we did, what motive is to impel the Conditioners to scorn delights and live laborious days in order that we, and posterity, may have what we like? Their duty? But that is only the *Tao*, which they may decide to impose on us, but which cannot be valid for them. If they accept it, then they are no longer the makers of conscience but still its subjects, and their final conquest over Nature has not really happened. The preservation of the species? But why should the species be preserved? One of the questions before them is whether this feeling for posterity (they know well how it is produced) shall be continued or not. However far they go back, or down, they can find no ground to stand on. Every motive they try to act on becomes at once a *petitio*. It is not that they are bad men. They are not men at all. Stepping outside the *Tao*, they have stepped into the void. Nor are their subjects necessarily unhappy men. They are not men at all: they are artefacts. Man's final conquest has proved to be the abolition of Man.

Yet the Conditioners will act. When I said just now that all motives fail them, I should have said all motives except one. All motives that claim any validity other than that of their felt emotional weight at a given moment have failed them. Everything except the *sic volo, sic jubeo* has been explained away. But what never claimed objectivity cannot be destroyed by subjectivism. The impulse to scratch when I itch or to pull to pieces when I am inquisitive is immune from the solvent which is fatal to my justice, or honour, or care for posterity. When all that says 'it is good' has been debunked, what says 'I want' remains. It cannot be exploded or 'seen through' because it never had any pretensions. The Conditioners, therefore, must come to be motivated simply by their own pleasure. I am not here speaking of the corrupting influence of power nor expressing the fear that under it our Conditioners will degenerate. The very words *corrupt* and *degenerate* imply a doctrine of value and are therefore meaningless in this context. My point is that those who stand outside all judgements of value cannot have any ground for preferring one of their own impulses to another except the emotional strength of that impulse. We may legitimately hope that among the impulses which arise in minds thus emptied of all 'rational' or 'spiritual' motives, some will be benevolent. I am very doubtful myself whether the benevolent impulses, stripped of that preference and encouragement which the *Tao* teaches us to give them and left to their merely natural strength and frequency as psychological events, will have much influence. I am very doubtful whether history shows us one example of a man who, having stepped outside traditional morality and attained power, has used that power benevolently. I am inclined to think that the Conditioners will hate the conditioned. Though regarding as an illusion the artificial conscience which they produce in us their subjects, they will yet perceive that it creates in us an illusion of meaning for our lives which compares favourably with the futility of their own: and they will envy us as eunuchs envy men. But I do not insist on this, for it is mere conjecture. What is not conjecture is that our hope even of a 'conditioned' happiness rests on what is ordinarily called 'chance'—the chance that benevolent impulses may on the whole predominate in our Conditioners. For without the judgement 'Benevolence is good'—that is, without re-entering the *Tao*—they can have no ground for promoting or stabilizing their benevolent impulses rather than any others. By the logic of their position they must just take their impulses as they come, from chance. And Chance here means Nature. It is from heredity, digestion, the weather, and the association of ideas, that the motives of the Conditioners will spring. Their extreme rationalism, by 'seeing through' all rational motives, leaves them creatures of wholly irrational behaviour. If you will not obey the *Tao,* or else commit suicide, obedience to impulse (and therefore, in the long run, to mere 'nature') is the only course left open.

At the moment, then, of Man's victory over Nature, we find the whole human race subjected to some individual men, and those individuals subjected to that in themselves which is purely 'natural'—to their irrational impulses. Nature, untrammelled by values, rules the Conditioners and, through them, all humanity. Man's conquest of Nature turns out, in the moment of its consummation, to be Nature's conquest of Man. Every victory we seemed to win has led us, step by step, to this conclusion. All Nature's apparent reverses have been but tactical withdrawals. We thought we were beating her back when she was luring us on. What looked to us like hands held up in surrender was really the opening of arms to enfold us for ever. If the fully planned and conditioned world (with its *Tao* a mere product of the planning) comes into existence, Nature will be troubled no more by the restive species that rose in revolt against her so many millions of years ago, will be vexed no longer by its chatter of truth and mercy and beauty and happiness. *Ferum victorem cepit:* and if the eugenics are efficient enough there will be no second revolt, but all snug beneath the Conditioners, and the Conditioners beneath her, till the moon falls or the sun grows cold.

My point may be clearer to some if it is put in a different form. Nature is a word of varying meanings, which can best be understood if we consider its various opposites. The Natural is the opposite of the Artificial, the Civil, the Human, the Spiritual, and the Supernatural. The Artificial does not now concern us. If we take the rest of the list of opposites, however, I think we can get a rough idea of what men have meant by Nature and what it is they oppose to her. Nature seems to be the spatial and temporal, as distinct from what is less fully so or not so at all. She seems to be the world of quantity, as against the world of quality: of objects as against consciousness: of the bound, as against the wholly or partially autonomous: of that which knows no values as against that which both has and perceives value: of efficient causes (or, in some modern systems, of no causality at all) as against final causes. Now I take it that when we understand a thing analytically and then dominate and use it for our own convenience we reduce it to the level of 'Nature' in the sense that we suspend our judgements of value about it, ignore its final cause (if any), and treat it in terms of quantity. This repression of elements in what would otherwise be our total reaction to it is sometimes very noticeable and even painful: something has to be overcome before we can cut up a dead man or a live animal in a dissecting room. These objects *resist* the movement of the mind whereby we thrust them into the world of mere Nature. But in other instances too, a similar price is exacted for our analytical knowledge and manipulative power, even if we have ceased to count it. We do not look at trees either as Dryads or as beautiful objects while we cut them into beams: the first man who did so may have felt the price keenly, and the bleeding trees in Virgil and Spenser may be far-off echoes of that primeval sense of impiety. The stars lost their divinity as astronomy developed, and the Dying God has no place in chemical agriculture. To many, no doubt, this process is simply the gradual discovery that the real world is different from what we expected, and the old opposition to Galileo or to 'bodysnatchers' is simply obscurantism. But that is not the whole story. It is not the greatest of modern scientists who feel most sure that the object, stripped of its qualitative properties and reduced to mere quantity, is wholly real. Little scientists, and little unscientific followers of science, may think so. The great minds know very well that the object, so treated, is an artificial abstraction, that something of its reality has been lost.

From this point of view the conquest of Nature appears in a new light. We reduce things to mere Nature in *order that* we may 'conquer' them. We are always conquering Nature because 'Nature' is the name for what we have, to some extent, conquered. The price of conquest is to treat a thing as mere Nature. Every conquest over Nature increases her domain. The stars do not become Nature till we can weigh and measure them: the soul does not become Nature till we can psycho-analyse her. The wresting of powers from Nature is also the surrendering of things to Nature. As long as this process stops short of the final stage we may well hold that the gain outweighs the loss. But as soon as we take the final step of reducing our own species to the level of mere Nature, the whole process is stultified, for this time the being who stood to gain and the being who has been sacrificed are one and the same. This is one of the many instances where to carry a principle to what seems its logical conclusion produces absurdity. It is like the famous Irishman who found that a certain kind of stove reduced his fuel bill by half and thence concluded that two stoves of the same kind would enable him to warm his house with no fuel at all. It is the magician's bargain: give up our soul, get power in return. But once our souls, that is, our selves, have been given up, the power thus conferred will not belong to us. We shall in fact be the slaves and puppets of that to which we have given our souls. It is in Man's power to treat himself as a mere 'natural object' and his own judgements of value as raw material for scientific manipulation to alter at will. The objection to his doing so does not lie in the fact that this point of view (like one's first day in a dissecting room) is painful and shocking till we grow used to it. The pain and the shock are at most a warning and a symptom. The real objection is that if man chooses to treat himself as raw material, raw material he will be: not raw material to be manipulated, as he fondly imagined, by himself, but by mere appetite, that is, mere Nature, in the person of his dehumanized Conditioners.

We have been trying, like Lear, to have it both ways: to lay down our human prerogative and yet at the same time to retain it. It is impossible. Either we are rational spirit obliged for ever to obey the absolute values of the *Tao,* or else we are mere nature to be kneaded and cut into new shapes for the pleasures of masters who must, by hypothesis, have no motive but their own 'natural' impulses. Only the *Tao* provides a common human law of action which can over-arch rulers and ruled alike. A dogmatic belief in objective value is necessary to the very idea of a rule which is not tyranny or an obedience which is not slavery.

I am not here thinking solely, perhaps not even chiefly, of those who are our public enemies at the moment. The process which, if not checked, will abolish Man, goes on apace among Communists and Democrats no less than among Fascists. The methods may (at first) differ in brutality. But many a mild-eyed scientist in pince-nez, many a popular dramatist, many an amateur philosopher in our midst, means in the long run just the same as the Nazi rulers of Germany. Traditional values are to be 'debunked' and mankind to be cut out into some fresh shape at the will (which must, by hypothesis, be an arbitrary will) of some few lucky people in one lucky generation which has learned how to do it. The belief that we can invent 'ideologies' at pleasure, and the consequent treatment of mankind as mere ὕλη specimens, preparations, begins to affect our very language. Once we killed bad men: now we liquidate unsocial elements. Virtue has become *integration* and diligence *dynamism,* and boys likely to be worthy of a commission are 'potential officer material.' Most wonderful of all, the virtues of thrift and temperance, and even of ordinary intelligence, are *sales-resistance.*

The true significance of what is going on has been concealed by the use of the abstraction Man. Not that the word Man is necessarily a pure abstraction. In the *Tao* itself, as long as we remain within it, we find the concrete reality in which to participate is to be truly human: the real common will and common reason of humanity, alive, and growing like a tree, and branching out, as the situation varies, into ever new beauties and dignities of application. While we speak from within the *Tao* we can speak of Man having power over himself in a sense truly analogous to an individual's self-control. But the moment we step outside and regard the *Tao* as a mere subjective product, this possibility has disappeared. What is now common to all men is a mere abstract universal, an H.C.F., and Man's conquest of himself means simply the rule of the Conditioners over the conditioned human material, the world of post-humanity which, some knowingly and some unknowingly, nearly all men in all nations are at present labouring to produce.

Nothing I can say will prevent some people from describing this lecture as an attack on science. I deny the charge, of course: and real Natural Philosophers (there are some now alive) will perceive that in defending value I defend *inter alia* the value of knowledge, which must die like every other when its roots in the *Tao* are cut. But I can go further than that. I even suggest that from Science herself the cure might come. I have described as a 'magician's bargain' that process whereby man surrenders object after object, and finally himself, to Nature in return for power. And I meant what I said. The fact that the scientist has succeeded where the magician failed has put such a wide contrast between them in popular thought that the real story of the birth of Science is misunderstood. You will even find people who write about the sixteenth century as if Magic were a medieval survival and Science the new thing that came in to sweep it away. Those who have studied the period know better. There was very little magic in the Middle Ages: the sixteenth and seventeenth centuries are the high noon of magic. The serious magical endeavour and the serious scientific endeavour are twins: one was sickly and died, the other strong and throve. But they were twins. They were born of the same impulse. I allow that some (certainly not all) of the early scientists were actuated by a pure love of knowledge. But if we consider the temper of that age as a whole we can discern the impulse of which I speak. There is something which unites magic and applied science while separating both from the 'wisdom' of earlier ages. For the wise men of old the-cardinal problem had been how to conform the soul to reality, and the solution had been knowledge, self-discipline, and virtue. For magic and applied science alike the problem is how to subdue reality to the wishes of men: the solution is a technique; and both, in the practice of this technique, are ready to do things hitherto regarded as disgusting and impious—such as digging up and mutilating the dead. If we compare the chief trumpeter of the new era (Bacon) with Marlowe's Faustus, the similarity is striking. You will read in some critics that Faustus has a thirst for knowledge. In reality, he hardly mentions it. It is not truth he wants from his devils, but gold and guns and girls. 'All things that move between the quiet poles shall be at his command' and 'a sound magician is a mighty god.' In the same spirit Bacon condemns those who value knowledge as an end in itself: this, for him, is to use as a mistress for pleasure what ought to be a spouse for fruit. The true object is to extend Man's power to the performance of all things possible. He rejects magic because it does not work, but his goal is that of the magician. In Paracelsus the characters of magician and scientist are combined. No doubt those who really founded modern science were usually those whose love of truth exceeded their love of power; in every mixed movement the efficacy comes from the good elements not from the bad. But the presence of the bad elements is not irrelevant to the direction the efficacy takes. It might be going too far to say that the modern scientific movement was tainted from its birth: but I think it would be true to say that it was born in an unhealthy neighbourhood and at an inauspicious hour. Its triumphs may have been too rapid and purchased at too high a price: reconsideration, and something like repentance, may be required.

Is it, then, possible to imagine a new Natural Philosophy, continually conscious that the 'natural object' produced by analysis and abstraction is not reality but only a view, and always correcting the abstraction? I hardly know what I am asking for. I hear rumours that Goethe's approach to nature deserves fuller consideration—that even Dr. Steiner may have seen something that orthodox researchers have missed. The regenerate science which I have in mind would not do even to minerals and vegetables what modern science threatens to do to man himself. When it explained it would not explain away. When it spoke of the parts it would remember the whole. While studying the *It* it would not lose what Martin Buber calls the Thou-situation. The analogy between the *Tao* of Man and the instincts of an animal species would mean for it new light cast on the unknown thing, Instinct, by the inly known reality of conscience and not a reduction of conscience to the category of Instinct. Its followers would not be free with the words *only* and *merely*. In a word, it would conquer Nature without being at the same time conquered by her and buy knowledge at a lower cost than that of life. Perhaps I am asking impossibilities. Perhaps, in the nature of things, analytical understanding must always be a basilisk which kills what it sees and only sees by killing. But if the scientists themselves cannot arrest this process before it reaches the common Reason and kills that too, then someone else must arrest it. What I most fear is the reply that I am 'only one more' obscurantist, that this barrier, like all previous barriers set up against the advance of science, can be safely passed. Such a reply springs from the fatal serialism of the modern imagination—the image of infinite unilinear progression which so haunts our minds. Because we have to use numbers so much we tend to think of every process as if it must be like the numeral series, where every step, to all eternity, is the same kind of step as the one before. I implore you to remember the Irishman and his two stoves. There are progressions in which the last step is *sui generis*—incommensurable with the others—and in which to go the whole way is to undo all the labour of your previous journey. To reduce the *Tao* to a mere natural product is a step of that kind. Up to that point, the kind of explanation which explains things away may give us something, though at a heavy cost. But you cannot go on 'explaining away' for ever: you will find that you have explained explanation itself away. You cannot go on 'seeing through' things for ever. The whole point of seeing through something is to see something through it. It is good that the window should be transparent, because the street or garden beyond it is opaque. How if you saw through the garden too? It is no use trying to 'see through' first principles. If you see through everything, then everything is transparent. But a wholly transparent world is an invisible world. To 'see through' all things is the same as not to see.

PILGRIM AT TINKER CREEK

ANNIE DILLARD

Annie Dillard was born in 1945 in Pittsburgh where she grew up. Attendance at Hollins College brought her to the Roanoke Valley of Virginia. After receiving the B.A. degree in 1967 and the M.A. in 1968, she continued to live in the Valley.

She has served as a contributing editor of *Harper's Magazine* and a columnist for The Wilderness Society. She has authored nine other books, poetry as well as prose, including *Teaching a Stone to Talk* (1982), *An American Childhood* (1987), *The Writing Life* (1989) and *Mornings Like This* (1995).

Dillard describes herself as "no scientist," but as a "wanderer with a background in theology and a penchant for quirky facts. . . . I consider nature's facts—its beautiful and grotesque forms and events—in terms of their import to thought and their impetus to the spirit. In nature I find grace tangled in a rapture with violence; I find an intricate landscape whose forms are fringed in depth; I find mystery, newness, and a kind of exuberant, spendthrift energy."

Pilgrim at Tinker Creek (1974) is a personal account of a year of contemplation and explorations on foot in the author's own neighborhood. The book won a Pulitzer prize for general non-fiction.

1. What is the significance of the sycamore for Annie Dillard?

2. What advantage, if any, is there for young people in being sent off to a camp in the country for a week or two in summer?

3. Why does Dillard choose to base her thoughts on Tinker Creek rather than on Tinker Mountain? What is the role of the creek in her thoughts?

4. What is Dillard's reaction to the "Principle of Indeterminacy"?

PILGRIM AT TINKER CREEK

ANNIE DILLARD

Chapter 6

The Present

II

I am sitting under a sycamore by Tinker Creek. It is early spring, the day after I patted the puppy. I have come to the creek—the backyard stretch of the creek—in the middle of the day, to feel the delicate gathering of heat, real sun's heat, in the air, and to watch new water come down the creek. Don't expect more than this, and a mental ramble. I'm in the market for some present tense; I'm on the lookout, shopping around, more so every year. It's a seller's market—do you think I won't sell all that I have to buy it? Thomas Merton wrote, in a light passage in one of his Gethsemane journals: "Suggested emendation in the Lord's Prayer: Take out 'Thy Kingdom come' and substitute 'Give us time!'" But time is the one thing we have been given, and we have been given to time. Time gives us a whirl. We keep waking from a dream we can't recall, looking around in surprise, and lapsing back, for years on end. All I want to do is stay awake, keep my head up, prop my eyes open, with toothpicks, with trees.

Before me the creek is seventeen feet wide, splashing over random sandstone outcroppings and scattered rocks. I'm lucky; the creek is loud here, because of the rocks, and wild. In the low water of summer and fall I can cross to the opposite bank by leaping from stone to stone. Upstream is a wall of light split into planks by smooth sandstone ledges that cross the creek evenly, like steps. Downstream the live water before me stills, dies suddenly as if extinguished, and vanishes around a bend shaded summer and winter by overarching tulips, locusts, and Osage orange. Everywhere I look are creekside trees whose ascending boles against water and grass accent the vertical thrust of the land in this spot. The creek rests the eye, a haven, a breast; the two steep banks vault from the creek like wings. Not even the sycamore's crown can peek over the land in any direction.

My friend Rosanne Coggeshall, the poet, says that "sycamore" is the most intrinsically beautiful word in English. This sycamore is old; its lower bark is always dusty from years of floodwaters lapping up its trunk. Like many sycamores, too, it is quirky, given to flights and excursions. Its trunk lists over the creek at a dizzying angle, and from that trunk extends a long, skinny limb that spurts high over the opposite bank without branching. The creek reflects the speckled surface of this limb, pale even against the highest clouds, and that image pales whiter and thins as it crosses the creek, shatters in the riffles and melds together, quivering and mottled, like some enormous primeval reptile under the water.

I want to think about trees. Trees have a curious relationship to the subject of the present moment. There are many created things in the universe that outlive us, that outlive the sun, even, but I can't think about them. I live with trees.

There are creatures under our feet, creatures that live over our heads, but trees live quite convincingly in the same filament of air we inhabit, and, in addition, they extend impressively in both directions, up and down, shearing rock and fanning air, doing their real business just out of reach. A blind man's idea of hugeness is a tree. They have their sturdy bodies and special skills; they garner fresh water; they abide. This sycamore above me, below me, by Tinker Creek, is a case in point; the sight of it crowds my brain with an assortment of diverting thoughts, all as present to me as these slivers of pressure from grass on my elbow's skin. I want to come at the subject of the present by showing how consciousness dashes and ambles around the labyrinthine tracks of the mind, returning again and again, however briefly, to the senses: "If there were but one erect and solid standing tree in the woods, all creatures would go to rub against it and make sure of their footing." But so long as I stay in my thoughts, my foot slides under trees; I fall, or I dance.

Sycamores are among the last trees to go into leaf; in the fall, they are the first to shed. They make sweet food in green broadleaves for a while—leaves wide as plates—and then go wild and wave their long white arms. In ancient Rome men honored the sycamore—in the form of its cousin, the Oriental plane—by watering its roots with wine. Xerxes, I read, "halted his unwieldly army for days that he might contemplate to his satisfaction" the beauty of a single sycamore.

You are Xerxes in Persia. Your army spreads on a vast and arid peneplain . . . you call to you all your sad captains, and give the order to halt. You have seen the tree with the lights in it, haven't you? You must have. Xerxes buffeted on a plain, ambition drained in a puff. That fusillade halts any army in its tracks. Your men are bewildered; they lean on their spears, sucking the rinds of gourds. There is nothing to catch the eye in this flatness, nothing but a hollow, hammering sky, a waste of sedge in the lee of windblown rocks, a meagre ribbon of scrub willow tracing a slumbering watercourse . . . and that sycamore. You saw it; you still stand rapt and mute, exalted, remembering or not remembering over a period of days to shade your head with your robe.

"He had its form wrought upon a medal of gold to help him remember it the rest of his life." Your teeth are chattering; it is just before dawn and you have started briefly from your daze. "Goldsmith !" The goldsmith is sodden with sleep, surly. He lights his forge, he unrolls the dusty cotton wrapping from his half-forgotten stylus and tongs, he waits for the sun. We all ought to have a goldsmith following us around. But it goes without saying, doesn't it, Xerxes, that no gold medal worn around your neck will bring back the glad hour, keep those lights kindled so long as you live, forever present? Pascal saw it. He grabbed pen and paper; he managed to scrawl the one word, FEU; he wore that scrap of paper sewn in his shirt the rest of his life. I don't know what Pascal saw. I saw a cedar. Xerxes saw a sycamore.

These trees stir me. The past inserts a finger into a slit in the skin of the present, and pulls. I remember how sycamores grew—and presumably still grow—in the city, in Pittsburgh, even along the busiest streets. I used to spend hours in the backyard, thinking God knows what, and peeling the mottled bark of a sycamore, idly, littering the grass with dried lappets and strips, leaving the tree's trunk at eye level moist, thin-skinned and yellow—until someone would catch me at it from the kitchen window, and I would awake, and look at my work in astonishment, and think oh no, this time I've killed the sycamore for sure.

Here in Virginia the trees reach enormous proportions, especially in the lowlands on banksides. It is hard to understand how the same tree could thrive both choking along Pittsburgh's Penn Avenue and slogging knee-deep in Tinker Creek. Of course, come to think of it, I've done the same thing myself. Because a sycamore's primitive bark is not elastic but frangible, it sheds continuously as it grows; seen from a distance, a sycamore seems to grow in pallor and vulnerability as it grows in height; the bare uppermost branches are white against the sky.

The sky is deep and distant, laced with sycamore limbs like a hatching of crossed swords. I can scarcely see it; I'm not looking. I don't come to the creek for sky unmediated, but for shelter. My back rests on a steep bank under the sycamore; before me shines the creek—the creek which is about all the light I can stand—and beyond it rises the other bank, also steep, and planted in trees.

I have never understood why so many mystics of all creeds experience the presence of God on mountaintops. Aren't they afraid of being blown away? God said to Moses on Sinai that even the priests, who have access to the Lord, must hallow themselves, for fear that the Lord may break out against them. This is *the* fear. It often feels best to lay low, inconspicuous, instead of waving your spirit around from high places like a lightning rod. For if God is in one sense the igniter, a fireball that spins over the ground of continents, God is also in another sense the destroyer, lightning, blind power, impartial as the atmosphere. Or God is one "G." You get a comforting sense, in a curved, hollow place, of being vulnerable to only a relatively narrow column of God as air.

In the open, anything might happen. Dorothy Dunnett, the great medievalist, states categorically: "There is no reply, in clear terrain, to an archer in cover." Any copperhead anywhere is an archer in cover; how much more so is God! Invisibility is the all-time great "cover"; and that the one infinite power deals so extravagantly and unfathomably in death—death morning, noon, and night, all manner of death—makes that power an archer, there is no getting around it. And we the people are so vulnerable. Our bodies are shot with mortality. Our legs are fear and our arms are time. These chill humors seep through our capillaries, weighting each cell with an icy dab of nonbeing, and that dab grows and swells and sucks the cell dry. That is why physical courage is so important—it fills, as it were, the holes—and why it is so invigorating. The least brave act, chance taken and passage won, makes you feel loud as a child.

But it gets harder. The courage of children and beasts is a function of innocence. We let our bodies go the way of our fears. A teen-aged boy, king of the world, will spend weeks in front of a mirror perfecting some difficult trick with a lighter, a muscle, a tennis ball, a coin. Why do we lose interest in physical mastery? If I feel like turning cartwheels—and I do—why don't I learn to turn cartwheels, instead of regretting that I never learned as a child? We could all be aerialists like squirrels, divers like seals; we could be purely patient, perfectly fleet, walking on our hands even, if our living or stature required it. We can't even sit straight, or support our weary heads.

When we lose our innocence—when we start feeling the weight of the atmosphere and learn that there's death in the pot—we take leave of our senses. Only children can hear the song of the male house mouse. Only children keep their eyes open. The only thing they *have* got is sense; they have highly developed "input systems," admitting all data indiscriminately. Matt Spireng has collected thousands of arrowheads and spearheads; he says that if you really want to find arrowheads, you must walk with a child—a child will pick up *everything*. All my adult life I have wished to see the cemented case of a caddisfly larva. It took Sally Moore, the young daughter of friends, to find one on the pebbled bottom of a shallow stream on whose bank we sat side by side. "What's this?" she asked. That, I wanted to say as I recognized the prize she held, is a memento mori for people who read too much.

We found other caddisfly cases that day, Sally and I, after I had learned to focus so fine, and I saved one. It is a hollow cylinder three quarters of an inch long, a little masterpiece of masonry consisting entirely of cemented grains of coarse sand only one layer thick. Some of the sand grains are red, and it was by searching for this red that I learned to spot the cases. The caddisfly larva will use any bits it can find to fashion its house; in fact, entomologists have amused themselves by placing a naked larva in an aquarium furnished only with, say, red sand. When the larva has laid around its body several rows of red sand, the entomologist transfers it to another aquarium in which only white bits are available. The larva busily adds rows of white to the red wall, and then here comes the entomologist again, with a third and final aquarium full of blue sand. At any rate, the point I want to make is that this tiny immature creature responds to an instinct to put something between its flesh and a jagged world. If you give a "masonry mosaic" kind of caddisfly larva only large decayed leaves, that larva, confronted by something utterly novel, will nevertheless bite the leaves into shreds and rig those shreds into a case.

The general rule in nature is that live things are soft within and rigid without. We vertebrates are living dangerously, and we vertebrates are positively piteous, like so many peeled trees. This oft was thought, but ne'er so well expressed as by Pliny, who writes of nature, "To all the rest, given she hath sufficient to clad them everyone according to their kind: as namely, shells, cods, hard hides, pricks, shags, bristles, hair, down feathers, quills, scales, and fleeces of wool. The very trunks and stems of trees and plants, she hath defended with bark and rind, yea and the same sometimes double, against the injuries both of heat and cold: man alone, poor wretch, she hath laid all naked upon the bare earth, even on his birthday, to cry and wraule presently from the very first hour that he is born into the world."

I am sitting under a sycamore tree: I am soft-shell and peeled to the least puff of wind or smack of grit. The present of our life looks different under trees. Trees have dominion. I never killed that backyard sycamore; even its frailest inner bark was a shield. Trees do not accumulate life, but deadwood, like a thickening coat of mail. Their odds actually improve as they age. Some trees, like giant sequoias, are, practically speaking, immortal, vulnerable only to another ice age. They are not even susceptible to fire. Sequoia wood barely burns, and the bark is "nearly as fireproof as asbestos. The top of one sequoia, struck by lightning a few years ago during a July thunderstorm, smoldered quietly, without apparently damaging the tree, until it was put out by a snowstorm in October." Some trees sink taproots to rock; some spread wide mats of roots clutching at acres. They will not be blown. We run around under these obelisk-creatures, teetering on our soft, small feet. We are out on a jaunt, picnicking, fattening like puppies for our deaths. Shall I carve a name on this trunk? What if I fell in a forest: Would a tree hear?

I am sitting under a bankside sycamore; my mind is a slope. Arthur Koestler wrote, "In his review of the literature on the psychological present, Woodrow found that its maximum span is estimated to lie between 2.3 and 12 seconds." How did anyone measure that slide? As soon as you are conscious of it, it is gone. I repeat a phrase: the thin tops of mountains. Soon the thin tops of mountains erupt, as if volcanically, from my brain's core. I can see them; they are, surprisingly, serrate—scallopped like the blade of a kitchen knife—and brown as leaves. The serrated edges are so thin they are translucent; through the top of one side of the brown ridge I can see, in silhouette, a circling sharp-shinned hawk; through another, deep tenuous veins of metallic ore. This isn't Tinker Creek. Where do I live, anyway? I lose myself, I float.... I am in Persia, trying to order a watermelon in German. It's insane. The engineer has abandoned the control room, and an idiot is splicing the reels. What could I contribute to the "literature on the psychological present?" If I could remember to press the knob on the stopwatch, I wouldn't be in Persia. Before they invented the unit of the second, people used to time the lapse of short events on their pulses. Oh, but what about that heave in the wrist when I saw the tree with the lights in it, and my heart ceased, but I am still there?

Scenes drift across the screen from nowhere. I can never discover the connection between any one scene and what I am more consciously thinking, nor can I ever conjure the scene back in full vividness. It is like a ghost, in full-dress regalia, that wafts across the stage set unnoticed by the principle characters. It appears complete, in full color, wordless, though already receding: the tennis courts on Fifth Avenue in Pittsburgh, an equestrian statue in a Washington park, a basement dress shop in New York city—scenes that I thought meant nothing to me. These aren't still shots; the camera is always moving. And the scene is always just slipping out of sight, as if in spite of myself I were always just descending a hill, rounding a corner, stepping into the street with a companion who urges me on, while I look back over my shoulder at the sight which recedes, vanishes. The present of my consciousness is itself a mystery which is also always just rounding a bend like a floating branch borne by a flood. Where am I? But I'm not. "I will overturn, overturn, overturn, it: and it shall be no more...."

All right then. Pull yourself together. Is this where I'm spending my life, in the "reptile brain," this lamp at the top of the spine like a lighthouse flipping mad beams indiscriminately into the darkness, into the furred thoraxes of moths, onto the backs of leaping fishes and the wrecks of schooners? Come up a level; surface.

I am sitting under a sycamore by Tinker Creek. I am really here, alive on the intricate earth under trees. But under me, directly under the weight of my body on the grass, are other creatures, just as real, for whom also this moment, this tree, is "it." Take just the top inch of soil, the world squirming right under my palms. In the top inch of forest soil, biologists found "an average of 1,356 living creatures present in each square foot, including 865 mites, 265 springtails, 22 millipedes, 19 adult beetles and various numbers of 12 other forms.... Had an estimate also been made of the microscopic population, it might have ranged up to two billion bacteria and many millions of fungi, protozoa and algae—in a mere *teaspoonful* of soil." The chrysalids of butterflies linger here too, folded, rigid, and dreamless. I might as well include these creatures in this moment, as best I can. My ignoring them won't strip them of their reality, and admitting them, one by one, into my consciousness might heighten mine, might add their dim awareness to my human consciousness, such as it is, and set up a buzz, a vibration like the beating ripples a submerged muskrat makes on the water, from this particular moment, this tree. Hasidism has a tradition that one of man's purposes is to assist God in the work of redemption by "hallowing" the things of creation. By a tremendous heave of his spirit, the devout man frees the divine sparks trapped in the mute things of time; he uplifts the forms and moments of creation, bearing them aloft into that rare air and hallowing fire in which all clays must shatter and burst. Keeping the subsoil world under trees in mind, in intelligence, is the *least* I can do.

Earthworms in staggering processions lurch through the grit underfoot, gobbling downed leaves and spewing forth castings by the ton. Moles mine intricate tunnels in networks; there are often so many of these mole tunnels here by the creek that when I walk, every step is a letdown. A mole is almost entirely loose inside its skin, and enormously mighty. If you can catch a mole, it will, in addition to biting you memorably, leap from your hand in a single convulsive contraction and be gone as soon as you have it. You are never really able to see it; you only feel its surge and thrust against your palm, as if you held a beating heart in a paper bag. What could I not do if I had the power and will of a mole! But the mole churns earth.

Last summer some muskrats had a den under this tree's roots on the bank; I think they are still there now. Muskrats' wet fur rounds the domed clay walls of the den and slicks them smooth as any igloo. They strew the floor with plant husks and seeds, rut in repeated bursts, and sleep humped and soaking, huddled in balls. These, too, are part of what Buber calls "the infinite ethos of the moment."

I am not here yet; I can't shake that day on the interstate. My mind branches and shoots like a tree.

Under my spine, the sycamore roots suck watery salts. Root tips thrust and squirm between particles of soil, probing minutely; from their roving, burgeoning tissues spring infinitesimal root hairs, transparent and hollow, which affix themselves to specks of grit and sip. These runnels run silent and deep; the whole earth trembles, rent and fissured, hurled and drained. I wonder what happens to root systems when trees die. Do those spread blind networks starve, starve in the midst of plenty, and dessicate, clawing at specks?

Under the world's conifers—under the creekside cedar behind where I sit—a mantle of fungus wraps the soil in a weft, shooting out blind thread after frail thread of palest dissolved white. From root tip to root tip, root hair to root hair, these filaments loop and wind; the thought of them always reminds me of

Rimbaud's "I have stretched cords from steeple to steeple, garlands from window to window, chains of gold from star to star, and I dance." King David leaped and danced naked before the ark of the Lord in a barren desert. Here the very looped soil is an intricate throng of praise. Make connections; let rip; and dance where you can.

The insects and earthworms, moles, muskrats, roots and fungal strands are not all. An even frailer, dimmer movement, a pavane, is being performed deep under me now. The nymphs of cicadas are alive. You see their split skins, an inch long, brown, and translucent, curved and segmented like shrimp, stuck arching on the trunks of trees. And you see the adults occasionally, large and sturdy, with glittering black and green bodies, veined transparent wings folded over their backs, and artificial-looking, bright red eyes. But you never see the living nymphs. They are underground, clasping roots and sucking the sweet sap of trees.

In the South, the periodical cicada has a breeding cycle of thirteen years, instead of seventeen years as in the North. That a live creature spends thirteen consecutive years scrabbling around in the root systems of trees in the dark and damp—thirteen years!—is amply boggling for me. Four more years—or four less—wouldn't alter the picture a jot. In the dark of an April night the nymphs emerge, all at once, as many as eighty-four of them digging into the air from every square foot of ground. They inch up trees and bushes, shed their skins, and begin that hollow, shrill grind that lasts all summer. I guess as nymphs they never see the sun. Adults lay eggs in slits along twig bark; the hatched nymphs drop to the ground and burrow, vanish from the face of the earth, biding their time, for thirteen years. How many are under me now, wishing what? What would I think about for thirteen years? They curl, crawl, clutch at roots and suck, suck blinded, suck trees, rain or shine, heat or frost, year after groping year.

And under the cicadas, deeper down than the longest taproot, between and beneath the rounded black rocks and slanting slabs of sandstone in the earth, ground water is creeping. Ground water seeps and slides, across and down, across and down, leaking from here to there minutely, at the rate of a mile a year. What a tug of waters goes on! There are flings and pulls in every direction at every moment. The world is a wild wrestle under the grass: earth shall be moved.

What else is going on right this minute while ground water creeps under my feet? The galaxy is careening in a slow, muffled widening. If a million solar systems are born every hour, then surely hundreds burst into being as I shift my weight to the other elbow. The sun's surface is now exploding; other stars implode and vanish, heavy and black, out of sight. Meteorites are arcing to earth invisibly all day long. On the planet the winds are blowing: the polar easterlies, the westerlies, the northeast and southeast trades. Somewhere, someone under full sail is becalmed, in the horse latitudes, in the doldrums; in the northland, a trapper is maddened, crazed, by the eerie scent of the chinook, the snoweater, a wind that can melt two feet of snow in a day. The pampero blows, and the tramontane, and the Boro, sirocco, levanter, mistral. Lick a finger: feel the now.

Spring is seeping north, towards me and away from me, at sixteen miles a day. Caribou straggle across the tundra from the spruce-fir forests of the south, first the pregnant does, hurried, then the old and unmated does, then suddenly a massing of bucks, and finally the diseased and injured, one by one. Somewhere, people in airplanes are watching the sun set and peering down at clustered houselights, stricken. In the montana in Peru, on the ram-forested slopes of the Andes, a woman kneels in a dust clearing before a dark shelter of overlapping broadleaves; between her breasts hangs a cross of smooth sticks she peeled with her teeth and lashed with twistings of vine. Along estuary banks of tidal rivers all over the world, snails in black clusters like currants are gliding up and down the stems of reed and sedge, migrating every moment with the dip and swing of tides. Behind me, Tinker Mountain, and to my left, Dead Man Mountain, are eroding one thousandth of an inch a year.

The tomcat that used to wake me is dead; he was long since grist for an earthworm's casting, and is now the clear sap of a Pittsburgh sycamore, or the honeydew of aphids sucked from that sycamore's high twigs and sprayed in sticky drops on a stranger's car. A steer across the road stumbles into the creek to drink; he blinks; he laps; a floating leaf in the current catches against his hock and wrenches away. The giant water bug I saw is dead, long dead, and its moist gut and rigid casing are both, like the empty skin of the frog it sucked, dissolved, spread, still spreading right now, in the steer's capillaries, in the windblown smatter of clouds overhead, in the Sargasso Sea. The mockingbird that dropped furled from a roof . . . but this is no time to count my dead. That is nightwork. The dead are staring, underground, their sleeping heels in the air.

The sharks I saw are roving up and down the coast. If the sharks cease roving, if they still their twist and rest for a moment, they die. They need new water pushed into their gills; they need dance. Somewhere east of me, on another continent, it is sunset, and starlings in breathtaking bands are winding high in the sky to their evening roost. Under the water just around the bend downstream, the coot feels with its foot in the creek, rolling its round red eyes. In the house a spider slumbers at her wheel like a spinster curled in a corner all day long. The mantis egg cases are tied to the mock-orange hedge; within each case, within each egg, cells elongate, narrow, and split; cells bubble and curve inward, align, harden or hollow or stretch. The Polyphemus moth, its wings crushed to its back, crawls down the driveway, crawls down the driveway, crawls.... The snake whose skin I tossed away, whose homemade, personal skin is now tangled at the county dump—that snake in the woods by the quarry stirs now, quickens now, prodded under the leafmold by sunlight, by the probing root of May apple, the bud of bloodroot. And where are you now?

I stand. All the blood in my body crashes to my feet and instantly heaves to my head, so I blind and blush, as a tree blasts into leaf spouting water hurled up from roots. What happens to me? I stand before the sycamore dazed; I gaze at its giant trunk.

Big trees stir memories. You stand in their dimness, where the very light is blue, staring unfocused at the thickest part of the trunk as though it were a long, dim tunnel—: the Squirrel Hill tunnel. You're gone. The egg-shaped patch of light at the end of the blackened tunnel swells and looms; the sing of tire tread over brick reaches an ear-splitting crescendo; the light breaks over the hood, smack, and full on your face. You have achieved the past.

Eskimo shamans bound with sealskin thongs on the igloo floor used to leave their bodies, their skins, and swim "muscle-naked" like a flensed seal through the rock of continents, in order to placate an old woman who lived on the sea floor and sent or withheld game. When he fulfilled this excruciating mission, the Eskimo shaman would awake, returned to his skin exhausted from the dark ardors of flailing peeled through rock, and find himself in a lighted igloo, at a sort of party, among dear faces.

In the same way, having bored through a sycamore trunk and tunneled beneath a Pennsylvania mountain, I blink, awed by the yellow light, and find myself in a shady side of town, in a stripped dining room, dancing, years ago. There is a din of trumpets, upbeat and indistinct, like some movie score for a love scene played on a city balcony; there is an immeasurably distant light glowing from half-remembered faces.... I stir. The heave of my shoulders returns me to the present, to the tree, the sycamore, and I yank myself away, shove off and moving, seeking live water.

III

Live water heals memories. I look up the creek and here it comes, the future, being borne aloft as on a winding succession of laden trays. You may wake and look from the window and breathe the real air, and say, with satisfaction or with longing, "This is it." But if you look up the creek, if you look up the creek in any weather, your spirit fills, and you are saying, with an exulting rise of the lungs, "Here it comes!"

Here it comes. In the far distance I can see the concrete bridge where the road crosses the creek. Under that bridge and beyond it the water is flat and silent, blued by distance and stilled by depth. It is so much sky, a fallen shred caught in the cleft of banks. But it pours. The channel here is straight as an arrow; grace itself is an archer. Between the dangling wands of bankside willows, beneath the overarching limbs of tulip, walnut, and Osage orange, I see the creek pour down. It spills toward me streaming over a series of sandstone tiers, down, and down, and down. I feel as though I stand at the foot of an infinitely high staircase, down which some exuberant spirit is flinging tennis ball after tennis ball, eternally, and the one thing I want in the world is a tennis ball.

There must be something wrong with a creekside person who, all things being equal, chooses to face downstream. It's like fouling your own nest. For this and a leather couch they pay fifty dollars an hour? Tinker Creek doesn't back up, pushed up its own craw, from the Roanoke River; it flows down, easing, from the northern, unseen side of Tinker Mountain. "Gravity, to Copernicus, is the nostalgia of things to become spheres." This is a curious, tugged version of the great chain of being. Ease is the way of perfection, letting fall. But, as in the classic version of the great chain, the pure trickle that leaks from the unfathomable heart of Tinker Mountain, this Tinker Creek, widens, taking shape and cleaving banks, weighted with the live and intricate impurities of time, as it descends to me, to where I happen to find myself, in this intermediate spot, halfway between here and there. Look upstream. Just simply turn around; have you no will? The future is a spirit, or a distillation of *the* spirit, heading my way. It is north. The future is the light on the water; it comes, mediated, only on the skin of the real and present creek. My eyes can stand no brighter light than this; nor can they see without it, if only the undersides of leaves.

Trees are tough. They last, taproot and bark, and we soften at their feet. "For we are strangers before thee, and sojourners, as were all our fathers: our days on the earth are as a shadow, and there is none abiding." We can't take the lightning, the scourge of high places and rare airs. But we can take the light, the reflected light that shines up the valleys on creeks. Trees stir memories; live waters heal them. The creek is the mediator, benevolent, impartial, subsuming my shabbiest evils and dissolving them, transforming them into live moles, and shiners, and sycamore leaves. It is a place even my faithlessness hasn't offended; it still flashes for me, now and tomorrow, that intricate, innocent face. It waters an undeserving world, saturating cells with lodes of light. I stand by the creek over rock under trees.

It is sheer coincidence that my hunk of the creek is strewn with boulders. I never merited this grace, that when I face upstream I scent the virgin breath of mountains, I feel a spray of mist on my cheeks and lips, I hear a ceaseless splash and susurrus, a sound of water not merely poured smoothly down air to fill a steady pool, but tumbling live about, over, under, around, between, through an intricate speckling of rock. It is sheer coincidence that upstream from me the creek's bed is ridged in horizontal croppings of sandstone. I never merited this grace, that when I face upstream I see the light on the water careening towards me, inevitably, freely, down a graded series of terraces like the balanced winged platforms on an infinite, inexhaustible font. "Ho, if you are thirsty, come down to the water; ho, if you are hungry, come and sit and eat." This is the present, at last. I can pat the puppy any time I want. This is the now, this flickering, broken light, this air that the wind of the future presses down my throat, pumping me buoyant and giddy with praise.

My God, I look at the creek. It is the answer to Merton's prayer, "Give us time!" It never stops. If I seek the senses and skill of children, the information of a thousand books, the innocence of puppies, even the insights of my own city past, I do so only, solely, and entirely that I might look well at the creek. You don't run down the present, pursue it with baited hooks and nets. You wait for it, empty-handed, and you are filled. You'll have fish left over. The creek is the one great giver. It is, by definition, Christmas, the incarnation. This old rock planet gets the present for a present on its birthday every day.

Here is the word from a subatomic physicist: "Everything that has already happened is particles, everything in the future is waves." Let me twist his meaning. Here it comes. The particles are broken; the waves are translucent, laving, roiling with beauty like sharks. The present is the wave that explodes over my head, flinging the air with particles at the height of its breathless unroll; it is the live water and light that bears from undisclosed sources the freshest news, renewed and renewing, world without end.

* * * * *

Chapter 11

Stalking

III

Living this way by the creek, where the light appears and vanishes on the water, where muskrats surface and dive, and redwings scatter, I have come to know a special side of nature. I look to the mountains, and the mountains still slumber, blue and mute and rapt. I say, it gathers; the world abides. But I look to the creek, and I say: it scatters, it comes and goes. When I leave the house the sparrows flee and hush; on the banks of the creek jays scream in alarm, squirrels race for cover, tadpoles dive, frogs leap, snakes freeze, warblers vanish. Why do they hide? I will not hurt them. They simply do not want to be seen. "Nature," said Heraclitus, "is wont to hide herself." A fleeing mockingbird unfurls for a second a dazzling array of white fans . . . and disappears in the leaves. Shane! . . . Shane! Nature flashes the old mighty glance—the come-hither look—drops the handkerchief, turns tail, and is gone. The nature I know is old touch-and-go.

I wonder whether what I see and seem to understand about nature is merely one of the accidents of freedom, repeated by chance before my eyes, or whether it has any counterpart in the worlds beyond Tinker Creek. I find in quantum mechanics a world symbolically similar to my world at the creek.

Many of us are still living in the universe of Newtonian physics, and fondly imagine that real, hard scientists have no use for these misty ramblings, dealing as scientists do with the measurable and known. We think that at least the physical causes of physical events are perfectly knowable, and that, as the results of various experiments keep coming in, we gradually roll back the cloud of unknowing. We remove the veils one by one, painstakingly, adding knowledge to knowledge and whisking away veil after veil, until at last we reveal the nub of things, the sparkling equation from whom all blessings flow. Even wildman Emerson accepted the truly pathetic fallacy of the old science when he wrote grudgingly towards the end of his life, "When the microscope is improved, we shall have the cells analysed, and all will be electricity, or somewhat else." All we need to do is perfect our instruments and our methods, and we can collect enough data like birds on a string to predict physical events from physical causes.

But in 1927 Werner Heisenberg pulled out the rug, and our whole understanding of the universe toppled and collapsed. For some reason it has not yet trickled down to the man on the street that some physicists now are a bunch of wild-eyed, raving mystics. For they have perfected their instruments and methods just enough to whisk away the crucial veil, and what stands revealed is the Cheshire cat's grin.

The Principle of Indeterminacy, which saw the light in the summer of 1927, says in effect that you cannot know both a particle's velocity and position. You can guess statistically what any batch of electrons might do, but you cannot predict the career of any one particle. They seem to be as free as dragonflies. You can perfect your instruments and your methods till the cows come home, and you will never ever be able to measure this one basic thing. It cannot be done. The electron is a muskrat; it cannot be perfectly stalked. And nature is a fan dancer born with a fan; you can wrestle her down, throw her on the stage and grapple with her for the fan with all your might, but it will never quit her grip. She comes that way; the fan is attached.

It is not that we lack sufficient information to know both a particle's velocity and its position; that would have been a perfectly ordinary situation well within the understanding of classical physics. Rather, we know now for sure that there is no knowing. You can determine the position, and your figure for the velocity blurs into vagueness; or, you can determine the velocity, but whoops, there goes the position. The use of instruments and the very fact of an observer seem to bollix the observations; as a consequence, physicists are saying that they cannot study nature per se, but only their own investigation of nature. And I can only see bluegills within my own blue shadow, from which they immediately flee.

The Principle of Indeterminacy turned science inside-out. Suddenly determinism goes, causality goes, and we are left with a universe composed of what Eddington calls, "mind-stuff." Listen to these physicists: Sir James Jeans, Eddington's successor, invokes "fate," saying that the future "may rest on the knees of whatever gods there be." Eddington says that "the physical world is entirely abstract and without 'actuality' apart from its linkage to consciousness." Heisenberg himself says, "method and object can no longer be separated. *The scientific world-view has ceased to be a scientific view in the true sense of the word.*" Jeans says that science can no longer remain opposed to the notion of free will. Heisenberg says, "there is a higher power, not influenced by our wishes, which finally decides and judges." Eddington says that our dropping causality as a result of the Principle of Indeterminacy "leaves us with no clear distinction between the Natural and the Supernatural." And so forth.

These physicists are once again mystics, as Kepler was, standing on a rarefied mountain pass, gazing transfixed into an abyss of freedom. And they got there by experimental method and a few wild leaps such as Einstein made. What a pretty pass!

All this means is that the physical world as we understand it now is more like the touch-and-go creek world I see than it is like the abiding world of which the mountains seem to speak. The physicists' particles whiz and shift like rotifers in and out of my microscope's field, and that this valley's ring of granite mountains is an airy haze of those same particles I must believe. The whole universe is a swarm of those wild, wary energies, the sun that glistens from the wet hairs on a muskrat's back and the stars which the mountains obscure on the horizon but which catch from on high in Tinker Creek. It is all touch and go. The heron flaps away; the dragonfly departs at thirty miles an hour; the water strider vanishes under a screen of grass; the muskrat dives, and the ripples roll from the bank, and flatten, and cease altogether.

Moses said to God, "I beseech thee, shew me thy glory." And God said, "Thou canst not see my face: for there shall no man see me, and live." But he added, "There is a place by me, and thou shalt stand upon a rock: and it shall come to pass, while my glory passeth by, that I will put thee in a clift of the rock, and will cover thee with my hand while I pass by: And I will take away

mine hand, and thou shalt see my back parts: but my face shall not be seen."
So Moses went up on Mount Sinai, waited still in a clift of the rock, and saw
the back parts of God. Forty years later he went up on Mount Pisgah, and saw
the promised land across the Jordan, which he was to die without ever being
permitted to enter.

Just a glimpse, Moses: a clift in the rock here, a mountaintop there, and the
rest is denial and longing. You have to stalk everything. Everything scatters and
gathers; everything comes and goes like fish under a bridge. You have to stalk
the spirit, too. You can wait forgetful anywhere, for anywhere is the way of his
fleet passage, and hope to catch him by the tail and shout something in his ear
before he wrests away. Or you can pursue him wherever you dare, risking the
shrunken sinew in the hollow of the thigh; you can bang at the door all night till
the innkeeper relents, if he ever relents; and you can wail till you're hoarse or
worse the cry for incarnation always in John Knoepfle's poem: "and christ is red
rover . . . and the children are calling/come over come over." I sit on a bridge
as on Pisgah or Sinai, and I am both waiting becalmed in a clift of the rock and
banging with all my will, calling like a child beating on a door: Come on out!
. . . I know you're there.

And then occasionally the mountains part. The tree with the lights in it
appears, the mockingbird falls, and time unfurls across space like an oriflamme.
Now we rejoice. The news, after all, is not that muskrats are wary, but that they
can be seen. The hem of the robe was a Nobel Prize to Heisenberg; he did not
go home in disgust. I wait on the bridges and stalk along banks for those
moments I cannot predict, when a wave begins to surge under the water, and
ripples strengthen and pulse high across the creek and back again in a texture
that throbs. It is like the surfacing of an impulse, like the materialization of fish,
this rising, this coming to a head, like the ripening of nutmeats still in their
husks, ready to split open like buckeyes in a field, shining with newness.
"Surely the Lord is in this place; and I knew it not." The fleeing shreds I see,
the back parts, are a gift, an abundance. When Moses came down from the clift
in Mount Sinai, the people were afraid of him: the very skin on his face shone.

Do the Eskimos' faces shine, too? I lie in bed alert: I am with the Eskimos
on the tundra who are running after the click-footed caribou, running sleepless
and dazed for days, running spread out in scraggling lines across the
glacier-ground hummocks and reindeer moss, in sight of the ocean, under the
long-shadowed pale sun, running silent all night long.

THE BIOLOGICAL TIME BOMB

GORDON RATTRAY TAYLOR

Gordon Rattray Taylor (1911-1981) was born in Eastbourne, England. After completing his formal education at Trinity College, Cambridge, he began a career as a newspaper man and freelance writer. During World War II he was with the Monitoring Service and European News of the British Broadcasting Corporation, and then served in the Psychological Warfare Division of General Eisenhower's headquarters.

At the conclusion of the war, he returned to freelance writing. Then, after eight years (1958-1966) in devising and writing science programs for BBC television, the last three of which he was Chief Science Advisor, he devoted his full time to writing. His later books included *The Doomsday Book* (1970), *How to Avoid the Future* (1975), and *The Natural History of the Mind* (1979).

In *The Biological Time Bomb* (1968) he deals with the remarkable—and frightening—prospects for the future brought about by the revolution in biology.

1. What does Taylor mean by "the biological time bomb"?

2. To what extent have the biological developments that Taylor predicted already come to pass?

3. What are the desirable and undesirable consequences of the developments that Taylor predicts?

4. What biological developments does Taylor see as being of the order of the developments of the atomic bomb in physics?

5. What is the impact on society of rapid biological changes?

6. What is your reaction to Taylor's statement, "As the impact of the biological time-bomb begins to be felt, the haunted look of Dr. Frankenstein may gradually appear on the faces of the biologists."? How does this relate to the myth of Prometheus?

7. What kind of a society do you want?

THE BIOLOGICAL TIME BOMB

GORDON RATTRAY TAYLOR

Chapter 8
The Future, If Any

At a guess, there are about 200,000 biologists in the world, depending to some extent on how you define "biologist". The sensual man, reflecting on their hazardous activities, may well feel a sense of apprehension. The prospect of having to cope with a number of such innovations simultaneously takes on a nightmare quality, and prompts the question: is this all really a load of nonsense, mere science fiction divorced from present reality? And even if these procedures are technically possible, will they ever be more than laboratory curiosities?

If so, he has missed the point. We are not simply discussing a number of new procedures, but the fact that a revolution is occurring in biology. The things I have described are merely the salient points, the first-fruits of a breakthrough on a broad front. Naturally, biology still has numerous unsolved problems, just as physics has. But the degree of control now being achieved calls for a new relationship between biology and society. Just as physics and chemistry did in the past century, it will steadily bring about a totally new pattern of existence. Whether it will be a happier and more satisfying pattern is by no means obvious. and it is not even clear whether society can survive the strains which will be imposed.

Jacques Piccard, son of the inventor of the deep-diving bathyscaphe, told a symposium at the Stevens Institute at Hoboken, New Jersey, recently that he was "seriously doubtful" whether mankind would last out the century. Aside from the atomic threat, he stressed the "widespread; suicidal pollution affecting the air we breathe, the water we drink and the land we till". Our whole technology was to blame, he said. Superimposed on these stresses, the social stresses created by biology may prove a sizeable final straw.

The question of how soon they will be upon us therefore deserves careful attention.

Naturally, no one can predict the future with certitude and no doubt some of the advances about which we are now optimistic will prove impossible, or at any rate the solution will be found so far in the future as to be of little practical importance to us now. But it is equally certain that many of these advances will occur in the very near future. Indeed, many of the techniques described in Chapter 2, such as artificial inovulation, are available now. And as I write these lines comes news of a breakthrough on the transplantation front. Dr G. J. V. Nossal, the new director of the Walter and Eliza Hall Institute of Medical Research in Melbourne, has reported a method of desensitizing the body to specific foreign materials by injecting ever smaller pieces of the antigen. It appears that the extent of the immune response is related to the size of the invading molecules. But once the body has met a fragment of the antigen so small that the immune response does not occur, it subsequently ceases to produce antibody to the complete antigen molecule. On the strength of this, Nossal considers that organ transplantation can be perfected in the 1970's with control of cancer and other diseases following a decade or two later. He has called for a world-wide effort to purify antigens, to see if a molecule sufficiently small, and of the right structure to set up tolerance, can be developed. "If it does." he told the First International Congress of the Transplantation Society, "the stage is set for experiments in human beings to see if injection of antigens can induce tolerance in a transplant patient." There are also encouraging reports about tissue typing and anti-lymphocytic serum.

On the other hand, I would not personally place any sizeable bet on success in prolonging life, and, while I think it may well be possible to improve memory, I am somewhat skeptical of the possibility of transferring entire memories. Against this, the very recent discovery of a factor controlling nerve growth makes it look extremely probable that we could do something quite drastic about raising intelligence, provided treatment can be given in the foetal stage or the earliest weeks of life.

On page 205, I have ranged the possibilities in three groups: discoveries which are going to affect us within the next five or ten years, if they have not already begun to do so; those which should become practicable within some fifty years; and those which are remoter.

The group which affects all of us, and on which no delay can be brooked, includes, in addition to transplantation techniques, parthenogenetic birth, prolonged storage of human eggs and spermatozoa, arrested death, choice of sex of offspring and the mind-modifying drugs. Surely enough to cope with.

In phase two, I forecast, we shall see all these problems become more acute, with hibernation and arrested death for prolonged periods; unlimited transplantation possibilities; and a very wide range of mind-modifying techniques, not only drugs but electrical effects, imperceptible odours and the like. If the artificial placenta has not been perfected in phase one, it now will be and naturally produced offspring will be brought to term on it. In addition, we shall see the start of life-copying. Living organisms will be produced by putting together units of life derived mainly from breaking down living systems- into these organisms a steadily increasing proportion of fully synthesized material will be incorporated. An impact will be made on the problem of prolonging youthful vigour. Hibernation and other storage methods will become practical. The first cloned animals will be produced.

Not till phase three should I expect to see the synthesis of life, control of ageing or a disembodied human brain. Above all, I think that it will take at least this long for genetic engineering to become practical. But all these things should reach fruition, unless war or politics or disaster drastically change the present curve of development, within the lifetime of those now young, and a few of those who are not so young.

Table of Developments

The dates are those of technical achievement, not of general availability, which depends on social and economic considerations.

Phase One: by 1975
Extensive transplantation of limbs and organs
Test-tube fertilization of human eggs
Implantation of fertilized eggs in womb
Indefinite storage of eggs and spermatozoa
Choice of sex of offspring
Extensive power to postpone clinical death
Mind-modifying drugs: regulation of desire
Memory erasure
Imperfect artificial placenta
Artificial viruses

Phase Two: by 2000
Extensive mind modification and personality reconstruction
Enhancement *of* intelligence in men and animals
Memory injection and memory editing
Perfected artificial placenta and true baby-factory
Life-copying: reconstructed organisms
Hibernation and prolonged coma
Prolongation of youthful vigour
First cloned animals
Synthesis of unicellular organisms
Organ regeneration
Man-animal chimeras

Phase Three: after 2000
Control of ageing: extension of life span
Synthesis of complex living organisms
Disembodied brains
Brain-computer links
Gene insertion and deletion
Cloned people
Brain-brain links
Man-machine chimeras
Indefinite postponement of death

   A recent objective study of current trends arrived at not dissimilar conclusions. Eighty-two experts took part in the study, which was conducted by Olaf Helmer of the Rand Corporation and T. J. Gordon of Douglas Aircraft, who fed the forecasts back to the participants and refined the prediction. These specialists put drugs producing personality changes some sixteen years ahead but, more optimistic than me, expect to see primitive forms of life created in the laboratory by 1989 and the control of hereditary defects by gene engineering by 2000.

More cautious than me, they don't expect long-term coma until 2050, nor do they see intelligence being raised by drugs until 2012, with brain-computer links soon after. But, like me, they don't expect extension of life until the same date, when they foresee 50 years being added to the expectancy. They put regeneration of limbs and organs down for 2007. Rather oddly, to my mind, they don't see the breeding of intelligent animals (to replace human labour) until 2050: I should expect this to come earlier than drugs for raising human intelligence, since these drugs will probably be tried out on animals before they are used in man; indeed, this is already occurring.

So it seems certain that many of these advances will occur in the life-time of those now middle-aged and nearly all in the lifetime of those now young. But how far are they in fact problems?

It is rather easy to sensationalize the issues, and some writers have already done so. Thus A. Rosenfeld in *Life* suggests that women may go into a kind of supermarket containing day-old frozen embryos and shop around for the one they want. Presumably there will be a glamorized 4-colour 3-D picture of the adult expected on the pack, as when one buys a package of seeds. For my part, I think this most unlikely. We already have frozen semen, but it is not sold at the dime-stores or do-it-yourself shops. It is obtained only by doctors at their discretion, which they exercise with restraint. Anyone who wants an implanted embryo will no doubt have to take a similar course and persuade her doctor—though, as the process becomes familiar, little persuasion may be called for; it may be more like requesting a smallpox injection. But if any firm were to attempt marketing frozen semen, the state would intervene and a web of legal and conventional codes would be invoked to stop them. The firm's advertisements would be refused, and their other products might be boycotted. No firm of repute would risk tarnishing its image by unconsidered, headlong action in such a field.

However, the realities are alarming enough.

More realistically, we might distinguish between those advances which create problems which are probably within the scope of society to handle and those which, like the atom bomb in physics, create problems of a totally new order.

In the first category I would place such matters as specification of the sex of offspring, use of stored eggs and spermatozoa, and even the bringing of babies to term on artificial placentas. It is possible that the power to determine sex might lead to a gross disproportion of the two sexes, but not particularly likely, unless the technique becomes available to countries, like India and China, where sons are greatly preferred to daughters. Since this would in any case cause a limitation of population, the immediate effects would be desirable rather than otherwise. Professor Lederberg has expressed the view that the sex ratio might fluctuate violently, as a result of over-correction of a trend to one extreme, then the other. But with computers, adequate prediction should not prove difficult, and there is no evidence that more than a minority of the population would use such techniques.

Even the bringing of infants to term on artificial placentas does not pose insuperable problems. It is true that there is a real and important task in providing children thus born with the requisite parental love and care. And there is no moral justification for exposing even one child to an inadequate background in this respect. But the requirements are well understood, and the number of cases should be small. Most people will prefer to have children in the normal way, or, if that is not possible, by inovulation.

On the other hand, while discounting some of the wilder bogy-raising, there are developments which I have described which raise issues far more fundamental than these.

Four strike me as particularly fearsome. First, the development of techniques, probably quite near, for dramatically raising intelligence. Once a few highly intelligent children are born and have reached the age at which they win academic honours and get plum jobs, parents everywhere will begin to scream for the same treatment for their newborn or unborn babies. On grounds of national interest, the state may decide to foster such a trend. Once the level of intelligence rises widely, the educational system will have to be revised. Meanwhile, an elite group will have come into existence. However, perhaps the new race of super-minds will soon find the answers to the problems created by their own existence.

Secondly, a drastic extension of the life span or even of youthful vigour would cause tremendous social and economic repercussions. Medical services would have to be re-adjusted, retirement practices changed. Markets would alter. But in addition, the life of the young would suffer a severe impact from the existence of a preponderance of active older people. Already, the rub is felt by couples who do not inherit money from their parents until long after the phase at which it would be most useful. When parents survive to 80, their children may be over 50 before they inherit, and the costs of raising a family have been met. If survival to 150 occurs, with intermediate generations at 120, 90 and 60, most young couples will have not only grandparents, but great-grandparents and great-great-grandparents to visit, look after, and put up with.

The remaining two I will indicate more shortly, since they have already been discussed at length: the prospect of the indefinite postponement of death and the power to modify heredity. Economics cannot cope with the first, nor politics with the second.

Specific consequences

So what? That these changes represent a serious challenge even a threat, has now been asserted by so many statesmen of science as to amount to a cliché. The matter has been analysed in rather more detail by the late Lord Brain, the eminent English neurologist, in his book *Science and Man*. As he points out, as long ago as 1932 Alfred North Whitehead asserted, "A muddled state of mind is prevalent. The increased plasticity of the environment for mankind resulting from the advances in scientific technology, is being construed in terms of habits of thought which find their justification in the theory of a fixed environment."

"This truth", comments Lord Brain, "has been overwhelmingly illustrated by the history of the thirty years which have passed since Whitehead wrote these words. The potentialities of science and technology for the benefit of mankind as a whole are almost inconceivably great, but the preparations which we are making for their we and development are pitiably small."

An outstanding example of our failure to predict and prepare for the consequences of scientific development, he continues, has been population growth. Take, for instance, the demand for physicians. "It is clear that we shall need many more doctors in thirty years' time. This means more medical schools. It takes a minimum of fifteen years to turn a first-year medical student into a consultant." It follows that in every westernized country we must start increasing the intake without delay. We are not doing 50.

But the prophets who issue these blood-chilling warnings don't give us much to chew on; they remain unhelpfully vague about just how these changes might affect us, and what to do about it.

In this last chapter, then, let me try to spell out in more detail than most prophets care to risk just what I think the consequences of biological innovation might be.

Most authorities have laid stress on the moral implications, but these have a way of solving themselves. It is the moralists rather than morality who stand to suffer most. As Canon Tiberghien has said: "Moralists may have to pronounce upon these questions, but woe to the world if, when they are consulted, they cannot agree among themselves." Moral systems firmly based on the golden rule need not be affected, even if they may have to be rephrased, for humanism is rooted in a definition of man which biology has shown to be, to put it mildly, vulnerable. But moral systems which preserve pre-rational tribal taboos, because they are soothing to deeply ingrained unconscious prejudices, and seek to endorse them with divine authority, will simply be overtaken by events, as they have always been in moments of crisis. The institutions which support them will either transform themselves or become obsolete.

The aspect which, in my view, may well prove the most dramatically important is one to which little or no attention has so far been paid: I mean the politico-economic angle.

Before long, I predict, we shall see a tremendous demand developing for the kind of biomedical aids and services which I have described—to say nothing of others still to be devised. A great part of the nation's productive capacity will eventually be devoted to providing prosthetic devices, brain-treatments, transplant operations and so on. It is estimated that in the U.S.A. 1500 transplant operations *a day* may eventually be called for. If society is slow to meet this demand, the response could be violent. People are powerfully motivated where their health and survival and those of their children are concerned.

Some readers may reel that this problem can be left to solve itself; that, as the demand develops, the productive machinery will adapt accordingly. Such complacency, if it exists, is unjustified. The problem is already upon us. The productive machinery is sluggish in adapting. And people are dying in consequence, already.

The case of kidney dialysis deserves most careful attention, not only because it is important in itself, but also because it provides us with an indication of what is to come. It is but the first in a series of such situations. Let us look at the figures. In Great Britain, some 7000 people die of kidney disease each year. Let us exclude all people over 55 and under 16 and assume, conservatively, that only 2000 of these 7000 are suitable for treatment by dialysis which they would require twice a week. Even if each patient survived only five years, this would build up to some 10,000 patients on dialysis, and average survival might be much longer than this. The first 2000 would cost about £3,500,00 to maintain, and so on for larger numbers e.g. £17.5 m. for 10,000, a minimum estimate. The number would be reduced, of course, if some received kidney transplants—but a corresponding increase in special germ-free surgical facilities would be required. To provide surgical facilities capable of handling up to 2000 patients a year would call for an increase in current facilities of many thousands per cent, as well as the training of numerous surgical teams. There is no supply of idle surgeons, anaesthetist and nurses on which to draw for such an expansion. They would have to be recruited and trained *ab initio,* a process requiring many years.

In the case of the U.S.A. it has been estimated that the demand could build up to 20,000 (2000 ideal patients surviving an average of 10 years) or 150,000 (5000 patients a year surviving 30 years) people on dialysis. On the more conservative figure of 20,000 the cost might be $140 m. a year.

"What is actually happening is that only a minute fraction of the patients with irreversible renal failure get either dialysis or transplantation, on the one hand because of the lack of money and machines, or on the other because no suitable living donor is available and a cadaver kidney cannot be obtained in time. And so they die, often quite young." These are the words of Professor M. F. A. Woodruff and he adds: "I am aware of the magnitude o the problem, but I am amazed that so many people appear to be indifferent to this unnecessary loss of life."

This indifference, I believe, arises from ignorance Many of those affected still fail to realize that their lives and those of their friends and relatives, could actually be saved. When this realization strikes home, there could be E major public outcry. But all this refers only to the limited field of kidney replacement. When livers, limbs, endocrines and even hearts are added, the load will be beyond anything we can conceive. Society will have to decide whether it wants life and health more than motorways and moon-rockets, and may well prefer the former.

A sign of the times is the appearance in increasing numbers of patient associations—for sufferers from multiple sclerosis, and similar deadly diseases. Such organizations serve a useful purpose in seeing that opportunities for research and treatment are not neglected, and might become politically important, in the kind of way that trade unions have been politically important in the past. In the U.S.A. has been seen an even more interesting trend: the formation of societies for the extension of life, such as the Prolongevity Institute and The Society for Artificial Internal Organs.

Here we see a group of the public pressing for novel biomedical advances, in a manner analogous with the role of the American Rocketry Society and the British Interplanetary Society thirty years ago. Their initiatives led to the National Aeronautics and Space Administration. Will the initiative of these new societies lead to the establishment of a National Biomedical Administration?

Currently, it is often said that we lack a "mathematics of mercy" by which we can calculate who, of thousands of sufferers, should receive the privilege of being saved by scarce facilities In Seattle, where kidney dialysis has been pioneered, it has been thought necessary to form a committee of citizens to make these judgments. No doubt this has been motivated, at least in part, by the natural desire of doctors to reduce the terrible and most unfair strain of having to make such decisions single-handed. In Britain, a parallel situation has already arisen in Birmingham, and the Minister of Health has issued guidance on how he thinks these decisions should be handled. As more dialysis machines become available, this situation will be reproduced elsewhere. I find it difficult to believe that it will be accepted calmly by those concerned.

In making such decisions, the natural response is to set up criteria which eliminate as many cases as possible: absence of other disease, younger persons preferred to old, and so on. Such criteria, by making the decision automatic, remove the frightful onus of having to decide on the basis of one's total impression of the human beings concerned. If one knows, for instance, that one candidate is an instigator of racial hatred, while the other has devoted his life to the service of his fellows, it is natural to wish to save the latter rather than the former. Where the difference is less clear-cut the decision is harder.

The fact is, of course, that we do not need a mathematics of mercy—we just need more kidney-dialysis machines.

In the U.S.A. Dr Belding H. Scribner, declaring that it would "court disaster" not to bring such problems out into the open and face them squarely, devoted his presidential address to the American Society for Artificial Internal Organs to the moral and ethical problems exposed by four years' work with artificial kidneys in Seattle. During this time, he declared, more than 10,000 "ideal candidates" had died for lack of treatment. In the whole U.S.A. there were at that time (1964) between 50 and 100 people on treatment. Patients who can learn to treat themselves will survive, he said- others will die.

And he made the additional point that even for the patient whose disease is too far advanced for a cure, with dialysis he can die with dignity and a minimum of pain. Without dialysis, uraemia leads to a slow, agonizing death—"one of the most horrible known, sometimes involving many months of intense suffering and great expense".

Early in 1967 the British Minister of Health, Mr Kenneth Robinson, publicly announced that the British Health Service would provide kidney dialysis equipment as fast as staff to operate it and buildings to house it could be obtained, but that this would be necessarily slow. He revealed that the number of persons currently receiving treatment was 116! He envisaged that a further 60 or so might be treated by new units which were approaching completion.

Fewer than 200 out of a potential demand of at least 2000: this means 1800 people condemned to death in one year, owing to lack of forward planning by the Ministry of Health. (Dr H. de Wardener of Charing Cross Hospital Medical School says the space problem is a red herring.)

It is fascinating to me that this appalling announcement was greeted by the House of Commons and the public with the utmost calm. I believe that if in a quarter of a century's time any politician makes a similar confession of ineptitude, he will be howled out of office.

Unless we take action now, this kind of situation could be repeated on many other fronts. Probably the next one will be transplant surgery, and we shall suddenly discover that there are not nearly enough surgeons and sterile wards available to save not only kidney, but heart and lung patients who will die in consequence.

The questions which may have to be raised are: is the political machine adequate and is the economic machine adequate to handle this new kind of situation?

Governments are elected for terms of four or five years, and find it difficult to plan much further ahead. They can not move far ahead of public opinion, even if they wish, and are influenced by their desire to be returned to power at the next election. Moreover, they are composed of laymen who represent the electorate by their awareness of the current situation, not by their ability to foresee future situations. When they call in expert advice, they constantly reject it, as history repeatedly shows, if it goes against the needs of the moment.

A particularly critical instance of governments' inability to cope with large sociological issues is provided by the population problem. Governments always opt for population increase, since a decline in population creates immediate economic difficulties.

These developments may also profoundly challenge the role of industry. Industry is well adapted to supply relatively portable objects which can be sold at a fixed price. It could therefore manufacture heart and limb prostheses, for instance, very efficiently. It is not adapted to provide medical services, including treatments for improving intelligence or prolonging life and vigour. Though hospitals, in past times, were often started by private or charitable enterprise they have come in the modern world to be accepted as a public responsibility of city or state. But if the future brings biomedical services which are not strictly essential—brain treatments are a good example—will these be provided by state or private enterprise? If biomedicine becomes a major activity, it could make the state a major entrepreneur.

The new biomedicine may lead also to problems on the international as well as the national scale. The first issue is a moral one: is a country justified in providing for itself such super-services as brain-treatment or life-prolongation when, elsewhere, people are dying of malnutrition and the expectation of life is between 20 and 30 years? Even if they feel excused morally, politically this could become a difficult issue.

Moreover, the effect of such developments will inevitably be to increase the gap between developing and developed countries. If the latter raise their levels of intelligence, they will be able so much the more to outstrip the under-developed countries. The leaders of such countries will not be slow to take the point. The demand for the donation of know-how will be intense, and no doubt the leaders themselves will be the very first to submit themselves for intellectual and physical treatment. Late-comers *who* get even bigger mental and physical boosts from improved techniques will then be well placed to supplant the first-comers, and political success will depend on having the best doctors. Equally, political self-defence will depend on denying one's opponents such jet-assisted take-off. Medicine will be drawn into politics in a manner recalling the Renaissance—a charming prospect.

The instances just cited make the case for forward planning most vividly, since life and death are involved and the number of people concerned is rather large. The belief that the situation will eventually adjust itself is little consolation to those who are dying or to their relatives. The legal and social implications are less obviously dramatic and harder to quantify—a death appears in the national statistics, a lifetime of misery does not—but just as important in their way. The law remains uncertain, as we have seen, on many important points—even the simple question of whether a child born by artificial insemination is legitimate. If it takes the lawyers half a century to modernize the law so it can handle these new situations rationally and unambiguously, many thousands of people will go through unnecessary worry, expense and deprivation. There is absolutely no excuse for a policy of wait-and-see, but that is what is happening. To the best of my knowledge, no government or group of lawyers has taken any initiative to consider this problem, as it affects the private individual—though some steps have been taken towards protecting the medical profession, as we have seen earlier.

Legal issues may become dramatically important when man-animal chimeras are constructed. What will be the legal status of a creature with human chromosoma but animal appearance? And conversely? Human nature being what it is, men will be more horrified at the killing of a creature which looks like a man but is not, than when the reverse combination is the victim, though reason would suggest the opposite. How shall we define man? How man-like need one be to qualify for human benefits, including access to the retirement pension or to union membership? It is not fantasy to say that in our lifetime unions may be faced with competition from intelligent apes, which may make British coal-miners' objection to Polish miners, and American racial difficulties, look like child's play.

These are some of the immediately foreseeable consequences. There are others more remote and uncertain about which one cannot legislate yet; it remains to be seen whether, when the time comes, these will be dealt with any more deftly. One of the more serious of these, I suspect, may be the creation of elite groups, or haves and have-nots: privilege is always unpopular, but takes on peculiar importance when applied to life-prolongation or raising of intelligence. As I suggested in an earlier chapter, it may be only a decade before we have a supernaturally intelligent elite, with very little ability to find common ground with normal, unimproved men.

Social Cohesion

But in addition to specific effects of this kind, varying with the particular biological development under consideration, there are others of a more general nature, no less important because less tangible.

Chief of these is the fact that the outlook as a whole presages an unprecedented amount of change—change in customs and attitudes, change in capital provision and current expenditure, change in training and job allocation, change in the tasks and responsibilities of government and much more. Now there are limits to the amount of change which any society can absorb in a given time. A high rate of change creates stresses, even when the change is for the better. Man is a conservative animal, and the machinery of the law, social customs, technological provision are only modified slowly. We can see this if we consider, say, motor transport. We wait until roads are clogged with traffic before we consider building new ones. Then there is a prolonged period of discussion, funds are gradually made available, and so on. During all this response-lag, the situation gets worse. Often the remedy is already obsolete by the time it is applied.

The sluggish nature of social response is derived from the sluggish nature of the individual's response, and his tendency to hope that any problem, if ignored, will go away. In a slightly deeper sense, men never completely unlearn the assumptions and patterns acquired in youth, and progress depends upon their removal by death—a thing which has often been demonstrated in the history of science. It seems likely therefore that the rate at which society can change is keyed in some measure to the average life span. The rising trend of life span is increasing resistance to change, and any major increase would make adaptation far more difficult, perhaps fatally so.

Moreover, change is liable to be frustrating or disturbing in a personal sense. We see this in simple instances such as driving through a section of town we thought we knew and finding new one-way streets or overpasses have been created since we were last there. Man simplifies his life by establishing conventions: we say "how do you do" because it would be exhausting to devise a new phrase every time. We celebrate weddings or funerals in traditional ways for just the same reason. But when circumstances change, conventions become obsolete and we have to devise responses on the spur of the moment until new conventions are established. This can be stressful—as we realize when we find ourselves in a society whose conventions are unfamiliar to us. Biology is about to present us with a vast range of situations for which we have no accepted social responses. (How should one greet a cyborg?)

This is no place for a complete analysis of the consequences of a high rate of change, and I make these points merely to establish the distressing character of rapid social change. One might equally point to the painful economic effects. When a new technology replaces an old one, labour has to be retrained and transferred. But when the car replaced the horse, not every groom converted himself into a mechanic. Unemployment resulted- old skills were wasted; individual human beings felt rejected and unwanted. To be sure, change cannot be blocked entirely because it will have adverse effects on some. But it is also true that, if change is very rapid, the number of people in society whose lives are impoverished or made painful becomes large. How large a number can we, or should we tolerate? The wearing nature of industrial society, as we know it today, is largely a result of the high rate of technological innovation. But the social changes generated by biology may impose even greater pressures than do technological changes. Any considerable increase in the change-rate of society might subject the whole structure to severe strain, even bring about collapse.

Finally, while the rate of biological innovation during the next half-century looks like being high, many of the processes thus started will be slow in working themselves out, and the full consequences will not be revealed for several generations. Consequently, society's reaction time will be slow. If a particular hereditary modification proves a mistake, it may take generations to be sure of the fact and several generations more to undo or correct it. The undesirable consequences of prescribing thalidomide to pregnant women became clear within a few years and appropriate steps were taken. Imagine the situation if the problem had not become clear until thalidomide had been used for forty years, and if it had taken forty more to withdraw it again.

We are apt to assume that society exists in its own right: that it will carry on much as before regardless of what we as individuals do. But this is not so. When men live together in groups, they sacrifice certain liberties in exchange for the advantages of mutual aid. The isolated farmer may burn his house down if he wishes. The city dweller is prohibited from doing so, but receives instead the advantages of a fire service. And in general, society functions because people are willing to help it function. A railway can provide padded seating only if people refrain from ruining it, and so on. Of course there are laws which can be enforced against anti-social minorities, when they can be caught. But if the minority becomes too large, it becomes impossible to enforce them effectively. Society is maintained by a constant struggle to control these anti-social elements. When they become too numerous, anarchy results. The socially oriented citizens lose heart and themselves cease to co-operate. If the disorientation continues, the country loses its constructive drive and either disintegrates or is taken over by a more co-ordinated country. This process, so briefly indicated here, we may call *loss of social cohesion*. It has been necessary to outline it, since the problem is scarcely recognized and there is no phrase available to designate it unambiguously.

The kind of massive social disorientation which seems likely to result from the explosion of the biological time-bomb will, I predict, seriously undermine the already somewhat tenuous social cohesion of western countries. Detailed studies of the forces making for cohesion and loss of cohesion are in any case urgently needed, and it is by no means certain that the changes needed to improve cohesion, which may be radical, can be put into effect in time. Some of them at least concern the structure of the family and the attitudes it inculcates in early life: a lag of a generation is thus the minimum before a noticeable change can be effected, and it may well take two generations before the change is well established.

It will be interesting to see whether the dictatorships are able to cope more effectively with such problems. Thus far, they have been notably backward in applying the social sciences. Eventually, the question of whether capitalism or communism survives may depend on their initiative and skill in dealing with these matters.

Coupled with the disorientation of society is a disorientation of personality. In a world in which effort and outcome are not clearly linked—in which the conscientious man is rewarded with injustice and the selfish man gets what he wants—or one where the outcome seems a matter of chance, people lose the incentive to go on trying. Like experimental rats presented with confusing cues, they become neurotic and finally withdraw into a state of tense inactivity. There are already signs of such personal nihilism in society today. It is expressed as cynicism, materialism and a preference for small profits and quick returns. It certainly lies behind the protests and withdrawal from social norms of many of the younger generation—the so-called beatniks, hippies, flower-people and what-have-you. This has been called the Crisis of Consent.

The explosion of the biological time bomb, unless we take effective steps to channel its energy now, must inevitably foment this nihilism. The new prospects opened up will present people with choices which may prove onerous to take. Responsibility is exhausting.

Today tradition is in bad odour: to describe a practice as traditional immediately suggests that it is obsolete, either an amusing survival or actively harmful. But traditions are devices to simplify decisions. Without them, life becomes impossibly demanding. Our family structure (so different in different cultures) is traditional, and our laws give our traditions force and support. For the new decisions facing people in the post-bomb world, we need new traditions, and a new respect for tradition itself. The deliberate undermining of tradition is one of the forces undermining the cohesion of society.

That these gloomy prognostications are not too unrealistic is suggested by the extraordinary and quite unforeseen consequence which have already attended one biological advance: the synthesis of hallucinogens and brain stimulants. In the thirties, a writer peering into the future might have written of the day, not far off, when one would be able to go to the pharmacist and buy drugs which would stimulate you when tired, calm you when anxious or make you feel good. Indeed, at that time you could actually buy amphetamine sulphate, caffeine and, of course, alcohol for such purposes. What such a writer would not have foreseen would have been that these new drugs would in thirty years have been taken off the open market because a generation had grown up which was quite unable to use them moderately and sensibly.

How has it come about that individuals so devoid of normal good sense as to take sixty times the standard dose of amphetamine at one go have been brought to maturity—if that is the right word?

The instance dramatizes the current failure of our society to instil a social conscience into its members, and gives us a vivid insight into what the future may hold. It seems quite certain that the new powers generated by biology will have to be reserved for a mature and privileged group, to be rationed out only to those who can be relied upon not to misuse them. This is an anti-democratic process, and much to be regretted, but it seems to be the way the world is going.

Some scientists feel that the only sufficiently mature and intelligent group for such a role are the scientists themselves.

The Accursed Scientist

The day may be approaching when the public turns against science. Currently, the scientist is still the miracle-worker in the white coat, who provides drugs and anaesthetics to relieve our hurts, sources of power and light to ease our labour, and who understands even the secrets of atoms and the stars. But this is a comparatively recent stereotype and behind it lie two others. First, the vague, impractical dreamer who doesn't even know what day it is so immersed is he in knowledge for its own sake. And then, by extension, the mad engineer, applying his arcane knowledge regardless of the human consequences, causing disasters, manufacturing monsters, prepared even to move the earth from its course or extinguish the sun to test his theories.

To many, the scientist appears as a trouble-maker, poking his nose into things better left obscure, disturbing the established order—at best, a small boy tearing the wings off flies from curiosity, at worst the man whose hallooing sets off the avalanche.

The explosion of the first atom bomb drove a jagged crack through the superman image. Prom behind the mask of the beneficent father-figure, the mad engineer suddenly looked out grinning like a maniac.

As the impact of the biological time-bomb begins to be felt, the haunted look of Dr. Frankenstein may gradually appear on the faces of the biologists.

At the same time, the very successes of biology create a reputation which becomes steadily harder to maintain. As Professor Rostand has said: "Yes, of science everything is expected: people believe that, to it, all things are possible. It must make dwarfs grow tall, it must dispense eternal youth, it must supply wit to imbeciles, it must raise the dead."

The way in which the public looks at science has been gradually changing, however, in a different sense. In the nineteenth century it was seen primarily as a source of material wealth, and this is how it is still seen by many politicians and some of the more old-fashioned, socialistically inclined type of scientist. But it is increasingly appearing as a source of non-material progress. At the same time, it is being increasingly realized that both kinds of science bring problems in their train of a particularly awkward kind, which we are presently ill equipped to solve. The first kind of science has brought pollution of air and water and general damage to the environment. The second has brought the population problem, the arithmetic of mercy problem and others which are as yet barely recognized.

As this process continues science will begin to be seen in a very disenchanted way as the bringer of gifts which too often end by cancelling their own benefits. The activities of scientists, and their demands for money, will come to be scrutinized much more narrowly than at present, and from a quite different point of view. Instead of asking "Will this provide us with something we can export, or at least sell?" the question will become "Will this create for us problems which will nullify any advantage?"

And if really serious adverse conditions develop—there may well arise a solid opposition to science, an anti-scientism the extremer elements in which may demand the prohibition of all scientific activity except under special licence and direct supervision by non-scientific representatives of the state.

The first of the questions which the public is likely to put to the scientists, as the nature of what they are up to becomes clearer, is: why didn't you warn us what was in store?

Various biologists have, in fact, published warnings, though mostly in specialist periodicals, at closed meetings, or in books written at a technical level placing them beyond the comprehension of the ordinary man without a scientific vocabulary. The editor of a widely read general scientific journal said on television recently that he had tried to get scientists to write on these problems, but had been unable to find any who were willing. Some of the warnings sounded in specialist media I have quoted earlier in this book.

Virtually the only warning addressed to the general public in a popularly written book was supplied by Professor Rostand in his *Can Man be Modified?*, originally written in 1956 and available in English from 1959. He was, in fact, far ahead of most other scientists in foreseeing what was coming.

But while a few imaginative scientists have been trying to consider the implications of their work, the great majority never do so, but just carry on from day to day with the problem in hand, recking as little of the wider issues as a bank clerk does of monetary policy.

When pressed to justify himself, in face of the possible misuse of his discovery by society, the scientist generally replies that how knowledge is used is the responsibility of others. Aircraft, he may point out, can be used to drop bombs or to fly sick people to hospital. They are ethically neutral. The way in which they are used is decided by generals and politicians, not by scientists. Knowledge, itself, is always to the good.

This is true, as far as it goes; but it is also true that one does not put matches into the hands of children. Hitherto it has been assumed that the voting citizen and his elected representatives were not children—that is, that they were neither ignorant nor irresponsible. The discovery of nuclear weapons has raised in many minds a genuine doubt whether this is a realistic assumption. This is, socially, a most extraordinary fact, the great significance of which has not been properly appreciated as yet. So profound are the implications that people hesitate to drag them out into the open and face them. It casts in doubt the whole machinery of democracy. Since, if the state cannot be regarded as responsible, it is difficult to think of any persons or organization that is, one is forced to the conclusion that some knowledge is too dangerous to possess.

It is fashionable to bewail the split between the "two cultures" and to blame the non-scientist for his ignorance of major scientific principles. But Professor Bentley Glass has cogently argued that the cleavage between the two cultures, at least as far as the academic world is concerned arises "not so much because scientists are little interested in the arts, or because humanists are little conversant with the great scientific concepts of the twentieth century, as because the scientist is too blithely confident that more and more scientific knowledge will be good for man irrespective of its applications and too hopefully confident that others can cope with the ethical problems that science generates, or perhaps even to recognize their existence."

While this non-stop sentence (in full, it contains 113 words) is itself indicative of the difficulty scientists have in explaining themselves to the non-specialist, the point is a crucial one, and all the more striking because it is put by a biologist. Biologists, on the whole, prefer to bury their heads in the sand rather than to consider what they should do about the social implications of their own work.

As Dwight Ingle has pointed out, the biologist, and especially the human biologist, is likely to be subject to internal and external pressures, and therefore needs a more independent mind than his colleagues in other disciplines. "Here he must be more objective and better able to recognize his primitive emotions and the effect of his childhood indoctrination. He must, in short, be a highly evolved person. Very often he is." But one must add: and often he is not.

Promethean Situation

Man now possesses power which is so extreme as to be, at most, god-like. Prometheus dared to bring down fire from the abode of the gods and give this technique to men, for which he was severely punished. Fire, for all its benefit was a dangerous acquisition. The myth embodies (as is the function of myths) a lesson: great power constitutes a danger unless used with great wisdom and is therefore reserved to those who know all things and can foresee the consequences of using it. Today mankind is in a Promethean situation. It is precisely because we cannot see, in detail, the consequences of using the new biological powers that they constitute dangers. The fact that they might be used for benign purposes or so as to benefit man is not the point, for history shows us that man is far more likely to use power wrongly than rightly.

The fact that some knowledge is potentially dangerous has been recognized by the molecular biologist Professor van R. Potter of Madison, Wisconsin. The only solution to the problem of dangerous knowledge is, in his view, more knowledge. "From the disorder of unevenly developed branches of knowledge we must achieve some new kind o equilibrium." And he urges scientists to extend their studies of human adaptability and individuality, and to investigate further the nature of stress and in particular the concept of an optimum degree of stress.

One scientist, it must be conceded, has expressed his doubts even more concretely, but arrives at the contrary conclusion: that there are some things which should no be known.

This is Sir Macfarlane Burnet, the Australian scientist who won the Nobel award in 1960 for his work on tissue transplants. "It seems almost indecent", says this research scientist, "to hint that, as far as the advance of medicine is concerned, molecular biology may be an evil thing," and he concludes: "It is a hard thing for an experimental scientist to accept, but it is becoming all too evident that there are dangers in knowing what should not be known. But no one has ever heeded the words of a Cassandra." He argued that work in the field of molecular biology not only ignores possible medical aspects but exposes the world to terrifying dangers. Measles vaccines could be improved, a vaccine could be developed for infectious hepatitis—a major requirement which is still unfulfilled. The practice of culturing viruses and looking for new mutants creates a risk that a dangerous new mutant might escape and set off an epidemic, against which the population of the world would be helpless, since the natural defense systems would be unable to cope with it. "The human implications of what is going on in this sophisticated universe of tissue cultured cells, bacteria and viruses which can be grown at the expense of one or other are at best dubious and at worst frankly terrifying."

The appearance of a serologically unique virus of great virulence "is a very serious danger". If it escaped into circulation without being immediately dealt with the result could be an "almost unimaginable catastrophe . . . involving all the populous regions of the world".

Sir Macfarlane Burnet points out that we know very little about why some viruses or bacteria are so much more lethal than others. The strain of virus causing myxomatosis in rabbits is 99.7 per cent lethal—perhaps some newly produced virus affecting humans might be equally potent. Just as the one virtually wiped out the world's rabbit population, so the other might all but wipe out the world's human population.

There is also another, subtler danger. As I described in a previous chapter, viruses can enter cells, carrying with them genetic instructions which may become incorporated in the genetic material of the host. These messages are known as episomes. This information may remain in the cell for several generations in a "dormant" state, and suddenly—for reasons which are completely mysterious—may become effective. In bacteria such dormant information may kill the host cell when it is thus switched on, or- it may alter it radically.

At present we can only detect that this has happened if the episomal information kills the cell or makes it malignant.

How can we be sure, Sir Macfarlane Burnet asks, that we are not introducing episomes into the human genetic material in the course of molecular biological experiment? He leaves the implications to his professional readers to work out, but presumably they include anything from the sudden appearance of radical alterations in the human genotype—detectable, it might be, as the appearance of mutant forms, monsters, defective individuals, a sharp increase in malformations at birth and so on—to sudden outbursts of cancer or other, perhaps hitherto unknown, diseases. Just as bacterial cells suddenly dissolve into a pulp because the viral episome has become active, so perhaps human cells may suddenly collapse. We might see people age overnight, develop fulminating arthritis, or disseminated sclerosis. Indeed, some of the disease we see around us now may spring, for all we know, from such a case.

If there are things which should not be known, should we be prepared to place some discoveries in the ice box, refusing to make use of them until we were good and ready? Or should we go even further, and declare a moratorium on certain branches of research altogether? The possibility that we might at least pursue the first course has occurred to some scientists. Thus Sir George Pickering, considering the prospect of an indefinite extension of human life, has said: "I find this a terrifying prospect, and I am glad I shall be dead and will have ceased to make my own contributions to this catastrophe before it happens. However, we may ask ourselves whether it is not time to halt the programme of research and development which will make such a thing possible. The hint of such an idea by a man who has spent most of his adult life in research of this kind savours of intellectual treason. It is inhumane. It is at variance with the age-old ideas and ideals of the medical profession. Nevertheless, we should face up to the probable consequences of our ideas and ideals and be prepared to revise them."

Another scientist to whom the idea of deliberately refraining from applying knowledge—in a different field—has occurred is Marshall W. Nirenberg, the biochemical geneticist at the National Institutes of Health, whose forecast of 25 years for the realization of genetic surgery was cited in Chapter 6. Because man will have this knowledge before he can solve the moral and ethical problems which will be raised, Nirenberg holds that "When man becomes capable of instructing his own cells, he must refrain from doing so until he has sufficient wisdom to use this knowledge for the benefit of mankind. I state this problem well in advance of the need to solve it," he says in a letter to *Science,* "because decisions concerning the application of this knowledge must ultimately be made by society, and only an informed society can make such decisions wisely."

And Rostand has asked: "Is science reaching a frontier beyond which its progress might be more harmful than advantageous?" raising the question of whether a total moratorium on *all* research may not be called for.

Lord Brain, on the other hand, dismissed this possibility as impracticable, on the grounds that if we cannot foresee the consequences of scientific discoveries, we cannot foresee the consequences of not making them either. It follows that man "certainly has not the capacity to decide that some particular line of scientific research ought to be abandoned because of its supposed evil consequences for mankind". And he adds that to argue that knowledge can be a bad thing is a waste of time, since the impulse to know is an inherent part of human nature.

Who, it may be more relevant to ask, is to make the decision, in any case? Scientists themselves are hardly likely to be unbiased about such a notion, while commercial concerns doing biological research will be leery of even the ice-box angle. Such decisions will have, naturally, to be taken by governments—but governments feel kindly towards industry and its research efforts, and are unlikely to go very far in this direction. Some powerful and farsighted body is needed to advise them—a body so prestigious that they will think twice before refusing its advice. With the growth of the social sciences, it is just possible that a strong Social Sciences Council may emerge in some countries, such as the U.S.A., but it is hardly likely to gain sufficient status in time.

Actually, a more powerful argument for the impossibility of such a course is that, while one country might conceivably embark on such a course, world-wide agreement to it would never be obtained. And since without general agreement there would be no point in one country abstaining, they would not do so. It is the fact that there are, or may be, military advantages in biological knowledge which makes it highly unlikely that such research would ever be truly abandoned. At most it might be placed behind barbed wire.

If a moratorium is out of the question, the only alternative is for society to bend every effort towards making an adaptation to the new conditions. How could this be done?

Biological Slums

The principal social consequence of the mechanical revolution of the eighteenth century was the crowding of human beings into filthy, disease-ridden slums in the nineteenth—slums which our century spends a great deal of effort in gradually replacing with more civilized conditions. If the biological revolution is allowed to develop unsupervised it will create social conditions causing just as much misery in the twentieth century, which later generations will have to struggle to undo—if there are any later generations, and if they have the needed resources. But, unlike the industrial revolution, the results will not be confined to a few western countries: the whole world will probably become one vast biological slum, no whit less dreadful for being intangible.

One opening step might be the setting up a research corporation on the lines of the Rand Corporation: we might call it Strand, for Socio-Technological Research and Development. But obviously numerous and varied initiatives are required. Universities should be establishing chairs of social prediction. Philanthropists should be financing research studies. Legal, economic and theological bodies should be organizing conferences to consider the implications. But before this can occur, considerable propaganda is required to alert people to the problem. As yet, most people don't even know there is a biological revolution.

It is time scientists passed from uttering individual warnings couched in general terms to detailed consideration of specific issues. Some begin to realize this. Thus Professor Luria said, at the symposium on the future of medicine referred to below, "I would not think it premature . . . to establish committees on the genetic direction of human heredity."

The time is more than ripe, I submit, for such bodies as the National Academy of Sciences in the U.S.A., the Royal Society in Great Britain, and the equivalent bodies in Russia, France and elsewhere, to set up committees to consider how to handle the problem of responsibility in general, and the biological revolution in particular.

A sign of their dawning awareness of this new responsibility is the setting up of committees to consider questions of medical ethics and of experimentation on human beings. In 1966 the AMA held the first National Congress on ethics, after which the US Public Health Service gave a substantial financial grant to the

AAAS to investigate the latter problem, following public concern at experiments involving the implantation of cancer cells in hospital patients without their informed consent. The AAAS called in lawyers, sociologists, clinics and doctors to advise. But, as we have seen, the field is enormously wider than mere questions of medical ethics.

In his presidential address to the Royal Society in 1964, Sir Howard Florey raised the issue of the social responsibilities of science in a typically cautious manner. "Ought we as a society", he said, "to be considering how science and scientists can contribute to the great problem of bringing the human population into equilibrium with its surroundings?" and he added: "I have no doubt myself that we should try to lead scientific advances by positive action."

Lord Brain has put the matter more forthrightly. "Our present crises have been produced partly by the activities of scientists. Scientists must therefore seize every opportunity to bring home to those who make the practical decisions about the social organization, the urgency of the problems with which they are faced and their true nature; and, if they can, themselves contribute to their solution."

And, of course, however well scientists advise political leaders, there is no assurance that their advice will be put into effect. Nevertheless, the advice must be given. For the rest, it is, as H. G. Wells said, a race between education and catastrophe.

Encouragingly enough, there are signs of change of attitude. In the past few years, in several countries, individuals and groups have formed organizations for studying future trends in a systematic manner, taking both social and technological aspects into consideration. The American Academy of Arts and Sciences, in its journal *Daedalus* (Summer, 1967), published a number of studies of the year 2000 and the first major international meeting devoted to this subject was held in September 1967 under the title *Mankind 2000*. The book you are now reading is itself an indication of this growing awareness that the future cannot just be allowed to happen—but the speculations of individuals will have to give place to comprehensive and systematic studies by teams, using special techniques (such as the Delphi technique developed by the Rand Corporation) to reduce errors and biases and to refine their forecasts.

Conditions of Happiness

A primary difficulty in devising plans to meet the problems which biology is conjuring up is constituted by the fact that we have no clear or agreed idea of what kind of world we want. No doubt most people would vote for a social pattern much like the one they know, but devoid of its principal abuses. In the east, this would mean a world of cars and factories and Coca-Cola, without delinquency, ulcers. air pollution or crime. But investigation discloses that the advantages and disadvantages are reciprocally connected. We have air pollution precisely because we have cars and factories to produce goods. We have ulcers because we have a highly competitive productive system which monopolizes the bulk of the time of the bulk of the population. We have delinquency because this kind of footloose society, with its unrestricted communications system, weakens family control of the young. And so on.

These statements, of course, are mere headlines with which I seek to outline great areas in an attempt to establish a point of view. The actual causes of delinquency, for instance are complex and it is not my intention to oversimplify them. My point is the large one that all the features of a given society are functionally interconnected, and one cannot change one in isolation from the others.

If, then, we ask ourselves what kind of a society to aim for, on the assumption that we might make a radical change in the pattern, we find ourselves faced with a series of questions to which there are at present no quantitative answers. For example, at what level should we set the density of population so as to avoid either undue isolation or disagreeable overcrowding? In England, with its high population densities, as on the eastern seaboard of the U.S.A. between Boston and Washington, many of the pleasures of life are made difficult or impossible by an absurdly high population density. Yet there are many who are willing to push this process further (cf. Nigel Calder: *The Environment* Game, 1967). Or again, to what extent should we be willing to sacrifice the quality of the environment in order to consume goods? We are busy creating a world in which it is steadily easier to consume goods than to take our pleasure in the form of privacy, a slow pace of work, communion with nature, or doing a job which one enjoys.

Modern industrial methods are making possible a shorter working week, and some authorities have prophesied a working week of twenty hours before the end of the century, with an absolute prohibition on anyone working longer than perhaps thirty hours a week. But why do we have to play it this way? There is no fundamental reason why we should not use this productive margin to redesign the work to make it more interesting. It is quite conceivable that many people would prefer to put in thirty or even forty hours at an interesting task than twenty at a tedious one.

The trouble is, we have simply no method of getting out of the groove. Western society is set up in such a way that increases in productive efficiency automatically show up as more goods; by great efforts over more than half a century we have organized social forces which can cut the supply of goods so as to create more leisure. But to cut it so as to make the job interesting is a trick to perform which no machinery exists.

Then there are more intangible problems, represented by the fact that, in biological matters, we have to plan for several generations ahead. It is not a question of what society we want, but what kind of society will our descendants—who by definition will differ greatly from us—want?

Societies consist of people, and it takes a different kind of person to live comfortably in a different kind of society. And vice versa. The hyperactive citizen of today is bored when transferred to a slower-paced society. The slowerpaced man is anxious and unhappy when transferred to a hyperactive society. But this does mean that we must consider designing a society which we might find uncongenial, if we feel that man might adapt to it, and would be happier for doing so.

The root of our problem, pragmatically, is the absence of any means of measuring satisfaction. And our tendency to assume that an economically calculated "standard of living" is actually a measure of satisfaction. When we read that the output of manufactured goods reached a new peak, we usually assume this made people happier. But if it was achieved by sacrificing conditions of life which they greatly value, it may have made them, on balance, less happy.

And by "conditions" I do not mean merely extrinsic conditions like privacy in an unpolluted atmosphere, but also intrinsic conditions like the intensified level of anxiety, a frustrated emotional life, or an increase in crime.

Yet, as in the economic instance cited above, we have no machinery, existing or in view, capable of reconstructing our society. If it proves profitable to prolong the lives of the old, for instance, it is all Lombard Street to a china orange that we shall prolong them, regardless of what the change in the age-structure of the population may do to our culture. If it is profitable to make man-animal chimaeras, we shall make them. And if memory-deletion offers some appeal, memories will be deleted. The degree of imagination and effort needed to break out of this situation is probably beyond the imagination and flexibility of man, eastern or western to achieve.

Current indications are that the world is bent on going to hell in a handcart, and that is probably what it will do.

Professor Arnold Toynbee has described our situation as a failure of our emotional development to keep up with our intellectual development. But this is to misrepresent the problem. For there is no sense in which emotion can be expected to accumulate as knowledge does, nor are there emotional techniques which can be handed on ready made to the following generation. It is more to the point to say that sociological knowledge has not kept up with knowledge in the physical sciences, for there is at least some reason to believe that, with a profounder understanding of the relationship between culture and personality, one might shift the system in the direction of co-operativeness and social conscience and away from selfishness and aggression. Human societies display a rather wide range between these extremes.

But while primitive societies, which have not learned to challenge their own traditions, may live peaceably and agreeably, it is far from certain that societies with universal means of travel and intensive education can do so. Modern life, as we understand it, may mean an inevitable increase in the proportion of desocialized individuals. But no one can quarrel with the proposition that we urgently need to find out whether this is so, and to learn how to hold disruption to a minimum.

The basic answers lie for all to read in the works of wise men. Man is the measure; knowledge, without the corrective of charity, hath some nature of venom or malignity. It is the know-how for putting these principles into effect which is lacking.

THE *HUMAN* USE OF HUMAN BEINGS

NORBERT WIENER

Norbert Wiener (1894-1964) may be said to be the inventor of the science of cybernetics with the publication of his book, *Cybernetics* in 1948. In this he sought to bring together the fields of biology and engineering for the study of communications and control, with emphasis on feedback for making corrections. He was one of the pioneers in the development of high-speed electronic computers.

Wiener was born at Columbia, Missouri. He graduated from Tufts University at the age of fourteen, and received a Ph.D. from Harvard just four years later. He taught at the Massachusetts Institute of Technology from 1919 to 1960. His teaching style and seeming absent-mindedness were legendary at MIT. During World War I he did mathematical work at the Army's Aberdeen Proving Ground, and during World War II he helped develop the computer. In 1964 he received the National Medal of Science.

In addition to his scientific works, Wiener wrote several non-technical books. In *The Human Use of Human Beings* (1950) he sought "to explain the potentialities of the machines in fields which up to now have been taken to be purely human, and to warn against the dangers of a purely selfish exploitation of these possibilities."

1. What does Wiener mean by *the human use of human beings*?

2. What does Wiener consider the most essential difference between human beings and other animals?

3. What is the place of communication in developing an understanding of society?

4. How do mechanical means of communication compare with the biological?

5. What is the role of *feedback*? Upon what does it depend?

6. What are the important positive and negative consequences of the tremendous expansion of communications in the "information superhighway,"—Internet, e-mail, satellite telephonic connections and cellular telephones, fax machines, etc?

THE *HUMAN* USE OF HUMAN BEINGS

NORBERT WIENER

WHAT IS CYBERNETICS?

I HAVE BEEN OCCUPIED for many years with problems of communication engineering. These have led to the design and investigation of various sorts of communication machines, some of which have shown an uncanny ability to simulate human behavior, and thereby to throw light on the possible nature of human behavior. They have even shown the existence of a tremendous possibility of replacing human behavior, in many cases in which the human being is relatively slow and ineffective. We are thus in an immediate need of discussing the powers of these machines as they impinge on the human being, and the consequences of this new and fundamental revolution in technique.

To those of us who are engaged in constructive research and in invention, there is a serious moral risk of aggrandizing what we have accomplished. To the public, there is an equally serious moral risk of supposing that in stating new potentials of fact, we scientists and engineers are thereby justifying and even urging their exploitation at any costs. It will therefore be taken for granted by many that the attitude of an investigator who is aware of the great new possibilities of the machine age, when employed for the purpose of communication and control, will be to urge the prompt exploitation of this new "know-how" for the sake of the machine and for the minimization of the human element in life. This is most emphatically not the purpose of the present book.

The purpose of this book is both to explain the potentialities of the machine in fields which up to now have been taken to be purely human, and to warn against the dangers of a purely selfish exploitation of these possibilities in a world in which to human beings, human things are all-important.

That we shall have to change many details of our mode of life in the face of the new machines is certain; but these machines are secondary in all matters of value that concern us to the proper evaluation of human beings for their own sake and to their employment as human beings, and not as second-rate surrogates for possible machines of the future. The message of this book as well as its title is *the human use of human beings*.

The problem of the definition of man is an odd one. To say that man is a featherless biped is merely to put him in the same class as a plucked chicken, a kangaroo, or a jerboa. This is a rather heterogeneous group, and it can be extended to our heart's content without throwing any further light on the true nature of man. It will not do to say that man is an animal with a soul. Unfortunately, the existence of the soul, whatever it may mean, is not available to the scientific methods of behaviorism; and although the Church assures us that men have souls and dogs do not, an equally authoritative institution known as Buddhism holds a different view.

What does differentiate man from other animals in a way which leaves us not the slightest degree of doubt, is that he is a talking animal. The impulse to communicate with his fellow beings is so strong that not even the double deprivation of blindness and deafness can completely obliterate it. It is not only that with adequate training the blind deafmute may become a Laura Bridgman or a Helen Keller, but even more, that without any training whatever, a Helen Keller will make a desperate attempt to break the almost impregnable barrier which separates her from the rest of the world. There are animals besides man which are social, and live in a continuous relation to their fellow creatures, but there is none in whom this desire for communication, or rather this necessity for communication, is the guiding motive of their whole life. What then is this communication, which is so human and so essential? I shall devote this chapter, and indeed the greater part of this book to the introduction of concepts and theories contributing to the answer to this question.

One of the most interesting aspects of the world is that it can be considered to be made up of *patterns*. A pattern is essentially an arrangement. It is characterized by the order of the elements of which it is made, rather than by the intrinsic nature of these elements. Two patterns are identical if their relational structure can be put into a one-to-one correspondence, so that to each term of the one there corresponds a term of the other; and that to each relation of order between several terms of one, there corresponds a similar relation of order between the corresponding terms of the other. The simplest case of one-to-one correspondence is given by the ordinary process of counting. If I have five pennies in my pocket, and five apples in a basket, I can put my apples in a row, and lay one penny beside each. Each penny will correspond to one apple and one apple only, and each apple will correspond to one penny and one penny only.

However, the notion of one-to-one correspondence is not confined to finite sets, which can be given a number in the sense of elementary arithmetic. For example, the pattern of the sequence of whole numbers from 1 on is identical with that of the sequence of even numbers, since we can assign as a counterpart to each number its double, and since the before-and-after relations of the doubles will be the same as those of the original numbers. Again, a copy of a painting, if it is accurately made, will have the same pattern as the original, while a less perfect copy will have a pattern which is in some sense similar to that of the original.

The pattern of a thing may be spread out in space, as for example, the pattern of a wallpaper; or it may be distributed in time, as the pattern of a musical composition. The pattern of a musical composition again suggests the pattern of a telephone conversation, or the pattern of dots and dashes of a telegram. These two types of pattern are given the special designation of messages, not because their pattern itself differs in any way from the pattern of a musical composition, but because it is used in a somewhat different manner: namely, to convey information from one point to another, and even from one remote point to another.

A pattern which is conceived to convey information, or something transmissible from individual to individual, is not taken as an isolated phenomenon. To telegraph is to convey a message by the proper use of dots and dashes; and here it is necessary that these dots and dashes be a selection from among a set which contains other possibilities as well. If I am sending the letter *e*, it gains its meaning in part because I have not sent the letter o. If my only choice is to send the letter *e*, then the message is merely something that is either there or not there; and it conveys much less information.

In the early days of telephone engineering, the mere sending of a message was so much of a miracle that nobody asked how it should best be sent. The lines were able to take care of all the information forced on them, and the real difficulties were in the design of the terminal apparatus at the sending and receiving ends. Under these conditions, the problems concerning the maximum carrying capacity of telephone lines were not yet of any importance. However, as the art developed, and ways were found to compress several messages into a single line by the use of carriers and other similar means, economy in sending speech over the telephone lines began to develop an economic importance. Let me explain what we mean by "carriers" and by "carrier-telephony."

A mathematical theorem due to Fourier states that every motion within very broad limits can be represented as a sum of the very simplest sort of vibrations which give rise to pure musical notes. A way has been found to take an oscillation on an electric line, and to shift each one of the notes that make it up, by a certain constant pitch. In this manner, we may take a pattern in which several subsidiary patterns would otherwise be placed on top of each other, and separate them so that they are placed side by side in positions, and do not produce a mere confusion. Thus we may run three lines together in the typewriter in such a way that they are superimposed and blurred, or we may write them in their proper sequence, and keep them separate. This process of moving different messages into separate positions of pitch is known as *modulation*.

After modulation, the message may be sent over a line which is already carrying a message, if the displacement in pitch is sufficient. Under proper conditions, the message already transmitted and the new message will not affect one another; and it is possible to recover from the line both the original undisplaced message and the modulated message, in such a way that they go to separate terminal equipment. The modulated message may then be subjected to a process which is the inverse of modulation, and may be reduced to the form which it originally had before it was entrusted to the apparatus. Thus two messages may be sent along the same telephone line. By an extension of this process, many more than two messages may be sent over the same line. This process is known as carrier-telephony, and has vastly extended the usefulness of our telephone lines without any correspondingly great increase in investment.

Since the introduction of carrier methods, telephone lines have been used at a high efficiency of message transmission. Thus the question of how much information can be sent over a line has become significant, and with this, the measurement of information in general. This has been made more acute by the discovery that the very existence of electric currents in a line is the cause of what is called *line* noise, which blurs the messages, and offers an upper limit to their ability to carry information.

The earlier work on the theory of information was vitiated by the fact that it ignored noise-levels and other quantities of a somewhat random nature. It was only when the idea of randomness was fully understood, together with the applications of the related notions of probability, that the question of the carrying capacity of a telegraph or telephone line could even be asked intelligently. When this question was asked, it became clear that the problem of measuring the amount of information was of a piece with the related problem of the measurement of the regularity and irregularity of a pattern. It is quite clear that a haphazard sequence of symbols or a pattern which is purely haphazard can convey no information. Information thus must be in some way the measure of the regularity of a pattern, and in particular of the sort of pattern known as *time series*. By time series, I mean a pattern in which the parts are spread in time. This regularity is to a certain extent an abnormal thing. The irregular is always commoner than the regular. Therefore, whatever definition of information and its measure we shall introduce must be something which grows when the *a priori* probability of a pattern or a time series diminishes. We shall later find the proper numerical measure for the amount of information. This range of ideas was already familiar in the branch of physics known as statistical mechanics, and was associated with the famous second law of thermodynamics, which asserts that a system may lose order and regularity spontaneously, but that it practically never gains it.

A little later in this chapter, I shall give this law its proper statement in terms of the scientific notion of *entropy* which I shall then define. For the present this qualitative formulation of the law will suffice. The notion of information has proved to be subject to a similar law—that is, a message can lose order spontaneously in the act of transmission, but cannot gain it. For example, if one talks into a telephone with a great deal of line noise, and a great deal of loss of energy of the main message, the person at the other end may miss words that have been spoken, and may have to reconstruct them on the basis of the significant information of the context. Again, if a book is translated from one language into another, there does not exist that precise equivalence between the two languages which will permit the translation to have exactly the same meaning as the original. Under these conditions, the translator has only two alternatives: namely, to use phrases which are a little broader and vaguer than those of the original, and which certainly fail to contain its entire emotional context, or to falsify the original by introducing a message which is not precisely there, and which conveys his own meaning rather than that of the author. In either case, some of the author's meaning is lost.

An interesting application of the concept of amount of information is to the elaborate telegraph messages which are offered at Christmas or birthdays or other special occasions. The message may cover a whole page of text, but what is sent is just a code symbol such as *B7*, meaning the seventh coded message to be sent on birthdays. Such special messages are only possible because the sentiments expressed are merely conventional and repetitive. The moment the sender shows any originality in the sentiments he desires to convey, the reduced rates are no longer available. The meaning of the cheap-rate message is disproportionately small compared with the length of the message. We again see that the message is a transmitted pattern, which acquires its meaning by being a selection from a large number of possible patterns. The amount of meaning can be measured. It turns out that the less probable a message is, the more meaning it carries, which is entirely reasonable from the standpoint of our common sense.

We ordinarily think of a message as sent from human being to human being. This need not be the case at all. If, being lazy, instead of getting out of bed in the morning, I press a button which turns on the heat, closes the window, and starts an electric heating unit under the coffeepot, I am sending messages to all these pieces of apparatus. If on the other hand, the electric egg boiler starts a whistle going after a certain number of minutes, it is sending me a message. If the thermostat records that the room is too warm, and turns off the oil burner, the message may be said to be a method of control of the oil burner. Control, in other words, is nothing but the sending of messages which effectively change the behavior of the recipient.

It is this study of messages, and in particular of the effective messages of control, which constitutes the science of *Cybernetics,* which I christened in an earlier book. Its name signifies the art of pilot or steersman. Let it be noted that the word "governor" in a machine is simply the latinized Greek word for steersman.

It is the thesis of this book that society can only be understood through a study of the messages and the communication facilities which belong to it; and that in the future development of these messages and communication facilities, messages between man and machines, between machine and man, and between machine and machine, are destined to play an ever-increasing part.

To indicate the role of the message in man, let us compare human activity with activity of a very different sort; namely, the activity of the little figures which dance on the top of a music box. These figures dance in accordance with a pattern, but it is a pattern which is set in advance, and in which the past activity of the figures has practically nothing to do with the pattern of their future activity. There is a message, indeed; but it goes from the machinery of the music box to the figures, and stops there. The figures themselves have not a trace of any communication with the outer world, except this one-way stage of communication with the music box. They are blind, deaf, and dumb, and cannot vary their activity in the least from the conventionalized pattern.

Contrast with them the behavior of man, or indeed of any moderately intelligent animal such as a kitten. I call to the kitten and it looks up. I have sent it a message which it has received by its sensory organs, and which it registers in action. The kitten is hungry and lets out a pitiful wail. This time it is the sender of a message. The kitten bats at a swinging spool. The spool swings to the left, and the kitten catches it with its left paw. This time messages of a very complicated nature are both sent and received. The kitten is informed of the motion of its own paw by organs called proprioceptors or kinaesthetic organs. These organs are certain nerve end-bodies to be found in its joints, in its muscles, and in its tendons; and by means of nervous messages sent by these organs, the animal is aware of the actual position and tensions of its tissues. It is only through these organs that anything like a skill is possible, not to mention the extreme dexterity of the kitten.

I have contrasted the behavior of the little figures on the music box on the one hand, and the human and animal behavior on the other. It might be supposed that the music box was an example typical of all machine behavior, in contrast to the behavior of living organisms. This is not so. The older machines, and in particular the older attempts to produce automata, did in fact work on a closed clockwork basis. On the other hand, the machines of the present day possess sense organs; that is, receptors for messages coming from the outside. These may be as simple as photo-electric cells which change electrically when a light falls on them, and which can tell light from dark. They may be as complicated as a television set. They may measure a tension by the change it produces in the conductivity of a wire exposed to it. They may measure temperature by means of a thermocouple, which is an instrument consisting of two distinct metals in contact with one another through which a current flows when one of the points of contact is heated. Every instrument in the repertory of the scientific-instrument maker is a possible sense organ, and may be made to record its reading remotely through the intervention of appropriate electrical apparatus. Thus the machine which is conditioned by its relation to the external world, and by the things happening in the external world, is with us and has been with us for some time.

The machine which acts on the external world by means of messages is also familiar. The automatic photo-electric door opener is known to every person who has passed through the Pennsylvania Station in New York, and is used in many other buildings as well. When the message constituted by the interception of a beam of light is sent to the apparatus, this message actuates the door, and opens it so that the passenger may go through.

The steps between the actuation of a machine of this type by sense organs and its performance of a task may be as simple as in the case of the electric door; or it may be in fact of any desired degree of complexity. A complex action is one in which the combination of the data introduced, which we call the *input*, to obtain an effect on the outer world, which we call the *output*, may involve a large number of combinations. These are combinations, both of the data put in at the moment and of the records taken from the past stored data which we call the *memory*. These are recorded in the machine. The most complicated machines yet made which transform input data into output data are the highspeed electrical computing machines, of which I shall speak later in more detail. The determination of the mode of conduct of these machines is given through a special sort of input, which frequently consists of punched cards or tapes or of magnetized wires, and which determines the way in which the machine is going to act in one operation, as distinct from the way in which it might have acted in another. Because of the frequent use of punched or magnetic tape in the control, the data which are fed in, and which indicate the mode of operation of one of these machines for combining information, are called the *taping*. I illustrate the situation by means of the following conventionalized diagram.

I have said that man and the animal have a kinaesthetic sense, by which they keep a record of the position and tensions of their muscles. For any machine subject to a varied external environment, in order to act effectively it is necessary that information concerning the results of its own action be furnished to it as part of the information on which it must continue to act. For example, if we are running an elevator, it is not enough to open the outside door because the orders we have given should make the elevator be at that door at the time we open it. It is important that the release for opening the door be dependent on the fact that the elevator is actually at the door; otherwise something might have detained it, and the passenger might step into the empty shaft. This control of a machine on the basis of its *actual* performance rather than its *expected* performance is known as *feedback,* and involves sensory members which are actuated by motor members and perform the function of *tell-tales* or *monitors*—that is, of elements which indicate a performance.

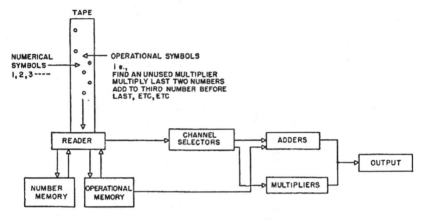

A TYPICAL TAPING SYSTEM

I have just mentioned the elevator as an example of feedback. There are other cases where feedback is even more essential. For example, a gun-pointer takes information from his instruments of observation, and conveys it to the gun. so that the latter will point in such a direction that the missile will pass through the moving target at some time. Now, the gun itself must be used under all conditions of weather. In some of these the grease is warm, and the gun swings easily and rapidly. Under other conditions the grease is frozen or mixed with sand, and the gun is slow to answer the orders given to it. If these orders are reinforced by an extra push given when the gun fails to respond easily to the orders and lags behind them, then the error of the gun-pointer will be decreased. In order to obtain a performance as uniform as possible, it is customary to put into the gun a control feedback element which reads the lag of the gun behind the position it should have according to the orders given it, and which uses this difference to give the gun an extra push.

It is true that precautions must be taken so that the push is not too hard, for if it is, the gun will swing past its proper position, and will have to be pulled back in a series of oscillations, which may well become wider and wider, and lead to a disastrous instability. If the feedback is controlled and kept within limits sufficiently stringent, this will not occur, and the existence of the feedback will increase the stability of performance of the gun. In other words, the performance will become less dependent on the frictional load; or what is the same thing, on the drag created by the stiffness of the grease.

Something very similar to this occurs in human action. If I pick up my cigar, I do not will to move any specific muscles. Indeed in many cases, I do not know what those muscles are. What I do is to turn into action a certain feedback mechanism; namely, a reflex in which the amount by which I have yet failed to pick up the cigar is turned into a new and increased order to the lagging muscles, whichever they may be. In this way, a fairly uniform voluntary command will enable the same task to be performed from widely varying initial positions, and irrespective of the decrease of contraction due to fatigue of the muscles. Similarly, when I drive a car, I do not follow out a series of commands dependent simply on a mental image of the road and the task I am doing. If I find the car swerving too much to the left, that causes me to turn it to the right; and if I find it swerving too much to the right, that causes me to pull it to the left. This depends on the actual performance of the car, and not simply on the road; and it allows me to drive with nearly equal efficiency a light Austin or a heavy truck, without having formed separate habits for the driving of the two. I shall have more to say about this in the chapter in this book on special machines, where we shall discuss the service that can be done to neuropathology by the study of machines with defects in performance similar to those occurring in the human mechanism.

It is my thesis that the operation of the living individual and the operation of some of the newer communication machines are precisely parallel. Both of them have sensory receptors as one stage in their cycle of operation: that is, in both of them there exists a special apparatus for collecting information from the outer world at low energy levels, and for making it available in the operation of the individual or of the machine. In both cases these external messages are not taken *neat,* but through the internal transforming powers of the apparatus, whether it be alive or dead. The information is then turned into a new form available for the further stages of performance. In both the animal and the machine this performance is made to be effective on the outer world. In both of them, their *performed* action on the outer world, and not merely their *intended* action, is reported back to the central regulatory apparatus. This complex of behavior is ignored by the average man, and in particular does not play the role that it should in our habitual analysis of society.

This is true whether we consider human beings alone, or in conjunction with types of automata which participate in a two-way relation with the world about them. In this, our view of society differs from the ideal of society which is held by many Fascists, Strong Men in Business, and Government. Similar men of ambition for power are not entirely unknown in scientific and educational institutions. Such people prefer an organization in which all orders come from above, and none return. The human beings under them have been reduced to the level of effectors for a supposedly higher nervous organism. I wish to devote this book to a protest against this inhuman use of human beings; for in my mind, any use of a human being in which less is demanded of him and less is attributed to him than his full status is a degradation and a waste. It is a degradation to a human being to chain him to an oar and use him as a source of power; but it is an almost equal degradation to assign him a purely repetitive task in a factory, which demands less than a millionth of his brain capacity. It is simpler to organize a factory or galley which uses individual human beings for a trivial fraction of their worth than it is to provide a world in which they can grow to their full stature. Those who suffer from a power complex find the mechanization of man a simple way to realize their ambitions. I say, that this easy path to power is in fact not only a rejection of everything that I consider to be of moral worth in the human race, but also a rejection of our now very tenuous opportunities for a considerable period of human survival.

The rest of this book is devoted to the development of this theme. In every chapter, we are studying either those respects in which the machine duplicates man, or those aspects of man which appear clearer in view of our study of the machine, or both. We begin with the two notions of *entropy* and of *progress:* notions which are completely necessary for the understanding of the orientation of man in the world, and notions which have been sadly misunderstood. We discuss the communicative behavior of man, as contrasted with that of the ant; and thereby are given a clearer idea of the function of learning in human society. Three more chapters are devoted to the problem of language, both in man and in the machine; and to those aspects of man in which human individuality resembles something essentially linguistic. We have a few words to say about law, and many to say about those widely misunderstood notions, secrecy and intellectual property. In the ninth chapter, we define and criticize the roles of those two priests of communication in the modern world: the literary intellectual and the scientist. The tenth and eleventh chapters are devoted to the machine, and to the great changes it has made and may be expected to make in the life of the human being of the present generation. Finally, we devote one chapter to the study of certain specific influences, in appearance very different from one another, and in nature very similar, which furnish the chief stumbling blocks to a proper understanding of what communication should mean to us, and to a proper development of communication itself.

COMPUTING MACHINERY AND INTELLIGENCE

A. M. TURING

Alan Mathison Turing (1912-1954) was one of the most provocative thinkers and writers on questions of so-called artificial intelligence during the mid-twentieth century. He was educated at Sherborne School and at King's College, Cambridge University. He was made a fellow of King's College in 1935. Throughout World War II he served in the British Foreign Office, and immediately afterward he joined the National Physics Laboratory where he served for three years. Then he was Reader in Mathematics at the University of Manchester from 1948 until his untimely death in 1954 at the age of forty-two. When only thirty-two years old (1946) he was made an Officer Order of the British Empire and five years later became a Fellow of the Royal Society.

Computing Machinery and Intelligence first appeared in the journal *Mind* in 1950.

1. What is the idea behind digital computers?

2. Do you think that computers can think? Can lower animals think? What do you mean by "think"?

3. How does Turing refute the common objections to the idea that a machine might think?

4. According to Turing, in what sense may a machine be said to think? Is this a useful assumption?

5. What is the "Turing test" or "Imitation Game" to determine whether or not a machine can think? Do you think it is valid? Do you think a machine ever will pass the test?

6. What are the implications for human society if machines *are* able to think?

COMPUTING MACHINERY AND INTELLIGENCE

A. M. TURING

1. The Imitation Game

I PROPOSE to consider the question, 'Can machines think?' This should begin with definitions of the meaning of the terms 'machine' and 'think.' The definitions might be framed so as to reflect so far as possible the normal use of the words, but this attitude is dangerous. If the meaning of the words 'machine' and 'think' are to be found by examining how they are commonly used it is difficult to escape the conclusion that the meaning and the answer to the question, 'Can machines think?' is to be sought in a statistical survey such as a Gallup poll. But this is absurd. Instead of attempting such a definition I shall replace the question by another, which is closely related to it and is expressed in relatively unambiguous words.

The new form of the problem can be described in terms of a game which we call the 'imitation game.' It is played with three people, a man (A), a woman (B), and an interrogator (c)who may be of either sex. The interrogator stays in a room apart from the other two. The object of the game for the interrogator is to determine which of the other two is the man and which is the woman. He knows them by labels X and Y, and at the end of the game he says either 'X is A and Y is B' or 'X is B and Y is A.' The interrogator is allowed to put questions to A and B thus:

C: Will X please tell me the length of his or her hair?

Now suppose X is actually A, then A must answer. It is A's object in the game to try and cause C to make the wrong identification. His answer might therefore be

'My hair is shingled, and the longest strands are about nine inches long.'

In order that tones of voice may not help the interrogator the answers should be written, or better still, typewritten. The ideal arrangement is to have a teleprinter communicating between the two rooms. Alternatively the question and answers can be repeated by an intermediary. The object of the game for the third player (B) is to help the interrogator. The best strategy for her is probably to give truthful answers. She can add such things as 'I am the woman, don't listen to him!' to her answers, but it will avail nothing as the man can make similar remarks.

We now ask the question, 'What will happen when a machine takes the part of A in this game?' Will the interrogator decide wrongly as often when the game is played like this as he does when the game is played between a man and a woman? These questions replace our original, 'Can machines think?'

2. Critique of The New Problem

As well as asking, 'What is the answer to this new form of the question,' one may ask, 'Is this new question a worthy one to investigate?' This latter question we investigate without further ado, thereby cutting short an infinite regress.

The new problem has the advantage of drawing a fairly sharp line between the physical and the intellectual capacities of a man. No engineer or chemist claims to be able to produce a material which is indistinguishable from the human skin. It is possible that at some time this might be done, but even supposing this invention available we should feel there was little point in trying to make a 'thinking machine' more human by dressing it up in such artificial flesh. The form in which we have set the problem reflects this fact in the condition which prevents the interrogator from seeing or touching the other competitors, or hearing their voices. Some other advantages of the proposed criterion may be shown up by specimen questions and answers. Thus:

Q: Please write me a sonnet on the subject of the Forth Bridge.

A: Count me out on this one. I never could write poetry.

Q: Add 34957 to 70764.

A: (Pause about 30 seconds and then give as answer) 105621.

Q: Do you play chess?

A: Yes.

Q: I have K at my K1, and no other pieces. You have only K at K6 and R at R1. It is your move. What do you play?

A: (After a pause of 15 seconds) R-R8 mate.

The question and answer method seems to be suitable for introducing almost any one of the fields of human endeavour that we wish to include. We do not wish to penalise the machine for its inability to shine in beauty competitions, nor to penalise a man for losing in a race against an aeroplane. The conditions of our game make these disabilities irrelevant. The 'witnesses' can brag, if they consider it advisable, as much as they please about their charms, strength or heroism, but the interrogator cannot demand practical demonstrations.

The game may perhaps be criticised on the ground that the odds are weighted too heavily against the machine. If the man were to try and pretend to be the machine he would clearly make a very poor showing. He would be given away at once by slowness and inaccuracy in arithmetic. May not machines carry out something which ought to be described as thinking but which is very different from what a man does? This objection is a very strong one, but at least we can say that if, nevertheless, a machine can be constructed to play the imitation game satisfactorily, we need not be troubled by this objection.

It might be urged that when playing the 'imitation game' the best strategy for the machine may possibly be something other than imitation of the behaviour of a man. This may be, but I think it is unlikely that there is any great effect of this kind. In any case there is no intention to investigate here the theory of the game, and it will be assumed that the best strategy is to try to provide answers that would naturally be given by a man.

3. The Machines Concerned in the Game!

The question which we put in § 1 will not be quite definite until we have specified what we mean by the word 'machine.' It is natural that we should wish to permit every kind of engineering technique to be used in our machines. We also wish to allow the possibility that an engineer or team of engineers may construct a machine which works, but whose manner of operation cannot be satisfactorily described by its constructors because they have applied a method which is largely experimental. Finally, we wish to exclude from the machines men born in the usual manner. It is difficult to frame the definitions so as to satisfy these three conditions. One might for instance insist that the team of engineers should be all of one sex, but this would not really be satisfactory, for it is probably possible to rear a complete individual from a single cell of the skin (say) of a man. To do so would be a feat of biological technique deserving of the very highest praise, but we would not be inclined to regard it as a case of 'constructing a thinking machine.' This prompts us to abandon the requirement that every kind of technique should be permitted. We are the more ready to do so in view of the fact that the present interest in 'thinking machines' has been aroused by a particular kind of machine, usually called an 'electronic computer' or 'digital computer.' Following this suggestion we only permit digital computers to take part in our game.

This restriction appears at first sight to be a very drastic one. I shall attempt to show that it is not so in reality. To do this necessitates a short account of the nature and properties of these computers.

It may also be said that this identification of machines with digital computers, like our criterion for 'thinking,' will only be unsatisfactory if (contrary to my belief), it turns out that digital computers are unable to give a good showing in the game.

There are already a number of digital computers in working order, and it may be asked, 'Why not try the experiment straight away? It would be easy to satisfy the conditions of the game. A number of interrogators could be used, and statistics compiled to show how often the right identification was given.' The short answer is that we are not asking whether all digital computers would do well in the game nor whether the computers at present available would do well, but whether there are imaginable computers which would do well. But this is only the short answer. We shall see this question in a different light later.

4. Digital Computers

The idea behind digital computers may be explained by saying that these machines are intended to carry out any operations which could be done by a human computer. The human computer is supposed to be following fixed rules; he has no authority to deviate from them in any detail. We may suppose that these rules are supplied in a book, which is altered whenever he is put on to a new job. He has also an unlimited supply of paper on which he does his calculations. He may also do his multiplications and additions on a 'desk machine,' but this is not important.

If we use the above explanation as a definition we shall be in danger of circularity of argument. We avoid this by giving an outline of the means by which the desired effect is achieved. A digital computer can usually be regarded as consisting of three parts:

(I) Store.
(ii) Executive unit.
(iii) Control.

The store is a store of information, and corresponds to the human computer's paper, whether this is the paper on which he does his calculations or that on which his book of rules is printed. In so far as the human computer does calculations in his head a part of the store will correspond to his memory.

The executive unit is the part which carries out the various individual operations involved in a calculation. What these individual operations are will vary from machine to machine. Usually fairly lengthy operations can be done such as 'Multiply 3540675445 by 7076345687' but in some machines only very simple ones such as 'Write down 0' are possible.

We have mentioned that the 'book of rules' supplied to the computer is replaced in the machine by a part of the store. It is then called the 'table of instructions.' It is the duty of the control to see that these instructions are obeyed correctly and in the right order. The control is so constructed that this necessarily happens.

The information in the store is usually broken up into packets of moderately small size. In one machine, for instance, a packet might consist of ten decimal digits. Numbers are assigned to the parts of the store in which the various packets *of* information are stored, in some systematic manner. A typical instruction might say—

'Add the number stored in position 6809 to that in 4302 and put the result back into the latter storage position.'

Needless to say it would not occur in the machine expressed in English. It would more likely be coded in a form such as 6809430217. Here 17 says which of various possible operations is to be performed on the two numbers. In this case the operation is that described above, viz. 'Add the number....' It will be noticed that the instruction takes up 10 digits and so forms one packet of information, very conveniently. The control will normally take the instructions to be obeyed in the order of the positions in which they are stored, but occasionally an instruction such as

'Now obey the instruction stored in position 5606, and continue from there' may be encountered, or again

'If position 4505 contains 0 obey next the instruction stored in 6707, otherwise continue straight on.'

Instructions of these latter types are very important because they make it possible for a sequence of operations to be repeated over and over again until some condition is fulfilled, but in doing so to obey, not fresh instructions on each repetition, but the same ones over and over again. To take a domestic analogy. Suppose Mother wants Tommy to call at the cobbler's every morning on his way to school to see if her shoes are done, she can ask him afresh every morning. Alternatively she can stick up a notice once and for all in the hall which he will see when he leaves for school and which tells him to call for the shoes, and also to destroy the notice when he comes back if he has the shoes with him.

The reader must accept it as a fact that digital computers can be constructed, and indeed have been constructed, according to the principles we have described, and that they can in fact mimic the actions of a human computer very closely.

The book of rules which we have described our human computer as using is of course a convenient fiction. Actual human computers really remember what they have got to do. If one wants to make a machine mimic the behaviour of the human computer in some complex operation one has to ask him how it is done, and then translate the answer into the form of an instruction table. Constructing instruction tables is usually described as 'programming.' To 'programme a machine to carry out the operation A' means to put the appropriate instruction table into the machine so that it will do A.

An interesting variant on the idea of a digital computer is a 'digital computer with a random element.' These have instructions involving the throwing of a die or some equivalent electronic process; one such instruction might for instance be, 'Throw the die and put the resulting number into store 1000.' Sometimes such a machine is described as having free will (though I would not use this phrase myself). It is not normally possible to determine from observing a machine whether it has a random element, for a similar effect can be produced by such devices as making the choices depend on the digits of the decimal for π.

Most actual digital computers have only a finite store. There is no theoretical difficulty in the idea of a computer with an unlimited store. Of course only a finite part can have been used at any one time. Likewise only a finite amount can have been constructed, but we can imagine more and more being added as required. Such computers have special theoretical interest and will be called infinitive capacity computers.

The idea of a digital computer is an old one. Charles Babbage, Lucasian Professor of Mathematics at Cambridge from 1828 to 1839, planned such a machine, called the Analytical Engine, but it was never completed. Although Babbage had all the essential ideas, his machine was not at that time such a very attractive prospect. The speed which would have been available would be definitely faster than a human computer but something like 100 times slower than the Manchester machine, itself one of the slower of the modern machines. The storage was to be purely mechanical, using wheels and cards.

The fact that Babbage's Analytical Engine was to be entirely mechanical will help us to rid ourselves of a superstition. Importance is often attached to the fact that modern digital computers are electrical, and that the nervous system also is electrical. Since Babbage's machine was not electrical, and since all digital computers are in a sense equivalent, we see that this use of electricity cannot be of theoretical importance. Of course electricity usually comes in where fast signalling is concerned, so that it is not surprising that we find it in both these connections. In the nervous system chemical phenomena are at least as important as electrical. In certain computers the storage system is mainly acoustic. The feature of using electricity is thus seen to be only a very superficial similarity. If we wish to find such similarities we should look rather for mathematical analogies of function.

5. Universality of Digital Computers

The digital computers considered in the last section may be classified amongst the 'discrete state machines.' These are the machines which move by sudden jumps or clicks from one quite definite state to another. These states are sufficiently different for the possibility of confusion between them to be ignored. Strictly speaking there are no such machines. Everything really moves continuously. But there are many kinds of machine which can profitably be *thought of* as being discrete state machines. For instance in considering the switches for a lighting system it is a convenient fiction that each switch must be definitely on or definitely off. There must be intermediate positions, but for most purposes we can forget about them. As an example of a discrete state machine we might consider a wheel which clicks round through 120° once a second, but may be stopped by a lever which can be operated from outside; in addition a lamp is to light in one of the positions of the wheel. This machine could be described abstractly as follows. The internal state of the machine (which is described by the position of the wheel) may be q_1, q^2 or q^3. There is an input signal i_0 or i_1 (position of lever). The internal state at any moment is determined by the last state and input signal according to the table

		Last State		
		q_1	q_2	q_3
	i_0	q_2	q_3	q_4
Input				
	i_1	q_1	q_2	q_3

The output signals, the only externally visible indication of the internal state (the light) are described by the table

State	$q1$	$q2$	$q3$
Output	0_0	0_0	0_1

This example is typical of discrete state machines. They can be described by such tables provided they have only a finite number of possible states.

It will seem that given the initial state of the machine and the input signals it is always possible to predict all future states. This is reminiscent of Laplace's view that from the complete state of the universe at one moment of time, as described by the positions and velocities of all particles, it should be possible to predict all future states. The prediction which we are considering is, however, rather nearer to practicability than that considered by Laplace. The system of the 'universe as a whole' is such that quite small errors in the initial conditions can have an overwhelming effect at a later time. The displacement of a single electron by a billionth of a centimetre at one moment might make the difference between a man being killed by an avalanche a year later, or escaping. It is an essential property of the mechanical systems which we have called 'discrete state machines' that this phenomenon does not occur. Even when we consider the actual physical machines instead of the idealised machines, reasonably accurate knowledge of the state at one moment yields reasonably accurate knowledge any number of steps later.

As we have mentioned, digital computers fall within the class of discrete state machines. But the number of states of which such a machine is capable is usually enormously large. For instance, the number for the machine now working at Manchester is about $2^{165,000}$, $i.e.$, about $10^{50,000}$. Compare this with our example of the clicking wheel described above, which had three states. It is not difficult to see why the number of states should be so immense. The computer includes a store corresponding to the paper used by a human computer. It must be possible to write into the store any one of the combinations of symbols which might have been written on the paper. For simplicity suppose that only digits from 0 to 9 are used as symbols. Variations in handwriting are ignored. Suppose the computer is allowed 100 sheets of paper each containing 50 lines each with room for 30 digits. Then the number of states is $10^{100 \times 50 \times 30}$, i.e., $10^{150,000}$. This is about the number of states of three Manchester machines put together. The logarithm to the base two of the number of states is usually called the 'storage capacity' of the machine. Thus the Manchester machine has a storage capacity of about 165,000 and the wheel machine of our example about 1·6. If two machines are put together their capacities must be added to obtain the capacity of the resultant machine. This leads to the possibility of statements such as 'The Manchester machine contains 64 magnetic tracks each with a capacity of 2560, eight electronic tubes with a capacity of 1280. Miscellaneous storage amounts to about 300 making a total of 174,380.'

Given the table corresponding to a discrete state machine it is possible to predict what it will do. There is no reason why this calculation should not be carried out by means of a digital computer. Provided it could be carried out sufficiently quickly the digital computer could mimic the behaviour of any discrete state machine. The imitation game could then be played with the machine in question (as B) and the mimicking digital computer (as A) and the interrogator would be unable to distinguish them. Of course the digital computer must have an adequate storage capacity as well as working sufficiently fast. Moreover, it must be programmed afresh for each new machine which it is desired to mimic.

This special property of digital computers, that they can mimic any discrete state machine, is described by saying that they are *universal* machines. The existence of machines with this property has the important consequence that, considerations of speed apart, it is unnecessary to design various new machines to do various computing processes. They can all be done with one digital computer, suitably programmed for each case. It will be seen that as a consequence of this all digital computers are in a sense equivalent.

We may now consider again the point raised at the end of § 3. It was suggested tentatively that the question, 'Can machines think?' should be replaced by 'Are there imaginable digital computers which would do well in the imitation game?' If we wish we can make this superficially more general and ask 'Are there discrete state machines which would do well?' But in view of the universality property we see that either of these questions is equivalent to this, 'Let us fix our attention on one particular digital computer C. Is it true that by modifying this computer to have an adequate storage, suitably increasing its speed of action, and providing it with an appropriate programme, C can be made to play satisfactorily the part of A in the imitation game, the part of B being taken by a man?'

6. Contrary Views on the Main Question

We may now consider the ground to have been cleared and we are ready to proceed to the debate on our question, 'Can machines think?' and the variant of it quoted at the end of the last section. We cannot altogether abandon the original form of the problem, for opinions will differ as to the appropriateness of the substitution and we must at least listen to what has to be said in this connexion.

It will simplify matters for the reader if I explain first my own beliefs in the matter. Consider first the more accurate form of the question. I believe that in about fifty years' time it will be possible to programme computers, with a storage capacity of about 10^9, to make them play the imitation game so well that an average interrogator will not have more than 70 per cent. chance of making the right identification after five minutes of questioning. The original question, 'Can machines think?' I believe to be too meaningless to deserve discussion. Nevertheless I believe that at the end of the century the use of words and general educated opinion will have altered so much that one will be able to speak of machines thinking without expecting to be contradicted. I believe further that no useful purpose is served by concealing these beliefs. The popular view that scientists proceed inexorably from well-established fact to well-established fact, never being influenced by any unproved conjecture, is quite mistaken. Provided it is made clear which are proved facts and which are conjectures, no harm can result. Conjectures are of great importance since they suggest useful lines of research.

I now proceed to consider opinions opposed to my own.

(I) *The Theological Objection.* Thinking is a function of man's immortal soul. God has given an immortal soul to every man and woman, but not to any other animal or to machines. Hence no animal or machine can think.

I am unable to accept any part of this, but will attempt to reply in theological terms. I should find the argument more convincing if animals were classed with men, for there is a greater difference, to my mind, between the typical animate and the inanimate than there is between man and the other animals. The arbitrary character of the orthodox view becomes clearer if we consider how it might appear to a member of some other religious community. How do Christians regard the Moslem view that women have no souls? But let us leave this point aside and return to the main argument. It appears to me that the argument quoted above implies a serious restriction of the omnipotence of the Almighty. It is admitted that there are certain things that He cannot do such as making one equal to two, but should we not believe that He has freedom to confer a soul on an elephant if He sees fit? We might expect that He would only exercise this power in conjunction with a mutation which provided the elephant with an appropriately improved brain to minister to the needs of this soul. An argument of exactly similar form may be made for the case of machines. It may seem different because it is more difficult to "swallow." But this really only means that we think it would be less likely that He would consider the circumstances suitable for conferring a soul. The circumstances in question are discussed in the rest of this paper. In attempting to construct such machines we should not be irreverently usurping His power of creating souls, any more than we are in the procreation of children: rather we are, in either case, instruments of His will providing mansions for the souls that He creates.

However, this is mere speculation. I am not very impressed with theological arguments whatever they may be used to support. Such arguments have often been found unsatisfactory in the past. In the time of Galileo it was argued that the texts, "And the sun stood still . . . and hasted not to go down about a whole day" (Joshua x. 13) and "He laid the foundations of the earth, that it should not move at any time" (Psalm cv. 5) 2 were an adequate refutation of the Copernican theory. With our present knowledge such an argument appears futile. When that knowledge was not available it made a quite different impression.

(2) *The 'Heads in the Sand' Objection.* "The consequences of machines thinking would be too dreadful. Let us hope and believe that they cannot do so." This argument is seldom expressed quite so openly as in the form above. But it affects most of us who think about it at all. We like to believe that Man is in some subtle way superior to the rest of creation. It is best if he can be shown to be *necessarily* superior, for then there is no danger of him losing his commanding position. The popularity of the theological argument is clearly connected with this feeling. It is likely to be quite strong in intellectual people, since they value the power of thinking more highly than others, and are more inclined to base their belief in the superiority of Man on this power.

I do not think that this argument is sufficiently substantial to require refutation. Consolation would be more appropriate: perhaps this should be sought in the transmigration of souls.

(3) *The Mathematical Objection.* There are a number of results of mathematical logic which can be used to show that there are limitations to the powers of discrete-state machines. The best known of these results is known as Godel's theorem, and shows that in any sufficiently powerful logical system statements can be formulated which can neither be proved nor disproved within the system, unless possibly the system itself is inconsistent. There are other, in some respects similar, results due to *Church, Kleene, Rosser,* and *Turing.* The latter result is the most convenient to consider, since it refers directly to machines, whereas the others can only be used in a comparatively indirect argument: for instance if Godel's theorem is to be used we need in addition to have some means of describing logical systems in terms of machines, and machines in terms of logical systems. The result in question refers to a type of machine which is essentially a digital computer with an infinite capacity. It states that there are certain things that such a machine cannot do. If it is rigged up to give answers to questions as in the imitation game, there will be some questions to which it will either give a wrong answer, or fail to give an answer at all however much time is allowed for a reply. There may, of course, be many such questions, and questions which cannot be answered by one machine may be satisfactorily answered by another. We are of course supposing for the present that the questions are of the kind to which an answer 'Yes' or 'No' is appropriate, rather than questions such as 'What do you think of Picasso?' The questions that we know the machines must fail on are of this type, "Consider the machine specified as follows.... Will this machine ever answer 'Yes' to any question?" The dots are to be replaced by a description of some machine in a standard form, which could be something like that used in § 5. When the machine described bears a certain comparatively simple relation to the machine which is under interrogation, it can be shown that the answer is either wrong or not forthcoming. This is the mathematical result: it is argued that it proves a disability of machines to which the human intellect is not subject.

The short answer to this argument is that although it is established that there are limitations to the powers of any particular machine, it has only been stated, without any sort of proof, that no such limitations apply to the human intellect. But I do not think this view can be dismissed quite so lightly. Whenever one of these machines is asked the appropriate critical question, and gives a definite answer, we know that this answer must be wrong, and this gives us a certain feeling of superiority. Is this feeling illusory? It is no doubt quite genuine, but I do not think too much importance should be attached to it. We too often give wrong answers to questions ourselves to be justified in being very pleased at such evidence of fallibility on the part of the machines. Further, our superiority can only be felt on such an occasion in relation to the one machine over which we have scored our petty triumph. There would be no question of triumphing simultaneously over all machines. In short, then, there might be men cleverer than any given machine, but then again there might be other machines cleverer again, and so on.

Those who hold to the mathematical argument would, I think, mostly be willing to accept the imitation game as a basis for discussion. Those who believe in the two previous objections would probably not be interested in any criteria.

(4) *The Argument from Consciousness.* This argument is very well expressed in *Professor Jefferson's* Lister Oration for 1949, from which I quote. "Not until a machine can write a sonnet or compose a concerto because of thoughts and emotions felt, and not by the chance fall of symbols, could we agree that machine equals brain—that is, not only write it but know that it had written it. No mechanism could feel (and not merely artificially signal, an easy contrivance) pleasure at its successes, grief when its valves fuse, be warmed by flattery be made miserable by its mistakes, be charmed by sex, be angry or depressed when it cannot get what it wants."

This argument appears to be a denial of the validity of our test. According to the most extreme form of this view the only way by which one could be sure that a machine thinks is to *be* the machine and to feel oneself thinking. One could then describe these feelings to the world, but of course no one would be justified in taking any notice. Likewise according to this view the only way to know that a *man* thinks is to be that particular man. It is in fact the solipsist point of view. It may be the most logical view to hold but it makes communication of ideas difficult. A is liable to believe 'A thinks but B does not' whilst B believes 'B thinks but A does not.' Instead of arguing continually over this point it is usual to have the polite convention that everyone thinks.

I am sure that Professor Jefferson does not wish to adopt the extreme and solipsist point of view. Probably he would be quite willing to accept the imitation game as a test. The game (with the player B omitted) is frequently used in practice under the name of *viva voce* to discover whether some one really understands something or has 'learnt it parrot fashion.' Let us listen in to a part of such a viva voce:

Interrogator: In the first line of your sonnet which reads 'Shall I compare thee to a summer's day,' would not 'a spring day' do as well or better?

Witness: It wouldn't scan.

Interrogator: How about 'a winter's day.' That would scan all right.

Witness: Yes, but nobody wants to be compared to a winter's day.

Interrogator: Would you say Mr. Pickwick reminded you of Christmas?

Witness: In a way.

Interrogator: Yet Christmas is a winter's day, and I do not think Mr. Pickwick would mind the comparison.

Witness: I don't think you're serious. By a winter's day one means a typical winter's day, rather than a special one like Christmas.

And so on. What would Professor Jefferson say if the sonnet-writing machine was able to answer like this in the *viva voce?* I do not know whether he would regard the machine as 'merely artificially signalling' these answers, but if the answers were as satisfactory and sustained as in the above passage I do not think he would describe it as 'an easy contrivance.' This phrase is, I think, intended to cover such devices as the inclusion in the machine of a record of someone reading a sonnet, with appropriate switching to turn it on from time to time.

In short then, I think that most of those who support the argument from consciousness could be persuaded to abandon it rather than be forced into the solipsist position. They will then probably be willing to accept our test.

I do not wish to give the impression that I think there is no mystery about consciousness. There is, for instance, something of a paradox connected with any attempt to localise it. But I do not think these mysteries necessarily need to be solved before we can answer the question with which we are concerned in this paper.

(5) *Arguments from Various Disabilities.* These arguments take the form, "I grant you that you can make machines do all the things you have mentioned but you will never be able to make one to do X." Numerous features X are suggested in this connexion. I offer a selection:

Be kind, resourceful, beautiful, friendly, have initiative, have a sense of humour, tell right from wrong, make mistakes, fall in love, enjoy strawberries and cream, make some one fall in love with it, learn from experience, use words properly, be the subject of its own thought, have as much diversity of behaviour as a man, do something really new.

No support is usually offered for these statements. I believe they are mostly founded on the principle of scientific induction. A man has seen thousands of machines in his lifetime. From what he sees of them he draws a number of general conclusions. They are ugly, each is designed for a very limited purpose, when required for a minutely different purpose they are useless, the variety of behaviour of any one of them is very small, etc., etc. Naturally he concludes that these are necessary properties of machines in general. Many of these limitations are associated with the very small storage capacity of most machines. (I am assuming that the idea of storage capacity is extended in some way to cover machines other than discrete-state machines. The exact definition does not matter as no mathematical accuracy is claimed in the present discussion.) A few years ago, when very little had been heard of digital computers, it was possible to elicit much incredulity concerning them, if one mentioned their properties without describing their construction. That was presumably due to a similar application of the principle of scientific induction. These applications of the principle are of course largely unconscious. When a burnt child fears the fire and shows that he fears it by avoiding it, I should say that he was applying scientific induction. (I could of course also describe his behaviour in many other ways.) The works and customs of mankind do not seem to be very suitable material to which to apply scientific induction. A very large part of space-time must be investigated, if reliable results are to be obtained. Otherwise we may (as most English children do) decide that everybody speaks English, and that it is silly to learn French.

There are, however, special remarks to be made about many of the disabilities that have been mentioned. The inability to enjoy strawberries and cream may have struck the reader as frivolous. Possibly a machine might be made to enjoy this delicious dish, but any attempt to make one do so would be idiotic. What is important about this disability is that it contributes to some of the other disabilities, *e.g.*, to the difficulty of the same kind of friendliness occurring between man and machine as between white man and white man, or between black man and black man.

The claim that "machines cannot make mistakes" seems a curious one. One is tempted to retort, "Are they any the worse for that?" But let us adopt a more sympathetic attitude, and try to see what is really meant. I think this criticism can be explained in terms of the imitation game. It is claimed that the interrogator could distinguish the machine from the man simply by setting them a number of problems in arithmetic. The machine would be unmasked because of its deadly accuracy. The reply to this is simple. The machine (programmed for playing the game) would not attempt to give the *right* answers to the arithmetic problems. It would deliberately introduce mistakes in a manner calculated to confuse the interrogator. A mechanical fault would probably show itself through an unsuitable decision as to what sort of a mistake to make in the arithmetic.

Even this interpretation of the criticism is not sufficiently sympathetic. But we cannot afford the space to go into it much further. It seems to me that this criticism depends on a confusion between two kinds of mistake. We may call them 'errors of functioning' and 'errors of conclusion.' Errors of functioning are due to some mechanical or electrical fault which causes the machine to behave otherwise than it was designed to do. In philosophical discussions one likes to ignore the possibility of such errors; one is therefore discussing 'abstract machines.' These abstract machines are mathematical fictions rather than physical objects. By definition they are incapable of errors of functioning. In this sense we can truly say that 'machines can never make mistakes.' Errors of conclusion can only arise when some meaning is attached to the output signals from the machine. The machine might, for instance, type out mathematical equations, or sentences in English. When a false proposition is typed we say that the machine has committed an error of conclusion. There is clearly no reason at all for saying that a machine cannot make this kind of mistake. It might do nothing but type out repeatedly '0 = 1.' To take a less perverse example, it might have some method for drawing conclusions by scientific induction. We must expect such a method to lead occasionally to erroneous results.

The claim that a machine cannot be the subject of its own thought can of course only be answered if it can be shown that the machine has *some* thought with *some* subject matter. Nevertheless, 'the subject matter of a machine's operations' does seem to mean something, at least to the people who deal with it. If, for instance, the machine was trying to find a solution of the equation $X^2 - 40x - 11 = O$ one would be tempted to describe this equation as part of the machine's subject matter at that moment. In this sort of sense a machine undoubtedly can be its own subject matter. It may be used to help in making up its own programmes, or to predict the effect of alterations in its own structure. By observing the results of its own behaviour it can modify its own programmes so as to achieve some purpose more effectively. These are possibilities of the near future, rather than Utopian dreams.

The criticism that a machine cannot have much diversity of behaviour is just a way of saying that it cannot have much storage capacity. Until fairly recently a storage capacity of even a thousand digits was very rare.

The criticisms that we are considering here are often disguised forms of the argument from consciousness. Usually if one maintains that a machine *can* do one of these things, and describes the kind of method that the machine could use, one will not make much of an impression. It is thought that the method (whatever it may be, for it must be mechanical) is really rather base.

(6) *Lady Lovelace's Objection.* Our most detailed information of Babbage's Analytical Engine comes from a memoir by *Lady Lovelace.* In it she states, "The Analytical Engine has no pretensions to *originate* anything. It can do *whatever we know how to order it* to perform" (her italics). This statement is quoted by *Hartree* who adds: "This does not imply that it may not be possible to construct electronic equipment which will 'think for itself,' or in which, in biological terms, one could set up a conditioned reflex, which would serve as a basis for 'learning.' Whether this is possible in principle or not is a stimulating and exciting question, suggested by some of these recent developments. But it did not seem that the machines constructed or projected at the time had this property."

I am in thorough agreement with Hartree over this. It will be noticed that he does not assert that the machines in question had not got the property, but rather that the evidence available to Lady Lovelace did not encourage her to believe that they had it. It is quite possible that the machines in question had in a sense got this property. For suppose that some discrete-state machine has the property. The Analytical Engine was a universal digital computer, so that, if its storage capacity and speed were adequate, it could by suitable programming be made to mimic the machine in question. Probably this argument did not occur to the Countess or to Babbage. In any case there was no obligation on them to claim all that could be claimed.

This whole question will be considered again under the heading of learning machines.

A variant of Lady Lovelace's objection states that a machine can 'never do anything really new.' This may be parried for a moment with the saw, 'There is nothing new under the sun.' Who can be certain that 'original work' that he has done was not simply the growth of the seed planted in him by teaching, or the effect of following well-known general principles. A better variant of the objection says that a machine can never 'take us by surprise.' This statement is a more direct challenge and can be met directly. Machines take me by surprise with great frequency. This is largely because I do not do sufficient calculation to decide what to expect them to do, or rather because, although I do a calculation, I do it in a hurried, slipshod fashion, taking risks. Perhaps I say to myself, 'I suppose the voltage here ought to be the same as there: anyway let's assume it is.' Naturally I am often wrong, and the result is a surprise for me for by the time the experiment is done these assumptions have been forgotten. These admissions lay me open to lectures on the subject of my vicious ways, but do not throw any doubt on my credibility when I testify to the surprises I experience.

I do not expect this reply to silence my critic. He will probably say that such surprises are due to some creative mental act on my part, and reflect no credit on the machine. This leads us back to the argument from consciousness, and far from the idea of surprise. It is a line of argument we must consider closed, but it is perhaps worth remarking that the appreciation of something as surprising requires as much of a 'creative mental act' whether the surprising event originates from a man, a book, a machine or anything else.

The view that machines cannot give rise to surprises is due, I believe, to a fallacy to which philosophers and mathematicians are particularly subject. This is the assumption that as soon as a fact is presented to a mind all consequences of that fact spring into the mind simultaneously with it. It is a very useful assumption under many circumstances, but one too easily forgets that it is false. A natural consequence of doing so is that one then assumes that there is no virtue in the mere working out of consequences from data and general principles.

(7) *Argument from Continuity in the Nervous System.* The nervous system is certainly not a discrete-state machine. A small error in the information about the size of a nervous impulse impinging on a neuron, may make a large difference to the size of the outgoing impulse. It may be argued that, this being so, one cannot expect to be able to mimic the behaviour of the nervous system with a discrete-state system.

It is true that a discrete-state machine must be different from a continuous machine. But if we adhere to the conditions of the imitation game, the interrogator will not be able to take any advantage of this difference. The situation can be made clearer if we consider some other simpler continuous machine. A differential analyser will do very well. (A differential analyser is a certain kind of machine not of the discrete-state type used for some kinds of calculation.) Some of these provide their answers in a typed form, and so are suitable for taking part in the game. It would not be possible for a digital computer to predict exactly what answers the differential analyser would give to a problem, but it would be quite capable of giving the right sort of answer. For instance, if asked to give the value of π (actually about 3.1416) it would be reasonable to choose at random between the values 3.12, 3.13, 3.14, 3.15, 3.16 with the probabilities of 0.05, 0.15, 0.55, 0.19, 0.06 (say). Under these circumstances it would be very difficult for the interrogator to distinguish the differential analyser from the digital computer.

(8) *The Argument from Informality of Behaviour.* It is not possible to produce a set of rules purporting to describe what a man should do in every conceivable set of circumstances. One might for instance have a rule that one is to stop when one sees a red traffic light, and to go if one sees a green one, but what if by some fault both appear together? One may perhaps decide that it is safest to stop. But some further difficulty may well arise from this decision later. To attempt to provide rules of conduct to cover every eventuality, even those arising from traffic lights, appears to be impossible. With all this I agree.

From this it is argued that we cannot be machines. I shall try to reproduce the argument, but I fear I shall hardly do it justice. It seems to run something like this. 'If each man had a definite set of rules of conduct by which he regulated his life he would be no better than a machine. But there are no such rules, so men cannot be machines.' The undistributed middle is glaring. I do not think the argument is ever put quite like this, but I believe this is the argument used nevertheless. There may however be a certain confusion between 'rules of conduct' and 'laws of behaviour' to cloud the issue. By 'rules of conduct' I mean precepts such as 'Stop if you see red lights,' on which one can act, and of which one can be conscious. By 'laws of behaviour' I mean laws of nature as applied to a man's body such as 'if you pinch him he will squeak.' If we substitute 'laws of behaviour which regulate his life' for 'laws of conduct by which he regulates his life' in the argument quoted the undistributed middle is no longer insuperable. For we believe that it is not only true that being regulated by laws of behaviour implies being some sort of machine (though not necessarily a discrete-state machine), but that conversely being such a machine implies being regulated by such laws. However, we cannot so easily convince ourselves of the absence of complete laws of behaviour as of complete rules of conduct. The only way we know of for finding such laws is scientific observation, and we certainly know of no circumstances under which we could say, 'We have searched enough. There are no such laws.'

We can demonstrate more forcibly that any such statement would be unjustified. For suppose we could be sure of finding such laws if they existed. Then given a discrete-state machine it should certainly be possible to discover by observation sufficient about it to predict its future behaviour, and this within a reasonable time, say a thousand years. But this does not seem to be the case. I have set up on the Manchester computer a small programme using only 1000 units of storage, whereby the machine supplied with one sixteen figure number replies with another within two seconds. I would defy anyone to learn from these replies sufficient about the programme to be able to predict any replies to untried values.

(9) *The Argument from Extra-Sensory Perception.* I assume that the reader is familiar with the idea of extra-sensory perception, and the meaning of the four items of it, viz. telepathy, clairvoyance, precognition and psycho-kinesis. These disturbing phenomena seem to deny all our usual scientific ideas. How we should like to discredit them! Unfortunately the statistical evidence, at least for telepathy, is overwhelming. It is very difficult to rearrange one's ideas so as to fit these new facts in. Once one has accepted them it does not seem a very big step to believe in ghosts and bogies. The idea that our bodies move simply according to the known laws of physics, together with some others not yet discovered but somewhat similar, would be one of the first to go.

This argument is to my mind quite a strong one. One can say in reply that many scientific theories seem to remain workable in practice, in spite of clashing with E.S.P.; that in fact one can get along very nicely if one forgets about it. This is rather cold comfort, and one fears that thinking is just the kind of phenomenon where E.S.P. may be especially relevant.

A more specific argument based on E.S.P. might run as follows: "Let us play the imitation game, using as witnesses a man who is good as a telepathic receiver, and a digital computer. The interrogator can ask such questions as 'What suit does the card in my right hand belong to?' The man by telepathy or clairvoyance gives the right answer 130 times out of 400 cards. The machine can only guess at random, and perhaps gets 104 right, so the interrogator makes the right identification." There is an interesting possibility which opens here.

Suppose the digital computer contains a random number generator. Then it will be natural to use this to decide what answer to give. But then the random number generator will be subject to the psycho-kinetic powers of the interrogator. Perhaps this psycho-kinesis might cause the machine to guess right more often than would be expected on a probability calculation, so that the interrogator might still be unable to make the right identification. On the other hand, he might be able to guess right without any questioning, by clairvoyance. With E.S.P. anything may happen.

If telepathy is admitted it will be necessary to tighten our test up. The situation could be regarded as analogous to that which would occur if the interrogator were talking to himself and one of the competitors was listening with his ear to the wall. To put the competitors into a 'telepathy-proof room' would satisfy all requirements.

7. Learning Machines

The reader will have anticipated that I have no very convincing arguments of a positive nature to support my views. If I had I should not have taken such pains to point out the fallacies in contrary views. Such evidence as I have I shall now give.

Let us return for a moment to Lady Lovelace's objection, which stated that the machine can only do what we tell it to do. One could say that a man can 'inject' an idea into the machine, and that it will respond to a certain extent and then drop into quiescence, like a piano string struck by a hammer. Another simile would be an atomic pile of less than critical size: an injected idea is to correspond to a neutron entering the pile from without. Each such neutron will cause a certain disturbance which eventually dies away. If, however, the size of the pile is sufficiently increased, the disturbance caused by such an incoming neutron will very likely go on and on increasing until the whole pile is destroyed. Is there a corresponding phenomenon for minds, and is there one for machines? There does seem to be one for the human mind. The majority of them seem to be 'sub-critical,' i.e., to correspond in this analogy to piles of subcritical size. An idea presented to such a mind will on average give rise to less than one idea in reply. A smallish proportion are super-critical. An idea presented to such a mind may give rise to a whole 'theory' consisting of secondary, tertiary and more remote ideas. Animals minds seem to be very definitely sub-critical. Adhering to this analogy we ask, 'Can a machine be made to be super-critical?'

The 'skin of an onion' analogy is also helpful. In considering the functions of the mind or the brain we find certain operations which we can explain in purely mechanical terms. This we say does not correspond to the real mind: it is a sort of skin which we must strip off if we are to find the real mind. But then in what remains we find a further skin to be stripped off, and so on. Proceeding in this way do we ever come to the 'real' mind, or do we eventually come to the skin which has nothing in it? In the latter case the whole mind is mechanical. (It would not be a discrete-state machine however. We have discussed this.)

These last two paragraphs do not claim to be convincing arguments. They should rather be described as 'recitations tending to produce belief.'

The only really satisfactory support that can be given for the view expressed at the beginning of Sec. 6, will be that provided by waiting for the end of the century and then doing the experiment described. But what can we say in the meantime? What steps should be taken now if the experiment is to be successful?

As I have explained, the problem is mainly one of programming. Advances in engineering will have to be made too, but it seems unlikely that these will not be adequate for the requirements. Estimates of the storage capacity of the brain vary from 10^{10} to 10^{15} binary digits. I incline to the lower values and believe that only a very small fraction is used for the higher types of thinking. Most of it is probably used for the retention of visual impressions. I should be surprised if more than 10^9 was required for satisfactory playing of the imitation game, at any rate against a blind man. (Note—The capacity of the *Encyclopedia Britannica,* 11th edition, is 2 X 10^9.) A storage capacity of 10^7 would be a very practicable possibility even by present techniques. It is probably not necessary to increase the speed of operations of the machines at all. Parts of modern machines which can be regarded as analogues of nerve cells work about a thousand times faster than the latter. This should provide a 'margin of safety' which could cover losses of speed arising in many ways. Our problem then is to find out how to programme these machines to play the game. At my present rate of working I produce about a thousand digits of programme a day, so that about sixty workers, working steadily through the fifty years might accomplish the job, if nothing went into the waste-paper basket. Some more expeditious method seems desirable.

In the process of trying to imitate an adult human mind we are bound to think a good deal about the process which has brought it to the state that it is in. We may notice three components,

(a) The initial state of the mind, say at birth,
(b) The education to which it has been subjected,
(c) Other experience, not to be described as education, to which it has been subjected.

Instead of trying to produce a programme to simulate the adult mind, why not rather try to produce one which simulates the child's? If this were then subjected to an appropriate course of education one would obtain the adult brain. Presumably the child-brain is something like a note-book as one buys it from the stationers. Rather little mechanism, and lots of blank sheets. (Mechanism and writing are from our point of view almost synonymous.) Our hope is that there is so little mechanism in the child-brain that something like it can be easily programmed. The amount of work in the education we can assume, as a first approximation, to be much the same as for the human child.

We have thus divided our problem into two parts. The child-programme and the education process. These two remain very closely connected. We cannot expect to find a good child-machine at the first attempt. One must experiment with teaching one such machine and see how well it learns. One can then try another and see if it is better or worse. There is an obvious connection between this process and evolution, by the identifications

Structure of the child machine = Hereditary material
Changes   "   "   "   "   = Mutations
Natural selection = Judgment of the experimenter

One may hope, however, that this process will be more expeditious than evolution. The survival of the fittest is a slow method for measuring advantages. The experimenter, by the exercise of intelligence, should be able to speed it up. Equally important is the fact that he is not restricted to random mutations. If he can trace a cause for some weakness he can probably think of the kind of mutation which will improve it.

It will not be possible to apply exactly the same teaching process to the machine as to a normal child. It will not, for instance, be provided with legs, so that it could not be asked to go out and fill the coal scuttle. Possibly it might not have eyes. But however well these deficiencies might be overcome by clever engineering, one could not send the creature to school without the other children making excessive fun of it. It must be given some tuition. We need not be too concerned about the legs, eyes, etc. The example of Miss *Helen Keller* shows that education can take place provided that communication in both directions between teacher and pupil can take place by some means or other.

We normally associate punishments and rewards with the teaching process. Some simple child-machines can be constructed or programmed on this sort of principle. The machine has to be so constructed that events which shortly preceded the occurrence of a punishment-signal are unlikely to be repeated, whereas a reward-signal increased the probability of repetition of the events which led up to it. These definitions do not presuppose any feelings on the part of the machine. I have done some experiments with one such child-machine, and succeeded in teaching it a few things, but the teaching method was too unorthodox for the experiment to be considered really successful.

The use of punishments and rewards can at best be a part of the teaching process. Roughly speaking, if the teacher has no other means of communicating to the pupil, the amount of information which can reach him does not exceed the total number of rewards and punishments applied. By the time a child has learnt to repeat 'Casabianca' he would probably feel very sore indeed, if the text could only be discovered by a 'Twenty Questions' technique, every 'NO' taking the form of a blow. It is necessary therefore to have some other 'unemotional' channels of communication. If these are available it is possible to teach a machine by punishments and rewards to obey orders given in some language, *e.g.*, a symbolic language. These orders are to be transmitted through the 'unemotional' channels. The use of this language will diminish greatly the number of punishments and rewards required.

Opinions may vary as to the complexity which is suitable in the child machine. One might try to make it as simple as possible consistently with the general principles. Alternatively one might have a complete system of logical inference 'built in.' In the latter case the store would be largely occupied with definitions and propositions. The propositions would have various kinds of status, *e.g.*, well-established facts, conjectures, mathematically proved theorems, statements given by an authority, expressions having the logical form of proposition but not belief-value. Certain propositions may be described as 'imperatives.' The machine should be so constructed that as soon as an imperative is classed as 'well-established' the appropriate action automatically takes place. To illustrate this, suppose the teacher says to the machine, 'Do your homework now.' This may cause "Teacher says 'Do your homework now' " to be included amongst the well-established facts. Another such fact might be,

"Everything that Teacher says is true." Combining these may eventually lead to the imperative, 'Do your homework now,' being included amongst the well-established facts, and this, by the construction of the machine, will mean that the homework actually gets started, but the effect is very satisfactory. The processes of inference used by the machine need not be such as would satisfy the most exacting logicians. There might for instance be no hierarchy of types. But this need not mean that type fallacies will occur, any more than we are bound to fall over unfenced cliffs. Suitable imperatives (expressed within the systems, not forming part of the rules *of* the system) such as 'Do not use a class unless it is a subclass of one which has been mentioned by teacher' can have a similar effect to 'Do not go too near the edge.'

The imperatives that can be obeyed by a machine that has no limbs are bound to be of a rather intellectual character, as in the example (doing homework) given above. Important amongst such imperatives will be ones which regulate the order in which the rules of the logical system concerned are to be applied. For at each stage when one is using a logical system, there is a very large number of alternative steps, any of which one is permitted to apply, so far as obedience to the rules of the logical system is concerned. These choices make the difference between a brilliant and a footling reasoner, not the difference between a sound and a fallacious one. Propositions leading to imperatives of this kind might be "When Socrates is mentioned, use the syllogism in Barbara" or "If one method has been proved to be quicker than another, do not use the slower method." Some of these may be 'given by authority,' but others may be produced by the machine itself, e.g., by scientific induction.

The idea of a learning machine may appear paradoxical to some readers. How can the rules of operation of the machine change? They should describe completely how the machine will react whatever its history might be, whatever changes it might undergo. The rules are thus quite time-invariant. This is quite true. The explanation of the paradox is that the rules which get changed in the learning process are of a rather less pretentious kind, claiming only an ephemeral validity. The reader may draw a parallel with the Constitution of the United States.

An important feature of a learning machine is that its teacher will often be very largely ignorant of quite what is going on inside, although he may still be able to some extent to predict his pupil's behaviour. This should apply most strongly to the later education of a machine arising from a child-machine of well-tried design (or programme). This is in clear contrast with normal procedure when using a machine to do computations: one's object is then to have a clear mental picture of the state of the machine at each moment in the computation. This object can only be achieved with a struggle. The view that 'the machine can only do what we know how to order it to do,' appears strange in face of this. Most of the programmes which we can put into the machine will result in its doing something that we cannot make sense of at all, or which we regard as completely random behaviour. Intelligent behaviour presumably consists in a departure from the completely disciplined behaviour involved in computation, but a rather slight one, which does not give rise to random behaviour, or to pointless repetitive loops. Another important result of preparing our machine for its part in the imitation game by a process of teaching and learning is that 'human fallibility' is likely to be omitted in a rather natural way, i.e., without special 'coaching.' Processes that are learnt do not produce a hundred per cent. certainty of result; if they did they could not be unlearnt.

It is probably wise to include a random element in a learning machine. A random element is rather useful when we are searching for a solution of some problem. Suppose for instance we wanted to find a number between 50 and 200 which was equal to the square of the sum of its digits, we might start at 51 then try 52 and go on until we got a number that worked. Alternatively we might choose numbers at random until we got a good one. This method has the advantage that it is unnecessary to keep track of the values that have been tried, but the disadvantage that one may try the same one twice, but this is not very important if there are several solutions. The systematic method has the disadvantage that there may be an enormous block without any solutions in the region, which has to be investigated first. Now the learning process may be regarded as a search for a form of behaviour which will satisfy the teacher (or some other criterion). Since there is probably a very large number of satisfactory solutions the random method seems to be better than the systematic. It should be noticed that it is used in the analogous process of evolution. But there the systematic method is not possible. How could one keep track of the different genetical combinations that had been tried, so as to avoid trying them again?

We may hope that machines will eventually compete with men in all purely intellectual fields. But which are the best ones to start with? Even this is a difficult decision. Many people think that a very abstract activity, like the playing of chess, would be best. It can also be maintained that it is best to provide the machine with the best sense organs that money can buy, and then teach it to understand and speak English. This process could follow the normal teaching of a child. Things would be pointed out and named, etc. Again I do not know what the right answer is, but I think both approaches should be tried.

We can only see a short distance ahead, but we can see plenty there that needs to be done.